The Economic History of Singapore

The Economic History of Singapore

Keen Meng Choy and Ichiro Sugimoto

NUS PRESS
SINGAPORE

Published by:

NUS Press
National University of Singapore
AS3-01-02, 3 Arts Link
Singapore 117569

Fax: (65) 6774-0652
E-mail: nusbooks@nus.edu.sg
Website: http://nuspress.nus.edu.sg

print ISBN: 978-981-325-323-0 (hardback)
ePDF: 978-981-325-324-7

National Library Board, Singapore Cataloguing in Publication Data
Name(s): Choy, Keen-Meng. | Sugimoto, Ichirō, author.
Title: The economic history of Singapore / Keen Meng Choy and Ichiro Sugimoto.
Description: Singapore : NUS Press, 2026.
Identifier(s): ISBN 978-981-325-323-0 (hardback) | 978-981-325-324-7 (ePDF)
Subject(s): LCSH: Economic development--Singapore. | Singapore--Economic conditions.
Classification: DDC 330.95957--dc23

Cover images:
(top) Dr Goh Keng Swee tours the Malaysia Mosquito Spiral Manufacturing Co factory at the Jurong Industrial Estate, April 1965. Ministry of Information and the Arts Collection, courtesy of National Archives of Singapore.
(bottom) View of the harbour, mid-19th century, artist unknown, collection of the National Museum of Singapore, National Heritage Board. Gift of Lim K. Tan.

Typeset by: Ogma Solutions Pvt Ltd
Printed by: Integrated Books International

Contents

List of Tables

List of Figures

List of Maps

List of Weights, Measures and Exchange Rates

Weights

1 long tonne = 2,240 lb = 1016.046 kg = 16.8 pikul
1 metric tonne = 2,204.62lb = 1000 kg =16.5347 pikul
1 pikul = 133⅓ lb ≈ 60.5 kg = 100 kati
1 kati (catty) = 1⅓ lb = 0.01 pikul = 16 tahil= 0.6048 kg
1 lb = 0.0075 pikul = 0.755987 kati

Measures

1 gallon = 4.54609 litres = 4.54609 cubic decimetres
1 foot = 0.3048 metre
1 yard = 3 feet = 0.9144 metre
1 mile = 1,760 yards = 5,280 feet = 1,609.344 metres
1 acre = 0.404685642 hectare

Exchange Rates

SPD1 ≈ 2.27–2.29 rupees (SPD = Spanish dollar)
£100 = SPD367 (1820)
£100 = SPD435 (1850)
£100 = SPD470 (1870)
£100 = SPD587 (1890)
£100 = SPD729 (1893)
£100 = SPD661 (1900)
£1 was divided into 20 shillings (s.) and each shilling into 12 pennies (d.).
$1 = 2s. 4d. = £0.117 (1906) ($ = Straits dollar)

Preface

To the colonial historian Richard Winstedt is due a bland if otherwise accurate assertion: "The history of Singapore is written mainly in statistics". As a corollary, the economic history of Singapore is indeed yet to be written, except again in its statistics. An important reference, W.G. Huff's *The Economic Growth of Singapore* (1994), focuses only on the twentieth century and adopts a thematic rather than chronological approach. The present book fills this glaring gap in the literature on the economic miracle that is Singapore by tracing its development through the ancient, colonial and modern epochs. Its chronological parameters extend from *circa* 1300 to the present; the inherently ambiguous task of periodisation is determined by the phases of economic growth in the respective timeframes under consideration. The book presents a scholarly and chronological account of the city-state's economic history that synthesises and adds to our knowledge of the past; in so doing, it may illuminate the nation's future. Adopting a narrative, albeit analytical approach, it covers macroeconomic events, microeconomic occurrences, living standards and socio-economic welfare, all of which are not discussed in detail in extant histories of Singapore such as Mary Turnbull's classic *History of Modern Singapore* (2009). The book's intended audience comprises historians, teachers and students; we also hope it will be of interest to the general public.

This book has been long in the making. Its genesis can be traced to the year 2007 when the authors met at a conference at which the second author presented his work on the reconstructed national income accounts of colonial Singapore. While that could have provided the initial motivation for the book, the idea for it germinated only at an *izakaya* in Shinjuku, Tokyo over glasses of beer. But caught up in our professional careers, the project came to fruition only five years ago when writing began. In the interim, we published three journal articles on the economic history of Singapore, material from which has been included in this book together with historical GDP statistics. Planning and conceptualisation took place in late 2020 when the first author spent a semester as a Visiting Professor in the Faculty of Economics at Soka University, where a major part of the book was written. A second stint in the same position during the winter of 2022 led to the drafting and redrafting of various chapters. He is grateful to the university and Deans Jyunichi Kanzaka and Isao Takagi for their kind hospitality during these visits.

Although we rely to a large extent on historical data to tell the economic story of Singapore, our view is that statistics almost certainly do not provide a complete picture. Despite our quantitative approach, moreover, we do not subscribe to the cliometric view that the task of economic history is the fructification of economic theory or that it is a type of applied economics. Rather, our aim is the more modest one of narrating historical events of economic significance as they unfolded and refraining as much as possible from passing judgement. In this respect, the British colonial authorities truly deserved their reputation as meticulous record-keepers. Where primary documents, information and data from the colonial archives or contemporary accounts have been compiled or documented, we rely on a careful reading of them to discern the underlying narrative. These materials are gathered from the Lee Kong Chian Reference Library in Singapore, the National Archives of Singapore and the National Archives of Malaysia, whose staff we would like to acknowledge for their assistance. When secondary sources are available, we consult these rather than return to the primary material; in many cases however, we have had to fill in gaps through resorting to the latter or newspaper articles. The full possibilities of Western travelogues, memoirs and anecdotal vignettes are also exploited to reconstruct the reality of the past and to convey memorable images.

The plethora of statistics on Singapore available to us as economic historians does not mean that they are free from error. Quite often, these are lacunose data which require patching by interpolation or other techniques. The accuracy or bias of the colonial statistics cited is also difficult to ascertain with any degree of certainty. The early censuses of population were not always accurate, and sometimes rife with mistakes, while the same can be said of other data; in particular, trade figures were not complete due to Singapore's free port status and smuggling activities. Difficulties in social measurement also stemmed from the migratory and multicultural nature of the population, the lack of manpower dedicated to the collection of statistics and the impenetrability of the island's interior in the early days. After Singapore became a Crown Colony in 1867, it was often lumped together with the Straits Settlements or British Malaya in the published statistics, and many researchers (including ourselves) have had to ingeniously (or ingenuously) separate them. By contrast, the modern period is replete with much improved and more reliable data, so we use them with less reservation. Where footnotes do not indicate the source, the economic and social statistics for this period are extracted from the Singapore Department of Statistics website.

In acknowledging our further debts of gratitude for the book, we would like to express our deep appreciation to Atsushi Kobayashi of Tokyo University for making available his comprehensive dataset on Singapore's trade in the 19th century. The dataset consists of the export and import quantities and prices of 23 prominent commodities in Singapore's trade, including regional primary products, foodstuffs, opium, cotton and silk piece goods. The prices (and quantities) are obtained from local commercial newspapers from 1831 to 1864 and can therefore be viewed as wholesale prices.

The research grants given by the Japanese government have facilitated our project. These are a series of Grants-in-Aid for Scientific Research (C) and carry the reference numbers 21830131 (2009–10), 23530422 (2011–13), 26380442 (2014–17), 17K03861 (2017–21) and 20K01800 (2020–24).

Peter Schoppert, Gerald Jackson and Lena Qua at NUS Press showed interest in the book early on and we are grateful to them for shepherding us through the exacting publication process, including giving us valuable comments. In addition, we thank Gerald and his company Bookwerk for drawing the maps found in the book. And of course, we are deeply indebted to our editor Barnard Turner for greatly improving the text and exposition.

Lastly, we thank our families, friends and colleagues for their moral support during the writing of the book.

Keen Meng Choy
Ichiro Sugimoto
October 2025

Prologue

In the various phases of its economic history, Singapore has been a regional port city, an entrepôt, a staple port and a global city. These roles were not unique to specific periods but tended to evolve and overlap such that in transitioning to a new era, the city generally continued to fulfil the economic functions of the previous period. Thus, when Singapore became a staple port in the late 19th century, it remained an entrepôt of some importance. Even in the 21st century when it transformed into a global city, the re-export trade was still conducted—albeit for a different mix of commodities. Throughout the different epochs, Singapore in its various roles has stayed as a totally open economy, connected to the world via trade, investment, human migration, the exchange of ideas and, in the latest phase, technological links and knowledge networks. In this sense, the island has existed as a global city at least since the early 19th century. It grew and prospered by leveraging on the world economy, underpinned by the long-held principle of free trade.

For the whole of its history, Singapore's survival was predicated on being economically relevant and useful to the region or the world, as the case may be. In its early incarnation in the 14th century as an autonomous port city, it fulfilled the need for a commercial emporium in the Southeast Asian region to conduct the flourishing trade with China and countries farther afield. Lying at the heart of the region, Temasek, as it was then known, inherited this role from Palembang during the ascendancy of the Srivijaya empire and subsequently relinquished it to the Melaka kingdom. As a regional emporium, the port city exchanged the native produce of the Malay Peninsula and Eastern Archipelago for the manufactured products of China and India. Singapore therefore existed for the sole reason of servicing the trade with China that opened up during the Song dynasty. As a collecting centre, it was able to supply the Straits produce demanded by the Celestial Kingdom.

After a long period of economic dormancy from the 15th to the 18th centuries the rediscovery of Singapore in 1819 was due almost entirely to the vision and exertions of one man—Sir Thomas Stamford Raffles. Yet its timing during the dawning era of Western imperialism was opportunistic, as the British East India Company sought to engage its Dutch rival in the maritime trade of the East Indies. Singapore at the time was seen as a fallback for the opium-for-tea trade between India and China. But that did not transpire and instead, the city grew rapidly to become the premier entrepôt of Southeast Asia. In the early 19th century, it also went through a relatively brief agricultural period during which the cultivation of gambier and pepper on the island was a major economic activity that attracted the earliest immigrants from China. As it turned out, this period became the first of only two episodes in Singapore's economic history in which commerce with the region and the world did not predominate.

By the mid-19th century, however, the island had relegated agricultural pursuits to the neighbouring state of Johor and turned to international trade as the means of livelihood. In this role, Singapore's economic function was threefold: intermediation of the East–West long-distance trade, the circulation of indigenous commodities within Southeast Asia, and the distribution of manufactured goods to the region. Except for the farther reach of the produce trade all the way to Europe, enabled by the presence of Western agency houses in the city which organised and financed Singapore's commerce, these activities were not that different from those in the bygone Temasek era. Other new actors during this period were the Chinese middlemen who, acting as factotums, linked native producers in the region with the Western firms.

As a part of the Straits Settlements, Singapore became a Crown Colony in 1867—an event that more or less coincided with two other momentous developments. First, the opening of the Suez Canal in 1869 and the introduction of steamships led to a fall in the cost of maritime transportation. Second, the British political advance into Malaya in 1874 enabled the country's rich tin resources to be mined on a commercial scale and exported through Singapore. Hence, the city transformed into a staple port *par excellence*, a role it would assume for the next 70 years. Tin would bring about a new prosperity and attract massive immigration from China, while at the same time extending Singapore's economic hinterland from just the state of Johor to include the whole of Malaya. Domestically, the increase in population resulted in a more diverse labour market and the emergence of modern occupations, while at the same time forcing the colonial government to improve the city's social infrastructure. In the last 30 years of the 19th century, Singapore's trade flows accelerated on account of both staple and entrepôt exports.

Alongside the advent of rubber as Malaya's next major staple product in the early 20th century, the Dutch East Indies became a second hinterland for Singapore, where smallholder cultivators of rubber added significantly to supply. Unlike the Chinese-dominated tin industry, the rubber industry in Malaya was a Western enterprise right from the outset. The agency houses in Singapore took on the tasks of financing investment in, and the management of, large plantations on behalf of listed companies in Britain. The migrant labour needed for the rubber estates came from India, who like the Chinese immigrants before them altered the country's demographic make-up. Compared with tin, rubber provided greater wealth for Malaya and Singapore because of its more extensive economic interlinkages; in particular, it transformed Singapore into the most important centre in the region for the processing and export of milled rubber to the West. A further indirect benefit was the expansion and modernisation of Singapore's port to accommodate increased trade volumes. In addition, the rubber industry created Chinese tycoons who were then able to diversify into other economic areas, especially banking. The long boom associated with rubber therefore resulted in the further commercialisation and financialisation of Singapore until it was interrupted by the Great Depression of the early 1930s.

Following the end of the Second World War, Singapore sought to obtain self-government and eventually independence from Britain. Concurrently, it was confronted with the decline of the staple and entrepôt trades as neighbouring countries established direct shipping links with faraway markets and set up their own primary processing industries. Thus forced to industrialise so as to provide jobs for its burgeoning population, Singapore initially opted for an import substitution policy in conjunction with a merger with Malaya. The attempt failed, however, compelling the independent nation's leaders to resort to foreign investment and multinationals to launch its manufacturing drive. This export-oriented industrialisation strategy was spectacularly successful, turning the island into a major production base for companies from the United States, Europe and East Asia. Singapore's venture into manufacturing in the modern era was thus only the second time in its history that trade and commercial activities did not serve as the sole engine of economic growth. After weathering a recession in the mid-1980s, the city also became a services hub for the region and its financial centre. During the 1990s, both the manufacturing and service sectors upgraded into more capital-intensive and high value-added activities, resulting in an improvement in living standards that was enhanced by the state's comprehensive provision of education, health and housing amenities.

Having attained developed country status by the end of the 20th century, Singapore at the turn of the new millennium harboured an even more ambitious goal: to become a global city. To this end, the city's physical landscape was given a facelift with new iconic buildings and entertainment venues. As Singapore aimed to compete in the league of places like London and New York, it assiduously cultivated foreign talent from all over the world while at the same time changing the focus in industrial policy to a knowledge-based and innovation-driven economy. In this global city configuration, Singapore continued to be firmly embedded within the international system of production fragmentation. Apart from remaining a major crossroads of international trade, its role was to serve as a regional headquarters and logistical centre for multinationals to direct economic activities and coordinate supply chains in Asia. In addition, it became a high-technology manufacturing platform and services hub. Hence, Singapore's status as a global city was undergirded by its ability to secure a pivotal position within changing economic geographies defined by transnational corporations' global production networks. This was in turn dependent on a highly successful developmental state that was able to build the hard and "soft" infrastructures required to enhance global connectivity and attract global resource flows.

In narrating Singapore's economic development over the ages, the chapters in this book focus on describing *how* the city succeeded throughout the different phases of its existence. *Why* it succeeded is a more difficult question to answer. Possible explanations can be found in considering the work of great men coupled with enlightened political leadership, pragmatism in responding to change, the absence of policy choices given the country's smallness and vulnerability, and pure luck. In all of these scenarios, agents of historical change in Singapore were driven by an overriding instinct for economic survival. This observation explains the underlying logic of many of the country's policy decisions and institutional development. From a social Darwinian perspective, Singapore got the basics right because it had to get them right or else perish.

Furthermore, as the book makes clear, its political and business leaders either had to live by their wits, as during the colonial period, or, in the modern era, were imbued with a crisis consciousness. For most of the time, they have had to take economic policy decisions in highly constrained environments, leaving them with little choice but to tackle problems head-on and creatively. The constant external challenges faced by the country therefore made for pragmatism and adaptability in policymaking. Another way to put these ideas across is that in Singapore, the factors that conditioned the actions taken by economic agents at critical historical junctures made for the correct choices. We therefore believe the city's economic success was ultimately due to its specific historical circumstances and imperatives.

Countries do not grow rich by chance. The current level of prosperity in Singapore is the result of long-run processes and long-standing political and economic features. This of course is an illustration of path dependence in history. As a satellite of the British empire, Singapore benefitted from being an integral part of its vast colonial economy. The city inherited a formidable physical infrastructure, global economic networks and legal-institutional arrangements that were to stand it in good stead when independence came. So the adage "to those who have, will be given" seems appropriate here. Economic policies matter too, especially in the modern period, although this contention begs the question of why the correct policies were chosen and brings us back to the "survival of the fittest" reasoning. But luck cannot be said to be totally absent, if only because Singapore had as its coloniser the most advanced and richest country in the world at the time. The island was lucky to be situated where it is and lucky to have had Stamford Raffles and Lee Kuan Yew. Counterfactually speaking, the country's economic history in modern times would probably have turned out very differently if the Communists had taken power in the 1950s.

In terms of historiography, it is best to view Singapore's economic progress over the *longue durée* as a hybrid between linear and cyclic processes, but without teleological momentum. That is to say, cycles of trade and commerce recurred in Singapore's economic history; nevertheless, there was a progression through time as foundations were laid for the next phase. This progress was however disjointed and punctuated by a long hiatus. In this framing, the timeless constant was the island's geographical location, which provides the setting for the passage of historical economic events, or *histoire événementielle*. Spatial-temporal dependence is most evident in the transition from colonial rule to political independence but it also operates as we move from the present to the future because of the irreversible investments made in physical infrastructure, buildings, machinery, equipment and human capabilities acquired through education and training.

If this hypothesis is correct, there is no reason why Singapore cannot continue to survive and thrive as long as it keeps adapting to changing external circumstances and reinventing itself. Hence, the future Singapore will be a continuously evolving and historically contingent entity; that, however, does not rule out the possibility of "history repeating itself". Indeed, the future may well resemble the past, as revealed by several recurrent themes in the economic history narrated in this book.

The first theme traced in the book is that Singapore has flourished regardless of the form of governance, and whether or not it existed as an independent polity or as a part of a larger entity. Thus, it has been independent only during the Temasek and modern periods; in between, it was ruled first by the East India Company and then as a Crown Colony of the British empire, and for a short period, as part of Malaysia. Yet despite these variations, the city consistently excelled. During the oppressive period when it was governed from India, it thrived because the merchant community vigorously and successfully resisted the imposition of trade duties and the use of the Indian rupee currency. In the colonial period, Singapore was given considerable autonomy to formulate its own policies; when this was not the case, during the merger with Malaysia, it chose to leave. The withdrawal from Malaysia turned out to be a blessing in disguise that allowed Singapore's leaders the freedom to pursue their own economic policies.

A second theme is that due to its small size, the island had always depended on one dominant or a few major commodities to prosper. When it was known as Temasek, it specialised in exporting lakawood, hornbill casques and blackwood, for which it was famous. During the early colonial era, the planting and marketing of gambier were dominant, followed by the trading and export of tin and rubber later on. In modern times, the production of electronic goods enabled the city-state to raise incomes and living standards substantially. In wave after wave of economic development brought on by technological progress, Singapore was able to capitalise on the rise in global demand for its products. A historicist dynamic in the dialectical sense seemed to be at work, in that the decline of one commodity was followed soon after by another that led to a new growth phase. The city was therefore fortunate that Straits produce and tin deposits existed in abundance in its neighbouring regions and that rubber plantations flourished in their tropical soils; in the most recent case of electronics, Singapore and other East Asian countries were the beneficiaries of the phenomenon of multinational outsourcing in the advanced industrial economies.

The third but by no means last recurring theme in Singapore's economic history is investment in physical infrastructure and social capital. Such outlays have been a feature of the city's success story since colonial days, regardless of whether they were undertaken by the public or private sector. Social services were no doubt neglected in the early 19th century but these gradually improved over time. And when the privately owned port facilities became antiquated at the turn of the 20th century, the colonial government intervened to take control of the port and to undertake much needed investment. State provision of infrastructure and human capital investment in education and healthcare have become even more marked in the modern period. The nation's leaders recognised that Singapore has no resources other than its people, excellent location and natural harbour, and hence these expenditures were necessary to give the city-state a competitive edge. There are other sequences of events that have played out similarly in the different epochs covered in the book.

The ultimate objective of the book is to unravel the enigma of Singapore. The reader is enjoined to ask the dual questions of "What is Singapore?" and "What will it be?". Notwithstanding tremendous advances in technology, Singapore's fundamental economic functions have not changed much during its evolution from regional entrepôt in the 14th century, to colonial port city in the 19th and 20th centuries, and finally to a global city-state in the 21st century. Reflecting continuity in change, its role has always been to serve as the intermediary in the exchange of tradable goods and services between and within Southeast Asia, China and India on the one hand and the Western world on the other. In this context, Singapore transformed the region, but was itself transformed in the process. The increasing servicisation of its economy suggests that Singapore may be returning to its roots, once the manufacturing phase passes. This raises the question of what, by learning from the past, may be conjectured of the future. One key lesson is that the "tyranny of distance" will still matter despite globalisation, hyper-globalisation or deglobalisation, as present trends suggest. If this prognosis turns out to be correct, Singapore's destiny is to remain with Southeast Asia as its economic hub. Stretching the logic a bit further, the city has been the metropolis and *de facto* capital of the region at least since the colonial period and it could very well become the *de jure* capital in time to come.

What of the not too distant future? Singapore looks set to continue being a manufacturing-cum-service economy; the line between these two types of activity has blurred with the servicisation of manufacturing. It will continue to depend on the world economy to grow with all the vagaries this brings. But there is nothing it can do about these fluctuations except learning how to live with periodic recessions, financial crises and epidemics. By the same token, Singapore will continue to rely heavily on multinationals, government-linked companies and foreign labour for its economic survival, a long-standing weakness of the economy that has not been remedied. Its short record to date as a knowledge-based economy founded on research and development is similarly a work-in-progress, and the city-state still has some way to go to become an innovation hub. Whatever the outcome on this score, Singapore will face the dilemma of being simultaneously a global city and a nation-state: the conflict between the requirements of being a cosmopolis and the demands of a local citizenry will surface from time to time. The inherent tension between these two identities was not present when Singapore was a colony since the overarching objective of the British rulers was economic development, resulting in the persistence of a poor underclass. But as a nation now, the country cannot neglect the economic well-being of its less successful denizens. A failure to resolve the income inequality problem would lead to a weakening of the social cohesion that has helped the city-state to succeed so far. But if the past is any guide to the future, Singapore will successfully overcome this and other new challenges that may arise.

Chapter 1 | Regional Port City, 1299–1396

To fully appreciate the economic history of Singapore, we have to venture back in time to the pre-modern epoch and begin with the island's location in both its geographical and historical contexts. Such a *longue durée* approach integrates space and time in a unified narrative that spans more than seven hundred years, extending through the colonial and up to the modern eras. The geographical boundaries of Singapore's economic past are terraqueous, extending to island and mainland Southeast Asia, its seas and climatic conditions. Most important of all was the command of the maritime trade route between East and West, from China to India and Persia. The historical contours have similarly been shaped by the impact of external events and more particularly, by the entanglements of Singapore, as a independent or colonial state, with the polities of the Malay world, amidst the rise and fall of successive commercial emporia.[1] Technological and economic changes over the centuries have not altered these *immobilisés* in place and time.

Geographical Background and Early History

The defining features of Singapore and the region around it are the tropical heat and humidity. Lying one-and-a-half degrees above the Equator, the island stands at the southern extremity of the Straits of Melaka, straddling the Indian Ocean on one side and the South China Sea on the other. In consequence, it occupies a geographically and economically strategic position in Southeast Asia and is also blessed with a natural deep harbour port. The coastline is indented by the estuaries of several rivers, the most important of which is the Singapore River. Singapore's present total land area is 735.7 square kilometres, of which one-fifth has been reclaimed from the sea. Almost all of the current population of six million people live on the main island, although the nation's territory includes the surrounding islets. Owing to Singapore's geographical position and maritime exposure, the climate is tropical rainforest: there is uniformly high temperature, abundant precipitation all through the year and no absolute distinction of seasons. The thermometer ranges from 28°C to 33°C on most days, fluctuating with the occurrence of showers which tend to be short but occasionally heavy. A coolness descends in the night and early morning when the

[1] C.O. Blagden, "Singapore Prior to 1819", in *One Hundred Years of Singapore,* vol. I, ed. W. Makepeace, G.E. Brooke and R. St.J. Braddell (London: John Murray, 1921), p. 5; P. Regnier, *Singapore, City-State in Southeast Asia* (Honolulu: University of Hawaii Press, 1991), pp. 1–2.

temperature drops to 24°C, even while the heat of the day is alleviated by rainfall and an ever present sea breeze.

With an unremarkable land topography made up mainly of granitic hills, ridges and flat alluvial soils, the geographical constant that has had the greatest import on Singapore's economic history is the sea around the island, together with the monsoon winds that lash it. As an ancient saying goes, "The land divides but the sea unites". The maritime communication afforded by the seas and the monsoon winds had for the longest time been the only means of reaching Singapore (Map 1). These winds blow in a southwesterly direction from June to September and a northeasterly direction from November to February, converging centripetally on Singapore and bringing drier and wetter seasons with them. The former monsoon is caused by the rush of cool air from central Asia where pressure is high towards the warmer and lower pressure tropical oceans and Australasia, while the latter results when the pattern reverses.

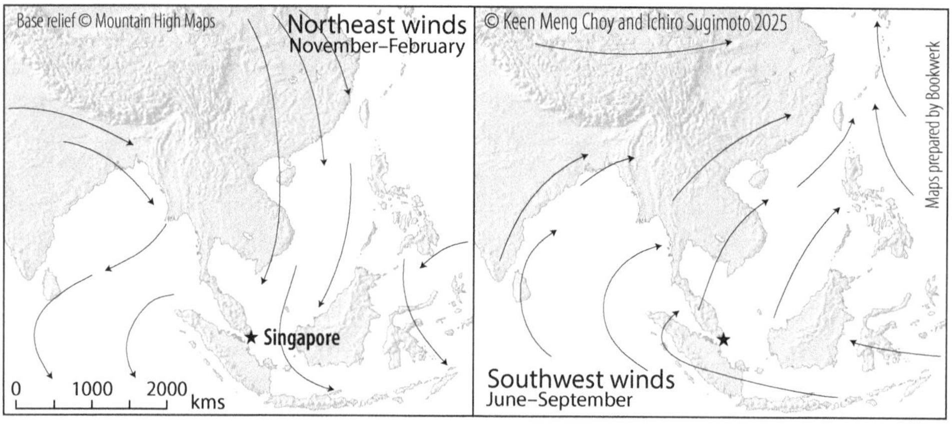

Map 1. The Monsoon Winds in Asia.

During the southwest monsoon, the obstruction of the winds by the mountains of Sumatra gives rise to the "Sumatra squalls" that used to terrorise sailors. Heralded by the beckoning dark clouds from the south coast, they buffet the island with their strong gusts, thunder and showers. This notwithstanding, the regularity of the monsoonal winds very early on opened up the possibility of maritime trade in the Southeast Asian subcontinent extending to the Bay of Bengal, aided by the iso-directional flow of ocean currents. Hence, these winds were also called "trade winds", propelling ships from the Indian Ocean to the East Indies and junks from China towards the Eastern Archipelago. In the age of sailing ships, Singapore was a convenient stopover to replenish supplies and the ideal resting place as mariners waited for the winds to change.

Much the same can be said, writ large, of the geographical landscape and climatic conditions of Southeast Asia as of Singapore; indeed, it is the influence of a homogeneous climate of constant sunlight and heavy rainfall that confers the plenitude, luxuriance and variety of the Malay Archipelago's natural products, in turn giving rise to trade. There are however regional variations in the geographic environment spawned by the ring of fire that encircles the islands making up Sumatra, Java, Sulawesi and the Philippines due to the subduction of the Australian tectonic plate, rendering them susceptible to seismic activity. Yet these are the regions with the most fertile volcanic soils and hence the densest populations; elsewhere, the rich and variegated fauna attracted sparser human settlements. On mainland Southeast Asia, the higher elevation and presence of a dry season created forests suitable for supporting diverse populations of deer, elephants, tigers and rhinoceros, making the trade in derived animal products lucrative right from the beginning. Finally in the great river deltas of the Mekong and Chao Phraya, rice growing was enabled by the alternation of dry and wet seasons, combined with annual flooding. Thus, while the uniformity of produce due to the relatively homogeneous climate reduced the scope for economic exchange within and outside the region, geological heterogeneity and biodiversity enhanced it.

Of importance to Singapore's history is the scholarly conclusion that a great expansion of maritime trade took place from the 10th to the 14th centuries between China and the Malay Archipelago, not long after the advent of the Song dynasty. This event was initiated during the reign of Emperor Shenzong (r. 1068–85) and continued under the Yuan dynasty that succeeded the Song. Overcoming the Confucian prejudice against commerce, a shift in Chinese imperial trade policy was instituted against a backdrop of wider economic reforms. The statesman Wang Anshi in particular made far-reaching changes to improve the state's fiscal management by reducing military expenditure and increasing revenue through monopolies and foreign trade, all carried out in an economy undergoing rapid monetisation.[2] To this end, the ban on the export of copper coins from China was lifted in 1074, alongside a large increase in the domestic money supply. Restrictions governing foreign trade, including importantly the previous ban on private trade, were relaxed in 1090 in an effort to woo foreign merchants from the *Nan-hai* (that is, Southeast Asia, literally the South Seas) and beyond to China's coastal ports to trade in novel products. These inducements led to an increase in maritime trade with the Malay Archipelago to heights not seen since the Tang period. As a result, the Song state collected enormous revenues from taxes on seafaring vessels, import tariffs and the monopoly in selected products.[3]

The booming trade with China could be effected only if there were a main entrepôt in the region serving as a commercial emporium. Ever since the seventh century, the port of Palembang in South Sumatra had performed both this role and that of the political capital of the thalassocratic Srivijaya empire which ruled most of the Eastern Archipelago. At the sub-regional level, smaller local ports served as collecting centres and feeder points.[4] To Palembang were brought the native commodities of Southeast Asia such as spices, aromatic woods, rhinoceros horns, ivory, birds' nests and tin, while Chinese products such as ceramics, porcelain, silk, satin, sulphur, copper, iron, salt and sugar were delivered there in return.[5] The Sino-Malay trade in those days was in turn linked to the long-distance

---

[2] R. von Glahn, *The Economic History of China: From Antiquity to the Nineteenth Century* (Cambridge University Press, 2016), pp. 236–7.

[3] G. Wade, "An Early Age of Commerce in Southeast Asia, 900–1300 CE", *Journal of Southeast Asian Studies* 40, 2 (2009): 224.

[4] Ng Chin Keong, *Boundaries and Beyond: China's Maritime Southeast in Late Imperial Times* (Singapore: NUS Press, 2017), p. 26.

[5] P. Wheatley, *The Golden Khersonese: Studies in the Historical Geography of the Malay Peninsula Before A.D. 1500* (Kuala Lumpur: University of Malaya Press, 1961), pp. 73–4.

East–West trade through the Maritime Silk Road, the seaborne version of the overland Silk Road.[6] This global maritime trade network with its smaller regional arteries extended from China to Southeast Asia, then to the Indian subcontinent, and thenceforth to the Arabian Peninsula and Europe.

The Malay Archipelago proved to be central to the Maritime Silk Road after Arab and Persian traders established extensive trade linkages between Asia and the Middle East via the ports of the Indian subcontinent. They carried African and Western Asian products like gems, frankincense, pearls and cloves to coastal China in exchange for spices, fragrances, ceramics, silk, tea and iron wares.[7] These developments subsequently ushered in what has been called an "Early Age of Commerce" in Southeast Asia that lasted from *circa* 900 to 1300.[8] The onset of this epoch spurred political, economic and social changes throughout the Malay region and populations expanded. The centralising hegemony of Srivijaya was weakened as a result, allowing newly autonomous port polities to emerge. Palembang increasingly found its role usurped by these ports which traded directly with China. After its late capital of Jambi was sacked in 1275, the Srivijaya empire went into decline and it was succeeded by the Java-based Majapahit empire in the late thirteenth century. This is where Singapore comes into the story.

The Economy of Temasek

Extant sources tell us that Singapore's known economic history began with a kingdom located on the island seven hundred years ago, purportedly founded by a prince from Sumatra. That it existed as an independent port city with a succession of sovereign rulers and was given the name Temasek (sea town) is also beyond doubt. Open to historical conjecture are however the nature and extent of its trade with polities both neighbouring and more distant, as well as the scope of its economic activity. Evidence on this activity is scant; archaeological artefacts inform our current knowledge but other traces of material culture vanished when the port was sacked by invading forces from the Majapahit empire a mere century after its establishment, following attacks by the Siamese kingdom.[9] Just as Temasek came into being as a result of the need for a commercial hub in the region after Palembang's decline to exploit the trade opportunities with China, the vacuum left by its demise was filled by Melaka, in turn apparently founded by the last ruler of Temasek.

In terms of its urban layout, Temasek was built very much in the mould of classical Malay port cities, modelled in particular on the Srivijayan capital of Palembang.[10] Its key

---

[6] von Glahn, *Economic History of China*, pp. 270–1.

[7] Ng Chin Keong, "At the Crossroads of the Maritime Silk Route", in *Maritime Heritage of Singapore*, ed. Aileen Lau and Laure Lau (Singapore: Subtree, 2005), p. 64; J.A.E. Morley, "The Arabs and the Eastern Trade", *Journal of the Malayan Branch of the Royal Asiatic Society* 22, 1 (1849): 145.

[8] Wade, "An Early Age of Commerce", pp. 221–65. See however a dissenting view by V. Lieberman, "Maritime Influences in Southeast Asia, c. 900–1300: Some Further Thoughts", *Journal of Southeast Asian Studies* 41, 3 (2010): 529–39.

[9] Victor R. Savage, *Lion City Narratives: Singapore Through Western Eyes* (Singapore: World Scientific, 2022), pp. 63, 64–5.

[10] Kwa Chong Guan, Derek Heng and Tan Tai Yong, *Singapore: A 700-Year History* (Singapore: National Archives of Singapore, 2009), pp. 37–8.

features would have included a hill, a foothill plain and a river basin well suited to religious, political and economic activities. From what is known, it has been postulated that Temasek was a "port of trade" where the international exchange of goods was undertaken by the ruler and his emissaries through a system of tributes and equivalences of value, rather than calculations of market prices.[11] Whether or not this was the case, it is not possible to arrive at an estimate of the volume or value of goods traded by the port city. The aggregate value of economic output in Temasek is also unquantifiable. However, the breath if not the depth of this *ancien regime* and the economic livelihood of its people can to a reasonable degree be inferred from documentary accounts and artefactual evidence.

The available evidence suggests that Temasek was an urbanised, thriving and densely populated settlement of traders, merchants and craftsmen who inhabited the foothill plain on the north bank of the Singapore River, overseen by a palace precinct on the site of present day Fort Canning Hill.[12] A *rialto* or market where foreign traders and locals met to exchange products is likely to have existed around the vicinity of the river.[13] The seasonal rhythms of economic life in Temasek and the seas around it would throb and ease with the arrivals of the monsoons, during which time the port would fill up with sailing ships big and small. Textual records further suggest that the Temasek ecumene could have extended to the southernmost tip of the island where bands of local pirates and *orang laut* (sea nomads) appeared to have lived side-by-side with a Chinese community.[14]

The total population of Temasek is uncertain, although an estimate derived from archaeological discoveries suggests a few thousand, possibly up to 10,000 inhabitants.[15] This would place the settlement as a port of immense size in its time and place; contemporaneous port polities such as Aceh in North Sumatra had a population of only 2,000 to 3,000.[16] The large population is itself a clear sign of wealth, matching up well with the evidence provided by archaeological artefacts.[17]

It is likely that the urban population of Temasek grew through immigration to accommodate the diversity of economic activity carried out on the island. In fact, the large quantity and heterogeneity of material remnants that were unearthed around the Singapore River basin—ceramics, stoneware, earthenware pottery, glassware, jewellery and Chinese copper coins—and their distribution patterns attest to the co-existence of plutocratic and plebeian sub-populations in Temasek, who enjoyed a generally high, albeit differentiated, level of per capita consumption. Specifically, the discovery on Fort Canning Hill of gold

[11] J.N. Miksic, "14th-Century Singapore: A Port of Trade", in *Early Singapore: 1300s–1819*, ed. J.N. Miksic and Cheryl-Ann Low Mei Gek (Singapore: Singapore History Museum, 2004), pp. 42–3.

[12] Derek Heng, "Reconstructing Banzu, A Fourteenth Century Port Settlement in Singapore", *Journal of the Malayan Branch of the Royal Asiatic Society* 75, 1 (2002): 72.

[13] F. Braudel, *The Mediterranean and the Mediterranean World in the Age of Phillip II*, vol. I (University of California Press, 1966), pp. 313, 315.

[14] Wheatley, *The Golden Khersonese*, p. 82.

[15] J.N. Miksic, "Temasik to Singapura: Singapore in the 14th to 15th Centuries", in *Singapore from Temasek to the 21st Century: Reinventing the Global City*, ed. K. Hack, J. Margolin with K. Delaye (Singapore: NUS Press, 2010), p. 110.

[16] Heng, "Reconstructing Banzu", p. 75.

[17] M. McCormick, *Origins of the European Economy* (Cambridge University Press, 2001), p. 30; Braudel, *The Mediterranean*, pp. 322, 325–8, 334–8.

ornaments as well as high-quality and rare artefacts made in China testifies to the presence of an elite with luxurious tastes.[18]

It would appear that the economy of Temasek in the 14th century was anchored on all the main tiers of productive activity: primary, secondary and tertiary. Accounts dating from the early 19th century—including John Crawfurd's celebrated morning stroll around Fort Canning Hill in 1822—stating that the southern slope of the hill was planted with fruit trees provide a hint of limited agricultural activity, although in view of the relatively small area inhabited and infertility of the soil, rice and victuals were probably imported.[19] Temasek's residents and the orang laut could have exported one or two vegetable and fruit crops, but they certainly harvested for sale forest and marine products such as hornbill casques, lakawood, tin, tortoise shells, sea slugs and sea cucumbers.[20] The first two of these native products of Southeast Asia were available in abundance in the island itself and the rest in Temasek's immediate neighbourhoods of Johor and the Riau Archipelago.[21] In addition, the Portuguese apothecary Tome Pires reported that Temasek boasted an exclusive product called blackwood used for making furniture.[22]

The port appears to have enjoyed a wide product range of goods. The early 14th century Chinese trader Wang Dayuan, whose travel account is a key textual source on Temasek, mentioned the distilling of rice wine at the port.[23] Moreover, the decorations and shapes of native pottery found in excavation sites in Singapore indicate a provenance that could be Temasek itself or the surrounding region.[24] Trade appears to have also allowed the port city to engage in pre-industrial manufacturing through the import of materials. The thousands of glass beads of varying colours and shards of glass vessels excavated from one specific location at Fort Canning Hill are especially intriguing for the intimation that bead-working and recycling of glassware to manufacture decorative items such as necklaces, bracelets and bangles took place, presumably by skilled craftsmen in the royal precinct.[25] On the river plain, copper and bronze working by artisans has been posited, based on the discovery of

[18] Miksic, "Temasik to Singapura", p. 121.

[19] J. Crawfurd, *Journal of an Embassy from the Governor-General of India to the Courts of Bangkok and Cochin-China,* vol. 1 (London: Colbum, 1828), p. 47; Derek Heng, "Casting Singapore's History in the Longue Durée", in *Singapore from Temasek to the 21st Century*, ed. Hack, Margolin with Delaye, p. 62. A similar account to Crawfurd's was provided by Munshi Abdullah, Raffles' Malay teacher and interpreter, in his *Hikayat Abdullah*, trans. A.R. Hill (Kuala Lumpur: Malaysian Branch of the Royal Asiatic Society, 2009), p. 168. However, a contemporary source noted that "The fields are barren and there is little padi". Wheatley, *The Golden Khersonese*, p. 82.

[20] Heng, "Reconstructing Banzu", p. 80; Miksic, "Temasik to Singapura", p. 123.

[21] Wheatley, *The Golden Khersonese*, p. 87.

[22] Tome Pires, *The Suma Oriental of Tome Pires: An Account of the East, From the Red Sea to Japan, Written in Malacca and India in 1512–1515,* vol. 1, trans. Armando Cortesao (London: The Hakluyt Society, 1944), p. 123.

[23] Wheatley, *The Golden Khersonese*, p. 83.

[24] J.N. Miksic, *Singapore and the Silk Road of the Sea, 1300–1800* (Singapore: NUS Press and National Museum of Singapore, 2013), pp. 266–7.

[25] Miksic, "Temasik to Singapura", pp. 122, 127.

copper prills, wire fragments, bronze and copper fish hooks, bronze bars and bells.[26] This strongly indicates that industrial workshops existed at the time.

Some scholars of Singapore's antiquity have even postulated that Chinese copper coins were melted down by the inhabitants of Temasek to be recast into other products. This claim was based on the discovery of numerous copper coins found in the Singapore River area, dating mostly from the Northern Song period. While it is known that the large-scale export of copper coins from China to Southeast Asia occurred during the late 11th century, the question of the precise role they played in the Sino-Malay trade and the exact monetary functions they performed in Temasek are still unsettled.[27] Nevertheless, the findings bear witness to the monetised and developed nature of Temasek's economy, although barter trade would also have been common. Archaeological data from elsewhere point to the widespread adoption of these coins for market transactions and official payments following their significant inflow into the region.[28] Furthermore, their use in commercial exchange in Temasek and at least one other roughly contemporaneous port city, Kota Cina on the northeastern coast of Sumatra, can be ascertained from both archaeological and shipwreck data. In these two port settlements, Chinese copper coins were most likely used as a means of exchange in transactions between local residents and traders from China who arrived and departed annually in keeping with the monsoon seasons.[29] Both these ports hosted substantial Chinese populations, which would have facilitated the adoption of the copper currency. Unlike Kota Cina however, in Temasek Chinese coinage was not the exclusive trade currency, as evidenced by small quantities of Vietnamese and Javanese coin finds. Moreover, it seems that the use of copper coinage was not restricted to external commerce but as in other parts of the region, extended to domestic transactions, given the wide geographical distribution of the coin discoveries at both the hill and river sites.

The Trade of Temasek

Archaeological investigations carried out in Singapore during the last few decades enable us to infer the broad patterns of Temasek's trade in the 14th century. From the ceramic and pottery assemblages found at locations in close proximity to Singapore, several conclusions on the port's trade connections and the reach of its economic sphere can be drawn. But further excavations at other key ports of the Malay Archipelago will be needed to obtain a statistically defensible assessment of the size and significance of the trade carried out at Temasek.[30] One must also be aware of the potential biases of archaeological finds due to differential preservation of artefacts and the non-randomness of excavation and shipwreck sites.

---

[26] Shah Alam M. Zaini, *Metal Finds and Metal-Working at the Parliament House Complex, Singapore* (Ann Arbor: University of Michigan, 1997), p. 27.

[27] Derek Heng, "Export Commodity and Regional Currency: The Role of Chinese Copper Coins in the Melaka Straits, Tenth to Fourteenth Centuries", *Journal of Southeast Asian Studies* 37, 2 (2006): 179–80.

[28] J. Wisseman-Christie, "Money and Its Uses in the Javanese States of the Ninth to Fifteenth Centuries A.D.", *Journal of the Economic and Social History of the Orient* 39, 3 (1996), pp. 243–86.

[29] Clement Liew and P. Wilson, *A History of Money in Singapore* (Singapore: Talisman, 2021), p. 13.

[30] The other ports include Kota Cina, Palembang and Pengkalan Bujang in Kedah.

That said, archaeologists and historians have hypothesised that Temasek was an important regional trade entrepôt astride the Maritime Silk Road, serving a dual role as an export centre for indigenous products and as an import and distribution centre of foreign commodities.[31] The reason for this is not difficult to grasp: the polity was situated along the shortest East-West shipping lane past the Bengal littoral and through the Straits of Melaka, as compared to the longer and more hazardous journey down the west coast of Sumatra and through the Sunda Straits. Therefore, the material base of Temasek's economy was ultimately commerce, not agriculture or industry, and its affluence was the outcome of trade growth and market expansion. As an augury of what was to come in the 19th century, Temasek during its short existence served as an intermediary of both the East–West trade and intraregional commerce. In this role, it acted as a gateway into the international and regional economic system for its immediate area.[32] Hence, it was a cosmopolitan, multicultural and pluri-religious emporium.[33] Product-wise, the port facilitated the exchange of the indigenous jungle and sea products of the Malay Peninsula and the Riau Archipelago for a range of goods from China and textiles from India, which were used for both utilitarian and ceremonial purposes. Not even when the first Ming emperor banned private trade in 1368 was Temasek's commerce disrupted, for Chinese from the southern parts of the country simply resettled in Southeast Asia wherein they continued to facilitate the tributary trade that replaced the private commerce.[34]

The archaeological deposits in Singapore are about evenly divided between locally made and imported items.[35] While this should not be construed as a sign of balanced trade, it serves to highlight the complementary nature of domestic production and imports. With respect to export markets, Temasek probably shipped a variety of commodities to China, India, Sri Lanka, Indonesia, Thailand and Vietnam. Documentary sources reveal that diplomatic missions were dispatched to China and Vietnam to maintain friendly trade relations, much as in modern times.[36] Pottery, jewellery and other imported artefacts sourced from some of these markets have also been unearthed. However, it is not known whether Temasek's manufactured products were intended purely for domestic consumption or exported.[37]

Of all the markets, China was the most important. A highly developed trade network existed between Temasek and South China, involving a variegated range of products and commodities.[38] Wang Dayuan had stated that China imported native products from

[31] N. Norruddin, "*Sejarah Melayu*: Beginnings of Singapura", in *On Paper: Singapore Before 1867* (Singapore: National Library Board, 2019), p. 12.

[32] Heng, "Casting Singapore's History", p. 64.

[33] A. Reid, *A History of Southeast Asia: Critical Crossroads* (Wiley Blackwell, 2015), p. 65.

[34] F. Gipouloux, *The Asian Mediterranean: Port Cities and Trading Networks in China, Japan and Southeast Asia, 13th–21st Century* (Cheltenham: Edward Elgar, 2011), pp. 102–4.

[35] Miksic, *Singapore and the Silk Road*, p. 289.

[36] Ibid., pp. 181–2.

[37] J.N. Miksic, "Recent Archaeological Excavations in Singapore: A Comparison of Three Fourteenth-Century Sites", *Bulletin of the Indo-Pacific Prehistory Association* 20 (2000): 5.

[38] Derek Heng, "Economic Networks Between the Malay Region and the Hinterlands of Quanzhou and Guangzhou", in *Early Singapore*, ed. Miksic and Low, pp. 83–4; Ng, *Boundaries and Beyond*, p. 8.

Temasek and exported gold, satin, cotton cloth, porcelain and iron and copper pots.[39] Other imports were spices like nutmeg, cloves and pepper as well as sulphur.[40] In the case of exports, by far the largest category of artefacts discovered was that of ceramics from the Yuan and early Ming dynasties, consisting of porcelain, stoneware and earthenware. More simply decorated variants of these types have been found in the Riau Islands and Kota Cina, suggesting that a portion of Temasek's imports were re-exported. Most of the ceramics were kitchen wares such as dishes, bowls and basins used by the common people. As mentioned, the high-quality porcelain probably belonged to the ruling elite, since these wares were unearthed at the hill sites.

Stoneware jars, reminiscent of the amphorae used in the ancient Western world, have also been found in abundance in Singapore. Initially thought to have contained mercury—a highly sought after item in China—they are now believed to be used (or reused) as containers for a variety of foodstuffs.[41] The putative Chinese commodities transported in these storage jars were rice and rice wine, sugar and salt, all of which were already produced indigenously in the Malay Archipelago. The logical inference is that the Chinese varieties competed with the local products based on quality and maybe price, thus enabling the denizens of Temasek and others in the region to enjoy a greater variety of food items at competitive prices. Frequently, the Chinese substitutes could be produced at lower cost because of the more advanced methods used and the presence of economies of scale. Chinese producers also tailored their products to suit the preferences of their Southeast Asian consumers.[42]

As a result of the functions carried out by Temasek, the economies of the Malay Archipelago became integrated with that of Southern China, a development that was to be repeated in the early 21st century. For example, Fujian province was known to be a major producer of the glutinous rice used in making rice wine. The omnipresent jars would be suitable vessels for transporting this wine to Southeast Asia and their widespread distribution has led to the postulation that the product was in high demand by both the elite and masses.[43] The relative proximity of the maritime ports of Quanzhou and Guangzhou in China to ceramic kiln districts implies that, during the Yuan period, a substantial proportion of economic activity in these ports and the surrounding areas depended on the export trade to Southeast Asian markets.[44]

Singapura in the Age of Commerce

Singapore's golden age in ancient times came to an abrupt end in the final years of the 14th century. Temasek was renamed Singapura and continued to exist first as a vassal of the Melaka kingdom and later, in a shrunken role as a naval outpost of the succeeding Johor-

---

[39] Wheatley, *The Golden Khersonese*, p. 87.

[40] Ng, "At the Crossroads", pp. 65–6.

[41] Heng, "Economic Networks", pp. 79–80, 82, 86.

[42] B.W. Andaya and L.Y. Andaya, *A History of Early Southeast Asia, 1400–1830* (Cambridge University Press, 2015), pp. 30–1.

[43] Heng, "Economic Networks", p. 82.

[44] Miksic, *Singapore and the Silk Road*, p. 323.

Riau-Lingga sultanate.[45] Archaeological finds at the Kallang River estuary to the north of the port city, dated to the late Ming dynasty, bear witness to human habitation and trade, but on a scale that was far removed from the glory of Temasek.[46] In the early 17th century, the waters around Singapore became the battleground for the contest between Dutch and Portuguese forces for control of the Asian maritime trade.[47] After that, Singapore was historically barren and almost completely uninhabited—a *terra nullius*—for more than two hundred years until it was rediscovered in 1819.

Meanwhile, Southeast Asia entered its Age of Commerce when, under the Ming Yongle Emperor (r. 1402–25), the maritime trade between China and Southeast Asia experienced a renaissance into the 15th century, spearheaded by official tribute missions.[48] The fabled voyages of the Chinese Admiral Zheng He to Southeast Asia and Africa that were accompanied by private merchants are emblematic of these state-sponsored expeditions, following the repeal of the ban on foreign trade.[49] The admiral and his entourage stopped at Temasek in 1409 but the place was already deserted by then.[50] Instead, its successor Melaka as a vassal state of China exploited and benefitted tremendously from the tributary system, as did Ayutthaya in the Siamese kingdom, Java, and Pasai in north Sumatra. This long trade boom fuelled by maritime expansion started in about 1400, ebbed and flowed intermittently in the following century, and then peaked in the first three decades of the 1600s. In its early stage, the upswing was sustained by China's huge appetite for spices, especially pepper.[51] The end of the expansion, when it came in the mid-17th century was marked by an economic crisis in Europe and generalised declines in international trade and the concomitant flow of bullion to Asia, exacerbated by Dutch monopolistic practices.[52]

Concurrently with the Age of Commerce, the quest for spices in the 16th century led the rising European powers—first the Portuguese, then the Dutch, and later the English—to embark on voyages of discovery to India and the East Indies. The rivalries between these imperialist nations were such that there was no possibility of peaceful trading and co-existence—each had to drive the other out of the region to survive.[53] It was through these successive hegemonies to monopolise and divert the highly profitable spice trade, of which pepper was the most important, that Southeast Asia's products very early on

---

[45] Arthur Lim Joo-Jock, "Geographical Setting", in *A History of Singapore*, ed. Ernest Chew and Edwin Lee (Singapore: Oxford University Press, 1991), pp. 5–6.

[46] Blagden, "Singapore Prior to 1819", p. 4.

[47] Kwa, Heng and Tan, *Singapore: A 700-Year History*, pp. 73–5.

[48] A. Reid, "An 'Age of Commerce' in Southeast Asian History", *Modern Asian Studies* 24, 1 (1990): 5–6, 11.

[49] von Glahn, *Economic History of China*, pp. 287–8.

[50] L. Levathes, *When China Ruled the Seas: The Treasure Fleet of the Dragon Throne 1405–1433* (New York: Simon and Schuster, 1994), pp. 98–102.

[51] Ng, *Boundaries and Beyond*, pp. 7–8.

[52] von Glahn, *Economic History of China*, p. 310.

[53] K.N. Chaudhuri, "The World-System East Longitude 20°: The European Role in Asia 1500–1750", *Review (Fernand Braudel Centre)* 5, 2 (1981): 229.

found their way into world markets.[54] In return for the exports of pepper from Java and Sumatra, nutmeg, mace and cloves from the Moluccas, silk and sugar from Vietnam as well as other products like aromatic woods, tortoise shells and pearls, the region received cloth from India, silver from the Americas and Japan, and copper cash, ceramics and silk from China.[55] In both East and West, the consumer revolution that commenced in the late 18th century further stimulated popular mass demand for these products and for other luxuries such as coffee and tea.[56] Singapura was conspicuously absent from this commerce, but the expanded trade flows established the foundation for the port's spectacular revival, as it transited from the early modern period to the historical conjuncture of the 19th century.

54 A. Reid, "Humans and Forests in Pre-Colonial Southeast Asia", in *Nature and the Orient: The Environmental History of South and Southeast Asia*, ed. R.H. Grove, V. Damodaran and S. Sangwan (Delhi: Delhi University Press, 1998), p. 112.

55 Reid, "An 'Age of Commerce'", p. 10.

56 K. Pomeranz, *The Great Divergence: China, Europe, and the Making of the Modern World Economy* (Princeton University Press, 2000), pp. 115–7.

Chapter 2 | The Early Years, 1819–30

By the time Singapura was woken up in the early 19th century from its long slumber, the world around it had changed dramatically. After the disastrous crisis that afflicted Southeast Asia as it exited the Age of Commerce in the mid-17th century, the region retreated from maritime trade for the next one hundred years even as European colonisation began to encroach, with stealth and purposeful agency, into the erstwhile maritime ports of the previous age, making them enclaves of foreign monopolised trade. Southeast Asia was again on the cusp of historical change, this time brought on by the era of imperialism.

The chronological division adopted in this and the following two chapters is artificial but convenient; no schema of periodisation will completely fit our purposes. Nonetheless, the first decade of Singapore's founding by Stamford Raffles provides the natural start to our narrative for the colonial period. During these years, the foundations of early prosperity were laid. Following the Anglo-Dutch Treaty of 1824 which settled the respective spheres of influence and activity of the two European powers in the Malay Archipelago, and in which the British yielded Bencoolen while the Dutch gave up their claims on Singapore and Melaka, these two settlements were amalgamated with Penang to form the Presidency of the Straits Settlements in 1826. In 1830, the Presidency was abolished and the Settlements were reduced to the status of a Residency under the Bengal Presidency in India. Thereafter, the administrative *status quo* remained essentially unchanged until 1867.

Raffles and Singapore

For historians, the question of whether in this period Singapore was discovered by chance or by design must be of great interest.[1] What we do know is that the Governor-General of India, Lord Hastings, had instructed the servants of the East India Company (EIC)—an English agency which had been granted a Royal Charter to trade in the East since 1600—to establish a station that commanded the southern entrance of the Straits of Melaka and could serve as a fallback for the China tea and opium trade.[2] Penang, which had been acquired by the EIC in 1786, had failed to live up to expectations of being a naval arsenal by dint of its situation far up north of the Straits while Melaka had been returned to the

[1] F. Swettenham, *British Malaya: An Account of the Origin and Progress of British Influence in Malaya* (London: George Allen and Unwin, 1948), pp. 66, 69–71.

[2] *Straits Settlements Records*, L.10, 6 Feb. 1819.

Dutch in 1816.[3] Yet it is also the case that Thomas Stamford Raffles disobeyed his superior in founding Singapore—rather than the Riau Islands or Johor—in February 1819, and overruled his deputy William Farquhar in choosing it rather than the Karimun Islands to the southwest of Singapore as the site of a trading outpost.[4] As feared by Lord Hastings, Raffles' action had incurred the displeasure of the British government which was trying to avoid any misunderstanding with the Dutch. Moreover, the EIC did not view Raffles' percipient undertaking as the geopolitical coup that it was. As Raffles had studied the history of the Malay Archipelago, did he then believe he was reviving the commercial glory of an ancient port after seeing its locational and topographical advantages?[5] Did he envisage "cloth[ing] the teeming millions of Southeast Asians and Chinese in British cotton dress" or was he simply the imperialist, *par excellence*?[6] We will never know, except to say with hindsight that the trade which was subsequently attracted to the port "consisted of the traffic which the very existence of Singapore had evoked".[7] That is to say, Singapore did not merely establish itself as a node of the existing Southeast Asian trade networks, but also created new trade opportunities.[8]

The economic imperatives themselves are clear enough: the EIC wanted the spices and native products of Southeast Asia to help pay for Chinese tea and stop the haemorrhage of gold and silver from Britain. Furthermore, Raffles and his Honourable Company wanted to break the Dutch hegemony and monopoly on trade in the East Indies enforced since 1700 by the Vereenigde Oostindische Compagnie (VOC), the Netherlands' equivalent of the EIC, from which it and subsequently the Dutch government derived much revenue. In addition, the British government faced rising pressure from home manufacturers, especially of textiles, to open up new markets in the Far East, as the Napoleonic and Independence Wars had led France and the United States to impose tariffs on British goods. As the most powerful nation to emerge from the Congress of Vienna in 1815, Britain enjoyed unchallenged supremacy at sea, with a growing merchant marine and

---

[3] M.H. Murfett, J.N. Miksic, B.P. Farrell and Chiang Ming Shun, *Between Two Oceans: A Military History of Singapore from First Settlement to Final British Withdrawal* (Singapore: Oxford University Press, 1999), p. 37. The EIC had temporarily taken the station over to prevent it from falling into French hands during the Napoleonic Wars.

[4] D. Moore and J. Moore, *The First 150 Years of Singapore* (Singapore: Donald Moore Press, 1969), pp. 11–15; Swettenham, *British Malaya*, pp. 69–70; C.O. Blagden, "The Foundation of the Settlement", in *One Hundred Years of Singapore*, vol. I, ed. Makepeace, Brooke and Braddell, p. 7; Kwa, Heng and Tan, *Singapore: A 700-Year History*, p. 86.

[5] Miksic, *Singapore and the Silk Road*, pp. 2–3, 5; Blagden, "The Foundation of the Settlement", p. 8. Apparently, Raffles did not know about the natural deep water port that was later to become Keppel Harbour. J.E. Abshire, *The History of Singapore* (Santa Barbara, CA: Greenwood, 2011), pp. 39–40.

[6] Wong Lin Ken, "Singapore: Its Growth as an Entrepôt Port, 1819–1941", *Journal of Southeast Asian Studies* 9, 1 (1978): 52–3; Moore and Moore, *The First 150 Years*, p. 24; Savage, *Lion City Narratives*, p. 83.

[7] Wong Lin Ken, *The Trade of Singapore, 1819–1869* (Kuala Lumpur: The Malaysian Branch of the Royal Asiatic Society, 2003), pp. 159, 194–204.

[8] Tan Tai Yong, "Early Entrepôt Portal—Trade and Founding of Singapore", in Lau and Lau, *Maritime Heritage of Singapore*, p. 88.

commercial shipping presence.[9] The new industrialists in England were aided by such mercantile and shipping interests in the Far East, with whom they formed an alliance of private trade and cotton interests.

Singapore would therefore not have emerged if the historical circumstances had been different. By the same token, its obscurity before 1819 merits attention. As an eminent scholar of Singapore's economic history put it, "no historian has yet adequately explained why Singapore failed to be a major trading centre before the nineteenth century".[10] While, as we saw in the previous chapter, it had become a trading port in the 14th century, the puzzle remains: why was Singapore left untouched in the two centuries preceding 1819, a period of crisis after the end of the Age of Commerce? Moreover, given the strategic location of Singapore, rivalry between the Dutch and the Portuguese should have led to its colonisation sooner or later.[11] That this did not happen set the stage for Singapore's rejuvenation, for Raffles would not have been able to sign the treaty with the Temenggong Abdul Rahman of Singapore and Sultan Hussein Shah of Johor (the *de facto* and *de jure* rulers of Singapore, respectively) on 6 February 1819 to set up a trading post if the island had been more than an immaterial satellite of the Johor-Riau-Lingga kingdom. As it was, the Dutch had already forestalled Raffles by obtaining possession of Riau in 1818 but had not laid any claim to Singapore even though they hotly disputed Raffles' action.[12] In short, Singapore's second founding was the result of a complex conjunction of individual, economic and political events—neither an accident of history nor preordained.

Be that as it may, Raffles was prescient in his foreknowledge that Singapore would rise to great importance; the initial measures he took, that resulted in its subsequent economic success, were almost self-fulfilling.[13] These can be broadly divided into trade policy, town planning and administration. Regarding the first aspect, of utmost importance for Singapore's economic take-off is Raffles' liberal political economy. The *Zeitgeist* of the times where trade policy was concerned was mercantilist; after all, the Corn Laws were repealed in Britain only in 1846. As an economic-ideological movement, free trade emerged as a doctrine of political economists in the late 18th century and gathered momentum after the Napoleonic Wars ended in 1815.[14] But not until the 1830s did economic liberalism burst forth as a crusading passion and the views of Adam Smith gained ascendancy; Raffles was a man ahead of his time.[15]

---

[9] D.R. SarDesai, *British Trade and Expansion in Southeast Asia, 1830–1914* (New Delhi: Allied, 1977), p. 12; D. Brunero, "Maritime Goes Global: The British Maritime Empire in Asia", in *Empire in Asia: A New Global History, Volume Two, The Long Nineteenth Century*, ed. D. Brunero and B.P. Farrell (London: Bloomsbury Academic, 2018), pp. 249–50, 255.

[10] Attributed to Wong Lin Ken, as quoted in Kwa, Heng and Tan, *Singapore: A 700-Year History*, p. 8.

[11] Ibid., pp. 63–4, 74–8. As mentioned, the two European powers clashed in the sea off Singapore in 1603.

[12] Moore and Moore, *The First 150 Years*, pp. 29–31.

[13] Ibid., pp. 30–1.

[14] C.P. Kindleberger, "The Rise of Free Trade in Western Europe, 1820–1875", *The Journal of Economic History* 35, 1 (1975): 27, 31, 50.

[15] SarDesai, *British Trade and Expansion*, p. 13.

Raffles was also a visionary and an innovator who saw in the progressivity of free trade a means to emancipate the peoples of the East Indies from their backwardness and poverty, not to mention the cruelties of Dutch rule.[16] Before leaving the island, he thus instructed the newly appointed Resident William Farquhar to encourage trade by not imposing any customs dues or port duties for the time being. Farquhar was also to devise a good watering place for the needs of shipping vessels, which was accomplished by building a reservoir and aqueduct near the foot of Fort Canning Hill.[17] A small fort on the hill overlooking the settlement was to be constructed, coastal batteries were to be erected to protect shipping, a European artillery unit with a garrison was to be maintained and a bridge was to be constructed across the Singapore River.[18] The land between the Singapore River and Rochor Street was to be reserved for public use.

On Raffles' departure in 1819, Farquhar took it upon himself to oversee the early development of the fledgling outpost. He obtained food and other supplies from Melaka, where he had good connections, and military reinforcements from Penang, which were slow in arriving as the station's Governor, out of jealousy, tried to scupper Raffles' project. Farquhar then set about to clear the land on the northeast bank of the river where the commoners of ancient Temasek had dwelled.[19] This plain was the palimpsest of Singapore on which the town was to be sited. With the arrival of building materials and tools shipped by Raffles from Penang, Farquhar situated the cantonments for the military troops at the eastern foot of the hill, on what is now the Stamford Road side.[20] However, he gave in to pressure from the merchant community to build their warehouses and homes along the north bank of the Singapore River which was earmarked for the government, at their own risk and against Raffles' preference for the beach at Kampong Glam where twelve lots were reserved for sale to Europeans.[21] Fortunately for later generations, he retained an open space that fronted the sea to the east—the Esplanade.[22]

On his final trip to Singapore in October 1822, following an absence of three years and a string of personal tragedies, Raffles was furious with Farquhar over the way he had administered the settlement. The differences between the two men eventually led Raffles to relieve Farquhar of his appointment in 1823. Apart from the issuances of land allocation, and without proper titles at that, the latter had given out licences for opium, liquor and

---

16 L.A. Mills, C.M. Turnbull and D.K. Bassett, "British Malaya, 1824–67", *Journal of the Malayan Branch of the Royal Asiatic Society*, 33, 3 (1960): 62.

17 *Straits Settlements Records*, L.10, 6 Feb. 1819, 2 Sept. 1819.

18 W. Makepeace, "Singapore Defences", in *One Hundred Years of Singapore*, vol. I, ed. Makepeace, Brooke and Braddell, p. 377; *Straits Settlements Records*, L.10, 6 Feb. 1819, 25 June 1819.

19 B. Nunn, "Some Account of Our Governors and Civil Service", in *One Hundred Years of Singapore*, vol. I, ed. Makepeace, Brooke and Braddell, p. 75.

20 *Straits Settlements Records*, L.10, 26 May 1819; J. Cameron, *Our Tropical Possessions in Malayan India: Being a Descriptive Account of Singapore, Penang, Province Wellesley, and Malacca; Their Peoples, Products, Commerce, and Government* (London: Smith, Elder and Co, 1865), p. 15.

21 Leong Foke Meng, "Early Land Transactions in Singapore: The Real Estates of William Farquhar (1774–1839), John Crawfurd (1783–1868), and Their Families", *Journal of the Malaysian Branch of the Royal Asiatic Society* 77, 1 (2004): 23–4; C.B. Buckley, *An Anecdotal History of Singapore* (Singapore: Fraser and Neave, 1902), pp. 56–7.

22 Swettenham, *British Malaya*, p. 75.

gambling dens in order to raise badly needed revenue to pay the salaries of government personnel, including the rudimentary police force. Coming from an older generation than Raffles and more in tune with native practices, Farquhar was of the opinion that the abolition of longstanding traditional institutions such as slavery and gaming would create widespread dissatisfaction amongst the people; rather than prohibit such activities, it would be wiser to license them.[23] To unravel Farquhar's haphazard assignment of land, Raffles went about redesigning the town and co-opted a planning committee to assist him and provide feedback from the native sub-populations. Even though it was based on Raffles' guidelines, the town plan that resulted became known as the Jackson Plan, as it was drawn up by Lieutenant Philip Jackson, Assistant Engineer of the Bengal Artillery.[24] He also supervised the construction of the first wooden drawbridge across the Singapore River that Raffles had proposed in 1819, then known as Presentment Bridge.[25]

The Jackson plan is dated 1823 and its most striking feature is a grid layout for the road network that has survived to this day, as stipulated by Raffles and possibly reflecting a peculiarly British notion of order and regularity.[26] It also shows a sharply demarcated segregation of ethnic groups not only according to their perceived economic value but also for socio-political reasons, evincing a conscious policy of "divide-and-rule", to be carried out in the first instance by separate chiefs appointed for each tribe.[27] The merchants were given priority over artisans in selecting a suitable commercial site and no agricultural activity was to be carried out in the town.[28] An area called Commercial Square (later renamed Raffles Place) on the southwest bank of the Singapore River was levelled and designated for trading activities. Adjacent to the square, the swampy land was filled in and named Boat Quay, to which the European and Chinese merchants were relocated after receiving compensation for their previous premises on the north bank.[29] In deference to the sanctuary occupied by the rulers of ancient Singapore, Fort Canning Hill was Raffles' choice for the seat of government, and there he had his residence built. At the foot of the hill, he had the first Botanic Garden in Singapore planted.[30] Given the EIC's limited lease

[23] J. Kathirithamby-Wells, "Early Singapore and the Inception of a British Administrative Tradition in the Straits Settlements (1819–1832)", *Journal of the Malaysian Branch of the Royal Asiatic Society* 42, 2 (1969): 64.

[24] H.F. Pearson, "Lt. Jackson's Plan of Singapore", *Journal of the Malaysian Branch of the Royal Asiatic Society* 42, 1 (1969): 161–5.

[25] Kwa Chong Guan, "Jackson Plan", in *On Paper: Singapore Before 1867*, p. 118.

[26] M. Jayapal, *Old Singapore* (Oxford University Press, 1992), p. 6; F.J. Hallifax, "Municipal Government", in *One Hundred Years of Singapore,* vol. I, ed. Makepeace, Brooke and Braddell, p. 323; Teo Siew Eng, "Planning Principles in Pre- and Post-Independence Singapore", *The Town Planning Review* 63, 2 (1992), p. 165.

[27] "Notices of Singapore", *The Journal of the Indian Archipelago and Eastern Asia*, ed. J.R. Logan, 7 (1853): 333; S. Dobbs, *The Singapore River: A Social History 1819–2002* (Singapore: Singapore University Press, 2003), p. 22.

[28] Moore and Moore, *The First 150 Years*, pp. 82–8.

[29] *Straits Settlements Records*, L.17, Feb. 1823.

[30] Savage, *Lion City Narratives*, pp. 108, 120, 139, 348. The garden was initially called the Botanical and Experimental Garden.

on the southern stretch of the island, the boundaries of the Jackson plan were demarcated by the land between the sea, the Singapore River and the Kallang River (Map 2).[31]

The sight of prosperous Singapore, his only "political child", gave Raffles renewed determination to forge "perfection in this one small place" instead of pursuing his grand dream of reviving the past glory of Java and Sumatra.[32] Indisputably, the greatest legacy of the founder of Singapore is the ideological lodestone of free trade, or what others have called his "commercial Charter of Freedom".[33] Even if one doubts his free trade credentials on the ground that he advocated it only as a pragmatic measure to get Singapore going, the fact remains that the principle has been permanently enshrined up to the present day.[34] During the concluding weeks of his stay, Raffles also drafted a constitution for Singapore based on the principles of "free trade and equal rights to all, with protection of property and person".[35] Repudiating Farquhar's policies, he promulgated administrative reforms, including notably the abolition of slavery and the prohibition of gaming, though the second of these would not outlast him.[36]

Raffles also set up a registry for the protection of landed property and the prevention of disputes through a record of all appropriations and transfers of land.[37] The land tenure system instituted for Singapore allowed all races to purchase land and hence have a stake in the development of the town—an idea that was to be revived in the modern era.[38] In the matter of administration, Raffles favoured a small and efficient establishment in which each civil servant was entrusted with precisely defined duties and powers.[39] He transplanted English law to Singapore and instituted trial by jury, appointing 12 Europeans to serve as public magistrates for petty crimes and civil cases.[40] But Raffles' efforts at laying the institutional foundations for the rule of law and property rights did not come to fruition until well after the second Resident, John Crawfurd, secured the cession of the entire island to the EIC from the Malay rulers in August 1824.

---

31 To be more precise, the territory of the EIC was bordered on the west by Tanjong Malang, on the east by Tanjong Katong, and extended as far inland as a cannon shot. Abshire, *History of Singapore*, pp. 41–2.

32 Moore and Moore, *The First 150 Years*, pp. 80, 81; C.M. Turnbull, *A History of Modern Singapore: 1819–2005* (Singapore: NUS Press, 2009), pp. 36–7.

33 Turnbull, *History of Modern Singapore*, p. 40; F.M. Luscombe, *Singapore, 1819–1930* (Singapore: C.A. Ribeiro, 1930), p. 36.

34 Such doubt has been expressed by SarDesai, *British Trade and Expansion*, pp. 36–40.

35 Quoted in Buckley, *An Anecdotal History*, p. 78.

36 "The amount of work which he accomplished in 1822–23 was as varied as it was colossal". Mills, Turnbull and Bassett, "British Malaya", p. 76; Kathirithamby-Wells, *Early Singapore*, pp. 48–73.

37 *Straits Settlements Records*, L.17, 1 Jan. 1823.

38 Savage, *Lion City Narratives*, p. 104.

39 Kathirithamby-Wells, *Early Singapore*, pp. 50–1.

40 Turnbull, *History of Modern Singapore*, p. 40; B. Nunn, "Some Account of Our Governors", p. 76. Raffles respected indigenous custom and law in matters relating to religion, marriage and inheritance. Edwin Lee, "The Colonial Legacy", in *Management of Success: The Moulding of Modern Singapore*, ed. K.S. Sandhu and P. Wheatley (Singapore: Institute of Southeast Asian Studies, 1989), p. 6.

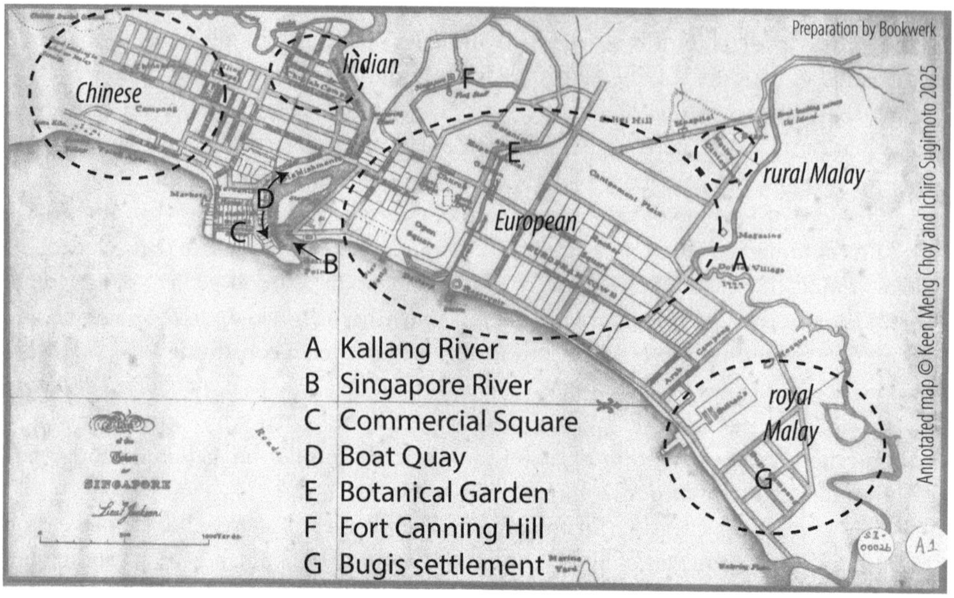

Map 2. The Jackson Plan of Singapore, 1823.

Source: Courtesy of the National Archives of Singapore [Accession number SP002981]. Annotations by the authors.

A medical doctor by training, Crawfurd was capable and painstaking in his administration of the settlement from 1823 to 1826, following its transfer to the Bengal government after Raffles returned to England. Under Crawfurd, Singapore achieved substantial progress in town development as well as legal and judicial administration. In 1827, 300 permanent land titles were issued to replace the grants given out by Raffles, covering land at Boat Quay, Circular Road, Market Street, Malacca Street, Philip Street, Telok Ayer Street, High Street, Hill Street and Beach Road.[41] In the same year, the Court of Judicature was established in the Straits Settlements, consisting of the Governor, the Resident Councillor of each settlement and a Recorder who proceeded on circuit to hold court at the three settlements.[42] Another of Crawfurd's enduring legacies is the systematic compilation of trade statistics detailing Singapore's imports and exports starting from 1823.

Early Trade Successes

Raffles in establishing his outpost had avowed: "Our object is not territory but trade".[43] As things turned out, trade followed the protection afforded by the British flag; soon after its establishment, Singapore attracted traders from the Malay Peninsula, the Dutch East

[41] Leong, *Early Land Transactions in Singapore*, p. 25; J. Lornie, "Land Tenure", in *One Hundred Years of Singapore*, vol. I, ed. Makepeace, Brooke and Braddell, p. 304; Savage, *Lion City Narratives*, pp. 110–1.

[42] *Singapore Chronicle and Commercial Register*, 5 Sept. 1827; *The Singapore Free Press and Mercantile Advertiser*, 24 Oct. 1844.

[43] Quoted in Turnbull, *History of Modern Singapore*, p. 38.

Indies, Borneo and the Philippines as well as from China, Siam and Cochin-China.[44] Permanently settled Straits-born Chinese from the Riau Islands, the Sumatran coast, Penang and especially Melaka flocked to its shores with their enterprise and capital, drawn by the appeal of free trade and new business opportunities.[45] There was also an exodus of Malays from Melaka who disliked the Dutch and were attracted by high wages in the new settlement; these immigrants were joined by Bugis and Javanese.[46] Raffles was delighted by the reception given to his infant outpost and wrote to his cousin in July 1820: "My settlement continues to thrive most wonderfully; it is all and everything I could wish and if no untimely fate awaits it, promises to become the emporium and the pride of the East".[47]

The growth of Singapore's trade reflected its instant success. In April 1820, barely a year after the outpost was founded, Raffles in his exuberance reported that the imports and exports on native craft alone exceeded four million Spanish dollars (SPD).[48] This seems to be overstated as the Master Attendant's list of imports and exports sent to him by Farquhar a year later showed that their values for the period beginning 1 April 1820 and ending 30 April 1821 amounted to only SPD885,881 and SPD914,638, respectively.[49] Another estimate stated the value of trade in the eighteen months from May 2020 to October 2021 at five million Spanish dollars, with three-fifths accounted for by native crafts and the rest by square-rigged vessels (that is, European sailing ships).[50] These differing estimates are explained by the fact that no regular account was kept of Singapore's trade before 1823. At any rate, in the first two-and-a-half years, no fewer than 2,889 vessels called at the harbour.[51] Some stopped at Singapore only for refreshments and water supplies, or to gather trade information. The commodities traded included esoteric products such as elephant ivory and sharks' fins as well as mundane goods such as Java mats and iron pans. The ten most valuable commodities were opium (by far the

44 *Straits Settlements Records*, L.10, 2 Nov. 1819. Cochin-China was the name for the southern part of Vietnam.

45 Mark Ravinder Frost, "Emporium in Imperio: Nanyang Networks and the Straits Chinese in Singapore, 1819–1914", *Journal of Southeast Asian Studies* 36, 1 (2005): 36.

46 Hill, *Hikayat Abdullah*, pp. 132–6; H. Marriott, "The Peoples of Singapore: Inhabitants and Population", in *One Hundred Years of Singapore*, vol. I, ed. Makepeace, Brooke and Braddell, p. 343; Elinah Abdullah, "Malay/Muslim Patterns of Settlement and Trade in the First 50 Years", in *Malays/Muslims in Singapore: Selected Readings in History, 1819–1965*, ed. Khoo Kay Kim, Elinah Abdullah and Wan Meng Hao (Pelanduk Publications, 2006), pp. 81, 94.

47 Quoted in Turnbull, *History of Modern Singapore*, p. 32.

48 Mills, Turnbull and Bassett, "British Malaya", p. 76. All currency figures in this and the following chapters are in Spanish silver dollars (SPD) unless otherwise stated; the silver coins were minted in Spanish America and used up to about the turn of the 20th century.

49 C.D. Cowan, "Early Penang & the Rise of Singapore 1805–1832", *Journal of the Malayan Branch of the Royal Asiatic Society* 23, 2 (1950): 114, 117.

50 J. Phipps, *A Practical Treatise on the China and Eastern Trade: Comprising the Commerce of Great Britain and India, Particularly Bengal and Singapore, with China and the Eastern Islands* (London: Wm. H. Allen, 1836), pp. 262, 263.

51 T.J. Newbold, *Political and Statistical Account of the British Settlements in the Straits of Malacca viz., Pinang, Malacca and Singapore; with a History of the Malayan States on the Peninsula of Malacca, in Two Volumes* (London: John Murray, 1839), pp. 112–7, 290.

most valuable), followed by rice, sugar, gambier, pepper, birds' nests, tin, China ware, raw silk and cloth.

By 1822, the value of Singapore's total trade had risen to SPD8,568,151. In a report to the EIC's Court of Directors, Raffles singled out a few key goods which would continue to play a critical role in the port's subsequent trade. He disclosed that Singapore exported 359 chests of opium, shipped 17,431 pikuls of pepper and imported SPD265,054 worth of British piece goods.[52] In 1824–25, trade increased further to SPD13,519,137, more than double the value at Penang and eight times that of Malacca. Singapore in 1825 accounted for nearly two-thirds of the trade that was conducted in the Straits Settlements; in 1830, this proportion had increased to over four-fifths.[53] These figures suggest, *prima facie*, that Singapore not only garnered the trade that used to be conducted at the nearby Riau Islands before the settlement was founded, but also captured large slices of Penang's and Melaka's commerce.[54] Small wonder then that the Governor of the Straits Settlements declared in 1830 that Singapore had "annihilated" the trade of Malacca, and "bade fair to annihilate that of Penang also".[55]

In 1830, the trade of Penang amounted to only SPD3,149,151, having fallen from a peak of SPD6,500,000 in 1822, and it regained the 1810 level only in 1844.[56] Compared to Singapore and even Melaka, it had always been disadvantaged by virtue of its location near the northern entrance to the Straits of Melaka, far away from the centre of gravity of the East Indian trade. Consequently, it had in the main served the commerce of north and east Sumatra—Aceh in particular—the west coast of the northern Malay Peninsula as well as the ports of the Indian littoral, and this part of its trade base remained after Singapore was founded.[57] However, a significant proportion of Penang's custom was diverted to the new settlement as ships which would have unloaded there no longer did so, not least because the journey up the Straits was hazardous due to pirate attacks and the Sumatra squalls. Thus, Penang in effect became a feeder port of Singapore; its exports shrank as shipping tonnage fell and its India trade was hit by competition from British cotton goods (Figure 1).

---

[52] *Straits Settlements Records*, L.2, 15 Jan. 1823. A chest of Bengal opium weighs about 140 lbs; a pikul is a local measure of weight equal to approximately 133.3 lbs (c. 60.5 kg).

[53] T. Braddell, *Statistics of the British Possessions in the Straits of Malacca: With Explanatory Notes* (Pinang, 1861), Abstract statement of value of trade at Pinang, Singapore and Malacca in £ Sterling.

[54] P.J. Begbie, *The Malayan Peninsula: Embracing Its History, Manners and Customs of the Inhabitants, Politics, Natural History, Etc. From Its Earliest Records* (Vepery Mission Press, 1834), pp. 318–9; British Military Administration, *The Entrepôt Trade of Singapore* (Singapore, 1945), p. 6.

[55] Quoted in Mills, Turnbull and Bassett, "British Malaya", p. 224.

[56] Mills, Turnbull and Bassett, "British Malaya", pp. 224, 225; R. St.J. Braddell, "A Short History of the Colony", in *One Hundred Years of Singapore*, vol. I, ed. Makepeace, Brooke and Braddell, pp. 23–4.

[57] Cowan, "Early Penang", pp. 12, 14–16.

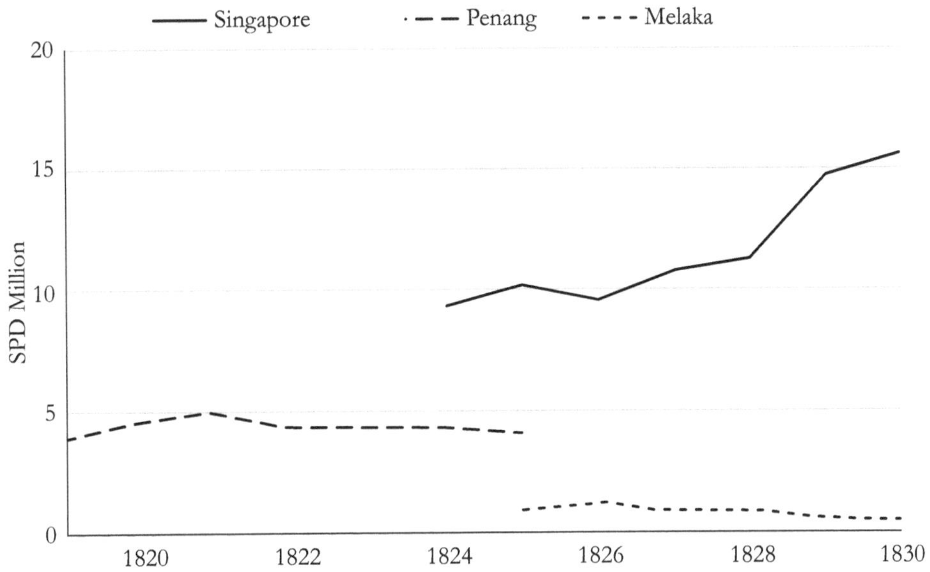

Figure 1. Trade of the Straits Settlements, 1819–30

Source: T. Braddell, *Statistics of the British Possessions*, Abstract statement of value of trade at Pinang, Singapore and Malacca in £ Sterling.

Melaka, which had already seen its commerce decline during Dutch rule before 1824, suffered a fatal blow to its trade because of its close proximity to Singapore.[58] Merchant vessels flocked to the latter port with no levies or harbour restrictions; added to this, Melaka's shallow harbour was silting up. Its trade decreased gradually until a revival took place in 1844.[59] A traveller remarked thus of Melaka in 1829: "Melaka … is no longer of the slightest importance, either as a military position or as a trading mart. Penang, at one end of the Straits, and Singapore at the other, have destroyed its prosperity".[60] Nonetheless, Singapore's capture of Penang's and Melaka's commerce did not mean that inter-settlement trade came to a standstill. In 1828–29, it still amounted to SPD1,025,981, involving largely the exchange of cotton goods between Singapore and Penang, the former being the centre for British textiles and the latter for Indian cloth. In addition, Singapore also obtained the Straits produce of the Malay Peninsula and tin sourced from Junkceylon (Phuket) and Sungai Ujong (Seremban) from its sister settlements and exported opium to them.

Before analysing the trade patterns of Singapore, a discussion of Dutch commercial policy in the Eastern Archipelago is helpful. Although the Anglo-Dutch Treaty of 1784 forced the Dutch to allow British ships the free navigation of the Archipelago's waters, they proceeded to reinstate their monopolies and discriminatory practices when their territories were reoccupied in 1816. Additionally, they took steps to secure the ports in the region,

---

[58] Nordin Hussin, *Trade and Society in the Straits of Melaka: Dutch Melaka and English Penang, 1780–1830* (Singapore: NUS Press, 2007), pp. 24–5; Begbie, *The Malayan Peninsula*, p. 370.

[59] R. St.J. Braddell, "The Good Old Days", in *One Hundred Years of Singapore*, vol. II, ed. Makepeace, Brooke and Braddell, p. 24.

[60] G.F. Davidson, *Trade and Travel in the Far East; or Recollections of Twenty-One Years Passed in Java, Singapore, Australia, and China* (London: Maiden and Malcolm, 1846), p. 94.

including through agreements with native chiefs, to prevent the British from forming settlements. When Java was under British rule between 1811 and 1815, private traders and India-based merchant houses selling English cotton goods had succeeded in making inroads into its huge market.[61] To regain their share, the Dutch introduced a differential tariff which imposed a duty of 6 per cent on the invoice price plus 60 per cent on goods imported in British vessels whilst Dutch ships paid 6 per cent plus 30 per cent. In 1818, British vessels were forced to pay a higher tariff of 12 per cent of the invoiced value of goods, double that on Dutch ships; a year later, products imported from the Netherlands were totally exempted from duties.

Despite these punitive actions, the Dutch could not stop British cloth manufacturers from virtually capturing the Java market by 1823. English textiles succeeded, even though they entailed higher duties and transport costs, both because their prices were falling on the back of productivity gains and because manufacturers in the country tailored their products to Javanese tastes.[62] But Belgium too had an advanced textile industry and after the territory was incorporated into the Netherlands following the end of the Napoleonic Wars, the Dutch had an interest in promoting Flemish textiles. In 1824, the Dutch government set up the Nederlandsche Handel-Maatschappij (NHM), an import and export agency, with the objective of expanding Belgian cloth exports to Java using Dutch shipping. The NHM was also given priority over non-Dutch firms in the Archipelago trade. In the same year, English cotton and woollen goods were subjected to a higher tariff of 25 per cent on the Batavia (Jakarta) price if imported directly, and 35 per cent if shipped from Singapore. The measure was intended to counter the large transshipment trade at Singapore and it had the desired effect: the influx of British cotton into Java from the port fell drastically, although that sourced directly from Britain continued to grow.[63] By 1829, the NHM had succeeded in reducing the share of English cotton to 30 per cent.[64] In spite of protestations by the English merchants and the British government to the Dutch, the latter stood their ground. The Javanese branch of Singapore's trade suffered as a consequence, falling from SPD1,487,865 in 1823–24 to SPD1,122,824 in 1829–30.[65] Still, an impressive range of products was imported from Java, including pepper, coffee, tobacco, spirits, gambier, rattan, sandalwood and indigo. In addition, there was a lively smuggling trade in opium from Singapore to Java that was conducted clandestinely by Arab traders in vessels flying the Dutch flag.[66] Overall, Singapore ran a persistent trade deficit with Java during the period 1824–30.

The decline in Javanese traffic was nevertheless compensated by the significant growth in Singapore's trade with other places in the East Indies under Dutch control. Raffles

[61] A. van der Kraan, *A Contest for the Java Cotton Trade, 1811–40: An Episode in Anglo-Dutch Rivalry* (University of Hull, Centre for South-East Asian Studies, 1998), pp. 11–13, 20.

[62] Ibid., pp. 12–13, 21.

[63] Wong, *The Trade of Singapore*, p. 50; SarDesai, *British Trade and Expansion*, p. 42.

[64] A. Reid, "Southeast Asian Consumption of Indian and British Cotton Cloth, 1600–1850", in *How India Clothed the World: The World of South Asian Textiles, 1500–1850*, ed. G. Riello and Tirtankar Roy (Leiden: Brill, 2009), p. 49.

[65] Wong, *The Trade of Singapore*, Appendix A, Table X, p. 224. These figures and the rest in this section refer to merchandise trade, that is, excluding the trade in treasury or specie.

[66] Ibid., p. 74; Buckley, *An Anecdotal History*, p. 324.

was reputed to have said: "[Singapore] continued to rise as rapidly as the outstations of the Dutch declined".[67] This extensive commerce rose from SPD1,934,768 in 1823–24 to SPD2,769,906 in 1827–28 and included trade with the nearby Riau Islands, Sumatra and the Malay Peninsula, as well as the more distant Borneo, Bali and Celebes. The Riau and Straits circuits of this commerce are particularly notable, as the natives and Chinese involved in this *prahu pukat* (trawler boat) trade made multiple trips to Singapore every month, sheltered as they were from the full force of the monsoons.[68] The Peninsula's east coast trade was conducted in the same way, though the number of voyages was confined to four or five each year, while similar vessels were used in the smuggling trade with the Dutch islands.[69] The combined trade of the Malay coasts amounted to slightly less than a quarter of the total for insular Southeast Asia in 1828–29. Throughout the early colonial period, the east coast was much more important to Singapore than the west coast owing to imports of gold dust and tin from Pahang, and the export of opium and provisions to the Chinese miners there.

The areas farther away from Singapore supplied the full range of forest products and unique commodities such as camphor, sago, fish maws, *bêche de mer* (sea cucumber, also known as *trepang*), aloeswood, birds of paradise and mother of pearl. These commodities constitute an important sub-branch of regional commerce and were traded by the intrepid Bugis who had established colonies at various places in the Eastern Archipelago. These people were the seafaring traders from the Celebes and the Moluccas who usually arrived during the inter-monsoon months of September to November—the "Bugis season"—and departed with the onset of the northeast monsoon, sailing with cargoes of opium, tobacco, nankeen, woollens, iron goods and arms.[70] Vessels from Borneo also delivered products such as nutmeg and cinnamon, cloves and batik textiles.[71] The trade balances with each of the above places were in Singapore's favour except for the Riau Islands, suggesting that their importance as re-export markets for Western manufactured goods imported by Singapore exceeded that as sources of Archipelago produce.

In Sumatra where the political influence of the Dutch administration centred at Batavia was diffused, Singapore carried out a substantial trade with ports along the east coast such as Siak and Campar.[72] In the late 1820s, this commerce was valued at SPD361,434, about equally split between exports and imports. The main export items from Singapore were British manufactures, Indian textiles, Chinese ware and opium, while the most valuable import item was coffee from the Minangkabau district, which was brought to Singapore every month in small fleets of 10 to 12 prahus.[73] Other imports were rice, gambier, betel

[67] Quoted in Luscombe, *Singapore*, p. 28.

[68] Wong, *The Trade of Singapore*, p. 34.

[69] R. St.J. Braddell, "The Good Old Days", p. 473; *Singapore Free Press and Mercantile Advertiser*, 12 Jan. 1837.

[70] *Singapore Chronicle and Commercial Register*, 16 Dec. 1830.

[71] Moore and Moore, *The First 150 Years*, p. 179.

[72] C.M. Turnbull, *The Straits Settlements, 1826–67: Indian Presidency to Crown Colony* (London: The Athlone Press, 1972), p. 165.

[73] Wong Lin Ken, *The Trade of Singapore*, pp. 53–4.

nuts, tortoise shells, rhinoceros horns and rattan.[74] The absence of pepper from the list was due to Penang's closer proximity to the pepper ports of northern Sumatra, with which it had conducted a substantial trade for some time.

Singapore's early trade with Cochin-China represented the first commercial intercourse between that region and a British settlement in the Straits.[75] Unlike Siam, Cochin-China due to its eastward orientation had not traded with Penang, China having been its major trade partner. While the volume of the trade with Singapore up to 1830 was small by comparison with other regions, it centred on a commodity which was to feature much more prominently in the later colonial era—rice. By contrast, Singapore's trade with Siam flourished, reaching SPD648,236 in 1828–29, with Siamese junks calling routinely at the port instead of at Batavia as previously. The most valuable imports from the kingdom were sugar and rice, as well as salt and ivory.[76] Singapore sent British and Indian piece goods, copper, gold dust, rattan and sago to Siam. Over the period 1824–30, Singapore's cumulative merchandise trade surplus with Siam almost completely offset the deficit with Cochin-China.

As for China, Raffles had harboured great expectations that Singapore might become the springboard for the import of English cotton into the country through the Chinese junk traffic. This did not come to pass for the simple reason that China had an abundant supply of its own nankeen. Moreover, the cloth was superior in quality and cost compared to Manchester cotton goods.[77] Instead, Singapore's trade with China grew rapidly because of the convenience for private country traders and Chinese sailors of being able to obtain Straits produce from the port, thus attracting to it the custom of Batavia and Manila very quickly.[78] Manila was further disadvantaged by excessive duties on Chinese junks.[79] Articles loaded in Singapore were carried in both square-rigged vessels and junks to Canton (Guangzhou) and Amoy (Xiamen), at that time the chief ports in China for conducting external commerce after the Qing Emperor Yongzheng (r. 1722–35) liberalised trade in 1727. The other significant export from Singapore to China, and one that was the preserve of the EIC, was opium. An important leg of the Chinese junk traffic also took place between Singapore and Bangkok, conducted almost exclusively by Chinese traders.

In the reverse direction, the heavy Chinese junks sailed from the southern ports of China during the northeast monsoon and came equipped with large quantities of goods such as dried fruits, mushrooms, medicine, porcelain, earthenware, copper ware, cloth,

---

[74] *Singapore Chronicle and Commercial Register*, 12 Jan. 1832.

[75] Wong, *The Trade of Singapore*, p. 109.

[76] *Singapore Chronicle and Commercial Register*, 21 May 1829.

[77] M. Greenberg, *British Trade and the Opening of China, 1800–1842* (Cambridge University Press, 1951), p. 2; *Singapore Chronicle and Commercial Register*, 3 Dec. 1829.

[78] Wong, *The Trade of Singapore*, pp. 78–9; G.W. Earl, *The Eastern Seas, or Voyages and Adventures in the Indian Archipelago in 1832–33–34, Comprising A Tour of the Island of Java—Visits to Borneo, the Malaya Peninsula, Siam, &c; Also, an Account of the Present State of Singapore, with Observations of the Commercial Resources of the Archipelago* (London: Wm. H. Allen, 1837), pp. 23–4; Ng, *Boundaries and Beyond*, p. 49; Lee Yip Lin, "Chinese Junk Trade in Early Singapore", in *A General History of the Chinese in Singapore*, ed. Kwa Chong Guan and Kua Bak Lim (Singapore: World Scientific, 2019), p. 25; *Singapore Chronicle and Commercial Register*, 21 May 1829.

[79] Begbie, *The Malayan Peninsula*, p. 319.

silk, tea and sundry items like joss sticks; these goods were intended for consumption by the Chinese settlements in the region as well as for export to the West.[80] Their arrival always aroused great excitement among the Chinese residents of Singapore, as the crew laid out their goods and wares on the ship decks, making them floating bazaars. In addition, the junks brought relatives and friends who were emigrants from the home villages. For the return trip, the junks took on a full cargo of opium, British cloth, pepper, sea slugs, sea cucumbers, birds' nests and delicacies such as sharks' fins and fish maws, sailing directly back to China during the southwest monsoon.[81] Trade in these products harked back to past ages, including the heyday of Temasek. Singapore's trade with China dwarfed that with other Asian markets, reaching SPD3,450,459 by 1829–30, and it was heavily in China's favour; in 1830 for example, the deficit amounted to a staggering SPD2,190,785.

In comparison with other world markets, it is not surprising that the lion's share of Singapore's early trade was taken up by Britain. In 1823–24, this proportion amounted to 18 per cent and it rose to 31 per cent in 1829–30. Except for two years during this period, Singapore ran trade surpluses with its coloniser. In contrast, direct trade with continental Europe and North America was miniscule. Britain's main export products were cotton piece goods and woollens from the Lancashire industry, cotton twist, wines, iron, armaments and sundries.[82] Nearer to the Archipelago along the maritime route, Singapore's trade with the Indian presidencies of Calcutta, Madras and Bombay, and with the island of Ceylon, was worth a hefty SPD2,723,695 by 1830, or 16 per cent of the total. The imports from the sub-continent were principally opium, raw cotton, piece goods, rice, arrack and ebony while the exports to it were gold dust, pepper, spices, copper, tin and especially treasure goods. Cotton piece goods and opium featured the most prominently in imports, resulting in a continuous deficit in trade with the Indian region.

As suggested by the above exposition of trade patterns and composition, Singapore essentially intermediated three types of seaborne commerce: intraregional, global and redistributive.[83] First, it circulated indigenous commodities within Southeast Asia, including importantly the exports of rice and sugar from mainland to archipelagic Southeast Asia, and a contrary flow of spices and native products. This branch of Singapore's commerce was conducted chiefly by native vessels which collected raw produce from places that were inaccessible to Western shipping, to be sold, sorted, graded and repackaged at the Singapore mart.[84] In this regard, the smaller ports in the region performed the same economic function as the feeder ports did in ancient times. The commerce represented the regional entrepôt trade and is very broadly estimated to be slightly less than one-eighth of the trade at Singapore (Map 3).

---

80 Wong, *The Trade of Singapore*, p. 111; *Singapore Chronicle and Commercial Register*, 23 Apr. 1829.

81 Moore and Moore, *The First 150 Years*, pp. 177–8.

82 *Singapore Chronicle and Commercial Register*, 29 Dec. 1831.

83 This trichotomous classification is different from the one used by Wong Lin Ken, "Commercial Growth Before the Second World War", in *A History of Singapore*, ed. Chew and Lee, pp. 41–2. The different types of trade here are quantified by summing up export or import values (as the case may be) of the different countries and regions provided in Appendix A of Wong, *The Trade of Singapore*, pp. 207–56.

84 British Military Administration, *Entrepôt Trade*, pp. 13–14.

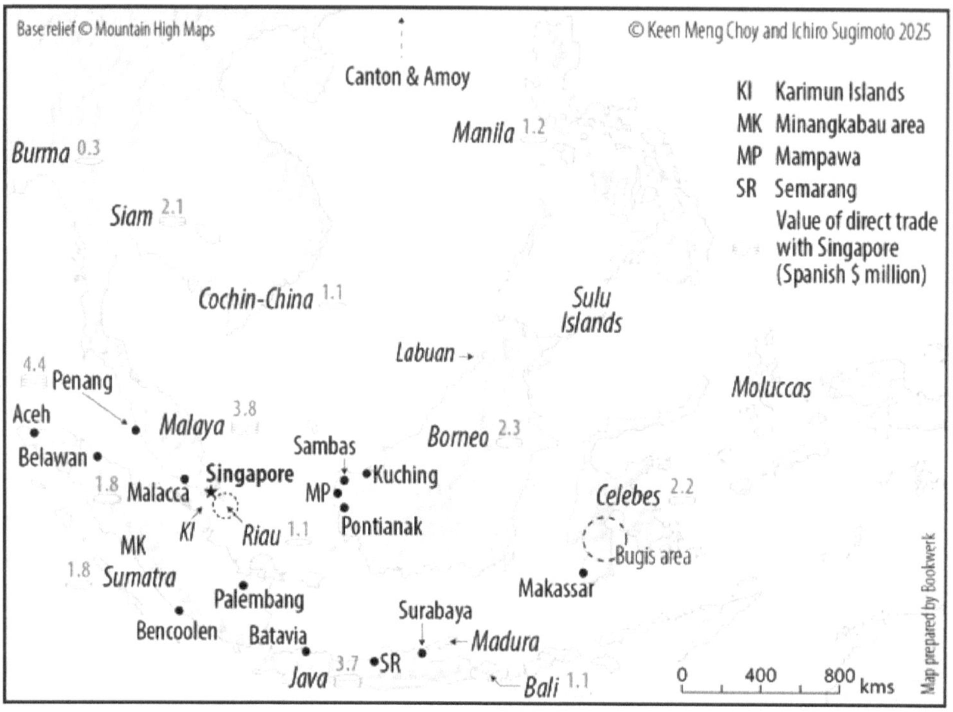

Map 3. Singapore's Trade with Southeast Asia, 1819–50.
Source: Based on data and a map supplied courtesy of Atsushi Kobayashi.

Second, as a commercial emporium, Singapore provided European (particularly British and Dutch), Chinese and Arab traders with the produce of the Archipelago, while facilitating the two-way exchange of European and Indian manufactures for the "exotic" products of China. This traffic began as a way to evade the EIC's monopoly on the China trade; in addition to the native products of the East Indies and the Malay Peninsula, it involved the exportation of ceramics and raw silk to Britain via Singapore, while some cotton and woollen goods flowed the other way in European country ships or Chinese junks. The commerce constituted the long-distance East–West exchange and it accounted for more than half of Singapore's port traffic. The third type of trade made up the remainder (about one-third), whereby Singapore distributed manufactures from Britain, Europe, India and China such as cotton goods, silk and ceramics to the region, which were bulk-broken before being reshipped. As an entrepôt-cum-emporium, Singapore's exports and imports were roughly balanced, the difference being imports retained for domestic consumption.

Population Growth

At the time Raffles arrived in Singapore, the swampy island with its jungles was not much more than a pirate haunt, mostly occupied by the orang laut who were descended from the sea nomads of the Temasek period. A generous estimate of the population of Singapore in 1819 would be 1,000 people, including the Temenggong's followers who had settled there with him eight years earlier and lived in small houses, although most accounts claimed a lower count.[85] It is also notable that there were already some Chinese on the island in 1819.[86] By 1821, the population had burgeoned to nearly 5,000 inhabitants, of whom close to 3,000 were Malays, more than 1,000 were Chinese and the rest a mix of Bugis, Indians and Europeans.[87]

Notwithstanding their shared *raison d'être* for emigrating to Singapore—making money—they were happy to confine themselves to separate living quarters, as instructed by Raffles. Thus, some Malays congregated in the Temenggong's village on the upper banks of the Singapore River, which later moved to Telok Blangah along the west coast, and others the area around the Sultan's palace in Kampong Glam next to the Kallang River estuary, where the Arab merchants were also accommodated and pirates gathered.[88] The Malay agricultural and fishing populations settled in the rural areas away from the town and along the coasts. To the southwest of the palace was the Bugis village, inhabited by settlers from the Riau Islands and the Celebes who were all traders.[89] The other major races and the Europeans ended up where Raffles had consigned them in the Jackson plan: the Chinese in the area to the south and west of the river, the Indians further upstream and the Europeans, the plain east of the river next to the Square.

The annual censuses conducted by Singapore's early administration from 1824 onwards up to 1830 reveal the extent of the outpost's economic progress in its first decade of existence, although the accuracy of the statistics collected may be questioned (Table 1).[90] Starting from 1824 when the settlement hosted 10,683 souls, the population increased by an average of 1,196 per year until 1830 when it reached 16,634.[91] Quite clearly, Singapore was attracting the most ambitious and enterprising people of the wider Asian region, not to mention itinerant traders, which already numbered 2,500 in 1823.[92] As in most immigrant societies, males predominated: there were nearly three men for every woman; the imbalance was much greater amongst the Chinese, being closer to 12 to 1.[93] From time

[85] Turnbull, *History of Modern Singapore*, p. 25; Swettenham, *British Malaya*, p. 78; Teo Siew-Eng and Victor R. Savage, "Singapore Landscape: A Historical Overview of Housing Image", in *A History of Singapore*, ed. Chew and Lee, p. 313. Newbold's estimate is 150 people and Phipps' number is 300. Newbold, *Political and Statistical Account*, p. 279; Phipps, *A Practical Treatise*, p. 280.

[86] Marriott, "The Peoples of Singapore", pp. 341, 344, 355.

[87] Turnbull, *History of Modern Singapore*, p. 32. Raffles claimed in June 1819 that the 5,000 mark had been reached and in August 1820, he further boasted that the settlement's population had increased to 10,000 or 12,000 people. Both assertions are almost certainly erroneous. S. Raffles, *Memoir of the Life and Public Services of Sir Thomas Stamford Raffles* (London: John Murray, 1830), pp. 383, 465–6.

[88] R. St.J. Braddell, "The Good Old Days", p. 469. It is worth noting that Raffles thought the Arab traders "keen, intelligent and adventurous". Morley, "The Arabs and the Eastern Trade", p. 163.

[89] Marriott, "The Peoples of Singapore", pp. 345, 347.

[90] Ibid., p. 348.

[91] Newbold, *Political and Statistical Account*, pp. 32–4, 283–4. The floating, convict and military populations, who were not counted in the early censuses, were estimated to number 4,400 in 1827. H. Marriott, "The Peoples of Singapore", p. 346.

[92] *The Asiatic Journal and Monthly Register for British India and its Dependencies* 20 (July–Dec. 1825), p. 468.

[93] Song Ong Siang, *One Hundred Years' History of the Chinese in Singapore, The Annotated Edition* (1923; Singapore: National Library Board and World Scientific, 2020), pp. 21–2.

to time, this lopsidedness elicited concern from the colonial authorities, though little was done to address it until the 20th century.[94]

Table 1. The Population of Singapore, 1824–30

	1824	1825	1826	1827	1828	1829	1830
Europeans	74	84	111	87	108	122	92
Indo-Britons	–	–	–	–	–	–	29
Native Christians	74	132	206	188	193	272	345
Armenians	16	9	18	19	25	24	23
Jews	–	–	–	–	–	–	9
Arabs	15	10	17	18	17	32	28
Malays	4,580	5,130	5,697	4,790	5,336	5,750	5,173
Chinese	3,317	3,828	4,279	6,088	6,210	7,575	6,555
Coromandel/Malabar Coasts	390	690	605	777	1,095	1,440	1,491
Hindustan and Bengal	366	226	384	244	294	455	422
Javanese	–	38	146	267	355	634	607
Bugis/Balinese, etc	1,851	1,704	1,442	1,242	1,252	1,360	1,860
Caffres[95]	–	–	2	5	–	–	–
Total	**10,683**	**11,851**	**12,907**	**13,725**	**14,885**	**16,664**	**16,634**

Source: Newbold, *Political and Statistical Account*, p. 283.

In 1824, Malays were still the most numerous among the racial groups, at 4,580 persons, thus making up the majority. However, their number rose only to 5,173 in 1830, an increase of about 600, while Chinese began to outnumber them in 1827, reaching 6,555 in 1830. The Bugis and Balinese communities also saw a large increase, to 1,860 people by the end of this period. Arab immigrants were few in number, with only 28 to be found in 1830. Indians from the Coromandel and Malabar coasts, Hindustan and Bengal tripled in number to 1,913. The other races present were Europeans, native Christians (that is, Eurasians), Javanese and others, who together totalled 1,105 persons at the end of the decade.

The physical segregation of the ethnic groups in Singapore for the purpose of political control extended to their economic functions and occupational status. Colonial policy restricted access to certain areas of economic activity, resulting in an ethnic division of labour. This outcome was not as rigid as it sounded, for "each nation, indeed, is found pursuing avocations which best accord with its tastes and habits".[96] For instance, the Malays were part of the Temenggong's entourage living off his patronage, or were small cultivators and orang laut who still relied on fishing and piracy for a livelihood. They were quite happy in their farms and fishing grounds, and most could obtain a subsistence

[94] S. Neal, *Singapore, Chinese Migration and the Making of the British Empire, 1819–67* (Martlesham, Suffolk: Boydell, 2019), p. 23.

[95] The few caffres found in Singapore refer to people without any religious belief from the lowest class of society.

[96] Earl, *The Eastern Seas*, p. 361.

living without working for fixed wages.[97] Some were employed as boatmen or sailors, vocations for which they were well-suited by custom and inclination.[98] Others ended up as woodcutters, house builders, carpenters and hawkers.[99] By contrast, the chief function of the Bugis, the "modern Phoenicians", was to deliver to Singapore the much sought after products of the Eastern Archipelago and take back in exchange opium, cotton goods and wares.[100] If not for the Bugis, British manufactures would not have found their way to the most isolated parts of the Archipelago.[101] In addition, there were Malay traders from Sumatra who called at the port regularly in their prahus to barter native products for opium and manufactured goods.

To the British authorities, Chinese migrants from the immediate region were welcomed because they provided valuable trading knowledge of local markets and prices. John Crawfurd had advised that the best way for inexperienced European merchants to do business with native traders was through "an intermediate class in whom both can repose confidence", namely the Straits Chinese from Melaka who could speak English and Malay, the *lingua franca* of the settlement.[102] Hence, the former relied on the latter as interlocutors and middlemen, or *compradores*, in the conduct of the long-distance trade.[103] These *Peranakan* Chinese were deemed to be better merchants than their counterparts from China by virtue of their familiarity with local and regional customs and the Asian way of doing business.[104] Like the Bugis, albeit operating mainly in the western sphere of the Archipelago and Borneo, Chinese merchants and dealers were relied upon to gather the Straits produce from, and distribute British manufactured products to, the interior parts of Singapore's extended hinterland. They also performed the indispensable function of assessing the creditworthiness of local traders and dealt in various Southeast Asian products on their own account.[105]

The early Chinese diaspora in Singapore was made up of male unskilled immigrants of peasant origin from southern China, a profile that had not altered late into the 19th century. Some were so-called "free labourers" who paid for their passage from China either on their own or by borrowing and could work for any employer they wished on arrival in Singapore. There were however others who had not the means to pay for their voyage and came as indentured labour under the "credit ticket" system. These immigrants were taken

---

97 K.S. Sandhu, *Indians in Malaya: Some Aspects of Their Immigration and Settlement (1786–1957)* (Cambridge University Press, 1969), p. 52.

98 Newbold, *Political and Statistical Account*, p. 280.

99 Marriott, "The Peoples of Singapore", p. 347; *Singapore Chronicle and Commercial Register*, 8 May 1834.

100 Wong, *The Trade of Singapore*, pp. 74–5.

101 G.W. Earl, "The Kri and Aru Islands", *The Journal of the Indian Archipelago and Eastern Asia*, ed. J.R. Logan, 7 (1853): 70.

102 Crawfurd, *Journal of an Embassy*, vol. 3, p. 263.

103 Yen Ching-Hwang, *A Social History of the Chinese in Singapore and Malaya: 1800–1911* (Singapore: Oxford University Press, 1986), p. 3.

104 Buckley, *An Anecdotal History*, p. 216.

105 A. Kobayashi, "The Role of Singapore in the Growth of Intra-Southeast Asian Trade, c.1820s–1852", *Southeast Asian Studies* 2, 3 (2013): 467–8.

on board goods-carrying ships sailing from China by labour brokers or captains of junks; on arrival, their passage money was paid by prospective employers and repayment was exacted through regular deductions from their wages.[106] Those who were artisans or craftsmen were quickly snapped up, with the profits pocketed by the broker or ship master. These parties also found employment for the rest by bargaining with the agents of employers.

In May 1823, Raffles published an Ordinance aimed at protecting such immigrants, stipulating that the amount of passage money was to be limited to 20 dollars and the period of service rendered in compensation thereof to not more than two years.[107] However, the law was not enforced and abuse within the system was rife from mid-century onwards when the credit ticket system evolved into a large-scale and lucrative "coolie trade".[108] Countless young men in rural China were enticed or tricked into emigrating and some died during the sea journey to Singapore from overcrowding and diseases, or were otherwise ill-treated. Those that could not be "sold" on arrival because they lacked skills or looked unhealthy were held against their will in temporary depots, rendering the system not too different from slavery. What drove these poor Chinese to put themselves through such ordeals were "the eager pursuit of gain", "pecuniary want" or "political necessity".[109] As labourers, they were "active, industrious, persevering" but "inveterate gamblers, and often addicted to smoking opium".

In contrast to Chinese migration which took place long before the period of Western colonisation, modern emigration from India commenced only with the establishment of British settlements in Southeast Asia. It began shortly after 1786 when Sir Francis Light founded Penang (then named Prince of Wales Island); by the end of the 18th century, there were nearly a thousand Indian immigrants working as agricultural labourers, shopkeepers and domestic servants on the island.[110] In Singapore, the first wave of migrants were sepoys (soldiers) in the employ of the EIC who together with an assorted company of milkmen, washermen and servants accompanied Raffles on his expedition in January 1819.[111] When Raffles came to Singapore for a second time from Penang in May 1819, a number of Indian businessmen followed him.

They were soon joined by Indian Muslim traders and shopkeepers from the Coromandel and Malabar coasts and the southern districts of Tamil Nadu, also known as the Chulias, who were attracted by the prospect of free trade, and whose presence in small

---

[106] Yen, *A Social History*, pp. 4–5.

[107] W.L. Blythe, "Historical Sketch of Chinese Labour in Malaya", *Journal of the Malayan Branch of the Royal Asiatic Society* 20, 1 (1947): 68–70.

[108] Yen, *A Social History*, pp. 6–8. The trade was also known as the "piglet" trade, which says much about how immigrants were treated.

[109] Newbold, *Political and Statistical Account*, pp. 10, 13. Nevertheless, the immigrants tended to be apolitical: "The Chinese do not mind who holds the cow as long as they can milk it".

[110] K.S. Sandhu, *Indian Migration and Population Change in Malaya, c.100–1957 A.D.: A Historical Geography*, Master of Arts Thesis (Department of Geography, The University of British Columbia, 1961), p. 196; Sandhu, *Indians in Malaya*, p. 47.

[111] J.B. Acharya, *Beyond the Myth: Indian Business Communities in Singapore* (Singapore: Institute of Southeast Asian Studies, 2011), pp. 25, 32.

numbers had long been ubiquitous in the Malay Archipelago.[112] Originally allocated land up the Singapore River, the Chulias subsequently spread out to Chulia Street, Cross Street and High Street, setting up shops and petty trading businesses that catered to their community.[113] The Tamil-speaking Klings also came from the Coromandel coast but they mostly served as general labourers, domestic servants or boatmen manning the *tongkangs* or lighters, who performed the quotidian task of transporting goods between ships anchored in the harbour and the wharfs on the Singapore River—the lifeblood and natural port of the town.[114] The busy commerce of the port was conducted along the whole river frontage and the waterfront where the private merchants' jetties were located and consisted of the ceaseless loading and unloading of cargoes brought by the tongkangs from the roads.

The year 1825 saw the arrival of a group of financiers from Madras, the Chettiars, well-known for their niche in money-lending.[115] In the early days before banks appeared on Singapore's financial scene, the Chettiars fulfilled the important function of extending loans to native traders and businessmen, especially those involved in the trade with India.[116] In fact, they continued to thrive right up to the 20th century on making credit available.[117] Another wave of Indians arriving in the same year were male convict labourers transferred from the British penal colony in Bencoolen following the retrocession of the settlement to the Dutch in 1824. These convicts originated mostly from North India and included thugs, dacoits, murderers and even political prisoners. The first batch of 200 prisoners came from both Bencoolen and Bengal and were confined to a godown by the Singapore River. Despite their criminal background, escapes were rare and convicts who showed good conduct could be employed on public works; later on, they could be promoted to become warders, in which capacity they supervised their fellow prisoners.[118] Raffles pioneered in Bencoolen the deployment of convicts in public works; in Singapore they were engaged in land filling and reclamation, roading and public building projects, such as the construction of Commercial Square, St. Andrew's Cathedral and Government House later on.[119] During the ensuing decades, the convicts were also called upon for mundane but no less necessary tasks like the killing of tigers in the jungle and the culling of stray dogs in the town, while some became hospital dressers and orderlies.

---

112 R. Rai, *Indians in Singapore 1819–1945: Diaspora in the Colonial Port City* (Oxford University Press, 2014), pp. 3–4.

113 Wong, "Commercial Growth", p. 62.

114 Earl, *The Eastern Seas*, p. 392; Marriott, "The Peoples of Singapore", p. 348; Dobbs, *The Singapore River*, p. 40. There is some controversy about the derogatory use of the term "Klings"; it is here used purely to give historical context.

115 Rai, *Indians in Singapore*, pp. 11–14, 15–16.

116 Kwa Chong Guan, Derek Heng, Peter Borschberg and Tan Tai Yong, *Seven Hundred Years: A History of Singapore* (Singapore: National Library Board and Marshall Cavendish Editions, 2019), pp. 211, 213–4.

117 Tan Tai Yong, "The Indian Ocean—Arab and Indian Traders", in *Maritime Heritage of Singapore*, ed. Lau and Lau, p. 28.

118 An audacious escape by 15 convicts took place in 1849 although 12 were recaptured. *The Straits Times*, 6 Nov. 1849, 13 Nov. 1849.

119 R. St.J. Braddell, "Crime: Its Punishment and Prevention", in *One Hundred Years of Singapore*, vol. I, ed. Makepeace, Brooke and Braddell, pp. 282–4.

The Europeans in Singapore stayed as a small elite community of a hundred residents or so, making up the differentiated levels of the colonial administration and merchant class. There was no civil service as such in the early days, only a few covenanted officers of the EIC, uncovenanted government servants and military officers.[120] The merchant class consisted of a curious mix of established traders who were the principals of merchant firms and who transacted business on their own account on the one hand, and young commercial assistants acting as agents for the European merchant houses on the other.[121] Nonetheless, the importance of the Europeans was disproportionate to their number, as they were the main providers of financial and human capital as well as of enterprise.[122] Almost all had extensive business dealings with the Chinese in regional and foreign goods while other English-speaking Straits Chinese and Eurasians worked as cashiers or clerks in merchant firms.[123] Educated Indians were also employed by the government as administrative and clerical staff, or as teachers.[124]

Fiscal Administration and Monetary System

A cardinal principle of the EIC's fiscal policy was the requirement that its eastern settlements be self-financing. Previously designated a "military outpost", Singapore after the Anglo-Dutch Treaty of 1824 was treated as a "commercial settlement". This meant that it had to earn its keep and not rely on funding from the Indian government.[125] As will be seen later, this policy presaged the principle subsequently adopted by the British colonial government of "living within one's means". It was imposed notwithstanding the pecuniary benefits that the Company derived from Singapore's existence, consisting of the profits on the opium trade, levies on cotton exports from India and commissions for the shipment of Straits articles to Britain. The local newspaper attempted to estimate the gains in 1827, reckoning them at no less than SPD58,000 a year.[126]

In this regard, Penang provided an instructive example for Singapore. It was founded as a free port but gave up the experiment in 1801, when it was forced to impose import and export duties of 5 per cent to cover the expenses of the settlement. The port town was then able to finance itself until it was made a Presidency of British India in 1805, whereupon its establishment became inflated and it had to be subsidised by India.[127] After the decision by the EIC to abandon it as a naval arsenal in 1810, the bureaucracy was sharply cut back but the annual deficit continued to grow steadily larger.[128] In 1816 when the government deficit was £81,448, a further retrenchment was ordered but Straits officials counter-argued

120 Nunn, "Some Account of Our Governors", p. 81.

121 Turnbull, *History of Modern Singapore*, pp. 34, 46; Newbold, *Political and Statistical Account*, p. 352.

122 Marriott, "The Peoples of Singapore", p. 347.

123 Earl, *The Eastern Seas*, p. 363.

124 Sandhu, *Indian Migration*, p. 216.

125 Nunn, "Some Account of Our Governors", p. 77; *Straits Settlements Records*, L.10, 26 Jan. 1820.

126 *Singapore Chronicle and Commercial Register*, 15 Mar. 1827.

127 Mills, Turnbull and Bassett, "*British Malaya*", p. 59; R. St.J. Braddell, "A Short History", p. 21.

128 Cowan, "Early Penang", pp. 5–6.

that Penang could prove its worth as a trading centre and a political outpost, bringing compensatory advantages to India.[129]

By 1821, however, this defence clearly could not be maintained, given the economic success of Singapore, while the deficit in Penang was as high as ever. The decline in the latter's trade caused a fall in its customs duties, on which the administration relied for half of its revenue, with the loss estimated at a total of SPD152,734 between 1821 and 1825.[130] Therefore, Penang's officials resisted both making the settlement a free port and an attempt to attain equal treatment with Singapore. On the contrary, after the two stations and Melaka were merged under its Presidency, they tried to extend the duty on the import of opium not produced in India (Turkey opium for example) to Singapore in 1827, at the rate of SPD6 per pound.[131] The merchants of Singapore protested vigorously and, to the chagrin of the local government in Penang, the Indian authorities ordered the suspension of all customs duties at the Straits Settlements, putting both Penang and Melaka on the same commercial footing as Singapore. Ironically then, this early attack on free trade had the opposite effect of entrenching the creed.

In contrast to Penang, Singapore right from the outset had to rely on raising revenue by means other than trade duties, or taxes on land and agriculture for that matter. As mentioned earlier, the wily Farquhar had devised a way to do so without violating the sacrosanct dictum of free trade by falling back on the time-tested method of taxing gaming, opium smoking and the consumption of spirits, seeking to gain advantage from the well-known vices of the Chinese population in Singapore and elsewhere in the region. He consulted Raffles in November 1819 on his plan but, not receiving a reply until March 1820, went ahead to institute "revenue farms" ("vice farms") for these activities.[132] Under this system, copied from the Dutch and practised in Penang and Bencoolen before Singapore was occupied, retailers of prepared opium and liquor had to bid for the right to sell their goods while those intending to operate gambling tables were taxed to provide the wherewithal for street cleaning and maintenance.[133] In effect, the government delegated its taxing authority to the private sector, and by so doing dispensed with the administrative burden. The farms also absolved the authorities from having to deal with the Chinese and evaded the problem of corruption.[134] In the first year, they generated SPD395 from opium, SPD100 from arrack (spirits) and SPD95 from gaming, which were partly used to foot policing expenses. Half a year later, Farquhar introduced port levies on visiting ships to augment the revenue.

The subsequent fate of these measures imparted a sardonic twist to Singapore's early history of fiscal management. During his last visit in May 1823, Raffles banned all forms of gambling and cock-fighting on the grounds that these were "highly destructive to the morals and happiness of the people" and "inconsistent with the principles of good

[129] In 1820, £100 was worth SPD367 (see the list of exchange rates at the front of the book).

[130] Cowan, "Early Penang", pp. 13–14; Buckley, *An Anecdotal History*, p. 180.

[131] *Straits Settlements Records*, N.3, 12 July 1827, 2 Oct. 1827.

[132] *Straits Settlements Records*, L.10, 2 Nov. 1819, 20 Mar. 1820.

[133] Buckley, *An Anecdotal History*, pp. 59–63.

[134] Cameron, *Our Tropical Possessions in Malayan India*, pp. 210–1.

government".[135] He retained the anchorage and port clearance fees but revised them to incorporate graduated rates in accordance with the tonnage of vessels; for example, ships of 500 tons or more paid SPD12, square-rigged vessels SPD6 and native prahus at most SPD5. However, on taking over from Farquhar, Crawfurd terminated the vessel charges and suspended the prohibition on gambling, arguing that it was impossible to extirpate and as such, the government ought to regulate and benefit from it through generating revenue. He even reported to the Supreme Government in Bengal that "many of the lower classes had quitted the Settlement on account of being deprived of a customary amusement".[136]

While practising economy, Crawfurd was compelled to write to the Indian government for permission to embark urgently on some public works, building on the initial infrastructure laid down by Farquhar and Raffles. Farquhar in a letter to Raffles in the latter part of 1819 had alluded to a sum of SPD8,961 being expended on public construction and in a second memoir dated May 1821, he detailed the total costs of constructing roads, bridges, fortifications and military buildings from the station's establishment in 1819 to that point as SPD17,877.[137] Of this sum, about fifteen miles of road had been built at a cost of SPD6,447 while SPD2,500 was expended on aqueducts for the supply of water to ships and the town. Crawfurd's subsequent letter proposed and provided justification for the building of a water course and reservoir for shipping purposes costing SPD1,000 and a temporary prison costing SPD900, as the present building was too small and insecure.[138] He also proposed to spend SPD1,200 on dredging and clearing the harbour of silted sand, which the Bengal government authorised in March 1824.[139]

These projects were to be funded by the proceeds from the revenue farms which brought in an average annual amount of SPD22,448 in 1821 and 1822. Opium was the biggest contributor, followed by the gaming and arrack farms. In 1825, Crawfurd reported that he had revamped the system of tendering for the farm rights, by splitting each farm into differentially sized lots and offering them for auction to the highest bidders. This method, he claimed, had the advantages of encouraging competition, rendering collusion impracticable and increasing the government's revenue.[140] Crawfurd also replaced the pork farm with that on pawnbroking and instituted a new farm for the manufacture and sale of gunpowder.[141] He was vindicated by the revenue that was raised in 1824, which more than doubled to SPD60,672 from the previous year. Reversing the ranking of the vices in the initial years, the gambling farm generated SPD26,112 while opium brought in SPD23,100.

---

135 *The Asiatic Journal and Monthly Register for British India and its Dependencies* 16 (July–Dec., 1823): 360–1, 544–5.

136 Song, *One Hundred Years' History of the Chinese*, pp. 21–2.

137 *Straits Settlements Records*, L.10, 2 Nov. 1819; "Notices of Singapore", *The Journal of the Indian Archipelago and Eastern Asia*, ed. J.R. Logan, 9 (1855): 450–1.

138 Hallifax, "Municipal Government", pp. 326–7.

139 "Notices of Singapore", *The Journal of the Indian Archipelago and Eastern Asia*, ed. J.R. Logan, 8 (1854): 403–5; *Straits Settlements Records*, M.2, 5 Mar. 1824.

140 J. Crawfurd, "Remarks on the Excise Revenue", *The Journal of the Indian Archipelago and Eastern Asia*, ed. J.R. Logan, 8 (1854): 408–10.

141 Alvin Tan, *Singapore: A Very Short History—From Temasek to Tomorrow* (Singapore: Talisman, 2022), p. 25.

Opium revenues rose further in the next two years but stabilised at SPD24,600 in 1827, partly due to slower growth of the Chinese population.[142] For comparison, it is worth noting that Penang, with a much larger population, raised only SPD27,600 from the opium farms in 1824.[143] As Crawfurd noted, the disproportionate increases in Singapore could be explained by the consumption capacity of the Chinese, specifically of the class that comprised unmarried males from China.

Gaming revenue pulled back in 1827 in reaction to overbidding in the previous years; at any rate, the gambling farms were shut down in 1830 because of the social misery and destitution they caused, rather than the moral grounds on which Raffles had forbidden them.[144] They were never to be reinstated until the modern era, in spite of repeated calls for their return as a means of raising much needed revenue and eradicating corruption in the police force.[145] The spirits farm, held by the Indian merchants, showed more erratic changes from year to year because the capital investment required for distilling liquor was the heaviest amongst the farms; in 1827, they contributed SPD12,000 to total revenue. The pawnbroking farm brought in the smallest collection, at SPD1,332. In addition to the farm revenue, the government collected rents from houses and markets, as well as fines and fees. The two public markets located at the Chinese town and Malay quarters were occupied by fishmongers, vegetable vendors and fruit sellers, bringing in SPD4,000 in 1827.[146] *In toto*, the colonial revenue amounted to SPD76,452 in 1827, increasing to SPD84,504 by 1830.[147]

As far as government expenditure is concerned, the records for the early years are scanty but some figures on disbursements in 1827 are available (Table 2).[148] These show that the largest portion of the civil expenditure in that year was paid as salaries to colonial staff, notwithstanding Raffles' efforts to keep the bureaucracy lean. Learning from his experiences in Penang and Bencoolen, he left behind in 1823 a civilian establishment consisting of only the Resident, his assistant, the Master Attendant cum Store-keeper and the Chaplain, whose salaries and those of subordinate staff together with miscellaneous expenses amounted to a mere SPD3,500.[149] In addition, there was a small police force, headed by a son-in-law of William Farquhar, of 17 constables and two sergeants.[150] By 1827, however, a Deputy Resident Councillor, two Assistant Councillors, a Sheriff, a Superintendent of Lands as well as a Coroner had been appointed, supported by a large

---

142 "Revenues of Singapore", *The Journal of the Indian Archipelago and Eastern Asia*, ed. J.R. Logan, 8 (1854): 416.

143 T. Braddell, *Statistics of the British Possessions*, Table No. 7, Abstract Statement of the Population and Revenues of Prince of Wales Island from 1805–06 to 1823–24, in Dollars.

144 R. St.J. Braddell, "Crime", p. 264.

145 *The Singapore Free Press and Mercantile Advertiser*, 21 Jan. 1836, 19 Oct. 1865.

146 *Straits Settlements Records*, M.2, 9 Mar. 1827.

147 "Revenues of Singapore", *The Journal of the Indian Archipelago and Eastern Asia*, ed. J.R. Logan, 8 (1854): 415–9; *Singapore Chronicle and Commercial Register*, 22 Apr. 1830.

148 "Accounts, Respecting the Annual Revenues and Disbursements, Trade and Sales, of the East India Company", *House of Commons Parliamentary Papers*, 1830.

149 Buckley, *An Anecdotal History*, p. 107.

150 R. St.J. Braddell, "Crime", p. 244.

clerical staff. Further, Crawfurd's judicial reforms had added court and other staff expenses. The next most substantial items of expenditure were the stipends of SPD14,356 paid to the Sultan of Johor and the Temenggong, as agreed upon in the treaty negotiated by Crawfurd. In contrast, the combined spending on medical services, elementary schools and the police force amounted to a paltry SPD8,635.

Table 2. Singapore Government Expenditure, 1827

	SPD
Civil	
Resident Councillor	10,641
Deputy Resident Councillor	7,201
Assistant Resident Councillors	6,533
Resident and Record Office	4,554
Accountants and Treasury Office	1,082
Clerical Establishment	5,898
Botanical Garden and Post Office	1,115
Medical Establishment and Stores	3,482
Master Attendant's Department and Import/Export Office	9,464
Courts of Judicature and Requests, Registrar's Office, etc.	4,010
Sheriff's Office and Superintendent of Lands	2,999
Coroner	495
Police Establishment	4,219
Convict Establishment	2,577
Elementary Schools	925
Rent of Houses	2,198
Political	
Stipend of Sultan	12,029
Stipend of Temenggong	2,313
Total	81,735

Source: "Accounts, Respecting the Annual Revenues and Disbursements, Trade and Sales, of the East India Company", *House of Commons Parliamentary Papers*, 1830, p. 83.

From the time of its founding in 1819 to 1823, Singapore was an infant British settlement of transient immigrants with an uncertain future and its affairs were administered by Raffles in Bencoolen. Only after the Anglo-Dutch Treaty of March 1824 was signed was its political status secured as an Indian dependency and its economic future looked more promising, yet far from assured.[151] As far as local administrative expenses were concerned, Singapore became self-supporting as early as 1821 owing to the revenues from the farms.[152] It could therefore enjoy a degree of fiscal autonomy from the Indian government after

[151] R. St.J. Braddell, "A Short History", p. 20.

[152] Cowan, "Early Penang", p. 17; *The Singapore Free Press and Mercantile Advertiser*, 8 June 1843, 14 Sept. 1843, 12 Aug. 1858.

1824. In that year, coconut oil lamps supplied the first street lighting and three years later, drainage works for the town were undertaken, both initiated by town committees.[153]

After 1826, the first Governor of the Straits Settlements, Robert Fullerton, had to consider new measures to raise revenue and reduce disbursements, since Singapore's fiscal surplus was not large enough to cover the deficit at Penang, or for that matter to pay for its own military charges of SPD30,000 per annum which were borne by the Indian government.[154] This pattern of a surplus at Singapore and deficits at Penang and Melaka persisted for many years, at least until the early 1840s.[155] In 1829, Fullerton came up with the idea of new taxes on land, dwellings and wealth but the EIC's Directors in London had by then decided to downgrade the Straits Settlements from a Presidency to a Residency under the direction of the Bengal government.[156] In the process, the number of key officials in Singapore was reduced from 19 to 8, headed by a Resident Councillor who reported to the Governor of the Straits Settlements.[157] Nonetheless, Fullerton's proposed regulations on land taxation, including subjecting registration to a fee and the charging of quit rent, were implemented in 1830—measures that would be much maligned in later years.

On the related matter of the monetary system, Singapore also had some leeway to deviate from the policies of the Bengal Presidency, even though the Penang government had attempted to impose the use of the Sicca (or Calcutta) rupee when the settlement was under its Presidency.[158] In principle, this intervention was justified as the Sicca rupee was sovereign within British Indian Dominions; Singapore, like the rest, had to use it in administration and official transactions. In reality, Raffles had stipulated that the settlement's establishment be paid and accounts be kept in Spanish dollars, which had long been the medium of exchange in the Eastern Archipelago.[159] The reliance on the Spanish dollar was undergirded by the fact that it was also the *de facto* currency of international commerce until the mid-1820s when its scarcity forced merchants to use Dutch guilders as the main currency of trade within the region. After the 1830s, however, the Spanish dollar reasserted its dominance in regional and international trade. Thus, Singapore's choice of money reflected its development as the Archipelago's entrepôt.

At the bazaar, William Farquhar decided to accept as circulation currencies Dutch guilders, Java rupees and all British India rupees, except the Calcutta Siccas.[160] As in the Temasek era, these are all forms of specie money or metallic currencies. The Dutch copper *doits* were the money handled by the common people and therefore, the most popular in daily transactions, although other subsidiary currencies such as Chinese copper coins were

153 Kathirithamby-Wells, "Early Singapore", pp. 49, 69; "Drainage of Singapore Town", *The Journal of the Indian Archipelago and Eastern Asia*, ed. J.R. Logan, 8 (1854): 414–5; Hallifax, "Municipal Government", pp. 316–7, 325; *Straits Settlements Records*, Q.2, 17 Aug. 1827, 18 Aug. 1827, 2 Oct. 1827.

154 Cowan, "Early Penang", pp. 17–18.

155 *The Singapore Free Press and Mercantile Advertiser*, 29 July 1841.

156 Nunn, "Some Account of Our Governors", p. 82.

157 Turnbull, *The Straits Settlements*, p. 55.

158 Liew and Wilson, *A History of Money*, pp. 43, 45.

159 "Raffles' Instructions on Formation of Singapore", *The Journal of the Indian Archipelago and Eastern Asia*, ed. J.R. Logan, 7 (1853): 327–30.

160 Ibid. pp. 327–30.

also used. In 1828, the Mexican dollar and other South American dollars—named after their places of minting—were officially accepted in payments to the Treasury as equivalent in value to the Spanish dollar, thus mitigating its shortage.[161] This multitude of currencies in use, like in ancient times, was the result of both Singapore's cosmopolitanism as well as the *laissez faire* attitude of its administrators. But the complex calculations needed to exchange one currency for another, not to mention the losses occasioned by currency fluctuations, resulted in unpredictable transaction costs.[162] This led John Crawfurd to propose the creation of a local currency in 1823. His intent in doing so was not to supplant the Spanish silver dollar, which he declared "legitimate" currency (legal tender) for trade, but rather for the convenience and cost reduction that a single currency in smaller denominations and coinage would bring to the marketplace. However, nothing was done and it was more than two decades later that Singapore obtained its own currency.[163]

---

[161] *Singapore Chronicle and Commercial Register*, 22 May 1828.

[162] Liew and Wilson, *A History of Money*, pp. 44–5, 46.

[163] *Straits Settlement Records*, M.1, 24 Sept. 1824.

Chapter 3

Plantation Economy and Commercial Rivalry, 1831–45

Richard Winstedt, a colonial historian of Malaya, dismissed Singapore's history as "a scene of peaceful commercial development".[1] While too general, this statement could perhaps be an apt characterisation of the 1830s and the 1840s, the pedestrian though somewhat depressed decades following the port's establishment. If one peers into the period more carefully, however, much happened that would count as significant economic history. For one, Singapore developed plantation agriculture in a quite atypical manner. For another, beneath the veneer of peaceful trading relations, Anglo-Dutch rivalry persisted even while pirates around the waters of Singapore disrupted trade. On at least two occasions, threats to the settlement's existence emerged and vanished. As the population grew and job opportunities expanded, the city's physical and social infrastructures began to develop, building upon the early trade successes.

Gambier and Pepper Cultivation

Gambier is the extract prepared from the eponymous plant and is traditionally used for medicinal purposes and as a masticatory to be chewed with betel leaf, areca nut and lime, a practice that originated in India and spread to Southeast Asia.[2] In the early 19th century, it started to be utilised as a tanning and dyeing agent for cotton, wool, silk and leather, giving rise to an industrial demand. Consequently, the price of gambier in world markets tripled between 1831 and early 1834, from an average of SPD1.50 to SPD4.50 per pikul.[3] In 1835, Britain rescinded the duty on the article's import, thus giving the gambier trade a boost.[4] The price of pepper rose in tandem with that of gambier, as the two commodities shared a symbiotic relationship: composted gambier leaves could be used as a fertiliser for pepper plants and they were often grown together within the same plantation in the ratio of one acre of pepper to ten acres of gambier. Pepper vines required

---

[1] R.O. Winstedt, *Malaya and Its History*, 1948, 7th edition (London: 1966), p. 61.

[2] Lim Guan Hock, "Gambier and Early Development of Singapore", in *A General History of the Chinese*, ed. Kwa and Kua, p. 36.

[3] The prices cited are from ibid., p. 40.

[4] C.A. Trocki, "The Origins of the Kangchu System 1740–1860", *Journal of the Malaysian Branch of the Royal Asiatic Society* 49, 2 (1976): 49.

continuous nurture, keeping the labour force in productive employment in between gambier maturation cycles.

The lush jungles of Singapore provided the supply of firewood needed for boiling the gambier leaves, leaving behind the extract which was allowed to cool and harden before being cut into small cubes and marketed.[5] Not by chance, gambier and pepper were the only two cash crops that had been found to flourish in Singapore, given its soil and climate, although at one time or another, cotton and sugarcane cultivation was being attempted during the "agricultural era" that lasted from the 1830s to the 1850s.[6] During this period, the British and European residents were much taken up with agricultural enterprise and experimentation with crops.[7] By contrast, the island was also well-suited for vegetable and fruit growing, which was undertaken by Chinese in market gardens at the back of the town—an activity that was carried on at least until the 1860s.[8] This local food supply was supplemented by imports mainly from the west coast of the Malay Peninsula.[9]

Nutmeg was cultivated in Singapore at about the same time as gambier and pepper, mostly by Europeans, albeit without the success that attended the latter. By the 1860s, however, the crop had all but disappeared from the island due to an unknown disease that spread from the plantations in Penang, as a result of which many British and Chinese nutmeg planters were reduced to ruin.[10] Originally grown in the Moluccas, the spice was introduced into Singapore by no less than Stamford Raffles himself.[11] At the height of the nutmeg mania, hundreds of acres of land for cultivation were purchased as far out as four or five miles from the town.[12] In 1848, 23 plantations were noted, many of which were in the Claymore and Tanglin areas.[13] These occupied 1,190 acres of land, with 71,400 nutmeg trees planted on them.[14] However, Singapore's output could not match Penang's, with the gross value of production in 1848 being SPD31,514, less than one-third of the latter, due in part to a lack of land and manure. Coconut plantations could also be found in Singapore well into the mid-century, especially in the Katong area. In 1849, coconut cultivation occupying 2,658 acres of land yielded a monetary value of SPD10,800.[15]

---

[5] *Singapore Chronicle and Commercial Register*, 1 May 1834.

[6] "Agriculture of Singapore", *The Journal of the Indian Archipelago and Eastern Asia*, ed. J.R. Logan, 3 (1849): 508–10; T.O. Crane, "Remarks on the Cultivation of Cotton in Singapore", *The Journal of the Indian Archipelago and Eastern Asia*, ed. J.R. Logan, 5 (1851): 120–4; Buckley, *An Anecdotal History*, pp. 420–1; H. Price, "Planting in Singapore", in *One Hundred Years of Singapore*, vol. II, ed. Makepeace, Brooke and Braddell, p. 83.

[7] Savage, *Lion City Narratives*, pp. 135–43, 145, 146.

[8] Earl, *The Eastern Seas*, p. 353; Song, *One Hundred Years' History of the Chinese*, pp. 194–5.

[9] *Singapore Chronicle and Commercial Register*, 12 Jan. 1832.

[10] Turnbull, *History of Modern Singapore*, p. 62.

[11] *Straits Settlements Records*, L.10, 18 Aug. 1819.

[12] Cameron, *Our Tropical Possessions in Malayan India*, pp. 30–2, 81–2.

[13] T. Oxley, "Some Account of the Nutmeg and Its Cultivation", *The Journal of the Indian Archipelago and Eastern Asia*, ed. J.R. Logan, 2 (1848): 659.

[14] T. Braddell, *Statistics of the British Possessions*, pp. 16–17.

[15] Buckley, *An Anecdotal History*, p. 502.

It is not known when gambier and pepper planting began in Singapore although in 1819, a number of Chinese were already cultivating gambier on the low hills near the town.[16] It has been conjectured that the planters came from the Riau Islands and in 1822, the Resident reported that some 20 gambier plantations were sold.[17] But the commencement of gambier cultivation on a large scale by the Chinese appears to be tied to the transfer of the gambier trade from those islands to Singapore in the late 1820s.[18] The end of the plantation economy is easier to date as the 15-year soil exhaustion cycle of gambier meant that by the late 1840s, the Chinese agriculturists had to shift their operations to the neighbouring Malayan state of Johor due to a shortage of land and firewood. This move was hastened by the government's land policy, specifically the decision to charge quit rents for the ground that the planters occupied, following the start of systematic land surveys in the interior of Singapore early in the decade.[19]

Before this change in colonial policy, Chinese cultivators operated by simply clearing a tract of land in the jungle and planting a part of it in gambier and another part in pepper, without so much as applying for a licence from the local authorities. Hence, they were squatters practising a form of shifting cultivation of a pair of "get-rich-quick" cash crops. It took three years for the pepper plants to mature and in the meantime, the fast-yielding gambier crop would generate an income.[20] When the soil became impoverished, the squatter cultivators would move to a fresh clearing and repeat the process.[21] The areas cultivated by the Chinese were typically small—of about 50 acres—though they appeared to have grown larger in later years.[22] The plantation owners obtained capital from the merchants and shopkeepers, or the *towkays*, in town, pledging the future plantation and its products as collateral for the loan. The implicit rate of interest charged on such borrowing was exorbitantly high, at about 12 per cent, since capital was scarce, the risk of failure high and the Europeans were deterred from financing the enterprise because of the uncertain legal status of the lands cultivated; moreover, the EIC forbade them from purchasing land.[23] Furthermore, the planters had to obtain food, clothes and supplies from the same creditors at inflated prices, with a commission on the agricultural output sold to them added for good measure.[24]

---

[16] W. Bartley, "Population of Singapore in 1819", *Journal of the Malaysian Branch of the Royal Asiatic Society* 42, 1 (1969): 112–3.

[17] Trocki, "Origins of the Kangchu System", p. 139; C.A. Trocki, *The Prince of Pirates: The Temenggongs and the Development of Johor and Singapore, 1784–1885* (Singapore: Singapore University Press, 1979), p. 92.

[18] Lim, "Gambier", p. 38.

[19] Trocki, *Prince of Pirates*, p. 98.

[20] J.C. Jackson, "Chinese Agricultural Pioneering in Singapore and Johore 1800–1917", *Journal of the Malaysian Branch of the Royal Asiatic Society* 38, 1 (1965): 80.

[21] J. Balestier, "View of the State of Agriculture in the British Possessions in the Straits of Malacca", *The Journal of the Indian Archipelago and Eastern Asia*, ed. J.R. Logan, 2 (1848): 143, 145–6.

[22] Trocki, *Prince of Pirates*, p. 141.

[23] J.T. Thomson, "General Report on the Residency of Singapore, Drawn up Principally with a View of Illustrating its Agricultural Statistics", *The Journal of the Indian Archipelago and Eastern Asia*, ed. J.R. Logan, 4 (1850): 39; *Singapore Chronicle and Commercial Register*, 22 May 1828.

[24] Lim, "Gambier", pp. 45–6; *Singapore Free Press*, 28 Mar. 1839.

The gambier and pepper cultivators relied for labour on emigrants from China who for the most part entered into engagements to work for a year, in lieu of payment for their passage money, and who in their turn had to purchase food, opium and provisions from the planter at extortionate prices. This almost always ensured, when gambling losses were added to the bill, that the labourers remained enslaved after the period of their indenture had expired. Each plantation, or *bangsal* as it was called, was worked by 3 to 11 men, depending on its size, and supervised by a headman. A typical wage for the agricultural labourer was SPD3–3.50 a month.[25] This remuneration apparently included a premium to cover the risk of being taken by tigers, which purportedly occurred at the rate of one man a day.[26] The tiger menace became so deadly in the 1840s that some plantations had to be abandoned because no Chinese would live in them.[27]

Javanese and Boyanese were sometimes recruited as labourers, especially on the nutmeg and coconut plantations where the work was light, and were paid a lower wage of SPD2.50–3.00 a month.[28] Nevertheless, nominal wages fluctuated with product prices, going up in good times and declining in downturns, thus partially insulating plantation owners through a flexi-wage system. The method of farming gambier was both labour-intensive and primitive, requiring only the hoe.[29] On average, the smaller plantations produced 110 pikuls of gambier and 50 pikuls of pepper in a year while the largest plantations produced about 210 pikuls of gambier and 125–150 pikuls of pepper.[30] A detailed estimate made in 1851 showed that at the prevailing gambier price of SPD1.45 per pikul and pepper price of SPD4.50 per pikul, even a relatively large plantation of 200 acres with an annual output of 170 pikuls of gambier and 70 pikuls of pepper and employing eight men would make a profit of only SPD73.[31] The best run plantations earned somewhat more, especially when the gambier price rose in world markets; even so, the maximum profit obtained was at most SPD400.[32] Consequently, many cultivators earned only a small income while others remained either perennially indebted to the Chinese financiers in town or absconded altogether.[33]

---

[25] J.T. Thomson, "General Report on the Residency of Singapore, Drawn up Principally with a View of Illustrating its Agricultural Statistics", *The Journal of the Indian Archipelago and Eastern Asia*, ed. J.R. Logan, 3 (1849): 747. Another source stated that the wage was slightly higher at SPD4.00 per month. Buckley, *An Anecdotal History*, p. 337.

[26] Cameron, *Our Tropical Possessions in Malayan India*, pp. 90–4; Savage, *Lion City Narratives*, pp. 132–5. This claim is not improbable since in 1840, five men were killed in eight days and many deaths went unreported. Buckley, *An Anecdotal History*, p. 220.

[27] Song, *One Hundred Years' History of the Chinese*, p. 88; Davidson, *Trade and Travel in the Far East*, pp. 51–2.

[28] Cameron, *Our Tropical Possessions in Malayan India*, pp. 90–4.

[29] Balestier, "View of the State of Agriculture", p. 150.

[30] Lim, "Gambier", pp. 43–4, 53–4; Song, *One Hundred Years' History of the Chinese*, pp. 51–2.

[31] *The Straits Times*, 28 Jan. 1851.

[32] *The Singapore Free Press and Mercantile Advertiser*, 28 Mar. 1839.

[33] Jackson, "Chinese Agricultural Pioneering", pp. 81–2.

Exploitative as the system of financier-planter and planter-labourer relations may seem, the early agricultural colonisation of Singapore was achieved by its means. And while the squatter cultivators were justly blamed for depleting the soil and deforesting the island, it was through their labour that Singapore was cleared of thick jungles and opened up. In 1836, the total area devoted to gambier and pepper cultivation in Singapore was 2,350 acres, going up to 5,000 acres in 1840.[34] As the planters abandoned exhausted land nearer the city in the districts of Toa Payoh and Ang Mo Kio, they cleared new ground by pushing further into the northern and western interior, including the hilly areas around Bukit Timah, Thomson Road and Mandai, and later into virgin territories such as Yio Chu Kang and Chua Chu Kang, in which the toponym *kang* signifies a port.[35] By 1848, there were 600 gambier and pepper plantations, employing about 6,000 labourers and the areas planted with gambier and pepper were 24,220 acres and 2,614 acres, respectively.[36]

Production of gambier rose accordingly from 10,549 pikuls in 1834 to 22,000 pikuls in 1836 and further to 80,000 pikuls in 1848; that of pepper was given as 10,000 pikuls in 1836 and was likely around 36,000 pikuls in 1848.[37] Since gambier and pepper were export-oriented crops destined for both global and regional markets (Britain, India and the Celebes were the top three destinations in 1836), the increases in output were mirrored in the trade statistics. Excluding shipments to Penang and Melaka, gambier exports were 37,306 pikuls in 1836 and 87,178 pikuls in 1840, earning Singapore SPD54,670 and SPD236,785, respectively (Figure 2).[38] In 1849, shipments rose to a record 140,667 pikuls.[39] On average, the gambier sourced mainly from Bintan island in the Riau Archipelago through the *prahu pukat* trade made up about one-third of all exports.[40] As a proportion of total export value, these quantities were insignificant (less than 3 per cent), but the importance of the plantation economy lay in its salutary effects on Singapore's early growth. It generated employment for immigrant labourers, which in turn contributed to population expansion and to the fiscal revenue generated through the vice farms mentioned in the previous chapter.[41]

---

34 Ibid., p. 78.

35 K. Yamashita, "Residential Segregation of Chinese Dialect Groups in Singapore: with Focus on the Period Before ca. 1970", *Geographical Review of Japan* 59 (Ser. B), 2 (1986): 88; Low Siow Chek, *Gambier-and-Pepper Planting in Singapore, 1819–1860*, Academic Exercise (University of Malaya, 1955), p. 12.

36 Turnbull, *History of Modern Singapore*, p. 63; Thomson, *General Report*, 1850, p. 219.

37 Buckley, *An Anecdotal History*, pp. 241, 307.

38 Newbold, *Political and Statistical Account*, pp. 297, 320; C.P. Holloway, *Tabular Statements of the Commerce of Singapore during the Years 1823/24 to 1839/40 Inclusive* (Singapore, 1842), pp. 2, 4. The data for gambier and pepper exports are extracted from the price currents published in *The Singapore Free Press and Mercantile Advertiser* (courtesy of Atsushi Kobayashi).

39 T. Braddell, *Statistics of the British Possessions*, p. 17.

40 *The Singapore Free Press and Mercantile Advertiser*, 29 Dec. 1836.

41 Trocki, *Prince of Pirates*, pp. 95–6; Wong, "Commercial Growth", p. 54.

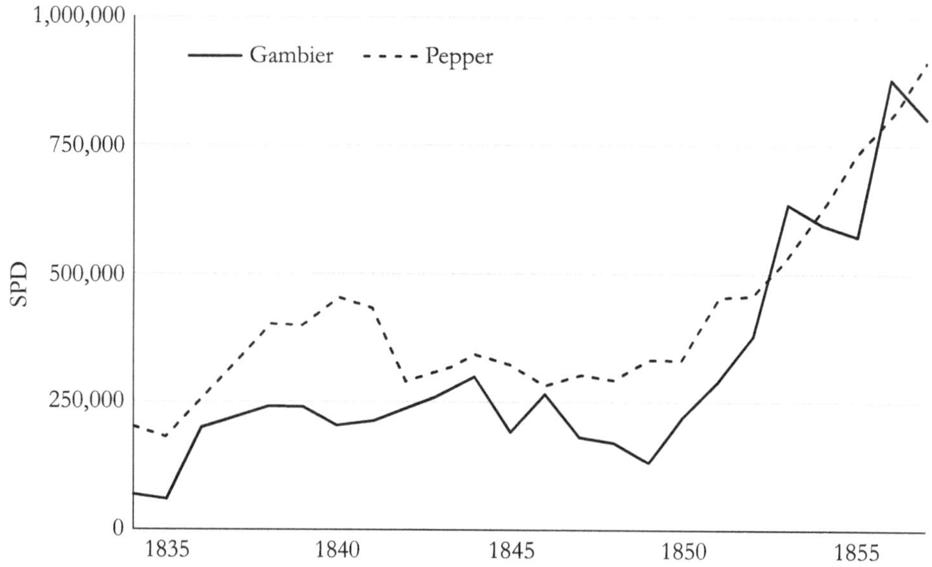

Figure 2. Gambier and Pepper Exports from Singapore, 1834–57
Source: Based on data supplied courtesy of Atsushi Kobayashi.

The demise of the plantation economy in Singapore can be dated to the passing of the Straits Land Act in 1839, which allowed the colonial government not only to declare all occupied lands not held under a grant or title as liable to assessment but also to evict squatter cultivators. Prior to that, a land act had been enacted in 1830 as part of Governor Fullerton's tax reforms to make agricultural land outside the limits of Singapore town available for cultivation on renewable 15-year leases.[42] The land was subject to an annual quit rent of SPD3 or SPD6 per acre depending on location while the rate within the town limits was SPD10 an acre, all of which assessments were considered to be high.[43] The act was revised in 1837 to lengthen the initial lease period to 20 years and make it renewable for another 30 years. However, it was a dead letter because potential lessees could add value to the land under lease only from the yield on trees planted, some of which had gestation periods of 10 to 15 years, leaving little time for the cultivator to be compensated for his investment.[44] Moreover, the law encouraged speculation in large tracts of land and the planting of exhausting crops such as gambier and pepper. The 1839 Land Act waived rent in the first two years, but due to the lack of long-term property rights, there were still few takers.

[42] Low, *Gambier-and-Pepper Planting*, pp. 39–40.

[43] Lornie, "Land Tenure", pp. 304–5, 307–8; Savage, *Lion City Narratives*, pp. 143, 144.

[44] Turnbull, *Straits Settlements*, p. 141; Thomson, *General Report*, 1850, pp. 38, 217; Earl, *The Eastern Seas*, pp. 408–9.

Meanwhile, the surveys of Singapore's interior proceeded steadily under the supervision of the Government Surveyor John Turnbull Thomson who arrived in 1841.[45] As late as 1850, the ratio of cultivated to uncultivated land was still only about one to four despite the exertions of the Chinese agricultural pioneers.[46] Of the 34,949 acres under cultivation, three-quarters were devoted to gambier and pepper while nutmeg and coconut together accounted for slightly over one-tenth. As for revenue, the value of land leased for agricultural purposes was a mere SPD3,040 in 1845, two years after the government finally conceded to the long-standing demand by European would-be agriculturists for land to be granted in perpetuity, whereas the quit rent collected from town properties amounted to SPD15,494.[47] A decade later, however, the number of agricultural land titles issued had increased to 792 although by that time, agriculture in Singapore was already in decline.[48]

In 1844, with the first land surveys of the island's interior in hand, the government demanded that squatters pay between SPD1.80 to SPD3.60 per acre for a deed of sale to stay on the land that they were occupying, an amount that was considered excessive. Even though the surveys were motivated in part by frequent territorial disputes between the Chinese cultivators, this imposition alarmed them as they found it difficult to make a decent profit since the gambier price had dropped to SPD1.50 per pikul.[49] An exodus to Johor started in the mid-1840s and gathered momentum after 1855, at which date the colonial authorities issued threats to evict illegal planters. In the middle of 1845, 52 gambier plantations had already commenced at fertile river sites in the state, engaging altogether 500 labourers.[50] The planters in Singapore pleaded with the authorities for exemption from the payments, but to no avail, and were compelled to hasten the process of agricultural relocation to Johor.[51] Even so, gambier cultivation in Singapore was phased out very slowly: in 1855, 39,650 pikuls of gambier were still produced by 4,818 plantation workers.[52] From that time on, production of gambier declined gradually amid fluctuations in global demand and prices until the crop's cultivation ceased at the turn of the century with the rise of pineapples and rubber.[53]

Thus, Singapore had replaced the Riau Islands as the main trading centre and producer of gambier in the 1830s, only to lose the position to Johor after the 1860s. Nonetheless, the city remained the financial and commercial centre of gambier and pepper trading throughout the 19th century.[54] Teochew merchants in Singapore formed a cartel and

---

45 Thomson, *General Report*, 1850, pp. 206–9, 211, 219.

46 T. Braddell, *Statistics of the British Possessions*, p. 7.

47 *Singapore Chronicle and Commercial Register*, 26 Dec. 1833; *The Singapore Free Press and Mercantile Advertiser*, 7 Sept. 1837, 5 July 1838, 22 June 1843, 29 June 1843.

48 Lim, "Gambier", p. 51; Lornie, "Land Tenure", p. 311.

49 *The Singapore Free Press and Mercantile Advertiser*, 4 Nov. 1841.

50 Jackson, "Chinese Agricultural Pioneering", pp. 83–4.

51 Low, *Gambier-and-Pepper Planting*, pp. 38, 42–3.

52 Lim, "Gambier", pp. 56–7.

53 J.C. Jackson, *Planters and Speculators: Chinese and European Agricultural Enterprise in Malaya* (Kuala Lumpur: University of Malaya Press, 1968), pp. 84–6; Price, "Planting in Singapore", p. 80.

54 Trocki, *Prince of Pirates*, p. 116.

continued to finance the planters in Johor in return for a monopsony on the output.[55] In addition, the proximity of the new plantations made it convenient for Singapore to serve as the supplier of provisions and the marketer of the produce. Whereas gambier and pepper cultivation in Singapore was haphazardly undertaken and semi-legal, the system adopted in Johor was orderly. Cultivators were granted legal rights by the Temenggong, whose jurisdiction included Johor, to occupy the land and Chinese headmen, or *kangchu*, were appointed to oversee each river site.[56] By the early 1860s, the number of plantations in Johor had risen to 1,200, the worker count to 15,000, and more than one million Spanish dollars had been invested by Singapore Chinese.[57]

To close this discussion of an unusual episode in Singapore's economic history, mention should be made of the manufacture of sago as it represented the first known industrial enterprise of the colonial era, beginning as it did in 1824 and lasting until the early 20th century.[58] The sago tree was to be found across the whole length and breadth of the Eastern Archipelago, although Singapore imported its raw sago mainly from Sumatra and Borneo.[59] Once the pith of the sago palm landed at the Singapore River, it was brought to the nearby factories around the foot of Pearl's Hill (specifically, Sago Street and Sago Lane), where Chinese workers turned it into pearl sago, a translucent and glutinous grain that resulted from heating and coagulation. This production method of pearl sago, which originated in Melaka, was labour-intensive and inefficient. The raw sago was first given a thorough washing and drying, at which point it was ready for roasting in iron pans heated by open furnaces, which rendered it hard and tough. Around 20 to 30 men were employed in a factory, each paid between SPD2.50–4.00 and the best workers had a share in the profits. In 1849, there were 15 of these enterprises started by Chinese and two by Europeans, all small-scale in nature. In aggregate, they exported 28,700 pikuls of pearl sago worth SPD100,000 to Asia, Europe and America.

Trade, Credit and Agency Houses

In 1836, it was remarked that "the island can, as yet, have no indigenous productions; it is in fact a commercial emporium, probably will never be much more".[60] This observation serves as a fitting reminder that Singapore's primary means of livelihood resided in trade, the plantation economy notwithstanding. In this regard, the 1830s were a difficult time for the settlement's merchants owing to sluggish trade conditions and continued competition with the Dutch. Despite this, commercial development proceeded apace and Singapore's

---

[55] Song, *One Hundred Years' History of the Chinese*, p. 54.

[56] Jackson, *Planters and Speculators*, pp. 22–4, 84–5.

[57] P.J. Drake, *Merchants, Bankers, Governors: British Enterprise in Singapore and Malaya, 1786–1920* (Singapore: World Scientific, 2018), p. 62.

[58] *Singapore Chronicle and Commercial Register*, 1 Mar. 1827, 15 Mar. 1827; C.W. Darbishire, "Commerce and Currency", in *One Hundred Years of Singapore*, vol. II, ed. Makepeace, Brooke and Braddell, p. 29.

[59] J.R. Logan, "Sago", *The Journal of the Indian Archipelago and Eastern Asia*, ed. J.R. Logan, 3 (1849): 288–9, 302–6, 308–9.

[60] Phipps, *A Practical Treatise*, p. 262. The same comment was made by Begbie, *The Malayan Peninsula*, p. 353.

trade and financing institutions matured within a hierarchical structure, with the European mercantile firms known as "agency houses" at the apex, the Chinese traders in the middle and the native traders of the Eastern Archipelago at the base.[61]

The trade doldrums were basically caused by financial problems which led to the failure of all the main British merchant firms in Calcutta in a short span of the five years from 1830 to 1834.[62] The origins of these entities can be traced to the emergence of non-East India Company mercantile firms in London during the late 18th century which were engaged in the India–China trade, or "country trade", in which private merchants were permitted to participate. These firms were typically managed by ex-servants of the EIC who were given exclusive trading rights by the Company, in addition to the "privilege trade" or cargo space that was entitled to captains commanding the East Indiaman ships. Eventually, the East Asia agency houses, as they were called, fell into the hands of another group of "free traders" who were licensed to operate as merchants in India after the Company lost its trading monopoly there in 1813, again using the capital of the EIC's employees.

If the EIC was the spearhead of the British advance into Asia, the agency houses were the vehicle for the expansion of trade and colonial capitalism, and Singapore was the base for the country traders in the East Indies. The agency houses in London set up branches or sister agencies in Calcutta and other Indian presidencies to circumvent the EIC's remaining monopoly on the China trade and to engage in a wide range of commercial activities. These included dealing in local products, financing plantations, managing the financial affairs of wealthy Indian clients and providing remittance facilities for the Company's employees in the so-called "triangular trade" involving tea and opium. By 1790, 15 agency houses had been established in Calcutta and they also helped to facilitate the EIC's China trade by providing a front for the export of Indian opium to China in exchange for tea.[63] After the EIC was stripped of its commercial monopoly in India, the Company's share of the country trade became insignificant, taken over by the London agency houses and new firms set up in India to import British cotton goods. However, financial troubles began to fester for these houses and firms when the Company borrowed heavily to pay for the Anglo-Burmese war of 1824 to 1826, causing interest rates to rise. The debts of the Calcutta agency houses mounted, undermining confidence and triggering their collapse starting from 1830.

The financial debacle in Calcutta reverberated through the Straits ports, with Singapore being especially affected because of the extensive commercial connections that had been established early on between the agency houses in the two cities. Some of the Singapore agencies were initially set up as branches or agents of the London and Calcutta houses,

---

[61] Wong, "Commercial Growth", p. 62. Strictly speaking, the mercantile firms came to be known as agency houses only with the advent of rubber in the 20th century when they managed rubber companies on behalf of foreign firms.

[62] A. Webster, "The Strategies and Limits of Gentlemanly Capitalism: The London East India Agency Houses, Provincial Commercial Interests, and the Evolution of British Economic Policy in South and South East Asia 1800–50", *The Economic History Review*, New Series 59, 4 (2006); *The Singapore Free Press and Mercantile Advertiser*, 11 May 1837.

[63] Webster, "The Strategies and Limits of Gentlemanly Capitalism", p. 746; SarDesai, *British Trade and Expansion*, p. 27.

making up the backbone of the local mercantile community.[64] Others were established by independent Straits merchants and country traders, who formed small partnerships.[65] In 1821, the city already boasted eight merchant houses performing varied economic functions such as the processing, grading and exporting of Straits produce, transshipment, credit provision and bill discounting.[66] In addition, they acted as agents for shipping firms, banks and insurance companies. The products for re-export they specialised in were Straits produce, opium, tea and British manufactures, for which they earned 0.5–1 per cent in commission.[67] More often than not, trade was conducted on barter terms, with the agency houses exchanging consignments of cotton goods, manufactures and opium shipped from the West and India for the spices, sugar, foodstuffs and tin of the Archipelago.[68] Barter trade was also expedient because there was a perennial scarcity of silver currency.[69]

No formal credit institutions existed in Singapore at this time and all commerce was conducted through an interlinked trade and credit system. The agency houses were the main conduits through which working capital originating in London (underwritten by exporters or banks) flowed all the way down the different trading layers, from the local Chinese merchant to the petty Asian trader plying the remote corners of the Archipelago, to the outpost dealer and village shopkeeper who advanced goods to native producers.[70] The Western merchants first tapped on the short-term trade credit provided by London through bills of exchange with a maturity of six months, which they discharged from the proceeds of sales of Straits produce.[71] In turn, the Chinese merchants traded and speculated on the capital of the Europeans.[72] Under this set-up, they were issued loans by the agency houses in the form of promissory notes with maturities of two months that were mostly unsecured and carried a time-based interest rate, to be repaid in Straits produce.[73] In bad times, the repayment obligation was extended to three or even six months. Defaults were common and when India's insolvency law was applied to the Straits Settlements in 1848 at the request of the Singapore Chamber of Commerce, it had the unintended effect of encouraging delinquent traders to send their profits to China and declare themselves bankrupt.[74] The Chamber claimed that two-thirds to three-quarters of native failures in

---

64 "Notices of Singapore", *The Journal of the Indian Archipelago and Eastern Asia*, ed. J.R. Logan, 9 (1855): 468.

65 Drake, *Merchants, Bankers, Governors*, p. 7.

66 Wong, "Commercial Growth", pp. 60, 61; *The Asiatic Journal and Monthly Register for British India and its Dependencies* 8 (Jan.–June 1822): 620.

67 Loh Wen Fong, *The Singapore Houses of Agency, 1819–1900*, Academic Exercise (Department of History, University of Malaya, 1958), p. 5.

68 J.H. Drabble and P.J. Drake, "The British Agency Houses in Malaysia: Survival in a Changing World", *Journal of Southeast Asian Studies* 12, 2 (1981): 301, 303.

69 Wong, *The Trade of Singapore*, pp. 301–2; Liew and Wilson, *A History of Money*, pp. 47–9; *Singapore Chronicle and Commercial Register*, 15 Aug. 1835.

70 British Military Administration, *Entrepôt Trade*, pp. 15–17; Wong, "Commercial Growth", p. 61.

71 Drake, *Merchants, Bankers, Governors*, p. 14.

72 *Singapore Chronicle and Commercial Register*, 13 Aug. 1829.

73 Wong, *The Trade of Singapore*, p. 163.

74 Turnbull, *The Straits Settlements*, pp. 7–8; *The Straits Times*, 26 July 1848.

Singapore were fraudulent.[75] In any case, the delay entailed by court proceedings meant that there was seldom a resort to legal measures.[76] Despite repeated attempts by the European merchants to reduce the loan maturity period or to conduct trade using cash, the old system proved resilient and almost all remittances to Britain and India were still in native produce in the 1840s.[77]

The system worked well enough in good times when Chinese merchants with scant resources could borrow money, pay later and earn 2 per cent commission by trading in produce.[78] It obviated the need for banks in Singapore (though there was no lack of proposals to set one up in the 1830s), since the agency houses were well-placed to issue promissory notes, bills of exchange, and letters of credit to facilitate commercial transactions.[79] As with external trade, domestic transactions prior to the 1840s were settled either by barter or in cash—banknotes had yet to make their appearance. When cash was used, the specie required was imported by the agency houses while the EIC also sent consignments of Spanish dollars to the Singapore Treasury.[80] Indeed, there was an active trade in specie and bullion, particularly with India. Singapore was also used as a base by the EIC to move bullion to China as payment for trade transactions.

However, the informal credit system turned toxic when the Bengal financial crash came: borrowers took longer to repay or defaulted on their loans, creating a domino effect that resembled a modern financial cataclysm. Many Chinese merchants in Singapore went bankrupt but the local agency houses survived the crisis and there were still 17 British houses in Singapore in 1834, as well as one Portuguese, one German, one American and three Armenian firms.[81] A catalyst for the increase in the number of houses was the opening of the China trade to private traders in 1833 with the loss of the EIC's monopoly. In addition, existing houses survived by incorporating new partners when the old ones retired or died, or sometimes through amalgamations. The number of agency houses and merchant firms continued to rise to 43 by 1846, of which 20 were British and the rest a mix of nationalities.[82]

A brief description of the more prominent agency houses and their founders (Table 3) suffices to show the eclectic mix of merchants that congregated in Singapore. The independent merchants who set up their own firms in the 1820s were A.L. Johnston, a former mariner with the EIC; John Purvis who came from Canton; Jose D'Almeida, a

[75] *The Singapore Free Press and Mercantile Advertiser*, 8 Oct. 1935.

[76] *The Singapore Free Press and Mercantile Advertiser*, 29 Apr. 1858.

[77] Davidson, *Trade and Travel in the Far East*, p. 66; Darbishire, "Commerce and Currency", pp. 32–4; *Singapore Chronicle and Commercial Register*, 21 Feb. 1835.

[78] The Chinese therefore referred to this trade as the "ninety-eight per cent trade". Tan Gia Lim, *An Introduction to the Culture and History of the Teochews in Singapore* (Singapore: World Scientific, 2018), p. 54.

[79] Buckley, *An Anecdotal History*, pp. 226–7; Liew and Wilson, *A History of Money*, pp. 50–1; *Singapore Chronicle and Commercial Register*, 28 Feb. 1833.

[80] Liew and Wilson, *A History of Money*, pp. 40, 42.

[81] Trocki, *Prince of Pirates*, pp. 17, 68; Drake, *Merchants, Bankers, Governors*, pp. 6–7; Buckley, *An Anecdotal History*, p. 232.

[82] Turnbull, *History of Modern Singapore*, p. 58.

doctor who initially practised medicine in Singapore; T.O. Crane, a former land agent; and William Napier, who apparently established a partnership with Charles Scott in 1827, but claimed to be the first commercial firm in Singapore.[83] Syme and Co., Spottiswoode & Connolly and George Armstrong & Co. were also founded independently. Ker, Rawson & Co. was linked to a merchant firm in London and Liverpool while Alexander Guthrie and Edward Boustead both started out as agents of foreign mercantile firms. The rest of the houses were either agents of, or connected with, the London and Calcutta firms.

Table 3. List of Merchant Firms in Singapore, 1834

Name of Firm	Year Established
A.L. Johnston & Co.	1819/20
Guthrie & Co.	1821
George Amstrong & Co.	1822
John Purvis & Co.	1822
Syme & Co.	1823
Spottiswoode & Connolly	1824
Jose D'Almeida & Sons	1825
Maclaine Fraser & Co.	1825
Crane Bros.	1825
Maxwell & Co.	1827
Morgan Hunter & Co.	1827
Napier, Scott & Co.	1827
Thomas & Co.	1827
Ker, Rawson & Co.	1828
Boustead & Co.	1830
Hamilton, Gray & Co.	1832
Shaw, Whitehead & Co.	1834

Source: Drake, *Merchants, Bankers, Governors*, p. 7.

Patterns of Trade

Due to the trade and financial interlinkages with the Indian agency houses, Singapore entered into a decade-long slump after 1830, with the entrepôt trade being the most seriously affected although the redistribution business was not spared either. A robust recovery took place at the start of the 1840s and by 1844, the overall level of trade was 17 per cent higher compared to the beginning of the downturn. As a result of the earlier depressed conditions, there was little change in the port's markets and articles of trade. Singapore remained chiefly oriented towards the West and Southeast Asia, which accounted for 22 per cent and 34 per cent of the port's total trade, respectively, in 1844.[84] Within the

[83] Drake, *Merchants, Bankers, Governors*, pp. 7–8. A.L. Johnston & Co. is another claimant to the honour of being the first European firm in Singapore. Song, *One Hundred Years' History of the Chinese*, p. 105.

[84] Wong, "Singapore: Its Growth" p. 53.

Western bloc, Britain's share fell to 20 per cent, continental Europe's rose to over 2 per cent and that of the United States also increased, though it remained small.

Prior to 1836, the United States did not trade directly with Singapore because of an ambiguous clause in the Anglo-American Treaty of 1815. As the settlement was not founded at the time the treaty was made, the list of British Dominions in the Far East with which the Americans were allowed to trade—Calcutta, Madras, Bombay and Penang—could hardly have included it. The little clandestine exchange conducted with Singapore was channelled through the nearby ports at Riau and Batam island. Since American trade was coveted for the specie they brought to the region to purchase commodities, the local merchants in Singapore remonstrated with the British and United States governments.[85] This went unheeded until June 1836, when the trade was finally declared legal by the EIC Court of Directors, prompting no less than 17 American ships to call at the port before the year was through.[86] However, further restrictions, including the stipulation that American vessels could carry goods only directly to US ports, were relaxed only in 1840, which caused Singapore's trade with America to jump to SPD118,513 in the following year.

Southeast Asia's share of the trade with Singapore increased substantially in 1844 due to an increase in the volume of entrepôt business, to 16.6 per cent of overall trade from 10 per cent in 1829. The rise was partly offset by a decrease in the distributive trade, from 32.1 per cent to 27.7 per cent. Concomitantly, the proportion of the long-distance trade (defined as including the commerce between China and the West but excluding the junk trade with Southeast Asia) fell by 2 percentage points to 55.7 per cent. In aggregate, the values of the re-export and distributive flows, which can be taken to represent intraregional trade, sum to 44.3 per cent of total trade, consistent with the finding that the total size of intra-Asian trade in 1840 was comparable to the long-distance trade with the West.[87] This is to be expected in view of the fact that Singapore accounted for fully two-fifths of the trade taking place within Asia.[88] As such, its trade patterns were a microcosm of those in Asia at large.

As for product mix (Table 4), the changes in the 1830s were almost imperceptible, but there were several new facets. British cotton goods and woollens were better received in China, and betelnut and ebony were added to the list of Straits produce exports. Gambier and pepper began to feature more prominently in Singapore's exports to India while the island received saltpetre (used for making gunpowder) from the latter. Having acquired a dubious reputation as a regional centre for free trade in arms and ammunition, Singapore's imports from Britain included gunpowder, muskets, pistols, rifles and swords.[89] From the United States, it obtained a large quantity of Spanish silver dollars, which were mostly

[85] S. Ahmat, "American Trade with Singapore, 1819–65", *Journal of the Malaysian Branch of the Royal Asiatic Society* 38, 2 (1965): 242, 245–6, 254; *Straits Settlements Records*, A.68, 27 July 1830.

[86] *Singapore Chronicle and Commercial Register*, 7 Jan. 1837.

[87] K. Sugihara, "The Resurgence of Intra-Asian Trade, 1800–1850", in *How India Clothed the World*, ed. Riello and Roy, p. 158.

[88] Calculated from ibid., p. 151.

[89] Turnbull, *The Straits Settlements*, p. 179; Savage, *Lion City Narratives*, p. 233; *The Singapore Free Press and Mercantile Advertiser*, 1 Feb. 1838.

re-exported to India.[90] The product composition of the intraregional trade remained largely unchanged from the early period. For example, six out of the top ten products in Singapore's exports to Sumatra in 1828 were replicated in 1844, including European and Indian cotton goods, opium, salt and raw silk.[91] With Siam, six products were common to the two lists: European and Indian cotton goods, opium, rattan, woollens and beeswax. The product mix in the trade with Borneo and the Celebes exhibited somewhat greater variation between the two years, although cotton piece goods and opium maintained their dominance. Similarly, Singapore exchanged a richer range of goods with Java mainly through smugglers; this range included new products such as opium, raw silk, gunnies, saltpetre, tin and spices.

Table 4. The Trade of Singapore in the 1830s

Trading Partner	Exports To	Imports From
China	British cotton goods and woollen cloth, opium, betelnut, ebony, birds' nests, seaweed, tin, pepper	Tea, napkins, piece goods, sugar, porcelain, copperware, gold and silver dust, raw silk, cassia, tobacco, specie
India/Ceylon	Tin, gold, nankeen, porcelain, pepper, gambier, spices	Opium, rice, saltpetre, ebony, cotton, Indian piece goods, arrack, cordage
Britain	Antimony, tin, tea, gold, cassia, coffee, sugar, raw silk, hides, ivory, tortoise shells, beeswax, mother of pearl	Woollen piece goods, cotton twist, iron, arms, gunpowder, wines, various manufactures
Java	Piece goods from India, China and Europe, nankeen, iron, opium, raw silk, wheat, porcelain, iron ware, cordage, gunnies, saltpetre	European piece goods, *bêche de mer*, birds' nests, gold, indigo, rice, rattan, spices, benjamin, brass and copper ware, tin, tobacco, sandalwood, arrack
East Coast of Malay Peninsula	Rice, tobacco, opium, salt, salted fish, arms, iron tools, agricultural implements, piece goods, cotton twist	Gold, tin, pepper, Malay silk and cotton cloth, sugar, rattan
West Coast of Malay Peninsula	Rice, tobacco, opium, salt, salted fish, arms, iron tools, agricultural implements, piece goods, cotton twist	Beeswax, elephant ivory, ebony, hides, rattan, sago, cattle, poultry, fruit, vegetables
Siam	British and Indian piece goods, opium, woollen cloth, cotton twist, beeswax, betelnut, ebony, steel, iron, lead, rattan	Rice, sugar, ivory, oil, salt, iron pans, wood
Other East Indies islands	British, Indian and Malay piece goods, woollens, rice, iron, brass, porcelain, earthenware, opium, salt, raw silk, tobacco, gunpowder, cotton twist, iron, steel iron tools, agricultural implements	Gold, ebony, ivory, camphor, tin, mother of pearl, pearls, benjamin, tortoise shells, birds' plumes, diamonds, birds of paradise, beeswax, *bêche de mer*, coffee, spices, oils, pepper, rice, birds' nests, tobacco, wood, antimony

Source: Drake, *Merchants, Bankers, Governors*, pp. 11–12.

[90] *The Singapore Free Press and Mercantile Advertiser*, 18 Jan. 1838, 1 Feb. 1838.

[91] Kobayashi, "The Role of Singapore", p. 463.

The bulk of the intra-Asian trade consisted of food, opium and clothing.[92] Where the last is concerned, Singapore's redistributive trade in cloth was concentrated in Indian fabrics at the beginning of the 1830s, as exports of European cotton goods from the port to areas under Dutch influence were still hobbled by high tariffs. A quarter of the outward shipments of Indian piece goods in 1836 were sourced from Penang and concurrently, over a quarter of European cotton exports from Singapore went to the same settlement.[93] American cloth and jeans were also well received in the region but their circulation was initially handicapped by the restriction on its trade.[94] It was not until the 1840s that European cloth manufactures got the upper hand.[95] However, Singapore still exported SPD157,000 worth of Indian cloth to consumers in the Archipelago in 1844 (Figure 3).

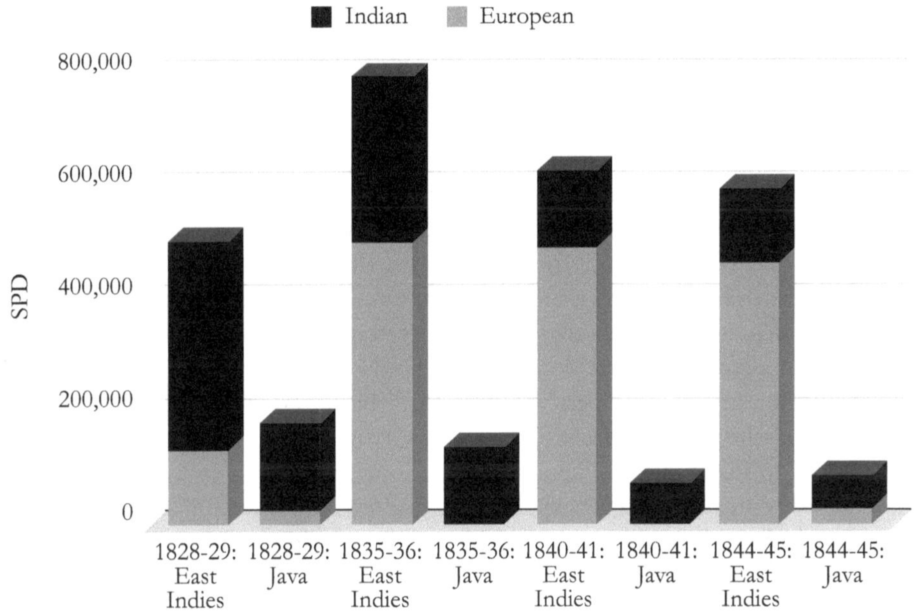

Figure 3. Cotton Goods Exports from Singapore to the Dutch East Indies, 1828–45
Note: Thc East Indies refer to the Outer Provinces, excluding Java and Madura.
Source: Wong, *The Trade of Singapore*, Appendix B, Table III, pp. 259–62.

As the general trading environment deteriorated in the 1830s, the nemesis of the British in the East Indies, the Dutch, again attempted to stifle the trade of the Straits Settlements through heavy duties and other restrictive measures. These actions were taken in spite of the Anglo-Dutch Treaty of 1824 stipulating that trade between the British and the Dutch

[92] Sugihara, "The Resurgence of Intra-Asian Trade", p. 162.

[93] Wong, *The Trade of Singapore*, Appendix B, Table III, p. 259; *The Singapore Free Press and Mercantile Advertiser*, 13 Oct. 1836.

[94] Ahmat, "American Trade with Singapore", p. 244.

[95] Reid, "Southeast Asian Consumption", p. 47.

would be conducted on the basis of "the most favoured nation".[96] The main target of the Dutch continued to be British cotton piece goods, which were subject to 10 per cent more duty if imported through Singapore. Although the Dutch succeeded in reducing the British share of the Java cotton trade by 1829, British manufacturers managed to recapture the market after Belgium seceded from the Netherlands in 1830, with the concomitant loss to the Dutch of the textile industry.[97] While the Dutch could have been expected to adopt illiberal measures to revive their economic fortunes, they went so far as to impose a prohibitive tariff of 70 per cent on imports of European cotton from ports east of the Cape of Good Hope in 1834, ostensibly as a wartime proclamation necessitated by the Belgian secession.[98] Later that year, the government at Batavia declared that European cotton goods would not be permitted to enter Dutch possessions unless they were first imported into the principal ports of Java, which were limited to Batavia, Semarang and Surabaya. Singapore was a clear victim of this policy as its exports of these goods to Java again plummeted from SPD22,286 in 1829 to SPD2,805 in 1836.[99] Total trade dropped to less than a million Spanish dollars in 1839, the lowest since 1827.

Despite petitions by the British merchants in Singapore and Java to their government, it only protested mildly to the Dutch authorities since it was hamstrung by political and strategic desiderata and not motivated purely by commercial interests in the Far East. Britain needed to maintain friendly relations with its ally the Dutch as a bulwark against the French state and was therefore hesitant to push its position too far.[100] As such, British policy represented a delicate balance between its European and Eastern strategies. Meanwhile, as a cosmetic concession, the Dutch raised the tariff on cotton goods made in Holland from zero to 12.5 per cent in 1836.[101] However, they secretly recompensed the Nederlandsche Handel-Maatschappij (NHM) the full amount of duty levied on Dutch goods to foster the development of the home industry.[102] In 1837, the duty on cotton goods routed through Singapore was equalised with direct imports from Britain at 25 per cent but new import levies were imposed on a wide range of products entering Java and Madura.[103] Finally in 1839, the prohibitive tariff on European piece goods was abolished following the Dutch-Belgian Treaty of that year. After a formal diplomatic protest was lodged by the British government in 1841, the port regulation of 1834 was also rescinded. By that time, however, the Dutch had regained their share of the Java

---

[96] T. Kawamura, "Trade, Finance and the 'Anglo-Dutch' International Order in Southeast Asia: The Case of the British Eastern Exchange Banks, 1870–1890", in *Singapore—Two Hundred Years of the Lion City*, ed. A. Webster and N.J. White (London: Routledge, 2020), p. 47.

[97] van der Kraan, *A Contest for the Java Cotton Trade*, pp. 24–5.

[98] Kobayashi, "The Role of Singapore", p. 460.

[99] Wong, *The Trade of Singapore*, Appendix B, Table III, p. 259.

[100] N. Tarling, "British Policy in the Malay Peninsula and Archipelago 1824–1871", *Journal of the Malayan Branch of the Royal Asiatic Society* 30, 3 (1957): 10.

[101] Wong, *The Trade of Singapore*, pp. 45, 49; *The Singapore Free Press and Mercantile Advertiser*, 9 June 1836.

[102] van der Kraan, *A Contest for the Java Cotton Trade*, pp. 50, 52; *The Singapore Free Press and Mercantile Advertiser*, 30 Mar. 1837.

[103] Kobayashi, "The Role of Singapore", pp. 459, 460; *The Singapore Free Press and Mercantile Advertiser*, 16 Nov. 1837.

cotton market, at 72 per cent.[104] Nevertheless, the concessions had the effect of boosting trade with the Straits Settlements, which partly explained the increases experienced by Penang and Melaka beginning in 1844.

The Rise of Free Ports

As it turned out, these concessions were a Pyrrhic victory for the Singapore mercantile community. Not long after, the Dutch followed through on the *laissez faire* policy forced upon it by making Makassar a free port in 1847. The view then abounded that Singapore would perish since the precious Bugis trade would be drawn away. In actual fact, the long-distance trade was partly insulated from Dutch policies at their native ports, since it hinged on the flow of goods between Singapore, Europe and India on the one hand, and China on the other.[105] At any rate, the fear proved to be unfounded for trade creation triumphed over trade diversion: Singapore's commerce was ultimately boosted by the liberalisation of trade in the region. That is to say, new free ports, both Dutch and British, did take away some custom from Singapore, but the additional impetus given to commerce and production by the policy of unfettered trade more than compensated for the loss. Raffles' vision for Singapore was finally realised—its very existence resulted in free trade in the Malay Archipelago and Dutch East Indies by the 1850s whereas prior to its founding, trade was heavily taxed and subject to all kinds of restrictions by colonial and native rulers alike.[106] Free trade was therefore Raffles' economic coup in the region.[107]

Makassar was not the first port that could be a potential rival of Singapore. Realising that their ports were losing out to Singapore because of the latter's free trade policy, the Dutch authorities decided to follow its example.[108] In 1829, they declared Riau a free port, followed by the outports of Pontianak and Sambas in West Borneo in 1834. These moves did not seem to have affected Singapore's trade much. Chinese traders from Singapore continued to conduct a robust exchange of goods with their counterparts in Brunei, Sambas, Mampawa and Pontianak, from whom they obtained gold dust and diamonds.[109] Hence, it is not surprising that local merchants welcomed the arrival of James ("Rajah") Brooke to form a ruling partnership with the Sultan of Brunei in Sarawak in 1841, a development that enjoyed the support of the British government. Brooke's plans to develop Sarawak as well as his vigorous efforts to stamp out the notorious pirates of the area were viewed as a great opportunity to open up the vast natural and mineral resources of Borneo for trade with Singapore.[110] Kuching quickly developed as an entrepôt for its immediate region and the hub for Singapore's trade in gutta percha and antimony ore with North Borneo. By 1845, the northwest coast of Borneo had overtaken Sumatra as the main source of the raw

---

104 van der Kraan, *A Contest for the Java Cotton Trade*, pp. 52–3.

105 J.H. Moor, *Notices of the Indian Archipelago and Adjacent Countries* (Singapore, 1837), p. 13.

106 Wong, "Commercial Growth", p. 47.

107 Savage, *Lion City Narratives*, pp. 100–1.

108 Darbishire, "Commerce and Currency", p. 31.

109 Wong, *The Trade of Singapore*, p. 89; *Singapore Chronicle and Commercial Register*, 1 Apr. 1837.

110 Cameron, *Our Tropical Possessions in Malayan India*, pp. 176–7.

sago which Singapore processed into pearl sago.[111] Later in the 1860s, Sarawak developed its own sago manufacturing industry that competed with Singapore in exporting pearl sago and sago flour directly to Britain.

All in, the induction of North Borneo into the Archipelago commerce was a plus for Singapore, as shown by a significant increase in the region's trade during the 1840s. However, a very different reaction from the mercantile and official communities greeted the move to make Labuan, an island off the northern coast of Borneo, part of British territory and a free port in late 1846.[112] After a crisis at the court, Rajah Brooke had acquired the island from the Sultan of Brunei to serve as a naval station for protecting British commercial interests in the region and suppressing piracy. But the Singapore parties saw it differently and fretted that the establishment of the settlement would spell the end of the region's trade with Singapore, or even of its emporium role. After all, Labuan is much closer to China and both the west and east coasts of Borneo were famous for their supply of commodities in high demand in that country, such as birds' nests, beeswax, tortoise shells and pearls.

The British authorities were more circumspect, looking instead to Labuan as a second Singapore.[113] The argument went that Labuan could garner the trade of the areas too far away from Singapore; furthermore, the discovery of rich coal deposits along the Borneo River had disposed some traders and the local press to lobby for a permanent settlement as it could function as a station for the steamers that were increasingly making their appearance in maritime communications.[114] In the event, Labuan turned out to have neither much strategic nor commercial value and in fact, its inaccessible location denied it the trade of eastern Borneo and the rich Sulu Islands. Efforts at coal mining also failed.[115] Instead, the island became a commercial dependency rather than a competitor of Singapore, importing opium and cotton goods from it.

Although the unease of Singapore merchants over Labuan was misplaced, their gloomy prognosis when the Dutch made Makassar a free port in 1847 was understandable. This decision was, ironically enough, partly motivated by the British takeover of Labuan. Compared to Labuan, Makassar occupies a more central location in the Eastern Archipelago and was expected to attract to it the trade of west Celebes, east Borneo, the Moluccas and Batavia.[116] Indeed, the risk that Makassar could pose to Singapore was already recognised as early as 1831.[117] Why would the Bugis bother to make the hazardous journey to Singapore when they had a free port to trade in at their doorstep? In this case, the pessimists were not

[111] Wong, *The Trade of Singapore*, pp. 90–1, 100–1.

[112] *The Straits Times*, 17 Oct. 1846.

[113] Wong, *The Trade of Singapore*, p. 95.

[114] Davidson, *Trade and Travel in the Far East*, pp. 294–6; Buckley, *An Anecdotal History*, p. 439.

[115] J.H. Drabble, *An Economic History of Malaysia, c. 1800–1990* (Basingstoke: Macmillan, 2000), p. 34.

[116] British Military Administration, *Entrepôt Trade*, p. 7; *The Straits Times*, 26 Sept. 1846.

[117] Moor, *Notices of the Indian Archipelago*, pp. 73–4.

entirely wrong: the number of Bugis ships calling at the port did decline after 1847.[118] Yet, Makassar's entrepôt trade could not match Singapore's even after the move.[119]

Another event that created a sense of foreboding in Singapore was the cession of Hong Kong to the British government after the latter won the first Opium War with China in 1842 and the Treaty of Nanking was signed. This landmark event in Sino-British history was triggered by the Qing government's concerted attempt in 1839 to interdict the illegal opium trade conducted at Canton, leading to retaliation by the British and the forcible opening of China to foreign trade. Four more "treaty ports" at Shanghai, Ningpo, Foochow and Amoy, in addition to Canton, were designated for trade and settlement by European merchants who were subject to foreign rather than Chinese laws, and tariffs were cut to nominal rates. At first, Singapore benefitted from being the point of supply for the British and Indian forces gathered there for the China expedition, and as a temporary opium depot after Canton was closed, both of which provided a mild stimulus to trade.[120]

When the drastic actions of the Chinese authorities prior to the Opium War threatened to extinguish the contraband opium trade, a Singapore-based merchant voiced the concern that the low price to which the drug had fallen would cause it to be dumped into the Archipelago, to the detriment of British cotton goods.[121] This contrasted with the positive sentiment expressed in 1833 when the British government decided, under pressure from shippers and home manufacturers, to end the EIC's monopoly of the China trade. At the time, the hope was that Singapore could become a depot for tea and other Chinese goods offered at lower prices than in Canton due to high duties and other charges there, saving free traders the hassle of proceeding to China.[122] Contrary to expectations, however, Singapore did not develop into a hub for the tea trade: its imports of tea from China in 1836 were a mere SPD57,509.[123] One reason why Singapore could not compete with traders who sailed directly from India or London to load tea in Canton was that the tea was delivered to Singapore by Chinese junks in bamboo containers, and hence was less fresh than that packed at Canton into air-tight chests.[124] Through direct shipping, tea traders also avoided Singapore middlemen's profits.[125]

Notwithstanding the failure of the tea trade, by the mid-1830s square-rigged vessels traversing the Singapore–Canton maritime route had become an important mode of shipping Western and Indian products to China. The statistics speak for themselves: in 1834, the country traders' proportion of the British trade with China had already exceeded one-half and in 1836, the total tonnage departing from Singapore to China was 66,023, carrying *inter alia* contraband opium that was worth SPD252,327 and European and

---

118 Wong, *The Trade of Singapore*, pp. 104–5; *The Straits Times*, 19 Dec. 1846, 12 Feb. 1848, 10 Jan. 1854.

119 Savage, *Lion City Narratives*, p. 229.

120 *The Singapore Free Press and Mercantile Advertiser*, 21 May 1840.

121 *The Singapore Free Press and Mercantile Advertiser*, 27 June 1839.

122 *Singapore Chronicle and Commercial Register*, 24 Apr. 1834, 28 Aug. 1834.

123 Newbold, *Political and Statistical Account*, p. 306; Darbishire, "Commerce and Currency", p. 27.

124 Burnett, *East Indies*, p. 148; *Singapore Chronicle and Commercial Register*, 28 Aug. 1834.

125 Moore and Moore, *The First 150 Years*, p. 167.

Indian cotton products valued at SPD80,456.[126] However, the 418 chests of opium exported to China from Singapore composed only a small fraction of the 30,202 chests shipped directly from India.[127] Three years later, at the start of the first Opium War (1839–42), shipments of Patna, Benares and Malwa opium had risen to SPD698,528 and cotton exports to SPD116,768.[128] The opium trade continued to grow in the following years but it stabilised after peaking in 1843.[129] The drug was initially brought to China in vessels of 500 to 800 tonnes and later on, by the opium clippers—a special type of craft that could beat windward against the monsoons and complete the journey to China in a shorter time—which carried the opium from India to Lintin Island on the Pearl River, initially via Singapore but later bypassing it.[130] From there, it was smuggled into China by peddlers.[131] Opium was also procured by small Chinese junks of 150 to 300 tonnes which sailed to Singapore expressly for the purpose of purchasing the drug, paying for it in silver.[132]

With the opening of Hong Kong and more Chinese ports to free trade after 1842, concern again arose that Singapore would be bypassed.[133] Hong Kong—and to a lesser extent, Canton—became the entrepôts for the China trade as well as depots for the unrestricted and untaxed transshipment of opium and Western manufactures to ports along the China coast.[134] The prophecy was proclaimed that Singapore's commerce had reached its apogee and would stagnate thereafter. Its future looked less bright than at any time in its short history.[135] Yet the fear turned out to be unjustified. Singapore continued to serve the Archipelago markets, a geographical division of functions between it and Hong Kong that was to be repeated time and again in the next two centuries. It became the opium centre of Southeast Asia, serving in particular the peripatetic colonies of Chinese labourers in the region.[136] In 1836, a larger share of Singapore's total opium exports equivalent to SPD537,891 already went to the Malay Peninsula, Java, Borneo, the Celebes, Cochin-China and Siam (Figure 4).[137] In subsequent years, the quantity of the drug re-exported to the region continued to increase.[138]

---

[126] Greenberg, *British Trade and the Opening of China*, pp. 96–7, 98–9, 175; Wong, *The Trade of Singapore*, Table Ia, Appendix C, p. 276; Newbold, *Political and Statistical Account*, p. 325.

[127] Wong, *The Trade of Singapore*, p. 114.

[128] Holloway, *Tabular Statements*, p. 19.

[129] Turnbull, *The Straits Settlements*, pp. 176–7; Lee, "Chinese Junk Trade", pp. 28, 29; *The Singapore Free Press and Mercantile Advertiser*, 2 June 1842.

[130] H. Derks, *History of the Opium Problem: The Assault on the East, ca. 1600–1950* (Leiden: Brill, 2012), p. 64; Abshire, *History of Singapore*, p. 60.

[131] Moore and Moore, *The First 150 Years*, p. 192.

[132] Buckley, *An Anecdotal History*, p. 323.

[133] Davidson, *Trade and Travel in the Far East*, pp. 67–9.

[134] Wong, "Singapore: Its Growth", p. 53.

[135] Moore and Moore, *The First 150 Years*, p. 177.

[136] C.A. Trocki, *Opium and Empire: Chinese Society in Colonial Singapore, 1800–1910* (Ithaca: Cornell University Press, 1990), pp. 50–5.

[137] Newbold, *Political and Statistical Account*, p. 306.

[138] Wong, *The Trade of Singapore*, Appendix B, Table IX, pp. 274–5.

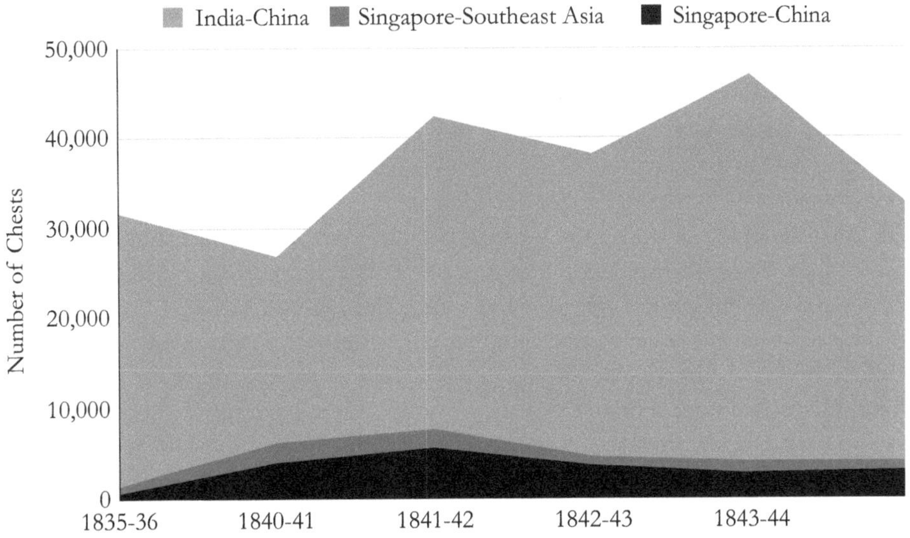

Figure 4. Opium Exports to China and Southeast Asia, 1835–45
Source: Wong, *The Trade of Singapore*, pp. 114–5, Appendix B, Table IX, pp. 274–5.

Singapore was therefore insulated from the full commercial consequences of the Opium War. In fact, the number of Chinese junks, which were the main carriers of opium, tea and cotton goods arriving at and departing from Singapore, increased rather than decreased immediately after the war.[139] European piece goods exported to China via Singapore rose to a record SPD280,103 in 1844. The import of Chinese tea to be transshipped to Britain suffered a more ignominious fate, having been reduced to naught by 1848. The port's transshipment of silk products from China to the West was also adversely affected by the increase in direct shipping to Britain.[140] Still, Singapore's overall trade with China increased instead of stagnating as predicted, accounting for 21.7 per cent of the total in 1844. This outcome was due to China's increased commercial intercourse with British and foreign traders at the treaty ports, leading to the incipient integration of its economy with global markets.[141] It was a matter of simple geography: as more square-rigged vessels called at these ports, more ships also stopped at Singapore to discharge cargo and pick up Straits articles and other products. The growth of the China market also enticed more European mercantile firms to set up business in Singapore: six new firms were registered, while some of the existing agency houses opened offices at the treaty ports.[142] However, the once glorious Chinese junk trade was displaced although its death was to be slow as Western shipping only gradually penetrated into China's harbours and inland rivers.[143] Following the second Opium War of 1856–60, the number of junks coming to Singapore

---

[139] Ibid., Appendix C, Table Ib, p. 276.

[140] Turnbull, *The Straits Settlements*, p. 177.

[141] von Glahn, *Economic History of China*, p. 392; *The Singapore Free Press and Mercantile Advertiser*, 26 Oct. 1843.

[142] *The Straits Times*, 18 Nov. 1846.

[143] *The Singapore Free Press and Mercantile Advertiser*, 2 Jan. 1845.

reached a high of 143 in 1857 before declining to 19 in 1866, supplanted by square-rigged vessels that carried insured cargo.[144]

In concluding this narrative, it is worth pondering the reasons for Singapore's trade success and the factors that perpetuated it in the face of adversity and competition. Most contemporary observers attributed the rise of Singapore to its geographical location. This point is obvious but it needs elaboration. First and foremost is the fact that Singapore lies in the maritime path of ships sailing between India and China (or Cochin-China). Even vessels passing through the Sunda Straits or the Straits of Makassar on their way to the Celebes and the Philippines would come within close distance of it.[145] Second and not less important, native vessels found Singapore's position most convenient as they ferried products from the Eastern Archipelago and Borneo, or from Siam, Cochin-China and China. However, location in and of itself obviously cannot guarantee success—the Riau and Karimun Islands provide the counterfactual confirmation: the Dutch had early on recognised their potential but they did not blossom into ports of any significance. Hence, Raffles' free trade policy, as well as the merchants and officials who upheld it, must be given the credit they deserve.

At a deeper level, Raffles succeeded in fusing Chinese trade networks in the region with British economic practices under the rubric of a free market economy, whereby government intervention was practically limited to the revenue farms: "it was Sino-Western enterprise, in a colonial enclave dedicated to *laissez faire*, that made Singapore the premier port of Southeast Asia before World War II".[146] Importantly, *laissez faire* here also means the unrestricted movement of people and unfettered trade. The relationship between the Europeans and Chinese was one of symbiosis: each provided something the other lacked—the former the global connections and lines of credit to Britain and the latter, intimate knowledge of the Archipelago and extensive regional links.[147] This mutual dependence was the reason for the resilience of the Anglo-Chinese trade and credit nexus in the entrepôt business.

In modern economic phraseology, it was the combined human capital and entrepreneurship of the Europeans and Chinese that made Singapore such a huge success; by the same token, Labuan failed because it was deprived of European enterprise even though Chinese traders settled there.[148] Singapore also triumphed over Makassar because of its first-mover advantage in free trade and the variety of commodities and choice of final markets which were available at the port and which, coupled with low transaction costs, continued to entice traders. These "thick market externalities" played a crucial role in matching sellers to buyers, on both the spatial and temporal dimensions. They were in turn the result of network effects, whereby the more trade attracted by Singapore, the more trade it brought.

---

[144] Lee, "Chinese Junk Trade", pp. 29–30; Wong, *The Trade of Singapore*, pp. 122–4, Appendix C, Table Ib, p. 276.

[145] Wong, "Commercial Growth", pp. 195, 196–7.

[146] Wong, "Singapore: Its Growth", p. 84.

[147] Drake, *Merchants, Bankers, Governors*, p. 9.

[148] Wong, *The Trade of Singapore*, p. 94.

Population, Occupational Structure and Secret Societies

In the previous chapter, we noted the rapid growth of Singapore's population to a shade below 17,000 souls in 1830. A decade later, it had more than doubled to 39,681 people.[149] Of these, the floating population of traders had risen to 4,000 and there were now 1,182 convicts in the settlement. Chinese formed a slim majority of the population, with 51 out of every 100 persons belonging to that ethnicity, their numbers having been expanded by immigrants labouring in the gambier and pepper plantations, who were estimated to number 3,000 in 1835.[150] In the 1830s, the coolies who arrived from China in junks and square-rigged vessels and who were known as *sinkheh* (literally new guests), averaged 5,000 per annum, though not all found work in Singapore as many went to the gambier, pepper and coffee plantations as well as the gold and tin mines in the Malay Peninsula and the Dutch East Indies.[151] The next most populous community in 1840 were the Malays, many of whom originated from neighbouring areas, followed by the Indians, Bugis, Javanese and Balinese. The Bugis population in Singapore began to decline after Makassar was made a free port but Javanese migrants continued to arrive as labourers, traders and craftsmen.[152] Singapore maintained its cosmopolitan appeal, although the minority races such as Arabs, Armenians and Siamese did not exceed 50 persons each. This preponderance of natives and immigrants and the scarcity of European inhabitants made Singapore a typical colonial port town.[153]

In describing occupational structure in the labour market, one could adopt a nomenclature based on class or identify economic function with race. The approaches are not mutually exclusive but given the colonial setting and extensive labour immigration to Singapore, the second approach is more pertinent. The Malays had fanned out from the Kampong Glam area to the country districts to cultivate fruit, farm and fish but none worked in the plantations. According to the census of 1840, four out of five Malays resided in the country rather than the town, typically in attap-roofed houses raised on stilts.[154] Many of them made a living by hawking vegetables, poultry and fruit in the town, which earned them the compliments of being "simple and docile" and "pliant [and] obedient" by the Europeans.[155] The rest remained tied to the traditional occupations of boatmen and woodcutters, and a small number were employed in government service.

The Klings from southern India boasted a more diverse occupational structure in 1840, working as traders, shopkeepers, teamakers, cooks, peons, syces, bullock cart drivers, boatmen and washermen.[156] The last occupation in this list was exclusive to the race, and

---

[149] Holloway, *Tabular Statements*, p. 51.

[150] Trocki, "Origins of the Kangchu System", p. 140; *Singapore Chronicle and Commercial Register*, 24 Jan. 1835.

[151] *The Journal of the Indian Archipelago and Eastern Asia*, ed. J.R. Logan, 9 (1855): 113–4; Marriott, "The Peoples of Singapore", p. 350; *Singapore Chronicle and Commercial Register*, 23 Apr. 1829.

[152] Kwa, Heng, Borschberg and Tan, *Seven Hundred Years*, pp. 208–9.

[153] Hussin, *Trade and Society*, pp. 123–5.

[154] Holloway, *Tabular Statements*, p. 51.

[155] Cameron, *Our Tropical Possessions in Malayan India*, pp. 134–5; Savage, *Lion City Narratives*, pp. 267–8; *The Singapore Free Press and Mercantile Advertiser*, 24 Aug. 1849.

[156] Rai, *Indians in Singapore*, pp. 23–4, 28. Syces were stable grooms who looked after horses.

these "dhoby men" could be found at the junction of Bras Basah and Orchard Roads, to where they had moved from their earlier location at Stamford Canal. Described as "easy to manage" and "tractable and steady" in their work but "desperately litigious", the Klings were also overwhelmingly represented in the police force, the lower ranks of the civil establishment, and in public works where they laboured alongside the Indian convicts.[157] By contrast, the migrants originating from Hindustan (present day Uttar Pradesh) held a dominant position in the dairy business.[158] Together with the Punjabis, they were the earliest sepoys in Singapore and since they originated from northern India, had been erroneously labelled as "Bengalis". These milkmen settled early on at Kandang Kerbau (meaning buffalo shed) because of the availability of grass and water and were instrumental in the creation of the adjacent Serangoon Road as an Indian enclave. Bordered by the Rochor Canal, the area attracted other Indian migrants due to its proximity to and accessibility from the town.[159] Unlike the other native races, almost all the Klings and Bengalis lived within the limits of the town bounded by the Rochor River and Mount Sophia, just three miles from east to west and one mile inland (the boundary was extended to the Kallang River in 1856).[160] The southern limit was Telok Ayer, where all manner of vessels were under construction by shipwrights, including a European shipbuilding yard.[161]

In 1845, it was noted that there were 3,609 houses in the town, which were mainly occupied by the Indians and Chinese.[162] Nearly two-thirds of the Chinese in the settlement resided in the town area.[163] The Boat Quay area was where the Chinese merchants involved in the import and export business and their warehouses were located. Behind the neat rows of godowns on the river were double-storeyed brick shophouses occupied by the wholesale and retail traders; these houses had red-tiled roofs and sheltered verandahs for pedestrians—the famed "five-foot way". Along the great thoroughfare formed by North and South Bridge Roads which met at the Elgin Bridge located at the site of the former Presentment Bridge, a veritable range of merchandise could be purchased: European wares of all descriptions from the Kling and Parsee stores and glass and crockery from the Chinese shops.[164] These goods were bought from the European merchant houses through auctions.[165]

---

157 Kwa, Heng, Borschberg and Tan, *Seven Hundred Years*, p. 212; Savage, *Lion City Narratives*, p. 281; *The Singapore Free Press and Mercantile Advertiser*, 9 Dec. 1841.

158 R. Rai, "Sepoys, Convicts and the 'Bazaar' Contingent: The Emergence and Exclusion of 'Hindustani' Pioneers at the Singapore Frontier", *Journal of Southeast Asian Studies* 35, 1 (2004): 2, 16.

159 *Serangoon Road: A Pictorial History* (Singapore: Educational Publications Bureau, 1983).

160 Jayapal, *Old Singapore*, p. 10; *The Singapore Free Press and Mercantile Advertiser*, 8 Dec. 1836, 18 Dec. 1856.

161 R. St.J. Braddell, "The Good Old Days", p. 485; R. St.J. Braddell, "Crime", p. 579.

162 Mok Ly Yng, "Plan of Singapore Town and Adjoining Districts", in *On Paper: Singapore Before 1867*, p. 147.

163 Turnbull, *Straits Settlements*, p. 37; Siah U Chin, "General Sketch of the Numbers, Tribes, and Avocations of the Chinese in Singapore", *The Journal of the Indian Archipelago and Eastern Asia*, ed. J.R. Logan, 2 (1848): 288.

164 Jayapal, *Old Singapore*, pp. 11, 13; Begbie, *The Malayan Peninsula*, p. 352; Cameron, *Our Tropical Possessions in Malayan India*, p. 60–1.

165 *The Singapore Free Press and Mercantile Advertiser*, 8 Oct. 1935.

The Chinese, it was said, "occupy a position in the social scale in the Straits decidedly inferior to the Europeans, but superior to all other classes of the native population".[166] But without the Chinese, there would be no European settlement to speak of, for they were, *inter alia*, the shoemakers, tailors, barbers, bakers, carpenters, blacksmiths and bricklayers.[167] Although the division of labour along ethnic lines was not watertight, it extended to dialect groups (or *bang*) within the Chinese community. These groups were differentiated by the province or district from which they originated in China, which were in the main the southern provinces that conducted the foreign trade, namely, Fukien, Kwangtung, the island of Hainan and the Portuguese enclave of Macao. In Singapore, economic discrimination between the groups arose due to native place ties, dialect barriers and occupational specialisation, in addition to a certain "clannishness" in business dealings.[168] Raffles' town plan also subdivided the Chinese population according to dialect lines, with the result that the Fukien immigrants tended to congregate around Amoy and Telok Ayer Streets, while those from Kwangtung concentrated in Boat Quay and Tanjong Pagar.[169] Taking the different groups as a whole, a distinct Chinatown had emerged to the southwest of the Singapore River. In 1836, it was the largest ethnic district in Singapore with more than 13,700 Chinese settlers.[170]

The association of dialect groups with particular vocations dated back to the early days of Singapore and is arguably the most notable feature of the labour market—the result of a complex socio-economic process of competition and exclusion, amongst other geography-specific factors.[171] Once established, however, it was perpetuated by the apprentice system whereby craftsmen and employers took on kinsmen or young workers of the same dialect group to learn their trades. Many of these undertakings were family-run enterprises, so that the widespread practice of sons in the family taking over their fathers' businesses acted as another factor that reinforced the dialect group–occupational correspondences. These artificial barriers to entry in a given profession were therefore the result of socio-cultural factors rather than exogenously imposed. Nonetheless, it was still possible to break into a trade, as shown by a commonality of occupations between several dialect groups.

In 1848, a list of the various occupations held by native-born and immigrant Chinese was supplied by a prominent gambier planter and dealer (Table 5).[172] A large number of trades were covered, though a couple only under broad headings, and the list confirmed the existence of dialect group–occupation classifications. Several features are worthy of

---

166 "Notes on the Chinese in the Straits", *The Journal of the Indian Archipelago and Eastern Asia*, ed. J.R. Logan, 9 (1855): 120; *Singapore Chronicle and Commercial Register*, 8 May 1834.

167 It was declared that "the Chinese are everything", being employed in over 100 occupations. J.D. Vaughan, *The Manners and Customs of the Chinese of the Straits Settlements* (Singapore: Mission Press, 1879), p. 16.

168 Members of a clan share the same surname.

169 S. Dobbs, *The Singapore River*, p. 24.

170 Lim Tin Seng, "Coolies, Triads and Pimps: Chinatown in Former Times", *BiblioAsia* 11, 3 (2015): 3.

171 Cheng Lim Keak, "*Bang* Specialisation of the Chinese Community in Singapore", in *A General History of the Chinese*, ed. Kwa and Kua, p. 311–2; Yen, *A Social History*, p. 4.

172 "Notes on Chinese in the Straits", p. 116; Siah, "General Sketch", p. 290. The enumeration of the total number of Chinese in Singapore in the first article was apparently an overestimate, as shown by the census of 1849. Marriott, "The Peoples of Singapore", p. 350.

note. First, the Straits Chinese and the Hokkiens originating from Amoy and other places in Fukien province were predominantly traders and shopkeepers, partly on account of their early arrival in Southeast Asia, or agriculturists. They constituted the most respectable and wealthy portion of the Chinese population.[173] Second, gambier and pepper cultivation was almost completely monopolised by the Teochews from Swatow and its vicinity in Kwangtung province, the most numerous of the dialect groups, more than half of whom were engaged in it either as planters or labourers. The Teochews were also keen traders and held a prominent position in the marine products, piece goods and rice trades.[174] Third, the Chinese from Canton and neighbouring towns and villages (including Macao) in Kwangtung province were the most spread out in their choice of occupation, fully involved in half of the professions listed. Fourth, the Hakka people from the same province were almost as versatile as the Cantonese but seemed to be especially adept at carpentry and furniture making. In contrast, the minority Hainanese were narrowly concentrated in shopkeeping and domestic help. At the most general level, one could say that the Hokkiens and Teochews were the merchants and tillers of the soil while the Cantonese and Hakka were the artisans and handicraft makers.

Much ink has been spilled on the subject of the Chinese secret societies, or *hoeys* (in Mandarin, *hui*), and their relevance to economic organisation in Singapore. These started out as political societies in China with the objective of overthrowing Qing rule but in the different environment of the Straits and with changed economic circumstances, they degenerated into something more sinister. In Singapore, the societies at the beginning served as benevolent mutual aid groups, providing advice and protection to the sinkheh, helping them to find jobs and inducting the "new guests" into a brotherhood of fellow countrymen that served as a surrogate for family. The coolie brokers who arranged the journeys of sojourners from China were reputed to be senior members of the hoeys, as were the headmen in gambier and pepper plantations.[175] The hoeys were already noticed during Crawfurd's administration by the Malay scribe Munshi Abdullah, who referred to the society whose secret rituals he observed as the *Tan Tae Hoey* (heaven and earth association, or *tian di hui,* implying triad society).[176] It was akin to "Freemasonry, of which it is a perverted type" and was reputed to be headed by a Council of four officers, each of whom represented a major dialect group.[177] The society's members were bound by oath to protect and shield one another from the law.

---

[173] Vaughan, *The Manners and Customs*, p. 15; Marriott, "The Peoples of Singapore", pp. 345, 346.

[174] Cheng, "*Bang* Specialisation", p. 314.

[175] Yen, *A Social History*, pp. 112–4; Trocki, *Opium and Empire*, 1990, pp. 25–6.

[176] T. Braddell, "Concerning the Tan Tae Hoey in Singapore", *The Journal of the Indian Archipelago and Eastern Asia*, ed. J.R. Logan, 6 (1852): 545–55.

[177] Moore and Moore, *The First 150 Years*, pp. 203–4; Song, *One Hundred Years' History of the Chinese*, pp. 105–9.

Table 5. Occupations of the Singapore Chinese, 1848

	Melaka-born	Hokkien	Teochew	Cantonese	Hakka	Hainan
Shopkeeper/Trader	900	3,100	4,700	350	600	100
Gambier/Pepper Planter	–	–	10,000	400	–	–
Agriculturist	100	2,000	2,000	–	–	–
Sago Manufacturer	–	500	–	–	–	–
Boatman	–	930	660	–	–	–
Porter	–	800	–	–	–	–
Fisherman	–	200	600	–	–	–
Lime Burner	–	100	–	250	–	–
Charcoal Burner	–	–	140	–	–	–
Brickmaker	–	–	–	500	–	–
Bricklayer/Mason	–	100	–	–	–	–
Poulterer	–	700	100	500	–	–
Stone Cutter	–	–	150	–	–	–
House Carpenter	–	–	–	300	1,000	–
Cabinet Maker	–	–	–	1,000	300	–
Woodcutter/Sawyer	–	–	–	1,000	800	–
Ship/Boat Builder	–	–	–	400	–	–
Blacksmith	–	–	–	–	500	–
Goldsmith	–	–	–	–	100	–
Baker	–	–	–	200	–	–
Barber	–	–	50	200	100	–
Tailor/Shoemaker	–	–	–	400	400	–
House Servant	–	–	–	500	–	600
Waterman	–	250	–	–	–	–
Revenue Peon/Preparers of Arrack and Opium	–	70	–	–	–	–
Total	1,000	9,000	19,000	6,000	4,000	700

Source: "Notes on Chinese in the Straits", p. 116.

Among other depredations, this society was responsible for gang robberies and burglaries in the town.[178] Its members resided in the jungles of the interior, out of reach of the authorities, combining their legitimate status of gambier cultivators in the day with nocturnal lawlessness.[179] In the 1830s, the membership of the Tan Tae Hoey expanded in tandem with immigration to 5,000–6,000 members.[180] During the 1850s, the society divided into two rival offshoots that were organised along dialect lines—the Ghee Hin and

[178] R. St.J. Braddell, "Crime", p. 245; *Straits Settlements Records*, A.68, 2 Mar. 1830.

[179] Marriott, "The Peoples of Singapore", pp. 347–8; Song, *One Hundred Years' History of the Chinese*, pp. 40–1, 82, 84.

[180] Moore and Moore, *The First 150 Years*, pp. 203–4.

Ghee Hok—as well as the Ghee Sin, Ghee Kee and Hai San.[181] The new dynamic was the principal cause of troubles including sporadic fights and riots, prompting the British residents of Singapore to demand their suppression.[182] The worst of the riots, one that lasted ten days, transpired in May 1854, with a heavy loss of property and 600 lives, purportedly sparked by a trivial dispute between the Hokkiens and Teochews belonging to rival secret societies.[183] The shops, godowns and houses in the town all closed as the police and military patrolled the streets, but the disturbances spread from the town to the country areas where there was heavy fighting with many casualties.[184] The situation quietened down only after European residents and the officers of ships lying in the harbour were sworn in as special constables and sent to the countryside to quell the disturbances, with help from Malays loyal to the Temenggong.[185]

In the aftermath of the incident, some hoey members were charged with rioting and plunder but the colonial government took no action to suppress the triads because of the self-governing mechanism they provided for dispute resolution within the Chinese immigrant community. On the one hand, they had been accused of creating an *imperium in imperio* and posing a serious challenge to law and order, but on the other they were viewed as a stabilising force.[186] The local government basically accepted the existence of the secret societies as an integral part of the Chinese social structure, with their control and sway over the community encompassing almost every facet of life in the settlement. In the absence of any formal political organisation, the heads of the hoeys acted as their *de facto* political leadership and occasionally also as dialect clan leaders.

The brotherhoods thus fostered economic and social solidarity amongst the immigrant population. However, the triads were also the economically motivated source of conflict in Chinese society, since they were deeply involved with the revenue farms and coolie trade.[187] The consequent quarrels and turf wars between rival societies running protection rackets, as well as frequent murders, earned Singapore the epithets of a "frontier town" and "Oriental Chicago".[188] Yet it should be pointed out that the Chinese were concurrently members of lawful dialect associations and clan organisations, which also performed welfare, religious, arbitration and even educational roles without giving any trouble to

---

[181] Edwin Lee, *The British as Rulers Governing Multiracial Singapore 1867–1914* (Singapore: Singapore University Press, 1991), pp. 25, 111, 113.

[182] Vaughan, *The Manners and Customs*, p. 99.

[183] Song, *One Hundred Years' History of the Chinese*, pp. 126–30; Turnbull, *The Straits Settlements*, pp. 115–6; *Straits Settlements Records*, V.19, 12 May 1854; *The Straits Times*, 9 May 1854, 16 May 1854.

[184] R. St.J. Braddell, "Crime", p. 247.

[185] Lee, *The British as Rulers*, pp. 37–8.

[186] Yen, *A Social History*, p. 115; *The Straits Times*, 25 Oct. 1853.

[187] Mak Lau Fong, *The Sociology of Secret Societies: A Study of Chinese Secret Societies in Singapore and Peninsular Malaysia* (Kuala Lumpur: Oxford University Press, 1981), pp. 45–52. It has been claimed that the hoeys and other social organisations were formed for primarily economic purposes and that the hoeys were effectively economic brotherhoods. While this view is not entirely mistaken, it disregards the many non-economic functions that they performed. Trocki, *Opium and Empire*, pp. 11–19.

[188] A. Pereira, "Triads and Riots: Threats to Singapore's Social Stability", in *Past Times: A Social History of Singapore*, ed. Chan Kwok Bun and Tong Chee Kiong (Singapore: Times Editions, 2003), pp. 124–5; Moore and Moore, *The First 150 Years*, p. 157–8.

the government, notwithstanding colonial officials' mislabelling of these bodies as secret societies.[189] Two early and prominent clan associations in Singapore were the Ngee Ann Kongsi and Hokkien Huay Kuan, founded by Teochews and Hokkiens respectively.[190]

Although the Indians were not in any way notorious for forming secret societies as they lacked the propensity for combination of the Chinese, the 1850s found the British worrying about the activities of the newly formed Red Flag and White Flag societies. It was said that these organisations were inspired by the leaders of the convicts in Singapore and thus were imported from India.[191] The members of the two societies were drawn from a wide spectrum of Tamil Muslims, Hindus, *Jawi Peranakan* (a mixed race of Indians and Malays) and even Malays. Like the Chinese hoeys, the two societies were initially focused on providing assistance at religious ceremonies and organising Muslim processions through the streets of Singapore; over time however, they resorted to illegal activities.[192] The criminal returns compiled by the colonial authorities showed that in 1846, one in four Klings were charged with some offence but only one in twelve Chinese were similarly indicted, despite the proliferation of Chinese secret societies.[193] Since the street processions often provided the occasion for disturbances in which convicts were involved and which were decried by the Europeans, the British authorities passed laws in 1856 that gave them the power to stop them. This prerogative was seldom exercised until the conflict between the Red Flag and White Flag groups broke into the open during the 1860s, prompting the government to ban processions in 1865.

The occupational status of the Europeans did not change during their second decade in Singapore. They continued to specialise in the long-distance trade, the adjunct to the commercial capitalism they practised. By the 1830s, they had moved out from the town into suburbs in Tanglin and Cairnhill and the hillocks, occupying large garden houses and mansions.[194] In 1840, the tightly knit community numbered only 167 people, made up of 102 males and 65 females. Another four to five hundred sailors as well as itinerant traders might be found at the port.[195] The new breed of Europeans present on the island were the agriculturists who owned the nutmeg and coconut plantations. As compared with the apathetic Chinese and other natives who were content to go about the business of life, the British merchants played an active semi-political role, the most prominent amongst them being appointed as (unremunerated) magistrates and members of the town Municipal Committee.[196] They also sat on the Grand Juries that did not restrict themselves to taking judicial decisions but also made critical "presentments" on public affairs, including conditions at the gaol, town sanitation and the administration of justice. Given

---

189 Yen, *A Social History*, passim; Mark Ravinder Frost and Yu-Mei Balasingamchow, *Singapore: A Biography* (Singapore: Editions Didier Millet, 2009), p. 175.

190 Tan, *A Very Short History*, p. 37.

191 Lee, *The British as Rulers*, pp. 168–9, 170–1.

192 Rai, *Indians in Singapore*, pp. 49–50, 52–4.

193 *The Straits Times*, 19 Feb. 1850.

194 Teo and Savage, "Singapore Landscape", p. 317.

195 J.T. Thomson, *Some Glimpses into Life in the Far East* (London, 1864), p. 202; *The Singapore Free Press and Mercantile Advertiser*, 1 June 1865.

196 Turnbull, *Straits Settlements*, p. 23.

these roles, the British were invariably the organisers of public meetings that provided a forum for the mercantile community to express dissent over colonial policies, particularly those emanating from the Bengal government, an endeavour that was often supported by the local press.

An important institutional development that took place in February 1837 was the establishment of a Chamber of Commerce by the principal European merchants in Singapore. Despite their self-perceived superiority, the British were liberal enough to admit two Chinese merchants as members of the General Committee, in addition to one American, one Arab and one Armenian merchant.[197] The aims of the Chamber were to protect free trade in the Straits Settlements, collect commercial information, arbitrate in trade disputes, and represent the mercantile community in liaisons with the colonial government. On its formation, the Chamber immediately took up with the relevant authorities the issue of Dutch trade restrictions on the import of British manufactured goods into Java and more generally, actions to suppress British commerce.[198] A further complaint was the Dutch attempt to subjugate the pepper ports on both the west and east coasts of Sumatra that were under native rulers, with the objective of blocking their trade with Singapore and Penang.[199] In subsequent years, the Chamber remained the vanguard against Dutch attempts to expand their political and economic influence in the Eastern Archipelago.

Infrastructure and Piracy

In the early 1830s, the state of infrastructure in Singapore town belied that of a successful port and was unbefitting of a city that was made the permanent seat of the Straits Settlements government in 1832, taking over from Penang. The comment was made that "the Europeans settled at Singapore are apt to censure the East India Company for allowing the bridges and other public works to fall into decay".[200] Such neglect appeared to be a feature of most Asian colonial towns but above all, it was the result of administering the colony on a shoestring budget. Furthermore, the EIC viewed the settlement as a financial burden and had ordered a reduction of public expenses in all its Presidencies in 1827, including Singapore. This attitude became entrenched after the Company had to give up its monopoly of the China trade in 1833.

Since the implementation of Raffles' town plan, little effort had been made at urban construction except to attend to repairs of government and military buildings.[201] The morphology and basic appearance of the town had taken shape in 1830 with a Courthouse and Post Office on the northeast bank of the Singapore River, a jail near the Chinese

---

197 Newbold, *Political and Statistical Account*, pp. 391–6; *The Singapore Free Press and Mercantile Advertiser*, 23 Feb. 1837, 9 Mar. 1837.

198 Moore and Moore, *The First 150 Years*, pp. 176–7.

199 *Straits Settlements Records*, R.5, 21 July 1838, 20 Nov. 1838.

200 Earl, *The Eastern Seas*, pp. 405–6.

201 *Straits Settlements Records*, A.62, Oct. 1829.

settlement and ornamental European houses at the Esplanade and Beach Road.[202] A motley of churches dotted the European town to the north while the Asian town to the south was the location of the native temples and mosque.[203] Beginning in 1829, the local magistrates of the Court, acting on behalf of the colonial government, resolved to levy an assessment of 5 per cent on the rents of all houses in the town for the purpose of making repairs to and cleaning of the roads.[204] The rate was raised to 8½ per cent in 1840 but reduced to 8 per cent in 1843.[205] The most remunerative assessments were brought in by properties situated in the commercial heart of the settlement along and around the Singapore River, namely Commercial Square, Boat Quay, Telok Ayer and Market Street. In 1838, local taxation was extended to country dwellers and to the modes of land transport at the time—pony-drawn palanquin carriages, four-wheeler open carriages and bullock carts pulled by buffaloes—as well as cattle.[206] The latter levies provided an assured base for revenue extraction since they were imposed on the primary means for the transportation of people and goods.[207]

Things began to change for the better when the architect George Coleman, who had designed Raffles' house at Fort Canning Hill, was appointed Superintendent of Public Works in 1833. Prior to this, he had carried out detailed surveys of the town and harbour area and designed many private houses with skill and good taste.[208] His architectural style was in the Greco-Roman tradition and can still be seen around the street that is eponymously named as well the Civil District, including the Armenian Church, St. Andrew's Church (subsequently rebuilt) and the Courthouse (now part of the Old Parliament Complex). As Superintendent of Public Works, Coleman deployed convict labour to work on public buildings and infrastructural projects such as the clearing of jungle, draining of mangrove swamps and construction of roads.[209] The convicts were judged to be so desirable and the work so plentiful that in 1838, the Governor of the Straits Settlements requested 500 more to be sent to Singapore from either Bengal or Madras.[210] As a result, the number employed on public works nearly tripled during Coleman's career in Singapore, reaching over 1,200 by 1840.[211] It was by Coleman's and the prisoners' labour that town roads were laid and the interior of the island made accessible through two roads leading to Bukit Timah and Serangoon; in 1845, the Bukit Timah road was extended all the way to Kranji. The road

---

202 Luscombe, *Singapore*, pp. 34–5; *Straits Settlements Records*, A.62, 19 Sept. 1828, 10 Dec. 1828, 25 Feb. 1829.

203 Savage, *Lion City Narratives*, pp. 106–7, 180.

204 *Singapore Chronicle and Commercial Register*, 5 Nov. 1829, 12 July 1832, 16 Jan. 1834.

205 Hallifax, "Municipal Government", p. 318; *Straits Settlements Records*, Z.15, 11 Jan. 1843.

206 *The Singapore Free Press and Mercantile Advertiser*, 30 Aug. 1838, 30 Jan. 1840.

207 *The Land Transport of Singapore: From Early Times to the Present*, Revised Edition (Singapore: Educational Publications Bureau, 1984), pp. 4, 25.

208 T.H.H. Hancock, *Coleman's Singapore* (Royal Asiatic Society in association with Pelanduk Publications, 1986), pp. 12–65, 66, 69.

209 *Straits Settlements Records*, Z.6, 3 Aug. 1830.

210 *Straits Settlements Records*, R.5, 10 Dec. 1838.

211 Buckley, *An Anecdotal History*, pp. 227, 430.

allowed gambier planters to convey their output to the harbour more economically on land, instead of via boats around the island.[212]

Apart from urban growth resulting from a rising population, the key impetus for the improvement of public infrastructure in the latter half of the thirties came from the increase in the fiscal capacity of the local colonial government. As in the 1820s, the recurrent surplus in the state coffers meant that Singapore could spend more freely on construction projects than was the case in Penang or Melaka.[213] The revenue from the farms stagnated in the first half of the decade due to the trade recession, but it picked up after 1834.[214] In 1836, it had increased to SPD106,812 with about half derived from opium alone. Disbursements grew at a slower rate by virtue of the fixed costs incurred by the colonial establishment and judiciary. As a result, the surplus excluding military and convict costs came up to SPD9,712 in the same year.[215] In addition, the municipal revenue had increased over time to the extent that a favourable balance of SPD1,142 was obtained in 1837 after the police and night watchmen expenses were accounted for.[216] In 1841, the police force had expanded to include a Superintendent, 14 officers and more than 110 constables.[217]

Even when the status of Singapore was undecided before 1824, the private merchants had built offices and godowns made of brick and plaster along Boat Quay and Clarke Quay on land acquired from the government. During the time of Raffles, Farquhar and Crawfurd, certificates of occupation and location tickets were issued for perpetual leases of 999 years.[218] In 1837 when revised land regulations were drawn up under the direction of the Indian government, the leases on town land were shortened to 99 years.[219] The prices obtained for these shorter leases were initially low compared to the perpetual ones, but they increased over time. According to the town surveyor, each lot sold for SPD1,600 to SPD2,000 or more per acre in 1850.[220] But no matter how much the merchants and shop owners were willing to fork out for their premises, they refused to pay for what was arguably the most important public good in early colonial Singapore—efforts to suppress piracy. This was not a case of the "free rider" problem: the trading community as a whole was adamant that the Indian government be responsible for anti-piracy measures.

Piracy in the Malay Archipelago was a perennial menace. During the Temasek era, Wang Dayuan had recorded that Dragon's Tooth Gate (Keppel Harbour) was the lair of Malay pirates, who, with up to three hundred boats at a time, pounced on their victims sailing eastward.[221] Given the geology of the Archipelago with its immense clusters of

---

[212] It was estimated that it cost five cents per pikul to transport gambier and pepper by carts and seven to eight cents by boat. *The Straits Times*, 28 Jan. 1851.

[213] *The Singapore Free Press and Mercantile Advertiser*, 28 Jan. 1836, 4 Feb. 1836.

[214] Newbold, *Political and Statistical Account*, p. 381.

[215] *The Singapore Free Press and Mercantile Advertiser*, 28 Jan. 1836.

[216] *The Singapore Free Press and Mercantile Advertiser*, 15 Feb. 1838.

[217] R. St.J. Braddell, "Crime", p. 244.

[218] Lornie, "Land Tenure", pp. 302, 306–7.

[219] Song, *One Hundred Years' History of the Chinese*, pp. 35–6; Cameron, *Our Tropical Possessions in Malayan India*, pp. 52–3.

[220] Thomson, *General Report*, 1850, p. 209.

[221] Wheatley, *The Golden Khersonese*, p. 82.

islands, creeks and channels, that piracy should have survived through the ages is only to be expected.[222] As Singapore prospered, the loot became more bountiful.[223] Moreover, the easy access to arms and ammunition at the Singapore port aggravated the problem.[224] When Raffles left instructions for John Crawfurd on leaving Singapore in 1823, he had stated categorically that "The suppression of piracy in the seas of the Archipelago...I would call [to] your attention. It would be extremely desirable that a general plan having this in view were [to be] put in force in conjunction with the government of Prince of Wales Island [Penang], the Dutch authorities and the principal native independent states".[225] He added that although attacks on European vessels had been rare since the British took control of the Straits of Melaka, those on native vessels continued, especially in the waters between Melaka and Penang, to the extent that 50 ships were deterred from coming to Singapore each year. The solution, he suggested, was to request the Supreme Government in India to send an accompanying convoy from Penang.

That suggestion never came to pass; in fact, the government of the Straits Settlements was quite ineffective in protecting the native trade owing to the lack of a naval force while Admiralty Jurisdiction for the Straits courts to prosecute suspected pirates was given only in 1837.[226] The best that the authorities could do was to delegate the problem to local Malay chieftains in the Straits of Melaka and the Riau Islands.[227] It was for example no secret that the Temenggong's followers, ensconced in the safety of their concealed inlet at Telok Blangah, were engaged in piracy with his protection and blessing.[228] The chieftains were made to answer for such acts committed by their men in areas under their jurisdiction, of which there were numerous, including in the Dutch-controlled seas. Estimates of the number of bandits in the region range from 7,000 to 10,000 and they plundered in groups of 40 to 60 prahus of 40 to 50 feet in length equipped with pounder and swivel guns, each manned by 20 to 30 armed men.[229] They were not confined to the waters of the Straits and the surrounding islands but also infested the east coast of the Malay Peninsula and west Borneo.[230] Acts of piracy were even committed in broad daylight within sight of the Singapore seafront and the bounty sold in town.[231] The boats used by the much feared Balanini pirates from the Sulu Islands and the Illanun pirates originating in Mindanao were

---

[222] G.E. Brooke, "Piracy", in *One Hundred Years of Singapore,* vol. I, ed. Makepeace, Brooke and Braddell, p. 290.

[223] Moore and Moore, *The First 150 Years*, p. 152.

[224] Turnbull, *The Straits Settlements*, p. 244.

[225] "Letter of Instructions to Mr Crawfurd on Raffles' Departure", *The Journal of the Indian Archipelago and Eastern Asia*, ed. J.R. Logan, 7 (1853): 341.

[226] Brooke, "Piracy", pp. 291, 293; *The Singapore Free Press and Mercantile Advertiser*, 5 Oct. 1837.

[227] *Straits Settlements Records*, Z.6, 28 July 1830.

[228] *Singapore Chronicle and Commercial Register*, 11 Apr. 1835.

[229] "The Piracy and Slave Trade of the Indian Archipelago", *The Journal of the Indian Archipelago and Eastern Asia*, ed. J.R. Logan, 4 (1849): 46.

[230] *Straits Settlements Records*, Z.6, 30 July 1830.

[231] Turnbull, *The Straits Settlements*, p. 245.

even larger and could carry up to 80 men.[232] These marauders made predatory excursions to the western seas during the favourable monsoon season.[233]

Anyhow, it was left to the local government to undertake, from time to time, campaigns against these sea raiders and their hideouts. The first known expedition was mounted in 1822 and it captured 50 pirate prahus.[234] As ordered by Raffles, John Crawfurd in 1823 hired a boat to fight the pirates but the enterprise failed.[235] His successor in 1827 proposed the purchase of two small gunboats to cruise for bandits in the neighbourhood of Singapore, which received assent from Calcutta although only one gunboat was eventually acquired.[236] After subsiding in the late 1820s, piracy picked up again in the early 1830s. In 1832, following losses of SPD15,000 to SPD20,000 each year, a coterie of Chinese merchants organised a fleet of four well-armed vigilante boats to patrol the approaches to Singapore harbour and they managed to sink one pirate prahu.[237] A year later, a British man-of-war destroyed a pirate haunt on the Karimun Islands near Singapore.[238] The Straits Settlements government also built two sailing ships armed with guns to deal with the problem but they were not up to the task.[239] Even effective measures could not keep the buccaneers at bay for long.

In 1835, the scourge was so bad that it caused trade to fall off and forced the Governor of the Straits Settlements to plead for a naval vessel to be sent from India.[240] Concurrently, the European merchants in Singapore petitioned the Bengal authorities for action to be taken but when it was proposed that an *ad valorem* duty of 2½ per cent be levied on exports and imports to provide the necessary funds for a flotilla and a customs house, they baulked at the idea and protested to the British government.[241] Some merchants believed that the duties were a pretext for raising additional funds, not necessarily for fighting piracy. Although the proposed levy was withdrawn, the Indian government obliged the request for naval and manpower reinforcements by sending two sailing vessels and a schooner in 1836.[242] This was followed by a steamer in 1837 as well as gunboats and ships from the Royal Navy.[243] Given their superior speed, the steamers were highly effective in flushing

---

232 S. St. John, "Piracy in the Indian Archipelago", *The Journal of the Indian Archipelago and Eastern Asia*, ed. J.R. Logan, 3 (1849): 253.

233 *The Singapore Free Press and Mercantile Advertiser*, 14 Jan. 1836.

234 St. John, "Piracy in the Indian Archipelago", p. 254.

235 Brooke, "Piracy", pp. 290, 293.

236 Murfett, Miksic, Farrell and Chiang, *Between Two Oceans*, p. 50; *Straits Settlements Records*, N.1, 27 Jan. 1827, 6 Mar. 1827, 16 Mar. 1827, 30 Mar. 1827.

237 A. Webster, "Singapore, the Straits Settlements and the Politics of Imperial Commerce, 1819–1867", in *Singapore—Two Hundred Years of the Lion City*, ed. Webster and White, p. 128; *Singapore Chronicle and Commercial Register*, 7 June 1832.

238 Earl, *The Eastern Seas*, p. 388.

239 Song, *One Hundred Years' History of the Chinese*, p. 45.

240 Turnbull, *The Straits Settlements*, pp. 246, 407.

241 Newbold, *Political and Statistical Account*, p. 359; *Singapore Chronicle and Commercial Register*, 16 Jan. 1836.

242 Brooke, "Piracy", pp. 294, 296–7.

243 Tan, "Early Entrepôt Portal", p. 93.

out pirates from their lairs and destroying their boats.[244] In conjunction with enhanced surveillance and cooperation from the Dutch authorities, the naval reinforcements were decisive in putting the problem to rest for the next ten years, notwithstanding occasional reports of piracy incidents in the press and several further engagements with pirate bands.[245] Indeed, this success prompted the Temenggong's son and successor to turn pirate hunter (as well as gambier overlord, since it was he who issued the licences in Johor), rendering the waters around Singapore even safer.[246]

However, the problem of piracy resurfaced in the 1850s, this time in the Gulf of Siam and the South China Sea where unarmed junks and boats were frequently preyed on by Chinese pirate fleets.[247] At 70 to 150 tonnes and manned by 100 to 200 men, the pirate junks were much larger than the native prahus and they were able to prey on larger boats than those attacked by earlier pirate gangs.[248] These attacks severely damaged Singapore's trade with Siam and Cochin-China, as well as with China, while the Chinese pirates were audacious enough to use the port as a rendezvous for their nefarious activities and for procuring arms and munitions.[249] Despite appeals for assistance from India and the British government, none was forthcoming except for a largely ineffective law passed in 1857 conferring the power to search ships and arrest suspected pirates.[250] In the meantime, the authorities in Singapore detained suspicious junks at the harbour and dispatched steamers to look out for pirate junks, while the British China squadron carried out expeditions around the Chinese coast.[251] The bane lingered on into the 1860s and was only subjugated a decade later with the help of the Chinese government and the extension of British influence in Malaya.[252]

Social Development

Singapore's social development in the early decades was as stunted as its physical infrastructure. It should be remembered that the EIC was a for-profit organisation

---

244 A. Wright and H.A. Cartwright, eds., *Twentieth Century Impressions of British Malaya: Its History, People, Commerce, Industries, and Resources*, Abridged Edition (Singapore: Graham Brash, 1989), p. 42; Frost and Balasingamchow, *Singapore*, pp. 113–7; *Straits Settlements Records*, R.5, 15 June 1838; *The Singapore Free Press and Mercantile Advertiser*, 18 May 1837, 1 June 1837.

245 Mills, Turnbull and Bassett, "British Malaya", pp. 274–7; "Piracy and the Slave Trade of the Indian Archipelago", *The Journal of the Indian Archipelago and Eastern Asia*, ed. J.R. Logan, 4 (1850): 734–46; *Straits Settlements Records*, R.6, 30 July 1840; *The Singapore Free Press and Mercantile Advertiser*, 12 Apr. 1838, 22 Apr. 1841.

246 Turnbull, *History of Modern Singapore*, p. 69; Trocki, *Prince of Pirates*, pp. 88–90.

247 Turnbull, *The Straits Settlements*, pp. 250–1; Song, *One Hundred Years' History of the Chinese*, p. 130.

248 Mills, Turnbull and Bassett, "British Malaya", pp. 264–5; Abshire, *History of Singapore*, p. 51.

249 *Report on the Administration of the Straits Settlements During the Year 1855–56*, pp. 27–8; *The Singapore Free Press and Mercantile Advertiser*, 27 Sept. 1855.

250 Buckley, *An Anecdotal History*, p. 253; *Annual Report on the Administration of the Straits Settlements During the Year 1858–59*, p. 68.

251 Moore and Moore, *The First 150 Years*, pp. 296–8; *Straits Settlements Records*, V.19, 6 Apr. 1854.

252 Drake, *Merchants, Bankers, Governors*, p. 31; *The Singapore Free Press and Mercantile Advertiser*, 13 June 1861.

and its main objective in the Far East was commerce; therefore, the well-being of inhabitants was of only secondary importance, if at all.[253] While drawing criticism from the Grand Jury, such a policy explains the governing authorities' neglect of educational and healthcare needs until late in the 19th century.[254] In 1843, for instance, spending on education amounted to less than SPD2,000 for the whole year, though healthcare spending fared better at SPD8,536.[255] To be sure, demand for education was lacking since the population consisted mostly of transient immigrants while the natives showed lukewarm interest at best.[256]

The neglect of education is nevertheless indefensible in light of another lasting legacy of Stamford Raffles, namely his plan to establish a Singapore Institution for the purpose of educating the region's native elites, instructing the EIC's servants in native languages, and advancing and disseminating knowledge on the Malay Archipelago.[257] As much as these aims were practical, Raffles conceived of his project in moralistic terms—the revival of the ancient civilisations of Southeast Asia and the enlightenment of its peoples through the spread of Western liberal values: "I am anxious to do all the good I can here".[258] Furthermore, he saw education not as an imposition of Western and Christian culture, but rather as a way to advance local cultures and traditions. To these ends, personal donations from him, the Sultan, the Temenggong and even William Farquhar together with public subscriptions were collected amounting to SPD17,495. The key officers of the institution were appointed, comprising a Board of Trustees, President, Vice President, a librarian and professors of various subjects and languages. Raffles himself laid the foundation stone of the Institution on land near the sea he allotted in June 1823 but somehow the plan to make Singapore the intellectual centre of the Malay Archipelago fell through when Raffles passed away in 1826.[259] Apart from a shortage of funds, the EIC wavered on its earlier commitment to provide a grant of SPD300 each month and asked for a feasibility study, which John Crawfurd provided in 1826; despite his support for setting up the Institution, albeit on a far less ambitious scale, the project was not seen through by the trustees. The monthly grant was withheld and the uncompleted school building fell into disuse.[260]

[253] T.R. Doraisamy, *150 Years of Education in Singapore* (Singapore: Teachers' Training College Publications Board, 1969), p. 7.

[254] C. Bazell, "Education in Singapore", in *One Hundred Years of Singapore*, vol. I, ed. Makepeace, Brooke and Braddell, p. 8; *The Singapore Free Press and Mercantile Advertiser*, 20 Jan. 1859.

[255] *The Singapore Free Press and Mercantile Advertiser*, 8 June 1843.

[256] *Annual Report on the Administration of the Straits Settlements During the Year 1858–59*, p. 68.

[257] "Notices of Singapore, Singapore Institution", *The Journal of the Indian Archipelago and Eastern Asia*, ed. J.R. Logan, 8 (1849): 408.

[258] Quoted in Moore and Moore, *The First 150 Years*, p. 98; Savage, *Lion City Narratives*, pp. 101–2, 340.

[259] Newbold, *Political and Statistical Account*, p. 289; Luscombe, *Singapore*, p. 50.

[260] *The Asiatic Journal and Monthly Register for British India and its Dependencies* 8 (Jul–Dec 1824): 17; Lim Peng Han, "English Schools and School Libraries Before the Second World War: A Singapore Perspective", *Singapore Journal of Library & Information Management* 37 (2008): 63; *Singapore Chronicle and Commercial Register*, 20 Dec. 1832.

Meanwhile in 1834, Singapore's first English public school was started in a planks-and-attap building on High Street by the Anglican chaplain of the settlement, Reverend Fred Darrah, with support from the public through donations and subscriptions.[261] Known as the Singapore Free School, it consisted of language departments with native masters, as well as a central department which European children could attend. It initially enrolled 74 students in English, Chinese, Malay and Tamil classes.[262] Before this, education in Singapore was limited to vernacular instruction, specifically Malay schools offering Koran classes and Chinese schools offering Chinese writing and abacus classes.[263] In 1837, there were over a score of these schools operated by missionaries, religious bodies and clan associations with more than 200 students enrolled.[264] Later in 1854, the Chinese community established the Chui Ying Institution or Chinese Free School to provide an orthodox Confucian education to 100 boys.[265] There was also a free boarding school for Malays run by the Christian missionary Reverend Benjamin Keasberry, which had 50 male and female pupils in 1860 who were taught useful trades like printing, lithography, needle work and embroidery.[266]

In 1836, the organisers of a drive to raise funds for a memorial to Raffles decided that the money collected would be best utilised by reviving the Institution project.[267] George Coleman was engaged to complete the unfinished school premises in Bras Basah and to add two new wings at a total cost of SPD11,530.[268] On learning this, Reverend Darrah decided to transfer his students to the proposed building in 1837, although it was only fully completed in 1841. Going initially by the name of the Singapore Institution Free School, it operated as an elementary school with around 170 boys in attendance, and not the institution of higher learning that Raffles envisaged. As both Crawfurd and the press pointed out, it was impracticable to set up a college when the foundations for elementary education were hardly in place.[269] The colonial government provided a liberal allowance to the school, supplemented by voluntary subscriptions, while the better-off students paid modest fees ranging from twenty-five cents to one Spanish dollar per month.[270] However, the Chinese, Tamil and even the Malay classes at the school were poorly attended and

---

261 Bazell, "Education in Singapore", pp. 431–2; *Singapore Chronicle and Commercial Register*, 8 May 1834.

262 Lim Peng Han, "Elementary Malay Vernacular Schools and School Libraries in Singapore under British Colonial Rule, 1819–1941", *School Libraries Worldwide* 14, 1 (2008): p. 74; Hancock, *Coleman's Singapore*, p. 80.

263 Doraisamy, *150 Years of Education*, p. 6; Bazell, "Education in Singapore", p. 431.

264 *The Singapore Free Press and Mercantile Advertiser*, 7 Sept. 1837.

265 Lim Guan Hock, "Development of Chinese Education in Singapore (1819–1979)", in *A General History of the Chinese*, ed. Kwa and Kua, pp. 422–3.

266 Turnbull, *History of Modern Singapore*, p. 79; *Annual Report on the Administration of the Straits Settlements, During the Year 1859–60*, p. 12; *Straits Settlements Annual Report*, vol. 1, ed. R.L. Jarman, (Archive Editions, 1998), p. 218. This publication will be referenced as *Straits Settlements Annual Report.*

267 Bazell, "Education in Singapore", pp. 430, 432.

268 *The Singapore Free Press and Mercantile Advertiser*, 26 May 1836. The original design of the institution was by Lieutenant Philip Jackson. Teo and Savage, "Singapore Landscape", pp. 313–4, 320.

269 *The Singapore Free Press and Mercantile Advertiser*, 19 May 1836.

270 *Straits Settlements Records*, R.5, 26 Feb. 1839; *The Straits Times*, 3 Jan. 1854.

most closed down.[271] The English class that remained was divided into an upper division with four classes and a lower division, offering subjects such as arithmetic, geometry, trigonometry, history, writing and drawing.[272] Overall, the standard of education was low and the aim was merely to churn out graduates to serve as clerks in government departments or mercantile houses. In 1844, the Singapore Institution added a girls' school with a small enrolment, managed by a committee of eight ladies.[273]

The only other English school of note which was founded during the early colonial period was the Christian Brothers school St. Joseph's Institution. Funded in part by the French government as well as by public subscriptions, the school was opened in a disused church in 1852 by the priest Father Jean-Marie Beurel, who recruited three Brothers from France as the first teachers.[274] While Roman Catholic in character, the school was "open to everyone, whatever his creed may be". In 1855, it had a daily attendance of more than 130 pupils and was especially favoured by Europeans and Eurasians.[275] Providing a gratuitous education for boys in its initial years, the school began to charge fees only in 1863. St. Joseph's shifted to a new home three years later at Bras Basah, at which time it became the first school in Singapore to receive a grant-in-aid from the colonial government. Father Beurel was also instrumental in establishing the Convent of the Holy Infant Jesus for girls in 1854, including purchasing a house for this purpose at the intersection of Victoria Street and Bras Basah Road.[276] The Convent was administered by four Sisters and took in female orphans; like St. Joseph's Institution, it was attended mainly by English-speaking girls.

The rudimentary state of education aside, social conditions in early Singapore were appalling. Problems of housing, congestion, sanitation and disease were left to sort themselves out.[277] Notwithstanding Singapore's reputation for a salubrious climate and the near absence of deaths among Europeans from tropical illnesses, a large number of Chinese immigrants were stricken with diseases and malnutrition.[278] Many arrived in Singapore penniless and if they could not find employment or fell sick, there was no social safety net; whatever welfare services that existed were confined to the benevolence of a few Chinese merchants and Europeans.[279] Those who could not avail themselves of such services had to literally beg, borrow or steal, which explained the numerous beggars on the streets of Singapore and frequent robberies.[280] In view of the lack of social services, the local

---

[271] Turnbull, *The Straits Settlements*, p. 226; Doraisamy, *150 Years of Education*, p. 22. The Chinese classes that were stopped were in the Cantonese and Teochew dialects while the Hokkien class continued. Bazell, "Education in Singapore", p. 435.

[272] Bazell, "Education in Singapore", p. 436.

[273] *The Singapore Free Press and Mercantile Advertiser*, 10 Oct. 1844.

[274] Turnbull, *Straits Settlements*, pp. 227–8; Bazell, "Education in Singapore", pp. 443, 452, 453, 454.

[275] *The Singapore Free Press and Mercantile Advertiser*, 10 Apr. 1856.

[276] Buckley, *An Anecdotal History*, pp. 265–6.

[277] Frost and Balasingamchow, *Singapore*, p. 162.

[278] Earl, *The Eastern Seas*, pp. 353–4; Davidson, *Trade and Travel in the Far East*, pp. 40, 66–7; G.E. Brooke, "Medical Work and Institutions", in *One Hundred Years of Singapore*, vol. I, ed. Makepeace, Brooke and Braddell, pp. 491–2.

[279] Turnbull, *The Straits Settlements*, p. 213; *The Straits Times*, 23 Sept. 1845, 30 Sept. 1845.

[280] *Singapore Chronicle and Commercial Register*, 10 May 1832.

populace was left very much to its own devices when it came to caring for the sick and the infirm. Initially, no hospitals for civilians were available, only a few private practitioners and dispensaries.[281] Understandably then, the Asian communities preferred to seek their own ethnic medical practitioners.[282]

Nevertheless, a military hospital with medical staff drawn from the EIC had been built at the cantonment for the troops in Selegie Road; by 1822, it was also tending to sick European sailors who called at the port. It was rebuilt twice during the decade on the same premises and was called the General Hospital.[283] By 1830, the building was in such a state of decay that no one would seek admission except those in the direst circumstances. Despite agitation for a new hospital to be constructed for Europeans, including sick sailors, the government held firm in its belief that a hospital should be funded by public contributions.[284] In 1838, the merchants petitioned the government, again without success. The Resident Councillor also brought to the attention of his superiors in India the plight of destitute European seamen who were shipwrecked and brought to Singapore, or otherwise abandoned by Masters of Vessels, but his call fell on deaf ears.[285] It was only after the outbreak of cholera among British naval officers three years later that the administration was spurred to co-fund the construction cost of a new General Hospital at Pearl's Hill by providing SPD4,800, with a balance of SPD2,700 coming from donations.[286] Also known as the European Seamen's Hospital, it began to admit a small number of patients in late 1845, treating the common illnesses of the day such as fever, smallpox and cholera.

Concurrently with the establishment of the military hospital, the administration of William Farquhar erected a shed in the cantonment for the purpose of treating and housing the sick and starving beggars of Singapore.[287] The money for running the home came from the revenue farms, and the Assistant Surgeon in charge of the military hospital doubled up in this infirmary. Initially, the cost of administering this so-called Pauper Hospital was minimal but as admissions increased, a request for additional government funds was denied as it was felt the local rich Chinese should support the hospital. In 1828, no further patients were admitted due to a lack of funds and only four Chinese were left in the cots.

In response to a presentment of the Grand Jury in the following year objecting to "the miserable and disgusting objects" to be seen all over the town, the Governor decided to follow the precedent set by Penang, which had imposed a tax on the sale of pork to support a Poor House.[288] The EIC Court of Directors in London approved the plan, whereupon

281 Brooke, "Medical Work", pp. 487–9, 490, 497.

282 Ooi Giok Ling, "British Colonial Healthcare Development and the Persistence of Ethnic Medicine in Peninsular Malaysia and Singapore", *Southeast Asian Studies* 29, 2 (1991): 163.

283 Y.K. Lee, "Private Practitioners and Private Hospitals in Early Singapore (1819–1872)", *Singapore Medical Journal* 46, 9 (2005): 489–91.

284 *Singapore Chronicle and Commercial Register*, 16 May 1833.

285 Moore and Moore, *The First 150 Years*, p. 243; Brooke, "Medical Work", pp. 494, 497; *Straits Settlements Records*, R.6, 9 Dec. 1840.

286 *Straits Settlements Records*, Z.15, 30 Nov. 1842, 3 May 1843.

287 Y.K. Lee, "The Pauper Hospital in Early Singapore, Part I, 1819–1829", *Singapore Medical Journal* 14, 1 (1973): 49, 50.

288 Brooke, "Medical Work", pp. 492–3.

the pork farm was put up for auction in April 1830. With the revenue collected, the number of patients in the Pauper Hospital increased to about 70 to 80 persons in the following year, made up not just of Chinese but also Europeans, convicts and lepers. The revenue exceeded the hospital's expenses of about SPD300 per month and after calls from the public, SPD11,417 was eventually utilised for the construction of a new Poor House at the corner of Stamford Road.[289] But after it was completed in 1834, the government appropriated the building for the purpose of a convict jail and relocated the paupers in an attap house instead, causing considerable indignation among the local residents.

In 1837, the Governor-General of India suddenly ordered the abolition of the pork farm in Singapore for surprisingly cogent economic reasons. This was the second time the farm had been cancelled, the first being by John Crawfurd in 1823 on the grounds that it was morally wrong to tax essential foodstuffs.[290] His view was echoed by the Governor-General, although the latter's decision was based on arguments of inequity and inefficiency: first, it is unfair to tax one segment of the population (the pork-eating Chinese) to support the rest; and second, a tax on the "most useful, industrious, intelligent and skilful part of our population" would discourage work effort.[291] There was probably a further reason: from 1832 to 1837, the pork farm raised only SPD39,720 from an estimated 9,000 consumers of pork while the opium farm generated SPD262,549 and the arrack farm $122,338.[292] Therefore, the revenue loss from abolishing the pork farm was not as detrimental to the general revenue as might be expected. The Governor-General also ordered the Poor House section of the Pauper Hospital to be shut, as it housed mostly sick and decrepit Chinese from the Riau Islands, and only chronic cases were to be admitted.

The local newspaper chastised the decisions and the wealthy Chinese in Singapore who would do nothing to help their poor countrymen.[293] The abolition of the pork farm did away with the objective for which it had been established—generating funds for feeding and housing the destitute, the homeless and the diseased of Singapore. Pleas to the Supreme Government were made to reinstate the farm by both the press and the Grand Jury, with the tacit approval of the Chinese community which purportedly did not look on the farm as a tax.[294] But the appeals were futile and as a result of the Pauper Hospital being deprived of its regular source of income, the quality of medical care deteriorated. By 1843, conditions were so bad that the Governor contemplated a law to force the rich to support the poor. He consulted Tan Tock Seng, one of the wealthiest and most influential Chinese in Singapore, who promptly offered to build a new Pauper Hospital at a cost not

---

289 Y.K. Lee, "The Pauper Hospital in Early Singapore, Part II, 1830–1839", *Singapore Medical Journal* 15, 1 (1974): 72–4, 76; T. Braddell, *Statistics of the British Possessions*, p. 47; *Singapore Chronicle and Commercial Register*, 17 Mar. 1831.

290 Turnbull, *The Straits Settlements*, p. 199.

291 Lee, "The Pauper Hospital, Part II", pp. 78–9. Ironically, the price of pork went up after the farm was abolished. Brooke, "Medical Work", p. 494.

292 T. Braddell, *Statistics of the British Possessions*, pp. 46–7.

293 *The Singapore Free Press and Mercantile Advertiser*, 21 Sept. 1837.

294 *The Straits Times*, 21 Oct. 1845.

exceeding SPD5,000 at Pearl's Hill.[295] Tan Tock Seng's munificence set an early example of the principles of philanthropy and self-help in the Chinese community. His action was to be followed by many others later in constructing schools and social amenities. As a businessman, he erected an elegant block of shophouses next to the commodious New Market in 1845 located at the upper stretch of Boat Quay, also known as the Ellenborough Market.[296] Before it opened, Singapore only had the two public markets alluded to earlier—the Lau Pa Sat or Old Market at Telok Ayer built in 1825 and the Kampong Glam Market. The Ellenborough Market was also called the Teochew Market on account of the predominance of vendors and traders from that dialect group who rented stalls that sold seafood and related products.

The foundation stone of the new Pauper Hospital, subsequently renamed Tan Tock Seng Hospital, was laid in July 1844, one month after that of the European Seamen's Hospital on the same hill. It was the first hospital in Singapore to be built from private funds, although the maintenance costs and recurrent expenses were to be borne by the government. However, when the hospital was finally occupied in 1849, the government considered imposing a new tax to pay for the operational expenses of SPD6,000 a year but was dissuaded from doing this by the residents of Singapore.[297] In the year from April 1849 to March 1850, the hospital treated 451 patients of whom 102 died; the mortality rate rose to one-third in 1853 when 752 patients were admitted because many of them were already in the last stage of disease.[298] The infant mortality rate was also high, at 347 per one thousand live-births.[299] Conditions at the overcrowded hospital were also not helped by bad ventilation and worse, the air was poisoned by a nearby swamp that was used as a garbage dump.[300]

Nevertheless, the situation gradually improved in the 1850s. The Indian government provided a modest grant to the hospital to employ additional medical staff and pay for medicine, following a law passed in 1850 to prevent the entry into Singapore of paupers and beggars from the Dutch settlements.[301] A successful appeal for public donations and monthly subscriptions catered to the diet of patients.[302] Tan Kim Cheng, the son of the hospital's founder, generously donated money in 1854 for alterations and additions to the main hospital building to alleviate the overcrowding problem.[303] Three years later, the government decided to move the Pauper Hospital to a site at the junction of Balestier and

[295] Y.K. Lee, "The Pauper Hospital in Early Singapore, Part III, 1840–1849, Section I", *Singapore Medical Journal* 16, 2 (1975): 107–9. Tan Tock Seng eventually spent $7,000 to construct the hospital while another Chinese merchant bequeathed $2,000. Brooke, "Medical Work", p. 495; Moore and Moore, *The First 150 Years*, p. 245.

[296] Buckley, *An Anecdotal History*, pp. 430, 441; *The Straits Times*, 15 July 1845.

[297] Buckley, *An Anecdotal History*, p. 408.

[298] Y.K. Lee, "The Pauper Hospital in Early Singapore, Part IV, 1850–1859, Section I", *Singapore Medical Journal* 16, 4 (1975): 272; *The Straits Times*, 5 July 1853, 11 July 1854.

[299] Tan, "Health and Welfare", in *A History of Singapore*, ed. Chew and Lee, p. 340.

[300] Turnbull, *The Straits Settlements*, p. 214.

[301] Lee, "The Pauper Hospital, Part IV", p. 270; *The Straits Times*, 30 July 1850.

[302] Song, *One Hundred Years' History of the Chinese*, p. 93.

[303] *The Straits Times*, 11 July 1854.

Serangoon Roads to make way for military fortifications and barracks at Pearl's Hill.[304] The new hospital was occupied in 1861, and it had a female ward paid for by Tan Tock Seng's widow and a ward for lepers.[305] With better air quality at the new location, the mortality rate fell in consequence.[306]

Since the European Seamen's Hospital was also situated on Pearl's Hill, its patients too had to be relocated to temporary quarters near Armenian Street before transferring to a new hospital at Kandang Kerbau in 1860, which had a mental health facility (lunatic asylum) attached.[307] Prior to that year, the mentally ill were housed in a building located at the site of the original Pauper Hospital in Bras Basah Road.[308] The new hospital had wards for Europeans, police officers and natives, and admitted both male and female patients, though its location was not considered ideal due to the swampy land nearby. Still, it started to treat gynaecological conditions and childbirth in 1865, thus becoming the precursor to the present KK Women's and Children's Hospital.[309]

---

304 Y.K. Lee, "Singapore's Pauper and Tan Tock Seng Hospitals, Part Three, The New Hospital, 1860", *Journal of the Malaysian Branch of the Royal Asiatic Society* 49, 2 (1976): 171–2; *Straits Settlements Records*, Z.33, 6 May 1857.

305 *150 Years of Caring: The Legacy of Tan Tock Seng Hospital* (Singapore: Tan Tock Seng Hospital, 1994), pp. 22–3.

306 Turnbull, *The Straits Settlements*, p. 215.

307 Y.K. Lee, "The 1926 General Hospital, Singapore", *Annals of the Academy of Medicine, Singapore* 34, 6 (2005): 56C; Brooke, "Medical Work", pp. 497, 498, 499; *Straits Settlements Records*, V.27, 10 Nov. 1859.

308 *Straits Settlements Records*, R.6, 28 Nov. 1840.

309 *Straits Settlements Records*, V.29, 5 Dec. 1859.

Chapter 4 From Trade Entrepôt to Crown Colony, 1846–66

The previous chapters have reviewed Singapore's early economic development, largely achieved through the dual growth engines of trade and agriculture. This chapter discusses how Singapore in the final analysis can be said to have been created for the purpose of trade, as it transformed into the premier entrepôt of Southeast Asia and performed functions that were not too different from those of its Temasek days. Accordingly, the chapter begins by examining the resulting changes in its patterns of trade and inquiring into the recurrent commercial fluctuations around a longer-term growth trend, as well as their underlying causes. Next, the key political and economic developments of the tumultuous 1850s and 1860s leading to the incorporation of the Straits Settlements as a Colony of the British Crown in 1867 are narrated. The state of infrastructure and the public finances on the eve of the transfer are reviewed. Finally, with the help of wage and price data, we assess the standard of living in Singapore during the early colonial era.

Commercial Growth and Diversification

After the 1840s, Singapore's commercial development and economic role changed. It effectively abrogated agricultural enterprise, leaving that to the neighbouring areas, and gained a comparative advantage instead in providing premier entrepôt trade services, from which the local merchants derived a handsome income.[1] By the 1850s, the level of merchandise trade had doubled from the first decade of Singapore's founding. In order to picture the scale of commercial development over the decades, the following shipping statistics are illuminating: the total number of ships and merchant vessels arriving at and departing from the port increased from 4,062 in 1829 to 6,646 in 1866, with the rise in the number of square-rigged vessels overwhelming the increase in native vessels in the ratio of six to one.[2] Total tonnage increased more than proportionately from 298,880 tonnes to 1,248,987 tonnes, implying that larger vessels called at Singapore as time went by.

[1] A. Kobayashi, "Price Fluctuations and Growth Patterns in Singapore's Trade, 1831–1913", *Australian Economic History Review* 57, 1 (2017): 108–10.

[2] Wong, *The Trade of Singapore*, Appendix C, Tables Ia to XXII, pp. 276–93.

As to the extent of the trade increase between 1823, when systematic trade data were first collected, and 1866, the year before the Straits Settlements were converted into a Colony of the British Empire, Singapore's foreign commerce in nominal terms expanded by nearly six times, from SPD11,417,036 to SPD64,554,435.[3] The compound growth rate implied was 3.6 per cent per annum. In real terms, the rate of growth was actually higher, at 4 per cent per annum, due to declines in the export and import price indices from 1831 to 1852.[4] Thereafter, prices gradually reverted to just below their starting levels by 1866. One explanation for the deflationary trend is the debasement of Latin American silver coins after the 1820s. However, an examination of the prices of key commodities in the price indices suggests that it was the falling cost of British cotton manufactured goods that dominated price fluctuations.[5] As we have observed, cheaper English cloth eventually drove Indian textiles out of the Southeast Asian market.

The reasons for these impressive advances were manifold, the first being the more liberal policies implemented by the Dutch and the opening of China to international commerce in the aftermath of the Opium Wars, both of which gave a boost to trade in Asia. In Europe, the end of the Napoleonic Wars in 1815 had ushered in a period of unprecedented peace, at least until the political disturbances in 1848. Perhaps most significantly, the first half of the 19th century, before the advent of colonial mining and plantation enterprise in Southeast Asia, was a time of vibrant trade expansion within the region itself.[6] This growth was driven by multilateral trading networks within Asia that were centred on Singapore, as described earlier.[7] Concurrently, Singapore's trade patterns shifted; however, contrary to what is believed, the port did not intermediate a greater proportion of the intercontinental trade in regional produce.[8] In fact, the proportion of long-distance commerce in overall trade fell further to 51 per cent in 1866 from 56 per cent in 1844 (Table 6). By contrast, intraregional commerce expanded in both absolute and relative terms. Specifically, the combined share of the entrepôt and redistribution trades rose to 49 per cent of the total value of trade transactions in 1866, compared to 44 per cent in 1844; the increase from 1829 was more marked, by 6.7 percentage points. Thus, Singapore transformed into the trade entrepôt *par excellence* of Southeast Asia, while continuing to intermediate the East–West trade.

---

[3] Wong, *The Trade of Singapore*, Appendix A, Table XXVII, p. 254. The nominal trade data include treasure.

[4] For the computation of real merchandise trade, we rely on the datasets of trade quantities and prices compiled by Atsushi Kobayashi. Given the similarity between Singapore's export and import items owing to its entrepôt role, the export and import price indices tended to move together.

[5] Kobayashi, "Price Fluctuations", p. 119. Despite the decline in manufactured goods prices, the terms-of-trade for Singapore did not improve as the goods were also re-exported at lower prices.

[6] Sugihara, "Resurgence of Intra-Asian Trade", passim.

[7] Kobayashi, "The Role of Singapore", pp. 453–7, 471–2.

[8] Kobayashi, "Price Fluctuations", p. 109.

Table 6. Distribution of Singapore's Trade Branches, Various Years

	Entrepôt	Long-Distance	Redistribution	Total
1829	1,769,832	10,236,842	5,676,160	17,682,834
Proportion of total	10.0%	57.9%	32.1%	100%
1844	3,527,130	11,842,680	5,895,690	21,265,500
Proportion of total	16.6%	55.7%	27.7%	100%
1866	6,662,020	25,464,814	17,569,678	49,696,512
Proportion of total	13.4%	51.2%	35.4%	100%

Note: Absolute trade figures are in Spanish dollars (SPD).

Source: Authors' calculations based on the export and import data for different countries and regions in Appendix A of Wong, *The Trade of Singapore*, pp. 207–56.

In a reflection of this shift, the importance of Britain and India to Singapore's commerce diminished, with their shares declining to about 18 per cent each in 1866. By contrast, the stronger Asian orientation can be seen for example in the case of Java, which had a share in Singapore's total trade of 6.5 per cent in 1866, in part the result of the more open trading environment in the East Indies after 1847.[9] Following the Netherlands' annexation of large parts of Sumatra, a treaty was concluded with Britain in 1871 giving British and Dutch merchants equal trading rights on the island.[10] Therefore, it may be surmised that the political stability the Dutch brought to the Archipelago was to Singapore's ultimate advantage. On the mainland, the combined trade of Burma, Cambodia, Cochin-China and Siam with Singapore increased from less than SPD1 million in 1844 to nearly SPD7 million in 1866. Together, they accounted for 12.2 per cent of its total trade in the later year, by which time the British had established their colony in Burma while the French had seized Cochin-China. Siam too was persuaded to sign the Bowring Treaty with Britain in 1855, which dismantled the royal monopoly on trade, replaced the heavy tonnage duty with a flat 3 per cent import duty and put British ships on an equal footing with Siamese vessels.[11] It was not at all a coincidence that the sequence of events that led to the treaty was initiated by Singapore-based merchants, who adverted the Supreme Government in India to the matter in 1848 and again in 1851.[12] All in, Singapore's export and import markets were more diversified at the end of Indian rule.

An analysis based on a broad classification of Singapore's export commodities reinforces the foregoing conclusions (Figure 5). In 1866, the proportion of regional foodstuffs in total exports was roughly unchanged compared to 1844.[13] These included rice, pepper, sugar, coffee and tobacco. Asian products, consisting of opium, raw silk and silk piece goods, declined in importance due to a further reduction in the shipments of Chinese silk products to the West, which had started after the EIC lost its China monopoly in 1833. In the 1850s, the decline was exacerbated by the adverse impact of the Taiping Rebellion on

[9] Wong, *The Trade of Singapore*, Appendix A, Table XXVIII, p. 255.

[10] Kawamura, "Trade, Finance and the 'Anglo-Dutch' International Order", pp. 49, 68.

[11] *The Singapore Free Press and Mercantile Advertiser*, 3 May 1855, 17 May 1855.

[12] Wong, *The Trade of Singapore*, p. 144; *The Straits Times*, 4 Feb. 1851.

[13] Kobayashi, "Price Fluctuations", p. 116.

silk production in Central China.[14] The value of raw silk re-exported from Singapore fell from SPD1,385,964 in 1831 to SPD50,455 in 1844 and dwindled to virtually nothing by 1866.[15] At the same time, the greater concessions gained by the foreign powers after the second Opium War (1856–60) had increased direct trade between China and the West, thus causing its share in Singapore's trade to fall to 14 per cent in 1866, from 22 per cent in 1844. By the later year, Singapore's participation in the China opium trade was also negligible, amounting to only 900 chests, compared to direct imports from India of 76,863 chests. Nevertheless, opium exports to Southeast Asia continued to rise, from 1,415 chests in 1844 to 2,641 chests in 1856 before falling back to 2,150 chests in 1866.[16]

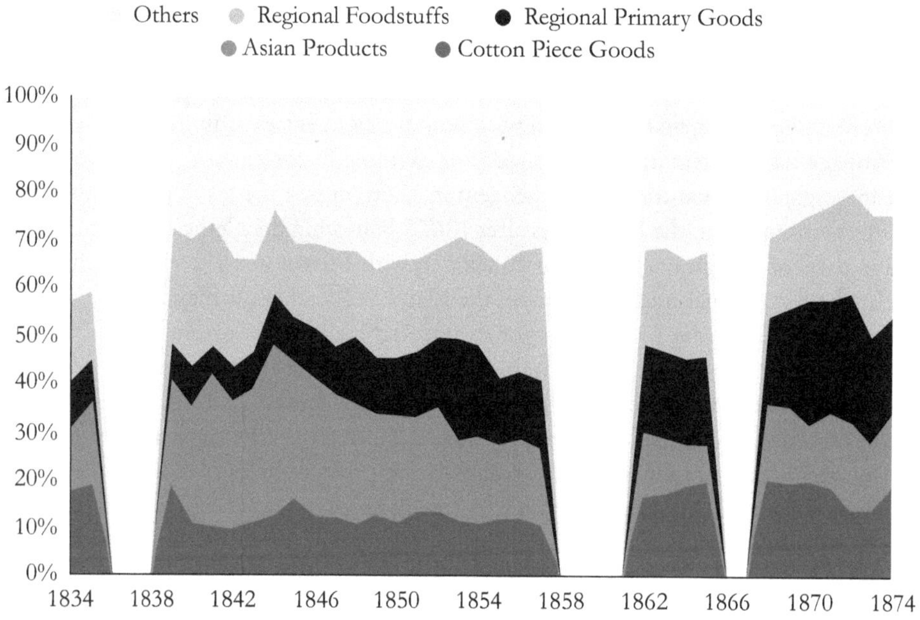

Figure 5. Commodity Composition of Singapore's Exports, 1834–74
Source: Based on data supplied courtesy of Atsushi Kobayashi.

The re-export of cotton goods to the region became more important. Up to the 1830s, imports of piece goods from India had dominated the regional market due to their high quality and great variety of colours; subsequently, luxurious fabrics and coarse cloth became more popular.[17] By 1866 however, European piece goods had triumphed—Singapore's circulation of Indian cloth was just 2.6 per cent of the total.[18] British textiles from Lancashire and Manchester in particular had finally driven out Indian cloth from Southeast Asia by virtue of their lower prices and improved quality. The output and trade

14 von Glahn, *Economic History of China*, p. 374.

15 Wong, *The Trade of Singapore*, pp. 119–20, Appendix A, Table XXVIII, p. 256.

16 Ibid., p. 116, Appendix B, Table IX, pp. 274–5.

17 A. Kobayashi, "The Origins of Singapore's Economic Prosperity, c. 1800–1874", in *Singapore—Two Hundred Years of the Lion City*, ed. Webster and White, pp. 19–20.

18 A. Reid, "Southeast Asian Consumption", pp. 42–4, 47–8.

in Indian cotton goods had also stagnated during the rule of the EIC, at a time when factory production of cloth in England was advancing rapidly. Java was the last bastion of Indian cotton goods for Singapore partly due to the Dutch prohibitive tariffs on European piece goods in the 1830s but it took only SPD13,504 worth in 1866.[19] In that year, the Dutch East Indies as a whole, inclusive of Borneo and Sumatra, accounted for fully one quarter of Singapore's re-exports of European piece goods. Another one-fifth went to the Malay Peninsula while the rest was shipped to Siam, Cochin-China and China (Figure 6).

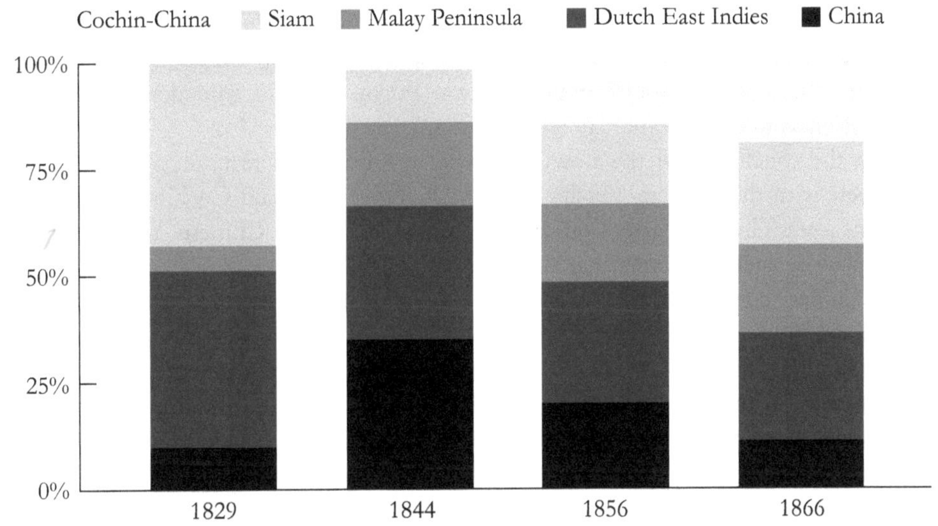

Figure 6. European Cotton Goods Exports from Singapore, Various Years
Source: Wong, *The Trade of Singapore*, p. 127, Appendix B, Tables III, IV and V.

As regards the last three destinations, the shares of Siam and Cochin-China in Singapore's cotton trade increased significantly between 1844 and 1866, but that of China declined. These diverging trends were to some extent caused by an increase in direct imports of British and European cotton goods into China, which grew by more than one-and-a-half times, whereas Singapore's corresponding exports to China increased by only 73 per cent.[20] However, the enlargement of the Siamese and Cochin-Chinese markets more than compensated for slower growth in the trade with China, so that Singapore's overall cotton exports still expanded more than fourfold during the same period. With a share of close to 24 per cent, Siam was the single biggest market for Singapore while Cochin-China accounted for 19 per cent.

The million Spanish dollars' worth of European cotton goods that Singapore exported to Siam in 1866 made up the bulk of that country's cloth imports, with the remainder sourced from India and Penang.[21] Before 1855, this trade was virtually monopolised by Chinese merchants in Bangkok who either owned or hired square-rigged vessels belonging to the Siam royal family to transport the cotton goods, which displaced the traditional

[19] Wong, *The Trade of Singapore*, Appendix B, Table III, p. 262.

[20] Ibid., p. 127.

[21] A. Reid, "Southeast Asian Consumption", p. 50.

Siamese junks.[22] In return, Singapore imported large quantities of sugar from Siam, although a noticeable decline took place after 1857, resulting in bilateral trade deficits for Siam. Similarly, Cochin-China was a major market for Singapore even after 1859 when the French intervened in the south of the country and despite their efforts to garner the commercial opportunities for themselves by establishing a direct trade route to Europe. The resultant trade loss to Singapore was more than offset by the opening of the port of Saigon in 1860 by the French colonists, wherein only a tonnage duty and import duty on opium was imposed. In 1866, Singapore shipped European cotton goods to the value of SPD858,628, which constituted 61 per cent of total imports into the country.[23] Again this was handled by Chinese merchants who traded on the credit obtained from European merchants. The key commodity imported from Saigon was rice, intended for domestic consumption as well as re-export to adjacent countries.

With the conclusion of the Bowring Treaty, the European firms in Singapore tried to compete with the Chinese merchants in the lucrative Siam and Cochin-China trades, albeit unsuccessfully. The latter's dominance was based on the Chinese "trade diaspora" made up of business networks that had been established for decades or even centuries, linking Chinese communities all over Southeast Asia through kith, kin, clan and dialect ties.[24] The 1860s also saw intense competition amongst the agency houses.[25] In 1867, their number had increased to 60, of which seven were German firms, three French, two Dutch, one Swiss and the rest British.[26] Since the capital needed for trading was minimal, natural barriers to entry were low; after the first German firm, Behn Meyer, was established in 1840, the others followed.[27] The German houses offered the stiffest competition to the British by undercutting prices, over-extending credit and providing shipping services. In 1865, there was one German merchant vessel to every two British ships in the harbour whereas in 1857, the proportion had been one to eleven.[28]

Apart from a greater diversity of mercantile firms, the British agency houses faced new competition from the commercial banks. While the houses had performed a valuable financing function in the early decades, they found that this mainstay of their business and that of remittances were being taken away as one bank after another established branches in Singapore, beginning with the Union Bank of Calcutta in 1840, followed by the Oriental Bank in 1846, the Chartered Mercantile Bank of India, London and China in 1855 and the Chartered Bank of India, Australia and China in 1859.[29] In the 1860s, the Asiatic Banking Corporation and the Commercial Bank of India were also established.[30] These institutions made their presence felt by occupying imposing edifices at Raffles Place, where

[22] Wong, *The Trade of Singapore*, pp. 147–50.

[23] Ibid., Appendix B, Table IV, p. 263.

[24] Ibid., pp. 83, 167; P.D. Curtin, *Cross-Cultural Trade in World History* (Cambridge University Press, 1984).

[25] Buckley, *An Anecdotal History*, p. 711.

[26] Turnbull, *The Straits Settlements*, p. 187.

[27] Moore and Moore, *The First 150 Years*, p. 239.

[28] *The Singapore Free Press and Mercantile Advertiser*, 27 Apr. 1865.

[29] Liew and Wilson, *A History of Money*, pp. 50–2.

[30] Drake, *Merchants, Bankers, Governors*, p. 25.

the European merchant firms, their warehouses and shipping offices were also situated.[31] Amongst them, the British exchange banks, by drawing funds from head offices in London, were able to provide the agency houses with more competitive loans for financing the exports of Straits produce and imports of opium, cotton goods and other manufactured products, although they generally refrained from extending long-term credit.[32] In contrast, the Chinese merchants did not have direct access to the credit extended by these banks and continued to rely on barter trade.

In Singapore, the banks could accept deposits, make short-term loans and transact in currency and remittances.[33] They cashed bills of exchange and dealt in promissory notes, which functioned like paper money and saved bearers the trouble of holding specie. The banks also issued banknotes, thus alleviating the scarcity of currency; they were therefore a welcomed feature of the commercial structure of Singapore at mid-century.[34] All banks issuing notes were required to keep in reserve bullion or specie an amount equal to one-third of the value of the banknotes issued. Furthermore, the banks' links with the international remittance system enabled them to play a critical role in settling the balance of payments, thus taking over a function performed by the EIC. Gold was imported from China to pay for Singapore's trade surplus with it, which was then re-exported together with silver to India and Southeast Asia to finance the trade deficits with these regions. In the early 1860s, silver was also imported from Britain to arbitrage movements in gold and silver prices, resulting in another source of profits for the exchange banks.[35]

The agency houses did not have the comparable expertise and economies of scale of the banks and two of the earliest mercantile firms, Jose D'Almeida & Co. and John Purvis & Co., failed in 1864 during a trade recession amid bankruptcies of Chinese firms, linked as they were by the credit system. The crisis was said to be the worst in Singapore's history and the press put the blame squarely on excessive credit creation by both the agency houses and the banks, it being said that "a coolie has only to put on a *baju* (shirt) and go to European godowns, when he will obtain as much goods on credit as he wishes".[36] The banks were not insulated from the dire conditions either, with the Chartered Bank and the Mercantile Bank experiencing mild runs.[37] In those early days, public confidence in paper money was not wholly secure and panic spread quickly among the Chinese when the Chettiars refused to accept it for payments.[38] In 1866, the collapse of several banks in London and India wiped out three banks in Singapore established in the earlier part of the decade—the Asiatic Banking Corporation, the Commercial Bank of India and the Bank of Hindustan,

[31] Savage, *Lion City Narratives*, p. 198; *The Straits Times Weekly Issue*, 14 Feb. 1887.

[32] Lee, "The Colonial Legacy", p. 10.

[33] Liew and Wilson, *A History of Money*, pp. 51–2, 74–6; *The Singapore Free Press and Mercantile Advertiser*, 26 Nov. 1840, 24 Feb. 1859.

[34] Drake, *Merchants, Bankers, Governors*, pp. 27–8; *The Straits Times*, 11 Nov. 1851.

[35] A. Kobayashi, "International Bimetallism and Silver Absorption in Singapore, 1840–73", *The Economic History Review* 72, 2 (2019): 595–617.

[36] *The Singapore Free Press and Mercantile Advertiser*, 19 May 1864.

[37] Drake, *Merchants, Bankers, Governors*, pp. 27–9; Song, *One Hundred Years' History of the Chinese*, p. 184.

[38] *The Singapore Free Press and Mercantile Advertiser*, 9 June 1864.

China and Japan.[39] Before that in 1843, the Union Bank of Calcutta had also suspended operations after its headquarters ran into trouble. Nevertheless, the public's confidence in the banks grew over time and in 1880, they had in circulation a total of SPD2.5 million worth of notes, which effectively supplemented silver dollars as a form of money.

Trade Cycles

Although trade grew steadily in the first 50 years of Singapore's existence, this growth should not be mistaken to be uniform. Rather, commercial progress came in spurts and spells of varying duration and depth. This section explicates the factors that caused trade to fluctuate around its long-run growth trend discussed in the previous section. During the initial decades, a spurt of growth occurred in the late 1820s and another took place in the early 1840s; in between and just after these episodes, trade basically stagnated. Then followed a faster pace of expansion starting from 1850 and lasting till the end of the period covered in this chapter due to the developments mentioned earlier, as shown by the smooth trend curve (the lighter line in Figure 7).[40] But here again, trade cycles are still discernible, with a peak occurring in 1858 and a trough in 1861. Thereafter, trade activity picked up and was headed for another peak in the later part of the decade.

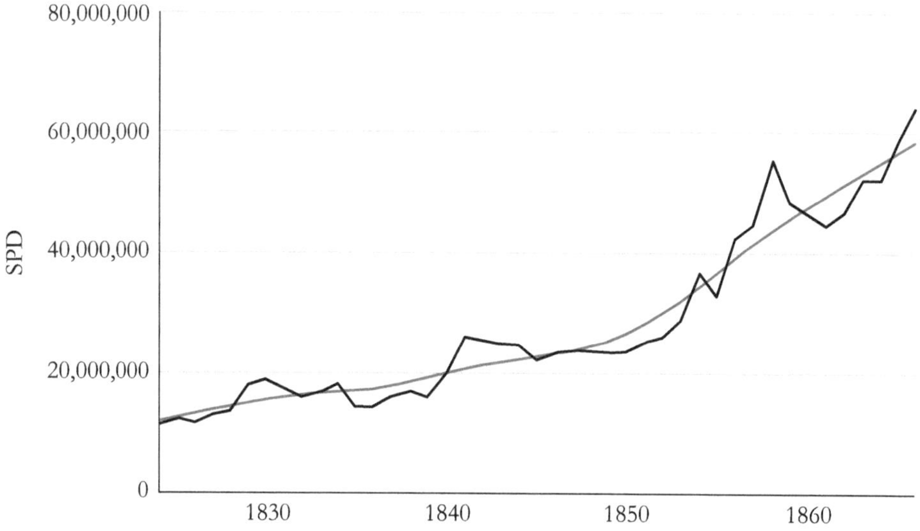

Figure 7. Trends and Cycles in Singapore's Trade, 1824–69
Source: Wong, *The Trade of Singapore*, Appendix A, Table XXVII and authors' calculations.

Given Singapore's heavy dependence on foreign trade and the absence of domestic economic events of great consequence, the cycles were invariably caused by external events outside its control. Moreover, its status as an outpost of the EIC did not offer much scope for policies to mitigate the negative impact on the domestic economy. The year-to-year fluctuations in the entrepôt commerce, including wild swings in opium and commodity

[39] Liew and Wilson, *A History of Money*, pp. 51, 76–7, 78–80.

[40] The trend in the series is estimated using the Hodrick-Prescott filter.

prices, were well noted by contemporaries who described the business of riding on them as "a long drudgery which men enter upon in their youth and leave in their old age".[41] During the early period, the trade upturn occurring in 1828 and subsequent downturn in the 1830s can be attributed to the speculative boom and bust in indigo by the agency houses in Calcutta, as alluded to before. The price of indigo had risen dramatically in 1824, encouraging production of the dye and high-risk lending by the houses. Once the inevitable collapse came, it bankrupted all the large agency houses with knock-on effects on the trade and economy of Singapore that persisted for almost a decade, aggravated by commercial downturns in both Britain and America during 1836–37.[42]

The next upswing in the early forties was precipitated by the first Opium War (1839–42) between Britain and China, in the wake of which commerce settled down again in the mid-1840s into "the quiet, monotonous prosperity of steady, moderate, or even low prices, with little of the excitement of speculation".[43] The dullness of trade seems to have reached a low point in late 1849, with the press laying the blame on the "stagnant and unhealthy state of European commerce", no doubt due to the revolutions in the previous year and the associated political upheavals.[44] At the beginning of the 1850s, economic conditions began to improve amidst a revival of confidence in the local mercantile community.[45] Trade conditions in 1853 were described thus: "Notwithstanding the existence of various circumstances which were calculated to exercise an unfavourable influence on the trade of Singapore during the year...our commercial prosperity continues unabated".[46] The trade cycle in the latter half of the 1850s is especially interesting on account of its sharp movement from peak to trough. After several boom years, confidence again evaporated following the Indian Mutiny of 1857 and the situation was aggravated by a general slump in European trade and the second Opium War in China.[47] However, the weakness in overall economic conditions was mitigated by vigorous construction activity in both the public and private sectors. The economic torpor persisted until the trade crisis of the mid-sixties, after which a recovery took hold.

Policy Conflicts with India: The Transfer

The year 1857 was a turning point in Singapore's political history, even though the momentous events associated with this date were primarily economic in origin. The mutiny of the sepoys in India against British rule in May that year, and which was finally put down in 1858, was instrumental in leading to the closure of the East India Company, almost 60 years after its Dutch counterpart was dissolved. The Indian Mutiny also effectively ended the regime that had ruled Singapore and its sister stations for close to four decades;

---

41 Quoted in Turnbull, *The Straits Settlements*, p. 58; Trocki, *Opium and Empire*, pp. 57–63.

42 *The Singapore Free Press and Mercantile Advertiser*, 31 Aug. 1837, 14 Sept. 1837.

43 Buckley, *An Anecdotal History*, p. 441.

44 *The Straits Times*, 18 Sept. 1849.

45 Turnbull, *The Straits Settlements*, pp. 186, 324.

46 Buckley, *An Anecdotal History*, p. 579.

47 *The Singapore Free Press and Mercantile Advertiser*, 6 Jan. 1859.

oversight of the Straits Settlements was given to the newly created India Office of the British government.

One would think that this hardly made a difference as the EIC, after losing all its trade concessions in 1833, was a governing and not a commercial entity anyway, merely administering India and its dependencies as an agent of the British government. But the Company's blighted economic administration of Singapore and the constant clash of interests that resulted were the reasons why, when the Calcutta merchants petitioned the British Parliament to transfer India from the EIC to the direct rule of the Crown in 1857, the European community in Singapore seized the opportunity to do the same, asking specifically not to be governed by a delegated authority in India.[48] The animosity towards the Bengal government had built up from the mid-fifties, notwithstanding the warmly received visit of the then Governor-General Lord Dalhousie in 1850, at which occasion it was commented that "His Lordship has gained some knowledge, from personal observation, of the circumstances of the Settlement...better aids to a mutual understanding than could be accomplished by petitions, memorials and dispatches".[49] The Straits Settlements were placed directly under the Supreme Government of India after the visit, though it did not lead to any material change and resulted only in disappointment.[50]

The grievances voiced by the transfer activists were plenty and wide-ranging, from aborted attempts at taxation and stifling land regulations to the forced adoption of the Indian rupee as the official currency.[51] Underlying the specific grouses was the singular sentiment that conditions in the Straits Settlements were vastly different from those in India, and measures tailored to the latter were usually ill-fitted to the Straits.[52] As another Governor-General of India, Lord Canning, had perceptively pointed out, the port was inhabited principally by Chinese, "imbued with a strong tendency to self-government, and [they] are, therefore, the very opposite of our Indian fellow subjects".[53] Furthermore, Singapore's trade with China exceeded that with India and its economic well-being was increasingly more dependent on events in the Far East than in India and the West.[54] While it is true that the higher authorities in London—the Company's Court of Directors and the British government's Board of Control—tended to be more sympathetic to Straits concerns, especially when supported by the lobbying of home manufacturers and shippers, they did not always side with the local merchants and colonial officials in the Straits in

---

[48] *The Singapore Free Press and Mercantile Advertiser*, 15 Oct. 1857.

[49] *The Singapore Free Press and Mercantile Advertiser*, 5 Mar. 1850.

[50] Turnbull, *The Straits Settlements*, pp. 324–5. Lord Dalhousie's fruitless visit is commemorated by the Obelisk next to the Victoria Memorial Hall.

[51] An alternative view is presented in A. Abraham, "The Transfer of the Straits Settlements: A Revisionist Approach to the Study of Colonial Law and Administration", *Journal of the Hong Kong Branch of the Royal Asiatic Society* 42 (2002): 1–33. The article argues that many of these issues were more or less resolved and questions whether the transfer to the Colonial Office represented the public will. Indeed, opinion on the move was not unanimous. B. Nunn, "Some Account of Our Governors", p. 92.

[52] This position was eloquently expressed by John Crawfurd, who represented the interests of the Straits mercantile community on his return to England. Buckley, *An Anecdotal History*, pp. 472–4.

[53] Quoted in Buckley, *An Anecdotal History*, p. 765.

[54] Ibid., p. 761.

making policy decisions.[55] Besides, the time and distance taken for letters and dispatches to get to or from London, made worse by the dilatoriness of the Indian government, resulted in a policy lag that was highly detrimental to the Straits Settlements.

The different circumstances of the Settlements were the primary reason why the fiscal policy of the EIC as applied to them was misplaced: where public investments in physical and human capital were needed for a thriving and growing port like Singapore, they were not forthcoming due to the refusal of the Indian government to provide the necessary funds. The narrow tax base and the resistance of the local merchants to property taxes also rendered it impossible to raise the money domestically. The need for institutional development in the areas of administration, the judicial system and policing had increased as Singapore grew more prosperous but this was also neglected by the Company.[56] As for monetary policy, the Indian authorities attempted to enforce uniformity within two highly disparate regions and currency zones through its repeated attempts to enforce the use of the rupee as the sole legal tender in India's dependencies, when no historical or economic basis existed for any form of monetary union whatsoever.

On the threat posed by the Bengal government to Singapore's free trade status, the press had acidly observed in 1837 after the outcry over the customs duties for fighting piracy that the government had legislated for the Straits Settlements "either in ignorance of their real wants or in a spirit of the most profound indifference as to their welfare".[57] In 1851, at a time when trade was turning around, Calcutta decided to impose a stamp duty in the Straits, ostensibly to replace the revenue foregone from the proposed abolishment of the *sirih* tax farm.[58] The Governor opposed the measure, arguing that the duty was unnecessary because the Straits Settlements paid their own expenses, exclusive of the cost of troops and convicts which should rightly be defrayed by India.[59] The farm was abolished in 1852 and the stamp duty was also aborted when the Singapore and Penang merchants petitioned the Governor-General of India and the Court of Directors, claiming that it would be a hindrance to trade, since purchases and sales in the Straits were largely made on credit. Nevertheless, the incident left them with the uneasy feeling that this would not be the last time that the Indian government interfered in Straits affairs. True enough, another futile attempt, this time with support from the Governor, was made in 1857 to raise revenue by levying port dues.[60] Taking the concept of free trade to its extreme by refraining even from port clearance or anchorage fees, Raffles' and Crawfurd's worthy successors in merchant circles objected successfully that the measure would be highly injurious to trade.

---

55 *The Singapore Free Press and Mercantile Advertiser*, 2 Feb. 1837.

56 *The Straits Times*, 15 Feb. 1853.

57 *The Singapore Free Press and Mercantile Advertiser*, 30 Nov. 1837.

58 *The Straits Times*, 23 Sept. 1851. Sirih is the betel leaf used as a wrapper for chewing areca nuts and was farmed from 1830.

59 *Straits Settlements Records*, R.15, 8 July 1850; *The Straits Times*, 23 Sept. 1851.

60 Buckley, *An Anecdotal History*, pp. 699–700; *The Singapore Free Press and Mercantile Advertiser*, 7 Jan. 1858.

As pointed out previously, Singapore had persisted in using the Spanish dollar in international trade despite being a Residency under Bengal. Following Penang's unsuccessful bid at enforcing the use of the Sicca rupee in 1827, the next aborted attempt to impose the Indian currency on the Straits Settlements was in 1837.[61] A decade later when the widespread circulation of debased and counterfeit Dutch copper doits threatened to destabilise trade, the merchant community revived John Crawfurd's proposal of 1823 for a copper coinage for the Straits Settlements to be issued in fractions of a dollar (one cent, half cent and quarter cent).[62] The EIC finally gave in to the request and decided to outlaw the doits but demand for the new money exceeded supply and complaints were often voiced about a scarcity of the new coinage. The third episode of interference, that took place in 1854, issued from a law passed in the Indian Legislative Council mandating that a new copper currency, to be minted in fractions of a rupee such that it was interchangeable with fractions of a dollar, be used in all receipts and disbursements by the local Treasury.[63] To the people of the Straits, this renewed attempt to introduce the "barbarous monetary system of India" was yet another insidious move to drive out other currencies, including the Spanish dollar.[64] Since Singapore's founding, the Sicca rupee was never used except as a unit of account; the dollar and the Dutch doit by the law of custom were legal coins, and used.[65] However, the local merchants this time failed to stop the currency bill from being passed into law, although it was repealed three years later and the supremacy of the Spanish dollar was restored.[66] Proving their point, however, was the fact that less than 2,500 rupees were issued to the public out of the 50,000 rupees received from India in 1855.[67]

Despite this concession, the damage was done and the press warned that the incident would lead to agitation to split off the Straits Settlements from British India.[68] This prognostication was rather prescient, for things came to a head in 1857. The year began inauspiciously with the native population expressing their unhappiness at the Conservancy and Police Act enacted by the Legislative Council of India in the previous year.[69] Also referred to as the Municipal Ordinance, this legislation, consisting of related acts, provided for the formal establishment of a Municipal Council in Singapore with the authority to collect rent on town properties and transport taxes, which had hitherto accrued to the colonial government.[70] One of the acts also provided for the election of three of the

[61] Liew and Wilson, *A History of Money*, pp. 52–3, 56–8.

[62] *The Straits Times*, 25 Nov. 1846.

[63] Drake, *Merchants, Bankers, Governors*, pp. 26–7; *The Singapore Free Press and Mercantile Advertiser*, 19 Oct. 1837; *The Straits Times*, 10 Oct. 1854.

[64] *The Singapore Free Press and Mercantile Advertiser*, 8 Oct. 1935.

[65] Buckley, *An Anecdotal History*, p. 596; *The Straits Times*, 21 Dec. 1852.

[66] *Straits Settlements Records*, Z.33, 24 Apr. 1857.

[67] *Straits Settlements Annual Report*, vol. 1, p. 18.

[68] *The Singapore Free Press and Mercantile Advertiser*, 16 Aug. 1855.

[69] Song, *One Hundred Years' History of the Chinese*, pp. 152–4; *The Singapore Free Press and Mercantile Advertiser*, 8 Jan. 1857.

[70] Turnbull, *The Straits Settlements*, p. 87. Before the act came into being, the conservancy of the town was in the charge of the Municipal Committee composed of two government officers and three residents. *Report on the Administration of the Straits Settlements During the Year 1855–56*, pp. 18–19.

five Municipal Commissioners by ratepayers, the other two being nominated by the government.[71] Why the natives resented a law that put public services in the town on a firm basis is unclear although apparently, it was due to misconceptions of its purview. In what might be the first general strike in Singapore, the Chinese and Indians closed their shops for a day while the Kling boatmen and syces refused to work.[72] The strike was followed by a minor disturbance involving the Tamil Muslims in Singapore and violent rebellions by the Chinese in Sarawak and Penang, all of which arose from perceived oppression by the British and their government.[73] But it was the Bengal government's decision to transport Indian mutineers and hardened convicts to the Settlements that was the proverbial straw which broke the camel's back.[74] The Europeans had complained that Singapore was used as a dumping ground for the "scum and refuse" of the British Empire, and fear mounted over their personal safety.[75] In August, that year overlapping with the Muslim month of Muharram, the alarm worsened to the extent that several European families took refuge on board ships.[76]

Following the petition for transfer of the Straits Settlements to the Colonial Office, the idea was quickly picked up by the press in Singapore and Penang. The political agitation for Crown Colony status, it is worth noting, was led by the European merchants in Singapore and supported by the Governor of the Straits Settlements, with their native counterparts scarcely playing any role, as evidenced by the fact that there was only one Chinese signatory to the petition.[77] The apathy reflected the sentiment that the native populations were indifferent as to who their rulers were, as long as they enjoyed the protection of the British. Moreover, the mercantile community in Penang decided not to be party to the move.[78] This abstinence appeared to be rather odd, considering that businessmen in both settlements had usually joined forces to remonstrate against official decisions affecting their livelihood.

However, it was only after a decade of persistent lobbying by the Singapore activists and protracted wrangling between British officials—at the India Office, the Colonial Office, the Treasury and the War Office—over the financial terms of divorce from India that the Straits Settlements were reconstituted as a Crown Colony on 1 April 1867. The most vexatious issue that held back the transfer was that of external defence: who was to pay for the military fortifications being constructed in Singapore at the time and the cost of new barracks at Tanglin to accommodate Indian infantrymen and a regiment of

---

71 *The Singapore Free Press and Mercantile Advertiser*, 10 July 1856.

72 *Report on the Administration of the Straits Settlements During the Year 1856–57*, Appendix No. 2, p. iv.

73 *Straits Settlements Records*, U.32, 20 Feb. 1857; *The Singapore Free Press and Mercantile Advertiser*, 12 Feb. 1857, 26 Mar. 1857.

74 *The Singapore Free Press and Mercantile Advertiser*, 19 Nov. 1857, 10 Dec. 1857, 27 May 1858.

75 Turnbull, *The Straits Settlements*, pp. 347, 351; *The Singapore Free Press and Mercantile Advertiser*, 25 July 1851.

76 Turnbull, *History of Modern Singapore*, p. 86; *Report on the Administration of the Straits Settlements During the Year 1857–58*, p. 5.

77 Song, *One Hundred Years' History of the Chinese*, pp. 202–3; Turnbull, *The Straits Settlements*, pp. 351, 379.

78 *The Singapore Free Press and Mercantile Advertiser*, 22 Oct. 1857.

British artillery.[79] The advocates of transfer argued that the extensive fortifications would be ineffective against a sea-based attack and the port could realistically be defended only by a naval force. Moreover, the revenue was sufficient for the maintenance of a garrison of reasonable size that would meet the needs of the settlement.[80]

Nevertheless, the British Treasury was not convinced of the Straits Settlements' ability to pay for both its civil and military expenses and was unwilling to take on a new colony unless it was financially solvent.[81] The Singapore merchants and their friends in England presented a wealth of statistics to show that the revenue exceeded civil expenditure and was "elastic", by which they meant that it was expected to increase further with trade, and that savings could be made that would contribute to defraying military charges.[82] To ascertain the veracity of these arguments, the Colonial Office despatched Sir Hercules Robinson, the Governor of Hong Kong, to Singapore in late 1863 to report on the financial position of the Straits Settlements. After the visit, he conveyed to London his finding that the local revenues were indeed sufficient to cover the military expenses and expressed support for the transfer.[83] However, he discovered a skeleton in the cupboard: the outstanding public debt consisting of loans made by the Indian government to the Straits government in the form of bonds bearing interest at 4 per cent.[84] Although the India Office was not opposed to divesting the Straits Settlements, disagreement over this issue was to further delay the transfer.

The British government's stance on defence expenditure seemed facile, since the Straits Settlements as a whole had been self-financing and India footed only the military and convict charges, which typically amounted to about half of the revenue. The problem was the refusal of the British authorities to recognise Singapore as a military base, in spite of the port's pivotal location, resulting in the neglect of its defence.[85] The inadequacy of Singapore's military capabilities was realised, not least by the mercantile community, but it was felt that an external attack on the town was only a remote possibility.[86] When Raffles had first established the outpost, the EIC had hesitated to condone his action, even though British policy in the Malay Peninsula and the Eastern Archipelago had always been to protect, on the one hand, its empire in India against French incursions and on the other, until 1833, the exclusive China trade.[87] After Singapore flourished as a commercial emporium, its potential role as a naval station was still not acknowledged even though it was used as a *point d'appui* for the China expedition during the first Opium War. This long-

[79] Mills, Turnbull and Bassett, "British Malaya", pp. 324–5; Moore and Moore, *The First 150 Years*, pp. 318–9.

[80] Buckley, *An Anecdotal History*, pp. 770, 775–8.

[81] Frost and Balasingamchow, *Singapore*, pp. 128–9; Turnbull, *History of Modern Singapore*, p. 87.

[82] Buckley, *An Anecdotal History*, pp. 768–70, 772. It is interesting to note that Lord Canning expressed a similar view. Swettenham, "British Malaya", pp. 105, 107.

[83] Mills, Turnbull and Bassett, "British Malaya", pp. 322–4.

[84] Turnbull, *The Straits Settlements*, p. 372.

[85] *The Singapore Free Press and Mercantile Advertiser*, 5 May 1859.

[86] Turnbull, *The Straits Settlements*, pp. 234, 236; *The Singapore Free Press and Mercantile Advertiser*, 8 Oct. 1835.

[87] Tarling, "British Policy", p. 9.

standing attitude explains why all substantive attempts to protect the settlement never got past the proposal stage and why the British government was reluctant to pay for the Straits Settlements' defence—both the sunk costs of the fortifications and barracks as well as the maintenance costs.[88]

Following the outbreak of the Indian Mutiny, however, detailed plans were drawn up to construct defensive fortifications on Pearl's Hill and Fort Canning Hill, the latter site complete with arsenal, powder house and barracks, at a cost of SPD176,996.[89] Sea coast defences and a line of batteries and forts on the islands facing the southern coast of Singapore (including Fort Siloso at Sentosa) were also proposed.[90] Once again, these works were to be executed by convicts, the whole body of which was mobilised for this purpose.[91] The fortress on Government Hill was completed in early 1861 and named Fort Canning while Fort Fullerton, built in 1830 at the mouth of the Singapore River, was enlarged and armed with pounder guns and mortars.[92] Similar armaments had been installed at Mount Palmer and Mount Faber in 1855 to protect Keppel Harbour.[93] The Indian government's motives for undertaking these projects were ambiguous, though it was likely that the fortifications at Pearl's Hill directly overlooking the Chinese town, and at Fort Canning with guns pointed inland, were intended to be a refuge for the European population in the event of an internal uprising.[94] In mid-1861, the government abruptly ordered a stop to all military construction work, leaving some of the fortifications unfinished. In 1864, the British government ignored a suggestion by the Governor-General of India that Singapore, instead of Hong Kong, be made the strategic centre for the British Empire in the Far East, as a counterweight to French expansion.[95] However, it performed a *volte face* two years later with the decision to transfer some European troops from Hong Kong to Singapore on account of the latter's healthier climate.

The way was therefore cleared for the transfer, since the India Office had earlier agreed to bear the expenses of constructing the military works and to assume the debt incurred by the EIC administration.[96] The Indian government would also recompense the convict expenditure from the date of transfer and the penal establishment in Singapore was to be removed no later than three years after the transfer.[97] But the Straits Settlements still ended up having to pay almost the full military cost, or £59,300 out of £66,000 per year, mainly to maintain a garrison of 1,024 men.[98] Had they foreseen this, the residents might not

[88] Murfett, Miksic, Farrell and Chiang, *Between Two Oceans*, pp. 44–5.

[89] Ibid., p. 72.

[90] Turnbull, *The Straits Settlements*, p. 237.

[91] *Annual Report on the Administration of the Straits Settlements During the Year 1858–59*, p. 55.

[92] Makepeace, "Singapore Defences", pp. 379–80; *The Singapore Free Press and Mercantile Advertiser*, 12 May 1859.

[93] Kwa, Heng and Tan, *Singapore: A 700-Year History*, pp. 142, 144–5.

[94] Cameron, *Our Tropical Possessions in Malayan India*, p. 242.

[95] Turnbull, *The Straits Settlements*, pp. 240–1.

[96] Ibid., pp. 374, 375; *The Singapore Free Press and Mercantile Advertiser*, 10 Apr. 1862.

[97] *The Singapore Free Press and Mercantile Advertiser*, 26 July 1866.

[98] Makepeace, "Singapore Defences", p. 381. The amount in local currency was equal to about SPD264,610.

have objected to the "arbitrary, impolitic, and inexpedient" income tax mooted in 1860, which would have balanced the local budget—including the military contribution—and facilitated an earlier transfer.[99] For better or worse, the Governor-General of India decided not to extend the new income tax act to the Straits and also shelved the introduction of a stamp duty on commercial transactions.[100] The stamp duty exemption turned out to be temporary and it was imposed in 1863 amid a chorus of protests even though the revenue raised helped to assure the British government of Singapore's financial viability.[101]

Public Works and Finance

By1850, Singapore's public infrastructure had become dilapidated again with the passage of time and the infusion of immigrants. The Bengal government initially refused to advance money for something as essential as a town drainage scheme, thus endangering the inhabitants' health with "pestilential odours".[102] It was left to the Municipal Committee in 1854 to hire an external consultant to drain a section of the town for the sum of SPD6,706; in the following year, the Indian government agreed to a loan for the purpose, to be charged at 4 per cent interest per annum and the drainage works commenced in March 1856.[103] The vexing problem of supplying adequate water to town residents, which had a long history beginning with Crawfurd's reservoir proposal in 1823 that was never carried out, was temporarily addressed by the construction of four additional wells funded by the wealthy Arab merchant Syed Ali Aljunied.[104] In 1861, the local government commenced work on an ambitious plan to introduce a supply of pure water into the town of Singapore, which however was subsequently plagued by a whole series of problems.

Although the government did its best to maintain the existing public utilities in good order, frequent complaints poured in about the state of the roads and bridges.[105] In 1843, it was recorded that a paltry SPD1,900 was spent on roads; a second bridge to relieve the congestion at the Presentment Bridge was constructed only in 1840 and named after George Coleman.[106] Furthermore, there was no fire brigade in the early years but only a single fire engine manned by the police, with the result that huge losses of property were incurred in periodic conflagrations.[107] These occurred in 1830 in Chinatown around

---

99 *The Singapore Free Press and Mercantile Advertiser*, 26 July 1860.

100 Turnbull, *History of Modern Singapore*, pp. 88–9; *The Singapore Free Press and Mercantile Advertiser*, 3 Jan. 1861.

101 *Straits Settlements Records*, U.44, 27 Aug. 1862; *The Singapore Free Press and Mercantile Advertiser*, 7 Aug. 1862, 11 Dec. 1862.

102 Turnbull, *The Straits Settlements*, p. 40; *The Straits Times*, 30 Apr. 1850; *The Singapore Free Press and Mercantile Advertiser*, 4 Oct. 1855.

103 *The Straits Times*, 18 July 1854; *The Singapore Free Press and Mercantile Advertiser*, 8 Mar. 1855, 12 Apr. 1855, 17 July 1856.

104 Buckley, *An Anecdotal History*, pp. 547–8.

105 Ibid., pp. 395, 464–5; *The Straits Times*, 1 Mar. 1853.

106 Hallifax, "Municipal Government", p. 323. Coleman Bridge was widened in 1845 to allow for the passage of carriages.

107 Ibid., pp. 336–7.

the vicinity of Phillip Street and Market Street, 1847 in Kampung Glam and 1852 in Kampung Java.[108] After one more fire engine was acquired by the Municipal Council in 1859 and following another fire in 1869, the Europeans formed a Volunteer Fire Brigade and in 1886, the wealthy Hokkien merchant Cheang Hong Lim created his own private brigade to protect his property.

The single notable achievement in public works during the first half of the 1850s was the completion of the Horsburgh Lighthouse in 1851, a project that had been first mooted 14 years prior.[109] This is a granite structure built by John Turnbull Thomson using hired Chinese labour on an outcrop of rocks called Pedra Branca located at the easternmost point of the entrance to the Singapore Straits.[110] Standing at nearly 97 feet above sea level and throwing a light beam up to 15 nautical miles, it was a veritable feat of engineering and was hailed by the local press as "the first Pharos of the Eastern seas".[111] A rudimentary cost-benefit calculation shows the immeasurable economic benefit of the lighthouse: while it cost SPD24,627 to construct, the loss of cargo and property from vessels sunk near that area from 1841 to 1851 amounted to SPD500,000 on average per annum.[112] Nor was the yearly recurrent cost of operating the lighthouse of SPD5,856 prohibitive by any means, and it was eventually decided to recover the expense (and the initial investment) from dues on ships leaving the Indian and Straits ports for China and vessels passing by the lighthouse, native boats excluded.[113] Revolving every night from sunset to sunrise, Horsburgh's light was a fitting beacon to free trade and the eminent hydrographer to whose memory it was dedicated. Another monument to free trade, perhaps more appropriately named, was the Raffles Lighthouse at Coney Island (Pulau Satumu) near the western entrance to the Straits which was lighted in November 1855 at a cost of SPD3,000.[114]

As trade improved over the decade, the Indian government became more sympathetic to requests to upgrade Singapore's physical infrastructure, although public works were temporarily halted after the mutiny in India.[115] It has already been mentioned that new General and Pauper hospitals were constructed in the later part of the 1850s. In 1854, the government decided to build a new Town Hall "commensurate with the commercial importance of Singapore" to replace the old Assembly Rooms located at the foot of Fort Canning Hill which had previously been used for public meetings and had fallen into

---

108 Song, *One Hundred Years' History of the Chinese*, pp. 38–9, 211–3, 307; Frost and Balasingamchow, *Singapore*, p. 102; *The Singapore Free Press and Merchandise Advertiser*, 18 Feb. 1847; *Straits Times Overland Journal*, 16 Mar. 1869; *The Straits Times*, 10 Apr. 1869.

109 *Singapore Chronicle and Commercial Register*, 14 Jan. 1837; *The Singapore Free Press and Mercantile Advertiser*, 9 Feb. 1837.

110 J.T. Thomson, "Account of the Horsburgh Light-house", *The Journal of the Indian Archipelago and Eastern Asia*, ed. J.R. Logan, 6 (1852): 385, 465.

111 *The Singapore Free Press and Mercantile Advertiser*, 3 Oct. 1851.

112 Buckley, *An Anecdotal History*, p. 519.

113 *The Straits Times*, 4 May 1852, 1 Feb. 1853, 6 June 1854.

114 *Straits Settlements Records*, Z.27, 7 July 1853; *The Singapore Free Press and Mercantile Advertiser*, 10 Jan. 1856. The latter report mentions that the lighthouse, "built on the Coney...will prove highly useful to vessels entering or leaving the harbour of Singapore in the night-time".

115 *The Singapore Free Press and Mercantile Advertiser*, 10 Sept. 1857.

disrepair.[116] It proposed to co-fund the estimated construction costs of SPD5,000–6,000 with the public; in November of that year, public subscriptions amounted to SPD5,089. By the time the foundation stone was laid in 1855, the Supreme Government in India had agreed to a contribution of SPD3,000 for its construction. In the same year, it sanctioned the building of the new church, now known as St. Andrew's Cathedral, by convict labour and using bricks and cement made at the government kilns at Serangoon Road by prisoners.[117] The Governor also approved a plan forwarded by private entrepreneurs in 1860 to reclaim land from the sea in front of Telok Ayer Street—the first proposed reclamation project in Singapore's history.[118] However, the undertaking became a reality only in the 1880s when the colonial government embarked on an ambitious plan to link Keppel Harbour to Boat Quay.[119]

By the time Singapore was declared a Crown Colony, the town's infrastructure had improved considerably. Apart from the Town Hall (now Victoria Theatre) which was completed in 1861 at a cost of SPD25,500, or four times the original estimate, new roads were constructed to connect existing ones and more police stations were established in various locations across the island, including along the Singapore Straits to prevent piracy.[120] After court trials had been moved in 1839 from the first Courthouse to a temporary shed next to a shipyard, the noise from which often drowned out the proceedings, the newly established Supreme Court of Judicature found a home in the refurbished public offices at Empress Place in 1867.[121] A seawall fronting the roadsteads at the estuary of the Singapore River was built in 1864 and named Collyer Quay after the engineer who planned the defence fortifications in 1858. In 1867, an important step was taken towards solving the problem of a stable water supply to the town with the completion of MacRitchie Reservoir and the laying of water pipes in the town.[122]

Following the enactment of the Municipal Ordinance in 1856, the newly and partially elected Municipal Council executed its mandate zealously by initiating the construction of iron bridges over the Singapore and Kallang Rivers and making extensive improvements to the roads and drains.[123] The feeble oil lamps in the town were converted to gas lighting by the Singapore Gas Company in 1864 and by the late sixties, native shops and dwelling

---

[116] Buckley, *An Anecdotal History*, pp. 608, 613, 621; *The Straits Times*, 31 Oct. 1854.

[117] *The Singapore Free Press and Mercantile Advertiser*, 8 Oct. 1935.

[118] *Straits Settlements Records*, V.29, 5 Jan. 1860, U.39, 11 Jan. 1860.

[119] *Straits Settlements Annual Report*, vol. 2, pp. 401, 406.

[120] Buckley, *An Anecdotal History*, p. 670; *Straits Settlements Records*, V.29, 5 Mar. 1860; *Straits Settlements Annual Report*, vol. 1, pp. 411, 586, 779–80.

[121] Turnbull, *History of Modern Singapore*, p. 88; *The Singapore Free Press and Mercantile Advertiser*, 21 Apr. 1859, 31 May 1866.

[122] *The Singapore Free Press and Mercantile Advertiser*, 21 Sept. 1865.

[123] *Report on the Administration of the Straits Settlements During the Year 1856–57*, p. 20; *Straits Settlements Annual Report*, vol. 1, p. 426; *The Singapore Free Press and Mercantile Advertiser*, 15 Apr. 1858, 15 July 1858, 2 Sept. 1858,14 Oct. 1858.

houses in the town which could afford to pay had also switched to gas.[124] The Municipal Council further took on the role of public regulator, in accordance with the wide-ranging authority granted to it by the Conservancy Act of 1856. Its first action was to take the sago producers to task for dumping sago waste product haphazardly around their premises, stipulating that such refuse must be drained away into the river or disposed outside of the town.[125] The Council also issued licences to candle makers, to be revoked if their business created a fire hazard.[126]

Reflecting the heavy charges for new public works, the Municipal Council operated on a budget of SPD137,818 in 1859, while the colonial government's amounted to SPD284,300.[127] The bulk of the revenue needed to pay for the upgrading of public facilities came from a 10 per cent assessment on the annual values of all houses and buildings (SPD50,731 collected from about 7,016 houses), a 5 per cent property tax on land owned (SPD5,045) and multi-tiered taxes on hackney carriages, bullock carts and horses (SPD16,058 from, *inter alia*, 589 carriages and 600 carts).[128] Fees and fines levied at the Magistrate's Courts, which were not insubstantial, also accrued to the Municipal coffers. Still, the activism of the newly elected Council resulted in rare deficits in both 1858 and 1859, bringing it to the verge of bankruptcy and forcing it to borrow from not only the public but also the colonial government.[129] However, the municipality's accounts were in the black again by 1860, showing a surplus of SPD12,000.[130] Uses of the funds in 1859 were highly varied and went beyond the normal purview of municipal responsibilities. On top of road maintenance and town cleaning (SPD30,660), the Municipal Council undertook public works (SPD42,124), acquired a fire engine (SPD674) and paid the salaries of the police force (SPD41,190), which had grown in line with the population and improved in efficiency.[131] This last outlay had long been an anomaly and a bugbear with the city's residents, who argued that the maintenance of law and order was a colonial responsibility.[132]

---

124 Buckley, *An Anecdotal History*, pp. 42, 710; O. Cavenagh, *Reminiscences of an Indian Official* (London: W.H. Allen, 1884), pp. 353–4; *Straits Settlements Records*, U.39, 11 Jan. 1860; *The Singapore Free Press and Mercantile Advertiser*, 21 June 1866. The gas company was bought over by the Municipality in 1900. Hallifax, "Municipal Government", pp. 330–1.

125 *The Singapore Free Press and Mercantile Advertiser*, 15 Apr. 1858.

126 *The Singapore Free Press and Mercantile Advertiser*, 20 May 1858.

127 T. Braddell, *Statistics of the British Possessions*, Table No. 14, Receipts for 1859–60 in £ Sterling, Table No. 20, Statement Shewing the Actual Receipts and Disbursements of the Municipal Funds, at Each Station in the Straits Settlements, for 1859.

128 Ibid., p. 42; *Straits Settlements Annual Report*, vol. 1, pp. 242–3, 300–1.

129 *Annual Report on the Administration of the Straits Settlements During the Year 1858–59*, pp. 72–3; *Straits Settlements Annual Report*, vol. 1, pp. 168–9, 225–6; *The Singapore Free Press and Mercantile Advertiser*, 16 June 1859, 26 Jan. 1860.

130 *Straits Settlements Annual Report*, vol. 1, pp. 272–3.

131 *Report on the Administration of the Straits Settlements During the Year 1855–56*, pp. 5–6; *The Singapore Free Press and Mercantile Advertiser*, 8 Oct. 1935.

132 *Report on the Administration of the Straits Settlements During the Year 1857–58*, p. 4; *The Singapore Free Press and Mercantile Advertiser*, 7 Aug. 1856. The Commissioner of Police and his deputy were remunerated by the colonial government. *Straits Settlements Records*, Z.33, 24 Apr. 1857.

The abovementioned improvements in public infrastructure would not have materialised without the use of convict workers. Indeed, as mentioned previously, many works of public utility would not have been executed had convict labour not been available.[133] Convicts did yeoman service in Singapore by providing the main source of manpower for these and other works and did so with a net social saving, so they must be considered to be beneficial from the economic point of view.[134] Many of them were artisans such as masons, blacksmiths and stonecutters, in addition to general labourers.[135] Putting aside conflicting claims about their productivity relative to free labour, as well as skill differences, a straightforward calculation will give a rough idea of the surplus value they created.[136] In 1858, the number of transported convicts from India in the Straits Settlements had increased to 4,172, of whom 2,199 were incarcerated in Singapore.[137] The going wage rate at the time was about SPD5 a month for an unskilled Indian labourer, so the imputed wages of the convict labourers would be SPD131,940 per annum.[138] Subtracting the expenditure for provisions, clothing and general maintenance of SPD56,669, the labour cost saving in that year alone would have amounted to SPD75,271.[139] If the manufacture of bricks, tiles and cement by the prisoners were accounted for, their net economic gain would be higher still.[140]

The use of convict labour helps to explain why the colonial government in Singapore was able to finance the large spate of military and public projects started in 1858. In that year, the fiscal accounts showed a huge jump in disbursements for public works to SPD9,546 from an average of SPD918 per annum in 1851–56 and they remained high in the subsequent years.[141] As the money for these projects came partly from the India Office, the British Treasury accused it of moral hazard in the run-up to the transfer of the Straits Settlements to the Colonial Office. The Treasury claimed that since the India officials knew that the move was probable, they went ahead to spend.[142] But this charge ignored the fact that the local government's revenue had increased with population growth: the number of residents on Singapore island roughly doubled between 1840 and 1860—with two-thirds of the rise coming from the Chinese population—and the farm tax revenue similarly

---

133 *Report on the Administration of the Straits Settlements During the Year 1855–56*, pp. 24–5.

134 Moore and Moore, *The First 150 Years*, pp. 298–9; *The Singapore Free Press and Mercantile Advertiser*, 16 Feb. 1860.

135 *Report on the Administration of the Straits Settlements During the Year 1856–57*, p. 8.

136 In the Governor's report for 1857–58, convict labour was valued at two-thirds that of free labour but the same report claimed that the quality of convict work was not inferior. *Straits Settlements Annual Report*, vol. 1, p. 122.

137 T. Braddell, *Statistics of the British Possessions*, Appendix No. 3, Convict Returns, taken from the *Administration Reports of the Local Government, Straits Settlements*.

138 Turnbull, *The Straits Settlements*, p. 47; Thomson, "Account of the Horsburgh Light-house", p. 433; *Straits Settlements Annual Report*, vol. 1, p. 151.

139 T. Braddell, *Statistics of the British Possessions*, Appendix No. 3, Convict Returns, taken from the *Administration Reports of the Local Government, Straits Settlements*.

140 *Straits Settlements Annual Report*, vol. 1, p. 156.

141 T. Braddell, *Statistics of the British Possessions*, Table No. 19, Disbursements in £ Sterling.

142 Mills, Turnbull and Bassett, "British Malaya", p. 322.

increased to SPD213,603.[143] Moreover, the revenue had been augmented greatly since 1857 because of two changes in farm administration. First, an agreement was concluded with the Temenggong to allow the farmers in Singapore to tender concurrently for the opium and arrack farms in Johor, whereby the farmers would receive 22.5 per cent of the proceeds.[144] Second, the farms were auctioned for a period of two years, renewable for a third year, instead of annually.[145] The census of 1860 stated that there were 144 opium shops, 87 spirit shops and 11 toddy outlets on the island.[146]

As it turned out, Singapore's public finances were in a healthy state on the eve of the transfer to direct colonial rule.[147] In 1866, total revenue amounted to SPD489,908, collected largely from the excise farms and the stamp duty imposed in 1863 which between them accounted for more than SPD380,000 (Table 7). Incidentally, the initial protest by the merchants against the duty died down quickly as they simply passed it on to their clients.[148] Land and forest revenue derived from quit and ground rents, transfer fees and the sale of agricultural land and permits to cut timber contributed SPD16,646. Law and justice, which covered fees paid to the Courts and the proceeds from the sale of articles made by local prisoners, added SPD20,903. Under marine, the chief item was lighthouse dues while the receipts for public works were bloated by part of the public benefactor Tan Kim Seng's contribution towards waterworks.[149] The miscellaneous revenue came mainly from pawnbroker licences.[150]

On the expenditure side of the financial ledger, the primary disbursements were for public works and the expenses of government departments. Legal and judicial services were also costly and exceeded the fees collected. The large marine charge reflected repairs to government vessels and the purchase of a boat. Allowances were paid mainly to the heirs of the Sultan of Johor, who remained as *pensionnaires* of the British government.[151] Thanks to the new stamp tax, Singapore could use the large operating surplus to nearly cover the military charge but not the convict expenses, although the charge swallowed up one-half of the revenue and was a source of dissatisfaction in the mercantile community.[152]

A comparison with the public finances four decades before, in 1827, shows how far Singapore had come. The total expenditure then was less than a third of what it was in 1866, with the principal spending being on establishments. Although the salaries of

---

[143] *Report on the Administration of the Straits Settlements During the Year 1857–58*, p. 2.

[144] *Straits Settlements Records*, U.32, 19 Dec. 1856; *Straits Settlements Annual Report*, vol. 1, pp. 115, 116.

[145] *Report on the Administration of the Straits Settlements During the Year 1857–58*, p. 2.

[146] *Straits Settlements Annual Report*, vol. 1, pp. 242–3.

[147] The financial data is from *Straits Settlements Annual Report*, vol. 1, pp. 680–5, 697–701. Some smaller items have been consolidated into the broad categories.

[148] Cameron, *Our Tropical Possessions in Malayan India*, p. 229.

[149] Tan Kim Seng first offered the donation of $13,000 in 1858 but the money was never used for its designated purpose and was instead expended on the memorial fountain that stands on Queen Elizabeth Walk. *Straits Settlements Records*, S.26, 9 Mar. 1858, V.29, 7 Dec. 1859; Song, *One Hundred Years' History of the Chinese*, pp. 71–2, 292.

[150] The pawnbroking business was liberalised in 1856, allowing anyone to open a shop without restrictions of any kind on the payment of a fee. *Straits Settlements Records*, U.32, 5 Dec. 1856.

[151] *Proceedings of the Legislative Council of the Straits Settlements*, 17 Sep. 1868.

[152] Makepeace, "Singapore Defences", p. 380.

civil servants continued to be substantial in 1866, public works featured prominently as an expenditure item; in 1827, there was hardly any expenditure on such works. Social spending on education and healthcare increased fivefold, though they still accounted for only 8 per cent of total expenditure (excluding military and convict charges). In 1866, the cost of providing legal services and dispensing justice had also ballooned.

Table 7. Singapore Public Finances, 1866

	SPD
Revenue	
Excise Farms	310,321
Land and Forests	16,646
Stamp Duty	69,727
Law and Justice	20,903
Public Works	9,695
Marine	16,969
Miscellaneous	45,647
Total	*489,908*
Expenditure	
Collection of Revenue	9,514
Allowances under Treaties	4,545
Public Works	89,396
Salaries and Expenses of Departments	43,046
Law and Justice	51,659
Marine	44,595
Retiree Allowances and Grants in Charity	922
Education and Medical Services	21,434
Miscellaneous	2,708
Total	*267,819*
Military and Convict	
Military Charges	244,308
Convict Expenses	46,697
Overall Deficit	**68,916**

Source: *Straits Settlements Annual Report*, vol. 1, pp. 680–5, 697–701.

Performing a similar retrospective for government revenue shows that, during the entire early colonial period, it was dominated by rising collections from the excise taxes and predominantly, the opium farm (Figure 8).[153] This heavy dependence on opium as the

[153] The data on the excise revenue are from Cameron, *Our Tropical Possessions in Malayan India*, p. 225 for 1821–25; Newbold, *Political and Statistical Account*, p. 381 for 1826–37; T. Braddell, *Statistics of the British Possessions*, Table No. 13, Farm Revenue at the Three Stations in Sterling Pounds for 1838–60; and *The Singapore Free Press and Mercantile Advertiser* and *The Straits Times*, passim for 1861–66. The gaming and pork farm revenues are not shown as they existed only for short periods. Further, the sirih farm, which started in 1830, was abolished in 1852. The sharp decline in opium revenue that occurred in 1862 was caused by the termination of the practice of auctioning the Singapore farms conjointly with those in Johor.

source of a consumption tax paid almost exclusively by the Chinese community raises questions of equity with respect to the apportionment of the tax burden among the local populace. That this method of revenue collection was also regressive cannot be doubted, since opium was widely consumed by the poorest in society. If municipal taxation were also considered, the burden of government exactions shouldered by the Chinese was even higher, since a large majority of property ratepayers were the wealthier amongst them.[154] In all fairness, the Indian government had also obligingly borne the cost of defence even though it stood to gain nothing from it. This leaves us with the conclusion that the sole beneficiaries of the system were the Europeans, who already enjoyed a high living standard and yet evaded their share of the tax burden by repeatedly invoking the principle, or pretext depending on how one views the issue, of free trade. Without a tax base that expanded with economic activity, excepting the new stamp duty, the Chinese by default provided the fiscal foundation of the colonial state, a situation that was not remedied until the modern era.

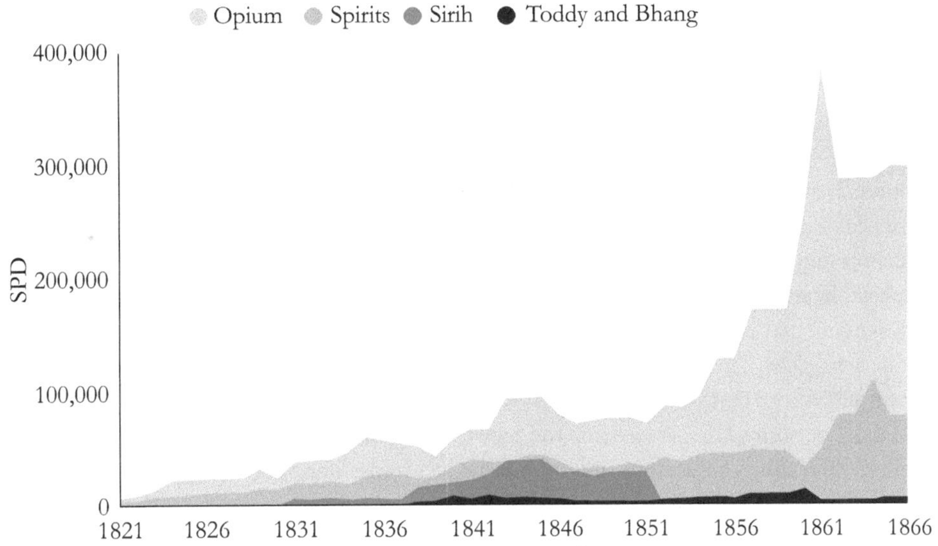

Figure 8. Revenue Farm Receipts in Singapore, 1821–66

Sources: Cameron, *Our Tropical Possessions in Malayan India*, p. 225; Newbold, *Political and Statistical Account*, p. 381; T. Braddell, *Statistics of the British Possessions*, Table No. 13, Farm Revenue at the Three Stations in Sterling Pounds; *The Singapore Free Press and Mercantile Advertiser*; *The Straits Times*.

Wages and the Standard of Living

Historical wage data have been called the "DNA of an economy".[155] In this section, such information is used to gauge the standard of living during the early colonial period. Notwithstanding its paucity in Singapore, we are able to find benchmark nominal wages at certain points in time beginning from the 1830s. As it is often the case that historical

[154] *The Singapore Free Press and Mercantile Advertiser*, 6 Nov. 1856.

[155] J.L. van Zanden, "The Skill Premium and the 'Great Divergence'", *European Review of Economic History* 13, 1 (2009): 221.

nominal wages tended to be unchanged for relatively long periods, the problem of missing data is alleviated. Furthermore, ethnic variation in the money wages paid to workers of different races has compelled us to use averages in the analysis. In particular, the dispersion in the wage distribution was most accentuated between Chinese and other native workers. For example, an unskilled Chinese worker reportedly earned SPD6 a month in 1834, while the Indian labourer received SPD4 and a Malay, SPD2.50.[156] The wage variation was greater for skilled workers such as carpenters. As far as we can tell, these differentials were due to perceived (or actual) differences in the (marginal) productivities of labourers and not to ethnic segmentation in the labour market.[157] Similarly, the persistence of occupations along dialect group lines discussed earlier should not be taken as a sign of labour market inefficiency, but rather as a sort of associative specialisation in the choice of jobs.

The nominal wage data that can be found were drawn from disparate sources and different professions, a procedure which, strictly speaking, renders intertemporal comparisons invalid. But the data are still worth studying for the hints they provide on the broad movements in nominal wages over time, thereby making possible an examination of changes in living standards. Moreover, a distinction is made between unskilled and skilled wages.[158] In the census of 1849, which returned a Singapore population of 59,043, the local government enumerated for the first time the occupations of all adult inhabitants of Singapore in a sixfold classification of merchants and clerks, mechanics, agriculturists, labourers, servants and miscellaneous.[159] General labourers in the construction and service sectors constituted the largest class at 13,991 persons, followed by agriculturists at 10,088, which presumably counted gambier plantation owners and labourers as well as workers in vegetable and fruit farms.[160] By 1871 however, the share of the primary sector in total employment had declined to 8 per cent as the gambier and pepper industry went into decline while the share of the tertiary sector increased due to the growth of the entrepôt economy.[161] If the first two categories of workers in the census are taken as skilled and the rest unskilled, only 8.5 per cent of the labour force of 37,785 workers would be skilled labourers, but this is an underestimate since skilled tradesmen such as blacksmiths, masons and carpenters were classified as labourers.

---

156 *Singapore Chronicle and Commercial Register*, 8 May 1834.

157 The differences dated from the time of John Crawfurd, who attempted to quantify the efficiency of Chinese workers. According to him, the labour of the 8,595 Chinese labourers in 1830 was equivalent to the work of 37,000 ordinary men. Crawfurd, *Journal of an Embassy*, vol. 1, p. 30.

158 For the 1830s, the monthly wages of agricultural labourers are taken as a proxy for unskilled wages and that of workers in sago manufacturing as a proxy for skilled labour. The unskilled wages in the 1840s and 1850s pertained to general labourers. As for skilled labour, the monthly wages cited were based on artisans' earnings in the 1840s, and the average of masons' and stone cutters' wages in the 1850s. Nominal wage statistics in the 1860s were the daily wages of predial workers and construction artisans, representing unskilled and skilled labourers, respectively, multiplied by 25 days to obtain the monthly wages.

159 Marriott, "The Peoples of Singapore", p. 350; *The Straits Times*, 26 Feb. 1850.

160 The total number of agricultural workers of all races in the census is lower than the count for Chinese workers discussed in the last chapter because the occupational classifications are not comparable.

161 Leung Yuen Sang, "The Economic Life of the Chinese in Late Nineteenth-century Singapore", in *Early Chinese Immigrant Societies: Case Studies from North America and British Southeast Asia*, ed. Lee Lai To (Singapore: Heineman Asia, 1988), p. 140.

Patchy though the decennial wage data are (Table 8), they suggest a steady increase in the remuneration of labourers in Singapore over the three decades from the 1830s to the 1850s, accompanied by a sharp rise in the skill premium during the 1840s. In the 1860s, nominal wages declined somewhat due to the recession in the late fifties and early sixties. The reason for rising wages before that was likely to have been the persistent and generalised shortage of labour in the settlement. Despite immigrant arrivals from China numbering over 10,000 per annum in the mid-1850s, official documents show a constant reference to a lack of labour.[162] It is also almost certain that the shortage of workers was exacerbated by the undertaking of extensive construction works in the fifties.

Table 8. Skilled and Unskilled Monthly Wages in Singapore, 1830s–60s

	1830s	**1840s**	**1850s**	**1860s**
Unskilled	SPD3.00	SPD4.50	SPD5.85	SPD5.00
Skilled	SPD4.00	SPD11.50	SPD12.00	SPD10.00

Sources: Thomson, *General Report*, 1849, p. 747; *The Singapore Free Press and Mercantile Advertiser*, 29 Oct. 1835; Newbold, *Political and Statistical Account*, pp. 14, 15; Turnbull, *The Straits Settlements*, p. 47; Thomson, "Account of the Horsburgh Light-house", p. 433; *Straits Settlements Blue Book*, 1868, p. 463; Logan, "Sago", p. 306.

Living standards in the past are usually gauged by deflating nominal wages by the average level of consumer prices to obtain a measure of the real wage. However, this could not be done for early to mid-19th century Singapore due to a lack of detailed information on typical consumption baskets and retail prices. Yet we do know from anecdotal accounts that the basic items of consumption during that period were rice, clothing and housing—encompassing the Malthusian necessaries of life—as well as opium in the case of Chinese labourers. While the wealthier classes like the local-born Peranakans and Europeans could afford to eat pork or beef regularly, the working class, both Chinese and Malays, consumed meat only on festive days and at weddings.[163] For most labourers, rice with salted fish or vegetables was the staple meal and could be had for a few cents a day.[164] The attire of a coolie was simple and unadorned—short trousers, sandals and a baju. As for housing, the rents of shophouses in the town area ranged from SPD10–15 per month in the 1880s while the mansions and villas occupied by European expatriates cost about SPD60.[165] Most single Chinese workers shared rooms in the shophouses, thus lowering substantially the cost of housing. Overall, the average worker probably spent SPD2.50 to SPD4.50 on food, clothes and rent in a month, leaving him with a few dollars to spare.

---

[162] Cameron, *Our Tropical Possessions in Malayan India*, p. 149; Buckley, *An Anecdotal History*, pp. 426, 642.

[163] Selina Ching Chan, "Consuming Food: Structuring Social Life and Creating Social Relationships", in *Past Times*, ed. Chan and Tong, pp. 124–5. The consumption of the upper-class in Singapore was highly unrepresentative of commoners in Singapore. For example, in the 1860s, an established public servant was estimated to require a salary of SPD446 per month for the upkeep of his wife, children and servants, as well as to maintain his lavish lifestyle. *The Singapore Free Press and Mercantile Advertiser*, 9 Nov. 1865.

[164] Vaughan, *The Manners and Customs*, p. 9.

[165] Leung, "The Economic Life of the Chinese", pp. 132, 148.

As an alternative to the construction of real wages based on an average worker's consumption basket, we can evaluate the general standard of living in Singapore by calculating the so-called "rice wage" or the quantity of rice that could be bought with his money wage.[166] This is a crude, albeit relatively robust, methodology that has been used in the historical literature to measure the purchasing power of wages, since rice is the basic wage good and it accounted for the largest share of a labourer's expenditure.[167] The graph (Figure 9) shows that the rice wage increased significantly from the 1830s to the 1850s but decreased in the 1860s, mirroring the trend in nominal wages. The price of rice was benign during the first two decades and then rose in the fifties before stabilising in the first half of the sixties. As a consequence, the rice wage of unskilled labourers ended up where it began, though that of skilled workers was higher by the end of the period. In the 1860s, the former could hypothetically purchase only about three pikuls of rice using a month's wage whereas the latter could obtain double that.

Figure 9. Singapore Rice Wage, 1830s–60s

Source: Based on data supplied courtesy of Atsushi Kobayashi and authors' calculations.

Therefore, living standards in Singapore did not deteriorate during the early colonial period despite uncontrolled immigration—they improved in most years. Indeed, it was claimed that "The condition of the poor man in this colony is exceedingly happy despite the increasing economic polarisation between rich and poor—he requires little clothing and very little money to make him comfortable".[168] A pointed statement of living standards was also made by the local newspaper in 1834: "[The Chinese immigrant] finds immediate

---

[166] The rice price is extracted from the price currents published in the *Singapore Free Press and Commercial Advertiser* for the benchmark dates (courtesy of Atsushi Kobayashi).

[167] J. Bassino and Debin Ma, "Japanese Unskilled Wages in International Perspective, 1741–1913", *Research in Economic History* 23 (2005); P. Parthasarathi, "Rethinking Wages and Competitiveness in the Eighteenth Century: Britain and South India", *Past and Present* 158 (1998).

[168] Vaughan, *The Manners and Customs*, p. 11.

employment in a congenial climate, and in a country where the wages of labour is [*sic*] three times as high as in China, and the necessaries of life one half cheaper".[169] Although it is difficult to verify relative wage levels, the prices of rice and clothing were conceivably lower in Singapore than in China by virtue of the large trade in these commodities that passed through the port. With respect to India, it was asserted that both the cost of living and nominal wages were higher in Singapore.[170]

Another indication of a relatively high living standard in Singapore, compared to that in China, is found in the remittances made by Chinese immigrant workers. Most workers could save and repatriate part of their earnings to support family members back home. The remittances could be in the form of cash or goods, sent to China via the junks returning during the southwest monsoon season.[171] A class of men would perform this task for a commission, said to be 10 per cent, although sometimes fellow villagers were willing to do it for free.[172] Alternatively, they would use the money entrusted to them to speculate in the ship's return cargo and transmit the same amount to the intended recipients, regardless of profit or loss. Depending on general business conditions, the total amount repatriated each year varied from SPD30,000 to SPD70,000 in the late 1840s.[173] The higher figure was equivalent to the average amount of annual revenue the government collected from the opium farm during that period.

The sick and the unemployed aside, the indigent in Singapore were those who expended their wages on opium smoking, gambling or visits to brothels. Consumption of opium amongst the Chinese was widespread, though the British considered it to be merely a vice like drinking alcohol and hence felt no compulsion to ban it, especially considering its importance as the mainstay of government revenue. Governor Fullerton had opined in 1824 that "The vicious propensities of mankind are the fittest objects of taxation".[174] This assertion does not detract from the fact that its incidence fell almost completely on one ethnic group just as the tax on the pork farm did. A contemporary estimate of the number of opium smokers in 1848 was 15,000, which implied that over half of the Chinese population were addicted to the drug, after discounting a small number of Javanese and Bugis who also used it.[175] A survey of Chinese inmates at Tan Tock Seng Hospital in 1851 depicted a worse situation: three-quarters of them were addicts.[176]

---

169 *Singapore Chronicle and Commercial Register*, 8 May 1834.

170 Moore and Moore, *The First 150 Years*, p. 320.

171 Wong, *The Trade of Singapore*, p. 113.

172 "Annual Remittances by Chinese Immigrants in Singapore to Their Families in China", *The Journal of the Indian Archipelago and Eastern Asia*, ed. J.R. Logan, 1 (1847): 35; Song, *One Hundred Years' History of the Chinese*, p. 110.

173 Vaughan, *The Manners and Customs*, p. 36.

174 Quoted in Turnbull, *The Straits Settlements*, p. 198.

175 R. Little, "On the Habitual Use of Opium in Singapore", *The Journal of the Indian Archipelago and Eastern Asia*, ed. J.R. Logan, 2 (1848): 65–6.

176 Lee, "The Pauper Hospital, Part IV", p. 279.

The secondary defence of the authorities in legalising this "moral curse attended with great and deep physical evils" was the belief that even if the habit was ineradicable, strict regulation would discourage it.[177] The number of shops selling opium and their opening hours were controlled by the Governor of the Straits Settlements but these rules were mostly observed in the breach.[178] In 1848, the number of licensed shops, or *papan merah* (red board) as they were colloquially known in reference to their signboards, were restricted to 45, but there were unlicensed shops to be found wherever there was a congregation of Chinese.[179] Those most prone to opium smoking were engaged in strenuous physical work, such as coolies, boatmen, construction artisans and agricultural workers. Others such as tailors and shoemakers had a far lower proportion of users in their ranks. At the individual level, opium consumed most of the workman's wages. For example, in a house of correction with 44 Chinese, 35 were excessive opium smokers; 17 of them earned an average monthly wage of SPD4.50 but spent SPD5.90 on the drug—that was the reason they turned to petty crime.[180]

To conclude the discussion, it is necessary to point out that the improvement in living standards during the early colonial period was not confined to Singapore but diffused widely in the Eastern Archipelago: an account can be found of "how new boats were being constructed in almost every creek of eastern Borneo and western Celebes, how people were moving from the interior to the coasts to trade, and whereas ten years before only the Dyak chiefs could afford to wear sarongs, now they were worn by even the poorest along the coast of Borneo".[181] Elsewhere in the region, the people were also better off as a result of the extension of trade to practically every corner of maritime and mainland Southeast Asia within the reach of Singapore: "The Javanese and Siamese bring their rice, sugar and coffee...the various products [...] concentrate at Singapore for distribution over the whole of the habitable globe".[182] Burgeoning consumption demand in the interiors of the region stimulated trade and vice versa, in a mutually reinforcing virtuous circle. Hence, Stamford Raffles' dream of lifting the peoples of the Eastern Archipelago from backwardness was achieved through Singapore.

---

177 "Gambling and Opium Smoking in the Straits of Malacca", *The Journal of the Indian Archipelago and Eastern Asia*, ed. J.R. Logan, New Series 1 (1856): 81.

178 Turnbull, *The Straits Settlements*, p. 220.

179 Little, "On the Habitual Use of Opium", pp. 17, 20, 42.

180 Leung, "The Economic Life of the Chinese", p. 151.

181 Quoted by Turnbull, *The Straits Settlements*, p. 164.

182 Quoted by N. Tarling, *Singapore Chronicles: Colonial Singapore* (Singapore: Institute of Policy Studies and Straits Times Press, 2015), p. 21; Wong, *The Trade of Singapore*, p. 85.

Chapter 5 Acquiring an Economic Hinterland, 1867–74

As in the Temasek era, Singapore's economic progress during the early colonial period was grounded on Adam Smith's motive forces of growth: the expansion of markets and the specialisation of labour. By the middle of the 19th century however, the gains had more or less been exhausted and further economic expansion had to come from new technological breakthroughs. Fortunately for Singapore, the invention of the steamship and the electric telegraph overcame the barrier of distance, resulting in an unprecedented increase in productivity and globalisation.

This chapter supplies the bridge between Singapore's early economic history and its transition to a new epoch. We begin by documenting the profound impact of steamships and—of equally momentous significance—the opening of the Suez Canal, on Singapore's long-distance maritime trade. These developments reduced transportation costs and greatly aided the forward march of imperialism.[1] From 1867, as part of a new Crown Colony of the British Empire, Singapore instituted a host of governance and socio-economic changes which would influence the future for years to come. Contemporaneously, a series of events led to British political intervention in the Malay Peninsula, resulting in Singapore's acquisition of an economic hinterland.

The Steamship and the Suez Canal

The "age of steam", beginning from the mid-19th century, provided the *primum movens* for Singapore's next phase of economic development. Like the Internet today, steam power is a "general purpose technology" that can be harnessed to different uses. As applied to intercontinental transportation, the advent of the steamship gave a renewed impetus to the growth of international trade by reducing travelling time and lowering shipping costs. Furthermore, since steamships did not have to rely on wind power, the tides and the monsoons, they could make more than a single voyage in a year. Together with the opening of the Suez Canal in 1869 which reduced the distance between London and Singapore by more than 3,000 miles (nearly 30 per cent), a voyage from England that took four to five months in the days of sail—and mail transmission roughly twice that time—was shortened

[1] C. Knick Harley, "Ocean Freight Rates and Productivity, 1740–1913: The Primacy of Mechanical Invention Reaffirmed", *The Journal of Economic History* 48, 4 (1988): 853.

by more than half to about 45 days.[2] In effect, the changeover from sail via the Cape of Good Hope to steam through the Suez Canal doubled the profitability of Singapore's merchant enterprises.[3]

The first steamer to call at the port of Singapore was the S.S. *Van der Capellan*, a Dutch vessel, in April 1827. After its appearance, a scheme was mooted in 1838 for the establishment of a steamship service between Singapore, Batavia, Melaka, Penang and Calcutta, but it was an idea whose time had not come.[4] By the 1840s, however, steamships were arriving regularly at New Harbour on the southern perimeter of the island (renamed Keppel Harbour in 1900 after Sir Henry Keppel who purportedly first charted its waters).[5] As a harbinger of the new age, the three stations of the Straits Settlements were connected by a steamship service in 1843. Apart from delivering cargo and replenishing stores and provisions, the steamers used Singapore's deep harbour port as a coal fuelling and watering station. In 1845, after its regular steamer service was extended to Malaya, Singapore and China, the Peninsular and Oriental Steam Navigation Company (P&O) carried the first mail from London to Singapore in 41 days.[6]

As a result of these developments, the cost of shipping to Singapore declined in tandem with a worldwide fall in freight rates. However, the adoption of the steam engine in ocean shipping was only one of several innovations which reduced freight costs. The large number of sailing ships built before 1850 was another, and so were technical changes in ship construction after 1869. In fact, the shift from wooden sailing ships to metal steamships took place gradually and only following an extended period of competition between the two modes of transport.[7] The latter did not supplant the former immediately because the hold of steam vessels that had to be devoted to fuel, rather than cargo or passengers, increased in proportion to the length of a voyage. Against this, for a given weight, they could carry twice the load of sail ships.[8] The Suez Canal also provided an advantage to steamers, not so much because of the shorter distance to traverse but due to the fact that large sailing ships could not use it owing to the lack of wind and navigational hazards. But it was only with the coal-saving improvements made in steamship technology (the compound engine and the screw propeller in particular) in the late 19th century that steam ultimately triumphed over sail in the early 20th century, although the tea and opium clippers were already done away with by the 1870s.[9]

---

[2] Chiang Hai Ding, *A History of Straits Settlements Foreign Trade, 1870–1915* (Singapore: National Museum, 1978), pp. 70–1; *The Straits Times*, 5 Mar. 1870.

[3] G. Bogaars, "The Effect of the Opening of the Suez Canal on the Trade and Development of Singapore", *Journal of the Malaysian Branch of the Royal Asiatic Society* 42, 1 (1969): 106; *The Straits Times*, 1 May 1869.

[4] Wright and Cartwright, *Twentieth Century Impressions*, p. 42; Moore and Moore, *The First 150 Years*, pp. 186–7, 219–20.

[5] It has been contended that this harbour was discovered earlier by others. Savage, *Lion City Narratives*, p. 125.

[6] R. Waterson, "Gathering Speed: Transport and the Pace of Life", in *Past Times*, ed. Chan and Tong, p. 104.

[7] Harley, "Ocean Freight Rates and Productivity", pp. 861, 865.

[8] Moore and Moore, *The First 150 Years*, p. 253.

[9] R. St.J. Braddell, "The Good Old Days", pp. 516–7; Abshire, *History of Singapore*, p. 60.

Telegraphic communication commenced at about the same time. Beginning with the first undersea electric cable laid between Singapore and Batavia in November 1859, communication with the rest of the world followed: in 1870, a telegraphic link was established with India, and thereafter with Britain and Europe.[10] A year later, the link was extended via Java to Australia, and to Hong Kong and Saigon, paralleling a steam service between the same places, with Singapore serving as the junction between East and West.[11] The arrival of the telegraph drastically quickened the pace of information and news flow on prices and freight, thus allowing for a larger volume of transactions at lower risk. And by enabling almost instantaneous communication between the agency houses and merchants in Singapore and the heart of global commerce in London, new opportunities to make money through more efficient trades emerged.

Where port infrastructure is concerned, the P&O had constructed the first pier at New Harbour in 1852 and the Patent Slip and Dock Company built two graving docks there in 1859 and 1869.[12] A rival to this company, the Tanjong Pagar Dock Company, added a wharf in 1866 and constructed Singapore's first dry dock, the Victoria Dock, in 1868.[13] A decade later, it built the Albert Dock.[14] Both companies were formed with capital and entrepreneurship provided by the agency houses; apart from maintaining docking facilities, they engaged in ship repair. Smaller wharves were also built by private merchant firms on the southern coast and on Pulau Brani, where the Royal Navy had a coal depot. Ocean-going shipping rapidly migrated to New Harbour from the Singapore River which, however, remained as the preferred landing place for native boats and coastal steamers. At the risk of oversimplifying, it could be said that the centre of gravity of Singapore's trade and with it the long-distance commerce moved to New Harbour, while the river and Boat Quay catered to the intraregional exchange of Straits produce, rice and textiles conducted by the Chinese traders, all the way up to the modern period. With this change, shipwrights and ship chandlers, as well as shipyards, repaired to the vicinity of the island's southern shore from Boat Quay; in the 1860s, two robust steamships were built at the new port.[15] In contrast, the Singapore River was over-congested and had little room for expansion. Over the years, the huge increase in traffic and cargo had resulted in the constant silting up of the riverbed, a long-standing problem dating from the residency of John Crawfurd who, recognising the strategic importance of trade, proposed measures to address it.[16] Since

---

[10] Wright and Cartwright, *Twentieth Century Impressions*, p. 45; *Annual Report on the Administration of the Straits Settlements During the Year 1859–60*, p. 13. The line with Java broke down due to a technical fault and was reconnected only in 1870.

[11] W. Makepeace, "The Machinery of Commerce", in *One Hundred Years of Singapore*, vol. II, ed. Makepeace, Brooke and Braddell, pp. 167–8.

[12] Bogaars, "The Effect of the Opening of the Suez Canal", pp. 234–5; *Singapore Port History* (Maritime Museum, Port of Singapore Authority, 1982), p. 5; *The Singapore Free Press and Mercantile Advertiser*, 1 Mar. 1866.

[13] Drake, *Merchants, Bankers, Governors*, p. 49.

[14] *The Straits Times Weekly Issue*, 11 June 1884.

[15] *The Singapore Free Press and Mercantile Advertiser*, 12 Jan. 1865.

[16] Dobbs, *The Singapore River*, pp. 52–3, 54–6; Darbishire, "Commerce and Currency", p. 39.

then, dredging works had become the responsibility of the local government and were carried out on an *ad hoc* basis to keep the waterway open to vessels.[17]

As the Western merchants were long ensconced in Raffles Place, the adjunct to Boat Quay, the need for a one-and-a-half mile transport route to New Harbour led to competing plans to link them. A railway line was proposed by two rival private companies, the first associated with the Tanjong Pagar Dock Company and the second with the Patent Dock and Slip Company, both owners of wharves at New Harbour.[18] The government initially favoured the second company as it proposed a longer line.[19] After hearing extensive arguments and evidence from both sides, the Legislative Council decided first, that the line should be built by a private firm since its benefits accrued to the dock companies and second, that the promoters of the longer line be given the concession.[20] However, the decisions were overturned by the Secretary of State for the Colonies, who directed the railway line to be undertaken by the government. The companies saw this as interference with private enterprise and claimed that the government could not manage the railway efficiently. Other commentators counter-argued that since the line would facilitate the transport of mail and passengers, public ownership was justified. In the end, the authorities settled for the paving of two new roads—Robinson and Anson Roads—along which goods were transferred by bullock carts from the warehouses at the river to the harbour and vice versa, and subsequently also Keppel Road to connect Tanjong Pagar to Telok Blangah (a railway line and a tramway came much later).[21]

Singapore's economic fluorescence at the beginning of the 1870s is therefore explained by demand and supply factors coming together—the switch to steam vessels on the one hand and the provision of harbour and communications facilities on the other.[22] In addition, Singapore was fortunate in that its coloniser, through a stroke of geological luck, was favoured by the abundant coal supplies that were needed to power steam engines. From 62,835 tonnes in 1870, coal imports into Singapore increased to 251,720 tonnes in 1874, including good-quality coal mined in South Wales that generated more heat per tonne.[23] The port therefore became an agent of steam globalisation in East Asia. At the same time, technological breakthroughs and the cutting of the Suez Canal led to a profound transformation in the nature of Singapore's trade and its broader role in the

[17] *Straits Settlements Annual Report*, vol. 4, pp. 462–3; *The Straits Times Weekly Issue*, 16 Feb. 1884.

[18] *Proceedings of the Legislative Council of the Straits Settlements*, 12 June 1871.

[19] Moore and Moore, *The First 150 Years*, pp. 375–81; *Proceedings of the Legislative Council of the Straits Settlements*, 29 May 1871.

[20] *Proceedings of the Legislative Council of the Straits Settlements*, 19 June 1871, 18 Sept. 1871.

[21] Bogaars, "The Effect of the Opening of the Suez Canal", pp. 237–42; J.R. Nicholson, "The Tanjong Pagar Dock Company", in *One Hundred Years of Singapore*, vol. II, ed. Makepeace, Brooke and Braddell, p. 6; Drake, *Merchants, Bankers, Governors*, pp. 49–51; *The Straits Times*, 13 Mar. 1869; *Straits Times Overland Journal*, 15 Feb. 1871; *The Straits Times Weekly Issue*, 9 Jan. 1886.

[22] *Straits Times Overland Journal*, 4 Jan. 1870.

[23] Bogaars, "The Effect of the Opening of the Suez Canal", Appendix 6, p. 250; J. Darwin, *Unlocking the World: Port Cities and Globalization in the Age of Steam, 1830–1930* (Allen Lane, 2020), pp. 80–156.

regional and global economic order.[24] The canal had a salutary effect: since ships did not have to round the Cape of Good Hope, they now routinely used the Straits of Melaka as the main route to the Far East instead of the Sunda Straits, which meant stopping at Singapore.[25] The steamship revolution also made Singapore an essential node in the chain of British colonial ports and coaling stations which stretched from Gibraltar, through Malta, Suez, Aden, Trincomalee and on to Hong Kong.[26] This was a truly Euro-Asian economic network of networks, as a result of which Singapore became integrated into Britain's emerging maritime empire.

In performing this nodal function, Singapore acquired all the accoutrements of a port city, more so than in its previous phase of development: steamship companies and shipping agents, specialised import and export businesses, bankers and insurers, and coaling agencies, just to list a few. These earned it the sobriquet of the "Clapham Junction of the East", after the major railway station and transport hub in south London.[27] Less obvious, steamships brought a new breed of Westerners to Singapore—the colonial tourist, whose increasing numbers catalysed the construction of first-class hotels like the Hotel de l'Europe, the Adelphi Hotel and Raffles Hotel. The refuelling of steamers at New Harbour gave rise to a new class of workers that complemented the Kling boatmen, namely coal-heavers whose job was to load the bunkers of ships with coal by the basket. This physically demanding, filthy and unhealthy work was performed mainly by Chinese coolies. The other occupation that was created was lascar, a term of Indian origin denoting the native seamen who crewed steaming vessels east of Suez.

What then was the impact of the foregoing developments on Singapore's trade? Conventional economic historiography maintains that the period from 1870 to 1914 marked the birth of the first era of trade globalisation ushered in by steamships. Between these two years, the world experienced an unprecedented acceleration in the growth of international trade and financial flows that raised the trade-to-GDP ratio from about 10 per cent to over 20 per cent.[28] However, it is less recognised that this globalisation was uneven across regions, benefitting some more than others owing to the asymmetric time and cost savings that resulted from the adoption of steam, which were in turn determined by location and wind patterns.[29] In this respect, Singapore was a clear winner, as can be seen directly from the trade data. In 1867, its total commerce was valued at SPD66,884,630 and in 1874, this had risen to SPD88,395,868, representing an increase of one-third in a matter of seven years.[30] In 1870 alone, imports grew by more than SPD7 million and

---

[24] Joseph Conrad in *The End of the Tether* (1902) wrote: "[The Suez Canal] had let in upon the East a flood of new ships, new men, new methods of trade. It had changed the face of the Eastern seas". Quoted in M. Wise, *Travellers' Tales of Old Singapore* (Singapore: Marshall Cavendish Editions, 2018), p. 18.

[25] *The Straits Times*, 1 Jan. 1870.

[26] Turnbull, *History of Modern Singapore*, p. 100.

[27] Frost and Balasingamchow, *Singapore*, pp. 134–5, 140–1.

[28] A. Estevadeordal, B. Frantz and A. M. Taylor, "The Rise and Fall of World Trade, 1870–1939", *The Quarterly Journal of Economics* 118, 2 (2003): 360.

[29] L. Pascali, "The Wind of Change: Maritime Technology, Trade, and Economic Development", *The American Economic Review* 107, 9 (2017): 2821–54.

[30] Wong, *The Trade of Singapore*, Appendix A, Table XXVII, p. 254.

exports by nearly SPD5 million. The increase in shipping tonnage at the port of 43 per cent in the six years after the transfer to colonial rule, compared to the six years before, was equally impressive.[31] In fact, 1870 was an *annus mirabilis*, as the aggregate tonnage of steamers calling at the port exceeded that of sailing ships for the first time.[32] While these achievements are remarkable in themselves, it is only with hindsight that the jump in trade volume in the early seventies is identified as a structural break. The increased steamship traffic eliminated whatever excess capacity existed in wharf and docking facilities during the pre-Suez period.

Since the transition from sail to steam unfolded over a period of time, the long-distance trade did not overshadow the regional commerce immediately. By 1875, however, Britain's share of Singapore's trade had increased to 22 per cent from 18 per cent in 1866; in comparison, a medium-haul destination like India maintained its proportion of 18 per cent.[33] English cotton goods imports led the way, rising from a mere SPD8,528 in 1870 to SPD273,049 in 1875, while machinery imports also grew.[34] Apart from Britain, France and Germany contributed to the growth in Singapore's commerce.[35] German trade expanded with the increased presence of its agency houses: from the late 1860s to the early 1870s, over a dozen more set up in Singapore.[36] Quite apart from the introduction of steamships and the opening of the Suez Canal, Germany had emerged as an industrial power, eager to stake its claim to Asian commerce. After the Civil War ended, the United States also availed itself of the fall in international freight rates to increase its trade with the Far East, including the import of gambier and sago from Singapore.

The effects of the decline in shipping costs on Singapore's trade with China and Hong Kong are more ambiguous for three reasons. First, as alluded to in the previous chapter, commercial intercourse with China fell away somewhat after the second Opium War, as the Celestial Kingdom opened up further to the West. Second, Hong Kong had come to serve as the trade gateway to China. Third, steamships gave a further impetus to direct shipping from Europe to China, while affording no advantage to the sailing route between Singapore and China. In the late 1860s, steamers voyaging between Britain and China, even via the Cape of Good Hope, made the journey in just 65 days.[37] These were the ships of the P&O and the Ocean Steamship Company, which were the most economical carriers, while feeder vessels belonging to other companies cruised China's inland rivers and eastern coast.[38] The impact of these factors was to keep the level of Singapore's exports to China

---

[31] *Straits Settlements Annual Report*, vol. 2, p. 205.

[32] *Singapore Port History*, p. 7. Due to the lack of detailed shipping returns for 1870 and 1871, it could only be inferred that steamer tonnage overtook that of sailing ships sometime between 1869 and 1872. Bogaars, "The Effect of the Opening of the Suez Canal", p. 213.

[33] *Straits Settlements Annual Report*, vol. 2, pp. 177, 286.

[34] Bogaars, "The Effect of the Opening of the Suez Canal", Appendix 7, p. 251.

[35] *Straits Times Overland Journal*, 3 May 1873.

[36] Bogaars, "The Effect of the Opening of the Suez Canal", pp. 222–3; *The Straits Times Weekly Issue*, 24 Sept. 1890.

[37] Bogaars, "The Effect of the Opening of the Suez Canal", pp. 231–2.

[38] F.E. Hyde, "British Shipping Companies and East and South-East Asia, 1860–1939", in *The Economic Development of South-East Asia*, ed. C.D. Cowan (1964; Routledge, 2012), pp. 27–8, 30.

and Hong Kong broadly unchanged through the 1870s, which implied that their shares in total trade actually fell.

The entrepôt trade—the collection and circulation of commodities within the region—was not at first affected by the advent of steam navigation, being still carried out by coastal shipping. During the 1870s, the trade in Straits produce continued to make gains in both value and volume.[39] However, staple commodities began to make an initial appearance in 1872, when Singapore imported and re-exported SPD3,813,661 worth of tin and SPD1,413,478 worth of gutta percha, on top of opium to the value of SPD6,131,190.[40] The geography of the trade with the immediate region did not change much, save for one notable development. As the French imperialists tightened their hold on Cochin-China, including imposing an export duty on rice, the country's trade with Singapore contracted by 86 per cent in the seventies, unravelling the gains of the previous decade.[41] Notwithstanding this, Singapore managed to double its re-exports of rice to the Southeast Asian region by sourcing them from Siam instead. The redistribution of Western manufactures showed a further absolute, though not relative, increase in the 1870s, as evinced by the trade in cotton piece goods. In 1870, Singapore imported SPD5,492,704 worth of such goods and exported SPD3,821,580; in 1876, these quantities had increased to SPD5,726,038 and SPD4,578,806 respectively.[42] The cotton goods were redistributed to the region mainly by native sailing vessels, many of which were owned by the Chinese in Singapore and flew British colours. It was only in the 1880s that it was economically viable for steamships to run between Singapore, Bangkok and other regional ports.[43]

Governance and Socio-Economic Reforms

It will be recalled that the exigent reasons for transferring the Straits Settlements to the British Crown were to obtain a measure of self-governance and also to throw off the shackles of Indian rule. If this was the primary desideratum, the move must be judged a qualified success. The vociferous mercantile community in Singapore was given a semi-autonomous constitution after the changeover to colonial rule, but only a limited say in the politics of governance. Devolution of authority took the form of the creation of a Legislative Council staffed in the majority by senior government appointees, with the public represented by four "Unofficials" nominated by the Governor (later increased to six, including one Chinese merchant).[44] This certainly was not "the greatest political event which has occurred

[39] W.G. Huff, *The Economic Growth of Singapore: Trade and Development in the Twentieth Century* (Cambridge University Press, 1994), Appendix Table A.1, pp. 373, 378, 379.

[40] *Straits Settlements Annual Report*, vol. 2, p. 151.

[41] Bogaars, "The Effect of the Opening of the Suez Canal", p. 228; *The Straits Times*, 5 Oct. 1878.

[42] Bogaars, "The Effect of the Opening of the Suez Canal", p. 225.

[43] Hyde, "British Shipping Companies", pp. 30–1; Chiang, *History of Straits Settlements Foreign Trade*, p. 52.

[44] *Proceedings of the Legislative Council of the Straits Settlements*, 23 May 1870; *The Straits Times*, 1 Jan. 1870. The nominees were all associated with British and European business interests and the prominent Chinese merchant appointed was Whampoa. Song, *One Hundred Years' History of the Chinese*, pp. 218–9.

since the foundation of the settlement".[45] For one thing, the native population remained indifferent to the change of government, as they were to the transfer movement; only the European elite was excited by the prospect of representative government even though they were not given the franchise. For another, many of the outstanding grievances of the local merchants had already been redressed by the time of transfer.[46] Lastly, no real power was transferred from the home authorities to the local government, especially where it concerned the external relations of the Straits Settlements with the native Malay states.[47]

The Governor of the Straits Settlements reigned supreme with the help of the Executive Council—a sort of kitchen cabinet consisting of senior officials and the officer commanding the troops—subject only to overrule by the Secretary of State for the Colonies in London. He had the power to initiate legislation, veto bills and ignore decisions taken by the Legislative Council, although the members of the Council could freely debate and vote on issues, including public expenditure and finance. The first governor of the new Colony, Sir Harry Ord, tasked to introduce the colonial system into the Straits Settlements, set out at once to weed out the inefficiencies and deficiencies that had accumulated under Indian administration, including the emasculated establishment that resulted from the retrenchment of 1830.[48] The reform of the judicial system was the most contentious, as the Recorder, with the support of the Unofficials in the Legislative Council, insisted on the principle of independence of the courts.[49] In the event, a Supreme Court was established, the judiciary was brought into line and the new Chief Justice was made to answer to the Governor.[50] In 1873, one of the last vestiges of the early period, the Grand Jury, was abolished by Ord, which seemed an uncontroversial move given the formation of the Legislative Council, but the Unofficials promptly resigned in protest against the decision after unsuccessfully petitioning the Secretary of State for the Colonies.[51]

One of the first acts of the new Governor pertained to currency. On the day that Singapore, along with the other Straits Settlements, became a Crown Colony, the Mexican dollar, which had supplanted the Spanish dollar, and the Peruvian, Bolivian and Hong Kong silver dollars with their system of decimalised currency were declared to be legal tender.[52] Public accounts were to be kept in dollars and cents.[53] The legal tender status of the Indian rupee and other subsidiary coins was revoked in the same year. This was followed by the minting in Britain of a Straits Settlements subsidiary coinage in denominations of 5, 10 and 20 cents in 1871, a move initiated by the Legislative Council and regarded as one

---

45 *The Straits Times*, 21 Mar. 1867, quoted in Turnbull, *History of Modern Singapore*, p. 94.

46 Drake, *Merchants, Bankers, Governors*, pp. 35–6.

47 *The Straits Times*, 12 Feb. 1870.

48 Turnbull, *The Straits Settlements*, pp. 55–6, 75, 381.

49 *Proceedings of the Legislative Council of the Straits Settlements*, 8 June 1868.

50 Turnbull, *History of Modern Singapore*, pp. 95–6; Lee, "The Colonial Legacy", p. 6.

51 *Straits Times Overland Journal*, 4 Oct. 1873.

52 Liew and Wilson, *A History of Money*, pp. 71–4; Lee Sheng-Yi, *The Monetary and Banking Development of Singapore and Malaysia*, Third Edition (Singapore: Singapore University Press, 1990), p. 7; *Proceedings of the Legislative Council of the Straits Settlements*, 1 Apr. 1867.

53 W. Makepeace, "The Legislative Council", in *One Hundred Years of Singapore*, vol. I, ed. Makepeace, Brooke and Braddell, p. 150.

of its early tangible achievements in self-rule. As the most prolific lawmaker in Singapore's history, Ord further introduced a whole host of legislation and ordinances dealing with shipping, immigrants, bankruptcy, law and order, contagious diseases and public health and security.[54] Even inveterate Chinese gamblers were not left out with the passing of the strict Gaming Ordinance in 1870 to deal with unlawful gaming in all its forms, including illegal lotteries.[55] The Governor's achievements were all the more sterling considering the opposition of the Unofficials—the same Europeans who had agitated for transfer—to many of these laws on the basis that they interfered with free trade and unrestricted immigration.

Ord reorganised the machinery of government to cope with the demands from the rise in trade and "replace[d] a quaint and informal administration with an efficient and somewhat formal administration".[56] The system of recruiting personnel at all levels, described as "a collection of military officers and gentlemen sent haphazard from Bengal", was rescinded and a clearer division of duties between different government departments was instituted.[57] The key departments performing economic roles were the Treasury, which was responsible for the receipt and expenditure of public funds, the Land Revenue Department, the Registrar General's Department that collected all statistics on births, marriages, deaths and companies, and the Auditor General's Department.[58] In 1872, a new Department of Public Works was created with the Colonial Engineer as its head, whereas previously this duty had been performed by the Superintendent of Convicts.[59] After prolonged consultations with the Colonial Office and the Legislative Council, Ord came up with plans to professionalise the Straits civil service by raising pay, retiring old employees and recruiting promising young men in Britain to be trained for important government posts.[60] This last cadet scheme of recruitment entailed the study by successful candidates of the Malay language or Chinese dialects for a number of years. While taking time to bear fruit, the changes initiated by Ord provided the foundation for a modern bureaucratic state.

In 1872, five years after the agreement on cost-sharing of military expenses, the Imperial Government in Britain consented to pay about half of the garrison costs in Singapore while at the same time reducing the garrison's size slightly from 1,200 to 1,019 men.[61] The military expenditure was therefore brought down to £51,595 (SPD242,497) in 1872–73 from £59,300 (SPD278,710) and further to £50,845 (SPD238,972) from 1874 to 1889.[62] In any case, the revenue expanded greatly with increases in trade and population, especially

[54] *Straits Settlements Annual Report*, vol. 2, pp. 3–4, 27–9, 202; *Straits Times Overland Journal*, 4 Jan. 1871.

[55] R. St.J. Braddell, "Crime", p. 265; *Proceedings of the Legislative Council of the Straits Settlements*, 27 Oct. 1870; *Straits Times Overland Journal*, 20 Dec. 1870, 9 Sept. 1871.

[56] R. Nagendiram, *The Straits Settlements, 1867–1874*, Master's Thesis (Australian National University, 1976), p. ii.

[57] Nunn, "Some Account of Our Governors", pp. 93–4.

[58] Lee, *The British as Rulers*, p. xv.

[59] R. St.J. Braddell, "Crime", p. 284.

[60] Nagendiram, *The Straits Settlements*, pp. 138–66; Drake, *Merchants, Bankers, Governors*, pp. 70–1.

[61] Murfett, Miksic, Farrell and Chiang, *Between Two Oceans*, p. 95; *Proceedings of the Legislative Council of the Straits Settlements*, 21 Sept. 1868, 26 Sept. 1872; *Straits Settlements Annual Report*, vol. 2, pp. 138, 147.

[62] Makepeace, "Singapore Defences", p. 399.

from the farms, and no new taxes were required to balance the accounts in spite of a much larger administration.[63] If the Colony had not paid its way under Indian rule, it now did: the Straits government ran substantial surpluses in the early 1870s.[64] In a veiled attempt to redistribute the tax burden, however, Ord antagonised the merchants in the early days of his administration by hinting that customs duties or income taxes might one day be needed to supplement the revenue, thus souring his relationship with them for the rest of his tenure and prompting a rebuke from the Colonial Office.[65] He claimed that the Europeans accounted for less than one-tenth of the Colony's revenue, which the press disputed on the grounds that they had to pay higher wages to workers as a consequence of the revenue farms.[66]

The Straits expenditure was curtailed on another account. Singapore's status as the major penal colony in the Eastern settlements, including for Chinese convicts from Hong Kong during a spell in the late forties to mid-fifties, came to an end in 1873 as part of the arrangement for transfer to home rule. In fact, no convicts from India were transported to Singapore after 1860 as a result of the petition of 1857.[67] In 1870, the last Indian convict in the Straits Settlements was removed to the Andaman Islands, leaving only 33 prisoners from Ceylon who finally left three years later.[68] Those whose term of imprisonment had come to an end merged into the population, earning a living as artisans, cow keepers, cart drivers, and the like. Although complaints of labour shortage persisted, a large influx of Chinese labourers had eased the situation and kept a lid on wages. Furthermore, the ambitious military and civil works embarked on in the late fifties had been completed and the government was finding it hard to find sufficient work for convicts.[69] The exception was the palatial residence that Ord ordered to be built for him, the new Government House (the present Istana), which replaced Raffles' wooden cottage. Completed in 1869, this elegant neo-Palladian structure was designed and built by John Frederick Adolphus McNair, the Superintendent of Convicts, at a princely sum of SPD185,000 against an initial estimate of SPD100,000, drawing much criticism and flak.[70]

Although Ord initially neglected public works, he later oversaw the reconstruction of the Chinatown Market and Ellenborough Market, the construction of a new Post Office at Fullerton Square, the building of new roads and bridges as well as the erection of a

63 *Straits Settlements Annual Report*, vol. 2, pp. 33, 37, 47–8; *The Straits Times*, 15 May 1869.

64 R. St.J. Braddell, "A Short History", p. 24; *Proceedings of the Legislative Council of the Straits Settlements*, 17 May 1871; *The Straits Times*, 2 Nov. 1872.

65 Turnbull, *History of Modern Singapore*, p. 96; J. Legge, "The Colonial Office and Governor Ord", *Journal of Southeast Asian Studies* 29, 1 (1998): 4; Drake, *Merchants, Bankers, Governors*, pp. 40–1; *Straits Settlements Annual Report*, vol. 2, p. 4.

66 *Straits Settlements Annual Report*, vol. 2, pp. 37–8; *The Straits Times*, 25 June 1870.

67 C.M. Turnbull, "Convicts in the Straits Settlements 1826–1867", *Journal of the Malaysian Branch of the Royal Asiatic Society* 43, 1 (1970): 99, 103.

68 Nagendiram, *The Straits Settlements*, p. 174.

69 *The Straits Times*, 27 Mar. 1869.

70 *The Straits Settlements and the Colonial System* (London: Alfred Boot, 1873); *Proceedings of the Legislative Council of the Straits Settlements*, 31 July 1867; *The Straits Times*, 13 Mar. 1869.

lighthouse in the Straits of Melaka.[71] His administration also brought to fruition a project that improved the town's sanitary conditions and the comfort of its residents—the ill-fated waterworks which at long last were completed in 1877 at a cost of SPD61,769, after a series of blunders dating back to the previous government.[72] In contrast, the Municipal Council, the only institution that was untouched by the Governor's zeal for reform, focused on maintenance of the town rather than new public works. The only major project it undertook was the erection in 1869 at a cost of SPD93,000 of Cavenagh Bridge, named after the previous governor, to commemorate Crown Colony status. The bridge dispensed with the quarter cent fare for the ferry service to cross the Singapore River from the business district to the government offices and resulted in further development of the river's south side.[73]

The end of the penal colony in the Straits Settlements had demographic repercussions. It was one factor that led to a drop in the local Indian population between 1860 and 1871.[74] According to the first decennial census taken under the Crown Colony administration, the number of Indians in Singapore was 10,313 in the later year, one-fifth lower than in the earlier year.[75] The other cause of the decline was the proactive policy taken by the Bengal government in 1864 to regulate Indian emigration by allowing movement of labour only to specified places which complied with its requirements on worker protection. The Straits Settlements was not one of them; furthermore, following reports of abuse, the Madras Presidency put an embargo on the migration of Tamils to the Straits in 1870. But clandestine operators sprang up to operate a system that resembled the Chinese credit ticket in its essential features. The Straits government pleaded with the Indian authorities to lift the restrictions, promising that workers who came to the Straits would be well looked after.[76] This was assented to, but only after various safeguards were instituted, including inspection of plantation estates by colonial officials, and an act was passed providing for them, which was eventually effected in 1877.[77] However, the ordinance was repealed in 1885, making Indian emigration to the Straits free although protective measures were still in place.[78]

---

[71] *Straits Settlements Annual Report*, vol. 2, p. 203; *The Straits Times*, 14 Aug. 1869, 8 June 1872; *Straits Times Overland Journal*, 19 Nov. 1873.

[72] *Straits Settlements Records*, V.29, 21 Nov. 1859; *Proceedings of the Legislative Council of the Straits Settlements*, 27 June 1870, 16 June 1873, 23 June 1873; *Straits Settlements Annual Report*, vol. 2, p. 324; *The Straits Times*, 17 July 1869, 5 Feb. 1870, 18 May 1872.

[73] Jayapal, *Old Singapore*, p. 30; Hallifax, "Municipal Government", p. 324; *The Straits Times*, 24 July 1869, 23 Apr. 1870, 11 June 1870.

[74] Rai, *Indians in Singapore*, pp. 58, 70, 72–3.

[75] Saw Swee-Hock, *The Population of Singapore*, Third Edition (Singapore: Institute of Southeast Asian Studies, 2012), p. 29; T. Braddell, *Statistics of the British Possessions*, Table No.1, Census Returns of Several Stations of the Straits Settlements.

[76] *Proceedings of the Legislative Council of the Straits Settlements*, 4 July 1872.

[77] *Proceedings of the Legislative Council of the Straits Settlements*, 5 Feb. 1876; *The Straits Times*, 26 Feb. 1876.

[78] *Straits Settlements Annual Report*, vol. 3, p. 16; *The Straits Times Weekly Issue*, 5 Mar. 1883, 16 Aug. 1883.

In 1871, Singapore's overall population had nearly reached the 100,000 mark.[79] In stark contrast to India's restrictive stance, the Qing government's relaxation of the imperial edict prohibiting emigration of Chinese in 1860, the suppression of the Taiping rebellion in China in 1864 as well as natural disasters had driven large numbers of pauperised peasants and political refugees to Singapore. What had been a trickle during Indian rule soon became a flood, with 30,000 Chinese immigrants arriving each year by the mid-1870s, many of them on passenger steamers operated by foreign companies in China who worked with local recruiting agents.[80] The phenomenal increase in population that resulted prompted Governor Ord to introduce bills regulating the importation of immigrants and the provision of protection to them, in the same way that Raffles had done half a century earlier. The key pieces of legislation were the Passenger Ships Ordinance of 1867 (later amended to cover only Chinese ships) which controlled the number of passengers carried in a ship, space per passenger, provision of food, etc. and the Chinese Immigration Bill of 1873 which was aimed at preventing the kidnapping of sinkhehs and forced relocation to Sumatra and other places, where it was rumoured that labourers were ill-treated.[81]

The Immigration Bill was the outcome of petitions by the Chinese merchants and it sought to register new arrivals from China and keep tabs on them for two years by issuing them with a ticket.[82] Unfortunately, it was passed but never implemented because of objections by the European merchants that it would raise the cost of labour; the Colonial Office was also opposed to it.[83] The coolie trade continued to be subject to abuses such as contract manipulation and false promises of pay and conditions.[84] Due to strong demand for labour, the coolie brokers made a profit of SPD3 to SPD6 for each man brought in.[85] Following another petition from the public in 1876, a committee was set up to inquire into the condition of Chinese labour in the Colony. The result of its deliberation was the establishment of a Chinese Protectorate, a move that was to irrevocably transform the relationship of the Chinese community with their colonial master as well as the character of Chinese society in Singapore itself.

The appointee to this new office was William Pickering who, being the first European official who could converse in Chinese dialects, remedied a serious difficulty that had been pointed out by a colonial official in 1857: "At present, there is a population of 70,000

---

79 Saw, *Population of Singapore*, p. 9.

80 Turnbull, *History of Modern Singapore*, p. 97.

81 Song, *One Hundred Years' History of the Chinese*, pp. 244–5; *The Straits Times*, 24 Apr. 1869, 28 Nov. 1874; *The Singapore Free Press and Mercantile Advertiser*, 8 Oct. 1935. In the preceding decades, the junks that brought Chinese immigrants to Singapore frequently ran out of food and water, resulting in a large number of deaths. Brooke, "Medical Work", p. 492.

82 W. Blythe, *The Impact of Chinese Secret Societies in Malaya: A Historical Study* (Oxford University Press, 1969), pp. 168–71; *Proceedings of the Legislative Council of the Straits Settlements*, 10 Dec. 1867, 9 Sept. 1873, 17 Oct. 1873; *The Straits Times*, 17 June 1876.

83 Lee, *The British as Rulers*, pp. 61–3, 76–7; *The Straits Times*, 16 Jan. 1875.

84 S. Neal, *Chinese Migration*, p. 19; *The Straits Times*, 9 Mar. 1872.

85 The cost of the passage ranged mostly from SPD7 to SPD12, depending on the port of embarkation, but could be as high as SPD17. P.C. Campbell, *Chinese Coolie Emigration to Countries Within the British Empire* (Taipei: Ch'eng Wen Press, 1971), pp. 3–4; *Proceedings of the Legislative Council*, "Annual Report of the Protector of Chinese for the Year 1878", 1879, Appendix 12, p. xlvii.

Chinamen in Singapore, and not a single European who understands their language".[86] The first and foremost task of the Protectorate was to offer protection to Chinese immigrants from the moment they landed in Singapore. On arrival, they would be received by Chinese-speaking colonial officers and told about the existence of the Protectorate where they could seek help and not be coerced into joining a hoey.[87] Registration of employment contracts and the details of employers was carried out for those who found ready jobs. Those who did not were brought to licensed depots which were visited and inspected by Protectorate staff on a regular basis, where they could be detained only for a total of ten days. With the implementation of these measures, the objectives of the Immigration Bill of 1873 were achieved.

Inevitably, by virtue of the regular intercourse between the Protectorate and the Chinese population in the settlement on all matters affecting them, Pickering's mission expanded from the protection of immigrants to the control of the secret societies—one of the few issues that had not been addressed by the transfer to direct rule. During the early part of Ord's tenure as Governor, an Act for the Better Preservation of the Peace was passed in 1867 to give the Straits government greater summary powers to deal with the triads, including importantly the banishment of secret society office-bearers.[88] After riots broke out in Penang between the members of two secret societies, the Dangerous Societies Suppression Ordinance was also enacted in 1869 to render it compulsory for all associations with ten or more members to be registered while magistrates and police officers obtained the right to attend society meetings.[89] Moreover, the hoeys would be answerable and liable for any damage which might result from riots orchestrated by them.[90] The Governor had stated then that the intent of the legislation was that "the moral effect... on the people would be a sufficient check on the turbulent without its being necessary to exercise the repressive powers which they confer".[91]

The registration exercise showed that there were six societies considered as dangerous in Singapore with a total membership of 11,507, the large majority of whom belonged to the Ghee Hin and Ghee Hok triads.[92] This figure actually understated the extent of secret society membership as some triads evaded the ordinance and others produced

[86] Quoted in Wise, *Travellers' Tales*, p. 308. While he was not wrong in his claim, the official was mistaken about the number of Chinese, which according to the census of 1860 numbered only 50,043.

[87] Ng Siew Hoong, "The Chinese Protectorate in Singapore, 1877–1900", *Journal of Southeast Asian History* 2, 1 (1961): 83–4; Lee, *The British as Rulers*, pp. 71, 78. The official committee inquiring into labour conditions noted that "the majority of Chinamen who come to work in these settlements return to their country not knowing clearly whether there is a government in them or not". Quoted in Frost and Balasingamchow, *Singapore*, p. 163.

[88] Blythe, *The Impact of Chinese Secret Societies*, p. 129; *Proceedings of the Legislative Council of the Straits Settlements*, 12 Aug. 1867; *Straits Times Overland Journal*, 2 Jan. 1873.

[89] Turnbull, *History of Modern Singapore*, pp. 96–7; R. St.J. Braddell, "Crime", pp. 276–7; *The Straits Times*, 18 Dec. 1869.

[90] *Proceedings of the Legislative Council of the Straits Settlements*, 15 Nov. 1869, 24 Nov. 1869.

[91] *Straits Settlements Annual Report*, vol. 2, p. 68.

[92] Nagendiram, *The Straits Settlements*, p. 232; *The Straits Times*, 11 Nov. 1876.

fake records for inspection.[93] The veil of secrecy and inner workings of the hoeys were impossible to penetrate, a fact made painfully clear to the government during the "post office riots" of December 1876. This disturbance was triggered by the government's move to set up a sub-post office for the Chinese to send letters and remittances to China, with the intention of collecting revenue as well as to prevent exchange rate manipulation by private remisiers.[94] Finding their business taken away and construing the move as interference by the government, the remittance agencies or "letter shops" run by Teochew men instigated the riots, in all likelihood with the help of the brotherhoods and their corps of fighting men, also known as *samseng*.[95] Prior to this disturbance, a series of riots had also broken out between Hokkiens and Teochews belonging to rival secret societies during the period from 1871 to 1873.

When the Chinese Protectorate was set up, Pickering was concurrently made the Registrar of Societies, in which capacity he personally witnessed, as had Munshi Abdullah a half century before, an initiation ceremony of the Ghee Hin society.[96] After learning their *modus operandi,* Pickering slowly reformed the headmen of the hoeys and usurped their authority in affording protection to the Chinese.[97] He was greatly assisted in these tasks by the high respect and esteem that the Chinese community had for him, presumably derived from his language ability and his interactions with them since he had been appointed the government interpreter in 1872. In particular, he used the headmen of the brotherhoods to maintain order among their unruly underlings, replicating at the hoey level a strategy that had been employed by previous administrations to resolve disturbances through influential Chinese merchants (who were, *ipso facto*, secret society leaders).[98] Triad members were re-registered under headmen in different districts and potential troublemakers could therefore be summoned at short notice to the Protectorate.[99]

Pickering's method for harnessing the organisational resources of the triads to the cause of public order can be judged from the following quotation : "It is nevertheless a question whether the Thien-Ti-Hui (Triad Society) might not with some radical reformations, be made conducive to the order and tranquillity of a country inhabited by a large Chinese

---

[93] Moore and Moore, *The First 150 Years*, pp. 413, 418–9; Song, *One Hundred Years' History of the Chinese*, pp. 253–4, 256–7, 258–9.

[94] *Proceedings of the Legislative Council of the Straits Settlements*, 1879, Appendix 31, pp. ccclxx–ccclxxvii.

[95] Blythe, *The Impact of Chinese Secret Societies*, p. 201; Lee, *The British as Rulers*, pp. 26, 38–9, 43–7; *Straits Times Overland Journal*, 29 Mar. 1871; *The Straits Times*, 16 Dec. 1876, 23 Dec. 1876.

[96] Mak Lau Fong, "Chinese Secret Societies in the Nineteenth-century Straits Settlements", in *Early Chinese Immigrant Societies*, ed. Lee, p. 232.

[97] L. Comber, "Chinese Secret Societies in Malaya; An Introduction", *Journal of the Malayan Branch of the Royal Asiatic Society* 29, 1 (1956): 154.

[98] Lee, *The British as Rulers*, pp. 28–9. Another method used earlier to control the triads was to appoint their headmen as special constables to police members. Song, *One Hundred Years' History of the Chinese*, pp. 205–6, 221–2.

[99] Ng Siew Hoong, "The Chinese Protectorate in Singapore", pp. 90–1; *Proceedings of the Legislative Council of the Straits Settlements*, 1878, Appendix 6, "Annual Report of the Protector of Chinese for the Year 1877".

population".[100] Pickering encouraged the secret society leaders to inform him of goings-on in the Chinese community and succeeded in getting them to refer their quarrels and financial disputes to the Protectorate for arbitration.[101] The coolies too would rather go to him to settle petty quarrels and small debts than to the triads or the courts.[102] By 1880, the Protectorate had become, in the eyes of the Chinese, the alternative to government by the brotherhood.[103] Years later, a commentator would remark that "if the police are the Government's right arm in suppressing crime, then the Protectorate is its very powerful left arm".[104] Ironically though, the effectiveness of the Chinese Protectorate resulted in a weakening of the headmen's influence over their members.[105]

The chief weapon available to the colonial government for dealing with the recalcitrant secret societies was the deportation of their headmen to China, where they were sometimes treated as rebels and peremptorily executed by Qing officials.[106] But Straits-born Chinese who were naturalised British subjects could not be so banished and their young members joined the hoeys or set up their own "Baba Clubs" during the 1880s, giving much trouble to the government through fights and other misdeeds.[107] In response, a law was passed prohibiting secret societies from having any Straits-born Chinese or naturalised British subjects as members.[108] Meanwhile, members of blacklisted societies went underground and carried on their criminal activities—operating gambling houses in particular—under the front of registered benevolent associations.[109] Pickering had warned that professionally organised gambling was a danger to the peace as it was likely to give rise to quarrels and fights between the triads. Still, as a testament to the success of his approach, there were no serious riots from the time Pickering became Protector of Chinese in 1877 until 1888 when he retired after being attacked by an axe-wielding triad member.

In that year, forcible action taken by the municipal inspectors to clear the five-foot ways of the merchandise and wares of traders and peddlers in the Arab Street and Rochor Road areas sparked off another disturbance (aptly labelled the "verandah riots") that lasted two days, and the shops closed again.[110] In spite of Pickering's objection that the abolition of

---

100 W.A. Pickering, "Chinese Secret Societies and Their Origin", *Journal of the Straits Branch of the Royal Asiatic Society* 1 (1878): 66.

101 *Proceedings of the Legislative Council of the Straits Settlements*, "Annual Report of the Protector of Chinese for the Year 1878", 1879, Appendix 12, pp. xlv, xlix.

102 Lee, *The British as Rulers*, pp. 85, 135.

103 *The Straits Times*, 10 Apr. 1880.

104 R. St.J. Braddell, "Crime", pp. 277–8.

105 *Proceedings of the Legislative Council of the Straits Settlements*, Appendix 15, "Report on the Chinese Protectorate, Singapore for the Year 1880", 1881, pp. 89–90.

106 Lee, *The British as Rulers*, pp. 96–8, 119; Ng Siew Hoong, "The Chinese Protectorate in Singapore", pp. 92–3.

107 *The Straits Times Weekly Issue*, 20 Feb. 1886.

108 *Proceedings of the Legislative Council of the Straits Settlements*, 7 Mar. 1882, 24 Mar. 1885, 28 Apr. 1885.

109 Blythe, *The Impact of Chinese Secret Societies*, pp. 214–5; *The Straits Times Weekly Issue*, 28 Feb. 1887.

110 Song, *One Hundred Years' History of the Chinese*, pp. 335–6; J.D. Ross, *The Capital of a Little Empire, A Descriptive Study of a British Crown Colony in the Far East* (Kelly and Walsh, 1898), pp. 13–15.

the hoeys would leave the authorities with no medium of contact with the Chinese masses, the Governor decided that the policy of obtaining the collaboration of the headmen through trust and goodwill had gradually become ineffective and the time had come to suppress the hoeys once and for all.[111] He therefore sought and obtained approval from the Secretary of State for the Colonies to pass a law to ban dangerous secret societies in 1889, which came into effect the following year.[112] In their place, the Chinese Advisory Board with representatives from the different bangs was formed to act as a consultative body to the government on subjects or measures affecting the interest of the Chinese in the settlement.[113] After the ban, the crime rate decreased while cases of assault also fell.[114] However, the hoeys did not just disappear but continued to make their presence felt through rent-seeking activities even though their connections with the opium farms had been cut; these activities included extorting protection money from shop proprietors, blackmailing the operators of gambling houses, opium dens and brothels, and combating with each other over territories of control.[115] Indeed, they surfaced again in the modern era.

Singapore and the Malay States

One of the "evils" of the Indian regime decried by the press and the mercantile community in Singapore was the neglect of efforts by the Straits government to maintain friendly ties with the rulers of the native states in the Malay Peninsula.[116] The authorities were accused of ignoring the wise counsel of Stamford Raffles who had foreseen the need to "cultivate the friendship of these powers, and to establish a friendly intercourse with them".[117] After declaring in a June 1819 letter that the object for Singapore was trade, he had added almost casually that it was also the "fulcrum whence we may extend our influence politically as circumstances may hereafter require".[118] Raffles was just stating what appeared obvious to him: the preservation and expansion of British commercial ties with the Malay Peninsula and the Eastern Archipelago required the exercise of political power.

From the earliest days of the Straits Settlements' establishment, however, the EIC had maintained a strict policy of non-interference in the internal affairs of the Malay rulers on both coasts of the Peninsula; if anything, the Company was more concerned about the conduct of the Dutch in the Archipelago. From time to time, the Straits government did

---

111 Blythe, *The Impact of Chinese Secret Societies*, pp. 224–5; R. St.J. Braddell, "Crime", pp. 279–81; *The Straits Times Weekly Issue*, 7 Oct. 1889, 29 Apr. 1890. The Indian and Malay-dominated Red Flag and White Flag societies had been banned in 1882. Lee, *The British as Rulers*, p. 172.

112 *Proceedings of the Legislative Council of the Straits Settlements*, 7 Feb. 1889, 8 Feb. 1889, 21 Feb. 1889.

113 "Annual Report on the Chinese Protectorate, Singapore, for the Year 1889", in *Straits Settlements, Annual Reports for the Year 1889*, p. 188; *The Straits Times Weekly Issue*, 29 Apr. 1890.

114 *Straits Settlements Annual Report*, vol. 4, p. 4.

115 Abshire, *History of Singapore*, p. 71; Comber, "Chinese Secret Societies in Malaya", p. 155; "Annual Report on the Chinese Protectorate", in *Straits Settlements, Annual Reports for the Year 1895*, p. 165; *The Straits Times Weekly Issue*, 17 June 1891.

116 *The Singapore Free Press and Mercantile Advertiser*, 5 Apr. 1860.

117 *Straits Settlements Records*, L.10, 6 Feb. 1819.

118 Quoted in Turnbull, *History of Modern Singapore*, p. 38.

take the initiative to make commercial treaties with the Malay chiefs and visits to their states to address grievances or mediate in disputes. Even this was frowned upon by the Indian government, while the expansion of territory was out of the question.[119] The Settlements were treated as trading centres and as such, sufficed to meet the Company's commercial interests before 1833; after losing all its privileges in that year, it feared getting entangled in Malay politics. The EIC sanctioned limited British intervention only when trade treaties were openly violated or flagrant attacks were made on British subjects or interests. The use of British force was rare—though the threat of deploying it more common—and was subject to disapprobation by the Supreme Government and the home authorities. The India and Colonial Offices inherited the Company's position and stuck to it long after political and economic developments had rendered the policy untenable. In fact, Governor Ord was accorded even less discretion than his predecessors when he attempted to extend British influence in the native states.[120]

Anglo-Siamese relations in the first half of the 19th century provide a good illustration of these strictures. For a long time, Siam had claimed suzerainty over the northern Malay states of Kedah and Perak, thereby bedevilling not only the trade of Penang with the states but also its food supply.[121] In 1821, the kingdom carried out its aggressive designs on the states by invading and occupying Kedah. The Straits government, then based in Penang, allowed the deposed Sultan to seek refuge on the island but took no action even though some thought it was in the British interest to defend its ally Kedah (which had ceded Penang to the EIC in 1786).[122] Only when the adjoining state of Perak was threatened did the government make the Burney Treaty with Siam in 1826, which effectively recognised that Kedah was a tributary state of Siam and promised that Britain would not attack Kedah or let the ex-Sultan do so.[123] In return, Siam would not colonise Perak or Selangor and agreed not to interfere in the Straits Settlements' trade with Kedah. The treaty also included an understanding that the Siamese would not obstruct British commerce with its other tributary states of Trengganu and Kelantan on the eastern side of the Malay Peninsula. In light of the agreement, the Straits government went ahead to give an assurance of British protection to the Perak ruler, but this action was severely censured by the Indian government.[124] In 1831, the ex-Sultan conspired with his nephew and supporters in Penang to retake Kedah, forcing the Governor of the Straits Settlements to honour the treaty with Siam by blockading the coast of Kedah and deporting him to Melaka.

In the 1840s, it had become increasingly clear that the doctrine of non-interference was constraining the expansion of the Colony's trade and economic ties with the Malay Peninsula. Merchandise trade between Singapore and the east and west coasts came close

---

119 Mills, Turnbull and Bassett, "British Malaya", p. 203; Tarling, "British Policy", p. 32.

120 Moore and Moore, *The First 150 Years*, pp. 349–50.

121 Mills, Turnbull and Bassett, "British Malaya", p. 155.

122 R.O. Winstedt, "A History of Malaya", *Journal of the Malayan Branch of the Royal Asiatic Society* 13, 1 (1935): 183–97; Tarling, "British Policy", pp. 29, 35, 37–9.

123 Begbie, *The Malayan Peninsula*, pp. 114–8, 127–31. The treaty also expressly acknowledged British governance of Penang, 40 years after the island was ceded. R. St.J. Braddell, "A Short History", p. 15.

124 Mills, Turnbull and Bassett, "British Malaya", pp. 183–90.

to a million Spanish dollars in 1848 and the west coast had increased in importance.[125] More critically, external events had made it imperative for the Settlements, and Singapore in particular, to increase their commercial dealings with the Malay states.[126] The forced opening of China and Hong Kong had to some degree diverted Singapore's entrepôt trade and France's colonisation of Indo-China had the same effect. In the Eastern Archipelago, notwithstanding Singapore's inherent advantages, the opening of Dutch free ports and discrimination against British traders had taken away part of the native trade, as had increased activity by the Spanish in the Philippines.

At precisely the same time, a period of unrest and anarchy descended on the Peninsula states, the result of interminable succession disputes and fratricidal quarrels between royals.[127] Weakened central authority spawned independent petty chiefs who acted with impunity as robber barons along the rivers and pirate kings in the seas, levying exactions on trade and plundering cargo. Where civil wars raged, trade declined, as happened in Pahang in 1857 when two sons of the deceased Sultan started a protracted war of succession. The younger sibling came to Singapore where arms and ammunition could be bought to fit out an expedition to dethrone his elder brother and succeeded in briefly occupying Kuantan.[128] At this point, the Temenggong of Johor joined in the fray, raising a private mercenary force to try and drive the usurper out of Trengganu where he had obtained refuge and support from the state's ruler. The fighting disrupted both the overland and seaborne trade of Pahang with Singapore, worth SPD500,000 a year, and blocked access to its gold and tin deposits.[129] The Chinese merchants in Singapore stood to lose the most from the advances of money and supplies they had made to the miners and called on the Governor to act. As they had property estimated to be worth SPD80,000 in Pahang, he was persuaded to bombard Trengganu in 1862, where the insurgent forces were gathered. This action again met with disapproval from the India Office.[130] The long-running saga only ended in the following year when the younger brother emerged victorious.

Among the economic changes over the decades, the most consequential related to tin mining, in which the Chinese and the secret societies to which they belonged were to play a vital role in shaping the course of events.[131] Tin mining has a long history in the Malay Peninsula, which will be discussed more fully in the next chapter; in this section, the focus is on its role as a cause for conflict in the 1860s–70s. The enterprise began before mid-century in Sungai Ujong when the Malay rulers invited Chinese labourers to work the tin mines in the interior. In 1828, there were nearly 1,000 Chinese toiling in the mines in this area.[132] The melted tin was taxed by the chiefs and sent to nearby Melaka to be exported

[125] Wong, *Trade of Singapore*, Appendix A, Tables XIV, XVa, XVb, pp. 231–3.

[126] This argument was made by the Governor in 1863. Tarling, "British Policy", p. 78.

[127] Mills, Turnbull and Bassett, "British Malaya", pp. 203–5.

[128] Turnbull, *Straits Settlements*, pp. 291, 293; Swettenham, "British Malaya", p. 113.

[129] M.I. Knowles, *The Expansion of British Influence in the Malay Peninsula, 1867–1885: A Study in Nineteenth Century Imperialism*, Doctoral Thesis (University of Wisconsin, 1935), p. 31.

[130] Tarling, "British Policy", pp. 73–4.

[131] Comber, "Chinese Secret Societies in Malaya", p. 148.

[132] Chee Siew Nim, *Labour and Tin Mining in Malaya*, Data Paper No. 7, Southeast Asia Program, Department of Far Eastern Studies, Cornell University, 1953, pp. 1, 299–301.

by Chinese and European merchants, who also advanced funds for prospecting for the metal.[133] Following a disturbance, many of the Chinese were killed by natives and their property confiscated. Later in the 1840s, Raja Jumaat in nearby Lukut—a settlement then under the jurisdiction of Selangor—welcomed Chinese prospectors and miners again after tin was discovered in paying quantities in the district.[134]

In 1857, new mines were opened in Ampang in the Klang Valley by Raja Abdullah, the brother of Raja Jumaat, both of whom were of Bugis descent. Chinese miners poured in from Lukut, accompanied by traders who provided supplies and bought the tin for export, thus founding the settlement called Kuala Lumpur.[135] After a period of peace that prevailed up to the late 1860s, antagonism between the Chinese belonging to rival hoeys over the control of tin deposits and water rights erupted into the open when one of their headmen was murdered in 1869.[136] Meanwhile, fighting had broken out three years earlier among the Malay ruling elite in Selangor over the control of Klang and with it the tin revenue. The war that ensued was as much a power struggle between two royals—Tengku Kudin, who had gained control of Klang, and Raja Mahdi, based at Kuala Selangor—as a contest between Chinese secret societies.[137] The former was recognised as the Viceroy of Selangor by the British government and supported by the Sultan of Selangor, who had earlier given the rights to farm the revenue in Klang to two prominent Singapore merchants; the latter was assisted by a mercenary named Syed Mashor.[138] On the Chinese side of the war were the Hai San and Ghee Hin triads, headed respectively by Yap Ah Loy, the Chinese Kapitan of Kuala Lumpur, and Chong Chong. Yap Ah Loy was initially on amicable terms with Raja Mahdi but was forced to switch his allegiance to Tengku Kudin as the war proceeded. Each of the Chinese leaders raised fighting armies of 2,000–2,500 men and clashed repeatedly in Kuala Lumpur and the surrounding territory.[139] With the aid of troops sent from Pahang and the backing of Governor Ord, Tengku Kudin and Yap Ah Loy eventually prevailed over their rivals in 1873.[140]

For the Straits merchants who also took sides in the Selangor conflict, political intervention by the British had become inevitable in order to enforce economic contracts. They had invested in tin mines in the state and Negri Sembilan under concessions granted

---

133 T. Braddell, "Notes on Naning, with a Brief Notice of the Naning War", *The Journal of the Indian Archipelago and Eastern Asia*, ed. J.R. Logan, New Series I (1856): 227–9; Begbie, *The Malayan Peninsula*, pp. 407, 408.

134 S.M. Middlebrook, J.M. Gullick and C.A. Gibson-Hill, "Yap Ah Loy (1837–1885)", *Journal of the Malayan Branch of the Royal Asiatic Society* 24, 2 (1951): 14–15.

135 Ibid., pp. 18–19, 34–6.

136 Khoo Kay Kim, *The Western Malay States 1850–1873* (Kuala Lumpur: Oxford University Press, 1972), pp. 152–9, 176–7.

137 Winstedt, *A History of Malaya*, pp. 227–30.

138 The merchants were W.H. Read and Tan Kim Ching. J.G. Davidson later also obtained a concession to mine tin in Selangor.

139 Middlebrook, Gullick and Gibson-Hill, "Yap Ah Loy", pp. 53, 55–62.

140 Swettenham, *British Malaya*, p. 131.

by the Malay chiefs.[141] As a result of the war in Selangor, huge losses were sustained and their investments in other states were in jeopardy.[142] Furthermore, they were conscious of the Peninsula's still undeveloped mineral and agricultural wealth, which, under peaceful conditions, would provide a highly profitable outlet for their capital. The urgency of the situation was accentuated by the declining return on trading activities as a result of increased commercial rivalry between the agency houses in Singapore. On the merchants' prodding, Governor Ord, who had failed to settle the dispute on his own, pressed the British government in 1872—without success—to alter its policy of abstention in Malay affairs.[143] He was forced to inform the Singapore and Melaka merchants that they had invested in the Peninsula at their own risk and should not expect the British government to bail them out.[144] Earlier in 1868, the Colonial Office had unambiguously told Ord it wanted to keep clear of disorder in the native states as long as the peace of the Straits Settlements was not threatened and warned him against entering into formal negotiations or concluding any agreements unless it was sanctioned by the British government.[145]

But a *deus ex machina* was delivered to the merchants in 1873 by the worsening turmoil that engulfed the northern state of Perak. In the early 1840s, the Malay chieftain Long Jaafar had opened the first tin mines in Taiping by borrowing the capital from Penang merchants and recruiting Chinese labourers who organised themselves through secret societies.[146] The triads co-existed peacefully until the Larut Wars broke out in 1861, the *casus belli* of which was again a dispute over mining land between the two rival hoeys of Ghee Hin and Hai San, also known as the "Si Kuans" and "Go Kuans", made up mostly of Cantonese and Hakkas, respectively. The two factions were supplied with food and arms by competing groups of Chinese and European financiers in Penang who were eyeing Perak's rich tin resources.[147] Monopoly concessions on customs revenue, opium and liquor sales, and gambling rights were also at stake.[148] Intermittent conflicts between the triads throughout the 1860s culminated in another large-scale war in 1873, dragging the hapless Malay rulers into the strife. The rulers were split between a claimant to the Perak throne, Raja Abdullah, and Ngah Ibrahim, the son of Long Jaafar, who controlled the Larut mines.[149] From then on, Malay and Chinese political interests merged. Ngah Ibrahim was long associated with the Hai San society although he sided with whichever Chinese faction

141 Khoo Kay Kim, "The Origin of British Administration in Malaya", *Journal of the Malaysian Branch of the Royal Asiatic Society* 39, 1 (1966): 57–60; Khoo, *Western Malay States*, pp. 80, 107–8; Drake, *Merchants, Bankers, Governors*, pp. 32–4, 69.

142 *The Straits Times*, 11 May 1872, 17 Aug. 1872.

143 Swettenham, *British Malaya*, p. 115; Drake, *Merchants, Bankers, Governors*, pp. 44–6.

144 R. St.J. Braddell, "A Short History", p. 26.

145 Legge, "The Colonial Office and Governor Ord", pp. 6–7; E. Sadka, *The Protected Malay States 1874–1895* (Kuala Lumpur: University of Malaya Press, 1968), pp. 40–1.

146 Khoo, *Western Malay States*, pp. 67–70, 174.

147 Khoo Kay Kim, "Taiping (Larut): The Early History of a Mining Settlement", *Journal of the Malaysian Branch of the Royal Asiatic Society* 64, 1 (1991): 1–13; Swettenham, *British Malaya*, p. 124.

148 Comber, "Chinese Secret Societies in Malaya", p. 152.

149 Winstedt, *A History of Malaya*, pp. 230–3.

appeared to be stronger at the moment. Raja Abdullah depended on the strength of the Ghee Hin society and was endorsed by the Straits government.

As the anarchy up north got worse, the leading Chinese merchants in the Straits Settlements petitioned the British government to intervene to protect their trade and investments.[150] Adding to this call, Raja Abdullah appealed for British arbitration in Perak through his contact in Singapore while Tengku Kudin in Selangor insinuated that if the British would not intervene, he would seek the help of another government.[151] More alarmingly, the disorder in Perak threatened to spill over to the parent hoeys in neighbouring Penang. The British government began to reconsider its stance. Although the ostensible justification for intervention given by the Colonial Office when it came in 1874 was political, namely to pre-empt a similar move by Germany, the extension of British influence to the Malay Peninsula was ultimately an economic *fait accompli*.[152] Germany's intervention was merely rumoured; in fact, it was used as a bogey to secure the approval of the British Prime Minister for the change of policy, the real reason being that the Colonial Office was very much concerned with the development of Straits commerce.[153] In addition, pressure from the Europeans in Singapore and England who had economic stakes in the Peninsula also played a role in the change in British policy.

In a dispatch to Ord's successor Sir Andrew Clarke in September 1873, the Secretary of State for the Colonies declared that "Her Majesty's Government finds it incumbent to employ such influence as they may possess with the native princes to rescue, if possible, these fertile and productive countries from the ruin which must befall them if the present disorders continue unchecked".[154] With this directive, interpreted liberally by Clarke even though he was instructed only to investigate and report on the state of affairs in the feuding states, the British government's "forward policy" in Malaya was implemented.[155] By the Pangkor Agreement signed with the Perak chieftains in January 1874 on the eponymous island, Raja Abdullah was installed as Sultan of Perak and British indirect rule was imposed through the appointment of a Resident in the state. The Resident was to be accredited to the ruler's court and his advice had to be asked and acted upon in all questions other than those touching on Malay religion and customs, including the collection of revenue and state administration. Concurrently, the feud between the Chinese triads in Larut was put to an end by William Pickering, who as the British mediator equitably divided tin mining land between them.

In Selangor, the Straits government endorsed the Viceroy of Selangor's authority to govern the state following his victory over his enemies. An act of piracy and brutal murder of nine Melaka subjects off the Selangor coast then served as a pretext for the appointment

150 *Straits Times Overland Journal*, 14 June 1873.

151 Pickering, "Chinese Secret Societies", p. 19; Knowles, *The Expansion of British Influence*, pp. 85–7; Ernest Chew, "The Reasons for British Intervention in Malaya: Review and Reconsideration", *The Journal of Southeast Asian History* 6, 1 (1965): 84–6.

152 Knowles, *The Expansion of British Influence*, pp. 42–5.

153 Khoo, *The Origin of British Administration*, pp. 71–2.

154 Swettenham, *British Malaya*, pp. 174–5; Winstedt, *A History of Malaya*, pp. 233–5.

155 Nunn, "Some Account of Our Governors", pp. 97–8.

of a British Adviser and in 1875, a Resident.[156] Negri Sembilan was more difficult to deal with since there was a long-standing enmity between the two Malay chiefs in Sungai Ujong—the Dato' Klana, whom Governor Clarke recognised as the legitimate ruler of the state and the Dato' Bandar, an influential leader in the area. The Governor went with two men-of-war from Singapore in May 1874 to meet the chiefs of Sungai Ujong and Rembau at the fork of the Linggi River; in a show of authority, his forces blew up the stockade there. After this, it was thought that order would return; instead, a challenge was mounted by the Dato' Bandar against the Dato' Klana. As the former refused to submit to the Governor's ultimatum, a force of British soldiers and sailors was sent to rout him from his stronghold, compelling him to flee to Selangor. Thus, the troubles in Sungai Ujong were brought to an end and a British Resident was sent to assist the Dato' Klana in governing the state.

Through the agency of the Straits merchants and capitalists, Singapore acquired what it had sorely lacked in its first half-century and also what was desired by Raffles—a territorial and economic hinterland from which the key staples of tin and rubber were to spring.[157] Importantly, Malaya was a hinterland that shared with it a common British ruler, unlike the East Indies which were subject to the vagaries of Dutch policies. In 1896, Perak, Selangor, Negri Sembilan and Pahang (which appointed a British Resident in 1888) were brought together to form the Federated Malay States (FMS) and their Residents were made answerable to the Governor of the Straits Settlements.[158] The Governor also became High Commissioner of the FMS, although the states were given substantial autonomy to pursue their own affairs, through which move the entire territory became known as "British Malaya" and was administered by a single civil service from Singapore. Johor was not part of the FMS, remaining more or less independent and later becoming an Unfederated Malay State. In 1914, a British Adviser was appointed to the Johor court but in the preceding decades the traditional good relations between the state and Singapore had been maintained.[159] By the early 20th century therefore, Singapore's hinterland stretched from the Malay Peninsula across the sea to the British protectorates of North Borneo, Sarawak and Brunei. Counterfactual reasoning suggests that Singapore would probably have continued to flourish as a regional entrepôt and port of call had these events not transpired, but they set the city on an entirely different historical trajectory, as we will see in the next chapter.

---

[156] Swettenham, *British Malaya*, pp. 183–91; Winstedt, *A History of Malaya*, pp. 239–43.

[157] Swettenham, *British Malaya*, pp. 72–3.

[158] Turnbull, *History of Modern Singapore*, p. 109.

[159] Drake, *Merchants, Bankers, Governors*, p. 65.

Chapter 6

Rise of the Staple Port, 1875–99

Singapore's transition from East India Company rule to Crown Colony status can be viewed historiographically as coincident with the movement from its Straits period to its Malayan period.[1] This chapter shows that it could be equally well-characterised as a shift from being an entrepôt to a staple port. British political and economic colonisation made possible the large-scale production of tin in Peninsular Malaya, which became the basis of its wealth in the late 19th century. As Singapore was the key export outlet for the tin, it stood to benefit and the structure of its trade was permanently transformed. Staple trade led in turn to the forging of new economic linkages, stimulating the growth of the service sector.

Singapore's economic history in the late 19th century is therefore co-extensive with the history of its staple port. Between 1874, the year of the signing of the Pangkor Agreement, and the turn of the century, the city experienced a commercial boom that was underpinned by the processing of tin ore in the city and its shipment to a rapidly expanding world market. The dynamic nature of staple development set in motion a process of self-sustaining growth—fuelled by rising incomes and expectations—that drew in wave after wave of immigration in the last quarter of the century. In these circumstances, the Colony began the process of improving its social infrastructure to meet the needs of a growing population and heterogeneous labour force.

Staple-led Growth

At the broadest level, the staples hypothesis of export-led growth presents a macro-dynamic paradigm of economic development that is driven by the production of a staple, or a resource-intensive export commodity, in which a country has a comparative advantage. The key insight of the hypothesis is that rapidly growing demand for the staple product can draw increasing inputs and productive factors, thus keeping production costs low.[2] Concurrently, linkages or "spread effects" will appear within the domestic economy,

[1] K. Hack, "Framing Singapore's History", in *Studying Singapore's Past: C.M. Turnbull and the History of Modern Singapore*, ed. N. Tarling (Singapore: NUS Press, 2012), p. 23.

[2] M. Altman, "Staple Theory and Export-led Growth: Constructing Differential Growth", *Australian Economic History Review* 43, 3 (2003): 230–55.

stimulating commercialisation and industrial development in their wake.[3] The result is a rise in aggregate income, but the rate at which income per capita grows and its distribution will depend on the production technology of the staple, as well as the rate of capital formation and labour inflows to the staple producing region.[4]

As originally propounded by Canadian economic historians, the discovery of a staple product brings previously idle or undiscovered resources into use, thus creating a return through the channel of international trade.[5] Typically, staples come from the extractive or agricultural sectors of the economy and do not require elaborate processing before consignment. While originally formulated for Canada and Australia, the staples hypothesis is often compared with Hla Myint's formulation of the "vent-for-surplus" hypothesis derived from Adam Smith.[6] This theory attempts to explain the process by which underdeveloped countries were opened up to trade with Europe during the 19th century. In both hypotheses, surplus labour and natural resources are present in the first instance but are initially left unexploited. The function of trade is to provide a vent for the output that can be produced by these inputs, thereby creating new effective demand. The contribution of Western enterprise to economic development is mainly through improvements in transportation and communications, discoveries of new products and the supply of manufactured goods to the staple economies.

Later elaborations of the staples theory emphasised how the progress of the Canadian economy was due to the successful exploitation of a series of staples, beginning with cod, moving through fur, timber, wheat, ores, petroleum and metals.[7] The discovery of new primary resources, availability of immigrant labour, development of technology and shifts in world demand are the key forces that unleashed successive waves of staple growth. With this growth, resources move to more productive uses and new requirements for intermediate goods are generated. Unemployed or underemployed workers will be absorbed into the labour force and once domestic resources are fully utilised, the continuation of growth will depend on the ability to import factors of production (capital and workers). If the supply of foreign inputs is sufficiently elastic, costs of production are prevented from rising or may even fall, thus leading to an increase in supply, lower staple prices and a further rise in demand.

---

[3] M.H. Watkins, "A Staple Theory of Economic Growth", *Canadian Journal of Economics and Political Science* 29, 2 (1963): 141–58.

[4] R.E. Baldwin, "Patterns of Development in Newly Settled Regions", *Manchester School of Economic and Social Studies* 24, 2 (1956): 161–79; R.E. Caves, "Export-led Growth and the New Economic History", in *Trade, Balance of Payments, and Growth*, ed. J.N. Bhagwati, R.W. Jones, R.A. Mundell and J. Vanek (Amsterdam: North-Holland Publishing, 1971), pp. 403–42.

[5] H.A. Innis, *The Fur Trade in Canada: An Introduction to Canadian Economic History* (1930; rev. ed. Toronto: University of Toronto Press 1956); W.A. Mackintosh, "Economic Factors in Canadian History", *Canadian Historical Review* 4, 1 (1923): 12–25.

[6] H. Myint, "The 'Classical Theory' of International Trade and the Underdeveloped Countries", *Economic Journal* 68 (1958): 317–37.

[7] G.W. Bertram, "Economic Growth in Canadian Industry, 1870–1915: The Staple Model and the Take-off Hypothesis", *Canadian Journal of Economics and Political Science* 29, 2 (1963): 159–84.

Apart from being the leading sector of the economy, staple industries induce a general expansion of economic activity by raising consumption and investment levels through the creation of backward linkages, forward linkages and final demand linkages.[8] Backward and forward linkages refer respectively to the domestic production of inputs and capital goods for the growing export sector, and investment in industries that use the staple product as an input, including staple processing. Final demand linkages arise from the attendant increase in incomes, and more specifically from the creation of industries to supply locally made consumer goods to labourers in the staple sector. The spending of incomes causes growth in the domestic sector to expand in step with the export sector via multiplier-accelerator mechanisms—the higher the average level of income, the greater these spread effects or spillovers would be. In combination, all three types of linkages, if important and strong enough, tend to stimulate economic development and diversification into secondary industries around the staple export base.[9]

Although colonial Singapore was not an ideal-typical region, recently settled, to which the staples theory is usually applied, the hypothesis of export-led growth provides a compelling account of its rise as a staple port during the late 19th century.[10] Singapore was the "heartland" for the hinterland of British Malaya; to use a metaphor from the staples literature, Singapore was Vancouver while the Peninsula was British Columbia.[11] Even though staple production did not take place in Singapore, the city benefitted from the backward, forward and final demand linkages created in the course of staple-led growth in the hinterland through its role as the service centre and export outlet for the tin produced there. Thus, the development of the tin mining industry in Malaya (and the rubber industry later on) led to tertiary specialisation in Singapore as new services were demanded and supplied.

In this respect, Singapore was not unlike other major staple ports of the 19th century such as Colombo in Asia, São Paolo in South America and Lagos in Africa. Staples were the leading industries in their respective economic hinterlands, and they dominated the exports of these ports and formed the basis of local economies.[12] Favourable geography and efficient infrastructure played important roles in the rise of all these ports, as they did in Singapore: as the maritime gateway at the southern tip of the Malay Peninsula with metropolitan connections, it was the meeting point of the hinterland rail network for transporting tin ore with the port's oceanic links. The economic functions of the staple port were multifarious and centred on providing entrepreneurial, managerial, mercantile, financial, marketing, staple processing and exporting services. Since these functions could

---

[8] Watkins, "A Staple Theory", pp. 145–6.

[9] A.O. Hirschman, *The Strategy of Economic Development* (New Haven, CT: Yale University Press, 1958), pp. 100–4. He defines "importance" in terms of the net output of the new industries that might be created by backward or forward linkages and "strength" in terms of the probability that these industries would actually come into being.

[10] Keen Meng Choy and Ichiro Sugimoto, "Trade, the Staple Theory of Growth, and Fluctuations in Colonial Singapore, 1900–39", *Australian Economic History Review* 53, 2 (2013).

[11] T.A. Hutton, "The Innisian Core-Periphery Revisited: Vancouver's Changing Relationships with British Columbia's Staple Economy", *BC Studies: The British Columbian Quarterly* (1997): 69–100.

[12] Huff, *The Economic Growth of Singapore*, pp. 15, 16.

be performed at lower costs in such port cities due to their easier access to capital and labour, as well as agglomeration and urban economies, they had a comparative advantage over inland cities.[13] As a result of mutual dependence, traders and dealers in staple ports usually had a direct commercial and political interest in the hinterland, as we saw in the previous chapter. In Singapore, Chinese merchants were instrumental in the enterprise of tin mining in Malaya in the early decades of the industry while the European agency houses were involved in downstream functions.

To fully comprehend the transformation of Singapore into a staple port after 1874, we can contrast this role with the traditional functions it fulfilled as an entrepôt in the early colonial period. Both entrepôts and staple ports were successful port cities that hosted a substantial foreign merchant community with intimate knowledge of faraway markets and products.[14] But an entrepôt traded in a much larger and more diversified mix of products and was seldom dependent on the produce of its immediate neighbourhood. Geographical location mattered, but only to a certain extent: the port served a much bigger and more dispersed hinterland and its traders were only remotely and circuitously connected with producers and consumers.[15] By contrast, the *raison d'être* of a staple port was to collect and export only a few products from the nearby hinterland to select markets, paid for with imports of food and manufactures. Unlike the profits made from exchanging multitudinous products in an entrepôt, the gains that accrued to the staple port depended on the production process of the commodities it exported—to be specific, the substitutability of factor inputs. This reflected the fact that the technological requirements for producing a staple determined the scope and scale of the economic linkages associated with it. In the case of tin, the relative labour or capital intensity of production was the key determinant, while for rubber, the linkages hinged on the predominance of estate as opposed to smallholder production.

Tin and Its Linkages

Tin has been mined in the Malay Peninsula from the earliest times and it was the main source of supply in the Eastern Archipelago until the ore was discovered in Banka Island off the southeastern coast of Sumatra in the early 18th century.[16] Chinese and Dutch records show that tin was a major trade item of Melaka in the 15th to 17th centuries.[17] Before the second half of the 19th century however, the quantity of tin mined in the Peninsula was small and sporadic. Tin production began to rise appreciably only from the 1840s, as its price in London increased from £81 (SPD352) per tonne at the start of the decade to £152

[13] Hutton, "The Innisian Core-Periphery Revisited", p. 70.

[14] Darwin, *Unlocking the World*, pp. xxi–xxxix.

[15] Huff, *The Economic Growth of Singapore*, pp. 16–17.

[16] It is interesting to note that Stamford Raffles, while Lieutenant-Governor of Java in the 1810s, had plans to monopolise the Banka tin trade. H. Yamada, "The Origins of British Colonialization of Malaya with Special Reference to Its Tin", *The Developing Economies* 9, 3 (1971): 230–1.

[17] Yip Yat Hoong, *The Development of the Tin Mining Industry of Malaya* (Kuala Lumpur: University of Malaya Press, 1969), p. 56.

(SPD714) in 1872.[18] The even more rapid increase after this year can be attributed to a conjunction of factors: rising industrial demand in the West, discoveries of new deposits of tin ore and, after the pacification of the Malay native states and the consolidation of direct control over them, the development of administrative and physical infrastructure by the British colonial government.[19]

Beyond the many uses for tin alloy in pewterware, soldering and bearings, the growth in demand was primarily due to the expansion of the British tin plate industry, which supplied canned food producers and manufacturers of oil barrels with a sheet of iron or steel coated with tin. In the early 1860s, a huge stimulus was imparted to the tin canning industry by the American Civil War. With the discovery of oil in Pennsylvania in 1859, tin barrel output also increased by leaps and bounds. Soon after, production of tin at the Cornwall mines, which had supplied almost all of Britain's needs, began to fall off while rich deposits were discovered in Malaya around the Kinta Valley and the Klang Valley (the Ipoh and Kuala Lumpur regions respectively) in the 1880s.[20] Coupled with the repeal of all duties on metallic tin imported into Britain in 1853 following a reduction in the tariff rate in 1842 (implemented simultaneously with the imposition of differential tariffs to favour supplies from British territories), this discovery delivered a fillip to production in the Malay Peninsula.

The history of the tin mining industry in Malaya can be roughly divided into three phases according to the type of production technology employed. Prior to the mid-19th century, Malay mining methods were crude, requiring insignificant investment and little labour.[21] These included panning, usually carried out in lowland streams after heavy rains had washed the tin-bearing soil from the hills, or ground sluicing which entailed washing tin-bearing earth in a sluice box using water from a stream. A more sophisticated method involved digging relatively shallow sinking pits, sometimes with walls supported by wood and bamboo, to extract tin deposits that lay above the bedrock. Given the inefficiency of these methods of recovery, Malay tin mining was largely confined to shallow and easily accessible deposits near foothills and rivers.

From 1850 to the last decade of the 19th century, these primitive methods were replaced by open-cast tin mining. Chinese immigrant workers provided the main labour force, with 50 to 80 coolies working each mine. They operated with the blessings of the Malay chiefs, albeit without proper land titles, and moved rapidly from one section of rich tin land to another, much like the itinerant gambier and pepper cultivators in Singapore.[22] Such mines were highly labour-intensive as large numbers of coolies were required to manually excavate the ore-bearing soil using nothing more than a hoe and

---

[18] Wong Lin Ken, *The Malayan Tin Industry to 1914, with Special Reference to the States of Perak, Selangor, Negri Sembilan and Pahang* (The University of Arizona Press, 1965), Appendix A, Table (a), p. 243.

[19] *The Straits Times*, 1 May 1875, 8 May 1875.

[20] *The Straits Times Weekly Issue*, 3 June 1886.

[21] This discussion of mining methods draws on Francis Loh Kok-Wah, "Early Malay Tin Mining" and "Chinese Immigration and Tin Mining", in *Early Modern History, 1800–1940, The Encyclopedia of Malaysia*, ed. Cheah Boon Kheng (Singapore: Editions Didier Millet, 2001), pp. 20–1, 72–3.

[22] Mining leases extending to 21 years and subject to a royalty payment were introduced only in 1877. Wong, *The Malayan Tin Industry*, p. 54.

shovel and then carry it in rattan baskets balanced on a wooden pole for washing in sluice boxes. The capital expenditure needed to start an open-cast mine was therefore minimal as machinery was conspicuously absent, except for the wooden chain pump driven by a water wheel. This piece of equipment brought by the Chinese miners from their native country represented a technological advance of the time as it enabled water to be removed from deeper mine pits. Reflecting these factor proportions, the average cost of producing a pikul of tin amounted to SPD19 in 1880, of which the wage cost at SPD11 was the largest component while the capital cost was less than 50 cents.[23]

In 1877, the steam pump was first used in Taiping and it quickly replaced the chain pump in most mining areas.[24] It was another technical innovation that solved the problem of mine pits being flooded during the rainy seasons, even if it was much more expensive to install and maintain.[25] This was followed by the gravel pump, perfected by European engineers at the turn of the 20th century but used mainly by better-funded Chinese mining firms.[26] Gravel pump mining mechanised almost all the production processes through the use of hydraulic elevators and monitors, allowing mines of even greater depth and without a natural water source to be exploited. This mining technique was therefore more capital-intensive than open-cast tin mining but it still required a substantial labour input.

In the last and most capital-intensive phase, the tin dredge was introduced in 1912 from New Zealand and Australia by European concerns as only they had both the technical knowledge and financial resources needed to operate these large machines. In a stratagem that was also deployed for rubber later on, they tapped the capital market in London for the funds needed in these ventures.[27] Essentially a floating factory, a tin dredge works by scooping up bucket loads of tin-bearing soil at its front end, which then passes through an oscillating drum and a system of jigs and screens to extract the mineral before spewing out the waste material at the rear end. Although the tin dredge did not displace the gravel pump in soil with irregular bedrocks, it was superior in swampy areas and could reach deep tin ore strata that the other methods could not, including ground that had been incompletely worked by the Chinese miners. Moreover, it employed far fewer workers.[28] The average operating cost of dredging was one-half that of gravel pumping, indicating a very high productivity. As a result, European-operated dredges gradually replaced the older technologies and by 1930, Western firms were producing more tin in Malaya than the Chinese-owned mines did.

---

[23] Wong, *The Malayan Tin Industry*, pp. 64–5.

[24] Lim Chong Yah, *Economic Development of Modern Malaya* (Kuala Lumpur: Oxford University Press, 1967), pp. 47, 49–50; *The Straits Times Weekly Issue*, 3 June 1886.

[25] Wong, *The Malayan Tin Industry*, p. 57.

[26] Wong Lin Ken, "Western Enterprise and the Development of the Malayan Tin Industry to 1914", in *Economic Development*, ed. Cowan, pp. 139–40.

[27] Yip, *The Development of the Tin Mining Industry*, pp. 17, 88, 140–2, 149.

[28] It was claimed that a dredge could dig and treat in one day, with the help of 90 Chinese workers under European supervision, as much tin-bearing ore as the amount excavated by 2,000 coolies in a traditional mine. Ibid., p. 134.

Since the mining methods employed in the latter half of the 19th century were labour-intensive, capital requirements were limited to the advance of funds to prospect for tin by hiring workers and equipping them with digging tools and implements. As pre-shadowed in the last chapter, this investment came from the Chinese merchants in the Straits Settlements in the form of credit extended to mine owners and advancers, who bore the immediate risks of the undertaking.[29] The loans obtained by the mine owners were expended on fixed assets while advancers supplied the working capital. In some mines, the owner (or headman) could also be the advancer. Hence, the Straits capitalists were not directly involved in production but had a lien on the tin ore produced for export.[30] Foreign companies in general and British firms in particular, including some floated in Singapore, did not manage to make inroads into the Chinese-dominated tin industry even though European entrepreneurs were well aware of the stanniferous wealth of the Malay Peninsula.[31] After the failure of the first British company in 1875 due to insufficient public support despite obtaining tin mining concessions from the Malay chiefs in Selangor, British investors were more taken up by prospects in Australia, which had by then emerged as a major tin producer.[32]

Unwittingly, colonial administrators encouraged European firms to work mines with Western machinery and management methods by offering them incentives such as the alienation of mining land and a concession on the tin export duty. However, these efforts backfired because capital-intensive techniques were tailored for lode deposits (that is, ores impregnated in rocks) and therefore not suited to the alluvial tin found in Malaya.[33] In addition, the companies misspent large sums of money on highly-paid staff and boring for tin without success; most crucial of all, they could not recruit a large enough pool of labourers.[34] Western firms did no better on the east coast of the Peninsula, in particular Pahang. Renewed interest among British investors after the extension of the Residential system to the state led to the incorporation of new companies to mine tin and gold during 1889 and 1890.[35] In the event, only one firm, the Pahang Corporation, succeeded and

[29] Yip, *The Development of the Tin Mining Industry*, pp. 89–90.

[30] K.S. Jomo, *A Question of Class: Capital, the State and Uneven Development in Malaya* (New York: Monthly Review Press, 1988), p. 161.

[31] J. van Helten and G. Jones, "British Business in Malaysia and Singapore Since the 1870s", in *British Business in Asia since 1860*, ed. R.P.T. Davenport-Hines and G. Jones (Cambridge University Press, 1989), pp. 164–5.

[32] Wong, "Western Enterprise", pp. 33–6; Drake, *Merchants, Bankers, Governors*, pp. 62–3. Between 1882 and 1897, 35 companies were registered in the United Kingdom to mine tin in Malaya. There was also an unknown number of French and Australian ventures. Almost all were unsuccessful; in 1897, only three foreign companies were operating in Perak and Selangor. Drabble, *An Economic History of Malaysia*, p. 56.

[33] Yip, *The Development of the Tin Mining Industry*, pp. 95–9, 138; *The Straits Times Weekly Issue*, 5 Jan. 1884, 30 Sept. 1889. As Wong Lin Ken put it: "[the Western firms] made the costly mistake of confusing technology and large-scale operation with economic efficiency". Wong, "Western Enterprise", p. 151.

[34] *The Straits Times Weekly Issue*, 8 Oct. 1884.

[35] Wong, "Western Enterprise", pp. 140, 141–3.

that was because it had the exclusive right and the appropriate technology to work the rich Kuantan tin lodes.[36]

In contrast to European endeavours, the system of importation of immigrant workers from China gave the Chinese miners, organised in small units or *kongsi*, an unrivalled edge through access to an almost inexhaustible supply of labour. Once in Malaya, the immigrants were inducted into secret societies, transforming them into a highly disciplined, docile and lowly-paid labour force. This mass movement of people from southern China to the Malay Peninsula was the key element that made the vastly increased production of tin feasible. Whereas the total Chinese population in the Malay states was estimated at only 15,000–20,000 in 1830, it increased to 163,000 in 1891 and nearly doubled to 300,000 in the decade to 1901.[37] In fact, these stock figures actually masked the true extent of immigration flows into the tin-rich states: it has been reckoned that between 1881 and 1900, one-and-a-half million Chinese found their way to Perak and Selangor. An overall estimate of the number engaged in tin mining is not available but in the Larut district alone, there were 20,000 to 25,000 miners in 1862, which increased to 40,000 in 1872.[38] When the tin at Larut was exhausted, the miners moved south to the Kinta district, where 45,000 miners worked 850 mines occupying an area of 10,498 acres in 1889.[39] In Selangor, there were 51,000 Chinese in 1891, most presumably tin miners.[40]

The immigrants from China landed by boat in Singapore or Penang and came either unassisted (free labour) or via the credit ticket system (indentured labour). The latter were recruited by agents sent to the Chinese countryside by coolie brokers based in the southern ports, who liaised closely with their counterparts in Singapore.[41] An indentured mine labourer had to repay the expenses incurred for his importation over a period of a year, during which time his employer had to provide daily food, a mosquito net and personal apparel, including a sun-hat.[42] He was also given an annual wage (SPD42 in 1890), about half of which was to be deducted for the cost of his passage, inclusive of the broker's profit. But like their compatriots in gambier and pepper cultivation, most new arrivals never received this wage fully, if at all, or repaid their debt because they had to purchase opium and other non-food provisions at prices marked up by as much as 200–300 per cent from the mine advancer.[43] Under this so-called "truck system" imported from England, a labourer usually ended up being bound to his employer for much longer, especially if he chalked up gambling debts. Ironically, the immigrants still preferred to work in Chinese-owned rather than European mines in spite of this blatant exploitation precisely because they had access to a regular supply of opium and gambling facilities.[44] On the part of the

---

[36] *The Straits Times Weekly Issue*, 8 Dec. 1891.

[37] Yip, *The Development of the Tin Mining Industry*, pp. 66–7, 68, 69.

[38] Blythe, "Historical Sketch", p. 65.

[39] Lim, *Economic Development of Modern Malaya*, pp. 44–5; *The Straits Times Weekly Issue*, 18 Aug. 1891.

[40] Middlebrook, Gullick and Gibson-Hill, "Yap Ah Loy", p. 8.

[41] Campbell, *Chinese Coolie Emigration*, pp. 2–3; *The Straits Times*, 11 Nov. 1876.

[42] Blythe, "Historical Sketch", p. 79.

[43] Drabble, *An Economic History of Malaysia*, p. 55.

[44] Yip, *The Development of the Tin Mining Industry*, pp. 103–4.

mine advancer or owner, the enormous profits he garnered from the provision of supplies and the gambling farm augmented the money made from the mines. These sidelines also acted as a buffer during periods when the tin price fell to below break-even levels, allowing the Chinese mines to continue in business.

The truck system was usually operated in conjunction with the "tribute system"—the most prevalent form of economic organisation of Chinese mines—which was a kind of profit-sharing arrangement whereby the mine owner or advancer spread his risks among the labourers by giving them a portion of the tin mined, according to the number of days worked and after deducting advances, etc.[45] The owner himself would receive a tribute of a fixed percentage of the tin ore recovered, depending on the richness of the deposit, but usually 10 per cent. Wage payments to workers were therefore effected through their share of the profits and also in kind through the provision of food and tools. If the mine failed, a labourer would have earned his food at least and whatever advances he took; if it prospered, he would partake in the profits. In the mid-1890s, the implicit earnings, excluding food, of a tribute worker (including a risk premium) in a relatively rich Kinta mine were 70 to 80 cents when calculated on a daily basis, whereas those of a fixed wage labourer were only 36 cents per day.[46]

The tin produced by Chinese miners, or "Straits tin" as it was called, was initially sold at a discount to Banka tin but the price gap had closed by the 1860s as the Straits product improved steadily in quality. By that time, it had superseded both Cornish and Banka tin in many uses and in the 1880s, it became the preferred source for the British and American tin plate industries, just as Australian production was nearly exhausted.[47] Malayan tin output increased exponentially from the 1870s to the mid-1890s, after which the pace of its rise slowed. Of the increase in world tin production of 46 per cent between the seventies and the eighties, Malaya accounted for nearly three-quarters.[48] By 1883, it had become the world's largest tin-producing country, with an output of 16,957 tonnes, followed by the Dutch East Indies, Australia and Britain.[49] Despite a fall in the price of tin in the first half of the nineties, Malaya's supply continued to rise from 29,333 tonnes in 1889 to 54,667 tonnes in 1895.[50]

As a staple port, Singapore gave its hinterland tin producers access to markets in the West and thereby facilitated the emerging pattern of regional specialisation in primary commodity production.[51] In return, the city's merchants imported food and manufactures to be shipped in advance to the miners and which were usually repaid in tin. These transactions were conducted at prices for both the ore and supplies that were highly advantageous to the merchants, thus yielding an inflated interest charge on the credit

---

[45] Ibid., pp. 81–2; Blythe, "Historical Sketch", pp. 105–6. Even the bed-boards and clerks' wages were charged to the workers.

[46] Wong, *The Malayan Tin Industry*, pp. 99–100.

[47] Ibid., p. 29; Wong, "Western Enterprise", pp. 130, 134.

[48] Lim, *Economic Development of Modern Malaya*, pp. 42, 43.

[49] *The Straits Times Weekly Issue*, 1 Dec. 1883.

[50] Wright and Cartwright, *Twentieth Century Impressions*, p. 212.

[51] Huff, *The Economic Growth of Singapore*, pp. 49, 51.

extended.[52] Food sourced by Chinese traders, consisting mainly of rice and salted fish, which could be viewed as the key input into staple production, was unloaded by tongkangs at the Singapore River. Manufactured goods imported by the European agency houses came in ocean-going vessels calling at New Harbour. The profits from trading in these commodities therefore constituted the final consumption linkages generated by the tin industry. By the early 1890s, Singapore was catering to the needs of 87,000 miners in the Malay states.

Compared to the demand linkages, the backward and forward linkages of the Malayan tin industry were relatively unimportant and weak, which is true of most primary production.[53] The most productive backward linkage engendered by tin was the establishment of rail and road networks and shipping routes connecting the major mining towns and districts in Malaya with Singapore. The first rail tracks were laid by the colonial administration between Taiping and Port Weld (now known as Kuala Sepetang) in 1885, followed by similar links from Kuala Lumpur to Port Swettenham (now known as Port Klang) in 1889 and from Seremban to Port Dickson in 1891, to carry tin ore on water to Singapore and deliver foodstuffs and supplies required for the tin mining industry.[54] The shipping business was dominated by a large number of Chinese companies based in the Straits Settlements and the small steamers they deployed on these routes earned the nickname of "mosquito fleet".[55] Road construction lagged, although cart tracks running from the mining centres to navigable rivers already existed when the first British Residents were appointed in Perak and Selangor.[56] After the rail lines came into being, new roads leading to the train stations were constructed; like the railways themselves, they were financed partly by loans from the Straits government.

Between 1899 and 1904, the railway branch lines were linked up by a main trunk line running from Butterworth, opposite Penang, all the way to Melaka, and farther south to Johor Bahru by 1909, a distance of nearly five hundred miles (Map 4).[57] On reaching this last station, the tin was ferried across the Straits of Johor to Singapore by boats and coasters. It was only with the establishment of the rubber industry and the construction of the Causeway that the railway was finally extended to the island in 1923 with the terminus subsequently located at the new Tanjong Pagar station in 1932. However, the first railway line built in Singapore opened in 1903, connecting Tank Road to Kranji via Bukit Timah. Following several unsuccessful attempts by private enterprise to build a railway in the late 19th century, the government stepped in to finance its construction at a cost of SPD1,967,495, although the line was sold to the FMS government in 1918.[58] The

---

52 Ibid., pp. 57–60.

53 Ibid., p. 109.

54 Wright and Cartwright, *Twentieth Century Impressions*, p. 177.

55 Huff, *The Economic Growth of Singapore*, p. 65; K.G. Tregonning, "Straits Tin: A Brief Account of the First Seventy-Five Years of The Straits Trading Company, Limited", *Journal of the Malayan Branch of the Royal Asiatic Society* 36, 1 (1963): 94; *The Straits Times Weekly Issue*, 25 Oct. 1884; *The Straits Times Annual*, 1 Jan. 1968.

56 Lim, *Economic Development of Modern Malaya*, p. 276.

57 Ibid., pp. 272–3, 276–8; *Straits Settlements Annual Report*, vol. 6, p. 186.

58 *The Land Transport of Singapore*, pp. 37, 38.

railway facilitated the movement of people and goods and it was extended to the docks at Pasir Panjang in 1906, partially replacing the cumbersome oxcart carriage traffic.[59] In the mid-1920s after the Causeway was constructed, Singapore was directly linked to all the Malayan west coast towns through a road. Together with the steamship and telegraph, the city's communications infrastructure connecting it to its economic hinterland and to the world was therefore largely completed by the early 20th century.

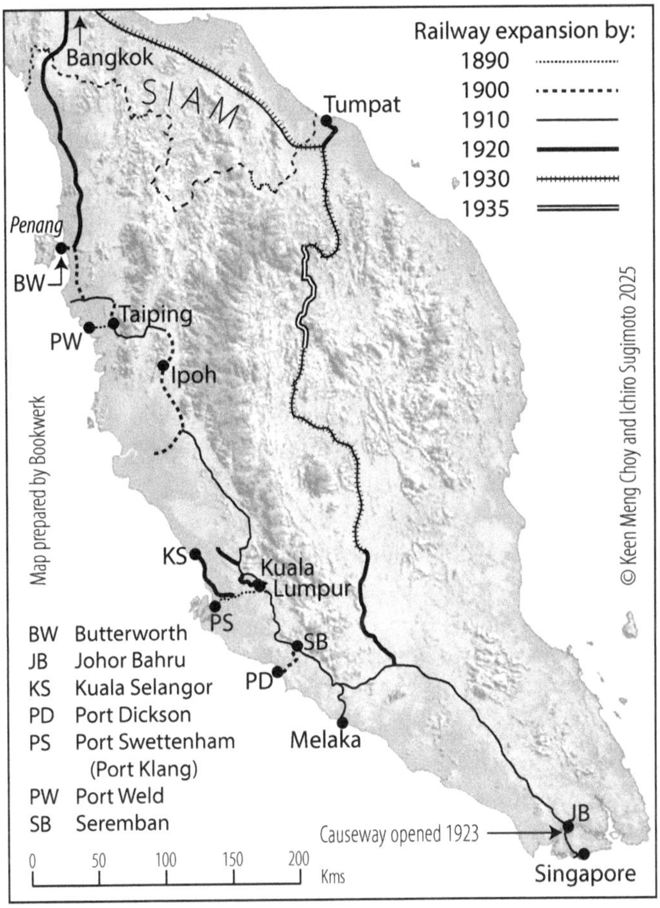

Map 4. Peninsular Malaya Railway System, 1890–1935.

Sources: Based on a Malayan rail map courtesy Wikimedia and informed by historical data from Huff, *The Economic Growth of Singapore*.

Before the mid-1880s, the sole forward linkage of the Malayan tin industry to Singapore was the marketing and export of processed tin. Through the 1850s and 1860s, the amount of slag metal sent to the port for export in return for the credit advanced by the merchants remained stagnant at about 500 tonnes, since most of the mined tin was shipped from Penang or Melaka.[60] Even when the trade took off in the 1870s, the smelting of tin ore

[59] Wright and Cartwright, *Twentieth Century Impressions*, p. 184; *Straits Settlements Annual Report*, vol. 5, p. 528; *The Straits Times Weekly Issue*, 6 Dec. 1886.

[60] Wong, *The Malayan Tin Industry*, pp. 30–1.

was still physically removed from its point of shipment, being processed *in loco* by mine owners or advancers in blast furnaces. However, there were two drawbacks to smelting in the west coast states: first, it recovered less refined metal owing to the technically inferior method adopted and second, the charcoal used as fuel was expensive and running out.[61] The smelted tin had to be further refined in the Straits ports before being exported. Given the complementarities between the smelting and exporting operations, it made more economic sense to smelt the ore in the Straits Settlements, in particular Singapore where coal was abundantly available through imports.

A major step towards this end was taken with the incorporation of the Straits Trading Company (STC) in 1887 by two European employees of merchant houses, James Sword and Herman[n] Muhlinghaus, who recognised the advantages that Singapore possessed. Along with a third partner, the two had started smelting works in Telok Anson in Perak state; when this enterprise failed, they turned to Singapore and selected a site on Pulau Brani next to Keppel Harbour, so as to obtain coal easily. In 1890, they installed a reverberatory furnace there that was capable of producing the purest quality tin, thus solving the problem of technical inefficiency that plagued the Malayan smelters.[62] By 1899, the STC smelters were producing 25,100 tonnes of tin or nearly two-thirds of Malayan output, contributing to one-third of global tin supply.[63] The company also smelted ore brought from Dutch-controlled Billiton (Belitung), an island south of Singapore, starting in 1897.[64]

Where the European companies had failed in tin extraction, the STC, due to superior technology and management, succeeded in breaking the Chinese monopoly of tin smelting. After obtaining concessions from the respective governments to export tin ore from the native states, which was previously forbidden, the company set up branches and buying stations in the Peninsula to make cash advances to and directly purchase the ore from mine owners, or through dealers.[65] Hence, it was able to cut out both the mine advancers and the Straits capitalists from the supply chain and gain a monopsony in the market. The STC also created economic linkages within Singapore by borrowing from the British banks for its circulating capital and selling the refined tin ingots to the European agency houses for export to the West. Although the diminished role of the credit-for-goods system reduced the profits of the city's merchants, they were still providing supplies to an estimated 100,000 miners at the turn of the century.

The Growth of Trade

In the 1870s, exports of refined tin from Singapore ratcheted up tenfold to more than 5,000 tonnes per annum.[66] The volume handled by the port increased further to an average

---

[61] Huff, *The Economic Growth of Singapore*, p. 60; Tregonning, "Straits Tin", p. 87.

[62] *The Straits Times Weekly Issue*, 12 Nov. 1890.

[63] Huff, *The Economic Growth of Singapore*, p. 62.

[64] Tregonning, "Straits Tin", pp. 98–9.

[65] Ibid., p. 97; Huff, *The Economic Growth of Singapore*, pp. 61–2; G.C. Allen and A.G. Donnithorne, *Western Enterprise in Indonesia and Malaya: A Study in Economic Development* (London: George Allen and Unwin, 1957), p. 161; *The Straits Times Weekly Issue*, 7 June 1892, 7 Sept. 1892.

[66] Huff, *The Economic Growth of Singapore*, Table A.2, p. 378.

of 10,491 tonnes each year in the eighties and 26,980 tonnes during the nineties. The outstanding success of the STC from 1890 meant that refined tin was increasingly exported from Singapore rather than the other two ports in the Straits Settlements.[67] Before a plant was opened there in 1897, Penang also re-exported tin ore to Singapore for smelting. At the end of the 19th century, the city's staple port had become the world's largest tin exporter. By then, the metal had grown to account for 20 per cent of the total value of exports, compared to just about 6 per cent in 1875.[68]

The principal markets for Straits tin shipped from Singapore and the other Settlements ports were few in number (Figure 10).[69] Prior to 1850, the large Asian economies of China and India absorbed most of the Malay Peninsula's output; in 1836 for instance, Singapore exported SPD117,386 worth of tin to China.[70] Thereafter, most of the trade flowed towards the Western industrial nations. Up to 1894, Britain was the largest market due to its position as the world's biggest tin plate producer and its share of Straits tin exports never fell below 40 per cent. During the late 1890s, it was briefly overtaken by the United States due to the higher demand for tin resulting from the implementation of a tariff policy, aimed at the protection of the nation's fledgling tin plate industry.[71] Apart from these two major markets, the European countries imported smaller quantities of tin from Malaya via Singapore. In comparison, the share of Asian countries fell to 10 per cent or less after the 1880s.

The rising trend in tin consignments was matched by an equally impressive increase in rice re-exports, from 65,870 tonnes in 1875 to 244,925 tonnes in 1899.[72] In the latter year, rice made up nearly a tenth of the value of merchandise exports. Located right at the centre of Southeast Asia, Singapore was the linchpin of the rice trade, serving as the intermediary between producers and consumers both inside and outside the region.[73] Fish exports increased from 56,014 pikuls to 727,489 pikuls, though its share in export value was still small at 3.5 per cent in 1900.[74] Rice was sourced mainly from Siam (51.5 per cent) and Burma (28.4 per cent) while salted and dried fish was imported from Siam (26.8 per cent) and Cochin-China (43.5 per cent).[75] These foodstuffs were largely re-exported to Malaya (55.2 per cent of rice) and the Dutch East Indies (76.1 per cent of fish).

---

67 *The Straits Times Weekly Issue*, 10 Aug.1892.

68 Huff, *The Economic Growth of Singapore*, Table A.1, p. 372.

69 The export destination data are from Wong, *The Malayan Tin Industry*, pp. 12, 212. Missing data for the period 1859–63 are linearly interpolated. Separate figures for shipments from Singapore are not available.

70 Wong, "Western Enterprise", p. 130; Khoo, *Western Malay States*, p. 56.

71 *The Straits Times Weekly Issue*, 7 July 1891.

72 Huff, *The Economic Growth of Singapore*, Table A.2, p. 378.

73 P.A. Coclanis, "Southeast Asia's Incorporation into the World Rice Market: A Revisionist View", *Journal of Southeast Asian Studies* 24, 2 (1993): 265–6.

74 Chiang, *History of Straits Settlements Foreign Trade*, Statistical Appendix XII, pp. 198, 200–1, 205.

75 Huff, *The Economic Growth of Singapore*, p. 55. Cochin-China hereafter refers to the region known as Indochina, after Siam ceded Laos to France in 1893.

In addition, opium was purchased from India while cotton piece goods came mainly from Britain; these were mostly sold to Singapore's immediate neighbours, Malaya and the Dutch East Indies (about one-fifth each for opium) and Siam (about one third of cotton goods). Another one-third of opium imports was sent to Hong Kong and China. Both of these trades exhibited tendencies in accordance with Engel's Law of Consumption.[76] As the region's incomes grew, it did not buy more clothing from, or through, Singapore: the quantity exported stagnated at about 2.6 million pieces in part because direct imports from Britain were on the rise. Similarly, the amount of opium shipped out rose by only 2,849 chests in the last quarter of the 19th century, notwithstanding the substantial increase in the tin mining population in Malaya. While the drug made up 13.5 per cent of Singapore's exports in 1875, this proportion fell to only about 4.7 per cent in 1900.[77] In this case, there were extraneous reasons for the relatively small rise, which were declining supply from India, opium price increases and direct exports to consumers.

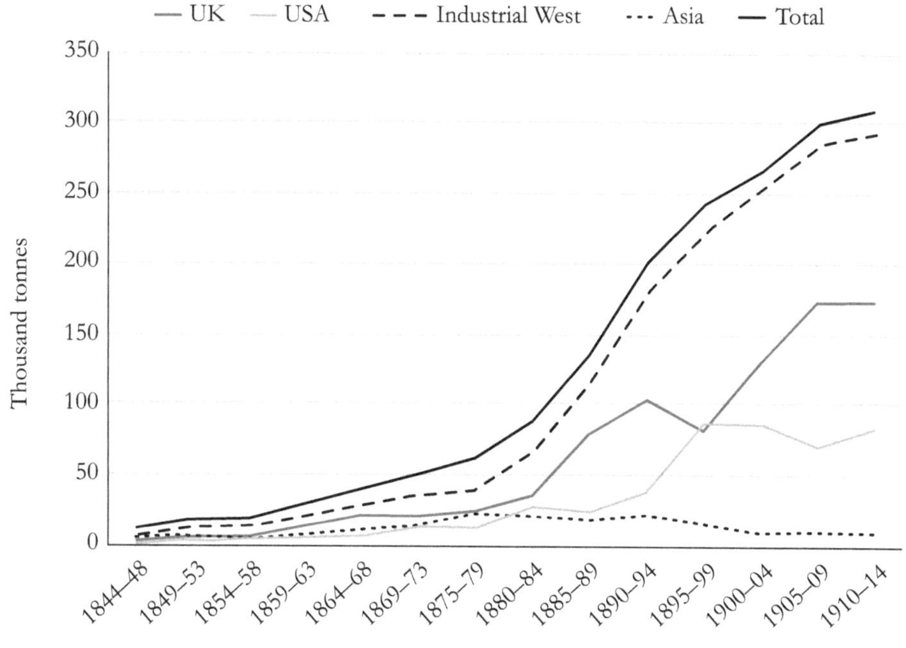

Figure 10. Malayan Tin Exports, 1844–1914
Source: Wong, *The Malayan Tin Industry*, pp. 12, 212.

Even as Singapore transformed itself into a staple port, the trade in Straits produce continued to grow as a result of rapidly rising demand from Continental Europe and the United States.[78] A portion of this new demand was due to Britain relinquishing its depot status of re-exporting produce to these countries.[79] The export value of 16 important

---

[76] The law states that as household income increases, the proportion spent on food and other basic necessities declines, even if the total amount spent on them increases.

[77] Chiang, *History of Straits Settlements Foreign Trade*, Statistical Appendix XII, pp. 118, 200, 201.

[78] *The Straits Times Weekly Issue*, 10 Sept. 1890.

[79] Chiang, *History of Straits Settlements Foreign Trade*, pp. 104–5.

tropical commodities increased from SPD10.7 million in 1875 to SPD48.7 million in 1899 and contributed nearly 30 per cent of export earnings in the later year.[80] Of these, the most important were gutta percha, rattan, gambier and pepper, sourced from the Dutch East Indies, Malaya and British Borneo.[81] Gutta percha exports alone shot up from SPD377,400 in 1875 to SPD11.6 million in 1899 while rattan exports went up from SPD548,607 to SPD4.37 million.[82] Imports from the East Indies in particular, including tobacco from Deli (Medan) in Sumatra, rose significantly due to the more liberal policies of the Dutch government.[83] The export side of the entrepôt trade was almost exclusively handled by the European merchants: in 1897, there were 20 European import-export firms (inclusive of agency houses) engaged in this business, as well as in the export of tin, and they had tripled in number a decade later.[84] The import side of the Straits produce trade continued to be the turf of Chinese traders, described as "an inexorable army of commercial travellers who probed, pushed and penetrated everywhere, collecting produce in exchange for food and manufactured goods".[85] The sundry list of goods supplied by the traders included items such as rice, salted fish, sugar, biscuits, matches and cotton goods.[86]

The trade credit system developed in the earlier years continued to function, with the Europeans obtaining loans from the banks and using them to finance Chinese wholesalers and retailers. However, learning from these businesses' long history of defaults, the British houses imposed shorter durations on the credit extended and more stringent terms than those of the European firms.[87] The maturity period of the loans also varied according to product: Straits produce one week; sugar and rice one month; hardware three months; and textiles four to six months.[88] By 1870 however, the practice of bartering products was on the decline, replaced by the direct conveyance of commodities to Singapore by native producers in coasting vessels and the sale of goods to them through agents located across the Archipelago.[89] Yet the problem of Chinese bankruptcies persisted. Following the introduction of the insolvency law in 1848, imprisonment for indebtedness was abolished in 1870 although bankrupts were not allowed to leave Singapore.[90] Again, the

---

80 Huff, *The Economic Growth of Singapore*, Table A.2, pp. 372–3. The 16 commodities were areca nuts, Borneo rubber, coffee, copra, coconut oil, gambier, groundnuts, gum, gutta percha, illipe nuts, nutmeg, pepper, rattan, sago, tapioca and tobacco.

81 Chiang, *History of Straits Settlements Foreign Trade*, Statistical Appendix XII, pp. 199, 203, 204. Gutta percha was used as insulation for electric cables and waterproof coating for submarine cables.

82 These statistics are extracted from the price currents published in *The Singapore Free Press and Mercantile Advertiser* (courtesy of Atsushi Kobayashi).

83 Wong, "Singapore: Its Growth", p. 62; *The Straits Times Weekly Issue*, 4 Feb. 1890, 24 Sept. 1890.

84 Chiang, *History of Straits Settlements Foreign Trade*, p. 47.

85 Ibid., p. 53.

86 *The Singapore Free Press and Mercantile Advertiser*, 8 Oct. 1935.

87 Chiang, *History of Straits Settlements Foreign Trade*, p. 42.

88 Cheng Lim-Keak, *Social Change and the Chinese in Singapore* (Singapore: Singapore University Press, 1985), p. 60.

89 Chiang, *History of Straits Settlements Foreign Trade*, pp. 51–2, 53–8.

90 *Proceedings of the Legislative Council of the Straits Settlements*, 30 Aug. 1870, 1 Dec. 1870. Imprisonment of debtors was reinstituted in 1896.

effect of the law was perverse, resulting in more and not fewer fraudulent practices—the Chinese devised ingenious means of evading bankruptcy by, for instance, falsifying accounts and trading in other people's names.[91] This last practice was especially vexatious because the European merchants could not ascertain the partners of a Chinese firm to which it granted credit. As a remedy, compulsory registration of firms, with the requirement for the details of partners, was proposed in 1888 but such a move never became law due to the opposition of Chinese and some European merchants, and so the issue lingered on into the early 20th century.[92]

To summarise the discussion so far, the major commodities that accounted for the bulk of Singapore's trade can be regrouped into those that entered into the East-to-West, West-to-East and intra-Asian merchandise flows.[93] Under this classification, the products categorised in the East-to-West flow are tin and the more important Straits produce, those in the West-to-East channel are cotton piece goods, and those exchanged in the intra-Asian trade are foodstuffs and opium. The movement of these goods from origin to destination, as described above, determined the geographical distribution of Singapore's key trading partners. A notable feature of the distribution is that Southeast Asia became the staple port's dominant trading region in the late 19th century, with a share of 45 per cent in 1873 and 51 per cent in 1899.[94] This development coincided with a period of rapid growth in intra-Asian trade.[95] Britain, Europe and North America contributed 29 per cent in the earlier year and 33 per cent in the later year. In contrast, China (including Hong Kong) and India, which had been important trade partners in the earlier era with a combined share of 26 per cent in 1873, accounted only for 20 per cent of Singapore's overall trade in 1899 (Table 9).

Within Southeast Asia, the share of Malaya in both imports and exports rose significantly from the mid-1870s owing to tin and its linkages, reaching 15.6 per cent and 10.2 per cent respectively in 1899.[96] The same is true of Siam where an absence of discriminatory or protective tariffs raised Singapore's export share to 8.4 per cent due to cotton goods and its import share to 8 per cent on account of rice. These figures represented 42 per cent and 37 per cent of Siam's import and export trade in 1899, respectively.[97] In sharp contrast, trade with Cochin-China continued to be curtailed by French commercial policies. In 1887, the general tariff of France was applied to Cochin-China, covering products ranging from clothing and machinery to matches, in order to disadvantage the British and German firms trading in the country.[98] This action had the

---

[91] *The Straits Times Weekly Issue*, 9 Jan. 1886, 11 Mar. 1890.

[92] Darbishire, "Commerce and Currency", pp. 41–2; *Proceedings of the Legislative Council of the Straits Settlements*, 1 Nov. 1905.

[93] This classification was used in Chiang, *History of Straits Settlements Foreign Trade*, pp. 84, 109, 112, 119–21. It corresponds broadly to the one in Chapters 2 and 4.

[94] Huff, *The Economic Growth of Singapore*, pp. 50, 52.

[95] H. Shimizu and H. Hirakawa, *Japan and Singapore in the World Economy: Japan's Economic Advance into Singapore, 1870–1965* (Routledge, 1999), p. 51.

[96] Huff, *The Economic Growth of Singapore*, pp. 50, 52; *The Straits Times Weekly Issue*, 10 Sept. 1890.

[97] Wong, "Singapore: Its Growth", p. 66.

[98] *The Straits Times Weekly Issue*, 24 Aug. 1887, 7 Sept. 1887.

effect of depressing trade with Singapore. With the further imposition of another tariff on exports from British colonies in 1892, cotton goods shipments plummeted from 517,905 pieces in that year to 132,720 pieces in the following year.[99] As a result, Cochin-China's share of Singapore's exports declined to only 1.8 per cent in 1899 and the city had to turn to Siam again for imports of rice and salted fish.[100] China's and Hong Kong's combined proportion of exports also fell to 8.9 per cent, although their import share was stable because of the rising demand for their goods from the increasing number of Chinese in the region. Continental Europe and the United States absorbed 12.5 per cent and 10.9 per cent of exports in 1899 while Britain's share dropped to 13.2 per cent. Overall, Singapore's trade with Southeast Asia was more or less balanced by century's end. It ran a trade surplus with the West, which was counterbalanced by a deficit with China, India and the rest of the world.

Table 9. Geographical Distribution of Singapore's Trade, 1873 and 1899

	Imports (%)			Exports (%)	
	1873	**1899**		**1873**	**1899**
Southeast Asia	43.1	52.6		48.0	49.0
Malay Peninsula	6.0	15.6		4.5	10.2
Dutch East India	15.2	16.4		20.5	20.6
British Borneo	1.0	1.7		1.4	1.5
Siam	4.5	8.0		6.5	8.4
Cochin-China	1.4	3.8		2.7	1.8
Burma	2.7	3.5		1.3	2.0
Others	12.3	3.6		11.1	4.5
The West	27.4	19.9		30.8	38.1
Britain	23.6	12.2		20.4	13.2
Europe	3.7	4.7		1.6	12.5
United States	0.1	0.4		8.8	10.9
Rest of the World	29.5	27.5		21.2	12.9
China (includes Hong Kong)	11.8	11.4		12.6	8.9
India	13.8	14.9		2.2	2.7
Others	3.9	1.2		6.4	1.3

Source: Huff, *The Economic Growth of Singapore*, pp. 50, 52.

Over the period from 1875 to 1899, the pace of increase in Singapore's overall trade accelerated compared to the early colonial period, to 6.3 per cent per annum on a compound basis. At the end of the century, total trade had increased to SPD185,393,199 and the amount of cargo and bunkers lifted by the port was unsurpassed in the Far East.[101]

[99] Chiang, *History of Straits Settlements Foreign Trade*, p. 98.

[100] Huff, *The Economic Growth of Singapore*, p. 52; Darbishire, "Commerce and Currency", pp. 40–1.

[101] *Straits Settlements Blue Book*, 1899, pp. U4–U5; Ross, *The Capital of a Little Empire*, p. 54.

A decomposition of the contributions to the yearly growth of total exports (Figure 11) shows that the major tropical commodities accounted for most of the gains observed, except in the second half of the 1880s when tin dominated and there was a large swing in other products. As in the earlier era, trade gyrations continued to recur every few years and they tended to be synchronised across commodities; in particular, the movements in Straits produce and foodstuffs were highly correlated. Peaks in export growth occurred in 1879, 1883, 1887 and 1894, and two troughs were recorded in 1885 and 1890. The recessionary episodes corresponded to periods when the prices of tin and Straits produce fell or there was a general depression in world trade.[102] This notwithstanding, the terms of trade for Singapore did not deteriorate and in fact improved slightly, since export and import prices tended to move in the same direction as a result of the city's entrepôt role.

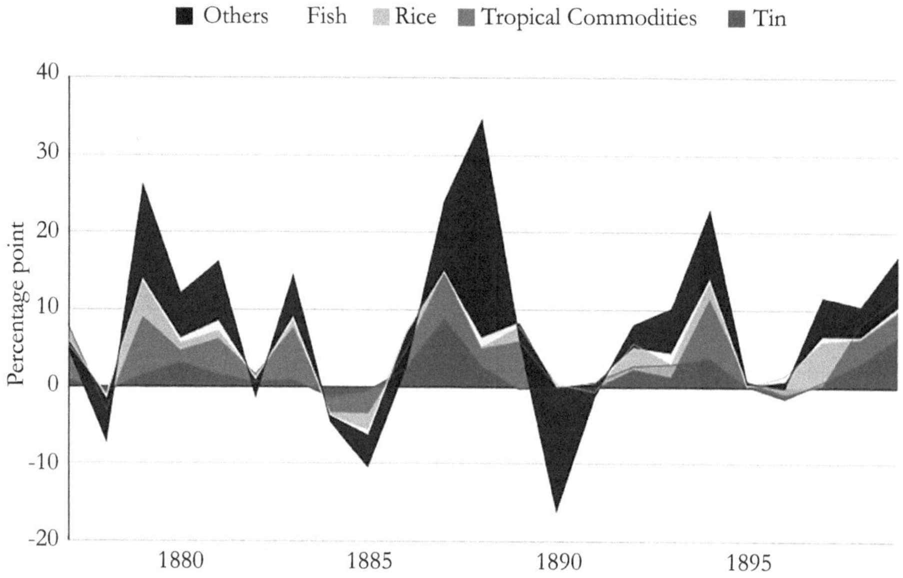

Figure 11. Decomposition of Singapore's Export Growth, 1875–99
Source: Huff, *The Economic Growth of Singapore*, Table A.1, pp. 372–3, Table A.2, pp. 378, 380 and authors' calculations.

A further comparison in real terms indicates that Singapore's trade performance surpassed the world's in the last 30 years of the 19th century, a period coinciding with trade globalisation.[103] World exports expanded at a rate of 2.9 per cent, lower than in Singapore.[104] Real merchandise exports from Singapore grew at an average annual rate of 5 per cent during 1870–1900, although this was slower than the increase in nominal terms due

[102] *Straits Settlements Annual Report*, vol. 3, p. 598, vol. 4, p. 304.

[103] The comparison has to be made in real terms to abstract from the use of different currencies, by converting Singapore's trade value in silver dollars into pounds sterling using prevailing exchange rates and deflating with the Sauerbeck-Statist price index. Huff, *The Economic Growth of Singapore*, p. 44.

[104] World trade data are obtained from the online appendix in G. Federico and A. Tena-Junguito, "World Trade, 1800–1938: A New Synthesis", *Revista de Historia Económica* 37, 1 (2019).

to the depreciation of the silver dollar as countries moved to the gold standard and silver production increased.[105] The city's outperformance can be attributed to several factors. First, the improvements in transport and communications benefitted Singapore disproportionately because of its location and excellent port infrastructure. They also resulted in an expansion of global markets and supply sources through increased shipping and telegraphic connections with ports in both East and West.[106] Second, the surge in tin exports and, concomitantly, the city's rise as a staple port provided a boost to trade that was not present in the entrepôt era, even while it continued to be a provider of commercial, warehousing and financial services to Southeast Asia and a distribution centre for goods. Third, Singapore became a crucial link in the growing interdependence between the industrial West and the primary exporting economies of Southeast Asia, where the extension of colonial rule brought political stability.[107]

Immigration, Population and Labour Force

One phenomenon implied by the staple growth hypothesis and amply borne out by the economic development of Malaya and Singapore was that of the massive waves of immigration that took place in the late 19th century. Labourers from China were needed so that the mineral resources of the sparsely populated native states could be exploited. Just as Singapore and Penang supplied the capital for tin mines, their ports were also the entry points for the influx of labour. Apart from the mines of Malaya, the coolies were headed for the coffee plantations of Sumatra and the tobacco estates of Borneo, but strong economic growth and the attendant need for labour led to a considerable number remaining in the two cities. The peopling of Singapore was therefore largely an outcome of these decades and the influx changed the demographic character of the city permanently. By 1891, Singapore had become a Chinese city, with nearly two-thirds of its population being of Peranakan origin or hailing from China.[108] As we will see, this preponderance of Chinese was to have far-reaching political consequences in the century that followed.

The system of importation of labour from China has been dealt with at length earlier and it had hardly altered since the first Chinese immigrants landed on Singapore's shore.[109] Suffice it to say that as the voyage down the South China Sea was now effected by steamers and chartered vessels, immigrants arrived at all times of the year and not just during the monsoon season.[110] Furthermore, conditions aboard ships improved compared to the days of sailing vessels and the passage and partial enforcement of a second Chinese Immigration Ordinance in 1877 helped to check the most egregious abuses of the system.[111] This

105 Chiang, *History of Straits Settlements Foreign Trade*, pp. 146, 148; Kobayashi, "Price Fluctuations", pp. 117–8; *The Straits Times*, 11 Mar. 1876, 28 Oct. 1876.

106 *The Straits Times Weekly Issue*, 10 Sept. 1890.

107 Wong, "Commercial Growth", pp. 50–2.

108 Marriott, "The Peoples of Singapore", p. 359; Savage, *Lion City Narratives*, p. 191.

109 Blythe, "Historical Sketch", pp. 68–74.

110 *The Straits Times*, 26 Oct. 1878.

111 Campbell, *Chinese Coolie Emigration*, pp. 10–12; *Straits Settlements Annual Report*, vol. 2, p. 320; *The Straits Times*, 29 Sept. 1877, 10 Apr. 1880.

law was revised in 1880 to incorporate improvements, most notably the establishment of government depots for the examination of immigrants on arrival.[112] In any event, the credit ticket system began to lose its importance from that decade on.[113] In 1887 when immigration hit a high, four out of five Chinese labourers arriving in Singapore were classified as "paid passengers", that is, they came unassisted or had their passage paid in advance; in 1895 when immigration peaked, the ratio was nine in ten.[114] Later still, the recruitment system shifted to one whereby employers in Malaya and Sumatra sent private agents to directly obtain workers from China, who were often relatives or fellow villagers.[115] Even so, the debt bondage inflicted by the credit ticket system was only legally abolished in 1914; the complementary truck system came to an earlier end, in 1908.[116]

Notwithstanding the progress made in improving the conditions of immigration, there were still blots on the system.[117] While being detained in the city's private lodging houses waiting to be selected by a prospective employer, some of the unpaid passengers were coerced to enter into contracts against their will by the depot-keepers, usually for less preferable work in Sumatra even though the terms were more attractive and included a cash advance.[118] Consequently, an official commission was appointed in 1890 to enquire into the state of labour in the Straits Settlements and FMS, and to propose solutions to the shortage of plantation labour in these places and British North Borneo.[119] Its key recommendation was to abolish the private lodging houses and the rapacious middlemen in the credit ticket system and replace them with government-run depots in Hong Kong and Swatow, the main ports of embarkation in China, as well as in Singapore. But the Protector of Chinese who succeeded William Pickering demurred to the proposal on the grounds that government lodging houses would be more costly to operate and at any rate, unlicensed depots would spring up.[120] Since the key objective of the commission was to encourage immigration and increase the supply of labour, the government in 1896 decided to fall back on licensing and regulating private lodging houses.[121]

The immigrants arriving in Singapore during the final decades of the 19th century can be divided into three streams and two distinct waves. The stream from China was overwhelming, that from India was much less numerous and migrants from the Malay Archipelago were comparatively negligible. In the 1880s and 1890s, annual immigrant arrivals from India to the Straits Settlements, who mostly landed in Penang, hovered at

---

[112] *Proceedings of the Legislative Council of the Straits Settlements*, 8 June 1880, 15 June 1880, 18 June 1880, 6 July 1880; *The Straits Times*, 29 May 1880.

[113] *The Straits Times Weekly Issue*, 26 Apr. 1884.

[114] Yip, *The Development of the Tin Mining Industry*, pp. 69–71, 77; Lee, *The British as Rulers*, p. 81.

[115] *The Straits Times Weekly Issue*, 23 May 1889.

[116] Jomo, *A Question of Class*, pp. 168–70; Wong, *The Malayan Tin Industry*, pp. 66–7.

[117] Joyce Ee, "Chinese Migration to Singapore, 1896–1941", *Journal of Southeast Asian History* 2, 1 (1961): 39–40.

[118] Blythe, "Historical Sketch", pp. 78–80, 83–4, 88.

[119] *The Straits Times Weekly Issue*, 8 Oct. 1890, 12 May 1891.

[120] Campbell, *Chinese Coolie Emigration*, pp. 16–18.

[121] *Straits Settlements Annual Report*, vol. 4, p. 318. In 1900, there were 46 such lodging houses, each holding up to 150 men. Huff, *The Economic Growth of Singapore*, p. 156.

10,000 to 20,000.[122] In contrast, coolies from China had increased steadily since the early seventies until the two waves of immigration were set in motion by a rise in the price of tin and a corresponding supply response in the Malayan mines (Figure 12).[123] The first occurred in the late eighties with the influx of labourers crossing the 100,000 mark in 1887 and the second crested when a record 150,000 immigrants came in 1895.[124] Thereafter, the influx ebbed as the tin price fell to a low of £60 per tonne in 1896 and direct immigration from China to Sumatra was established.[125]

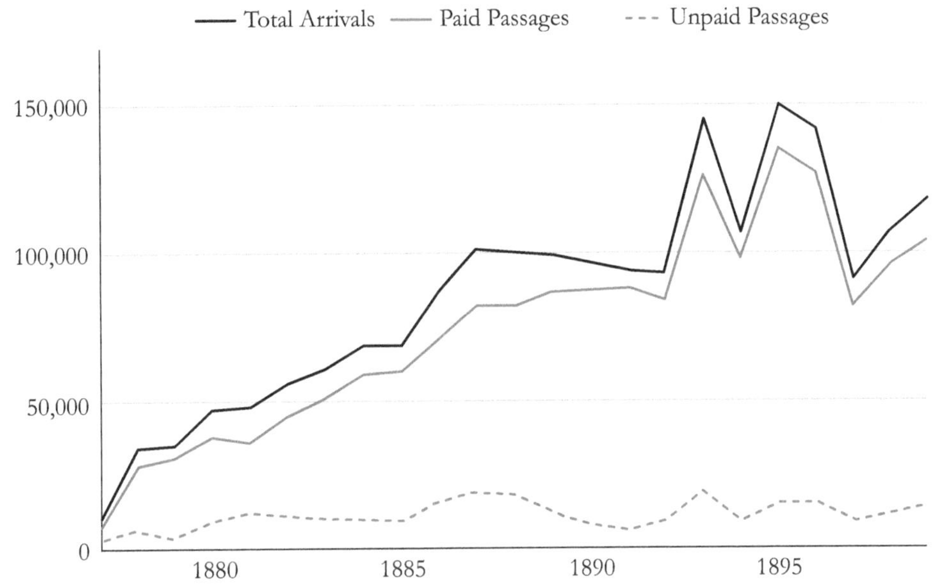

Figure 12. Immigration from China to Singapore, 1877–99
Source: Yip, *The Development of the Tin Mining Industry*, pp. 68, 70.

Of course, the large majority of immigrants landing in Singapore merely passed through the city into the Malay Peninsula, Penang, Melaka or the Dutch East Indies and there were also large numbers who returned to China every year.[126] Statistics on both flows are spotty, with the available data showing that returnees were much fewer in number compared to arrivals in the 1890s. The decennial population censuses of 1881, 1891 and 1901 revealed that net migration was positive over this period, rising from 74,798 in the eighties to 88,522 in the nineties.[127] These gains were the decisive factor behind the huge increase in Singapore's population, even though there was a natural reduction of 30,932 and 42,542 in these two decades respectively as deaths exceeded births by a large margin. In 1878, the crude birth rate was only 5 per 1,000 of the population and

122 Rai, *Indians in Singapore*, p. 74.

123 *The Straits Times*, 18 Nov. 1876.

124 Yip, *The Development of the Tin Mining Industry*, pp. 68, 70.

125 *The Straits Times Weekly Issue*, 29 Apr. 1890.

126 *The Straits Times Weekly Issue*, 20 Feb.1886.

127 Saw, *Population of Singapore*, pp. 11, 32.

the death rate was six times higher at 30 per 1,000 of population.[128] A decade later, the birth rate improved to 20 per 1,000 of population but this was still low since the number of indigenous inhabitants remained relatively small, almost all the immigrants in the city were single, and the sex ratio was lopsided, with three males for every female.[129] On the other hand, the death rate went up to 43 per 1,000 people due to diseases such as malaria, cholera, dysentery and beri-beri.[130]

Following the two waves of immigration, Singapore's population swelled to 184,554 in 1891 and 228,555 in 1901, implying an annual average growth rate between those two years of 3.6 per cent—high by historical standards.[131] The proportion of Chinese rose from 66 per cent to 72 per cent while Indians saw a fall in their representation even though their absolute number increased slightly. The ratio of Malays also went down from 20 per cent to 16 per cent. The definition of the Malay category used in the population census included migrants from the Archipelago such as Javanese, Boyanese, Acehnese and Bugis, who tended to be married couples with families or permanent settlers. In 1901, slightly over half of the Malay population in Singapore originated from various parts of the region.[132] Most lived in the outskirts, driven out of the city by rising property values. As for the wealthy Arab families who had long settled in the town, a few were active in the pilgrimage business that conveyed Muslims from all over the region to Mecca, a lucrative undertaking as can be gauged from the fact that 14,000 pilgrims passed through Singapore in 1900.[133] These Arab families not only acted as pilgrim brokers arranging tickets but also were owners of steamships.[134]

The polyglot mix of races that had populated Singapore in the early days, with their different social, cultural and religious practices, was still present, including Eurasians, Siamese, Armenians, Parsis and Jews, the last group owning many commercial and residential properties.[135] In a reflection of the prosperity of the times, Europeans doubled in number between 1881 and 1901, to a shade below 3,000. The community would be closer to 4,000 people if the floating population of traders, sailors and military personnel were added. British merchants who had made their fortunes in Singapore were also owners of property in land and houses, constituting a wealthy gentry.[136] The other Europeans in

---

128 *Straits Settlements Annual Report*, vol. 2, pp. 382–3. It was noted that both rates were likely to be understated due to deficiencies in the system of registration, which were only remedied in the late 1890s. *Straits Settlements Annual Report*, vol. 4, pp. 308, 318.

129 "Annual Report on the Registration of Births and Deaths in the Straits Settlements, for the Year 1888", in *Straits Settlements, Annual Reports for the Year 1888*, p. 123; *The Straits Times Weekly Issue*, 14 Feb. 1887.

130 "Annual Report on the Registration of Births and Deaths in the Straits Settlements, for the Year 1888", "Annual Medical Report on the Civil Hospitals of the Straits Settlements, for the Year 1888", in *Straits Settlements, Annual Reports for the Year 1888*, pp. 90, 124.

131 Marriott, "The Peoples of Singapore", p. 359; Huff, *The Economic Growth of Singapore*, pp. 150, 161, 166–7.

132 Kwa, Heng, Borschberg and Tan, *Seven Hundred Years*, p. 207.

133 Tan, "The Indian Ocean", p. 22.

134 Lee, *The British as Rulers*, pp. 165–6.

135 Kwa, Heng, Borschberg and Tan, *Seven Hundred Years*, pp. 210, 211; Marriott, "The Peoples of Singapore", p. 359.

136 Hussin, *Trade and Society in the Straits of Melaka*, pp. 273, 275.

the city led a comfortable or even lavish lifestyle, served by domestic servants.[137] Amongst them, the "Germans and Swiss take kindly to Singapore, and thrive apace ... [but] neither the Americans nor the French can make any headway".[138]

Like the Europeans, the established Chinese towkays in Singapore lived in luxury. They typically owned shops and warehouses in town and stayed in "large houses surrounded by high walls...where they eat the best of food".[139] The new Chinese sojourners to the island on the other hand mostly lived in penury, with many of them crowded into Chinatown. By the late 19th century, their dialect group affiliations had altered as a result of changing geographical patterns of emigration. However, the bangs' specialisation in economic activities persisted, as did their seclusion from each other: they "worshipped different deities in separate temples, laid their dead in different burial grounds, and attended different schools".[140] In 1891, the Hokkiens had become the most numerous group, forming 38 per cent of the Chinese sub-population and taking over the lead from the Teochews earlier in the century, whose proportion had fallen to 19 per cent.[141] The Cantonese constituted another 19 per cent whereas the Hakkas and Hainanese with ratios of 6 per cent and 7 per cent respectively retained their minority status. Immigration also brought new dialect groups into Singapore, notably the Hockchiu and Henghua from Fukien province.

Singapore's labour force in the late 19th century was the result of the mutually interacting forces of emigration and commercial growth, or "push" and "pull" factors.[142] In addition to push factors such as war, natural calamities, poverty and overpopulation in China, immigrants poured into Singapore because they were attracted by the prospect of earning a higher wage or starting a business.[143] The growth of the city and its bright lights drew more Chinese coolies to it, who in turn stimulated further expansion. Given this and an effective 100 per cent participation rate of foreign workers, the labour supply was a function of increasing population size. Nonetheless, this burgeoning labour force did not fully match the varied demand for workers due to a general lack of skills and because the different races remained compartmentalised in the allocation of the jobs available. The labour market segmentation that resulted was most evident in the commercial and civil sectors, but less so in the others.

A comprehensive listing of the occupations found in Singapore as reported in the census of 1881 will demonstrate the point.[144] Compared to the somewhat rudimentary list enumerated for the Chinese in 1848 (Table 5), the vocations available a third of a century later look distinctly modern (Table 10). Indeed, except for a few professions that were created later as a result of new inventions such as drivers, electricians, mechanics

---

137 Turnbull, *History of Modern Singapore*, pp. 125–6.

138 Ross, *The Capital of a Little Empire*, p. 69.

139 Savage, *Lion City Narratives*, p. 278.

140 Turnbull, *History of Modern Singapore*, p. 115.

141 Marriott, "The Peoples of Singapore", p. 362.

142 Frost and Balasingamchow, *Singapore*, pp. 150–1.

143 Huff, *The Economic Growth of Singapore*, pp. 151–2, 176; Ee, "Chinese Migration to Singapore", pp. 33–5.

144 *Census of the Straits Settlements 1881*, Singapore.

and telephone operators, the types of jobs available in the late 19th century were the same as those in the early 20th century.[145] There was now a thriving class of professionals who provided the full range of value-added services required of a staple port and they were invariably Europeans, especially British. Thus, the rise in the European population primarily reflected the proliferation of bankers, insurers, shipping agents, brokers, lawyers, accountants and managers. In 1881, there were more engineers, architects and surveyors working in the city, most of them also members of the European community. British residents staffed the growing civil and military establishments: in 1891, the number of positions at all echelons totalled no less than 500 and included new appointments such as treasurers, auditors, translators and marine officers.[146] The number of educators and medical officers also increased substantially.

Few natives were actively engaged in the internationalised commercial sector of the economy.[147] The numerous Chinese traders and wholesalers who conducted the entrepôt trade of the region, the labourers who toiled in the harbour and godowns as well as the Chettiars and money changers were at best on the periphery of this sector. Conversely, the British and Europeans, naturally enough, shunned domestically oriented occupations such as butchering, breeding/selling poultry, fishmongering, shopkeeping, pawnbroking and the upkeep of eating houses, which were dominated by the Chinese. A large number of Malays and Chinese could also be found in the agricultural sector—including over a thousand who were classified as padi planters—while a small number of Indians were general labourers in this sector. Occupations classified as industrial that subsumed artisans, craftsmen and makers of simple manufactured products like bricks, footwear, umbrellas, sago, confections and coffins, were also filled mostly by the Chinese.

The rest of Singapore's Chinese workers were engaged mostly in the personal service industries, putting aside a very small fraction in construction. They included barbers, tailors, water carriers, opium shop and lodging house keepers, opera troupe actors and actresses as well as funeral undertakers. However, information gleaned from the formation of occupational guilds indicates that dialect group involution was still apparent.[148] The Hokkiens continued to be prominent in trading and shopkeeping, though with the growth of the economy, they diversified into shipping and light industry. The Teochews maintained their grip on the import and re-export of Straits produce, rice, preserved and fresh fish and also ventured into the trade in vegetables, fruits and piece goods.[149] Male Cantonese and Hakka immigrants were mostly artisans and labourers as before, though some expanded into the restaurant and medicinal shop businesses.

To the extent that they were found in Singapore, female Cantonese were stereotyped as prostitutes and it was reported that there were a few thousand of them in the Chinatown area during the late 19th century.[150] In the 1870s, it was estimated that four out of five women who came to the city from China were sold into the prostitution trade and in 1877,

[145] Huff, *The Economic Growth of Singapore*, pp. 176–7.

[146] *Straits Settlements Blue Book*, 1891, pp. L15–L51.

[147] Huff, *The Economic Growth of Singapore*, p. 177.

[148] Mak Lau-Fong and Him M. Lai, "Occupational Structures of Chinese Immigrants in Early Malaya and North America", *Southeast Asian Journal of Social Science* 20, 1 (1992): 49, 50, 51, 55–7.

[149] Huff, *The Economic Growth of Singapore*, pp. 178–9.

[150] *Straits Times Weekly Issue*, 9 May 1893; *Pinang Gazette and Straits Chronicle*, 23 May 1894.

Table 10. Singapore Occupations, 1881

Professional	Poulterer	Gunsmith/Locksmith
Actor/Artist/Musician	Rice Merchant	Harness Maker/Saddler
Auctioneer	Rice Mill Owner	Jeweller/Goldsmith/Silversmith
Barrister/Attorney	Ship Chandler	Knife Maker
Chemist/Druggist	Spirit Shop Keeper	Labourer
Clerk	Timber Dealer	Lime Burner
Engineer/Architect/Surveyor	Toddy Shop Keeper	Mason/Bricklayer
Minister/Missionary	Vegetable Seller	Mat/Kajang/Basket Maker
Native Priest	**Agricultural**	Moulder
Nun/Catechist	Fruit Cultivator	Oil Manufacturer
Physician/Surgeon/Dentist	Gambier/Pepper Planter	Net Maker/Mender
Pilot	Planter/Manager of Estates	Painter
Schoolmaster/Schoolmistress	Market Gardener	Paper Lantern Maker
Telegraphist	Labourer	Plumber
Civil Servant	Paddy Planter	Potter
Police and Military Personnel	**Industrial**	Printer
Naval Staff	Attap Maker	Rattan Worker
Domestic	Baker/Miller	Rope Maker
Domestic Servant	Bamboo Worker	Sago Manufacturer
Commercial	Barber	Sail Maker
Boarding/Lodging House Keeper	Blacksmith	Sawyer
Bumboatman	Boatman	Seaman
Butcher/Pork Seller	Bookbinder	Seamoss/Seaweed Gatherers
Cake Maker/Seller	Boot/Shoemaker	Ship/Boat Builder
Cart/Hackney Carriage Owner	Brick Maker	Shell/Coral Seller
Charcoal Seller	Carpenter	Soap Boiler
Cloth Hawker	Carriage Builder/Cartwright	Stone Cutter
Curry Stuff Seller	Cart/Hackney Carriage Driver	Sugar Boiler
Eating House Keeper	Cattle Keeper/Milk Seller	Tailor/Dressmaker/Seamstress
Fishmonger	Cigar Maker/Tobacco Seller	Tin Smelterer
Fruit Seller	Coffin Maker	Tinsmith/Brazier
Grass Seller	Confectioner	Toddy Drawer
Hawker	Contractor/Builder	Umbrella Maker
Hotel/Tavern Keeper	Cooper	Undertaker/Tomb Builder
Mangrove Bark Seller	Diver	Washerman
Merchants' Agent/Broker	Dyer	Watchmaker
Money Changer	Engineer/Machinist	Watchman/Messengers
Oil Seller	Engine Driver/Fireman	Water Carrier
Opium Shop Keeper	Farrier/Shoeing Smith	Weaver
Pawnbroker	Firewood Seller	Woodcutter
Pig Dealer	Fisherman	Wood/Ivory Carver

Source: *Census of the Straits Settlements 1881*, Singapore there were 212 brothels.[151] They were joined in this occupation by *karayuki-san* or Japanese prostitutes who offered their services in Middle Road and Malay Street.[152] Domestic servants in British households and establishments were virtually all Hainanese—there were not enough of them even though they numbered nearly 13,000 in 1881.[153] The Hainanese also found a niche in bakeries, coffee shops and hotels' food and beverage operations.[154]

The Chinese who could not obtain steady jobs in the services industry piled into rickshaw pulling and hawking.[155] These two callings were the main receptacles for surplus labour and afforded a subsistence level of existence. Rickshaws were introduced into Singapore from Shanghai in 1880 and quickly became ubiquitous, competing for custom and road space with pony carts, private carriages and a public omnibus operated by hack gharries.[156] Pulling a rickshaw was a last resort occupation because the job was physically strenuous and no capital was needed to be a *jinriksha* coolie. The pullers rented the vehicles and earned as much as they could from a day's or night's work. Most of them belonged to the Hockchiu and Henghua dialect groups, on account of their late arrival in Singapore when the other bangs had already established themselves in their respective trades. Similarly, hawking requires little capital and this could be borrowed from shopkeepers or moneylenders. In the 1881 census, 1,125 Chinese and 202 Malays were listed as hawkers. For unemployed sinkheh, rickshaw pulling and hawking provided an informal safety net and the latter occupation provided job opportunities to all since segregation between dialect groups extended even to food.

Immigrants from India to Singapore, consisting by and large of Tamil labourers, satisfied the strong demand for manpower in transportation, public works, hospitals and the municipality.[157] About 1,300 were either owners or—more likely—drivers of carts and hackney carriages, supplemented by about 700 Malays. Some continued to work as lighter men, though by the end of the 19th century the Chinese had taken over the vocation and introduced their own colourful bumboats called *twakows*.[158] Indian and Ceylonese immigrants who had received an English education were employed as teachers and interpreters in the colonial administration or as supervisors.[159] Many worked as clerks in the business sector, although they were outnumbered by the Chinese, among whom more than 2,500 were in the same profession. Amongst the Malays too, an educated elite emerged comprising teachers, journalists and religious writers. From the early 1880s, Sikhs were recruited from Punjab to serve as police constables, prison wardens and security personnel

---

[151] Turnbull, *History of Modern Singapore*, pp. 86, 114; Lim, "Coolies, Triads and Pimps", p. 6.

[152] Savage, *Lion City Narratives*, pp. 202–3, 262.

[153] *The Straits Times Weekly Issue*, 19 Aug. 1886.

[154] Cheng, *Social Change*, p. 97.

[155] Huff, *The Economic Growth of Singapore*, pp. 173–5.

[156] Turnbull, *History of Modern Singapore*, p. 124; Hallifax, "Municipal Government", pp. 331–2; *The Straits Times*, 11 Sept. 1875; *The Straits Times Weekly Issue*, 25 June 1884. By 1884, 2,077 rickshaws were licensed. *Straits Settlements Annual Report*, vol. 3, p. 23.

[157] Rai, *Indians in Singapore*, pp. 76, 82, 96–9, 100–3.

[158] Turnbull, *History of Modern Singapore*, pp. 111–2; Ng Chin Keong, "The Maritime Chinese and Colonial Singapore 1819–1900", in *Maritime Heritage of Singapore*, ed. Lau and Lau, pp. 104, 108.

[159] *The Straits Times Weekly Issue*, 15 June 1892.

as they were deemed to be superior to Klings, who were accused of being susceptible to drink and bribery.[160] The Sikh contingent of the police force proved to be a great success and they have been ever since a vital component of the service. In 1890, a new and improved pay scale was introduced for these officers after an official commission enquired into the reasons for the difficulty in recruiting natives for the force, even though there were many Malay policemen.[161]

Education, Healthcare and Defence

The neglect of education in Singapore during the early period was remedied by the colonial government in the later part of the 19th century. But little progress was made in the initial years after the transfer even though the Colonial Office recognised that the standard of education was low.[162] A Select Committee was formed to report on the matter to the Legislative Council in 1870, but the government acted on only one of its recommendations, namely, appointing an Inspector of Schools to report on their conditions.[163] In 1873, there were just six English schools in Singapore, catering to 865 pupils.[164] Nevertheless, the authorities gradually implemented the other recommendations on reforming the grant-in-aid system, which applied to English schools, and extending and improving free Malay vernacular education.[165]

The last of these proposals made the fastest progress, with the establishment of the Kampong Glam Malay Branch School in 1876 as a "feeder" school to Raffles Institution, several new Malay schools in the early 1880s including at Pulau Tekong, Rochor, Tanjong Rhu, Siglap and Tanah Merah, as well as three vernacular Malay girls' schools in 1883 and 1884.[166] In 1876, a Malay College to provide a bilingual secondary education in Malay and English and to train schoolmasters was founded with support from the Maharajah of Johor (as the Temenggong was known by then).[167] Many Malay teachers were trained at the

---

160 R. St.J. Braddell, "Crime", pp. 251, 253–4; *The Straits Times Weekly Issue*, 4 May 1892.

161 *Proceedings of the Legislative Council of the Straits Settlements*, 1889, Appendix No. 8, pp. C31–7; "Annual Report on the Straits Settlements Police Force and on the State of Crime, for the Year 1890", in *Straits Settlements, Annual Reports for the Year 1890*, p. 515.

162 M. Erb, "Moulding a Nation: Education in Early Singapore", in *Past Times*, ed. Chan and Tong, p. 22; *Proceedings of the Legislative Council of the Straits Settlements*, 3 Oct. 1872.

163 Nagendiram, *The Straits Settlements*, pp. 257–62, 267–71; Turnbull, *History of Modern Singapore*, p. 128; *Straits Settlements Annual Report*, vol. 2, pp. 65–6; *The Straits Times*, 6 Nov. 1869.

164 *Proceedings of the Legislative Council of the Straits Settlements*, 1875, Appendix 13, "Report of the Inspector of Schools for the Year 1873", pp. xcviii, xcix.

165 Lim, "English Schools and School Libraries", pp. 64–5, 67.

166 Lim, "Elementary Malay Vernacular Schools", p. 76; *Proceedings of the Legislative Council of the Straits Settlements*, 1884, Appendix No. 13, "Annual Education Report, for the Year 1883", pp. C125–6, 1885, Appendix No. 21, pp. C149–51; *Straits Settlements Annual Report*, vol. 3, p. 13; *The Straits Times*, 1 Sept. 1877; *The Straits Times Weekly Issue*, 2 Aug. 1883.

167 Turnbull, *History of Modern Singapore*, p. 128; *Straits Settlements Annual Report*, vol. 2, p. 285.

college and despite the closure of some vernacular schools in 1893, a fifth of boys aged 15 and under were still attending them in 1901.[168]

As in the earlier decades, Chinese-medium education was left to the efforts of the philanthropists in the community. In 1884, there were altogether 51 Chinese schools, big and small, in Singapore run by the Chinese themselves, none of which was subject to government inspection.[169] Some of these schools were endowed by leaders of the community like Tan Kim Seng. In 1886, Gan Eng Seng opened the Anglo-Chinese Free School at his shophouses in Telok Ayer, offering both an English and Chinese education; in 1893, this school transferred to new premises capable of accommodating 300 boys.[170] Another free school was opened in Havelock Road by Cheang Hong Lim in 1892, named after his eldest son Cheang Jim Hean. The school received a government grant and had more than 100 pupils on its register in 1897 but closed in 1901 when the son died.[171] The Reverend A. Lamont of the Presbyterian Church also set up the Singapore Chinese Educational Institute to provide a continuing education for working Chinese who wanted to learn English and acquaint themselves with Western ideas.[172]

The colonial government did however set up two Anglo-Tamil schools and another, Our Lady of Lourdes Anglo-Tamil School, was founded in 1885.[173] Nonetheless, since the Tamil community in Singapore was small and demand was low, the schools eventually closed or were converted into English schools.[174] By comparison, the English-medium schools taught mostly by British masters were more successful.[175] By 1899, there were 14 such schools in Singapore, with three—Cross Street School, Victoria Bridge School and The Kampong Glam English Class—fully run by the government and the rest by Christian missions (Table 11). Altogether, they provided a primary education to 3,213 boys; only Raffles Institution offered secondary classes, starting from 1884, in part with the aim of becoming a high school for the elementary schools.[176] The lack of interest in secondary education was attributed to the tendency for students to cease further study after learning sufficient English to find work in the city, which was also the reason why the course of education had progressed so slowly in earlier decades.[177]

---

[168] Doraisamy, *150 Years of Education*, p. 26; *Straits Settlements Annual Report*, vol. 3, p. 13; *The Straits Times Weekly Issue*, 23 May 1889.

[169] Lim, "Development of Chinese Education", pp. 420, 424–5; *Proceedings of the Legislative Council of the Straits Settlements*, 1875, Appendix 13, "Report of the Inspector of Schools for the Year 1873", p. xcvii.

[170] Song, *One Hundred Years' History of the Chinese*, pp. 371–4, 386–7.

[171] Bazell, "Education in Singapore", pp. 448, 449–50.

[172] *The Straits Times Weekly Issue*, 16 Dec. 1891.

[173] Lim, "English Schools and School Libraries", pp. 65, 66; *Proceedings of the Legislative Council of the Straits Settlements*, 1885, Appendix No. 21, pp. C162–3, 1886, Appendix No. 17, pp. C192–3.

[174] Turnbull, *History of Modern Singapore*, p. 128.

[175] *The Straits Times*, 3 June 1876; *The Straits Times Weekly Issue*, 2 Aug. 1883, 12 Dec. 1887.

[176] Bazell, "Education in Singapore", p. 439; "Education", in *Annual Departmental Reports of the Straits Settlements for the Year 1899*, p. 136.

[177] *Straits Settlements Annual Report*, vol. 4, p. 449.

Most of the new English schools were set up in the 1870s, the notable exceptions being the Anglo-Chinese School established in 1886 by the American Methodist Mission and the Eastern School, which was founded in 1891 by Chinese educationists and taken over by the Presbyterian Church in 1895.[178] Within a few years of opening, the Anglo-Chinese School with its modern curriculum turned out to be so popular that its enrolment had increased to 400 students and it needed to extend the premises.[179] Another mission school, St. Andrew's School, was established in 1871 in Victoria Street and three years later it moved to Fort Canning Hill, where the church was used as a classroom. In terms of education for girls, three more schools were opened, including St. Anthony's Girls' School which had an enrolment of 437 in 1899. In 1883, Raffles Girls' School was relocated to a larger site with new buildings, after which attendance increased sharply.

Table 11. Singapore Boys' Schools, 1899

	Europeans/ Eurasians	Chinese	Malay	Indians/ Others	Total
Raffles Institution	96	209	15	12	332
St. Joseph's Institution	171	180	–	14	365
Eastern School	1	146	–	–	147
St. Andrew's School	2	92	1	–	95
St. Anthony's Boys' School	77	46	–	14	123
Anglo-Chinese School	81	233	6	41	361
Our Lady of Lourdes Anglo-Tamil School	–	6	–	7	13
American Mission Anglo-Tamil School	3	–	–	18	21
Geylang Mission School	–	12	–	–	12
Anglo-Chinese Free School	–	153	–	–	153
Cheang Jim Hean's Free School	–	64	–	–	64
Cross Street School	3	181	4	14	212
Victoria Bridge School	–	–	61	12	73
Kampong Glam Chinese Branch School	–	44	–	–	44

Source: Lim, "English Schools and School Libraries", p. 66.

Although the Straits government in Singapore felt compelled to play a role in educating the masses in light of the huge expansion in population and increased demand for new jobs, its policy was not one of directly providing the service. Except in the case of Malay vernacular education, the task was left to the missionary and private schools.

[178] Lim, "English Schools and School Libraries", pp. 65–6, 67. The Eastern School was subsequently handed over to the American Methodist Mission in 1900. "Education", in *Annual Departmental Reports of the Straits Settlements for the Year 1900*, p. 167.

[179] Bazell, "Education in Singapore", pp. 444–5, 455, 458; Frost and Balasingamchow, *Singapore*, pp. 183–4; *The Straits Times Weekly Issue*, 17 Dec. 1890, 11 Oct. 1892.

The authorities were content to be merely a partner in the enterprise.[180] To this end, the grant-in-aid system that was adopted in English schools after 1879 was based on results obtained at examinations and average attendance.[181] In that year, total government grants amounted to SPD15,321 out of an education budget of SPD38,396; SPD5,381 was given to Raffles Institution, by then the top English school in Singapore.[182] However, the system proved to be too oriented towards examination results and was subsequently replaced by grants based on general efficiency and for specific purposes such as the salaries of school teachers and maintenance of buildings.[183] In this new system that took effect in 1899, schools were classified into three grades according to their efficiency.[184] Primary schools were divided into six standards and both ordinary subjects like reading, writing and arithmetic and extra subjects such as history, geography, languages and music were offered to students; the grant given to a school for a student who passed in an extra subject was higher than that for an ordinary subject.[185]

Alongside these developments, two innovations were introduced that left long-lasting legacies on Singapore's educational system—the Queen's Scholarships in 1886 and the Cambridge Local Examinations in 1891.[186] Prior to this, government scholarships and industrial scholarships were awarded only for study in local schools.[187] The two Queen's Scholarships, each of which carried an annual stipend of £250 tenable for five years, enabled the *crème de la crème* among the young Straits-born Chinese to further their education at universities in England and return to Singapore as doctors, lawyers and professionals.[188] Lim Boon Keng and Song Ong Siang were two early beneficiaries of the scheme and they subsequently became *de facto* leaders and activists in the Chinese community.[189] Together, they established the Singapore Chinese Girls' School in 1899 to provide a modern education for women. The Senior Cambridge examination proved to be a reliable assessment of academic ability at the upper secondary level, so much so that it continues to this day.

---

180 Bazell, "Education in Singapore", pp. 450–1; Doraisamy, *150 Years of Education*, pp. 27, 36, 40; "Annual Education Report, for the Year 1886", in *Straits Settlements, Annual Reports for the Year 1886*, p. 141.

181 *Straits Settlements Annual Report*, vol. 2, p. 408.

182 *Straits Settlements Blue Book*, 1880, pp. C22, C24; *The Straits Times*, 12 June 1880. The amount given to Raffles Institution was fixed rather than based on the new criteria for grants. *Proceedings of the Legislative Council of the Straits Settlements*, 24 Aug. 1880.

183 *Straits Settlements Annual Report*, vol. 4, p. 527; *The Straits Times Weekly Issue*, 28 Apr. 1891.

184 *The Straits Times Weekly Issue*, 23 May 1889.

185 A seventh standard was added in 1891.

186 Turnbull, *History of Modern Singapore*, p. 129.

187 *Straits Settlements Annual Report*, vol. 4, p. 607; *The Straits Times Weekly Issue*, 20 June 1883.

188 The number of scholarships was reduced to one in 1907. *Straits Settlements Annual Report*, vol. 5, pp. 599–600.

189 Song, *One Hundred Years' History of the Chinese*, pp. 430–1, 494; *The Straits Times Weekly Issue*, 15 July 1891.

In healthcare, the situation also improved even though no new hospitals were added to the existing civil hospitals until the early 20th century.[190] After a cholera outbreak in 1873, the General Hospital, or European Seamen's Hospital as it was then called, was temporarily moved to its present site at Sepoy Lines along Outram Road, which stood on higher ground.[191] The move became permanent when a new hospital building was completed in 1882.[192] Meanwhile at Tan Tock Seng Hospital, the founder's grandson Tan Beng Swee constructed three new wards in 1879, bringing the total to 16, capable of accommodating 552 patients.[193] The Chinese community donated SPD15,503, augmenting the government aid of SPD20,400.[194] In 1880, overall government expenditure on medical and related expenses was a hefty SPD85,800, as a result of which health conditions at both hospitals and the quality of medical care improved.[195] The General Hospital treated 2,833 patients in 1891 while Tan Tock Seng Hospital admitted 5,656.[196] The mortality rate fell to 4.1 per cent at the former but was still high at 17.1 per cent at the latter because it treated natives with chronic illnesses.[197] In fact, the rate would have been even higher had the Chinese not had the predilection to send their terminally ill relatives and friends to the "death houses" at Sago Lane, which functioned both as hospices and morgues.[198] The quality of the water supplied at the hospitals was good, patients had adequate bathing facilities and the night soil was removed twice a day.[199] In general, socio-economic conditions in the city improved as a result of ordinances passed to vaccinate the population against smallpox, prevent the spread of cholera, and check venereal disease by registering brothels and mandating the medical examination of prostitutes.[200]

The pressure of population growth compelled the authorities to streamline their administration of the city. By the 1880s, the town of Singapore had grown large enough for a municipality to be created, divided into five wards containing 85 per cent of the population and separated from the rural districts.[201] The limits of the Municipality extended from Pasir Panjang to Napier Road, then to Bukit Timah Road and thenceforth to Thomson Road, Serangoon Road and Paya Lebar Road.[202] In 1887, a new Municipal Ordinance was

---

190 *The Straits Times*, 24 June 1876, 5 Aug. 1876.

191 *The First General Hospital: 175th Anniversary, 1821–1996* (Singapore: Singapore General Hospital, 1996), p. 26; *Proceedings of the Legislative Council of the Straits Settlements*, 1875, Appendix 9, "Annual Medical Report of the Civil Hospitals in the Straits Settlements, for the Year 1873", p. xxvii.

192 *The Straits Times Weekly Issue*, 5 July 1883.

193 *150 Years of Caring: The Legacy of Tan Tock Seng Hospital*, p. 26; Brooke, "Medical Work", p. 496.

194 *The Straits Times*, 5 June 1880.

195 *Straits Settlements Blue Book*, 1880, pp. C22, C24.

196 *Straits Settlements Blue Book*, 1891, p. AA2.

197 *The Straits Times Weekly Issue*, 7 July 1891.

198 Savage, *Lion City Narratives*, pp. 204–6.

199 *Straits Settlements Blue Book*, 1891, p. AA7.

200 Nagendiram, *The Straits Settlements*, pp. 273–7; *The Straits Times*, 4 June 1870, 17 Dec. 1870.

201 Y.K. Lee, *The Medical History of Early Singapore* (Tokyo: Southeast Asian Medical Information Center, 1978), p. 305; *The Straits Times Weekly Issue*, 3 Sept. 1884.

202 *The Straits Times Weekly Issue*, 5 Oct. 1887.

passed, superseding the ordinance of 1856 that first brought the Municipal Council into existence.[203] As with the earlier legislation, the representation on the Council under the new law was intended to be popular, with its constitution allowing for five members to be elected by ratepayers and five official members, including a salaried President selected by the Governor.[204] Moreover, a clause in the Ordinance stated that "all matters necessary for or conducive to the public safety, health and convenience" were to be a responsibility of the Municipal Council.[205]

Thus was born the Municipal Health Department, armed with an updated Infectious and Contagious Diseases Ordinance that gave the government powers to prevent and check the spread of epidemics and deal with rabies caused by stray dogs.[206] The lack of such a department had led to appalling living conditions in the city due to overcrowding, which in turn aided the spread of disease. The Department's first task was to visit facilities that could have a bearing on the sanitary state of the Municipality—cow sheds, slaughter houses, poultry and pig farms, sago manufactories, markets, the list went on.[207] Unlike in the case of the hospitals, the reports filed by the Health Officer were uniformly unfavourable; his main complaints regarded filthy conditions, poor ventilation and bad drainage.[208] There were swine kept within the municipal limits and fish unfit for consumption were sold in various markets. It was claimed that Asiatics set no store by sanitation and that their "incurably filthy and disorderly habits" exacerbated the spread of disease.[209] In response to the Health Officer's reports, the Municipality promulgated by-laws to supervise cow sheds, dairies, piggeries and poultry yards, in violation of which fines were imposed, which had the desired effect of improving the state of affairs.[210]

The indictment by the Health Officer seemed to have applied quite generally to sanitary conditions in the Colony.[211] Although a bill making it compulsory for residents to be vaccinated was passed in 1868, the colonial authorities had to institute health inspections on all arrivals at Singapore during the 1870s because the hordes of labourers descending on the city each year accentuated the spread of infectious diseases, especially

---

[203] *Proceedings of the Legislative Council of the Straits Settlements*, 2 May 1887, 18 Aug. 1887.

[204] Hallifax, "Municipal Government", p. 317; Wright and Cartwright, *Twentieth Century Impressions*, p. 237; Turnbull, *History of Modern Singapore*, p. 124; *The Straits Times Weekly Issue*, 25 May 1887.

[205] Lee, *Medical History*, p. 305.

[206] Hallifax, "Municipal Government", pp. 321–2; *Proceedings of the Legislative Council of the Straits Settlements*, 20 Oct. 1886, 30 Nov. 1886; *The Straits Times Weekly Issue*, 22 Nov. 1886. The first Contagious Diseases Ordinance was passed in 1870 and repealed in 1888. Tan, "Health and Welfare", p. 342.

[207] Lee, *Medical History*, p. 306.

[208] *The Straits Times Weekly Issue*, 20 June 1889.

[209] Quoted in Brenda S.A. Yeoh, "Urban Sanitation, Health and Water Supply in Late Nineteenth and Early Twentieth Century Colonial Singapore", *South East Asia Research* 1, 2 (1993): 153, 155–6; *The Straits Times Weekly Issue*, 18 May 1887.

[210] *The Straits Times Weekly Issue*, 26 Nov. 1889, 25 Feb. 1890, 7 May 1890, 10 Sept. 1890.

[211] *The Straits Times*, 17 July 1875; *The Straits Times Weekly Issue*, 13 Mar. 1886.

those brought from southern China.[212] Strict regulations were promulgated and in 1874, a quarantine station was set up on St. John's Island located a short distance from New Harbour, which became one of the world's largest quarantine stations in the early 20th century.[213] Singapore's mortality rate averaged 42 per 1,000 of population in the last years of the 19th century, above that of Hong Kong and India.[214] In overcrowded and unhealthy Chinatown, the heart of the city, disease including of the venereal type was rife, but given the stigma attached to hospitals, most residents referred themselves to *sinsehs* (that is, practitioners of traditional Chinese medicine) or sought free treatment at the Thong Chai Medical Institution which was set up in 1867 by Chinese merchants.[215] In the rickshaw quarters at Rochor Road and Queen Street, inadequate housing and the lack of a safe water supply facilitated the transmission of water-borne and infectious diseases that spread from person to person.[216] Apart from fevers of various kinds, the main killers were typhoid and cholera, both caused by drinking contaminated water from wells and other sources. Cholera in particular had made periodic visitations to the city, with epidemics breaking out in 1841, 1851, 1862 and 1873.[217]

The medical authorities in Singapore recognised that polluted water was a primary agent of propagating epidemic disease.[218] Hence, public health policy focused on providing a supply of pure water to every dwelling within the municipal limits. In order for the water to reach houses by gravitation, two service reservoirs had to be built at Mount Emily and Pearl's Hill in 1878 and 1898, respectively.[219] The completed waterworks were handed in 1878 to the Municipal Council, which levied a flat rate of 3 per cent on all properties in the town and an additional metered rate on households using water of 10 cents per 250 gallons.[220] However, the service was available only for 12 hours a day and had to be further curtailed during the dry season. Most critical of all, the supply of water was outstripped by demand due to population growth and increasing industrial usage at the

---

[212] J.F. Warren, *Rickshaw Coolie: A People's History of Singapore 1880–1940* (Singapore: NUS Press, 2003), p. 258; Ng, "Maritime Chinese", p. 106; *Proceedings of the Legislative Council of the Straits Settlements*, 16 Oct. 1868, 12 Nov. 1868, 17 May 1869; *The Straits Times*, 14 Aug. 1875; *The Straits Times Weekly Issue*, 19 July 1883.

[213] Huff, *The Economic Growth of Singapore*, pp. 46–7; Brooke, "Medical Work", pp. 505–6.

[214] Yeoh, "Urban Sanitation, Health and Water Supply", p. 145.

[215] J.F. Warren, *Ah Ku and Karayuki-san: Prostitution in Singapore 1870–1940* (Singapore: NUS Press, 2003), p. 129; Ooi, "British Colonial Healthcare Development", pp. 168–9; Savage, *Lion City Narratives*, pp. 191–2; "Annual Medical Report on the Civil Hospitals", in *Straits Settlements, Annual Reports for the Year 1895*, p. 563; *The Straits Times Weekly Issue*, 20 Aug. 1890.

[216] Warren, *Rickshaw Coolie*, p. 258.

[217] Brooke, "Medical Work", pp. 504–5.

[218] Yeoh, "Urban Sanitation, Health and Water Supply", pp. 145–6, 147–9. The competing medical view was the "miasma theory" which held that diseases such as malaria were caused mainly by poisons arising from the decomposition of organic matter in the soil under damp and humid conditions.

[219] Hallifax, "Municipal Government", pp. 327–8.

[220] *The Straits Times*, 23 Mar. 1878, 7 Aug. 1880. The town markets, with an annual income of SPD25,000, were also given over to the Municipality in 1876; by then, there was a market in Rochor and another one at Clyde Terrace selling uncooked food. Hallifax, "Municipal Government", p. 333; *The Straits Times*, 12 June 1875, 21 Aug. 1875.

docks and wharves. A plan was therefore proposed by the Municipality in 1900 to increase the water supply by channelling the flow from the upper portion of the Kallang River into MacRitchie Reservoir. For this purpose, the reservoir was enlarged in 1905 by raising its embankment and in 1910, a second reservoir next to it was built and named after the Municipal Engineer Robert Peirce.

These two reservoirs provided the city with nine million gallons of water a day but raising water supply capacity was not enough—it had to be accompanied by closing surface wells that were contaminated, which meant almost all wells in Singapore.[221] Beginning from 1897 therefore, the Municipal Health Department ordered wells to be closed, starting with the most congested areas of the town. The move was resented by the labouring classes and non-compliance with the directive was widespread, not least because well water was free while the water supplied by the Municipality had to be paid for.[222] It was precisely because of overconsumption that the authorities decided to conserve water use by charging for it through metering rather than a fixed payment. But this met with protests from lodging-house keepers, forcing the Municipality to reduce water rates from 40 cents to 20 cents per 1,000 gallons.

Apart from education and healthcare, the colonial government's spending on physical infrastructure in Singapore rose substantially during the 1880s, following the pause in building in the preceding decade. Two new bridges were added to the Singapore River—Ord Bridge in 1886 and Read Bridge in 1889.[223] A new prison on Pearl's Hill capable of incarcerating 736 criminals was ordered to be built by the Governor in 1878 at an estimated cost of SPD358,000 and was completed four years later.[224] The Telok Ayer land reclamation scheme, which entailed the levelling of coastal hills, finally started, with an initial sum of SPD105,779 expended on it in 1880. On completion, the cost of the project came up to SPD569,320 but one million dollars was expected from the sale of the 18 acres of ground recovered from the sea.[225] Furthermore, SPD300,000 had to be spent subsequently to build a seawall on the reclaimed land.[226] A landmark building, the Raffles Library and Museum at Stamford Road, was completed in the late eighties.[227] In 1886, a record sum of SPD685,365 was spent on public works and SPD25,354 on road building and repairs.[228]

Other demands on government expenditure in the final two decades of the 19th century related mostly to military and defence matters. The first of such calls on colonial revenue was SPD550,000 for the suppression of the disturbances in the Malay states—Perak,

---

[221] Yeoh, "Urban Sanitation, Health and Water Supply", pp. 149, 152–61.

[222] Water provided at public standpipes was not charged but delivery to households cost between half a cent to one cent for two buckets of approximately 16 gallons (c. 60 litres).

[223] Hallifax, "Municipal Government", p. 324.

[224] *Straits Settlements Annual Report*, vol. 2, pp. 372, 564; *The Straits Times*, 21 Dec. 1878; *The Straits Times Weekly Issue*, 7 June 1883, 20 Mar. 1886.

[225] Darbishire, "Commerce and Currency", p. 39; *Straits Settlements Annual Report*, vol. 2, p. 446, vol. 3, pp. 3–4, 171; *The Straits Times Weekly Issue*, 16 Aug. 1883, 4 Oct. 1883.

[226] *Straits Settlements Annual Report*, vol. 3, p. 585.

[227] Ibid., pp. 4, 10, 252, 436.

[228] Ibid., p. 170.

Selangor and Negri Sembilan—that was sparked off by the murder of the British Resident of Perak in 1875, to be paid back to the British government over three years starting from 1879.[229] Loans by the Straits government to the states for development purposes required additional funds and led to a deterioration in the Colony's financial position, forcing the government to take out a debenture issue of £100,000 (SPD470,000).[230] By the mid-1880s, however, the situation had improved considerably, with the revenue proving to be elastic while expenditure was capped.[231] The increases in government revenue were due to a large extent to the letting of the opium and spirit farms for three years at a time. The satisfactory finances induced the local press to declare that "what was most dubious before and some time after the transfer took place, the revenue has increased and prospered beyond all expectations".[232] In 1885, the credit balance of the Colony was SPD1,084,530, with about half of it in loans owed by the native states and the Straits municipalities and the rest invested in Indian government securities as a reserve contingency fund.[233]

The annual military expenditure of the Straits Settlements as a whole diverged very little from an average of SPD240,000 throughout the 1880s.[234] A series of expensive military fortifications was completed in Singapore, involving building forts on the islands overlooking Keppel Harbour to protect the docks and coal stores. The Imperial Government would provide the armaments, yet demanded in 1890 that the Colony double the military contribution to £100,000 (SPD587,000) per annum.[235] In support of the demand, it was pointed out that the contribution as a percentage of the revenue had dwindled from 38 per cent in 1858 to just 7 per cent in 1887.[236] Given the flourishing state of the Colony, it was asserted that the increased amount could be easily borne. Despite the protest of Unofficials in the Legislative Council that the Colony should not be expected to pay for more than half the cost of the garrison and the six dissenting votes on the issue, the British government's request was rammed through the chamber, carried by seven official votes.[237]

---

229 *Straits Settlements Annual Report*, vol. 2, pp. 446, 563; *The Straits Times*, 29 May 1880. The bulk of the payments were made to Perak and the amount to be repaid was eventually reduced by £20,000 (SPD117,400). *Proceedings of the Legislative Council of the Straits Settlements*, 1879, 20 May 1880, 22 Nov. 1881, Appendix 31, p. cclxiii.

230 *Straits Settlements Annual Report*, vol. 3, p. 654; *The Straits Times*, 16 Sept. 1876; *The Straits Times Weekly Issue*, 16 Aug. 1883. The loan was paid off in 1891.

231 *Straits Settlements Annual Report*, vol. 3, pp. 8, 167–8, 334.

232 *The Straits Times Weekly Issue*, 16 Aug. 1883.

233 *Straits Settlements Annual Report*, vol. 3, p. 86.

234 Ibid., passim.

235 Murfett, Miksic, Farrell and Chiang, *Between Two Oceans*, p. 120; Makepeace, "Singapore Defences", pp. 378, 380, 381–3, 399–400; Wright and Cartwright, *Twentieth Century Impressions*, pp. 48–9; *Straits Settlements Annual Report*, vol. 3, pp. 248, 584. In the 1890s, the defences at Fort Palmer and Fort Faber on the mainland were also strengthened.

236 *The Straits Times Weekly Issue*, 28 Jan. 1890.

237 *Proceedings of the Legislative Council of the Straits Settlements*, 1892, 11 Nov. 1892, 1 Dec. 1892, 2 Nov. 1893, Appendix No. 4, pp. C27–33, Appendix No. 18, pp. C257–67.

Already unfairly saddled with the war expenses of the native states, the local community reacted forcefully, resulting in the resignation in 1894 of three Unofficials in the Legislative Council and all the Justices of the Peace and members of the Chinese Advisory Board.[238] Not since the agitation for transfer to direct rule had the residents expressed such vehement dissent.[239] Their counter-argument was a variation on an old theme: Singapore was an Imperial coaling station and a material part of its defence cost should therefore be borne by the Empire.[240] One of the Unofficials pointed out that Hong Kong's contribution was only £40,000 while other British colonies paid even less or nothing.[241] Singapore had a smaller garrison than most of these colonies with an overall troop strength of only 1,515 but was made to pay the most just because it could afford to do so.[242] As a result of the protests, the military contribution was reduced to £80,000 for 1894 and £90,000 for 1895; the matter was finally settled in the following year when it was agreed that, excluding the cost of defence works which was to be borne by the Colony, the contribution would be 17½ per cent of the Straits Settlements' annual revenue.[243] By then, the increased contribution had already resulted in financial deficits in 1891 and 1892.[244] The straitened conditions of the finances forced the government into economic retrenchment and the shelving of public projects.[245] In 1899, the defence contribution rate was revised upwards retrospectively to 20 per cent although the Colony would be relieved of all expenses for buildings, works and allowances.[246] The amount in local currency of the military expenditure in that year came up to nearly SPD1 million.[247]

Notwithstanding all this, the government's finances were back in good shape and the public debt was zero at the end of the 19th century.[248] The balance of the loans made by the Colony to the FMS was repaid at the end of 1899.[249] The high price of tin revived trade and revenue more than doubled to SPD3,072,528; expenditure rose, but was limited to SPD2,655,574.[250] Spending on education had risen to 3.4 per cent of the overall budget from 2.7 per cent during the period 1867–85 while the proportion expended on healthcare

---

238 Turnbull, *History of Modern Singapore*, pp. 132–3; *Proceedings of the Legislative Council of the Straits Settlements*, 15 June 1880, 30 Dec. 1880.

239 *The Straits Times Weekly Issue*, 25 Feb. 1891, 11 Mar. 1891.

240 *The Straits Times Weekly Issue*, 28 Jan. 1890, 11 Feb. 1890, 25 Feb. 1890, 11 Mar. 1891.

241 Makepeace, "Singapore Defences", pp. 401–2.

242 Murfett, Miksic, Farrell and Chiang, *Between Two Oceans*, pp. 119–21.

243 *Proceedings of the Legislative Council of the Straits Settlements*, 31 Jan. 1899.

244 *Straits Settlements Annual Report*, vol. 3, pp. 609–11, vol. 4, p. 77.

245 *Straits Settlements Annual Report*, vol. 4, p. 78–9.

246 *Proceedings of the Legislative Council of the Straits Settlements*, 1899, 31 Jan. 1899, 14 Feb. 1899, 25 Apr. 1899, Appendix No. 8, pp. C47–50.

247 "Financial Report and Statements", in *Annual Departmental Reports of the Straits Settlements for the Year 1900*, p. 568.

248 Ross, *The Capital of a Little Empire*, p. 7.

249 *Straits Settlements Annual Report*, vol. 4, p. 540.

250 Ibid., pp. 459–60; *Straits Settlements Blue Book*, 1899, pp. C8, C9.

was even higher at 6.8 per cent.[251] No less than two-thirds of the revenue came from the opium and other farms, thanks to the increase in the Chinese population, while stamp duty continued to be the next most important contributor on account of trade expansion. Land revenue was also inflated by a rise in the value of commercial properties in the town.[252] The municipal finances were in equally good order in 1899, following continuous deficits in the late 1880s: a surplus of SPD136,404 was registered even though expenditure had risen about tenfold to just over one million dollars.[253] The much larger outlay reflected the evolution of municipal government in Singapore over the eight decades since its founding, from *ad hoc* committees set up to provide roads and drains to a local authority supplying water and regulating the city's sanitary conditions.[254]

251 "Annual Education Report, for the Year 1886", in *Straits Settlements, Annual Reports for the Year 1886*, p. 141; *Straits Settlements Blue Book*, 1899, pp. C21, C30–3.

252 Ross, *The Capital of a Little Empire*, pp. 15–16.

253 Wright and Cartwright, *Twentieth Century Impressions*, p. 48; *Straits Settlements Annual Report*, vol. 3, passim; *Straits Settlements Blue Book*, 1899, p. E3; *The Straits Times Weekly Issue*, 21 Jan. 1891.

254 Hallifax, "Municipal Government", pp. 316–7.

Chapter 7

The Late Colonial Economy, 1900–28

At the dawn of the 20th century, it appeared that by virtue of a historical turn of events, Singapore was destined to lose one staple product only to gain another. Tin was becoming increasingly scarce in Malaya as alluvial deposits were exhausted. But again, through the agency and location of Singapore, its port and hinterland acquired a second and more important staple—rubber. The rubber boom had all the essential hallmarks of staple development: discovery of a new crop, rising industrial demand and a rapid increase in production from an infusion of productive factors. Rubber brought about unprecedented prosperity, created novel industries and sustained the expansion of the Singaporean and Malayan economies until the start of the Second World War.

This transformation led to an increase in shipping volumes and necessitated a concomitant upgrading of Singapore's port infrastructure, which was not forthcoming from the private sector and required governmental intervention. However, the innovations of "modernity" in transport, communications and daily life—the motorcar, telephone and electricity—were the result of a *laissez faire* economy. These new inventions were introduced into Singapore during the interwar years (1919–39), a period that witnessed not only further progress in education and healthcare but also the modernisation of monetary and banking institutions following the stabilisation of the currency's value in 1906. The government's revenue base shifted for the first time since the city's founding, giving rise to a conservative fiscal policy.

The Rubber Boom: Staple Redux

In the last two decades of the 19th century, coffee became the main cash crop in European agricultural pursuits in Malaya, complementing the extractive tin industry. By the turn of the century, however, the export had lost favour to coffee from Brazil amidst falling prices and was also the victim of moths that devastated the trees.[1] It was soon replaced by rubber from the *Hevea Brasiliensis* plant, known as "para rubber", which by a quirk of fate also came from Brazil. The first rubber seeds outside Brazil were appropriated and brought to Kew Gardens in London in 1873, from where they were sent to India and Ceylon. Saplings of three varieties of the rubber plant from Ceylon reached the Botanic Gardens in Singapore in 1876 and another consignment arrived in 1877, some of which

[1] Moore and Moore, *The First 150 Years*, pp. 476–7.

were forwarded to Perak and subsequently distributed elsewhere in Malaya.[2] Nevertheless, rubber cultivation was not in vogue amongst European or Asian planters then because of a lack of demand, overshadowed by the profitable coffee industry.

The popularisation of the crop was the work of one man—the Director of the Botanic Gardens appointed in 1888, Henry Ridley. He was not only a fine botanist who invented the herring-bone method of tapping rubber without damaging the tree, but also a firm believer in the potential of rubber even before the motorcar was in production.[3] The story goes that he always kept a handful of rubber seeds in his waistcoat pocket and distributed them to the planters he met, or almost everybody else, in the belief that it would be the crop of the century. It matters very much for the economic histories of Singapore and Malaya that he was right and his importunity paid off, for rubber wrought a remaking of their economies that was both sweeping and phenomenal. As we will see, the economic linkages generated by rubber served as a powerful motor of commercialisation and financialisation in Singapore.

Some of the earliest rubber trees planted were in Ridley's backyard—Singapore itself. By 1905, 1,110 acres had been devoted to rubber in outlying districts such as Yishun and Sembawang, including areas where gambier and pepper cultivation had been abandoned.[4] Chinese entrepreneurs such as Tan Chay Yan and Lim Nee Soon decided to try their luck at the new cash crop, in lieu of or in conjunction with pineapples.[5] Just then, the price of rubber in the world market soared due to an increase in demand for raw rubber to manufacture pneumatic tyres for motorcars, following their invention late in the 19th century. Rubber was also needed to insulate electrical wires, apart from making gloves, shoes, hoses and bicycle tyres. From 2s. 3d. (two shillings and threepence) per pound of rubber in 1901, the price went up to 5s. 10½d. (five shillings and ten-and-a-half pence) in 1906, which marked the beginning of the rubber boom.[6] Global consumption of natural rubber increased from 710,000 tonnes in the 1900s to 1,880,000 tonnes in the 1910s, as the American automobile industry expanded after Henry Ford invented the factory assembly line in 1907.[7]

This intensification of demand induced planters from Singapore and in Malaya to cultivate the crop commercially along the west coast of the Peninsula, where land was in great abundance and the climate was congenial to rubber planting.[8] In 1902, 15,000 acres were under rubber; by 1905, 46,000 acres; and by 1909, 334,000 acres.[9] When the world war broke out in 1914, 1.1 million acres were devoted to the *Hevea* crop, the dramatic increase in acreage coming from both large estates and smallholdings. The war

---

[2] J.H. Drabble, *Rubber in Malaya 1876–1922* (Kuala Lumpur: Oxford University Press, 1973), pp. 3–5; *The Singapore Free Press and Mercantile Advertiser*, 8 Oct. 1935.

[3] Drabble, *Rubber in Malaya*, pp. 6–10.

[4] *Straits Settlements Blue Book*, 1905, pp. X2, X4.

[5] *Malaya Tribune*, 7 Mar. 1916; *The Singapore Free Press and Mercantile Advertiser*, 23 Mar. 1936.

[6] Lim, *Economic Development of Modern Malaya*, Appendix 3.1, p. 323.

[7] Drabble, *Rubber in Malaya*, p. 62.

[8] Lim, *Economic Development of Modern Malaya*, p. 92.

[9] J.H. Drabble, "Investment in the Rubber Industry in Malaya c. 1900–1922", *Journal of Southeast Asian Studies* 3, 2 (1972): 261.

also caused rubber prices to rise, which stimulated further investment in the industry. By 1922 when the first census of rubber acreage was taken, the area cultivated in the Peninsula had increased to 2.33 million acres bearing an output of 212,400 tonnes of rubber.[10] When the Second World War began, the area had reached 3.43 million acres, producing 360,100 tonnes. It was remarked that "no other branch of agriculture has ever developed so rapidly".[11]

Unlike tin, commercial rubber cultivation was carried out in Malaya in large-scale plantations owned by absentee British and European capitalists, although plots opened up by the Chinese and the smallholdings of Malay families contributed to supply. The estates were managed by the agency houses in Singapore, some of them with branches in Kuala Lumpur. These houses provided management and secretarial services to owners in the West which arose from the backward, forward and final demand linkages associated with the technological requirements of rubber plantations, namely, the importation of capital goods and labourers, the processing and transportation of rubber to Straits ports, and the provision of insurance and shipping services to Britain, Europe and the United States. The capital inputs into the rubber production process were machinery, vehicles, fertilisers, insecticides and of course, the initial capital to start a rubber estate, estimated at between £25–50 per acre for purchasing the land, clearing the jungle, planting the trees and tending to them before they matured.[12] At six years, the maturation period for rubber trees is long, during which time the return on capital was nil. In view of this, the colonial government of Malaya played an enabling role by providing security of land tenure, waivers of rents and duties, as well as cheap loans.

In addition, the agency houses had to provide for the needs of a large labour force in the estates by sourcing rice and foodstuffs from Chinese traders in Singapore. The provision of cotton and other manufactured goods they handled themselves from their long-established business lines and marketing connections. A substantial engineering industry also developed in Singapore to service estate equipment and to manufacture smaller items such as coagulating tanks, rubber mangles, cups and buckets.[13] To the extent that the rail and road networks in Malaya were already well developed by the time rubber came onto the scene (which also explained the location of rubber estates), the most profitable forward linkage left unexploited was rubber milling, which was handled by Singapore Chinese who set up numerous mills in the city and the Peninsula for this purpose.

The sourcing of financial capital from Britain was given a huge impetus when the rubber price briefly hit 12s. 9d. per pound in 1910 and the London Stock Exchange rallied on the

[10] Lim, *Economic Development of Modern Malaya,* Appendix 4.3, pp. 328, 329.

[11] P.T. Bauer, *The Rubber Industry: A Study in Competition and Monopoly* (Harvard University Press, 1948), p. 25.

[12] Nazrin Shah, *Charting the Economy: Early 20th Century Malaya and Contemporary Malaysian Contrasts* (Oxford University Press, 2017), p. 30. The initial cost stated here can be contrasted with the early view that, for proprietary owners, "the expenses of a rubber estate will be very small. No machinery and no skilled labour are required". Drabble, *Rubber in Malaya,* p. 21.

[13] Huff, *The Economic Growth of Singapore,* pp. 198, 200, 216–7.

euphoria over the new economic crop.[14] This proved to be no bubble, as the joint-stock companies, floated with the help of the agency houses, channelled the massive investment required for setting up plantations into Singapore to substitute for the bank loans that were not forthcoming.[15] Major tyre manufacturers in Europe and America also invested in rubber production.[16] Raising the required capital was not difficult since the agencies had a good reputation among the British investing public and Malaya was effectively part of the British Empire; besides, there were no restrictions on foreign capital inflow. At the peak of the boom in 1910, capital flows into Singapore amounted to £8 million, about one-third of which was mobilised by the agency houses and the rest by issuing houses in London.[17] By 1913 when the rate of flotation slowed down, 373 estates had been established in Malaya through this investment. During the 1910s, the rubber companies paid annual dividends of 20–80 per cent and the accumulated return on investment exceeded 500 per cent.[18] The ploughing back of profits in turn provided another source of capital for the further expansion of the industry.[19]

Concurrently, the agency houses were incorporated as limited liability companies to shoulder the greatly increased risks of the rubber enterprises.[20] These incorporated entities included, *inter alia*, Boustead and Company, Harrisons and Crosfield, Guthrie and Company, Paterson, Simons and Company, Adamson, Gilfillan and Company and A.C. Harper and Company, a few of these being formed from mergers of merchant firms. Thus, the agency houses in Singapore underwent a process of diversification in the early 20th century, from acting as intermediaries of the long-distance entrepôt trade to also being managers of agricultural enterprises in Malaya. The houses had whole ownership of some of the plantations and were the majority shareholders in others. Before this, there were only two known involvements of the houses in commercial agriculture: Guthrie had started nutmeg cultivation in Singapore in the 1830s and Ker, Rawson and Company had assisted and represented the Temenggong of Johor in the gambier and pepper industry.

The shift in business model was evident in the houses' trading activities: the Straits produce export business remained significant, but it diminished in importance compared to the import of capital goods.[21] Indeed, well-known agency houses like Sime Darby and Thomas Barlow and Company did not participate in the Straits produce trade at all. In other houses, the traditional dealings in manufactured goods like cottons, woollens, opium

[14] J.H. Drabble, "The Plantation Rubber Industry in Malaya up to 1922", *Journal of the Malaysian Branch of the Royal Asiatic Society* 40, 1 (1967): 55, 58. Capital also came into Malaya from Ceylon, with 18 companies floated between 1899 and 1907.

[15] Huff, *The Economic Growth of Singapore*, pp. 181–2.

[16] Abshire, *History of Singapore*, p. 62.

[17] R.T. Stillson, "The Financing of Malayan Rubber, 1905–1923", *The Economic History Review* 24, 4 (1971): 594.

[18] Nazrin Shah, *Charting the Economy*, p. 33; K. Rönnbäck, O. Broberg and S. Galli, "A Colonial Cash Cow: The Return on Investments in British Malaya, 1889–1969", *Cliometrica* 16, 1 (2022): 149–73.

[19] R. Findlay and M. Lundahl, "Natural Resources, Vent for Surplus, and the Staples Theory", in *From Classical Economics to Development Economics: Essays in Honor of Hla Myint*, ed. G. Meier (New York: St. Martin's Press, 1994), p. 76.

[20] Drabble and Drake, "The British Agency Houses in Malaysia", p. 307–8.

[21] Ibid., p. 308.

and spirits became a secondary activity, in part because the management and administration of rubber plantations—supervision of estate managers, the oversight of engineers and technicians and the preparation of accounts—entailed substantial resources.[22] The agency houses also undertook research and development; in bad times, they were expected to tide over the difficulties encountered by estates by continuing to provide working capital.[23]

The profits gained from performing these multiple roles were managerial and secretarial fees, commissions on supplies provided and payments for brokerage, freight and insurance services. These profits were boosted by the economies of scale that accrued to estate production, which came not so much from the size of an estate itself, defined as land having an area of 100 acres or more under one legal ownership, but from the collective scale of a number of plantations managed by an agency house. Large estates required control of ground conditions, a network of roads and drains, housing for estate labourers and processing factories.[24] Efficiencies in performing all these tasks were present particularly in the hiring of professional staff who could gain practical expertise by dealing with different estates, but also in input procurement and rubber marketing.

In view of the capital needs of rubber, Chinese plantations were seldom equal in size to the European estates; most were between 100 and 500 acres.[25] Some pioneering Chinese in the industry incorporated their companies locally and others sold them to the Western plantations, but ownership was generally diffused among individuals and partners. Many of the plantations were started by Straits merchants who had accumulated commercial wealth or were otherwise involved in growing gambier, tapioca and coffee in the hinterland. *In toto*, Chinese estates accounted for 18.5 per cent of the rubber cultivated area in 1932 (the Indian and Malay shares were negligible).[26] In these plantations, the typical practice was to grow rubber trees together with pineapples so as to ensure an income while the rubber trees matured, thus reducing startup costs to only a quarter of that incurred by European estates.[27]

While Chinese plantations also existed in Singapore, the venture quickly came up against the constraint of land, forcing their proprietors to move to Johor for the same reason that gambier cultivators had migrated during the previous century. In 1932, there were more than 300 estates owned by Singapore planters in Johor with varying sizes.[28] To reduce risk and the uncertainty associated with highly volatile rubber prices, the owners employed a system of sharecropping that was very similar to the tribute system in tin mining. Chinese immigrant coolies were recruited to work the rubber-pineapple plantations and were promised a share of 50 per cent in the profits realised from rubber sales plus a fixed wage of $1 per acre worked each month.[29] Effectively, the labourers were

[22] Allen and Donnithorne, *Western Enterprise in Indonesia and Malaya*, p. 113.

[23] Drabble and Drake, "The British Agency Houses in Malaysia", pp. 309–10.

[24] Drabble, "Investment in the Rubber Industry", p. 255.

[25] Jomo, *A Question of Class*, p. 184.

[26] Lim, *Economic Development of Modern Malaya*, Appendix 4.5, p. 331.

[27] Huff, *The Economic Growth of Singapore*, p. 190.

[28] Ibid., pp. 190, 191–2.

[29] The sign $ refers to the Straits dollar that was issued to replace the Spanish dollar in 1899.

forced to partially bear the cost of locking up capital for a long period, at a foregone interest rate estimated to be 20 per cent.

High rubber prices also drew into the industry Asian smallholders, whose acreage was less than 100 acres. Although they did not receive government assistance because their small plots were not deemed to be a form of commercial agriculture and they had no access to foreign capital, rubber smallholdings expanded rapidly in the 1910s to reach 918,000 acres in 1922, or 39 per cent of the total area under rubber in the Peninsula.[30] In 1929 when detailed statistics were first collected separately for estates and smallholdings, the output produced by the former was 245,000 tonnes and that by the latter was not far behind at 212,000 tonnes (Figure 13). Most smallholders were Malay peasants or immigrants from the Archipelago who used family labour to clear unused ground, typically three acres or less, and plant it with rubber.[31] Or they might divert land from rice fields and fruit orchards since the earnings from rubber were more attractive, without affecting subsistence production much.[32] Hardly any fixed expenditure was incurred except for rent (if new land were acquired), rubber seeds which were available at low cost and simple agricultural implements for tapping and latex processing.[33]

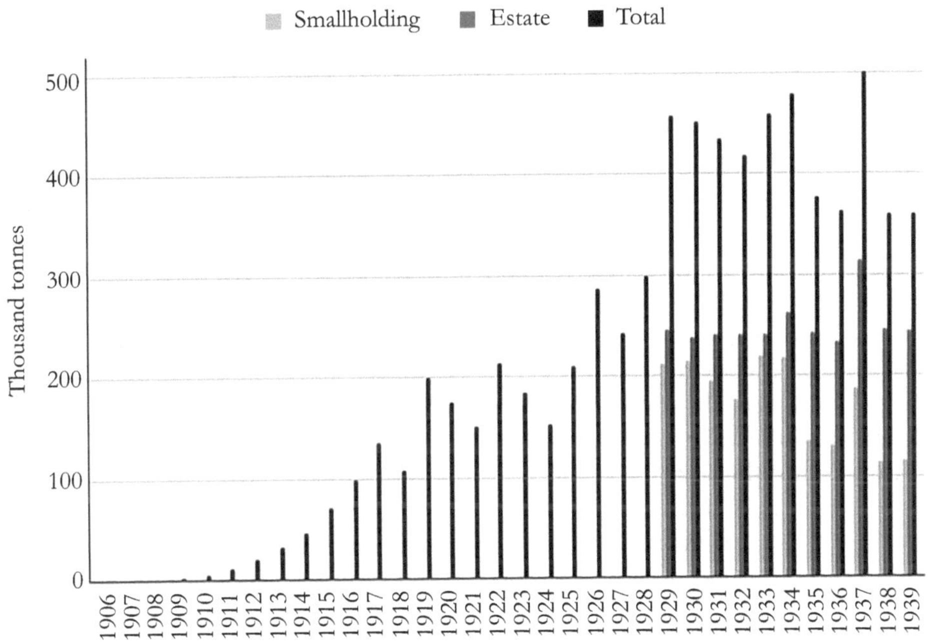

Figure 13. Malayan Rubber Production, 1906–39
Source: Lim, *Economic Development of Modern Malaya*, Appendix 4.3, pp. 328–9.

[30] Lim, *Economic Development of Modern Malaya*, p. 115, Appendix 4.3, p. 328.

[31] F. Benham, "The Rubber Industry", *Economica*, New Series 16, 64 (1949): 358; Drabble, "The Plantation Rubber Industry", p. 72.

[32] Jomo, *A Question of Class*, pp. 64–5.

[33] Findlay and Lundahl, "Natural Resources", pp. 76–7.

Hence, the Malays were drawn into the international export economy by the early 20th century. Their rudimentary production methods, however, did not generate any substantive linkage effects as smallholder rubber was sold for cash in the open market, although the bulk was eventually sent to Singapore for milling and export.[34] This was also the case with native smallholders in Sumatra and Borneo who added significantly to supply in the 1920s.[35] According to one estimate, Dutch East (Netherlands) Indies smallholding rubber acreage increased from 450,000 acres in 1922 to 1.65 million acres in 1929, with 128,000 tonnes of the output exported to Singapore.[36] Insofar as rubber was concerned therefore, the Dutch East Indies became a second hinterland for Singapore.

Estate production created more linkages for Singapore, but without necessarily leading to more economic efficiency compared to smallholder production. On the contrary, it has been argued that the smallholding was a more economic unit than most plantations in view of its lower costs of production.[37] Smallholders responded nimbly to rubber price decreases in that their supply was elastic, as they could turn to alternative sources of income such as growing rice and vegetables or getting a paid job. In contrast, the European estates were saddled with heavy overhead expenses—as the above comparison between them and the Chinese estates shows—as well as the high salaries paid to expatriate staff, which introduced a certain amount of inertia in their adjustments to price changes.[38] They also made mistakes in planting and weeding policy; specifically, the clean weeding practice followed up to the 1920s led to soil erosion and root diseases.[39] Therefore, smallholders were a formidable competitor to the large European estates, although it has been counter-argued that they neglected investment in the long run by not replanting rubber trees or planting new ones.

What enabled the European estates to thrive was the easy access to the supply of cheap imported labour. In the closing years of the 19th century, a shortage of workers again arose in the Straits Settlements and the FMS due to the ebbing of Chinese immigrant flows and the requirements of infrastructure development. The colonial administration introduced assistance for these immigrants in 1899, which led to an influx of over 200,000 Chinese in 1900 but this resulted only in an increase of the labour force in the tin mining industry in Malaya, from 186,337 in 1903 to 231,368 in 1907.[40] The workers required for the rubber plantations had therefore to be obtained from another labour reservoir in Asia—India. Earlier we remarked that Indian emigration was freed from most restrictions in 1885; still, an inflow of the magnitude required for the rubber industry, given an estimated labour-land ratio of one worker to two acres, required organised and coordinated action from the

[34] Stillson, "The Financing of Malayan Rubber", p. 591.

[35] Huff, *The Economic Growth of Singapore*, pp. 194–5, 203–4.

[36] *Rubber Growers' Association's Bulletin*, Feb. 1931.

[37] Bauer, *The Rubber Industry*, p. 206.

[38] Drabble, "Plantation Rubber Industry", pp. 73–4; Jomo, *A Question of Class*, p. 67.

[39] Benham, "The Rubber Industry", pp. 356, 366; *The Singapore Free Press and Mercantile Advertiser*, 10 Sept. 1908; *The Straits Budget*, 7 Jan. 1932.

[40] Drake, *Merchants, Bankers, Governors*, pp. 105–6, 110; "Chinese Protectorate", in *Annual Departmental Reports of the Straits Settlements for the Year 1900*, pp. 111, 116.

British authorities in both India and Singapore.[41] In 1907, partly in response to accusations that they were recruiting workers from the estates for its public works, the authorities in Singapore decided to subsidise the importation of Tamil workers from Madras and Ceylon to work on the rubber estates, since they were cheaper than Chinese labourers and easier to manage.[42] For this purpose, a Tamil Immigration Fund was set up, to which rubber planters contributed based on the number of days worked by the Indian labourers they employed. The Fund provided for the free passages of Indian immigrants to Malaya, inclusive of the train fare from their villages to embarkation ports.

Like their counterparts from China, Indians came to Malaya because of difficult economic conditions in their homeland, the result of the destruction of indigenous industry under the impact of colonialism and the dispossession of the rural classes.[43] Since the late 19th century, Tamil labourers had been arriving under an indentured labour system that bound them for one to three years to work in the European coffee plantations and public projects, notably road and railway construction.[44] Around the turn of the century and following criticism in India, indentured labour was replaced by the *kangany* system practised in Ceylon, similar to that for Chinese coolies, whereby rubber planters engaged men to recruit people from their own villages and paid them a commission for doing so.[45] The Indian villagers were sometimes enticed by rosy claims about wages and work conditions in Malaya.[46] It was actually a case of one evil substituting for another, as Indian estate labourers were not only supervised by but also indebted to the kangany, who acted as the intermediary between them and plantation owners, for recruitment costs and living expenses.[47] Hence, the system represented a form of debt bondage even though it generally worked well.[48] *En passant*, it should be mentioned that the system was also employed on a much smaller scale to obtain labourers for rubber plantations in Singapore, which had grown to include estates in Seletar and Mandai in the 1920s.

With the establishment of the Tamil Immigration Fund, however, Indians came as independent labourers, the kangany was bypassed and the system's importance declined progressively. Although the authorities were under pressure to keep wages down, Indian labourers did enjoy greater protection from their employers and better work and living conditions, especially in terms of sanitation and medical care, compared to Chinese

---

41 Drabble, *Rubber in Malaya*, pp. 53–5, 94. Another estimate put the ratio at one rubber tapper to four to five acres. Sandhu, *Indians in Malaya*, p. 51.

42 Sandhu, *Indians in Malaya*, pp. 56, 61–3; Rai, *Indians in Singapore*, pp. 68–9, 77, 79; *Proceedings of the Legislative Council of the Straits Settlements*, 17 June 1904, 2 Aug. 1907, 6 Sept. 1907. Assisted emigration actually started in 1887 when a steamship subsidy was given for transporting Indians to the Colony.

43 Sandhu, *Indians in Malaya*, pp. 31–43, 67.

44 Sandhu, *Indian Migration*, pp. 198, 225. Since wages were low, workers often stayed indentured for longer than three years.

45 Rai, *Indians in Singapore*, pp. 80–1, 88–9. The indenture system was banned in 1910.

46 Sandhu, *Indians in Malaya*, pp. 99–100.

47 Jomo, *A Question of Class*, pp. 188–9; *Straits Echo*, 4 July 1917; *Malaya Tribune*, 16 Jan. 1929.

48 *The Straits Budget*, 5 May 1916.

immigrant workers.[49] There were two reasons for this: first, Indians originated from another British colony whose government was concerned about their welfare in Malaya; second, it was easier to monitor labour conditions in large European estates, as opposed to the numerous and dispersed tin mines in which the Chinese toiled. In 1911, a Labour Department was established in the FMS specifically to look after the interests of Indian workers.

As a direct consequence of the rubber boom, the largest flows of Tamil immigrants to Malaya, who mostly disembarked in Penang, occurred in the second decade of the 20th century, when average annual arrivals more than doubled from the first decade to 90,000 persons, despite efforts by the Indian authorities to regulate the inflow.[50] Again as was the case with Chinese immigrants, the number of returnees was also large, since most of the immigrants came as short-term labourers and usually did not stay longer than two years.[51] It was estimated that about two-thirds of the immigrants were labourers, the other third being traders, professionals and others.[52] The resulting predominance of Indian estate workers in the rubber plantations was reflected in their numbers in both absolute and relative terms *vis-à-vis* other racial groups. From 43,824 in 1907, the pool of Tamil workers rose to 181,205 on the cusp of the Great Depression in 1929.[53] From the 1930s onwards, a significant proportion of these workers, estimated at between 25–45 per cent, were females, partly because of an increase in the employers' contribution rate for male labourers to the Immigration Fund.[54] As a percentage of the overall labour strength in the industry, Indian workers consistently fluctuated between 66 per cent and 78 per cent, with some employed as subordinate managerial, clerical and technical staff. Chinese, Javanese and other, mostly Malay, labourers made up the remainder.[55] The first of these groups were typically employed for jungle felling and land clearing while Javanese indentured labour, which was generally difficult to import due to onerous Dutch regulations, was used for all tasks.[56] In 1928, the total labour force in rubber planting was 223,044, whose supplies of food and provisions were obtained mostly from Singapore.

As for forward linkages, there were two that were crucial for the economic development of Singapore in the rubber era. The first was the establishment of an international market for rubber in the city and the second was the setting up of rubber mills to process the raw material imported from Malaya and the Dutch East Indies. The rubber market had humble beginnings in the 1911 decision of the Singapore Chamber of Commerce to form

---

49 Rai, *Indians in Singapore*, p. 195; A.A. Kamble, "Indians in the Plantation Industry of Malaya (Mid-19th to 20th Century)", *Proceedings of the Indian History Congress* 68, Part Two (2007): 1174; *Straits Echo*, 4 July 1917.

50 Sandhu, *Indian Migration*, p. 273; Abshire, *History of Singapore*, pp. 66–7.

51 "Labour Department", in *Annual Departmental Reports of the Straits Settlements for the Year 1913*, p. 33.

52 "Labour Department", in *Annual Departmental Reports of the Straits Settlements for the Year 1916*, p. 153.

53 Jomo, *A Question of Class*, pp. 190–1.

54 Kamble, "Indians in the Plantation Industry", pp. 1169–70, 1171; Sandhu, *Indians in Malaya*, pp. 97–8; *Proceedings of the Legislative Council of the Straits Settlements*, 11 Oct. 1926, 13 Dec. 1926.

55 *The Straits Budget*, 5 May 1916.

56 Huff, *The Economic Growth of Singapore*, p. 153; Sandhu, *Indians in Malaya*, pp. 55–6.

a Rubber Association for the purpose of holding auctions. Incidentally, in the same year a produce exchange was established by Chinese brokers to facilitate business with European merchants and to provide a meeting place at Change Alley for consultation and information exchange, following the establishment of the Chinese Chamber of Commerce in 1906.[57] Although initially overshadowed by the London market, the rubber auctions were given a huge boost when trading in London halted with the outbreak of the First World War in 1914 and American demand took off.[58] Singapore's advantages as a rubber market were its proximity to supply sources, which meant that it could take delivery of the commodity and make quicker payment to producers, while avoiding transshipment costs in London by sending the rubber directly to consumers.[59] By the time the war ended, Singapore was established as a global rubber trading, financing, processing and bulk shipping centre.[60] One quarter of world exports were sold there and four-fifths of the rubber produced in Malaya was re-exported through the city.[61]

These developments had a salutary effect on the growth of the services provided by Singapore by attracting to the city rubber brokers, rubber manufacturers' purchasing agents (representing tyre makers Dunlop, Firestone and Goodyear) and specialist firms from Britain, America and Japan, thus complementing the trading activities of the agency houses.[62] Local Chinese firms dealing in rubber also proliferated: by 1921, 21 rubber dealers were operating along the Singapore River.[63] During that decade, the agency houses turned to buying rubber directly from producers in Malaya to economise on transaction and transportation costs. The rubber bought was thus not brought into Singapore and the houses were able to procure the output of the estates not under their management and of smallholders without relying on middleman dealers. In this way, the agency houses wrested a part of the profits made by the rubber brokers and dealers in Singapore. Nonetheless, the latter continued to perform a price discovery function at the local auctions as well as executing overseas orders and forward sales by estates.[64]

Although the Chinese dealers and commission agents in Singapore lost out from the agencies' upcountry buying of rubber, they were able to make good this loss of business by handling the increasing quantities of wet rubber produced by Dutch East Indies smallholders in the 1920s and sent to Singapore for processing and export.[65] The Chinese were able to seize this opportunity because besides long-standing network contacts, they

57 Huff, *The Economic Growth of Singapore*, pp. 97–8; Song, *One Hundred Years' History of the Chinese*, pp. 559–62, 664; *The Straits Times*, 13 Apr. 1911. Change Alley was a famous shopping arcade and street for changing money that was frequented by visitors. Savage, *Lion City Narratives*, pp. 196–7.

58 *The Straits Times*, 28 Feb. 1914, 2 Sept. 1916.

59 *The Straits Times*, 7 July 1909.

60 V. Giacomin, "Singapore, Global City Ante Litteram in Early Twentieth Century Southeast Asia", in *Singapore—Two Hundred Years of the Lion City*, ed. Webster and White, pp. 69–70.

61 W.G. Huff, "The Development of the Rubber Market in Pre-World War II Singapore", *Journal of Southeast Asian Studies* 24, 2 (1993): 287.

62 Ibid., p. 288; Giacomin, "Singapore", p. 69; *The Straits Times*, 5 Aug. 1920.

63 Ng, "The Maritime Chinese", p. 112.

64 Huff, "The Development of the Rubber Market", pp. 294–6.

65 *The Straits Budget*, 18 Apr. 1924; *The Singapore Free Press and Mercantile Advertiser*, 10 Sept. 1924.

already had a ready-made credit-for-goods system in place in the Straits produce trade with Dutch East Indies suppliers.[66] Under a similar arrangement, they financed rubber production indirectly by advancing food and consumer goods to staple producers against future deliveries of rubber. The international rubber trade in Singapore facilitated these transactions and in turn, benefitted from them through a larger volume of imports. Before 1933, about three-quarters of the native rubber exported from the Dutch East Indies went to Singapore to be remilled.[67]

In some cases, the importers were themselves rubber millers; others sold the wet rubber to milling companies. Singapore soon established the biggest rubber milling industry in the region on the basis of the supply from the Netherlands Indies. Unlike in Malaya where Chinese millers treated smallholder rubber, there were no processing facilities there.[68] Along with the rise of this sector, there was a need for godowns and facilities for storing and grading rubber, the construction of which further stimulated economic growth. In 1925, 20 mills owned by Chinese had been set up in Singapore and by 1928, total employment in this labour-intensive industry might have reached 5,000 workers; in contrast, there were only three European mills in 1933.[69] The profit from milling was reported to be around $12.50 per tonne, or 12 per cent of the average value of a tonne of wet rubber. Before the 1920s, the re-export of processed rubber was mainly in the hands of the European firms but as the Chinese began processing Dutch East Indies imports in large quantities, they started to export the milled rubber themselves to foreign markets, although the former continued to dominate the export of high-grade rubber.[70] In the early 1930s, a substantial proportion of rubber shipments to the United States was by these millers.

When the rubber trees planted in the early 1910s attained maturity in the second half of the decade, Malaya became the world's largest producer, supplying more than half of the global market, and Singapore the largest exporter.[71] From the mid-twenties, however, imports of rubber from the Peninsula for re-export stagnated as the agency houses not only bought the commodity directly from estates and smallholders but also milled it for export from Malayan ports. Port Swettenham in particular had developed steamship facilities to compete with Singapore and was handling a large proportion of the rubber output from Lower Perak, Selangor and Negri Sembilan.[72] The volume imported into Singapore averaged around 100,000 tonnes annually, representing only about one-third of Malayan rubber production in 1925, most of it being the better quality output from Johor and the east coast, while imports from the Dutch East Indies were higher at 131,859 tonnes.[73]

---

[66] Huff, "The Development of the Rubber Market", pp. 298–9.

[67] Lim, *Economic Development of Modern Malaya*, p. 103.

[68] Lee Soo Ann, *From Colony to Nation: Continuity and Change in the Singapore Economy 1946–2006* (Singapore: Singapore Heritage Board), pp. 14–15.

[69] Huff, *The Economic Growth of Singapore*, pp. 205, 301.

[70] Lee, "The Colonial Legacy", p. 11. Chinese dealers also increasingly sourced, graded and exported copra and pepper. Wong, "Commercial Growth", pp. 60–1.

[71] Wong, "Singapore: Its Growth", p. 64.

[72] Chiang, *History of Straits Settlements Foreign Trade*, pp. 93–4; British Military Administration, *Entrepôt Trade*, p. 7.

[73] Huff, *The Economic Growth of Singapore*, pp. 196, 198.

Owing to Singapore's superior ocean-going shipping connections, about half of the rubber exported directly from Malaya was still transshipped there.

Even before the Chinese foray into rubber marketing, the commodity had become all-important in Singapore's exports. The contribution of rubber earnings to merchandise exports first exceeded that of tin in 1916, in which year 44,986 tonnes were shipped out.[74] Due to the increase in supply of rubber from the Dutch East Indies, the commodity's share in Singapore's total exports rose to a peak of 45.1 per cent in 1925. As the agency houses began to prioritise rubber at the expense of traditional commodities, the proportion of Straits produce in exports declined to 9.1 per cent in 1927 from 29.8 per cent at the start of the 20th century. In terms of volume, exports of Straits produce reached their zenith of 346,237 tonnes in 1910, after which they fluctuated around an average of 286,000 tonnes. However, their value in dollar terms fell in the 1930s due to declines in primary commodity prices. Moreover, as demand and supply evolved, there were some notable changes in the product mix, with increased trade in copra and coconut oil and reductions in pepper, rattan and gutta percha.[75] Less gambier and tapioca were exported as Malayan planters shifted to rubber growing.

In contrast to Straits produce, Singapore kept up the flows of food, clothing and opium to its hinterlands to satisfy robust final demand from rubber and tin producers. The quantity of rice re-exported increased by 55.4 per cent in 1927 compared to 1900, whereas dried and salted fish rose by 39.4 per cent.[76] Rice continued to find its largest markets in Malaya and the Dutch East Indies, which together took four-fifths of Singapore's re-exports. As in the preceding decades, these foodstuffs were brought into Singapore from Siam, Burma and Cochin-China by Chinese wholesalers who broke bulk and graded them before resale. As for cotton piece goods, their proportion in Singapore's exports dropped further to just 2.5 per cent in 1927, corroborating their status as an inferior good as posited in the preceding chapter. Opium too had become relatively less important in Singapore's intra-Asian trade in the early 20th century, its share having declined to about 5 per cent.[77]

On the imports side, Southeast Asia had become Singapore's most important trading bloc in the late 19th century. Rubber consolidated this trend and narrowed the port's import sources mainly to Malaya and the Dutch East Indies, with the next two largest import partners being Britain and Siam.[78] In 1927, 53 per cent of total imports came from the two neighbours; apart from rubber, these included tin, pineapples, sugar, copra, coffee and pepper (including black pepper, or "Singapore pepper").[79] The rubber and produce from the Dutch Indies were mostly supplied by Sumatra while Java and the other islands slipped out of Singapore's orbit. In the case of manufactured goods, about half was

[74] Ibid., p. 72, Appendix Table A.1, p. 374, Appendix Table A.2, pp. 378, 380.

[75] A.W. King, "Plantation and Agriculture in Malaya, with Notes on the Trade of Singapore", *The Geographical Journal* 93, 2 (1939): 148; *Straits Settlements Annual Report*, vol. 8, pp. 103–4.

[76] Huff, *The Economic Growth of Singapore*, pp. 78, 99, Appendix Table A.2, pp. 379, 381.

[77] A.J.H. Latham, "The Dynamics of Intra-Asian Trade, 1868–1913: The Great Entrepôts of Singapore and Hong Kong", in *Japanese Industrialization and the Asian Economy*, ed. A.J.H. Latham and H. Kawakatsu (Abingdon: Routledge, 1994), p. 152.

[78] Huff, *The Economic Growth of Singapore*, pp. 82, 84, 86; *Straits Settlements Annual Report*, vol. 9, p. 130.

[79] King, "Plantation and Agriculture in Malaya", pp. 145, 147–8.

imported from Britain and the other half from Europe (19.4 per cent), the United States (16.7 per cent) and Japan (14.1 per cent) in 1927.[80] A large proportion of the producer goods and consumer durables imported by Singapore was retained for domestic use. The rest went to the region, of which Malaya took nearly a third. The items sent there were mainly capital goods for the rubber estates and tin mines, but also consumer products demanded by rubber smallholders. Among the remaining markets, the Netherlands Indies was by far the most important, with Siam being another substantial destination. In the former, cigarettes replaced opium as the most important consumer good, outside of food and cotton goods, while other products were galvanised iron, tyres and tubes.

The system for importing manufactured goods had evolved from the practice in the 19th century of merchant houses accepting consignments and selling them for a commission to their acting as sole agents for manufacturers in the originating countries. Thus, different houses were associated with specific brands for which they were the exclusive distributors. New firms, sales offices of manufacturers and specialised engineering companies also appeared in the city to handle the import and regional distribution of novel industrial products like electrical appliances and machinery, motorcars and rubber tyres, sewing machines, photographic equipment and materials, and chemicals.[81] These new goods increasingly replaced textiles as the more important manufactured imports: the latter's share declined to just over a third in 1927 from one-half in 1913.[82] More homogeneous goods like cement, steel and bicycles were also brought in and distributed by merchant firms and general importers.

The most conspicuous effect of rubber on Singapore's export destinations was the rise of the United States as a major trading partner due to its booming automotive industry, which was the world's biggest buyer of natural rubber. From 1915 until the Great Depression, the United States' absorption of Malayan and Netherlands Indies rubber was never less than two-thirds and it reached four-fifths in some years. Next in importance was Britain, followed by Japan and Germany.[83] By 1927, the United States was the destination for 36.5 per cent of Singapore's overall exports; the proportions that went to Britain and Europe fell respectively to 5.7 per cent and 8.7 per cent, while China, Hong Kong and India faded into further insignificance.[84] However, the heavy dependence on the United States carried downsides. Its entry into the Great War in Europe in late 1917 led to the withdrawal of merchant ships and the imposition of quotas on Malayan rubber imports in May 1918 that halved the amounts taken in the previous year, causing stocks to pile up in Singapore.[85] As a result, the rubber price fell below the cost of production of most estates.[86] In the war's aftermath, a recession in 1921 again curtailed rubber exports, which fell by 11 per cent from their 1919 level. As in 1918, some rubber estates in the Peninsula

[80] Huff, *The Economic Growth of Singapore*, pp. 106–14, 115, 118, 258, 259–61, 262–3.

[81] *Straits Settlements Annual Report*, vol. 9, pp. 131–2.

[82] Huff, *The Economic Growth of Singapore*, pp. 114–5.

[83] Lim, *Economic Development of Modern Malaya*, Appendix 4.2, p. 327.

[84] Huff, *The Economic Growth of Singapore*, p. 81.

[85] Drabble, "Plantation Rubber Industry", pp. 67, 68–72, 77; *The Straits Budget*, 24 May 1918.

[86] W. Bartley, "Singapore and the Great War", in *One Hundred Years of Singapore*, vol. I, ed. Makepeace, Brooke and Braddell, p. 415.

voluntarily reduced their output.[87] By late 1921, however, it was clear that this strategy had not achieved the desired result of raising the world rubber price, in part because the scheme was not mandatory and producers outside Malaya, in particular those in the Dutch East Indies, did not follow suit. The price of rubber declined to a nadir of 9⅓d. per pound in 1922 as supply continued to increase owing to the large investments poured into the industry before the war.

Government intervention had become inevitable and it had to be on an international scale. The necessary action came about only in November 1922 after the Dutch made known that they would not cooperate with a proposed scheme but the British government decided to go ahead anyway with participation from Malayan and Ceylonese rubber growers, as well as British-owned plantations in the Dutch East Indies.[88] The Stevenson Scheme, as the price control measure was called, allotted individual quotas to all producers, of which a certain quantity, varying according to the ruling rubber price, could be exported at a minimum rate of duty.[89] Exports in excess of this amount would be subject to progressively higher rates of duty. The initial aim of the scheme was to reduce production to 60 per cent of the 1920 level, with a corresponding target price of 1s. 3d. per pound of rubber.[90] The Stevenson Scheme lasted until 1928 and the general verdict is that it was not very effective, mainly because of the Dutch East Indies' non-participation, which meant that almost a quarter of the world's rubber output was excluded in the first year of the scheme, and more in later years. Yet by restricting supply, it did help to keep rubber prices high for the better part of its period of operation, thus propping up the returns to capital and dividends of the large plantation companies.[91]

The Dutch benefitted from being a free rider. Moreover, the high prices galvanised new planting among native smallholders. The Netherlands Indies did however participate in the successor to the Stevenson Scheme, the International Rubber Regulation Agreement of 1934 to 1943, that also co-opted, in addition to the British colonies, Siam and Cochin-China.[92] The restrictions under this scheme operated differently as there was no price target, only a time-varying export quota expressed as a proportion of participating countries' production capacity and applied uniformly to all countries except the last two named above. Malaya was allocated an average annual quota of 560,000 tonnes over the first five years of the scheme's operation while the Netherlands Indies was given 429,000 tonnes.[93] In the five years preceding the scheme when there was no price control, Malaya's exports had averaged 442,189 tonnes per annum.[94]

---

87 Lim, *Economic Development of Modern Malaya,* pp. 75–6.

88 Drabble, "Plantation Rubber Industry", pp. 71–2.

89 *The Straits Budget,* 13 Oct. 1922; *Malaya Tribune,* 14 Oct. 1922.

90 Lim, *Economic Development of Modern Malaya,* pp. 76–8.

91 J.H. Drabble, *Malayan Rubber: The Interwar Years* (Basingstoke: Macmillan, 1991), p. 304; C.R. Whittlesey, "The Stevenson Plan: Some Conclusions and Observations", *Journal of Political Economy* 39, 4 (1931): 511–2; *The Straits Budget,* 19 Aug. 1926.

92 *Malaya Tribune,* 30 Apr. 1934, 20 Apr. 1935.

93 *Malaya Tribune,* 11 June 1934.

94 Drabble, *Malayan Rubber,* Appendix 3, p. 309.

At the individual country level, the allocation of the annual quota was left to the relevant authorities in charge. Based on the rationale that the European estates were more efficient in their technology and organisation, they were given higher production quotas than smallholdings, taken as a group. Even if the efficiency assumption was correct, this allocation seemed harsh on the smallholders as they together with the Chinese and Indian-owned estates had suffered in the recession of the early twenties and became heavily indebted as rubber earnings fell.[95] In late 1922, the Chettiars who lent money to Chinese planters had foreclosed on 20,000 acres of their estates. Moreover, smallholdings produced nearly half of the country's output in 1933 but they were assigned only 38 per cent of the shared quota.[96] It was claimed by critics that the fear of estates being outcompeted by smallholders with their much lower production costs was the reason for the discrimination, although ignorance on the government's part has been put forward as an alternative explanation.[97]

A Marxian perspective on the issue similarly maintains that smallholders were under-assessed by both restriction schemes even though they were the more efficient producers, and regards this underestimation as a manifestation of dominant class interests in Malayan rubber production, namely, British investors in large plantation companies.[98] According to this view, the colonial state was pressed by these capitalists to intervene at the expense of the smallholders by assigning to estates production allocations that were higher than would be justified by their average output per acre and conversely, allocations to smallholders below their average yield. Furthermore, the International Rubber Regulation Agreement forbade new planting of rubber except for one year in 1939–40.[99] The implication is that rubber output would have been higher in both Malaya and the Dutch East Indies if there had been no restrictions and Singapore would have gained by processing and exporting a larger volume of rubber, albeit at lower prices.

Shipping and Transport Infrastructure

The expansion of the rubber industry in the Malay Peninsula provides, after tin mining, a further illustration of staple-led growth. Following a technical breakthrough in the method of tapping rubber and with the British government playing a facilitating role, Western enterprise brought capital resources and organisational skills to bear on economic development in a thinly populated and relatively uncultivated region. A scarcity of labour was overcome by bringing in workers from densely populated areas, which led to an increase in production, the forging of economic linkages and the creation of new wealth. Along with rubber trading and milling, Singapore derived an additional benefit from the Malayan rubber industry—the modernisation of its shipping and transport infrastructure.

Not long after the advent of the steamship era, the city's Chinese businessmen took a decisive lead in establishing a regular network of steamers that plied between ports in the Eastern Archipelago. Such a move was totally in keeping with their interests in the Straits

---

95 Lim, *Economic Development of Modern Malaya*, pp. 76, 82, Appendix 4.3, p. 328.

96 Jomo, *A Question of Class*, p. 71.

97 Bauer, *The Rubber Industry*, p. 215; Benham, "The Rubber Industry", pp. 362–3.

98 Jomo, *A Question of Class*, pp. 67–9.

99 Benham, "The Rubber Industry", pp. 359–60.

produce trade and many of the shipowners had widespread mercantile dealings in the region. Moreover, entry costs into the shipping industry were relatively low compared to other investment outlets, as it was feasible to purchase second-hand tonnage.[100] As early as the 1860s, a number of Chinese firms already owned 120 of the 178 vessels registered in Singapore.[101] The more prominent among them were Wee Bin and Company (later becoming the Ho Hong Steamship Company) with 20 vessels, and the Bun Hin Line which owned 15 steamers.[102] All did a flourishing business in the inter-island coastal trade of the Dutch East Indies, carrying rice, machinery and consumer goods in exchange for tropical produce, though none attempted to compete with the international shipping concerns that conducted the long-distance trade.[103] The companies' other focus was on local shipping which carried tin ore from the ports of Malaya to Singapore and Penang (the "mosquito fleet" mentioned above).

During the 1880s, the Chinese shipowners in Singapore began to encounter competition from the ocean-going lines on the Dutch East Indies leg of their operations. Of the British-owned fleets that had entered the market, the most visible were those belonging to the P&O and the Ocean Steamship Company (OSC) of Alfred and Philip Holt (commonly known as the Blue Funnel Line) founded in 1865. In Southeast Asia, the agency of the latter carrier was handed to Walter Mansfield and Company based in Singapore.[104] The agency managed to build up in a relatively short time a fleet of small steamers running between Singapore, Bangkok, Deli (in Sumatra), Sandakan (in North Borneo) and other Dutch East Indies ports, carrying rice, tobacco, spices and sugar. Very quickly, the field became crowded as booming trade attracted increasing numbers of European shippers to operate in Singapore.[105] A total of 37 companies were officially listed as shipping businesses in 1888 but two firms in particular offered cut-throat competition to the British incumbents: the German Norddeutscher Lloyd line and the Dutch Koninklijke Paketvaart Maatschappij (KPM) line, a company formed to operate as an exclusive and national shipping line in the Netherlands Indies.[106] Both established feeder services in the Archipelago to their main line operations, although they stayed clear of the Peninsular tin trade. In 1891, the KPM had 27 steamers servicing the inter-coastal trade of the Dutch islands and Java.[107] As non-Dutch ships were excluded from this trade, the KPM was able to divert commerce from Singapore to Batavia and

---

[100] Huff, *The Economic Growth of Singapore*, pp. 65, 66–7.

[101] Song, *One Hundred Years' History of the Chinese*, pp. 173, 175.

[102] *The Straits Budget*, 16 Dec. 1903.

[103] *The Straits Times Weekly Issue*, 30 Sept. 1889.

[104] *The Singapore Free Press and Mercantile Advertiser*, 2 Jan. 1932.

[105] K.G. Tregonning, *Home Port Singapore: A History of Straits Steamship Company Limited 1890–1965* (Singapore: Oxford University Press, 1967), pp. 11–12.

[106] Huff, *The Economic Growth of Singapore*, p. 65; Turnbull, *History of Modern Singapore*, pp. 106–7; *The Singapore and Straits Directory*, 1888, pp. 165–6; *Straits Echo*, 18 Feb. 1907. Another prominent foreign carrier operating from Singapore was the French shipping company Messageries Maritimes; by the end of the century, the Western shipping lines were joined by firms from Japan. Lee, "The Colonial Legacy", pp. 8–9.

[107] *The Singapore Free Press and Mercantile Advertiser*, 8 Oct. 1935.

other ports in Java, including tobacco imports from Deli.[108] By early 1893, however, competition had given way to an agreement between the Ocean Steamship Company and the KPM to carve out the routes in the Archipelago, the former obtaining the right to sail to Java and the latter taking a share of the Sumatra and Penang trades.

With the setting up of the STC smelter in Singapore in 1890, the need for expanded shipping facilities gave rise to a rare instance of joint enterprise between Chinese and European merchants. In that year, several of these entrepreneurs came together to register the Straits Steamship Company (SSC), which in a sense was a sister company of the STC as it carried all the tin ore from Malaya to be smelted in Singapore and supplied a return flow of provisions and labourers.[109] The SSC initially confined its services to this activity, plying from Singapore to its sister settlements as well as the ports that had sprung up on the west coast of the Malay States, especially Port Weld and Telok Anson in northern Perak. During the early years of the 20th century, the company's coasters began to make regular runs to Port Swettenham and Port Dickson to collect rubber from the inland estates. Then between 1903 and 1911, it built six new ships to meet the burgeoning demand for passenger services between Singapore, Port Swettenham and Penang, which also ferried Chinese immigrants to the Peninsula. By the mid-1920s, the vessels owned by the SSC became known as the "White Fleet" and they served 53 ports in the region.[110]

At the start of the First World War, the Norddeutscher Lloyd line was liquidated as enemy property by the British authorities. The SSC was then asked by the OSC to take over the Bangkok and Borneo routes of the defunct line while the latter injected capital for building new steamers to replace the German ships and obtained in return a large stake in the SSC.[111] During the early 1920s, rubber's increasing importance in Singapore's trade led to a further expansion of the SSC's fleet—bespoke vessels tailored to the conditions of Southeast Asian trade—and imparted a boost to its profits.[112] The staple also brought about further structural changes in the regional shipping industry. First, the tonnage to and from Malaya and the Dutch East Indies increased by 237 per cent between 1913 and 1929.[113] Second, the industry became dominated by the SSC and the KPM after they edged out most of the Chinese firms owing to better capital endowments and greater resilience to the vicissitudes of the rubber industry.

In the twenties and thirties, the SSC acquired seven Chinese shipping lines. The first of two major takeovers was its purchase of the Eastern Shipping Company of Penang in 1922 with its fleet of 40, no doubt dilapidated, vessels.[114] This company had secured the contract of the Eastern Smelting Company for the carriage of tin ore from mines in the

---

[108] Hyde, "British Shipping Companies", pp. 37, 38; Chiang, *History of Straits Settlements Foreign Trade*, p. 95.

[109] Huff, *The Economic Growth of Singapore*, p. 67; Tregonning, *Home Port Singapore*, pp. 17–19, 20–3, 35–6.

[110] Lee, "The Colonial Legacy", p. 9.

[111] Hyde, "British Shipping Companies", p. 39; Huff, *The Economic Growth of Singapore*, p. 127; Tregonning, *Home Port Singapore*, pp. 45–6.

[112] Chiang, *History of Straits Settlements Foreign Trade*, p. 97.

[113] Huff, *The Economic Growth of Singapore*, pp. 137, 145–7.

[114] Tregonning, *Home Port Singapore*, pp. 56–9, 67–8.

Peninsula, the Siamese western coast and Burma to a smelter on the island that opened in 1897.[115] Since then, the two firms had jointly waged a contest with the STC-SSC partnership by diverting ores to Penang for processing and export, prompting the STC to set up a rival smelting works on the Province Wellesley coast opposite Penang harbour in 1902.[116] However, the Eastern Shipping Company fell victim to the severe recession of 1921, enabling the SSC to seize the opportunity to absorb its competitor. But by then, Penang was already smelting more ore than Singapore was.[117] During the Great Depression a decade later, the SSC secured its second major takeover through obtaining the management of the Ho Hong Steamship Company after acquiring the line's three ocean-going steamships, which allowed it to trade with China. Nevertheless, there was still competition between the SSC and the KPM: in spite of an agreement made in 1924 to divide up shipping routes and fix freight rates, the KPM succeeded in grabbing a part of its rival's business by wooing native traders in the Dutch East Indies and adding passenger services to its operations.[118] Consequently, Dutch vessels owned the lion's share of the regional shipping tonnage by 1928.[119]

The local and regional shipping industry therefore evolved from a monopolistically competitive position in the 19th century to essentially a duopoly in the 20th century. In contrast, the market structure of the long-haul shipping lines developed in a different direction. Although it was for all practical purposes an oligopoly in the early years, the ocean-going sector turned into a cartel at the turn of the century. This anti-competitive outcome was the result of the Straits Homeward Conference organised by the shipowners to eliminate, restrict and regulate the competition on the maritime routes from Singapore to Britain and Europe.[120] This conference came about in 1897 with the participation of 23 shipping lines and three merchant firms, later on increasing to seven which between them handled three-fifths of the homeward (to Britain and Europe) export trade.[121] With this agreement, shipping schedules were rationalised, freight rates were controlled and the participants undertook to provide sufficient cargo space on regular services. Enforcement of the Conference was effected by means of a deferred rebate given to exporters of tropical produce and tin, thereby securing their exclusive patronage. The rebate amounted to 5 per cent of the total freights paid by them on cargo carried in half a year, and would be forfeited if non-Conference shipping lines were utilised.[122] Loyalty was further enhanced through an additional secret rebate of 5 per cent, to be dispensed yearly to the participating merchant firms and shared among them if average freight rates exceeded stipulated

---

[115] Allen and Donnithorne, *Western Enterprise in Indonesia and Malaya*, pp. 159–60.

[116] Tregonning, "Straits Tin", p. 100.

[117] Wong, "Singapore: Its Growth", p. 72.

[118] Hyde, "British Shipping Companies", p. 42.

[119] Huff, *The Economic Growth of Singapore*, p. 124.

[120] Chiang, *History of Straits Settlements Foreign Trade*, pp. 124–5, 127–9.

[121] This was the third attempt to form a conference for homeward cargo following two previous unsuccessful initiatives. Huff, *The Economic Growth of Singapore*, p. 128.

[122] *Straits Echo*, 25 July 1911.

minimum amounts.[123] While deferred rebates are common to all shipping conferences, the secret rebate was unique to Singapore.

The economic rationale for the Straits Homeward Conference is not difficult to grasp, in view of the intense competition between shipping companies prior to its formation. As there was excess capacity on the homeward voyage—though not on the outward journey—freights were pushed down to very low levels, which could not provide an adequate return on the heavy investments made in steamships.[124] In this respect, the Conference enabled the participating shipping lines to behave as a joint monopolist and raise freight charges by reportedly 35 per cent.[125] Challenges to the system from dissentient merchant firms who chartered "tramp" steamers were neutralised by co-opting them into the secret rebate or, in the case of independent shipping lines that did not participate, by buying them out, as happened to two smaller companies.[126] By virtue of the secret rebate, the Conference actually created a second monopoly in the produce trade: merchant firms receiving the payment were able to drive out companies that did not (and were not shipping agents) by offering higher purchase prices.[127] Beginning in 1905, the Straits Homeward Conference was supplemented by the New York Freights Conference on routes from Singapore to the east coast of the United States, involving essentially the same merchant firms and working on similar principles.[128]

Meanwhile, the Straits Homeward Conference came under attack from various quarters.[129] The Registrar of Imports and Exports, as the representative of the colonial government, was a stern critic, accusing the cartel of throttling the trade of Singapore.[130] According to his calculations, the excess on freight paid in 1907 as a result of the Conferences—a measure of monopoly profits—amounted to £164,100.[131] The Singapore Chamber of Commerce, which had initially adopted an ambivalent attitude because its members included the parties to the secret rebate, joined the opposition to the Conference in 1907. At about this time, the British government set up a Royal Commission to enquire into the conferences in its colonies. The Commission's report in 1909, while pointing out the undesirable nature of the secret rebate, did not however recommend the dismantling of the system.[132]

---

123 *The Ring and the Book* (Singapore, 1908), p. 4. This is a compilation of newspaper articles highly critical of the Straits Homeward Conference that were published by *The Singapore Free Press and Mercantile Advertiser*. Shippers would already have received two rebates of 5 per cent during the year, paid on a six-monthly basis.

124 Chiang, *History of Straits Settlements Foreign Trade*, pp. 125–6, 129–30.

125 *The Ring and the Book*, p. 5; Huff, *The Economic Growth of Singapore*, pp. 128, 129, 131–3.

126 Tramp steamers had neither fixed schedules nor published ports of call.

127 *The Ring and the Book*, p. 19.

128 *Straits Echo*, 15 Dec. 1904.

129 Chiang, *History of Straits Settlements Foreign Trade*, pp. 131–3.

130 *The Ring and the Book*, pp. 29–30; *Proceedings of the Legislative Council of the Straits Settlements*, 1908, Appendix No. 27, pp. C95–109.

131 *Straits Settlements Annual Report*, vol. 5, pp. 682, 684–5.

132 *The Straits Times*, 29 June 1909.

In the same year, a petition signed by more than 700 firms, businessmen and professionals in Singapore was presented to the Legislative Council calling for action against the Straits Homeward Conference.[133] The result was the Freight and Steamship Ordinance of 1910 aiming to "protect shippers of goods from excessive charges and undue restrictions".[134] A duty of 20 per cent was levied on every bill of lading over $100 handled by Conference shipping agents while exporters could demand a rebate of 10 per cent from non-Conference lines at the end of a six-month period. However, the law did not come into operation but was superseded a year later by an agreement reached between the Straits government and the Conference shipping companies to abolish the secret rebate and allow exporters to freely choose shipping lines after three years.[135]

The issue was thus settled and it faded from the public gaze after 1911, but the debate over its merits continued for a long time. There were both detractors and supporters, even within the mercantile community.[136] On one side, it was claimed that the Straits Homeward Conference had stunted the development of Singapore's commerce and reduced its trade in Straits produce and cargo transshipment because freight rates were artificially increased to equal or exceed those in competing ports.[137] For the first time in its history, the Colony's free port status was held in abeyance.[138] Furthermore, the system was alleged to have led both to an increase of foreign shipping tonnage at the expense of Britain and to the development of ocean-going port facilities elsewhere in the Archipelago, resulting in a rise in direct shipments to Europe and America from places which had previously sent their goods to Singapore for sorting, grading and rebulking.[139] The supporters of the Conference, on the other hand, argued that the increase in the share of foreign tonnage was due to the growth of nationalism and subsidies given by governments to shipping companies, a practice that originated with France and was followed by other European countries as well as the United States and Japan.[140] This assertion was backed up by the Royal Commission, which stated that the Dutch especially attempted to develop trade in their colonies by subsidising the KPM. In terms of the benefits to Singapore, the Conference brought about the stability in freight rates desired by exporters and improved the quality of shipping services, both by ensuring adequate tonnage and through adding faster vessels.

Turning now to port infrastructure, our narrative will focus on the Tanjong Pagar Dock Company, which was established as the first limited liability company in Singapore in 1864. As stated earlier, it built Singapore's first dry dock and competed with the Patent Slip and Dock Company and other smaller shipyards in providing wharfage, dock and ship

[133] *Proceedings of the Legislative Council of the Straits Settlements*, 1910, Appendix No. 24, pp. C115–6.

[134] Chiang, *History of Straits Settlements Foreign Trade*, pp. 133–4; *Proceedings of the Legislative Council of the Straits Settlements*, 19 Aug. 1910, 14 Oct. 1910; *The Straits Budget*, 23 June 1910.

[135] *Proceedings of the Legislative Council of the Straits Settlements*, 1911, 21 July 1911, 13 Oct. 1911, Appendix No. 26, pp. C74–5; *Straits Echo*, 25 July 1911.

[136] *The Ring and the Book*, passim.

[137] Chiang, *History of Straits Settlements Foreign Trade*, pp. 131–2, 133, 142.

[138] *The Ring and the Book*, pp. 27–8.

[139] Huff, *The Economic Growth of Singapore*, pp. 134, 136–7.

[140] Chiang, *History of Straits Settlements Foreign Trade*, pp. 71, 135, 138, 140–2, 143.

repair facilities from 1866 to 1881.[141] In spite of the competition, it was recognised that the company was a good investment; it paid an annual dividend of 12 per cent in 1872 and thereafter, except for a few years, the dividend never fell below 10–14 per cent.[142] The company resolved the conflict between investor return and infrastructure development by issuing debenture bonds to build ancillary facilities such as machine, boiler and blacksmith shops, a foundry, godowns, a sawmill and a timber yard. In 1881, the two rival firms entered into a joint-purse agreement that allowed them to share dock and machine shop profits.[143] Following that, they proceeded to lease or acquire rival establishments, starting with a small dock on Pulau Brani and culminating with the purchase of the Borneo Company's wharf in 1885, which gave the Tanjong Pagar Dock Company a continuous line of wharves a mile-and-a-quarter long. Then in 1899, the Tanjong Pagar Dock Company obtained complete control of port facilities in Singapore by amalgamating with its partner, for which it paid $1.75 million (Map 5).[144]

The Tanjong Pagar Dock Company's domination meant that the port and hence the Colony's prosperity were in the hands of a private company whose accountability was to its shareholders. This would not matter as long as the company's and the public's interests coincided. During the decade 1890–1900, however, around half of the profits earned by the company were distributed as dividends rather than reinvested. By the time the amalgamation took place, the expansion of naval and commercial shipping in the Far East was beginning to overwhelm the company's facilities and this, combined with the increasing size and capacity of steamships, resulted in congestion and delays at the port.[145] Its wooden wharves were "shabby, outdated and congested" and badly in need of modernisation.[146] Even though Singapore ranked as the world's seventh largest port in terms of tonnage in 1903, an extension of the wharves and further development were clearly necessary to meet new demands for fuel and facilitate a quick turnover of cargo.[147] Plans and estimates were submitted to the company's management for consideration but they were aborted for various reasons.[148]

---

[141] G. Bogaars, *The Tanjong Pagar Dock Company, 1864–1905*, Memoirs of the Raffles Museum, No. 3 (Singapore, 1956), pp. 129–30, 157, 160, 161–2; Nicholson, "The Tanjong Pagar Dock Company", p. 4; *The Singapore Free Press and Mercantile Advertiser*, 5 May 1896, 8 Oct. 1935. The Patent Slip and Dock Company later changed its name to the New Harbour Dock Company.

[142] *Straits Times Overland Journal*, 26 Feb. 1874, 1 Mar. 1879; *Straits Budget*, 9 Mar. 1899.

[143] Bogaars, *The Tanjong Pagar Dock Company*, pp. 192–6; *Singapore Daily Times*, 13 May 1881.

[144] *The Straits Budget*, 8 Dec. 1899; *The Singapore Free Press and Mercantile Advertiser*, 18 Jan. 1900, 3 Feb. 1900. This was the second attempt to amalgamate the two companies, the first being unsuccessful in 1866. Nicholson, "The Tanjong Pagar Dock Company", p. 3.

[145] *The Singapore Free Press and Mercantile Advertiser*, 24 Aug. 1899, 18 Oct. 1900.

[146] Tan, *A Very Short History*, p. 36.

[147] Turnbull, *History of Modern Singapore*, p. 93; Huff, *The Economic Growth of Singapore*, pp. 137–9; Bogaars, *The Tanjong Pagar Dock Company*, pp. 216, 235.

[148] Nicholson, "The Tanjong Pagar Dock Company", pp. 10–12.

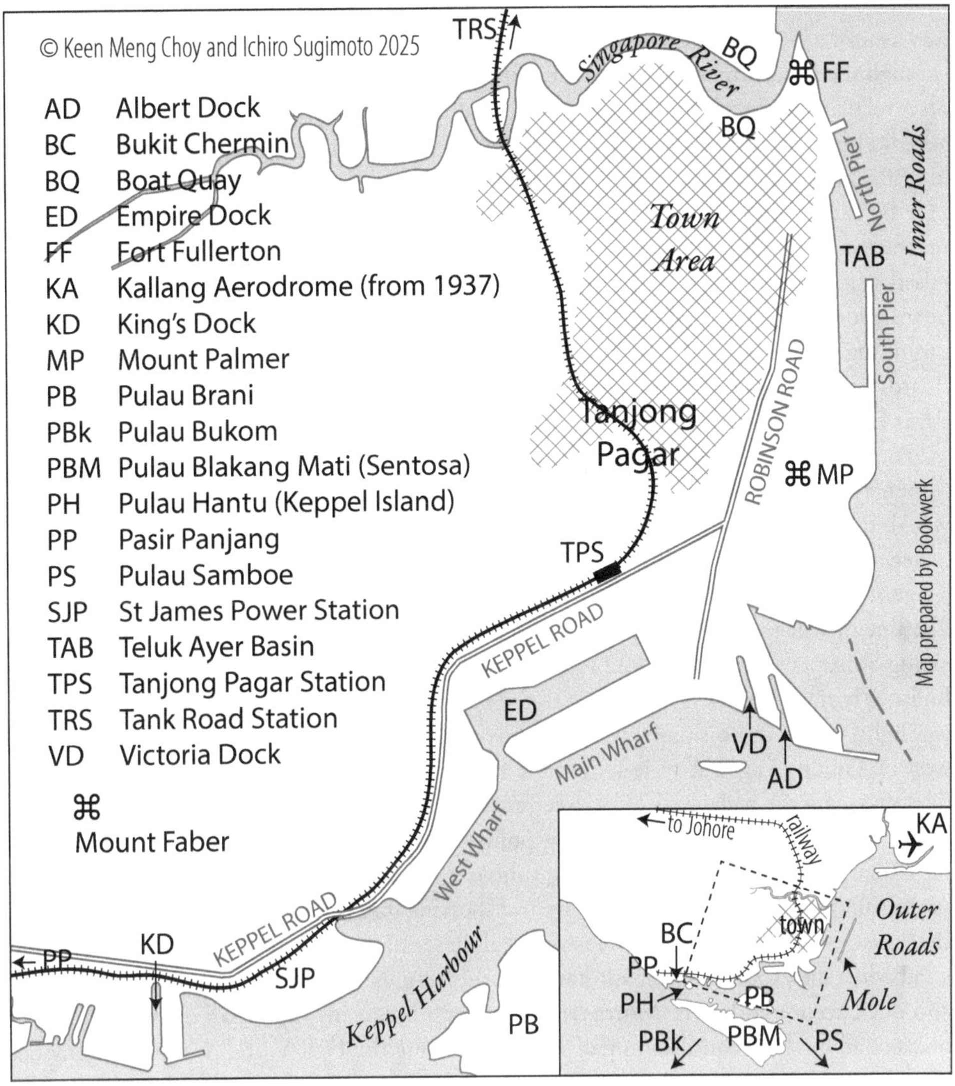

Map 5. Singapore River and Keppel Harbour, c. 1925.

Note: The squares with ovals at each corner represent military installments.

Source: Based on a series of historical maps of Singapore, especially the 1924 map of the Municipal Area, from the Singapore Land Authority collection, courtesy of the National Archives of Singapore.

When the directors of the company were finally ready to go ahead in 1904, the costs of redeveloping the port had risen to some $12 million and so a loan from the FMS government was requested, since the Peninsula stood to gain from improved port infrastructure in Singapore.[149] The matter was referred to the Colonial Office in London and its decision came in late 1904: the company was to be expropriated by the Straits Settlements government.[150] This drastic action was favoured by many in Singapore, including Chinese traders who found the port charges exorbitant, although the Governor

[149] Bogaars, *The Tanjong Pagar Dock Company*, pp. 235–6, 237, 240, 241–2.

[150] *Straits Echo*, 16 Jan. 1905; *The Singapore Free Press and Mercantile Advertiser*, 5 Oct. 1905.

was against it.[151] The alternative of giving the authorities some control of the company through the appointment of a director with veto power to its board proved to be infeasible. State regulation of a naturally monopolistic industry through, for example, a harbour trust, also did not seem to have been seriously contemplated, even though the idea was suggested in 1901 but quickly forgotten. With that, the Tanjong Pagar Dock Company was taken over by the government-appointed Tanjong Pagar Dock Board in July 1905. Following protracted arbitration proceedings, the compensation paid was £28,348,114, which was raised through a loan.[152] As most of the company directors were retained on the new board, works to modernise the harbour based on the existing blueprint were implemented beginning from 1907.[153] In 1913, the Straits government set up the Singapore Harbour Board to take over the management and control of the undertaking from the Tanjong Pagar Dock Board.[154]

Port infrastructure was much enhanced by the Singapore Harbour Board. The wharf frontage built of wood was replaced with concrete and steel structures, new storage facilities were built, and electric cranes and forklift trucks were introduced to save on manpower.[155] A new wet dock, named the King's Dock, was constructed in 1913 and the Empire Dock, a lagoon graving dock, was inaugurated in 1917 after a delay caused by the contractors.[156] The line of wharves was extended by building along the north shore of Keppel Harbour, giving Singapore a total of 9,822 feet of wharfage, nearly 8,000 feet of which were newly built. Wharfage fees were kept low as the capital expenditure incurred on construction was light, owing in no small part to the favourable geographical layout of the land to the west of Tanjong Pagar. A mile-long mole (a breakwater) made up of granite in the roads directly facing the reclaimed Telok Ayer Basin was completed in 1915, creating Inner and Outer Harbours as additional landing points for ocean-going vessels and local steamers to discharge and load cargo, including rubber.[157] During rough weather, the mole offered protection to the lighters and twakows transporting goods to and from the warehouses at the Singapore River and Keppel Harbour. All these enhancements stood Singapore in good stead when the export and transshipment of rubber greatly increased the demand for wharf and dock accommodation. Moreover, there was a boom in ship repair activities that was occasioned by the reconditioning of vessels following the First World War; these activities

---

[151] Huff, *The Economic Growth of Singapore*, pp. 139–40; Song, *One Hundred Years' History of the Chinese*, pp. 539–40.

[152] Wright and Cartwright, *Twentieth Century Impressions*, p. 221; *Proceedings of the Legislative Council of the Straits Settlements*, 20 Jan. 1905, 7 Apr. 1905; *Straits Settlements Annual Report*, vol. 5, pp. 594, 643–4; *The Straits Budget*, 6 July 1905.

[153] Nicholson, "The Tanjong Pagar Dock Company", pp. 14, 19.

[154] *Straits Settlements Annual Report*, vol. 6, p. 470.

[155] *Singapore Port History*, p. 14.

[156] Huff, *The Economic Growth of Singapore*, pp. 137, 139, 140, 142, 245–6; Nicholson, "The Tanjong Pagar Dock Company", pp. 14–15.

[157] *A Short History of the Port of Singapore with Particular Reference to the Undertakings of the Singapore Harbour Board* (Singapore: Fraser and Neave, 1922), p. 3; Swettenham, *British Malaya*, pp. 333–4; *Straits Settlements Annual Report*, vol. 7, pp. 7–8.

kept the dockyards busy and in turn boosted the Board's revenue in 1920.[158] Between 1913 and 1928, total inward and outward cargo at the wharves rose by 45 per cent.[159] In 1922, the operations of the Singapore Harbour Board entailed the employment of 11,000 Europeans and Asians.[160]

As for land transport, the introduction of the motor vehicle into Singapore in the early 20th century brought about revolutionary change. The number of private motorcars increased from 842 in 1915 to 3,506 in 1920, allowing more people to live away from the town but causing congestion.[161] Contemporaneously, the inauguration of lorries for transporting rubber and other goods led to the phasing out of bullock carts, whose manifold uses had included, beyond the conveyance of goods, carrying refuse, mail delivery and road rolling.[162] The town's Fire Brigade was motorised in 1907, replacing the horses in service since a professional brigade had been created in 1888.[163] By the 1930s, the sight of buffaloes and horses, imported from India, Java and Australia since the early days of Singapore's existence, was relatively rare. Small seven-seater mosquito buses without fixed stops also crowded out the carriages, gharries and rickshaws. These erstwhile forms of transport were not missed, for despite the great utility of the rickshaws for example, the town was crippled whenever the pullers went on strike, as in 1901 when the police tried to enforce obedience with road regulations.[164] As the number of rickshaws on the roads decreased from 8,376 in 1925 to 3,693 in 1939, they ceased to be a menace to other users, but their death knell was sounded only during the Japanese Occupation when trishaws were introduced.[165]

The motorcar did not flourish until much later as there were other improved modes of road transport. A steam tramway began operating in 1886 between the docks and Johnston's Pier.[166] However, the passenger service, which ran as far as Rochor, lasted for only three years before the whole works was bought over by the Tanjong Pagar Dock Company for the transport of goods, as it could not compete with the cheaper and more convenient rickshaws which charged only three cents for a half-mile.[167] In 1902, the Singapore Electric Tramway Company was formed; three years later, it was running six lines through the town, serving Keppel Road, North and South Bridge Roads, Crawford Street and Serangoon Road.[168] High fares and doubts about its usefulness notwithstanding,

[158] Huff, *The Economic Growth of Singapore*, p. 246; *Straits Settlements Annual Report*, vol. 8, p. 173; *The Singapore Free Press and Mercantile Advertiser*, 8 Oct. 1935.

[159] *The Straits Budget*, 17 Oct. 1929.

[160] *A Short History of the Port of Singapore*, p. 8.

[161] Turnbull, *History of Modern Singapore*, p. 140.

[162] *The Land Transport of Singapore*, pp. 57–8.

[163] Jayapal, *Old Singapore*, pp. 57, 59, 65; Waterson, "Gathering Speed", pp. 107, 111–3. Prior to 1888, the brigade was made up entirely of volunteers. *Proceedings of the Legislative Council of the Straits Settlements*, 1884, Appendix No. 29, p. C285.

[164] Wise, *Travellers' Tales*, pp. 308–33; Song, *One Hundred Years' History of the Chinese*, p. 471.

[165] Lee, "The Colonial Legacy", pp. 15–16.

[166] Wright and Cartwright, *Twentieth Century Impressions*, pp. 183–4; *The Straits Times Weekly Issue*, 6 May 1886. Johnston's Pier was where Clifford Pier used to be.

[167] Hallifax, "Municipal Government", p. 332; Wise, *Travellers' Tales*, p. 302.

[168] Waterson, "Gathering Speed", pp. 112–3.

the electric trams provided an alternative means of transport to dwellers in the outskirts, most of whom did not own a car.[169] The service was discontinued only in 1927 and replaced two years later by the more comfortable and faster trolley buses (also electric-powered but without rails) and petrol-driven omnibuses.[170]

By then, the motorcar was king of the roads, numbering 7,097 at the end of 1929 while the tally for lorries was 1,432.[171] The ascendance of the automobile gave rise to a variety of related trades and employment: car dealers, spare parts suppliers, service garages, mechanics and drivers.[172] In 1926, Ford built an automobile assembly plant in Singapore, the first in Southeast Asia. On the negative side, the proliferation of motorcars led to a deterioration in traffic conditions and a lack of parking spaces.[173] Travellers to Singapore at that time often remarked on the enormous amount of motor traffic in the city.[174] For instance, on a working day, nearly 5,000 cars passed across Anderson Bridge, the last of the colonial era bridges straddling the mouth of the Singapore River, erected in 1910 to relieve heavy traffic on Cavenagh Bridge.[175] To accommodate the increase in the car population, more and better roads were constructed—their length in the municipal areas alone was 140 miles in 1929, not to mention major arteries in the country districts such as East and West Coast Roads, Ayer Rajah Road and Changi Road.[176] Motorised transport provided the municipal government with a new source of revenue: in 1929, just over a million dollars was collected from licences on cars, lorries, buses and rickshaws.[177] Thus began the system of vehicle taxation that was to assume much greater importance in Singapore as the century progressed.

The Interwar Years Up To 1928

During the relatively prosperous interwar years before the Great Depression of the 1930s, the conveniences of modern life became more widely available in Singapore: the motorcar as just described, the telephone, radio and electricity.[178] Like many inventions of the industrial age, telephony began in Singapore in the late 19th century, specifically in 1879 with a trial connection made between Raffles Square and Tanjong Pagar using a telegraph

---

169 Jayapal, *Old Singapore*, p. 63; *Straits Settlements Annual Report*, vol. 5, p. 32; *The Singapore Free Press and Mercantile Advertiser*, 1 Aug. 1919, 13 Apr. 1920.

170 *The Land Transport of Singapore*, pp. 31, 81; *Malaya Tribune*, 16 Aug. 1926; *The Straits Budget*, 8 Sept. 1927.

171 *The Singapore Free Press and Mercantile Advertiser*, 29 Mar. 1930.

172 Huff, *The Economic Growth of Singapore*, pp. 214, 263; *Malayan Saturday Post*, 5 Oct. 1929.

173 *Proceedings of the Legislative Council of the Straits Settlements*, 1938, Appendix No. 76, pp. 397–445.

174 Savage, *Lion City Narratives*, p. 178.

175 Hallifax, "Municipal Government", p. 324; *The Straits Times*, 12 Mar. 1910; *The Singapore Free Press and Mercantile Advertiser*, 8 Oct. 1935.

176 "Public Works Department", in *Annual Departmental Reports of the Straits Settlements for the Year 1906*, p. 80; *Straits Settlements Blue Book*, 1929, Section 32, p. 32; *The Singapore Free Press and Mercantile Advertiser*, 23 Aug. 1921.

177 *The Singapore Free Press and Mercantile Advertiser*, 17 July 1930.

178 Frost and Balasingamchow, *Singapore*, pp. 179–81.

line.[179] It was the first use of the telephone in the Far East, barely three years after the device was invented.[180] In 1882, the merchants caught on to the innovation and the Oriental Telephone and Electric Company began to provide a wider service through a telephone switchboard exchange located in Prince Street with 60 lines connecting the major firms and banks in Singapore.[181] From the beginning of the 20th century onwards, the telephone became a more widespread mode of business communication and by 1907, 1,000 lines had been installed in businesses and government departments.[182] The first overseas connection was with Johor Bahru in 1898 but it was not until 1931 that Singapore was linked to the rest of Malaya.[183] Seven years later, the first call was made to London. Radio broadcasting was introduced to the public at about this time with the formation of the British Malaya Broadcasting Corporation in 1935, transforming the radio from a wireless device for enthusiasts into a household item.[184]

Electricity came to Singapore just one year earlier than the telephone, in 1878. The Tanjong Pagar Dock Company first introduced electric lighting in its docks and workshops, thereby extending working hours into the night.[185] The power was generated by three steam engines which cost the company $23,000 a year to maintain. In 1906, the town centre was provided with electricity and electric street lights, Raffles Place and Battery Road being among the earliest to be lit. The electricity was supplied to the Municipality by a station at Mackenzie Road owned by the Singapore Electric Tramway Company and transmitted by underground mains to a substation at Coleman Street.[186] Initially, the electricity tariff charged was 40 cents per kilowatt-hour but this was reduced to 25 cents later. One occupation that disappeared due to the diffusion of this new energy source amongst the population was the *punkah wallah* or Kling fan men, whose labour was substituted by the electric fan.[187]

By 1924, the station's load had reached its limit, but public demand was still rising. To satisfy it, the Municipal Commissioners entered into an agreement with the Singapore Harbour Board for a bulk supply of electric current from its generating station at Keppel Harbour.[188] In the meantime, plans were made to construct a new power station that could meet the needs of the whole island. Finally in 1927, the outskirts of the town received electricity for the first time with the opening of the St. James Power Station. With the addition of new machinery, the modern generating equipment installed there was capable

---

179 *The Straits Times*, 1 Apr. 1979.

180 *Keylines*, June 1990, p. 6.

181 *The Singapore Free Press and Mercantile Advertiser*, 8 Oct. 1935.

182 "Postal and Telegraph Department", in *Annual Departmental Reports of the Straits Settlements for the Year 1906*, p. 50.

183 *Proceedings of the Legislative Council of the Straits Settlements*, 26 Jan. 1931; *The Straits Budget*, 24 Apr. 1930; *The Straits Times*, 1 Apr. 1979.

184 Chua Ai Lin, "The Story of Singapore Radio, 1924–41", *BiblioAsia* 12, 1 (2016): 22–3, 26.

185 Koh Buck Song and Lee Geok Boi, *Brighter: Electricity in Singapore: From Beginning to Beyond* (Singapore: Energy Market Authority, 2011), p. 24.

186 *The Straits Budget*, 27 Oct. 1927; *The Singapore Free Press and Mercantile Advertiser*, 8 Oct. 1935.

187 *The Straits Budget*, 16 Oct. 1902; *The Straits Times*, 22 Oct. 1933.

188 *The Straits Budget*, 27 Oct. 1927.

of producing 10,000 kilowatts per day. The station was located next to the wharves to facilitate access to coal supplies for firing the engines and seawater for turning the turbines.[189] As a result of its opening, total electricity consumption in the island increased from 128,000 kilowatt hours in 1907 to 51 million kilowatt hours in 1939.[190] By 1930, the Singapore Municipality had spent nearly $44 million on water, electricity and gas undertakings on the island.[191]

In narrating the events of the interwar period with their transformations (especially the impact of modern technology just described), the place to begin is the First World War (1914–18) as it provides a point of comparison with subsequent developments in the first half of the 20th century. At the outset, it should be stated that overall, the war did not have much effect on economic conditions during the four years it lasted. This is surprising given Singapore's dependence on seaborne trade, which rendered it vulnerable to the shortage of shipping caused by the war.[192] Nevertheless, general restrictions on exports did lead to a decline in trade in the early months of the conflict. There was some panic buying of food and uneasiness among the residents, especially when the German SMS *Emden* sailed past Singapore, but it was not long before things went back to normal.[193] Thereafter, imports and exports of rice, dried fish and flour were strictly regulated. Trade with Germany and Austria-Hungary was prohibited, German ships in the harbour were seized and German firms in the city liquidated, including Behn Meyer—measures that would have long-lasting effects on Singapore's commercial landscape.[194]

Acting after the start of hostilities, the colonial government in August 1914 temporarily prohibited Chinese and Indian immigration and provided free passages home for coolies who were retrenched.[195] At the end of the year, 12,222 Chinese had been repatriated but the number in the following year fell to 1,100.[196] The total sum of money expended on war expenditures was close to $1 million, including the cost of sending new army recruits to Europe.[197] Of more significance in establishing a precedent for government intervention was the official decision, following the suspension of the London tin market, to purchase Malayan tin through the STC at a fixed price, on which a profit was realised in 1915 when the market recovered.[198] With the closure of markets for rubber in Europe and

---

189 Koh and Lee, *Brighter*, pp. 33–4.

190 Huff, *The Economic Growth of Singapore*, p. 210.

191 *Proceedings of the Legislative Council of the Straits Settlements*, 1930, 12 May 1930, Appendix No. 31, pp. C189–90.

192 Bartley, "Singapore and The Great War", pp. 405–8, 420–3.

193 Turnbull, *History of Modern Singapore*, p. 137; *Straits Settlements Annual Report*, vol. 7, p. 4; *Straits Echo*, 22 Jan. 1915. After destroying a large number of merchant ships, SMS *Emden* was sunk off the Cocos Islands.

194 *Straits Settlements Annual Report*, vol. 6, pp. 646–8.

195 Ee, "Chinese Migration to Singapore", p. 42; *Proceedings of the Legislative Council of the Straits Settlements*, 16 Apr. 1915.

196 *Straits Settlements Annual Report*, vol. 7, p. 6.

197 *Proceedings of the Legislative Council of the Straits Settlements*, 31 Mar. 1916.

198 Bartley, "Singapore and the Great War", pp. 407, 408; *Straits Settlements Annual Report*, vol. 6, pp. 643–4; *Straits Echo*, 6 Aug. 1914; *Malaya Tribune*, 7 Aug. 1914, 21 June 1915.

restrictions on merchant shipping, relief was also given to rubber planters in the form of advances. Nonetheless, rubber could still be shipped to the eastern United States along the Trans-Pacific route via the newly opened Panama Canal by relying partly on Japanese and American tonnage.[199] In late 1914, the German Fleet was destroyed off the Falklands and with that, the threat to local shipping was temporarily removed.

Indeed, not even the mutiny of Indian sepoys from the Fifth Light Infantry Regiment based in Singapore in February 1915 upset the relative calm that prevailed.[200] Unlike Chinese riots, the rebellion by a group of Indian Muslim soldiers from Punjab stationed at the Alexandra and Tanglin Barracks who were guarding German prisoners of war from the *Emden* was totally unexpected. It was however quickly suppressed with the help of allied naval crews and the mutineers summarily executed.[201] The incident did not stay in the public memory and neither did it lead to any major change in government policy, except for the compulsory registration of all Indians in Singapore. It was not until 1919, after the war ended, that the next important event took place, one that was to create more panic among the Singapore public—the rice crisis of 1919. The crisis was as much an indirect outcome of the war as it was a result of freak weather in the great "rice bowl" of Southeast Asia—Siam, Burma and Cochin-China—although speculative buying also played a role. The war had led to a scarcity of shipping and towards the last days of the conflict, the prices of various articles of food—beef, fish, vegetables, eggs and milk—had increased despite government price control of the last item.[202] In October 1918, the Indian government disallowed the export of rice from Burma to Singapore for distribution to the rest of the region as a worsening shortage caused its price to more than double from $6 to $15 a pikul.[203] At the start of 1919, the situation developed into a full-fledged crisis when it became apparent that drought had severely curtailed the harvests in Burma and Siam.[204] Singapore might not be able to feed its inhabitants, not to mention labourers in the Malay Peninsula dependent on it for their staple food.

Notwithstanding the charge by the press that the authorities were slow to recognise the impending food crisis, they quickly took control of the rice market in an effort to protect the local population.[205] In February 1919, following the imposition of price controls in Burma, a maximum price was fixed for Burmese rice.[206] In May, regulations were promulgated requiring all rice dealers to be licensed; both they and rice millers were

---

199 Huff, *The Economic Growth of Singapore*, p. 122; *The Straits Budget*, 6 Oct. 1916.

200 Turnbull, *History of Modern Singapore*, pp. 138–9; *Straits Settlements Annual Report*, vol. 7, pp. 8–10.

201 Kwa, Heng, Borschberg and Tan, *Seven Hundred Years*, p. 236; Bartley, "Singapore and the Great War", pp. 408–14; Abshire, *History of Singapore*, p. 80.

202 Song, *One Hundred Years' History of the Chinese*, pp. 786, 787–8; *Straits Settlements Annual Report*, vol. 7, pp. 155–6; *The Straits Budget*, 18 Apr. 1919.

203 P.H. Kratoska, "The British Empire and the Southeast Asian Rice Crisis of 1919–1921", *Modern Asian Studies* 24, 1 (1990): 125–6.

204 Huff, *The Economic Growth of Singapore*, pp. 72, 75; *The Straits Budget*, 11 Apr. 1919; *Malaya Tribune*, 18 June 1919.

205 *The Straits Budget*, 18 Apr. 1919.

206 Kratoska, "The British Empire and the Southeast Asian Rice Crisis", pp. 122–5, 130; *The Singapore Free Press and Mercantile Advertiser*, 27 Feb. 1919.

to furnish returns of their rice holdings.[207] Given the curtailment of imports from Burma, the government turned to Siam and Cochin-China for supplies. As a result, the prices of rice from both countries, which had increased after the introduction of controls in Burma, effectively doubled by the end of May. Two months later, the stocks of importers and wholesalers were impounded by the government.[208] After a riot broke out in Penang, the Straits government was forced, partly out of alarm, to extend price controls to Siamese and Cochin-Chinese rice as well in July 1919.[209] The ceilings on prices were enforced not by letting markets clear but through government subsidies to rice importers and distributors, thereby ensuring an adequate rice supply.[210] Still, there was hoarding of rice in December, prompting the colonial government to implement household rationing in Malaya, though not in the Straits Settlements.[211]

This move was motivated to some extent by the failure of the Siam rice crop in late 1919 and the decision of the authorities there to prohibit exports for 1920.[212] Rice re-exports from Singapore contracted sharply as the authorities prioritised the domestic market.[213] Fortunately, Burma had surplus grain to dispose of after India embarked on a policy of import substitution. For 1920 as a whole, the quantity purchased from Rangoon was 225,000 tonnes while Saigon provided another 111,000 tonnes. The price paid to avert starvation was punitive, however, because of continued shortages and unfavourable exchange rates: the total subsidy given to rice consumers by the Straits government was approximately $18 million.[214] Following bumper crops in Siam and Cochin-China, price controls were finally lifted in May 1921.[215] These two countries and Burma together exported more rice in that year than the previous one.[216]

Although the rice crisis had largely passed by 1921, it was a year of recession.[217] Following the brief post-war boom, a downturn began to materialise in the second half of 1920 in the industrial countries as the effects of disrupted trade channels manifested themselves. The slowdown in economic activity was aggravated by a general restriction of credit by banks in all parts of the world.[218] The Straits government had to support tin prices again by buying the metal in cooperation with the Dutch government in the Netherlands Indies.[219] This set the stage for British and European firms to re-enter the tin industry,

---

207 *Straits Echo*, 22 Apr. 1918; *The Straits Budget*, 16 May 1919.

208 *Straits Settlements Annual Report*, vol. 7, p. 309.

209 *The Straits Budget*, 20 June 1919, 4 July 1919.

210 *The Straits Times*, 12 Dec. 1919.

211 *Straits Settlements Annual Report*, vol. 7, p. 475.

212 Kratoska, "The British Empire and the Southeast Asian Rice Crisis", pp. 132, 134–40.

213 Huff, *The Economic Growth of Singapore*, p. 375.

214 *Straits Settlements Annual Report*, vol. 7, pp. 515, 622–5.

215 *The Straits Times*, 7 Feb. 1921.

216 V.D. Wickizer and M.K. Bennett, *The Rice Economy of Monsoon Asia* (Stanford University Press, 1941), Appendix Table IV, p. 320.

217 *Straits Settlements Annual Report*, vol. 7, pp. 461–3, 515–6; *The Straits Times*, 31 Dec. 1921.

218 Moore and Moore, *The First 150 Years*, pp. 574–5.

219 van Helten and Jones, "British Business in Malaysia and Singapore", pp. 167–8.

encouraged by policies on mining land favouring technically advanced methods and a reduction in the export duty on tin.[220] By 1929, the Malayan tin industry had taken on a distinctively different character. Except for gravel pumping, the old mining methods had been rendered technologically obsolete by the exhaustion of rich tin-bearing grounds and the widespread employment of the tin dredge.[221]

Chinese mines had yielded their commanding position in the industry to Western companies that relied on dredging methods to mine virgin swamp land, especially in the Kinta Valley. The Chinese mines employed about 59,000 workers mostly in gravel pump mining, compared to the 16,817 at work on 105 tin dredges.[222] However, they produced only half of the tin extracted in Malaya. The fall in the mining workforce reduced the food and provisions supplied by Singapore although this was more than compensated by the increase in rubber estate workers.[223] Singapore also benefitted from the forward linkage created by tin dredges through the establishment of engineering firms which imported, fabricated and serviced them.[224] As with rubber, the agency houses acted on behalf of Western tin companies based overseas.[225]

Unlike rubber, however, the first international tin control scheme came along only in 1931, followed by two others in succession starting from 1934 and 1937 and ending in 1941 with the outbreak of war in Asia. The initiative to restrict tin output in the 1930s was taken by the British firms in Malaya and it was they who profited from the schemes; the Chinese mine owners were not certain they wanted restriction at all although they eventually supported it.[226] The mechanism for implementing the restrictions was somewhat similar to but simpler than that in the case of rubber, each country being assigned a quota representing a fixed percentage of its production capacity. Using the level of output in 1929 as the basis, Malaya's capacity was 69,366 tonnes, which was thought to be an underestimation of its potential because new dredges had come into operation since that year. Bolivia and Nigeria were given more generous quotas despite their higher production costs.[227] The net result was a decline in the amount of tin smelted in Singapore despite the fact that the STC was buying ore from non-participating countries such as Siam and Cochin-China.[228] The situation was made worse after 1933 when the tin from the Dutch East Indies was sent to a smelter in Arnhem in the Netherlands for processing. As a result, Singapore's tin exports fell to 23,550 tonnes in 1934 from 43,352 tonnes in 1929.[229]

---

220 Allen and Donnithorne, *Western Enterprise in Indonesia and Malaya*, p. 152; Jomo, *A Question of Class*, pp. 171–2; Yip, *The Development of the Tin Mining Industry*, pp. 134–5.

221 Lim, *Economic Development of Modern Malaya*, pp. 50–1, 55–6.

222 Ibid., pp. 52, 53, 54; Yip, *The Development of the Tin Mining Industry*, p. 163; Allen and Donnithorne, *Western Enterprise in Indonesia and Malaya*, p. 162.

223 Jomo, *A Question of Class*, p. 164.

224 Huff, *The Economic Growth of Singapore*, p. 253.

225 Wong, "Commercial Growth", p. 59.

226 Yip, *The Development of the Tin Mining Industry*, pp. 168–9, 179–80, 184–5, 187–9, 265, 277–9.

227 Tregonning, "Straits Tin", p. 122.

228 Allen and Donnithorne, *Western Enterprise in Indonesia and Malaya*, pp. 160–1.

229 Huff, *The Economic Growth of Singapore*, Appendix Table A.2, p. 380.

As the linkages from tin weakened, a new commodity appeared on the scene, the last to emerge from the *Belle Époque*: petroleum. Although it is regarded as Singapore's third staple after tin and rubber, this is true only insofar as the product became a major export item. Demand for petroleum increased steadily from the beginning of the 20th century and especially during the First World War.[230] By the 1930s, petroleum revenues contributed 15 per cent on average to annual export earnings, excluding the sale—not deemed to be exports in the colonial trade statistics—of oil bunkers at the port.[231] There were three factors which accounted for the rise of Singapore as an oil centre.[232] First was the increasing penetration of motorcars in the Far East; second was the island's proximity to oilfields in Sumatra and Borneo; and third, the islands at the western entrance to the harbour afforded an ideal location to process oil into petroleum products for distribution to the region's consumers, particularly in Japan and Australia. Nonetheless, the statistical prominence of petroleum belied its economic significance even while it generated little employment. Although Singapore became the storage and distribution centre for mineral oils in the Far East, oil blending, like tin smelting, was effectively an offshore industry with minimal spillover effects onto the economy of the mainland—in both the literal and figurative senses.[233] The sole backward linkage that added to the existing port facilities was the construction of oil storage depots.

Towards the conclusion of the 19th century, the agency house Syme and Company had applied for a licence from the Municipal Council to install oil tanks at Bukit Chermin but was refused on the ground of the danger posed to the safety of the port.[234] It decided on Pulau Bukom instead, a small island situated advantageously near Keppel Harbour. The London oil company it acted for became the Shell Transport and Trading Company in 1897 after acquiring a large oilfield in Borneo.[235] This was one forerunner of Royal Dutch Shell, the other being the Royal Dutch Petroleum Company, which obtained an oil concession in Sumatra and installed storage facilities on the Dutch island of Pulau Samboe to the southeast of Singapore.[236] Rivalry between the two companies continued until 1903 when they set up a firm to jointly market petroleum and in 1908, they merged under the new name of Royal Dutch Shell.[237] The main competitors to the new concern were the Standard Oil Companies of New York and New Jersey, two American firms active in the region.[238] Following a series of mergers, the New York company metamorphosed into Mobil which to this day competes with Royal Dutch Shell.

---

230 Regnier, *Singapore*, p. 19.

231 Huff, *The Economic Growth of Singapore*, Appendix Table A.1, p. 374.

232 Ibid., pp. 239–40, 241–2.

233 King, "Plantation and Agriculture in Malaya", p. 146.

234 "The Mineral Oil Trade", in *One Hundred Years of Singapore*, vol. II, ed. Makepeace, Brooke and Braddell, p. 97; *Mid-day Herald*, 2 Mar. 1895.

235 *The Singapore Free Press and Mercantile Advertiser*, 23 Aug. 1900; *The Straits Times*, 8 May 1923.

236 Huff, *The Economic Growth of Singapore*, p. 239; *The Straits Times*, 26 July 1961.

237 "The Mineral Oil Trade", p. 98; *The Singapore Free Press and Mercantile Advertiser*, 2 Feb. 1907, 5 Mar. 1908.

238 *The Straits Budget*, 15 Dec. 1910.

Rice aside, petroleum was probably the only export commodity that was consumed in appreciable quantities in Singapore. In this respect, the constant price wars between the oil majors right up to the 1930s benefitted local consumers, who used kerosene for lighting and cooking and motor oil for automobiles.[239] Other than this, the petroleum distribution business reinforced Singapore's role as a port of call by making bunker fuel easily and conveniently available to the steamers that had switched from coal to oil.[240] From 1926, vessels discharging and loading cargo at the wharves could be simultaneously refuelled through pipelines connected with the oil storage tanks.[241] Singapore therefore evolved from a coaling depot into an oil bunkering centre. Another spin-off came from the repair of oil tankers and ships which called at the harbour. The two dominant regional shipping lines, the SSC and the KPM, availed themselves of this service even though they had their own shipyards elsewhere. In the final analysis, petroleum's contribution to Singapore's colonial economy was in the foundations it provided for the development of modern oil-related and ship repair industries in the post-war period.

We round up this review with an update of the progress made in the fields of education and health during the early 20th century. In the opening years of the century, two events of note relating to education transpired. In 1902, a commission was appointed to report on the system of education in the Straits Settlements and make recommendations.[242] With regard to English schooling, the most important measures carried out on the advice of the commission were the establishment of English medium primary schools and the assumption by the government of the Raffles Institution (including the Raffles Girls' School).[243] The trustees of the Institution had requested for the move because its management by a private body was unsatisfactory and a lack of funds precluded the recruitment of fully-qualified teachers from England.[244] Following this, science and commercial classes were started in 1903.[245] The number of places at St. Joseph's Institution and the Anglo-Chinese School were expanded through new building grants to accommodate the growing demand for an English education, which led to higher salaries than a vernacular one did.[246] As the colonial administration grew, more job opportunities began to open up to English-educated Asians,

---

239 *The Straits Budget*, 6 Mar. 1930; *Malaya Tribune*, 11 Jan. 1933.

240 Huff, *The Economic Growth of Singapore*, pp. 241, 244–5, 249.

241 *The Straits Budget*, 17 Oct. 1929.

242 Doraisamy, *150 Years of Education*, p. 28; *Straits Settlements Annual Report*, vol. 5, p. 102; *The Singapore Free Press and Mercantile Advertiser*, 12 June 1902.

243 S. Gopinathan, "Education", in *A History of Singapore*, ed. Chew and Lee, p. 269; *Straits Settlements Annual Report*, vol. 5, p. 184; "Education", in *Annual Departmental Reports of the Straits Settlements for the Year 1903*, p. 80; *The Straits Times*, 23 Dec. 1902.

244 Francis H.K. Wong and Gwee Yee Hean, eds., *Official Reports on Education: Straits Settlements and the Federated Malay States, 1870–1939* (Singapore: Pan Pacific Book Distributors, 1980), pp. 49–50. The same request had been made in 1890 but it was rejected by the government. Bazell, "Education in Singapore", pp. 441–2.

245 Bazell, "Education in Singapore", p. 442.

246 Doraisamy, *150 Years of Education*, p. 28; *Straits Settlements Annual Report*, vol. 5, p. 528; "Education", in *Annual Departmental Reports of the Straits Settlements for the Year 1903*, p. 79; *The Straits Times*, 31 May 1902.

especially in lower-ranking positions.[247] To address a lack of sufficiently qualified teachers, training courses outside of school hours were started in 1907.[248]

The other significant development concerns tertiary education. In 1904, a petition was addressed to the Governor of the Straits Settlements by the leading members of the Chinese and other Asian communities in Singapore requesting that a medical school be established.[249] It was stated that the doctors and surgeons to be trained in such a school would go a long way towards "a general comprehension of proper sanitary conditions and habits" among the natives.[250] The Governor replied by throwing the petitioners a challenge: if they could raise by subscription $71,000 to pay for scholarships and equipment, the authorities would provide the site and building and fund the staff.[251] To his surprise, $87,077 was collected in the Straits Settlements and Malaya.[252] The medical school came into being in July 1905 with an intake of 22 students—nine Chinese, twelve Indians and others, and one European; by 1941, its intake had increased to 40 students.[253] The school was renamed the King Edward VII Medical School in 1913, when dentistry degrees were first awarded, and the King Edward VII College of Medicine in 1920.[254]

In 1919, the centenary of Singapore's founding, a committee tasked to advise the government on a scheme for establishing the foundations for a university proposed the formation of Raffles College, which together with the medical school were the precursors of the University of Singapore.[255] However, the project was realised only a decade later after the necessary funds were raised from the public.[256] The government on its part provided the land and structures and a yearly grant of $50,000 towards the college's upkeep, while prominent merchants contributed further to the building fund. In 1929 when it opened at Bukit Timah, 79 students were admitted who were reading subjects in the sciences, mathematics, English language and literature, history, geography and education.[257] The estimated cost of study and residence at the college was $1,000 a year although most students were scholarship recipients.[258]

---

247 Frost and Balasingamchow, *Singapore*, p. 183.

248 *Proceedings of the Legislative Council of the Straits Settlements*, 1905, Appendix No. 54, C195–6; "Educational", in *Annual Departmental Reports of the Straits Settlements for the Year 1907*, p. 66.

249 Brooke, "Medical Work", p. 514; *Proceedings of the Legislative Council of the Straits Settlements*, 1905, Appendix No. 14, C37–39.

250 Song, *One Hundred Years' History of the Chinese*, pp. 529–30.

251 *The Straits Budget*, 19 Oct. 1904; *The Straits Times*, 4 Oct. 1913.

252 One donation came from a Chinese in Saigon.

253 Tan, "Health and Welfare", pp. 342, 343.

254 *Proceedings of the Legislative Council of the Straits Settlements*, 3 Oct. 1913, 31 Oct. 1913; "Education", in *Annual Departmental Reports of the Straits Settlements for the Year 1905*, p. 202; *Eastern Daily Mail and Straits Morning Advertiser*, 29 Sept. 1905.

255 Wong and Gwee, *Official Reports on Education*, pp. 8, 67, 69.

256 *Malayan Saturday Post*, 27 July 1929.

257 *The Straits Budget*, 18 Apr. 1929, 25 July 1929.

258 *The Straits Times*, 18 Jan. 1928.

In 1920, the system of grants to aided schools was revamped for the third time, putting them on par with government schools by subsidising the shortfall between revenue from fees and other sources and approved expenditure, and paying teachers at the same rate as those in government institutions.[259] The change in policy therefore recognised the status of aided schools as an integral part of the education system.[260] Altogether, 31 aided schools with an enrolment of 13,713 boys and girls benefitted from the new arrangement, which resulted in the amount of government grants increasing from $166,450 in 1917 to $529,294 in 1921. The demand for the education of girls also increased, in large part due to the work of the Convents and other missionary schools.[261] In addition, there were ten government schools with 4,539 pupils serving as feeder schools to the secondary classes at Raffles Institution and later on at Victoria School, including some opened in the new century such as the New Bridge Road School, Outram Road School and Pearl's Hill School.[262] In the early 1920s, a shortage of places and overcrowding in English schools also led to the founding of new elementary schools in Owen Road, Telok Kurau and other suburbs of the city.[263]

The Malay vernacular schools continued to be supported by the colonial governments in Singapore and Malaya. Although the Malay College in Singapore had closed in 1895, two new ones were opened in Melaka and Perak in 1900 and 1922 respectively.[264] Malay boys who entered vernacular schools could proceed to an English school after four years.[265] Before the outbreak of the Second World War, the total school population had increased to 72,000 pupils who were in attendance at 23 government and aided English schools and a much larger number of vernacular institutions.[266] The majority of teachers in the English schools were by now locally recruited and trained. After 1928, Raffles College supplied many of them and in 1934, graduates intending to become teachers had to undergo a fourth year of study.

Chinese schools in Singapore multiplied rapidly in the first two decades of the 20th century, which coincided with a period of political and social upheaval in China.[267] Under

259 Wong and Gwee, *Official Reports on Education*, pp. 7, 83, 117; "Educational", in *Annual Departmental Reports of the Straits Settlements for the Year 1922*, p. 226.

260 "Annual Report on Education in the Straits Settlements for the Year 1937", in *Annual Departmental Reports of the Straits Settlements for the Year 1937*, vol. II, p. 157.

261 "Education", in *Annual Departmental Reports of the Straits Settlements for the Year 1926*, p. 280.

262 Wong and Gwee, *Official Reports on Education*, p. 83; Doraisamy, *150 Years of Education*, pp. 37–8; Turnbull, *History of Modern Singapore*, p. 152; "Educational", in *Annual Departmental Reports of the Straits Settlements for the Year 1922*, pp. 70–1.

263 *Proceedings of the Legislative Council of the Straits Settlements*, 23 Apr. 1923, 28 May 1923, 29 Oct. 1923; "Education", in *Annual Departmental Reports of the Straits Settlements for the Year 1923*, p. 107.

264 Wong and Gwee, *Official Reports on Education*, pp. 4–5; "Education", in *Annual Departmental Reports of the Straits Settlements for the Year 1900*, pp. 172–4.

265 "Educational", in *Annual Departmental Reports of the Straits Settlements for the Year 1906*, pp. 220–1.

266 Doraisamy, *150 Years of Education*, pp. 41, 42; "Annual Report on Education in the Straits Settlements for the Year 1938", in *Annual Departmental Reports of the Straits Settlements for the Year 1938*, vol. II, Appendix I, p. 786.

267 Doraisamy, *150 Years of Education*, pp. 30–3; "Education", in *Annual Departmental Reports of the Straits Settlements for the Year 1921*, pp. 217–8.

its impact and with the infusion of new ideas, Chinese education in Singapore underwent a fundamental reorientation, abandoning the classical Chinese language and using Mandarin as the medium of instruction; the Confucian classics were also replaced with modern textbooks.[268] Along with these changes and with the formation of a Kuomintang branch in Singapore in 1912, there was a marked increase in political consciousness and loyalty to China amongst students and teachers.[269] The first Chinese secondary school, Hwa Chong, commenced in 1919, with more to follow in the next decade; by 1928, there were 247 Chinese schools in Singapore, both primary and secondary.[270] A small number of them received grant-in-aid from the government but many came under left-wing influence. Concerned about the rise of nationalism and to contain political activism in these schools, the authorities took measures to register all schools and teachers, close Chinese night schools and ban textbooks from China.[271]

We have seen that the emphasis in healthcare during the late 19th century was on the improvement of sanitary conditions in Singapore. The local government continued to pay attention to this problem in the early 20th century, but it also undertook to build new pauper and general hospitals. Recurrent outbreaks of beri-beri at Tan Tock Seng Hospital provided the motivation for a new hospital to be constructed on a hill in Moulmein Road, funded by the government and aided by a $50,000 donation from the business magnate Loke Yew.[272] On completion in 1909, the hospital had a capacity of 1,000 beds, good ventilation, corrugated iron roofs and cement floors.[273] In the following year, a special ward for the blind was erected after a donation was received from a Chinese person in Melaka.[274] This third Tan Tock Seng Hospital outlasted its predecessors, only finally moving to new premises in 1999.

The construction of a new Singapore General Hospital at Sepoy Lines also originated in somewhat serendipitous circumstances. An effort to improve the quality of teaching at the King Edward VII Medical School and to upgrade it into a College of Medicine led to the decision to rebuild the hospital and develop the surrounding area into a medical complex.[275] The new hospital, which cost $4.5 million to build, opened in 1926, fully equipped with male and female wards for different classes, a children's ward, X-ray rooms

---

[268] "Annual Report on Education in the Straits Settlements for the Year 1937", in *Annual Departmental Reports of the Straits Settlements for the Year 1937*, vol. II, pp. 167–8.

[269] Wong and Gwee, *Official Reports on Education*, p. 3; Lee, "The Colonial Legacy", p. 22.

[270] Turnbull, *History of Modern Singapore*, pp. 142–4.

[271] Tan, *A Very Short History*, p. 49; *Proceedings of the Legislative Council of the Straits Settlements*, 16 Mar. 1925, 24 Aug. 1925, 17 May 1926; "Education", in *Annual Departmental Reports of the Straits Settlements for the Year 1923*, pp. 120–1; "Education", in *Annual Departmental Reports of the Straits Settlements for the Year 1928*, pp. 239–40.

[272] *150 Years of Caring: The Legacy of Tan Tock Seng Hospital*, p. 27; Brooke, "Medical Work", p. 496.

[273] "Tan Tock Seng's Hospital", in *Annual Departmental Reports of the Straits Settlements for the Year 1909*, p. 21; *The Straits Times*, 1 Feb. 1909, 19 Mar. 1909.

[274] "Tan Tock Seng's Hospital", in *Annual Departmental Reports of the Straits Settlements for the Year 1910*, pp. 45–6.

[275] Lee, *The 1926 General Hospital*, p. 57C.

and operating theatres, altogether catering to 800 patients.[276] Meanwhile, the upgraded King Edward VII College of Medicine moved to a handsome new building nearby at the same time that a new hostel to accommodate 50 medical students at Tan Tock Seng Hospital opened.[277]

A privately supported Chinese hospital, the Kwong Wai Shiu Hospital, began to offer free Western and Chinese medical treatment in 1911 at the site of the old Tan Tock Seng Hospital, which it leased from the government.[278] By the end of the year, over 1,900 patients from three Cantonese prefectures, immigrants from which had donated to the hospital, had been admitted. Another private hospital, St. Andrew's Mission Hospital, was opened by the Anglican Church in 1913 and in 1923, it moved to a new building.[279] Given the prevalence of epidemics in Singapore, it is somewhat surprising that the first facility for treating infectious diseases was opened only in 1913 in Moulmein Road and later renamed Middleton Hospital, the precursor to the present National Centre for Infectious Diseases.[280] In 1924, the new Kandang Kerbau Hospital, that used to be a part of the old General Hospital and had served as a "lock hospital" for treating venereal disease in the 19th century, opened with 30 beds and 12 children's cots and in 1927, a dedicated hospital for treating mental patients, the Woodbridge Hospital, was built.[281] Together with the Maternity Hospital at Sepoy Lines, Kandang Kerbau Hospital continued to provide for the medical needs of women and children free of charge and was instrumental in lowering maternal and infant mortality rates. The infant mortality rate was high at 320 per 1,000 babies born in 1902 but it fell to 233 in 1919 after more midwives were trained and home visits by nurses began, and then to 159 in 1935 with the establishment of infant welfare centres dispensing advice to mothers.[282]

Several further developments impinging on health conditions in Singapore deserve a brief mention. Although the town's oldest public market, at Telok Ayer, had been rebuilt in 1894 and a new wing had been added to the Ellenborough Market in 1899, cleanliness and hygiene at the markets still left much to be desired into the new century and the

---

276 *The First General Hospital*, p. 30; *The Singapore Free Press and Mercantile Advertiser*, 29 Mar. 1926, 31 Mar. 1926; *The Straits Budget*, 1 Apr. 1926.

277 "Straits Settlements Medical Report", in *Annual Departmental Reports of the Straits Settlements for the Year 1924*, p. 667; "Straits Settlements Medical Report", in *Annual Departmental Reports of the Straits Settlements for the Year 1925*, pp. 569, 575.

278 *Proceedings of the Legislative Council of the Straits Settlements*, 22 Apr. 1910, 27 May 1910; *Straits Settlements Annual Report*, vol. 6, p. 383.

279 *Malaya Tribune*, 22 May 1923.

280 Brooke, "Medical Work", p. 506.

281 Y.K. Lee, "A Short History of Kandang Kerbau Hospital and the Maternity Services of Singapore", *Singapore Medical Journal* 3 (1990): 599, 606–7; Turnbull, *History of Modern Singapore*, p. 140.

282 Brooke, "Medical Work", p. 510; A. Booth, "Measuring Living Standards in Different Colonial Systems: Some Evidence from South East Asia, 1900–1942", *Modern Asian Studies* 46, 5 (2012): 1169; "Registration of Births and Deaths, Straits Settlements", in *Annual Departmental Reports of the Straits Settlements for the Year 1902*, Table K, p. 283; "Straits Settlements Medical Report", in *Annual Departmental Reports of the Straits Settlements for the Year 1913*, pp. 493–4; "Annual Report on the Registration of Births and Deaths in the Straits Settlements for the Year 1935", in *Annual Departmental Reports of the Straits Settlements for the Year 1935*, p. 523, Appendix J, p. 534.

Municipality had to take over their management in 1909 and 1910, respectively.[283] The government therefore gave up the lucrative farm revenue from these markets, though $300,000 was still collected each year from rentals of stalls. With regard to the disposal of refuse, incinerators had been acquired since 1889, but a modern sewerage system was put in place only from 1913. The project originated from a recommendation made by a government appointed public health expert, W.J. Simpson, in 1907.[284] It was a work-in-progress until the late twenties by which time virtually the whole municipal area was serviced by underground sewers.[285] Before that, household nightsoil was manually removed by municipal workers and Chinese syndicates who sold it to the vegetable farms for use as manure. In 1934, the Municipal Council replaced the existing sewerage system with a more up-to-date and cleaner purification method.[286]

The death rate fell to 31 per 1,000 of population in 1926 through a combination of benign influences including most importantly the near-universal provision of pure piped water.[287] The problem of water shortage that still recurred in the initial years of the 20th century during drought periods was decisively settled by the early 1930s with the addition of two reservoirs in Johor state located at Gunung Pulai and Pontian Kechil which piped the water across the Causeway to Singapore.[288] Lastly, after nearly a century of battling malaria based on the wrong prophylaxis (the miasma theory mentioned earlier), the role of the Anopheles mosquito in spreading the scourge was recognised; starting from 1911, campaigns were continuously carried out to eradicate the disease by destroying breeding grounds.[289]

Money, Banking and Fiscal Policy

In an earlier chapter, the functions of banks in the latter half of the 19th century were elucidated. Their entry into Singapore had macroeconomic consequences: the money supply was no longer determined solely by the net inflow of specie in the balance of payment for bullion, as in countries under a *de facto* silver standard. Prior to the issue of government paper currency, these institutions' banknotes served as an important

---

[283] Hallifax, "Municipal Government", pp. 333, 334; *Proceedings of the Legislative Council of the Straits Settlements*, 23 Feb. 1893.

[284] Yeoh, "Urban Sanitation, Health and Water Supply", pp. 165–6; Savage, *Lion City Narratives*, p. 195; *The Singapore Free Press and Mercantile Advertiser (Weekly)*, 13 June 1907; *The Straits Budget*, 13 June 1907, 20 June 1907; *Straits Echo*, 13 July 1907.

[285] Hallifax, "Municipal Government", pp. 325–6; *The Straits Times*, 2 Nov. 1923; *Morning Tribune*, 2 May 1936.

[286] *The Straits Budget*, 27 Sept. 1934.

[287] "Registration of Births and Deaths, Straits Settlements", in *Annual Departmental Reports of the Straits Settlements for the Year 1926*, Appendix F, p. 263.

[288] Yeoh, "Urban Sanitation, Health and Water Supply", pp. 149, 151–2; *Straits Settlements Annual Report*, vol. 9, pp. 331–2.

[289] Brooke, "Medical Work", pp. 490, 515–6; *Proceedings of the Legislative Council of the Straits Settlements*, 9 Feb. 1912; *The Singapore Free Press and Mercantile Advertiser*, 20 Aug. 1920; *The Singapore Free Press and Mercantile Advertiser (Weekly)*, 23 Feb. 1922, 15 Dec. 1926, 1 June 1927; *The Straits Budget*, 22 Oct. 1936.

component of the money supply—effectively as "quasi-money"—even though these were not legal tender. The use of banknotes and bills of exchange as paper money had become widespread in global commerce by the later part of the 19th century. The banks therefore expedited Singapore's transition to a fully monetised economy and alleviated the contractionary effect of a net outflow of specie, such as occurred when the price of silver depreciated in terms of gold from 1873 to 1893.[290] Despite the granting of legal tender status to the United States and Japanese dollars, silver coins were still scarce.[291] Hence in 1895, the mint at Bombay began the coinage of the British trade dollar to meet demand in the Eastern territories.[292]

However, the supply of the trade dollar was not under the control of the Straits government and could not be adjusted to changing trade conditions. In 1897, a request was accordingly made to the Colonial Office for a government note to be issued and circulated alongside banknotes.[293] In 1899 after approval was granted, the Board of Commissioners of Currency issued government currency notes that were interchangeable with banknotes and silver dollars.[294] These notes came in denominations of 5, 10, 20, 50 and 100 dollars; one dollar notes were issued in 1905.[295] In the first year after they were issued, the average monthly amount in circulation amounted to $5.5 million, while the corresponding value of banknotes was $6.7 million, an indication that the government notes were meeting a deficiency in the medium of exchange.[296] The currency notes were backed by a silver reserve amounting to two-thirds of their value and by securities for the remaining one-third, thus inaugurating the currency board system in Singapore.[297] Increasingly, however, the disadvantages of a monetary system based on silver became clear as one trading nation after another switched to the gold standard by the end of the 19th century. Two currents of thought arose: the first advocated gold as being indispensable for stability in the currency and therefore a necessary condition of trade; the second defended silver, or rather its depreciation, as the basis of the Colony's prosperity.[298]

The underlying cause of the decline in the silver price relative to gold was the greatly increased demand for the latter as a monetary reserve, which in turn was due to its discovery in large quantities after 1850.[299] This had the effect of lowering the exchange rate of the silver dollar to the pound sterling, since Britain had formally adopted the gold standard

---

290 P.J. Drake, "The Evolution of Money in Singapore since 1819", in Monetary Authority of Singapore, *Papers on Monetary Economics* (Singapore: Singapore University Press, 1981), pp. 5–6.

291 Liew and Wilson, *A History of Money*, pp. 89–92.

292 Lee, *The Monetary and Banking Development*, p. 8.

293 Drake, "The Evolution of Money", pp. 6–7, 8.

294 Liew and Wilson, *A History of Money*, pp. 92–6.

295 J.O. Anthonisz, *Currency Reform in the Straits Settlements* (London: R.W. Simpson, 1913), pp. 7, 8.

296 "Currency Note Issue", in *Annual Departmental Reports of the Straits Settlements for the Year 1900*, pp. 87–8.

297 The specie reserve was reduced to one-half in 1902, one-third in 1909, one-fifth in 1915 and one-tenth in 1923. *Proceedings of the Legislative Council of the Straits Settlements*, 28 May 1923.

298 Lee, *The Monetary and Banking Development*, pp. 8–10; Chiang, *History of Straits Settlements Foreign Trade*, pp. 146–7.

299 Chiang, *History of Straits Settlements Foreign Trade*, pp. 76–9, 147–8, 162, 163.

in 1819. The result was that the domestic silver dollar prices of the major commodities in Singapore's international trade remained relatively buoyant, as in the case of tin and copra, or were rising, as for gambier and pepper. In fact, the local price of tin would have increased in the 1890s had its world price in sterling not fallen. A less desirable effect of currency depreciation was the decline in the pound sterling value of British civil servants' salaries and remittances back to England. Additionally, since they consumed goods from the gold standard countries in Europe, their cost of living increased.[300] The issue became serious enough for the colonial government to implement schemes to reimburse its employees, the most generous being full exchange compensation for the salaries of all service grades in 1901.[301] The Municipality, the Tanjong Pagar Dock Company, the banks and some mercantile firms also paid exchange compensation.

The need for currency reform was given impetus in the early 20th century when countries in the region that traded with Singapore converted to the gold standard: Siam in 1902, the Philippines in 1903 and Cochin-China in 1904. By that time, trade with the gold regions had grown larger than that with the remaining countries on the silver standard.[302] In 1897, the Singapore Chamber of Commerce had already called on the government to adopt the gold standard, although the resolution was not unanimous since the opposing views on gold versus silver were mirrored in the Chamber's membership.[303] The Colonial Office formed a committee in 1902 to study the question and very quickly petitions poured in from firms, Chinese businessmen and employees asking for a gold standard.[304] Following the committee's report, the preliminary step of issuing a silver Straits dollar at par value with the Spanish dollar, and with the same weight and fineness as the British trade dollar was taken in 1903.[305] The import of Mexican and other silver dollars was prohibited and those in circulation were melted into bullion and demonetised.[306] In January 1906, with a view to its conversion into a gold standard currency, the value of the new Straits dollar was pegged to sterling at 2s. 4d.; this was close to the prevailing market rate in order to minimise disruptions to trade and contracts. Almost immediately thereafter, however, a run on gold in 1907 and 1908 depleted the local gold stock and in 1914, Britain abandoned the gold standard at the outbreak of war, effectively changing the basis of the Straits dollar to a sterling exchange standard.[307]

---

300 *The Singapore Free Press and Mercantile Advertiser*, 4 Dec. 1894.

301 *Proceedings of the Legislative Council of the Straits Settlements*, 20 Oct. 1894, 24 Sept. 1901, 3 May 1907, 21 May 1907; *Straits Settlements Annual Report*, vol. 4, p. 148, vol. 5, p. 166; *The Straits Independent and Penang Chronicle*, 10 Nov. 1894.

302 Chiang, *History of Straits Settlements Foreign Trade*, pp. 157, 160–1.

303 *Mid-day Herald and Daily*, 10 Nov. 1897.

304 Anthonisz, *Currency Reform in the Straits Settlements*, pp. 14–15, 36; *Proceedings of the Legislative Council of the Straits Settlements*, 29 May 1903.

305 *Proceedings of the Legislative Council of the Straits Settlements*, 3 July 1903; *The Singapore Free Press and Mercantile Advertiser*, 13 Nov. 1902; *The Straits Budget*, 14 May 1903; *Straits Echo*, 2 June 1903.

306 Lee, *The Monetary and Banking Development*, pp. 12–15.

307 *Proceedings of the Legislative Council of the Straits Settlements*, 28 May 1923, 3 Sept. 1923; *Straits Settlements Annual Report*, vol. 6, pp. 8, 65.

The inception of the Straits dollar and its fixed exchange rate eliminated the violent fluctuations under the silver standard that hampered trade, discouraged capital inflow and attracted exchange speculation.[308] The government currency notes also rendered privately issued banknotes superfluous, although these stayed in circulation throughout the early part of the 20th century. At the end of 1908, the amount of Straits dollars in circulation in the Colony and the FMS was $16,871,147, government paper notes $25,670,505 and banknotes $999,255.[309] By 1938, the quantity of banknotes had been further reduced to $134,985 while the total amount of currency had grown to $105,300,470.[310] In the intervening years, changes in the money supply were determined by the public demand for cash, with banks adjusting their silver reserves accordingly as backing for it. The amount of currency in circulation moved in tandem with the pace of economic activity in general and rubber prices in particular, and it was also affected by seasonal increases in the demand for money, such as during the Chinese New Year period.[311] When rubber prices rose during the First World War, currency notes increased by nearly 50 per cent in the two years from 1914 to 1916.[312] In the recession of the early twenties, the amount of currency in circulation was reduced by half from March 1920 to December 1921. During the Great Depression of the 1930s, an even larger decline in note circulation preceded the slump, falling from $163 million at the start of 1927 to a low of $61.5 million in September 1931 before gradually rising again.[313]

In the latter part of the 19th century, intermittent bank runs and failures had created instability in the local money supply and financial stress.[314] After the bank failures of the 1860s, another financial panic had occurred in the late 1870s and in 1884, the Oriental Bank was bankrupted after a run on its branch in Calcutta. Barely eight years later, the Mercantile Bank collapsed, leaving only the Chartered Bank and the Hong Kong and Shanghai Bank which came to Singapore in 1877 to issue banknotes until their Royal Charters expired in 1904 and 1908, respectively.[315] Without the authority to issue banknotes, these British exchange banks forfeited their profits from seigniorage. Nevertheless, the growth of the tin and rubber industries afforded them plenty of scope for expansion through the setting up of branches and agencies in Malayan towns.[316] The Chartered Bank opened offices at Taiping in 1884 and Kuala Lumpur in 1888 to cater to the tin mining industry and comparably the Hong Kong and Shanghai Bank expanded into Perak, Selangor and Johor through agencies in the early 20th century to finance rubber plantations. Although their main clientele in Singapore comprised the agency houses and European merchant firms, these banks also mediated the inflow of British

[308] Drake, *Merchants, Bankers, Governors*, pp. 83–4.

[309] *Straits Settlements Annual Report*, vol. 6, p. 65.

[310] *Straits Settlements Annual Report*, vol. 11, pp. 403–4.

[311] Huff, *The Economic Growth of Singapore*, p. 88.

[312] *Straits Settlements Annual Report*, vol. 7, pp. 56, 94, 111, 471, 599.

[313] *Straits Settlements Annual Report*, vol. 9, p. 162, vol. 10, pp. 8, 171, 326, 484.

[314] Liew and Wilson, *A History of Money*, pp. 63, 66, 77–9, 82–3, 84.

[315] Lee, *The Monetary and Banking Development*, pp. 11, 37, 41, 42.

[316] Kawamura, "Trade, Finance and the 'Anglo-Dutch' International Order", p. 52.

capital into the rubber industry and served as the colonial government's conduit for telegraphic funds transfer between Singapore and London. The Mercantile Bank had also played a major part in financing rice exports from Burma to Singapore.[317] New banks with headquarters in the Netherlands, the United States, Japan and Britain appeared in the 20th century: the Nederlandsch-Indische Handelsbank in 1901, the First National City Bank of New York which subsequently became Citibank in 1902, the Bank of Taiwan and the Yokohama Specie Bank in the interwar period and the Eastern Bank in 1928.

The most significant development in banking in the late colonial period was the formation of indigenous Chinese banks. The first was Kwong Yik Bank, founded in 1903 by the Cantonese gambier-cum-rubber planter and sponsor of the Kwong Wai Shiu Hospital, Wong Ah Fook, who paid his workers in his own promissory notes.[318] The Sze Hai Tong Bank followed in 1906, a conservative institution established by Teochew businessmen. Even though Kwong Yik Bank closed in 1913 after it ran into financial difficulties, that decade witnessed the rise of a troika of new Chinese banks founded by the Hokkien community: the Chinese Commercial Bank, the Ho Hong Bank and the Oversea-Chinese Bank. Being the first to be established in 1912, the Chinese Commercial Bank did much to popularise the use of current accounts among Chinese merchants and shopkeepers but had to be rescued by the government at the onset of the First World War.[319] The Ho Hong Bank was part of a conglomerate that had interests ranging from trading to rice milling to shipping. In 1917, it opened numerous branches in Malaya, the Dutch East Indies and Hong Kong and was the first among the local banks to engage in correspondent banking with important financial centres around the world.[320] Given this vast network, the Ho Hong Bank was also a pioneer in the foreign exchange business which had hitherto been the exclusive preserve of the Western banks. The last of the troika to be established in 1919, the Oversea-Chinese Bank, followed the Ho Hong Bank by opening regional offices and dealing in foreign exchange.

Other Chinese banks were established during the interwar years, including the United Chinese Bank, later named the United Overseas Bank (UOB), in 1935.[321] Their fundamental contribution to Singapore's economic development was to give credit access to Chinese borrowers, who were shunned by the Western banks. The founders and directors of these banks were nearly all businessmen who had accumulated wealth from the rubber industry and the managers employed were usually their relatives and associates.[322] All the Chinese banks were managed along modern Western lines—accepting deposits, making loans and advances, discounting trade bills and transacting foreign exchange. However, compared to the Western banks, they had much smaller capital and reserves. Due to the existence of

[317] van Helten and Jones, "British Business in Malaysia and Singapore", pp. 175–8.

[318] Tan Ee-Leong, "The Chinese Banks Incorporated in Singapore and the Federation of Malaya", *Journal of the Malaysian Branch of the Royal Asiatic Society* 42, 1 (1969): 257–68; Huff, *The Economic Growth of Singapore*, pp. 230–4; *Straits Echo*, 4 Aug. 1911.

[319] *Straits Echo*, 29 Aug. 1914.

[320] *The Straits Budget*, 6 June 1919; *Malaya Tribune*, 16 Oct. 1923.

[321] *Malaya Tribune*, 2 Oct. 1935.

[322] Huff, *The Economic Growth of Singapore*, pp. 88–9, 232–3; Lee, *The Monetary and Banking Development*, pp. 40–1, 46–7, 48–9.

overseas Chinese economic networks, they were more strongly oriented towards Southeast Asia and China. The Chinese banks were also conservative in their lending policy and insisted on adequate collateral but the volume of credit extended was highly procyclical and tended to contract during downturns, which aggravated recessions and eventually led to a major shakeout of the banking industry during the Great Depression.

In the realm of fiscal policy, there were new developments in the early 20th century. The most germane was the abolishment of the opium farm, which dated from the earliest days of Singapore's existence and had been the main contributor to government revenue throughout the 19th century. In 1900, it still accounted for 43 per cent of government revenue.[323] In that year, the government was given legislative approval to fix the retail price of opium.[324] Before that, the local price of the drug was effectively determined by global demand and supply since the Singapore market was too small to impact the larger regional trade in opium. The price had remained more or less constant throughout the 19th century and increased only in 1903 from $2.20 to $3 per tahil (Figure 14).[325] The demise of the farm in 1910 was presaged by the adoption of the report of the Straits Settlements Opium Commission convened by the government to inquire into the use of the drug, after anti-opium sentiment built up in Singapore at the turn of the century.[326] It recommended ending the opium farm, banning the sale of the drug to women and those under 18 years old, and suppressing its use in brothels.[327]

A government Monopolies Department was set up to take over the preparation and sale of opium, although private retail shops were allowed to co-exist with government-run outlets until 1926.[328] The department took over the farmers' buildings and factories, and continued to employ most of the existing staff.[329] It also exerted direct control over the retail price, which was raised to $4.80 per tahil in 1911 and $12.50 per tahil in 1920, where it more or less stayed until 1939. Although the department made a profit of $1.3 million in its first one-and-a-half years of operation, it was not sufficient to make up for the loss of farm rents even after the price increases.[330] The revenue had to be supplemented

323 Cheng U. Wen, "Opium in the Straits Settlements, 1867–1910", *Journal of Southeast Asian History* 2, 1 (1961): 52.

324 *Proceedings of the Legislative Council of the Straits Settlements*, 3 Apr. 1900, 21 May 1900.

325 One tahil is equivalent to about 1.33 lb. The opium price data from 1831 to 1913 are from Atsushi Kobayashi and those for the remaining years up to 1939 are from Keen Meng Choy and Ichiro Sugimoto, "Opium Consumption and Living Standards in Singapore, 1900–39", *Journal of Southeast Asian Studies* 54, 1 (2023).

326 *The Singapore Free Press and Mercantile Advertiser*, 25 July 1907.

327 Straits Settlements Opium Commission, *Proceedings of the Commission Appointed to Enquire Into Matters Relating to the Use of Opium in the Straits Settlements and the Federated Malay States*, vol. I, (Singapore: 1909); *The Straits Budget*, 7 Jan. 1909; *The Singapore Free Press and Mercantile Advertiser*, 28 Jan. 1909.

328 *Straits Settlements Annual Report*, vol. 6, pp. 193–4, 276; "Government Monopolies Department", in *Annual Departmental Reports of the Straits Settlements for the Year 1926*, p. 131.

329 "Government Monopolies Department", in *Annual Departmental Reports of the Straits Settlements for the Year 1910*, pp. 87–8.

330 *Proceedings of the Legislative Council of the Straits Settlements*, 1910, Appendix No. 50, pp. C218–21; *Straits Settlements Annual Report*, vol. 6, pp. 289, 377, 478, vol. 7, pp. 135, 280.

by import duties on petroleum and tobacco imposed in 1909 and 1916 respectively, as well as a tax on liquor that the government collected directly instead of through a farm.[331] By 1928, the liquor tax accounted for 10.6 per cent of total government revenue, import duties for 21.8 per cent and opium profits contributed 35.1 per cent.[332] In 1935, the combined gross revenue from the indirect taxes exceeded that from opium.[333]

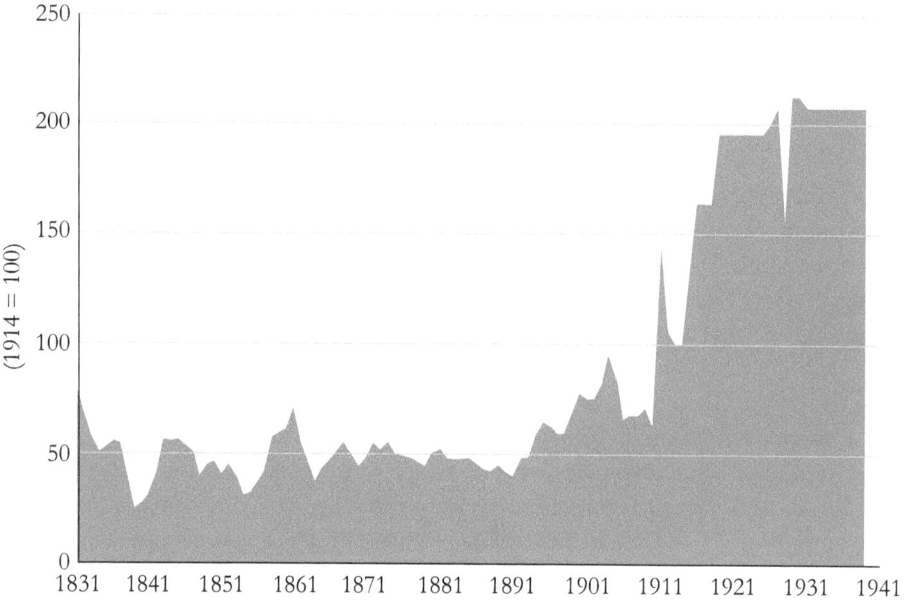

Figure 14. Singapore Opium Price Index, 1831–1939

Sources: Based on data supplied courtesy of Atsushi Kobayashi; Choy and Sugimoto, "Opium Consumption in Singapore", pp. 121–3.

As opium consumption fell gradually over the early decades of the 20th century due to the price increases and greater awareness of its effects, the government's revenue shrank progressively. Furthermore, Britain had signed up to the Hague Convention of 1912 that committed it to suppress the consumption of opium in its colonies within a given timeframe.[334] In 1925, the Governor of the Straits Settlements therefore proposed the establishment of the Opium Revenue Replacement Reserve Fund to provide a more sustainable source of income for the Colony, a precursor to the sovereign wealth fund

[331] *Straits Settlements Annual Report*, vol. 7, p. 93; *The Straits Budget*, 18 Nov. 1909, 2 Dec. 1909; *The Singapore Free Press and Mercantile Advertiser*, 2 Dec. 1909; *Straits Echo*, 19 June 1916.

[332] Ichiro Sugimoto and Tan Eu Chye, "Government Fiscal Behavior and Economic Growth of Singapore in the Twentieth Century", *The Singapore Economic Review* 56, 1 (2011): 25.

[333] "Report of the Department of Excise for the Year 1935", in *Annual Departmental Reports of the Straits Settlements for the Year 1935*, p. 455.

[334] H. Goto-Shibata, "Empire on the Cheap: The Control of Opium Smoking in the Straits Settlements, 1925–1939", *Modern Asian Studies* 40, 1 (2006): 62–3.

established in the modern period.[335] The fund started with seed money of $30 million drawn from accumulated government surpluses and the currency reserves.[336] At the time, the government's financial position was in an excellent state: its balance of assets over liabilities at the end of 1924 amounted to almost $67 million, with a large portion of it held in liquid assets.[337] Thereafter, one-tenth of the opium revenue was to be paid into the fund every year to be invested in the government securities of Britain, India and the Dominions.[338] It was expected that by the time the opium revenue dried up, the fund would have reached a size such that the annual investment income from it would prove to be a much needed supplement to general revenue. In 1939, the fund amount had grown to $56 million and it earned an estimated interest of $2.4 million.[339]

It has already been mentioned that the Great War did not much affect the economic life of Singapore. Indeed, the rise in tin and rubber prices made it possible for the Colony to contribute to the Imperial Government's war expenditure. The first half-yearly payment of £100,000 ($857,100) was made in 1916, followed by a yearly contribution of £200,000 ($1,714,200) up to 1921.[340] In addition, the Colony waived the excess of the annual military contributions over the cost of the garrison for several years and issued two bonds to help pay for and subsidise the cost of the war. Hence, the government was justified to claim that the Straits Settlements had "played [their] part well" in the war effort.[341] The military contributions were partly financed from government surpluses, the imposition of the tobacco duty, higher duties on liquor and an income tax.[342] From 1934 to 1938, the Colony again contributed $500,000 each year towards the cost of Imperial defence.[343] Notwithstanding this largesse, the British government requested that the Legislative Council consider an increase in the defence contribution in 1938.[344] In lieu of this, the Colony gave £1 million ($8,517,000) to Britain just before the outbreak of the Second World War in 1939 and again in 1940.[345]

---

335 *Proceedings of the Legislative Council of the Straits Settlements*, 24 Aug. 1925, 5 Oct. 1925; *Straits Settlements Annual Report*, vol. 8, pp. 405–6.

336 *The Straits Times*, 24 Aug. 1925; *The Singapore Free Press and Mercantile Advertiser (Weekly)*, 26 Aug. 1925.

337 *Straits Settlements Annual Report*, vol. 8, pp. 274, 359.

338 "Report on the Working of the Currency Department", in *Annual Departmental Reports of the Straits Settlements for the Year 1926*, Appendix D, pp. 60–1; *The Singapore Free Press and Mercantile Advertiser*, 6 Oct. 1925.

339 *Straits Settlements Annual Report*, vol. 11, pp. 451, 564.

340 *Proceedings of the Legislative Council of the Straits Settlements*, 16 June 1916; *Straits Settlements Annual Report*, vol. 7, pp. 94, 101, 143–4.

341 *Proceedings of the Legislative Council of the Straits Settlements*, 29 Sept. 1916, 27 May 1918; *Straits Settlements Annual Report*, vol. 7, pp. 215, 311.

342 *Straits Settlements Annual Report*, vol. 7, pp. 135–6, 143–4, 191.

343 *Proceedings of the Legislative Council of the Straits Settlements*, 12 Feb. 1934, 18 Feb. 1935, 17 Feb. 1936, 26 Apr. 1937, 14 Feb. 1938.

344 *Proceedings of the Legislative Council of the Straits Settlements*, 1938, Appendix No. 106, pp. C557–8.

345 *Proceedings of the Legislative Council of the Straits Settlements*, 24 Apr. 1939, 22 Apr. 1940; *Straits Settlements Annual Report*, vol. 11, pp. 438–9; *Morning Tribune*, 19 Apr. 1939.

From 1917 to 1919, a controversial one-off income tax was levied on residents, in part to raise funds for the war.[346] In 1910, an attempt had been made to impose such a tax but it was strongly opposed by the public.[347] Notwithstanding the alleged difficulty of collecting war funds from the Chinese, the representatives of the community came out in support of the income tax as the fairest imposition for the stated purpose, since it was levied only on incomes of $3,000 or more per annum at progressive rates of 1 to 6 per cent.[348] During 1917, $2.8 million was collected from income taxes, salary deductions, taxes on property and the interest on securities.[349] Of this, companies and associations were assessed at an average rate of 5.7 per cent and paid a total of $1.73 million. Individuals were taxed at an average rate of 4.3 per cent and paid $549,000, with the incidence falling most on the Europeans due to their higher incomes. For the Colony as a whole, a total sum of $12.77 million was raised by the war tax and £1.4 million was remitted to Britain.[350] The income tax was continued for three more years up to 1922 before it was ended by unanimous public opinion, as expressed by commercial bodies and the press.[351]

In conclusion, two principles of fiscal management could be discerned in the late colonial period. First is the philosophy of "living within one's means", borne out by the fact that throughout the period, there had not been a need for the British government to support the Colony financially.[352] To the contrary, fiscal surpluses were recorded in most years, so that funds could be lent to the FMS and the municipalities within their ambit.[353] For instance, the Singapore Municipality obtained a $2 million loan at interest of 4 per cent per annum for the town sewerage scheme and other works in 1913. Incidentally, that year saw its constitution changed to allow the Governor to nominate all the Commissioners.[354] Not all British colonies adhered to the philosophy, a notable example being India which borrowed heavily to finance its expenditure. Second, Singapore during the late colonial period could be described as a "night watchman state" and thus contrasted with the late 20th century concept of the "developmental state". The colonial government merely ensured public law and order and provided external security. It intervened only when the public interest was at stake, as when it expropriated the dockyards, and the state's

---

346 *Proceedings of the Legislative Council of the Straits Settlements*, 21 Jan. 1918, 30 Dec. 1918; *Straits Settlements Annual Report*, vol. 7, pp. 143–4, 156, 200, 300–1; *Straits Echo*, 21 June 1916.

347 "Interim Administration Report on the War Tax Ordinance, 1917", in *Annual Departmental Reports of the Straits Settlements for the Year 1918*, p. 251.

348 *The Straits Budget*, 1 Dec. 1916; *The Singapore Free Press and Mercantile Advertiser (Weekly)*, 11 Jan. 1917; *Straits Echo*, 21 Mar. 1917.

349 "Interim Administration Report on the War Tax Ordinance, 1917", in *Annual Departmental Reports of the Straits Settlements for the Year 1918*, pp. 254, 258, 260, 261–2.

350 "Administration Report on the War Tax Ordinance, 1919", in *Annual Departmental Reports of the Straits Settlements for the Year 1920*, p. 226.

351 Sugimoto and Tan, "Government Fiscal Behavior", p. 22; *Proceedings of the Legislative Council of the Straits Settlements*, 19 Jan. 1920, 19 Dec. 1921, 23 Jan. 1922, 23 Oct. 1922, 27 Nov. 1922.

352 Sugimoto and Tan, "Government Fiscal Behavior", pp. 20, 21, 28, 29–36.

353 *Proceedings of the Legislative Council of the Straits Settlements*, 29 June 1925; *Straits Settlements Annual Report*, passim.

354 *Proceedings of the Legislative Council of the Straits Settlements*, 1912, 1913, 15 Nov. 1912, 18 Apr. 1913, 27 June 1913, Appendix No. 28, pp. C132–3.

spending on social services in relation to the size of the population was modest. Given this, Wagner's Law postulating that the government sector would grow in tandem with economic development and the functions of a modern state was not observed in colonial Singapore, as there was no tendency for government spending to increase commensurately with the growth of the economy in the early 20th century.

Chapter 8 The Great Depression and Its Aftermath, 1929–39

We have witnessed in the previous two chapters how Singapore transformed itself from being an entrepôt for Asian trade into a staple port. The city's economic development during the early part of the 20th century gave it an almost unrivalled commercial importance in the British Empire. Ruling over large swathes of the world's population and oceans, the Empire reached its apogee during the reign of tin and rubber, elevating both Singapore and Malaya to a higher sphere of prosperity on account of the political hegemony and trade connections created by *Pax Britannica*. Singapore became an imperial city *par excellence* and the paragon of colonial power.[1]

The ups and downs in the staple trade persisted throughout the later colonial period—crisis alternating with prosperity in what seemed like an endless repetition and periods of commercial efflorescence followed by retrogression. The interwar years saw the growing amplification of these oscillations in economic activity, whereupon a spell of vigorous growth in the late twenties was terminated by a severe depression in the early thirties, which was made worse by structural changes in trade. Nevertheless, a modest economic revival followed, alongside a turn towards protectionism. These short-term fluctuations caused by staple cycles since 1870 amidst long-term changes in Singapore's standards of living are discussed in the last parts of this chapter.

The 1930s Slump

The economic disaster that befell Singapore and the world in the early 1930s, known as the Great Depression, can be understood only by contrasting it with the prosperity of the preceding decade. In the later part of the 1920s, the global economy and world trade enjoyed an unprecedented boom on the back of investor and consumer optimism and unbridled speculation in asset markets. The "roaring twenties" in the United States saw a golden age of growth that permeated to Singapore and Malaya. Singapore's foreign trade increased sharply in 1925 and stayed buoyant in the next two years: trade value over this period was 74 per cent higher compared to 1922–24.[2] Although rubber and tin prices retreated from their peaks in mid-decade, they remained relatively high.[3] The amount of

[1] Tan, *A Very Short History*, pp. 43–4; Savage, *Lion City Narratives*, p. xxxi.

[2] Huff, *The Economic Growth of Singapore*, Appendix Table A.1, p. 374.

[3] Lim, *Economic Development of Modern Malaya*, Appendix 2.3, p. 322, Appendix 3.1, p. 323.

tin exported through the port reached a maximum of 37,468 tonnes in 1927, while that of rubber exceeded 200,000 tonnes for the first time.[4] The thriving economy attracted record numbers of 174,795 Indian and 359,262 Chinese immigrants in 1926 and 1927 respectively.[5] About two-thirds of the latter remained in the Colony and Malaya.[6]

Domestically, the prosperity of the times was reflected in the rising prices of town and suburban lands.[7] A construction spree was underway in private buildings and houses, which was further bolstered by government projects such as the new General Post Office at Fullerton Square (the Fullerton Building), the Hill Street Police Station, Woodbridge Mental Hospital, the new Chinese Protectorate and Raffles College.[8] The crowning achievement in public works was the Municipal Offices, now known as City Hall, completed in 1929.[9] Totally paid for by the Municipal Council through a $22 million loan from the colonial government which was also expended on other works, the stately building with its Corinthian columns brought together for the first time the various departments under the Council.[10] The Municipality also rebuilt Elgin Bridge at the extravagant cost of $1 million in borrowed funds.[11] These new structures completed the transformation of Singapore into an "elegant city which reflected the mores and values of British control and administration".[12]

However, even before the New York stock market crash of October 1929 that heralded the start of the global depression, the malaise began in mid-1928 when the rubber price declined on the announcement that the Stevenson restriction scheme would be terminated in November.[13] The prices of tin and Straits produce followed suit, providing a sure sign of the impending downturn, while an index of the value of 20 principal exports declined.[14] Singapore's total trade fell by 17 per cent in 1928; as the recession worsened and countries began to impose tariffs and exchange controls, it dropped further by over a half between

4 Huff, *The Economic Growth of Singapore*, Appendix Table A.2, p. 380.

5 *Straits Settlements Annual Report*, vol. 8, p. 659, vol. 9, p. 153.

6 "Annual Report of the Statistical Office", in *Annual Departmental Reports of the Straits Settlements for the Year 1927*, Appendix, p. 31.

7 *Straits Settlements Annual Report*, vol. 9, p. 107; *The Singapore Free Press and Mercantile Advertiser*, 7 Feb. 1928.

8 *Straits Settlements Annual Report*, vol. 8, p. 568, vol. 9, pp. 14, 17, 140, 145; *The Straits Budget*, 28 June 1928; *Malayan Saturday Post*, 22 Dec. 1928.

9 Turnbull, *History of Modern Singapore*, p. 141; *Straits Settlements Annual Report*, vol. 9, p. 332; *The Singapore Free Press and Mercantile Advertiser (Weekly)*, 24 July 1929.

10 *Proceedings of the Legislative Council of the Straits Settlements*, 1925, 26 Oct. 1925, Appendix No. 67, C205–6; *The Straits Times*, 30 Apr. 1929. Of the loan amount, $1.75 million was appropriated for the building while part of the remainder was used to finance the Johor water reservoirs and the electrical power station at St. James.

11 *Proceedings of the Legislative Council of the Straits Settlements*, 29 Mar. 1926.

12 Jayapal, *Old Singapore*, p. 26.

13 *Straits Settlements Annual Report*, vol. 9, p. 261; *The Straits Budget*, 7 June 1928.

14 *Straits Settlements Annual Report*, vol. 9, p. 380.

1929 and 1932, with a concomitant decline in shipping traffic.[15] Rubber and tin exports declined even more in value terms over the same period due to contractions in American automobile and steel output. In September 1930, the Governor soberly declared that: "There is unfortunately at the present time a world-wide depression and Malaya has been hard hit by the sharp fall in the prices of tin and rubber".[16] The prices of both staple products dropped by 75 per cent over the course of the depression.[17] As a result, tin production in the Peninsula plummeted from 72,000 tonnes in 1929 to 29,000 tonnes in 1932.[18] The output of rubber fell by less but given their higher supply elasticity, that of smallholders declined by much more than estates.[19] The declines in staple production and exports generally lagged the fall in prices.[20]

The labour situation became dire in 1930, forcing the colonial government to restrict Chinese and Indian immigration, the latter partly by stopping the issuance of kangany licences.[21] An Immigration Restriction Ordinance had been passed in 1928, having as its objectives the prevention of unemployment and the rectification of the imbalance in the sex ratio by constraining the influx of unskilled male labourers.[22] The law was partly motivated by the record set in 1927 in the number of immigrants arriving at the city.[23] With the onset of the slump, the ordinance was used to impose quotas on male immigrants starting from August 1930; these quotas were tightened in the subsequent two years. Consequently, the number of adult men who came to Singapore dropped from 204,924 in 1929 to 18,741 in 1932.[24] In contrast, 215,193 women and children from China entered the Straits Settlements during this period.

Even so, unemployment in the city rose dramatically, including among Europeans as the agency houses and other firms dismissed staff.[25] In the local population, the worst hit were the menial labourers but many in steady wage employment such as clerks were also retrenched.[26] The commercial and financial sector, which included the staple and entrepôt

---

[15] Huff, *The Economic Growth of Singapore*, Appendix Table A.1, p. 374; W.G. Huff, "Entitlements, Destitution and Emigration in the 1930s Singapore Great Depression", *The Economic History Review* 54, 2 (2001): 290; *Straits Settlements Annual Report*, vol. 9, p. 388.

[16] *Straits Settlements Annual Report*, vol. 9, p. 449.

[17] Abshire, *History of Singapore*, p. 63.

[18] Lim, *Economic Development of Modern Malaya*, Appendix 2.1, p. 319, Appendix 4.3, p. 328.

[19] Benham, "The Rubber Industry", p. 363.

[20] Loh Kah Seng, "Beyond Rubber Prices: Negotiating the Great Depression in Singapore", *South East Asia Research* 14, 1 (2006): 10–11.

[21] *Proceedings of the Legislative Council of the Straits Settlements*, 25 Aug. 1930, 15 Oct. 1930; *Straits Settlements Annual Report*, vol. 9, pp. 449–50, vol. 10, p. 12.

[22] Turnbull, *History of Modern Singapore*, pp. 145–6; Ee, "Chinese Migration to Singapore", pp. 42–4; *Proceedings of the Legislative Council of the Straits Settlements*, 30 Jan. 1928, 7 May 1928; *The Singapore Free Press and Mercantile Advertiser*, 31 Jan. 1928.

[23] Moore and Moore, *The First 150 Years*, p. 491.

[24] *Straits Settlements Annual Report*, vol. 9, p. 420, vol. 10, pp. 65, 420, 551, 620.

[25] Huff, "Entitlements, Destitution and Emigration", pp. 300–1.

[26] Huff, *The Economic Growth of Singapore*, p. 175; Khoo Kay Kim, "The Great Depression: The Malaysian Context", in *The History of South-East, South and East Asia: Essays and Documents*, ed. Khoo Kay Kim (Kuala Lumpur: Oxford University Press, 1977), p. 89.

trades as well as banking, took the brunt of the depression, although it still provided employment to 19.2 per cent of the labour force in 1931.[27] The unemployment rate varied among the races, from as high as 57 per cent for Malays to 15.4 per cent for Indians, with the Europeans and Chinese somewhere in between.[28] Some idea of overall economic conditions can be gleaned from the fact that 1,977 workers were retrenched in a group of industries that employed 11,631 people.[29] Underemployment was also widespread as firms rationed out the work available through part-time arrangements or rotating shifts.[30] The situation was not helped by redundant Chinese and Indian workers from the Malay Peninsula who came to Singapore to look for work.[31] The devastated rubber and tin industries there laid off close to 200,000 workers during the depression years. Crimes committed in the city—robberies and cases of criminal intimidation—increased commensurately with the rise in unemployment and the number of beggars on the streets multiplied.[32]

As in the 19th century, the labour glut was partially absorbed in street hawking, giving rise to a new class of "slump hawkers".[33] The census of 1931, which recorded the population at 557,745, counted 22,725 hawkers and street sellers.[34] Still, the worsening scale of the unemployment problem and the fear of social unrest left the British authorities with no choice but to repatriate those who were out of work. In addition to Europeans, 197,087 Indians from both Malaya and Singapore were repatriated at government expense from 1929 to 1932.[35] The consequence was that a migrational surplus of 37,743 labourers in 1929 turned into a cumulative deficit of 230,684 in the following three years.[36] Since the Chinese were not British subjects, the initial policy of sending back only the decrepit and destitute labourers among them was extended to all unemployed workers in 1931.[37] Adding those who left on their own and Indian departures, this resulted in a fall of 60,000 in the city's population in 1933.

As the depression proceeded, nominal wages fell across the board and had it not been for the repatriation of Indian and Chinese labourers, the declines would have been more severe.[38] Fortunately, deflation in the prices of rice and other foodstuffs mitigated the fall in real wages and alleviated the suffering of workers. Thus, it has been suggested that the slump's impact was not uniformly harsh and many workers managed to negotiate its worst

[27] Huff, *The Economic Growth of Singapore*, Appendix Table A.10, pp. 407–9.

[28] Yeo Eng Leng, *Effects of Great Depression on Singapore*, Academic Exercise (History Department, University of Singapore, 1972), p. 20.

[29] *The Straits Times*, 30 Sept. 1930.

[30] Huff, "Entitlements, Destitution and Emigration", pp. 299–300, 303, 309–10, 312.

[31] Loh, "Beyond Rubber Prices", p. 17; *The Straits Times*, 30 Sept. 1930.

[32] *Proceedings of the Legislative Council of the Straits Settlements*, 1931, Appendix No. 85, p. C314.

[33] Huff, "Entitlements, Destitution and Emigration", pp. 307, 313–4.

[34] Huff, *The Economic Growth of Singapore*, pp. 407–9.

[35] *Straits Settlements Annual Report*, vol. 9, pp. 421, 553, 619–20, vol. 10, pp. 64–5; *Malaya Tribune*, 23 May 1931.

[36] Huff, "Entitlements, Destitution and Emigration", pp. 301, 311–3, 315.

[37] *The Straits Budget*, 9 Oct. 1930.

[38] Keen Meng Choy and Ichiro Sugimoto, "Staple Trade, Real Wages, and Living Standards in Singapore, 1870–1939", *Economic History of Developing Regions* 33, 1 (2018): 38–9.

effects.[39] This assertion was borne out by the case of government employees and municipal workers, whose wages were not reduced by as much as those in the private sector though they constituted only a relatively small proportion of the labour force.[40]

The international slump was rapidly transmitted to the local economy: 500 shops closed down in the second half of 1930 and bankruptcies went up by 50 per cent between 1929 and 1931.[41] As a sign of the economic malady, imports of passenger cars fell from 5,751 to 1,611.[42] Construction work dried up as the building boom fizzled out and property values deflated.[43] Pawnshops experienced a brisk business—more people were pledging articles for cash than redeeming them.[44] Given its sound fiscal position, the colonial government brought forward necessary public projects to ameliorate the situation and offer some relief to the unemployed, although it eschewed pure relief works.[45] As a result, fiscal deficits of $6.8 million and $18.1 million were incurred in 1930 and 1931 respectively, which were also caused in part by contractions in revenue.[46] But in 1932, whatever good this measure did was unravelled by a retrenchment policy that froze new hiring in the civil service, reduced government salaries and drastically cut back on public construction.[47] The overall aim was to achieve a 13 per cent reduction in recurrent expenditure, including on education and medical spending. These austerity measures returned the budget to surplus from 1932 onwards.

There were some notable victims of the Great Depression in Singapore. One was the bankruptcy of the firm started by the Sarkies Brothers, the owner of the Raffles and Sea View Hotels in the city and the E. & O. Hotel in Penang.[48] Owing to the plunge in commodity prices, millionaire rubber tycoons saw their wealth shrink.[49] Chinese firms were worse affected in comparison to European enterprises because they did not provide for reserves and lacked borrowing power.[50] Among the numerous company failures were

---

[39] Loh Kah Seng, "Records and Voices of Social History: The Case of the Great Depression in Singapore", *Southeast Asian Studies* 44, 1 (2006): 31.

[40] Loh, "Beyond Rubber Prices", pp. 16–17.

[41] Huff, "Entitlements, Destitution and Emigration", pp. 302–3.

[42] "The Foreign Trade of Malaya", in *Annual Departmental Reports of the Straits Settlements for the Year 1931*, Table XXIV, p. 366.

[43] *Straits Settlements Annual Report*, vol. 9, pp. 261, 434, 484, 567, vol. 10, p. 10.

[44] Loh, "Beyond Rubber Prices", p. 13.

[45] Huff, "Entitlements, Destitution and Emigration", pp. 314–5; *Malayan Saturday Post*, 11 Oct. 1930; *Malaya Tribune*, 13 Oct. 1931, 30 May 1933.

[46] *Straits Settlements Annual Report*, vol. 9, pp. 487, 699. The government covered its deficit in 1930 by using its reserves but did not do so in 1931. Liew and Wilson, *A History of Money*, p. 122.

[47] *Straits Settlements Annual Report*, vol. 10, pp. 126–7, 157–8, 167, 221, 271; *Malaya Tribune*, 26 Sept. 1932, 11 Oct. 1932; *The Straits Budget*, 29 Sept. 1932. The Municipality likewise implemented a salary cut, reductions in allowances and job retrenchments. Loh, "Beyond Rubber Prices", p. 17.

[48] "Annual Report of the Bankruptcy Department for the Year 1931", in *Annual Departmental Reports of the Straits Settlements for the Year 1931*, Appendix II, p. 913.

[49] Loh, "Beyond Rubber Prices", pp. 12–13.

[50] Huff, "Entitlements, Destitution and Emigration", p. 302; "Annual Report of the Bankruptcy Department for the Year 1931", in *Annual Departmental Reports of the Straits Settlements for the Year 1931*, Appendix II, pp. 919–41; *The Straits Budget*, 21 Nov. 1929; *Malaya Tribune*, 4 Oct. 1930, 1 Apr. 1931.

Chinese manufacturing firms making rubber products and export processing plants like rubber mills and sugar refineries. Another noteworthy failure was the pineapple industry, which had been established by Europeans in Singapore in the late 1880s. Later on, interplanting of the crop with rubber by Chinese growers had led to a significant increase in output, with cultivation extending to Johor in the 1930s.[51] The fruit was processed by Chinese-owned canneries which sprang up in Singapore and Johor and was marketed by the European merchant firms.[52] By the 1900s, canned pineapples figured considerably in exports to Britain; in 1929, their value exceeded $8 million, making Singapore the second largest exporter in the world after Hawaii.[53] During the First World War, the industry had ceased to exist for a time due to restrictions on imports into Britain.[54] In the 1930s slump, the low price to which the product had fallen led to the closure of two of the five canning factories in Singapore during the greater part of a year.[55]

Both the pineapple canning and the rubber manufacturing industries (making shoes, gloves and rickshaw tyres) were dominated by the Chinese magnate Tan Kah Kee.[56] At the height of his fortunes in the mid-1920s, his industrial conglomerate extended to rubber plantations and mills, a bicycle assembly plant, a leather tannery and biscuit, candy, chocolate, soap and toothpaste factories, which altogether employed 15,000 workers.[57] However, the depression dealt a fatal blow to his businesses, which began to flounder in 1931 and had to be kept going by large overdrafts from the banks.[58] As the slump persisted, the company was confronted with a liquidity crisis and its liabilities mounted due to falling demand for its products, Japanese competition and reduced earnings from rubber and pineapples.[59] By 1934, all of Tan Kah Kee's factories had shut down except for the biscuit factory with 400 workers.[60]

Another major casualty of the Great Depression was the Ho Hong group of companies founded by Lim Peng Siang.[61] In 1932, it was forced into a financial restructuring and its shipping line had to be taken over by the SSC, as mentioned in the previous chapter.[62] In 1934, the Ho Hong Cement Factory was closed down.[63] The Ho Hong Bank too was

---

51 King, "Plantation and Agriculture in Malaya", p. 141; Huff, *The Economic Growth of Singapore*, pp. 76–7, 192–3.

52 *The Singapore Free Press and Mercantile Advertiser*, 2 Jan. 1932.

53 Huff, *The Economic Growth of Singapore*, Appendix Table A.1, pp. 373, 375; Tan, *A Very Short History*, p. 45; *The Straits Times*, 15 June 1906; *The Singapore Free Press and Mercantile Advertiser*, 18 Nov. 1930.

54 W. Bartley, "Singapore and the Great War", p. 415.

55 *Straits Settlements Annual Report*, vol. 9, pp. 500–1; *Malaya Tribune*, 1 Apr. 1931.

56 *The Singapore Free Press and Mercantile Advertiser (Weekly)*, 22 June 1922, 14 July 1926; *The Straits Budget*, 13 June 1929.

57 Tan, *A Very Short History*, pp. 47–8; *The Straits Budget*, 22 Feb. 1934.

58 Huff, *The Economic Growth of Singapore*, pp. 226–8.

59 Loh, "Beyond Rubber Prices", p. 12.

60 *The Singapore Free Press and Mercantile Advertiser*, 17 Mar. 1934.

61 Song, *One Hundred Years' History of the Chinese*, pp. 169–72.

62 Huff, *The Economic Growth of Singapore*, pp. 147, 225, 234.

63 Kuo Huei-Ying, "Rescuing Businesses through Transnationalism: Embedded Chinese Enterprise and Nationalist Activities in Singapore in the 1930s", *Enterprise & Society*, 7, 1 (2006): 109.

dissolved through a merger with the Chinese Commercial Bank and the Oversea-Chinese Bank.[64] All three banks were severely affected by the slump, though to different degrees and in somewhat different ways. The Chinese Commercial Bank prudently cut back on lending after encountering problems on its overdrafts to Tan Kah Kee in 1930.[65] The Ho Hong Bank's concentration on the foreign exchange business was the cause of its downfall. The abandonment of the gold standard by Britain in 1931 and the downturn in business conditions led to heavy losses that almost wiped out its reserves. The Oversea-Chinese Bank experienced a run at its Rangoon branch, after which it initiated the merger plan. In 1932, the three banks combined to form the Oversea-Chinese Banking Corporation (OCBC) with a paid-up capital of $10 million. As a result of the merger, redundant bank branches were closed and staff dismissed.[66]

The collapse of rubber and tin exports during the Great Depression was aggravated by structural changes in Singapore's produce trade, with repercussions for both the European merchant houses and Chinese dealers. These were concerning enough for the Governor of the Straits Settlements to appoint a commission "to make a diligent and full inquiry into the trade of the Colony, the directions in which it has gained or lost, and the reasons for these gains or losses, and its future potentialities".[67] After summoning more than a hundred witnesses, the commission produced a comprehensive and detailed report which went beyond the trade in primary produce.

For a start, it rebutted criticisms voiced publicly that Singapore had lost the trade in Straits produce with the Dutch East Indies, eclipsed as it had been by rubber production.[68] On the contrary, the commission asserted that Singapore continued to be a collecting centre for produce from the Archipelago, this trade being still largely financed by the barter exchange of manufactured goods at fixed prices.[69] Hence, a deterioration in the terms of trade could be ruled out as a reason for any decline in the produce trade as these terms remained more or less unchanged in the early 20th century. As during the earlier colonial period, Singapore dealers secured a lien on the produce in return for advances of cash and provisions to outport middlemen.[70] The persistence of the credit-for-goods system accounted for the city's hold on Dutch East Indies producers and whatever was left of the trade with the more distant Celebes. In 1935, the Dutch East Indies accounted for 39 per cent of Singapore's imports, with Sumatra being the most important source.[71] The shipping conferences that operated in Singapore, and which had grown to cover routes

64 *The Singapore Free Press and Mercantile Advertiser*, 28 July 1932; *The Straits Budget*, 22 Sept. 1932.

65 Tan, "The Chinese Banks", pp. 261, 266, 268–9.

66 *The Singapore Free Press and Mercantile Advertiser*, 11 Aug. 1932.

67 *Report of the Commission appointed by His Excellency the Governor of the Straits Settlements to Enquire into and Report on the Trade of the Colony*, vol. 1 (Singapore: 1933–1934), p. 27. This document will hereafter be referred to as *Straits Settlements Trade Commission*.

68 *The Singapore Free Press and Mercantile Advertiser*, 17 May 1930; *Malaya Tribune*, 30 July 1934.

69 Wong, "Commercial Growth", p. 61.

70 *Straits Settlements Trade Commission*, pp. 41, 48–9.

71 King, "Plantation and Agriculture in Malaya", p. 145.

to Europe, Bombay, China and Japan, also enabled traders to offer the highest prices for produce in the region.[72]

One important factor that did affect the Straits produce trade was the development of direct shipping services between ports in the Dutch East Indies and markets in Europe and East Asia, leading to a shrinkage of the area from which produce was collected in Singapore.[73] This development was fostered by the construction of ocean wharves at Batavia, Surabaya, Palembang and Belawan, among other places.[74] The rise of Port Swettenham as an ocean port also encouraged Malayan traders to import manufactured goods without going through Singapore.[75] Concurrently, the establishment of direct maritime transport between the countries of mainland Asia and Western markets reduced Singapore's entrepôt and transshipment trades. As an illustration, the combined percentages of China and Hong Kong in the trade of the Straits Settlements fell from 10.6 per cent early in the century to 6.3 per cent for imports and from 7 per cent to 2.5 per cent in the case of exports. Trade with Cochin-China was adversely affected by the development of Saigon's port facilities and continued discrimination by the French authorities in the form of preferential rates for shipments by French vessels.[76]

The volume of the city's rice exports to its major markets had also declined as a result of direct imports from producing countries, which was precipitated to some extent by the colonial government's ban on rice re-exports during the crisis of 1921.[77] The rice trade with mainland Southeast Asia was conducted mostly in cash terms although Chinese firms bartered dried fish from Siam and Cochin-China for rice from Burma.[78] A similar fate had befallen some of Singapore's leading trade commodities. Coffee exports dwindled to just 2,568 tonnes in 1933 partly as a result of an embargo imposed by India while the gambier and black pepper trades shrunk to just over 10,000 tonnes as growers switched to rubber.[79] Exports of gum copal and rattan from the Celebes also declined markedly. These reductions were partially compensated by increased trade in copra and sago flour, which replaced pearl sago.

The shipping conferences in Singapore, while helping to secure Straits produce, had been alleged to be one of the causes of the decline in the produce trade. Refuting this claim, the commission cited evidence from witnesses that the conferences were viewed as beneficial to the trade of the Colony even though they charged higher freights than necessary to break even, charges which partially negated Singapore's advantages as a shipping port.[80] However, the conferences concentrated the produce trade in a small number of British and European

---

72 Huff, *The Economic Growth of Singapore*, p. 95.

73 British Military Administration, *Entrepôt Trade*, pp. 8–9; *Straits Settlements Trade Commission*, pp. 46–7, 232.

74 King, "Plantation and Agriculture in Malaya", p. 147.

75 *Straits Settlements Trade Commission*, p. 51.

76 British Military Administration, *Entrepôt Trade*, p. 14.

77 Huff, *The Economic Growth of Singapore*, pp. 90–1, 104–5; Wong, "Singapore: Its Growth", p. 79; King, "Plantation and Agriculture in Malaya", pp. 147, 148; *Straits Settlements Trade Commission*, p. 47.

78 *Straits Settlements Trade Commission*, p. 46.

79 Ibid., pp. 43–5.

80 Ibid., pp. 42, 76, 79, 83, 233.

firms that held shipping agencies, thus preventing Chinese firms from exporting to the West, although this did not imply a diminution in trade volumes.[81] Furthermore, the cartels offered a lower freight rate on cargo from the Dutch outports that was transshipped in Singapore through bills of lading, robbing the port of the profits and employment accruing from the processing of commodities.[82]

As for the SSC's control of regional shipping routes and its introduction of a deferred rebate to retain support, freights were kept reasonable by competition from a few remaining Chinese lines.[83] Much the same could be said about local shipping charges from and to Malaya due to the availability of rail and road networks as alternative means of transport. On the issue of port dues at the free landing sites provided by the government at Tanjong Rhu and the Rochor River, the commission was unequivocal in stating its opinion that they should not be imposed, lest "a charge which by itself was less than corresponding charges elsewhere might combine with other factors to turn a nicely balanced scale against us".[84] For the same reason, it deemed that a reimposition of the light dues abolished in 1912 was inadvisable.[85] Wharfage charges by the Singapore Harbour Board compared favourably with rival ports, even if they were not cheaper, while free storage facilities were available for transshipment goods.[86] In summary, the commission concluded that the Straits produce entrepôt trade continued to exist, notwithstanding higher freight charges and a smaller geographical hinterland.

Economic Revival and Imperial Preference

Having reached a trough in 1932, Singapore and Malaya began to recover from the economic depression in the following year. As on the way down, the revival was foreshadowed by an increase in the prices of rubber and tin, the latter aided by the restriction scheme that started in 1931.[87] This had the effect of making tapping of both estate and smallholder rubber in Malaya viable once more. In 1934, large estates were reported to be making profits again as the International Rubber Regulation Agreement kicked in and raised the rubber price.[88] As world trade started to increase in volume terms and Malaya's exports of its two main staples picked up, Singapore's

---

81 Huff, *The Economic Growth of Singapore*, p. 102.

82 British Military Administration, *Entrepôt Trade*, p. 15; *Straits Settlements Trade Commission*, pp. 93–4.

83 *Straits Settlements Trade Commission*, pp. 96, 99.

84 King, "Plantation and Agriculture in Malaya", pp. 144, 145; *Straits Settlements Trade Commission*, pp. 105–6.

85 *Proceedings of the Legislative Council of the Straits Settlements*, 1 Nov. 1912.

86 *Straits Settlements Trade Commission*, pp. 123–4, 127.

87 Lim, *Economic Development of Modern Malaya*, Appendix 2.3, p. 322, Appendix 3.1, p. 323; Yeo, *Effects of Great Depression*, pp. 7–8; *Straits Settlements Annual Report*, vol. 10, p. 150; *The Singapore Free Press and Mercantile Advertiser*, 22 June 1933.

88 *Straits Settlements Annual Report*, vol. 10, pp. 371–2.

merchandise exports and imports increased in value terms.[89] The local press announced the turn-around triumphantly by declaring in May 1934: "Set fair—for Prosperity".[90] Improvements in the domestic economy followed: people began spending again and Singapore shopkeepers filled their shelves with goods.[91] Property values in the town stabilised and gradually inched upwards in the mid-thirties.[92] Immigration also resumed and net arrivals of Chinese, Indian and Javanese labourers amounted to 103,900 for the year 1935.[93]

With the recovery in place in 1933, the Governor of the Straits Settlements, who was concurrently High Commissioner for the FMS, actively pressed for a customs union with Malaya as a means of promoting the manufacturing industry in Singapore.[94] The industrial development of the city up to that time had been insignificant, aside from the mainly Chinese-owned rubber and pineapple factories.[95] There were light industries producing import-substituting food and drinks (biscuits, cooking oil, sugar, aerated water, beer) and construction materials (bricks, tiles, cement, nails, pipes), sago factories, coconut oil mills, tanneries and sawmills, in addition to the traditional trades of woodworking, furniture making and tailoring.[96] Heavy industries hardly existed, save for one big firm that manufactured and repaired machinery for rubber estates, factories and tin mines. In 1931, 16 per cent of Singapore's labour force was engaged in manufacturing activities, although this figure is likely to have been underestimated.[97] Small factories were the norm, scattered all over the island and around the city centre in shophouses. This haphazard development led the town's planners to earmark the Kallang River Basin as an industrial area with facilities to attract manufacturers.[98] The river served as a natural harbour for junks and sailing vessels and was home to sawmill traders and shipyards building twakows.

The advantage afforded by a customs union with Malaya, which had imposed duties on re-exports from Singapore, was that manufactured and other goods imported into the latter for redistribution to the Peninsula would not be liable for duty regardless of their origin.[99] Hence, it was championed by importers but this latest and most serious

---

89 Huff, *The Economic Growth of Singapore*, Appendix Table A.1, p. 374; "The Foreign Trade of Malaya, 1933", in *Annual Departmental Reports of the Straits Settlements for the Year 1933*, p. 691; *The Straits Times*, 18 Aug. 1934.

90 *The Sunday Tribune (Singapore)*, 6 May 1934.

91 *The Straits Budget*, 27 Dec. 1934.

92 *Straits Settlements Annual Report*, vol. 10, p. 460.

93 *Straits Settlements Annual Report*, vol. 11, p. 103.

94 Huff, *The Economic Growth of Singapore*, pp. 212–4; *The Straits Times*, 2 Sept. 1931, 11 Jan. 1932. It has been suggested that another motivation for a customs union was for financially better off Singapore to aid Malaya, whose revenue from tin and rubber duties had fallen severely due to the depression. Liew and Wilson, *A History of Money*, pp. 122–3.

95 Lee, *From Colony to Nation*, pp. 14–15.

96 Wong, "Singapore: Its Growth", p. 76; *Straits Settlements Trade Commission*, pp. 145, 146.

97 Huff, *The Economic Growth of Singapore*, p. 209, Appendix Table A.10, p. 407.

98 *The Singapore Free Press and Mercantile Advertiser*, 15 Jan. 1932; *Malaya Tribune*, 13 Feb. 1935, 14 Mar. 1935.

99 Wong, "Singapore: Its Growth", pp. 74–7; *The Singapore Free Press and Mercantile Advertiser*, 28 July 1932.

challenge to free trade was almost unanimously opposed by all the representative bodies in Singapore, including a committee set up to consider the issue.[100] Apart from the jealously guarded freedom of trade, it was felt that Singapore's interests were "largely extra-Malayan", notwithstanding its increased economic ties with the FMS, a reference to the importance of the Netherlands Indies and other regional markets.[101] To enter into a customs union with common tariff rates and regulations was to reduce its status to that of a Malayan port and deprive it of the entrepôt trade.[102] By the same token, protection of local manufacturing industries was ruled out.[103] Moreover, wage costs in Singapore were relatively high, compared to Hong Kong for example, and the combined Singapore and Malayan market was not large by any standards.

The veer towards protectionism was not restricted to Singapore, for the British government abandoned the free trade policy practised since the mid-19th century in 1932 and established a system of Imperial Preference across the Empire. This action was taken in response to the Great Depression, whereby certain goods imported from and exported to the British Dominions (including India) and Colonies would enjoy preferential tariff rates or none at all for a period of five years. The system had its origins in the special tariff rates granted by the regions of recent settlement (that is, Canada, Australia and New Zealand) to British Empire producers in earlier decades.[104] It was preceded by the Empire Marketing Board created in 1926 to promote British and colonial products, including canned pineapples from Singapore.[105] With Imperial Preference, about four-fifths of all imports from the Empire were admitted duty-free into Britain while protective duties or quotas were imposed on the rest at preferential rates. The products affected were chiefly agricultural commodities such as wheat, butter, eggs, meat and fruits. On the whole, imports from the Colonies and Protectorates into Britain did increase after the system was implemented and the proportion of British exports that went to them also rose since reciprocating concessions were offered in some cases, though they were not mandatory.[106]

Imperial Preference was implemented in Malaya but not in Singapore, given its long-standing opposition to tariffs, except for preferential duties on liquor and tobacco imported from Britain and Northern Ireland.[107] The system hardly benefitted Malaya since its principal exports of tin and rubber had all along been the main sources for Britain and these commodities were not awarded preference anyway; all it did was to

---

[100] Huff, *The Economic Growth of Singapore*, pp. 109, 111, 213, 215, 266, 274–5; *Straits Settlements Trade Commission*, p. 163; *Malaya Tribune*, 31 Oct. 1932; *The Straits Times*, 26 Feb. 1935.

[101] British Military Administration, *Entrepôt Trade*, pp. 12–13; *The Straits Times*, 1 Nov. 1932; *Malaya Tribune*, 23 Feb. 1934.

[102] P.H. Kratoska, "Imperial Unity versus Local Autonomy: British Malaya and the Depression of the 1930s", in *Weathering the Storm: The Economies of Southeast Asia in the 1930s Depression*, ed. P. Boomgaard and I. Brown (Singapore: Institute of Southeast Asian Studies, 2000), pp. 272–3.

[103] *Straits Settlements Trade Commission*, pp. 140–50, 151–2, 163.

[104] D.L. Glickman, "The British Imperial Preference System", *The Quarterly Journal of Economics* 61, 3 (1947): 440–1, 443–9.

[105] Liew and Wilson, *A History of Money*, pp. 119–20, 125.

[106] British Military Administration, *Entrepôt Trade*, p. 9.

[107] *Straits Settlements Annual Report*, vol. 10, p. 24; *The Straits Budget*, 18 Apr. 1935.

raise the cost of living due to higher import duties on non-Empire goods.[108] Neither would the system help Singapore to industrialise as the Dominions and India did not grant it preference. Moreover, rubber goods imports were limited by Britain and canned pineapples by Canada.[109] Thus, being part of the British Empire did not confer any benefit in this instance. On the contrary, the Colony did the right thing by not participating in the 1932 Imperial Conference in Ottawa and hence, it did not experience an increase in the cost of basic necessities.[110]

The Imperial Preference system targeted mainly Japanese cotton piece goods.[111] During the First World War, Japanese trading companies had exploited the lull in Western business to establish import-export branches in Singapore and the number of Japanese ships on the Southeast Asia routes also increased enormously.[112] Many of these firms were bankrupted by the post-war recession in the early twenties but as further progress was made in industrialisation in Japan and productivity increased, cotton textiles and other manufactured goods were exported in significant quantities to Asia at the expense of British products.[113] For example, Japanese rubber shoes and bicycle tyres held predominant shares in the Malayan market.[114] During the Great Depression, Japan followed a number of industrialised countries in leaving the gold standard in December 1931, causing the yen to depreciate sharply and making Japanese goods relatively cheaper by up to 50 per cent.[115] Although Britain also went off the gold standard in the same year and the pound sterling lost value, the proportion of Lancashire piece goods in the imports of Singapore and Malaya was reduced to 25 per cent in 1932 from over 50 per cent in 1929, while the Japanese proportion increased to nearly 60 per cent.[116]

Owing to the presence of overseas Chinese merchants in Kobe, their counterparts in Singapore became the biggest distributor of Japanese cotton goods in the Eastern Archipelago and Siam.[117] The cheaper cotton goods appealed to the poorer classes in Malaya and were also well received in the Dutch East Indies where domestic substitutes were lacking.[118] When Imperial Preference was implemented in 1932, it failed to curtail the sales of Japanese products as Singapore remained outside the system and a large part

108 *Straits Settlements Trade Commission*, p. 159; *The Straits Times*, 6 Jan. 1934.

109 Yeo, *Effects of Great Depression*, p. 36; *Straits Settlements Trade Commission*, pp. 161–2; *The Singapore Free Press and Mercantile Advertiser*, 2 Apr. 1935.

110 Liew and Wilson, *A History of Money*, pp. 124–5.

111 *Singapore Daily News*, 13 Jan. 1933.

112 Shimizu and Hirakawa, *Japan and Singapore in the World Economy*, pp. 66–8, 72–3, 77–8, 81.

113 Wong, "Singapore: Its Growth", p. 77; Huff, *The Economic Growth of Singapore*, pp. 265–6; *Straits Settlements Trade Commission*, pp. 56–7, 64–70; *The Singapore Free Press and Mercantile Advertiser*, 10 June 1932.

114 Denis Koh Soo Jin and K. Tanaka, "Japanese Competition in the Trade of Malaya in the 1930s", *Southeast Asian Studies* 21, 4 (1984): 375, 378–9.

115 Kratoska, "Imperial Unity versus Local Autonomy", p. 274; *Straits Settlements Trade Commission*, p. 58.

116 Liew and Wilson, *A History of Money*, pp. 123–4.

117 Shimizu and Hirakawa, *Japan and Singapore in the World Economy*, pp. 52, 57, 61–6, 81.

118 Wong, "Singapore: Its Growth", p. 78; S. Shinya, "The Expansion of Japan's Cotton Textile Exports into Southeast Asia", in *International Commercial Rivalry in Southeast Asia in the Interwar Period*, ed. S. Shinya and M.C. Guerrero (Yale University Southeast Asia Studies, 1994), pp. 60–3.

of its re-exports went to non-Empire countries.[119] In Malaya, the preferential tariff rate on Empire textiles was 10 per cent as against the foreign rate of 20 per cent, but this advantage was negated by the price difference between Japanese and British textiles of about 90 per cent.[120] Not surprisingly then, the British agency houses in Singapore found themselves deprived of a long-standing business and the Chinese dealers in Circular Road who had distributed English piece goods since the previous century were forced to turn to Japanese goods instead.[121] Making things worse, bulk-broken British textile re-exports to Malaya were subject to an import duty of 20 per cent due to Imperial Preference.[122]

As a further measure to drive Japanese goods out of the market, quotas were imposed on all cotton and rayon piece goods imported from outside the British Empire into Singapore in June 1934.[123] The quota for each foreign importing country was based on its relative share of the domestic market for the period 1927–31.[124] In the year following the measure, Japanese imports were reduced by nearly 50 per cent while British imports went up by 35 per cent.[125] But again, the quotas did not have much effect on Singapore's re-exports of Japanese textiles to Malaya as they were exempted, although sales declined somewhat due to higher prices.[126] In the Netherlands Indies, however, restrictions imposed by the Dutch government sharply reduced imports from Singapore.

If anything, Chinese boycotts of Japanese products had a greater impact. These sporadic actions began in the late twenties in the face of Japan's military adventurism in China but gathered strength with the invasion of Manchuria in 1931 and the outbreak of the Sino-Japanese War in 1937.[127] Amidst anti-Japanese demonstrations, Chinese in Singapore and Malaya refused to patronise Japanese doctors, dentists and barbers while Chinese traders who broke the boycott had their shops damaged. In 1938, trade with Japan fell by nearly 70 per cent and the share of Japan in Singapore's merchandise imports declined from 29.5 per cent in 1934 to 16.2 per cent.[128] And while the Chinese importers and retailers suffered, their loss was the gain of Indian merchants who stepped in to re-export Japanese and Indian goods to Sumatra and Siam, where overseas Chinese did not constitute a large part of the population.[129] The larger Indian firms in this trade even opened offices and branches in Japan.

---

119 Huff, *The Economic Growth of Singapore*, p. 266.

120 Koh and Tanaka, "Japanese Competition", p. 383.

121 *Straits Settlements Trade Commission*, pp. 51–2.

122 *Straits Settlements Annual Report*, vol. 10, pp. 3–5; *The Straits Budget*, 29 Sept. 1932; *The Straits Times*, 22 Oct. 1933.

123 Shimizu and Hirakawa, *Japan and Singapore in the World Economy*, pp. 83–5; *The Singapore Free Press and Mercantile Advertiser*, 22 June 1934.

124 *Proceedings of the Legislative Council of the Straits Settlements*, 11 June 1934.

125 "Report on the Working and Effects of Quotas on Cotton and Artificial Silk Piece-Goods in Malaya and Sarawak during the period 1st January to 31st December, 1935", in *Annual Departmental Reports of the Straits Settlements for the Year 1935*, vol. I, pp. 483, 489.

126 Huff, *The Economic Growth of Singapore*, pp. 108–9, 110–1; *Malaya Tribune*, 15 Apr. 1935.

127 Turnbull, *History of Modern Singapore*, pp. 157–8; *The Straits Budget*, 26 Aug. 1937, 26 Jan. 1939.

128 Huff, *The Economic Growth of Singapore*, pp. 258, 268–9.

129 Shimizu and Hirakawa, *Japan and Singapore in the World Economy*, pp. 87–90; *Straits Settlements Trade Commission*, pp. 57, 59–61; *Malaya Tribune*, 28 Sept. 1938.

The response of the Western agency houses to the quotas was uncharacteristically meek and ambiguous because there was a division of interests and views within the British mercantile community.[130] On the one hand, it was argued that it was not Singapore's duty to rescue manufacturers of the mother country whose goods had become uncompetitive in Southeast Asian markets, a view echoed by the Unofficials on the Legislative Council.[131] On the other hand, there was a real fear that if left unchecked, Japanese firms would eventually take over the functions of importer and distributor from the agency houses.[132] Although a significant minority of its members were in favour of the quotas, the Singapore Chamber of Commerce protested to the colonial administration after the quotas were imposed but since they were decided as a matter of Imperial policy, nothing could be done. In the event, British Empire producers managed to recapture 58 per cent of the market for cotton piece goods by 1938 because of the Chinese boycott.

In the years leading up to the Second World War, Malaya's two principal staple industries were given a fillip by the global economic recovery. Motor vehicle production in the United States rebounded in mid-decade, sending rubber exports from the Peninsula to a record 467,000 tonnes in 1937 and at higher prices.[133] In the same year, export revenue from tin also attained a post-war high while the volume of refined petroleum shipments reached 700,000 tonnes.[134] As a result, Singapore's external trade value regained the level of 1930.[135] In 1938, however, exports of the two commodities suddenly dropped due to another recession in the United States, but they recovered in the following year.[136] The colonial government revived some of the public works postponed earlier in the decade, bidding up the prices of construction materials and labour.[137] These included the reconstruction of the main road across the island to the Johor Causeway that was heavily utilised by lorries transporting goods, Changi Prison, the Art Deco-styled Civil Aerodrome at Kallang (which opened in 1937) and the new and grand Supreme Court, which rose in 1939 on the site of the former Hotel de l'Europe that had declared bankruptcy during the slump.[138]

The loss of population during the Great Depression was more than made up in the second half of the 1930s even though quotas continued to be maintained on the entry of Chinese adult males under the Aliens Ordinance of 1933 and restrictions were placed on Chinese

[130] I. Brown, "The British Merchant Community in Singapore and Japanese Commercial Expansion in the 1930s", in *International Commercial Rivalry*, ed. Shinya and Guerrero, pp. 111–2, 114–5, 117–22.

[131] Kratoska, "Imperial Unity versus Local Autonomy", pp. 276–7.

[132] *Straits Settlements Trade Commission*, pp. 60–1, 63.

[133] Shah, *Charting the Economy*, pp. 116–8.

[134] Tan, *A Very Short History*, p. 45.

[135] Huff, *The Economic Growth of Singapore*, Appendix Table A.1, p. 374, Appendix Table A.2, p. 380.

[136] *Straits Settlements Annual Report*, vol. 11, p. 315.

[137] "Annual Report of the Public Works Department, Straits Settlements, for the Year 1937", in *Annual Departmental Reports of the Straits Settlements for the Year 1937*, vol. I, p. 469.

[138] Wise, *Travellers' Tales*, p. 339; *Straits Settlements Annual Report*, vol. 11, pp. 35–6, 155–6, 262; "Annual Report of the Public Works Department, Straits Settlements, for the Year 1937", in *Annual Departmental Reports of the Straits Settlements for the Year 1937*, vol. I, p. 475; *The Singapore Free Press and Mercantile Advertiser*, 4 Aug. 1939.

women in 1938 to ease the unemployment situation.[139] Singapore's population increased by an average of 5.8 per cent per annum from 1934 to 1939 due to new immigrants as well as natural increase.[140] Given the normalising of the sex ratio and policies to encourage more settled Chinese and Indian populations, the birth rate doubled from 23 per thousand in the late 1910s to 47 per thousand in 1936.[141] Over the same period, the death rate declined to 24 per 1,000 from about 44 per 1,000 as the health authorities brought the most common diseases under control. The combined impact of these developments was to increase the total population of Singapore to 727,564 in 1939.

Growth and Fluctuations: 1870 to 1939

As we have now come to the end of our historical narrative on the late colonial period, a review of Singapore's economic performance over the seven decades or so from 1870 to 1939 may be opportune. This is effected through a quantitative account of commercial growth and business fluctuations. Using statistical methods, growth rates and cycles are extracted from a set of reconstructed national income accounts for Singapore, composed of real GDP and related expenditure components.[142] The data reveal the time-varying pace of economic expansion during the period covered and also the accompanying cyclical gyrations. Generally speaking, both growth and fluctuations were predominantly caused by changes in trade.

The long-term expansion of the Singapore economy during the late colonial period was characterised by phases of acceleration, deceleration and even absolute declines. Average yearly growth rates calculated from the data suggest that economic activity in Singapore expanded robustly in the 1870s by 4 per cent per annum, accompanied by strong private consumption growth of 4.7 per cent and an increase in government spending (Table 12). Investment spending also increased sharply towards the end of the decade. In the 1880s, both real GDP and consumption growth slowed but tin exports took off. As Singapore was an entrepot as well as a staple port, exports and imports tended to move in tandem, though import growth typically exceeded export expansion.[143] Gross capital formation continued

[139] Ee, "Chinese Migration to Singapore", p. 44; *Straits Settlements Annual Report*, vol. 10, p. 204, vol. 11, pp. 322–3, 341–2. The quotas on Chinese males were accompanied by fees that immigrants had to pay on arrival in Singapore. Abshire, *History of Singapore*, p. 78.

[140] Ichiro Sugimoto, *Economic Growth of Singapore in the Twentieth Century: Historical GDP Estimates and Empirical Investigations* (Singapore: World Scientific, 2011), p. 49.

[141] Saw, *Population of Singapore*, pp. 9, 83; Kratoska, "Imperial Unity versus Local Autonomy", pp. 287–9; Brooke, "Medical Work", p. 511; "Annual Report on the Registration of Births and Deaths in the Straits Settlements for the Year 1936", in *Annual Departmental Reports of the Straits Settlements for the Year 1936*, Appendix B, p. 925, Appendix F, p. 928.

[142] The growth rates are the year-to-year changes in variables while the cycles are obtained through the use of the Hodrick-Prescott filter. The sources of the national income data are Sugimoto, *Economic Growth of Singapore* and Ichiro Sugimoto and Keen Meng Choy, "Reconstructing the National Accounts of a British Colony: New GDP Estimates for Singapore, 1870–1900", Mimeograph, 2023.

[143] The discrepancy was partly due to the fact that neither the bunkers and water sold to ships calling at the harbour nor the port revenues were accounted for in the exports data, an omission that was particularly conspicuous in the late 19th century.

to grow steadily in the eighties due to the colonial government's spending on infrastructure. In the 1890s, with the momentum in trade growth maintained, real GDP grew by 5.8 per cent on average each year. However, the increase in household spending slowed further to 1.1 per cent per annum due to a recession in the Malayan tin industry in the initial years of the decade, which also caused Singapore merchants to pull back their investments.

Table 12. Growth of GDP and Its Components, 1870s–1930s

	GDP (%)	**Private Consumption (%)**	**Government Consumption (%)**	**Gross Capital Formation (%)**	**Exports (%)**	**Imports (%)**
1870s	4.0	4.7	3.7	26.9	3.9	4.1
1880s	–3.3	3.5	5.0	16.1	4.3	5.9
1890s	5.8	1.1	4.4	5.9	4.4	3.5
1900s	5.0	2.6	4.7	13.1	0.3	0.2
1910s	1.7	1.7	1.7	2.9	5.8	5.8
1920s	6.0	6.4	8.0	5.9	5.1	5.2
1930s	5.1	4.9	2.4	7.4	-1.8	-1.6

Source: Authors' calculations.

Foreign trade stagnated in the first decade of the 20th century as both entrepôt and staple exports turned sluggish, aggravated by the operation of the Straits Homeward and other conferences. Nevertheless, annual GDP growth during this period was boosted by an increase in government consumption and a 13.1 per cent surge in investment spending, a portion of which went into rubber planting and the upgrading of port facilities. In the 1910s, the trend in growth rates of imports and exports accelerated to nearly 6 per cent despite the First World War, as demand for primary commodities shot up along with rising prices. However, gross capital formation in the rubber industry was held in check during the war years and consumer spending was sluggish.

Without a doubt, the 1920s turned out to be the best performing decade of the colonial era as real GDP grew at 6 per cent per annum and private consumption at 6.4 per cent. Capital accumulation recovered as large sums were expended on public infrastructure; the growth in government consumption also accelerated. Fixed investment outlays by private firms on machinery and equipment saw a sevenfold increase between 1923 and 1929, reflecting capital spending in the rubber milling and petroleum industries and demonstrating the presence of spread effects. After the downturn caused by the global recession of 1921, rubber exports continued to increase until 1928, partly on the back of demand from the automobile industry.[144] In the 1930s, GDP grew at a sprightly rate of 5.1 per cent per annum despite the depression during the early part of the decade.

For the entire period 1870–1939, the average annual rate of increase in Singapore's real GDP was 3.5 per cent per annum. The growth rates for the late 19th and early 20th century were 2.2 per cent and 4.5 per cent, respectively. This differential performance bears out the conventional belief that the rubber industry brought greater prosperity to Singapore than the tin industry had done due to the former's more extensive economic

[144] Abshire, *History of Singapore*, p. 65.

linkages. Nonetheless, GDP per capita grew at a slower rate of 1 per cent per annum over the whole period, with most of the progress occurring in the 1870s, 1900s and 1920s. The increase was especially marked during the rubber era, with real GDP per person rising from $182 in 1900 to $321 in 1939.

Like the early colonial period with its trade cycles, economic growth did not progress evenly from 1870 to 1939; on the contrary, it was volatile and suffered temporary setbacks from time to time (Figure 15). Real GDP was more volatile in the 19th century but the reverse is true for private consumption. Investment cycles were erratic in the 19th century but they became attenuated in the first decades of the 20th century. Trade cycles were also volatile and more severe; as such, they were an important cause of the fluctuations in GDP. Altogether, six trade downturns can be discerned—three in the tin era (1878, 1886, 1892) and another three in the rubber era (1914, 1921, 1932). These were years when staple prices fell, resulting in production cutbacks in Malaya. The most severe trade recessions that Singapore experienced were the ones in 1878 and 1921.

In the first decades of the 20th century, private consumption shrank when the rice crisis broke out in 1919–20. A consumer spending spree then started in the mid-twenties until the Great Depression hit Singapore with a vengeance in 1929. Nevertheless, the cutback in consumption was not any worse than in the recession of the early twenties. Amid a sharp fall in the rate of capital formation, external trade suffered a severe and prolonged decline. From 1929 to 1932, the level of real GDP fell by 9.4 per cent. By 1934, however, domestic demand had begun to turn around in a remarkable recovery. Exports also rebounded by mid-decade and subsequently benefitted from the international effort to stockpile tin and rubber ahead of the Second World War.

Both the long-term growth and short-run fluctuations in Singapore's real GDP over the seven decades can be explained by the staples hypothesis. With regard to the former, there was a direct positive link between trade performance and economic growth.[145] To be specific, the driving force of growth in the late 19th century was the expansion of exports brought about by tin and in the first decades of the 20th century, by rubber. Furthermore, the increases in staple export volumes led to an improvement in living standards, as discussed in the next section.[146] Trade accounted for four-fifths of the increase in output from 1871 to 1898 and three-fifths from 1900 to 1939. In this respect, not only growth in world demand but supply increases in Singapore's hinterlands in response to the rise in tin and rubber prices played an important role.[147] For example, during the rubber era from 1910 to 1929, the high prices fetched by the commodity in booms stimulated output from large estates and smallholders alike, which accounted for most of the increase in total exports. On the flipside, the collapse of rubber prices during the Great Depression triggered a contraction in supply, thus aggravating the curtailment of global demand.

Paradoxically, trade was also a source of economic instability due to the fact that exports were a most volatile component of GDP.[148] Changes in the economic conditions of the industrial countries were an important determinant of the demand for raw materials

[145] Choy and Sugimoto, "Trade, the Staple Theory of Growth", pp. 122–3.

[146] Choy and Sugimoto, "Staple Trade, Real Wages and Living Standards", pp. 36–7.

[147] Choy and Sugimoto, "Trade, the Staple Theory of Growth", pp. 134–7.

[148] Ibid., pp. 138–41.

produced by the Southeast Asian countries on the periphery of the world economy. These changes were also a cause of Singapore's trade and business cycles, although not the predominant one, except during the Great Depression. The major cause was instead the violent fluctuations in tin and rubber prices. Tin was not subject to control in the 19th century while the international regulation of rubber prices began only in the 1920s.

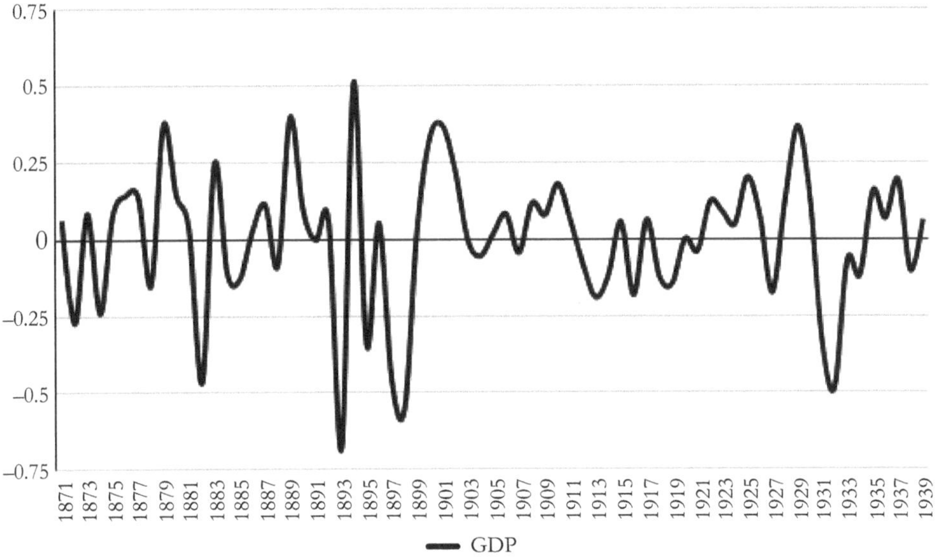

Fig. 15a

Fig. 15b

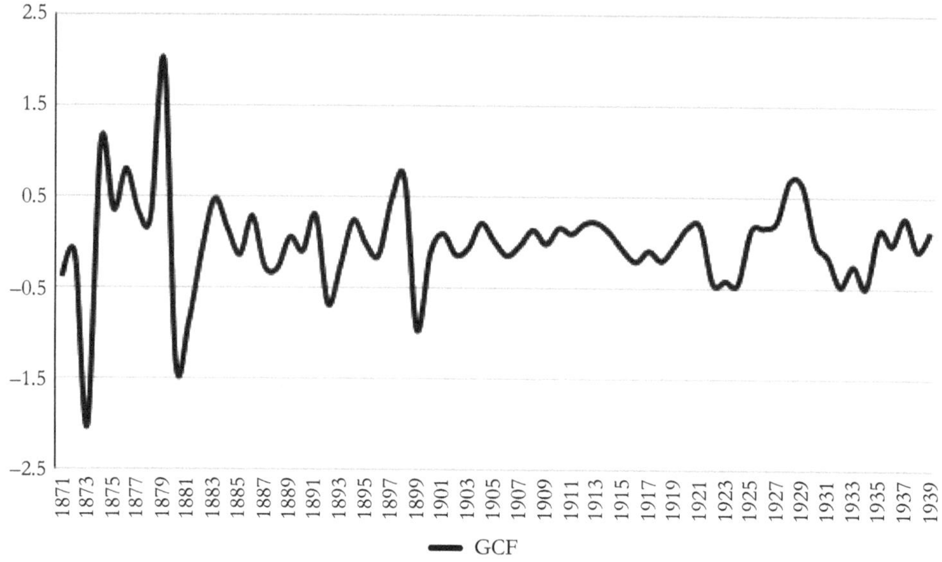

Fig. 15c

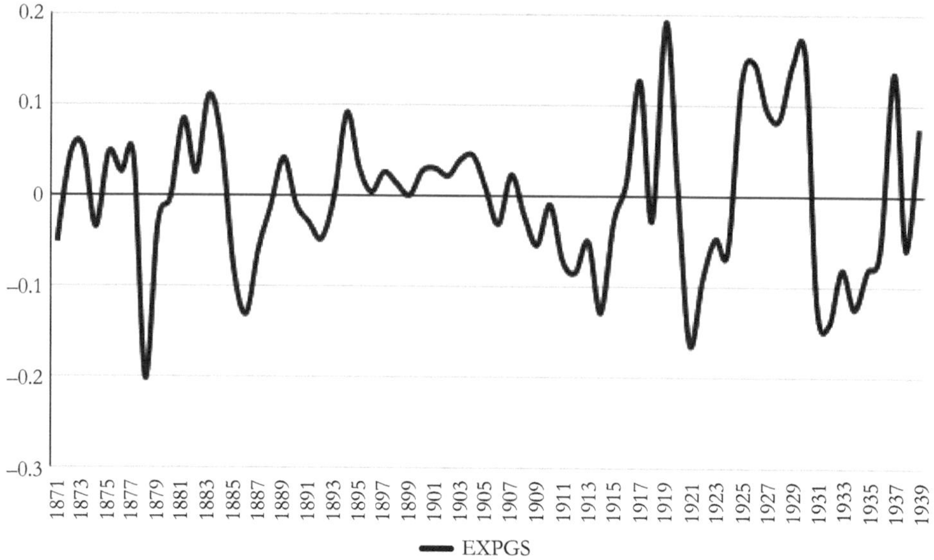

Fig. 15d

Figure 15. Business Cycles in Singapore's GDP (15a) and Its Components (15b–d), 1871–1939

Note: The unit for the vertical axis is a logarithm; GDP = Gross Domestic Product (Fig. 15a); PFCE = Private Final Consumption Expenditure (Fig. 15b); GCF = Gross Capital Formation (Fig. 15c); EXPGS = Exports of Goods and Services (Fig. 15d).

Source: Authors' calculations.

Consumption and Living Standards: 1870 to 1939

Following up on the discussion of material living standards in the early colonial era, a similar exercise will be carried out in this section for the later period from 1870 to 1939. Two complementary approaches are taken: the first is based on the availability, on a per capita basis, of the basic goods of food, clothing and housing as well as two "luxury" goods—the motorcar and the telephone. The second approach assesses the changes over time in a widely used measure of economic welfare, the real wage. In this instance, reconstructed nominal wage data are deflated by a consumer price index instead of by rice prices as before for the early period. This real wage is independent of the national income accounts and provides an alternative to GDP per capita as an indicator of living standards, with the advantage of ameliorating the problem of income inequality by measuring the purchasing power of the less well-off in society.[149] Furthermore, the real wage is more robust than the GDP measure as it takes into consideration the goods consumed by people.[150] It is of course subject to intrinsic problems such as the fact that nominal wages may not be an adequate guide to total household incomes, although this drawback applies more to the agrarian-based economies of Southeast Asia than urbanised Singapore.[151] There is also the previously noted phenomenon of nominal wage rigidity over long periods of time.

As the Chinese adage goes, "food is what matters for ordinary people"; it therefore figures prominently in attempts to gauge changes in living standards over time (Figure 16). Rice is the staple item in the Singaporean food consumption basket, taking up 35 per cent of expenditure, the other products being meat, fish, sugar, flour, milk and coffee, *inter alia*. In this respect, consumption of food amounted to $106 per person in 1870; by 1939, it had increased to $130. After rising modestly during the late 19th century, it experienced a gradual decline in the 1910s that culminated in the rice crisis at the end of the decade. Even at this low point, the average quantity of rice consumed by the Asian races was 335 kg per person per year, nearly twice the subsistence level of 172 kg.[152] Following that episode, food consumption commenced a steady rise in the 1920s which was interrupted by the slump in the early 1930s before it increased again in the last years of the period, indicating a substantial improvement in living standards over these last two decades. That said, consumption per capita differed widely between the ethnic groups in Singapore. Europeans on average spent $412 per person on food in a year, about five times that of the natives, amongst whom Indians had the highest per capita consumption, followed by the Chinese and the Malays.

Another widely cited measure of the quality of life is per capita purchases of clothing (Figure 16). Just as in the case of rice, Singapore was the major distribution centre for cotton piece goods in Southeast Asia, which meant that both goods could be obtained at the competitive prices prevailing in global markets. In fact, the city relied more than the

149 R.C. Allen, T. Bengtsson and M. Dribe, "'Introduction", in *Living Standards in the Past: New Perspectives on Well-being in Asia and Europe*, ed. R.C. Allen, T. Bengtsson and M. Dribe (Oxford University Press, 2005), p. 9.

150 Z. Chen and K. Peng, "Production, Consumption, and Living Standards", in *The Cambridge Economic History of China*, vol. I, ed. D. Ma and R. Von Glahn (Cambridge University Press, 2022), pp. 676–7.

151 Booth, "Measuring Living Standards", pp. 1171–81.

152 The subsistence level of rice consumption is based on real wage studies of living standards.

rest of the region on imports of cotton yarn, bleached cotton and silk piece goods to fulfil its needs. After allowing for re-exports, domestic consumption in Singapore (and British Malaya) appeared to be higher than in any other country in Asia.[153] The data show that the expenditure on clothing per person had risen from $21.50 at the start of the period to about $28 at the end. As the prices of piece goods from Britain and subsequently Japan fell by more than the general price level in the early part of the 20th century, this increase in spending actually underestimates the welfare gain to consumers. Once again, there were ethnic differences in the amount of clothing purchased; indeed, they were even wider than those for food.

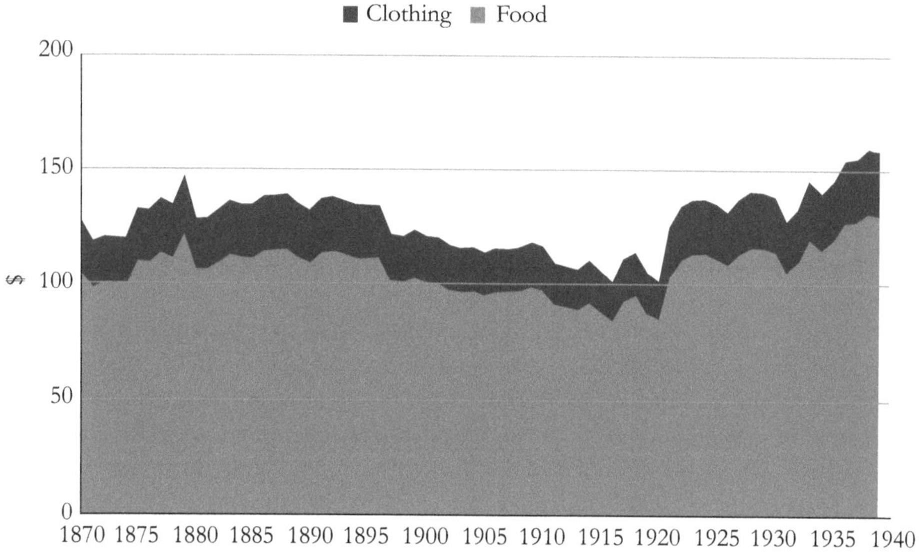

Figure 16. Per Capita Consumption of Food and Clothing in Singapore, 1870–1939
Source: Authors' calculations.

As for luxury goods, the number of motorcars registered per 10,000 people in the Singapore population was 24 in 1915 but this shot up to 85 in 1920. In 1929, the tally reached 122 per 1,000 and by 1938, it was 146.[154] The secular increase is evidence of rising affluence during the rubber era, even though the ownership of cars was restricted to the well-to-do. In contrast, the statistics for the number of telephone subscribers are less striking but they illustrate the impact of cyclical economic conditions on consumption. In the 1910s, fewer than one person in a thousand owned a telephone, but following the prosperous years of the twenties, the number jumped to eight. The Great Depression halted this upward trend, resulting in only seven subscribers per 1,000 in 1936. Going by these figures, the telephone was an even less affordable device than the motorcar—as a newspaper put it, "a private telephone is a luxury enjoyed by only a select few" in Singapore.[155]

With respect to housing, quantitative information is hard to come by but statistics on population density are available. From 1,926 in 1921, the number of persons to the

[153] Booth, "Measuring Living Standards", p. 1162.

[154] *The Sunday Tribune (Singapore)*, 12 Mar. 1939.

[155] *Morning Tribune*, 19 Mar. 1937.

square mile in the island increased to 3,227 in 1938.[156] In 1918, a commission set up by the colonial government to enquire into housing conditions had warned that there was a very serious shortage of houses and other dwelling units in Singapore.[157] Five years later, the number of new dwelling houses constructed by private builders numbered fewer than 2,000 and after adding the houses and quarters built by the government, the Municipality and the Singapore Harbour Board for their employees, they could house only 21,100 persons whereas the increase in population was 60,500. The commission also recommended the creation of a city improvement trust modelled after those in Bombay and Calcutta to carry out town planning and improvement schemes.[158] However, it was only in 1927 that such an independent body was set up, named the Singapore Improvement Trust (SIT), its objectives being to draw up a general improvement plan, condemn insanitary buildings, encourage new construction, clear slums and construct back lanes for houses.[159] The Trust was to be financed by a 2 per cent levy on the annual value of all houses, buildings, lands and tenements within the Municipality, according to which the government would match dollar for dollar. In the early years, it concentrated on the last two tasks with the result that large parts of Chinatown were provided with better ventilation and sanitation.[160] In all, 92 back lanes were opened and about 1,252 houses reconstructed to facilitate service maintenance and collection of refuse.[161] The Trust also constructed new roads and open spaces but it had less success with insanitary buildings because of owners' protests. Given the Trust's lack of funds, land was acquired for rehousing residents but the dwellings were constructed by private parties.[162]

According to the census of 1931, there were 39,200 occupied houses in the Singapore Municipality in that year.[163] Since four-fifths of the population lived in the town areas, overcrowding in a city with over half a million people was inevitable. Despite this, Chinese immigrants preferred to stay in shophouses, which had extra floors added to them and had undergone modifications and subdivision into cubicles.[164] On average, 11 residents were crammed into a single house (although the number in the rural areas was about half that) and whole families were crowded into one room. In view of the squalid housing conditions, the SIT was empowered to build houses and flats starting in 1930; building took place at Tiong Bahru, Balestier Road and Lavender Street, and the accommodation

---

156 *Straits Settlements Blue Book*, 1921, Section 15, p. 3, 1939, Section 15, p. 717.

157 *Proceedings of the Legislative Council of the Straits Settlements*, 1923, Appendix No. 57, pp. C146–50.

158 *The Singapore Free Press and Mercantile Advertiser*, 22 Aug. 1918; *The Straits Times*, 30 Aug. 1918.

159 *Proceedings of the Legislative Council of the Straits Settlements*, 7 Feb. 1927, 16 May 1927.

160 *The Singapore Free Press and Mercantile Advertiser*, 7 July 1934; *The Straits Budget*, 12 July 1934 ,1 July 1937.

161 Alan F.C. Choe, "The Early Years of Nation-Building: Reflections on Singapore's Urban History", in *50 Years of Urban Planning in Singapore*, ed. Heng Chye Kiang (Singapore: World Scientific, 2016), p. 6; *50,000 Up: Homes for the People* (Singapore: Housing and Development Board, 1965), pp. 19–20.

162 *The Singapore Free Press and Mercantile Advertiser (Weekly)*, 29 June 1927.

163 *Straits Settlements Blue Book*, 1939, Section 15, p. 718.

164 Teo and Savage, "Singapore Landscape", p. 324; Choe, "The Early Years of Nation-Building", p. 6.

was rented out at $20–25 a month.[165] However, the population increased so fast in the mid-thirties that the Trust was not able to keep pace with it.[166] In 1939, the Municipal Health Officer asserted that Singapore had only half the number of houses it required.[167] Urban living conditions were therefore far from desirable in the city and this was the root cause of the dire housing situation that prevailed in the post-war years.

Before discussing the long-term trend in the real wages of ordinary workers, it is instructive to review the pay of government servants and those working in private firms.[168] In 1931, the activities of public administration and defence engaged 29 per cent of the labour force in Singapore.[169] During that decade, clerks and interpreters were paid anything from $600 to $3,120 a year, around $2.60 to $12.50 a day, mainly on account of their knowledge of English. Teachers got more, from $8 to $14 per day. The daily wage of hospital assistants and storekeepers was $5 to $10; for carpenters and gardeners it was about $2.60 to $3.60. Police officers were paid $1–2 a day and at the lower echelons, peons and watchmen received $1–1.20. In the non-governmental sectors, agriculture employed 13.5 per cent of the labour force in 1931 and paid workers between 40–60 cents per day in 1938. The construction industry employed 2.4 per cent and labourers there earned between 50 cents and $1.30, the higher end being the wages of skilled workers such as masons. Workers in manufacturing enterprises, comprising 16 per cent of the workforce, received more, between 50 cents and $2.60; however, wages varied according to the type of industry—for instance, sago factory labourers earned between 40–75 cents while those in soap factories got up to $1. Industrial labourers like fitters, electricians and welders were also well remunerated, receiving between $1 and $3 in general. For workers in service occupations, domestic servants in European homes earned up to $40 a month or $1.50 per day; lorry drivers' wages were between 80 cents to $1.50 per diem; and lastly, workers in steam laundries received from 75 cents to $1.85.

Since the salaries of civil servants were higher than those of manual labourers and service workers in the private sector, it can be surmised that there was a wage premium on government jobs during the colonial period. For the purpose of calculating the average wages of workers in Singapore, such jobs are not taken into consideration since they cannot be compared with other countries. The wages of Europeans are also excluded as they were far above those of the Asians. As females joined the workforce only from the 1920s, the nominal wage data used pertain to male labourers in the construction, manufacturing and agricultural industries; given the premium placed on skills, a distinction is made between

[165] *Proceedings of the Legislative Council of the Straits Settlements*, 28 May 1934; *Morning Tribune*, 21 May 1937.

[166] *The Straits Budget*, 1 July 1937; *Morning Tribune*, 3 July 1937.

[167] *The Straits Budget*, 16 Mar. 1939.

[168] The salaries cited here are reported in the *Straits Settlements Blue Book*, 1938, passim. The daily salary is computed on the assumption of 250 working days a year.

[169] Huff, *The Economic Growth of Singapore*, Appendix Table A.10, pp. 407–9.

skilled and unskilled workers.[170] In order to calculate real wage indices, the nominal wage data are compared to the cost of living, that is, a consumer price index based on the typical spending patterns of the Asian working class in Singapore.[171]

The real wage indices suggest that living standards initially rose in the 1870s, fell during the early 1880s, and recovered somewhat up to the mid-1890s (Figure 17). Skilled labourers in the construction industry then experienced a long decline in their real wages which lasted until the outbreak of the First World War. This "wage climacteric" was partly brought about by the lower demand for labour resulting from sluggish trade volumes in the 1900s.[172] Tin exports had stagnated at about 30,000 tonnes, following a sharp rise from 1887 to 1895.[173] Immigration into Singapore exacerbated the downward pressure on remuneration rates: in 1901–11, the net inflow was about 136,000 people, which added more than 75,500 persons to the population after accounting for natural decrease (in 1901 the population was 228,555).[174] The real wage stabilised and even rose slightly during the First World War, but workmen's purchasing power shrank again during the rice crisis of 1919–20, with inflation rising to nearly 30 per cent on an annual basis.[175] Thereafter, the real wage rebounded, eradicating the losses of the previous 30 years. At the same time, the skill premium increased and stayed high.[176] Then came the Great Depression and generalised deflation, which saw food prices and rents decline the most, by close to one half.[177] Following the depression, another rapid recovery in real wages got underway from around 1931, lifting living standards to their interwar apex.

The long-term trend in the real wage for skilled workers can be viewed in relation to staple development. The timing of the two phases which saw real earnings increase coincided more or less with the rise of tin and rubber, *circa* 1874–1900 and 1910–29, respectively. During the tin phase, real wage increments were modest, amounting to 15–21 per cent between 1870 and 1893, in line with its limited spread effects. In contrast, the great rubber boom produced a much larger and more sustained improvement in the standard of living that persisted after the global depression ended: from its trough in 1920 to its peak in 1939, the skilled real wage increased by three times. Therefore, the more extensive and deeper linkages associated with rubber generated larger wage gains that

170 The wages of construction artisans (carpenters, joiners, blacksmiths and bricklayers) and from 1925, rubber factory workers are used as proxies for the earnings of skilled labour and the wages paid to predial workers in the nineteenth century and to rubber coolies and tappers in the 20th century serve as the measures of unskilled earnings. The data for the latter group of labourers are missing from 1901 to 1912.

171 The items included in the consumption basket are rice, salt, beef, mutton, pork, fish, sugar, wheat flour, milk, tea, coffee, tobacco, clothing, rent and miscellaneous items (which include soap and fuel). Sugimoto, *Economic Growth of Singapore*, gives a detailed account of the methodology used to construct the consumption basket. The real wage indices are computed by comparing the incomes of workers in a year with their expenditures, known as "welfare ratios" in the literature. A value of 100 therefore implies that incomes were just sufficient to pay for expenditures.

172 Choy and Sugimoto, "Staple Trade, Real Wages and Living Standards", pp. 36–7.

173 Huff, *The Economic Growth of Singapore*, Appendix Table A.2, pp. 378, 380.

174 Saw, *Population of Singapore*, p. 11.

175 Sugimoto, *The Economic Growth of Singapore*, p. 61.

176 Choy and Sugimoto, "Staple Trade, Real Wages and Living Standards", pp. 39, 40–2.

177 Loh, "Beyond Rubber Prices", p. 22.

trickled down to the working class. Viewed from the perspective of the staples theory, the wage climacteric from 1894 to 1913 was due to the lull between the eclipse of tin and the ascent of rubber—a period of relative economic stagnation in the Colony's history.

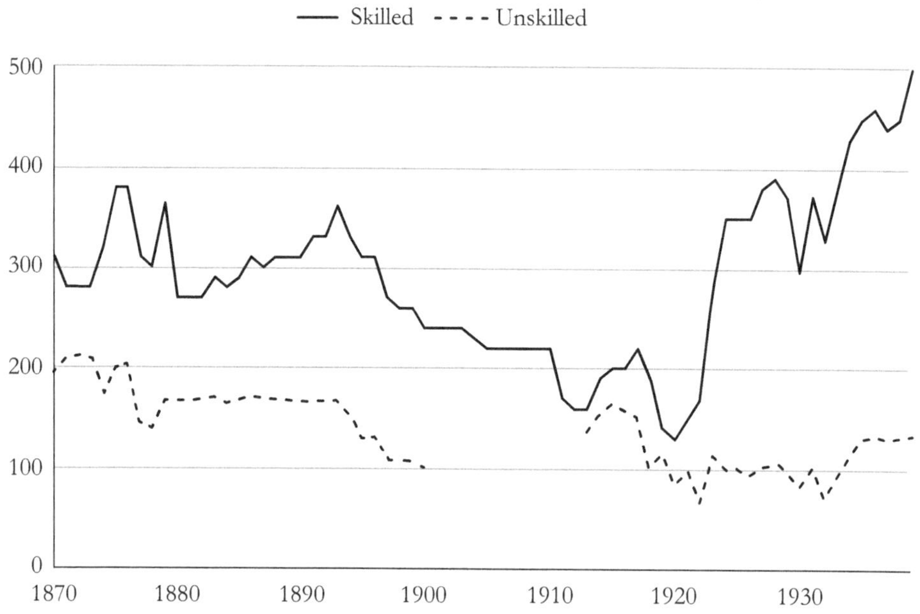

Figure 17. Skilled and Unskilled Real Wage Indices in Singapore, 1870–1939
Source: Keen Meng Choy and Ichiro Sugimoto, "Staple Trade, Real Wages and Living Standards".

The unskilled real wage (Figure 17) was relatively high for the most part of the 19th century, exceeding that of urban workers in East Asia and providing a powerful motive for immigration to Singapore.[178] As the wage climacteric set in, however, the living standards of unskilled workers deteriorated to the extent that they were hardly better off than their counterparts in China and worse off than those in Japan in the early 1910s. Thereafter, the unskilled real wage never regained its previous high level and in fact declined further in the early 1920s. In the mid-thirties, it recovered some ground on account of the renewed boom in rubber. Yet an underclass made up of coolies, rickshaw pullers and hawkers continued to exist in Singapore.[179] These hapless denizens constituted about one-fourth of total employment in 1931, many of them newly arrived immigrants to the city. Evidently, there was a substantial gap between the average standard of living in Singapore and that of people at the bottom of the income scale.

The living standards of the lowest rungs of society were also adversely affected by the consumption of opium. Of all the social ills that beset the Colony, this habit was the most pernicious. As in the previous century, users of the drug were found mostly, though not exclusively, among unskilled workers whose jobs were physically strenuous. For example, coal haulers at the wharves were thought to contain 60 per cent of smokers in their ranks

---

[178] Choy and Sugimoto, "Staple Trade, Real Wages and Living Standards", pp. 41–3.

[179] Huff, *The Economic Growth of Singapore*, p. 277, Appendix Table A.10, pp. 407–9.

while 80 per cent of rickshaw pullers were addicts, including those who used opium only at intervals.[180] In the Chinese population at large, a conservative estimate would put the proportion of opium smokers at one-third, implying that the number of users was 42,065 in 1911 and 56,559 in 1921.[181] For a majority of smokers, opium was a basic necessity, an essential sedative for them to perform their jobs. Nonetheless, except for a small hard core of addicts, they were moderate and not heavy users of opium who consumed only up to 2.3 grammes of the drug per day. Given inelastic demand, price increases did not have much of a dampening effect on aggregate opium consumption, which peaked in 1920 at a level equivalent to 10.7 per cent of private consumption spending. Apart from price, the quantity of opium consumed in any year depended on general economic conditions in the Colony: when tin and rubber production in Malaya boomed, wages were high and workers spent their extra money on the drug.[182]

While anti-opium campaigners in the Chinese community such as Lim Boon Keng agitated for the drug to be banned on health and moral grounds, the colonial government did not consider opium consumption to be a serious problem in Singapore. The specious arguments made to rationalise its continued use were that any effort to restrict it would encourage smuggling and that raising its price would drive addicts to resort to the more deleterious practice of injecting morphine.[183] In 1924 however, the local authorities were forced by increasing international pressure on the British government and the tide of public opinion to again inquire into the issue, resulting in the compulsory licensing of smokers and the rationing of opium supplies.[184] In 1936, the Governor of the Straits Settlements reported that opium addicts in Singapore did not number more than 35,000, or approximately 5 per cent of the Chinese population.[185] But it was not until 1943, during the Japanese occupation, that a complete ban on opium came into place.

A skilled worker in Singapore would have been able to afford a typical consumption basket of goods and services even if he smoked opium.[186] As for an unskilled labourer, the situation would depend on whether he was a moderate or light smoker (the latter is defined by consumption of no more than 1.1 grammes per day). Moderate smokers would struggle to survive as by the 1920s, their wages could cover only half of their expenses; by the 1930s, they would be spending almost all their earnings on the drug. However, even light smokers could not escape the poverty trap after the early twenties. There were mitigating factors to consider, however. Some unskilled labourers earned above the average wage and working more hours each day could also help addicts to make ends meet; for example,

---

180 Straits Settlements Opium Commission, *Proceedings of the Commission*, p. 12; Warren, *Rickshaw Coolie*, p. 242.

181 Choy and Sugimoto, "Opium Consumption", pp. 126–7.

182 Goto-Shibata, "Empire on the Cheap", p. 68.

183 Moore and Moore, *The First 150 Years*, pp. 530–1.

184 Cheng, "Opium in the Straits Settlements", pp. 52–75; British Malaya Opium Committee, *Proceedings of the Committee appointed by His Excellency the Governor and High Commissioner to Inquire into Matters Relating to the Use of Opium in British Malaya* (Singapore, 1924).

185 Goto-Shibata, "Empire on the Cheap", p. 77.

186 Choy and Sugimoto, "Opium Consumption", pp. 128–30.

rickshaw coolies usually earned more than $1 a day in the 1920s.[187] At the same time, smokers could react to higher opium prices by attempting to reduce their consumption or swallowing opium dross.[188] In the last resort, opium addicts had to borrow money or reduce their purchases of other goods, including food.

To substantiate the foregoing findings on living standards in Singapore, we compare levels of GDP per capita across several Asian countries (Figure 18).[189] These suggest that at the start of the 20th century, Singapore was richer than Japan, Taiwan and India. From 1911, its per capita GDP was also significantly higher than that in Korea and in all likelihood, China (data are unavailable). In 1912, however, Singapore relinquished its leading position to Japan. Malaya initially lagged behind but after the First World War overtook the rest except for Singapore and Japan. It caught up with Singapore during the boom of the late 1920s and its per capita income also declined less than the city's during the Great Depression. At the end of the era, in 1939, Singapore's GDP per capita again exceeded Malaya's but was lower than Japan's. The comparison here provides conclusive evidence that rubber had made Singapore and Malaya rich in the 20th century.

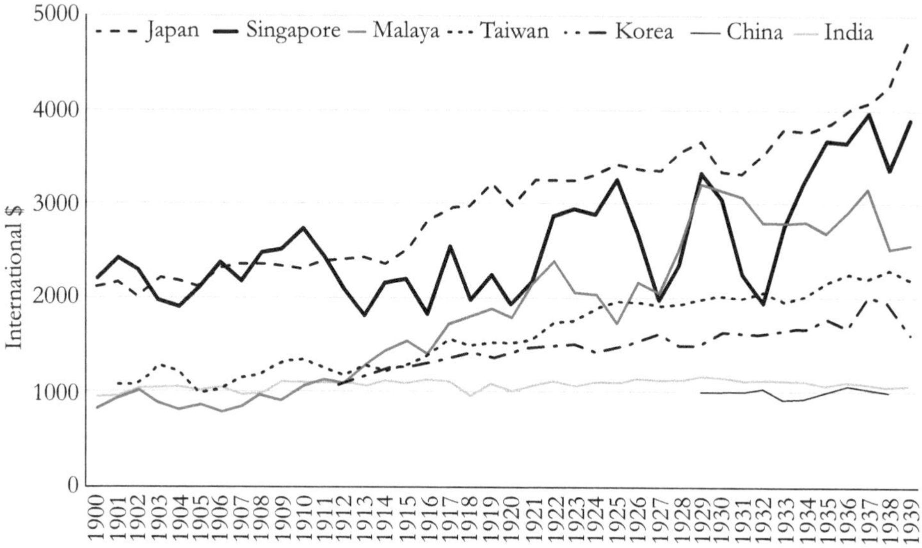

Figure 18. GDP Per Capita in Asian Countries, 1900–39

Note: The international dollar is based on the exchange rates of countries to the US dollar after adjusting for purchasing power parity.

Source: Maddison Project Database, Version 2020 (https://www.rug.nl/ggdc/historicaldevelopment/maddison/releases/maddison-project-database-2020?lang=en).

[187] Warren, *Rickshaw Coolie*, p. 246.

[188] Opium dross is the residuum remaining in the opium pipe after smoking.

[189] The GDP data are obtained from the Maddison Project database (https://www.rug.nl/ggdc/historicaldevelopment/maddison/releases/maddison-project-database-2020?lang=en) and have been converted into purchasing power parity terms to facilitate international comparisons.

Chapter 9

Wartime Economy, 1940–46

War came to the Far East in late 1941. For two decades before it broke out, Singapore had been made ready to face off any threat, turning the bustling commercial outpost into a key strategic asset of the British Empire. In the end though, the island's defences were found to be severely wanting. Following Japan's attack on the United States' military and naval bases at Pearl Harbor on 7 December 1941, it simultaneously commenced the invasion of Southeast Asia, beginning with Thailand. Singapore was bombed on the morning of the following day. The primary motivation for the conquest would appear to be economic, as Japan's vision was the concept of a "Greater East Asia Co-Prosperity Sphere"—a euphemism for a cooperative regional grouping of nations in the continent directed from Tokyo that would provide it with the natural resources and markets denied by the West.[1]

In stark contrast to the First World War, the Pacific War was an unprecedented social and economic calamity for Singapore and Malaya, compared with which the Great Depression was but a disruption. The economic devastation and human suffering inflicted by the conflict scarred the memories of those who lived through it but it also led to the end of colonialism and the reshaping of Singapore's political future. When the British forces surrendered the island on 15 February 1942, it was instantly given a Japanese name: Syonan, the "Light of the South". For the next three years, the economic mismanagement of the Japanese military administration served as a poignant lesson in governing an unfettered free market economy under wartime conditions. Despite concerted efforts to reorganise production and distribution, economic collapse was inevitable. Starvation was barely averted and food shortages gave rise to rationing and black markets. Most disastrous of all was the reckless printing of Japanese dollar notes and the resulting debasement of the currency. When the British returned, they had to take up to the end of the forties to repair the ravages of war.

Prelude to War: Singapore as Naval Base

At the Imperial Conference of Colonies and Dominions held in 1921 to decide on the defence of the British Empire after the end of the First World War, an ambitious plan was hatched for Singapore. In light of the shifting geopolitical balance of power in Asia as Japan

[1] W.G. [Gregg] Huff, *World War II and Southeast Asia: Economy and Society Under Japanese Occupation* (Cambridge University Press, 2020), pp. 6–7.

rose in economic and military strength, Singapore was to become the naval base for Britain's eastern possessions, or "Fortress Singapore".[2] The military fortifications which had last been built on the island in the 1880s were outmoded and the new base was envisaged to be the foundation of the Empire's defence, protecting the gateways to India and Australasia.[3] The colonial city was chosen over Hong Kong, Colombo and Sydney by virtue of its strategic location and as Hong Kong was vulnerable to a land-based attack and Colombo and Sydney were too distant for military action in the Far East theatre.[4] The Sembawang area at the northern tip of the island next to the Johor Strait was selected as the site of the anchorage for the British Navy's fleet. It was originally to have 10 graving docks, a floating dock, wharves, workshops, fuel tanks and storage facilities for the servicing, repair and retrofitting of naval warships, and would be capable of accommodating 20 capital ships and more than 200 vessels in all. Together with offices, housing for navy personnel, a hospital and a cinema, it would almost be a small town by itself. An airfield and seaplane base were also to be built in nearby Seletar.[5] Although the plan was subsequently downgraded to just a floating and graving dock and the ancillary facilities were drastically reduced, the total financial bill for the Imperial government still came up to £25.45 million. In fact, the actual cost was slightly higher since the notional value of the land ceded by the Straits Settlements government was $1.25 million or £145,833.[6]

Since the Colonies and Dominions in the Far East would benefit from the existence of a British naval base in Singapore, the New Zealand government contributed £1 million to help defray the expenses, Hong Kong gave £250,000 and the FMS were persuaded to give £2 million.[7] But in 1928, the Colony received a fright when the suspicion arose that it would be forced to pay the entire cost of the defence works—forts, batteries and other installations—and the additional garrisons that were necessary for the protection of the naval base.[8] The Legislative Council was asked by the Imperial government to vote on funds for the acquisition of land, buildings and artillery. A strong protest was forwarded to the British government by the Unofficial members of the Council stating that the benefits of the naval base would accrue primarily to India, Australia and New Zealand, and therefore it was unfair to burden local taxpayers with the cost of defending it. The counterargument by the War Office was disingenuous: since the danger to the island had increased enormously with the construction of the base, it should share in the expenses.[9] A more substantive justification was that Singapore would benefit economically from the project and attract more trade, while property values would be enhanced. The dispute

---

[2] Kwa, Heng, Borschberg and Tan, *Seven Hundred Years*, pp. 231–2.

[3] Abshire, *History of Singapore*, p. 83.

[4] Murfett, Miksic, Farrell and Chiang, *Between Two Oceans*, pp. 148, 153–4, 155–6; B. Clements, *The Fatal Fortress: The Guns and Fortifications of Singapore 1819–1953* (Barnsley: Pen and Sword Books, 2016), p. 90.

[5] Turnbull, *History of Modern Singapore*, pp. 170–1.

[6] *Malayan Saturday Post*, 29 Sept. 1928.

[7] W.D. McIntyre, "The Strategic Significance of Singapore, 1917–1942. The Naval Base and the Commonwealth", *Journal of Southeast Asian History* 10, 1 (1969): 90–1.

[8] *Malayan Saturday Post*, 29 Sept. 1928; *The Singapore Free Press and Mercantile Advertiser*, 14 Feb. 1938.

[9] *Malayan Saturday Post*, 12 Nov. 1927.

ended in 1932 when it was agreed that the Colony should pay $4 million each year for the purpose of Imperial defence and at the same time, expenditure on the local forces should not exceed $500,000 in any year.[10]

The construction of the facilities was sporadically halted by changes in home government policies and the Great Depression; in the process, delays resulted and a further downscaling of the project was ordered.[11] In 1931 however, it took on urgency as Japan invaded and occupied Manchuria.[12] Two years later, the British Imperial government allocated a sum of £1.5 million to install new artillery guns for protecting the naval base.[13] By 1935, the Singapore garrison had grown to over 3,000 including a full battalion of infantry manning gun emplacements and anti-aircraft installations.[14] In addition to Seletar Airbase, two new airfields were built at Tengah and Sembawang. In 1936, the labour force involved in building the naval base numbered 4,000 Chinese and Indians, entailing a weekly payroll bill of $60,000.[15] As inducements, they were provided with accommodation and paid wages slightly above the average prevailing elsewhere.[16]

In February 1938, the huge King George VI dry dock at Sembawang—the largest in the world at that time—was opened with great fanfare by the Governor of the Straits Settlements.[17] It was encircled by artillery defences at Changi, Pulau Tekong and Johor, the gun battery at this last place being financed by a gift from the Sultan of £500,000. Anti-aircraft guns were approved for the defence of the naval base and the airfield at Seletar in 1937, with nine alone guarding the huge oil fuel depot at the base.[18] These were complemented by strategic roads, reserves of war materials, emergency supplies and radio wireless stations.[19] Commenting on these facilities, the international and domestic media boasted that Singapore was the "Gibraltar of the East".[20] The entire naval base encompassed an area of 21 square miles and was constructed at a cost that far exceeded the initial estimate.[21]

The works had taken 15 years to complete; when they were finished, there was no fleet to defend the naval base. Britain by that time had become preoccupied with the threat from Nazi Germany in Europe. The "Singapore Strategy" in the event of hostilities was to deploy the navy from Britain; the voyage would take 42 days to reach Singapore. Unrealistic as the plan already was, this period before relief arrived was extended first to 70 days, then

---

10 *The Singapore Free Press and Mercantile Advertiser*, 14 Feb. 1938.

11 McIntyre, "The Strategic Significance of Singapore", pp. 75–83.

12 *The Sunday Tribune (Singapore)*, 17 Dec. 1933, 18 Mar. 1934.

13 Clements, *The Fatal Fortress*, p. 114.

14 Kwa, Heng, Borschberg and Tan, *Seven Hundred Years*, p. 238.

15 *The Straits Times Annual*, 1 Jan. 1936.

16 *The Singapore Free Press and Mercantile Advertiser*, 14 Feb. 1938.

17 Murfett, Miksic, Farrell and Chiang, *Between Two Oceans*, pp. 166–7; Clements, *The Fatal Fortress*, pp. 99, 123, 132; *The Straits Times Annual*, 1 Jan. 1938.

18 *The Straits Budget*, 27 Aug. 1936.

19 *The Straits Times Annual*, 1 Jan. 1936; *The Straits Budget*, 11 Mar. 1937.

20 Turnbull, *History of Modern Singapore*, p. 171.

21 Estimates of the final cost ranged from £30 million to £50 million. *The Singapore Free Press and Mercantile Advertiser*, 14 Feb. 1938.

90 days and finally to 180 days at the outset of the Second World War in September 1939.[22] Shrewd military observers at the time would have concluded that the strategy was unfeasible: in case of war in the Pacific, the number of battleships and vessels needed to defend British interests would exceed the capacity of the Sembawang base anyway. What actually happened was even more unthinkable: as the war in Europe proceeded and the British suffered setbacks, it became clear that no adequate fleet could be dispatched and the focus turned to the air force and the army instead, while recognising that the Malay Peninsula also had to be defended.[23] Therein lay the fatal flaw in the strategy—the existence of the base had always been predicated on the assumption that Britain would never be obliged to fight on two fronts at the same time.[24] But since it was, the Singapore naval base was as good as useless.

Troop reinforcements from Britain, India and Australia arrived in February 1941, followed by the battleships *Prince of Wales* and *Repulse*, accompanied by four destroyers.[25] But air power was conspicuously lacking and consisted only of 158 planes in airfields situated in northern Malaya, rendering the Peninsula and Singapore highly vulnerable to attack.[26] When the war started, these were swiftly destroyed by Japanese fighters as their land forces swept down the Malay Peninsula after landing on the northeast coast, aided by the extensive road and railway networks the British had built.[27] The weakness of the British defence strategy, a lack of coordination between military leaders and inexperienced troops enabled the battle-hardened Japanese soldiers to advance past Kuala Lumpur in mid-January 1942.[28] By the end of the month, the troops were amassed at Johor Bahru, ready to make the final onslaught on Singapore island to which the remaining British and Allied forces had withdrawn.[29]

Under cover of darkness, the Japanese landed on the northwest coast of Singapore on 8 February 1942.[30] With no coastal defences on the northern shore—they were mostly intended to protect the approaches to Keppel Harbour, with the gun arrays pointing out to sea—the abandoned naval base had to be destroyed to prevent it from falling into Japanese hands, going up in flames in the early days of February and prompting a senior military official to lament that "the whole reason for building and defending Singapore, which has cost so many million pounds, has now gone". He might have added that with the destruction of the base, the myth of British naval power and might in the Far East had

---

[22] Murfett, Miksic, Farrell and Chiang, *Between Two Oceans*, pp. 149–50, 154–5, 166.

[23] McIntyre, "The Strategic Significance of Singapore", pp. 84–5, 88; Tan, *A Very Short History*, p. 58. It was already realised in 1938 that the successful defence of Singapore was dependent upon the defence of Malaya as a whole, but this inference was largely ignored by the Imperial authorities. Murfett, Miksic, Farrell and Chiang, *Between Two Oceans*, pp. 165–6.

[24] Moore and Moore, *The First 150 Years*, p. 569.

[25] Kwa, Heng and Tan, *Singapore: A 700-Year History*, p. 150; Abshire, *History of Singapore*, p. 150.

[26] Turnbull, *History of Modern Singapore*, pp. 175, 178; Moore and Moore, *The First 150 Years*, p. 605.

[27] Abshire, *History of Singapore*, p. 85.

[28] Frost and Balasingamchow, *Singapore*, pp. 244, 258.

[29] Murfett, Miksic, Farrell and Chiang, *Between Two Oceans*, pp. 200–1, 215–6.

[30] Turnbull, *History of Modern Singapore*, pp. 184–5, 187–8, 189, 192; Moore and Moore, *The First 150 Years*, p. 620.

also been shattered.[31] Before that, engineers had drained the massive stocks of oil held in 40 storage tanks. The Governor ordered the destruction of rubber stockpiles, the STC's tin smelting plant at Pulau Brani and the fuel tanks at the other offshore islands. Allied forces then blew up the Causeway, cutting off water supply to Singapore from the Johor reservoirs, and ships around the waters of Singapore were scuttled.[32]

Strangely enough, the Singaporean public remained largely unperturbed about the imminence of war.[33] There was a strong belief among military commanders and the press that a Japanese invasion was unlikely as its army was bogged down by the campaign in China, and others thought that Japan would not win in any war.[34] The British residents had been busy socialising on New Year's Day after Malaya was invaded and soldiers did not show the slightest concern but continued to visit the bars and cabarets.[35] Shops, hotels and cinemas remained open and life went on as usual despite a huge influx of war refugees from Malaya and intense bombing from Japanese air raids.[36] The colonial government was partly to blame for not preparing the local population and failing to conduct evacuation exercises, out of fear of alarming the public.[37] Indeed, it seemed to have encouraged people to carry on with their activities as per normal, including sporting events.[38]

Moreover, the economy was booming on account of the strong demand for rubber and tin occasioned by the war. Singapore and Malaya were the "dollar arsenal", contributing to the war effort by keeping the funds and the commodities flowing.[39] Despite calls to curtail purchases of imported luxury goods to conserve shipping space and to reduce consumption, extravagance and wastage still prevailed.[40] In the expectation that reinforcements would soon arrive, the false sense of calm persisted even after the two British battleships were sunk off the coast of Trengganu on the third day of the Japanese invasion of Malaya (10 December 1941). This calm gave way to anxiety and tension only in the final days before the fall of Singapore in mid-February 1942.[41] On the morning after the surrender, as an eerie silence descended on the city, its residents woke up to their plight and prepared for the worst.

---

31 Savage, *Lion City Narratives*, pp. 41, 302–3.

32 *10 Years that Shaped a Nation* (Singapore: National Archives of Singapore, 2008), p. 39; P.H. Kratoska, *The Japanese Occupation of Malaya and Singapore, 1941–45: A Social and Economic History*, Second Edition (Singapore: NUS Press, 2018), pp. 167, 170.

33 Turnbull, *History of Modern Singapore*, pp. 173, 177, 183, 185; *The Singapore Free Press and Mercantile Advertiser*, 5 Aug. 1941.

34 *Malaya Tribune*, 2 Dec. 1941.

35 *Syonan Shimbun Fortnightly*, 4 Apr. 1942. The *Syonan Shimbun* was the name given by the Japanese to the *Straits Times* newspaper.

36 Liew and Wilson, *A History of Money*, pp. 141–2; The *Singapore Free Press and Mercantile Advertiser*, 31 Dec. 1941.

37 Murfett, Miksic, Farrell and Chiang, *Between Two Oceans*, p. 189; *The Sunday Tribune (Singapore)*, 28 Sept. 1941.

38 *Malaya Tribune*, 10 Dec. 1941.

39 Abshire, *History of Singapore*, p. 86.

40 *Malaya Tribune*, 1 Oct. 1941; *The Singapore Free Press and Mercantile Advertiser*, 13 Dec. 1941.

41 *The Straits Times*, 26 Jan. 1942.

Economic Reorganisation and Collapse

Apart from rounding up and executing suspected supporters of the Kuomintang and Communist Party of China—all Chinese—the Japanese military administration's priority in Syonan was to reorganise and revamp the economy. Its objectives were to facilitate the export of primary commodities needed by the military and achieve self-sufficiency.[42] Although Japanese leaders were fully aware of the strategic importance and economic value of Singapore and had even wanted it to be the capital of their empire in Southeast Asia, they had not made concrete plans before the invasion on how to administer the city.[43] In the early days of the occupation, the military authorities took a hard line on governance but they were soon tempered by the arrival of Japanese civilian bureaucrats.[44] A new government headed by a mayor was set up and municipal services were restarted.[45] Most shops had also reopened by the end of February 1942.[46]

In terms of the economy's *modus operandi*, the Japanese abandoned the *laissez faire* policy of the British, favouring instead direct control and monopolies as these were deemed to be efficient and less demanding on administrative resources.[47] Singapore's biggest asset was its port, so the authorities' first target of economic reorganisation was the shipping and transport infrastructure.[48] Not only would the island's functionality as a naval base and its ship repair facilities extend the reach of the Japanese fleet, but the proximity of the port to the Sumatra oilfields and its extensive oil storage facilities would be of strategic value. The Tanjong Pagar docks, the Sembawang naval base, Kallang Airport and the airfields at Seletar and Tengah were sequestered while large numbers of ships and lorries were requisitioned for military use.[49] The Japanese also commandeered privately owned cars without paying much compensation.[50]

In the city itself, the Singapore Gas Works was expropriated by the Japanese military administration though its output was severely curtailed, as was that of electricity, due to shortages of coal and lubricants.[51] From the pre-war level of 1.2 million cubic feet, gas capacity dropped to 500,000 cubic feet.[52] At the Syonan Steam Power Plant (St. James Power Station), the maximum amount of electric power that could be generated was a mere

---

[42] Kratoska, *Japanese Occupation*, p. 58.

[43] Tan, *A Very Short History*, p. 61.

[44] W.G. [Gregg] Huff and S. Majima, ed. and trans., *World War II Singapore: The Chōsabu Reports on Syonan* (Singapore: NUS Press, 2018), p. 8. This book contains valuable translations of economic reports on Syonan by a team of Japanese researchers and bureaucrats and will hereafter be referred to as *Chōsabu Reports*.

[45] Turnbull, *History of Modern Singapore*, pp. 196, 202; *Syonan Shimbun*, 16 Mar. 1942.

[46] *Syonan Shimbun*, 26 Feb. 1942.

[47] Shimizu and Hirakawa, *Japan and Singapore in the World Economy*, pp. 113, 135; Huff, *World War II and Southeast Asia*, p. 48.

[48] *Syonan Shimbun*, 10 Oct. 1942.

[49] *Chōsabu Reports*, p. 44. The Municipality also took over the operation of bus services in the city. *Syonan Shimbun*, 17 Mar. 1942.

[50] Chin Kee Onn, *Malaya Upside Down* (Singapore: Jitts, 1946), p. 86.

[51] Huff, *World War II and Southeast Asia*, pp. 197, 201.

[52] *Chōsabu Reports*, pp. 302–5.

14,200 kilowatt hours per day. The military amalgamated the Standard Oil Company and the Asiatic Petroleum Company and made its Oil Distribution Department responsible for the supply of gasoline.[53] The Japanese also monopolised the distribution of charcoal and firewood and, as the British had done, the production and sale of opium.[54] In the case of rubber, a syndicate of 18 Japanese firms operated through the Syonan Rubber Association, which functioned similarly as the local association that it replaced.

Next came the commercial businesses. In the distribution of food and consumer goods, the only option was to work through existing traders, which effectively meant reliance on the Chinese.[55] Towards the end of 1942, commercial firms in the same lines of business were grouped together into rationing associations known as *kumiai* and awarded quasi-monopolies in the trading of rice, meat, fish, vegetables, sugar and cloth.[56] The role of the kumiai included distributing supplies of foodstuffs to the heads of households in Syonan, with the amount each household received depending on the size of the family and age of its members.[57] According to a census conducted by the Municipality's Department of Commerce and Industry in May 1944, there were 8,025 local traders in the wholesale and retail sectors.[58] Of these, 1,120 were traders in staple foods that were rationed, namely rice, salt and sugar, of which 69 were wholesalers and 51 were specialist retailers catering to institutions and large customers such as food manufacturers and restaurants. The rest were general grocers selling uncontrolled foods. Supplementary foods such as meat, fish, vegetables and oil were also rationed and distributed by 320 appointed traders, including a large number of butchers and fishmongers. The vendors operating in controlled markets were organised in kongsis which shared profits with their employees, while some also sold foods on their own account. In addition, a number of individuals sold vegetables and fruits grown in Syonan.

In general commerce, the census found 5,207 traders engaged in activities ranging from selling liquor to tailoring and trading in machinery, electrical appliances and automobiles.[59] They were mostly small businesses with capital of less than $5,000 except for those selling intermediate goods; the most numerous were haberdashers and tobacco traders. Slightly over half of the owners had started business after the outbreak of war, suggesting a dearth of regular jobs. At the time of the census, most were not doing well due to a shortage of imported stocks, raw materials and parts. By contrast with local traders, Japanese traders who established businesses in Syonan operated with larger capital bases. Of the 95 firms present, 64 or two-thirds had capital of $10,000 or more and they also enjoyed a commensurately higher turnover; for example, the grocers and liquor sellers amongst them boasted average sales of over $50,000.[60] Cold Storage, a notable local grocer

---

[53] *Syonan Shimbun*, 30 Sept. 1942.

[54] Huff, *World War II and Southeast Asia*, pp. 64–5, 69.

[55] Ibid., p. 64; Turnbull, *History of Modern Singapore*, pp. 206–7.

[56] Kratoska, *Japanese Occupation*, p. 172; Shimizu and Hirakawa, *Japan and Singapore in the World Economy*, p. 127; *Syonan Shimbun*, 27 Nov. 1942.

[57] Eunice Thio, "The Syonan Years, 1942–1945", in *A History of Singapore*, ed. Chew and Lee, pp. 105–6.

[58] *Chōsabu Reports*, pp. 177–8, 181–4, 372, 379–81, 384.

[59] Ibid., pp. 184–9 and 203–5.

[60] Ibid., pp. 215–7 and 241–2.

established before the war, was now turned into a *butai* or military-linked company.[61] Two other prominent Japanese traders also deserve mention: Mitsubishi Corporation, which was granted a monopoly to import rice into Syonan and Malaya (renamed "Malai" by the Japanese) and Mitsui & Co., which was awarded the monopolies in sugar and salt.[62] Both had had branches in the city prior to the war and they competed with Chinese merchants and the European agency houses in the import-export business. During the occupation, they were able to dominate foreign trade.[63]

The smaller Japanese merchants were mostly haberdashers, watch sellers, leather goods vendors and building materials suppliers. There was also a retailer of electrical appliances and one firm dealing in machines and tools.[64] Only 16 of the Japanese businesses dated from before the war, ranging across a variety of trades including the provision of staple and supplementary foods and commercial wares. Many of the new firms were suppliers of goods to the military while some were restaurant, hotel and geisha house operators.[65] The others were *rikenyas*, opportunistic concession hunters, with personal connections to the military who came to Syonan to get rich by engaging in shady business deals and driving the Chinese out of business, sometimes through expropriation.[66] There were also three Japanese department stores, namely Daimaru, Matsuzakaya and Shirakiya which operated in various parts of Asia.[67] In Syonan, these trading companies procured military goods for the army, managed dormitories for Japanese soldiers and retailed goods at the Raffles Place premises that were formerly occupied by John Little, Robinson's and Whiteaway Laidlaw, respectively. Like their local counterparts, not all Japanese traders were prosperous, although food providers generally fared better than the rest.

After occupying Singapore, the Japanese military and *kaishas* (corporations) took over the engineering works, foundries and machine shops on the island largely intact (Map 6).[68] But they had to repair the naval base and harbour facilities due to the "scorched earth" policy of the British.[69] The repaired shipyards at Tanjong Pagar were given over to the management of Mitsubishi Heavy Industries.[70] As with the transport infrastructure, existing industrial facilities were adapted to military requirements. United Engineers, a large enterprise maintaining and repairing imported machinery for the rubber and tin

---

61 Lee Geok Boi, "Wartime Victuals", *BiblioAsia* 15, 1 (2019): 24.

62 Shimizu and Hirakawa, *Japan and Singapore in the World Economy*, p. 121; *Syonan Shimbun*, 14 Aug. 1942.

63 *Syonan Shimbun*, 10 Apr. 1943.

64 *Chōsabu Reports*, pp. 241–2.

65 Turnbull, *History of Modern Singapore*, p. 206; *Chōsabu Reports*, p. 21. Including manufacturing firms, there were altogether 130 Japanese companies in Syonan in May 1944. Shimizu and Hirakawa, *Japan and Singapore in the World Economy*, pp. 113, 123–7.

66 Y. Akashi, "Japanese Policy Towards the Malayan Chinese 1941–1945", *Journal of Southeast Asian Studies* 1, 2 (1970): 81–3.

67 *Syonan Shimbun*, 13 Sept. 1943.

68 W.G. [as Gregg] Huff and G. Huff, "The Second World War Occupation of Singapore", *Journal of Southeast Asian Studies* 51, 1–2 (2020): 258–61; Chin, *Malaya Upside Down*, pp. 83, 84.

69 Huff, *World War II and Southeast Asia*, p. 215; *Syonan Shimbun*, 18 June 1942.

70 Shimizu and Hirakawa, *Japan and Singapore in the World Economy*, pp. 135–7.

industries, was taken over by Mitsui Kozan Kabushiki Kaisha and converted to a factory making weapons and materials for railway construction.[71] Machinery was shipped from Japan to Singapore for the production of diesel engines while an automobile company turned trucks into armoured vehicles.

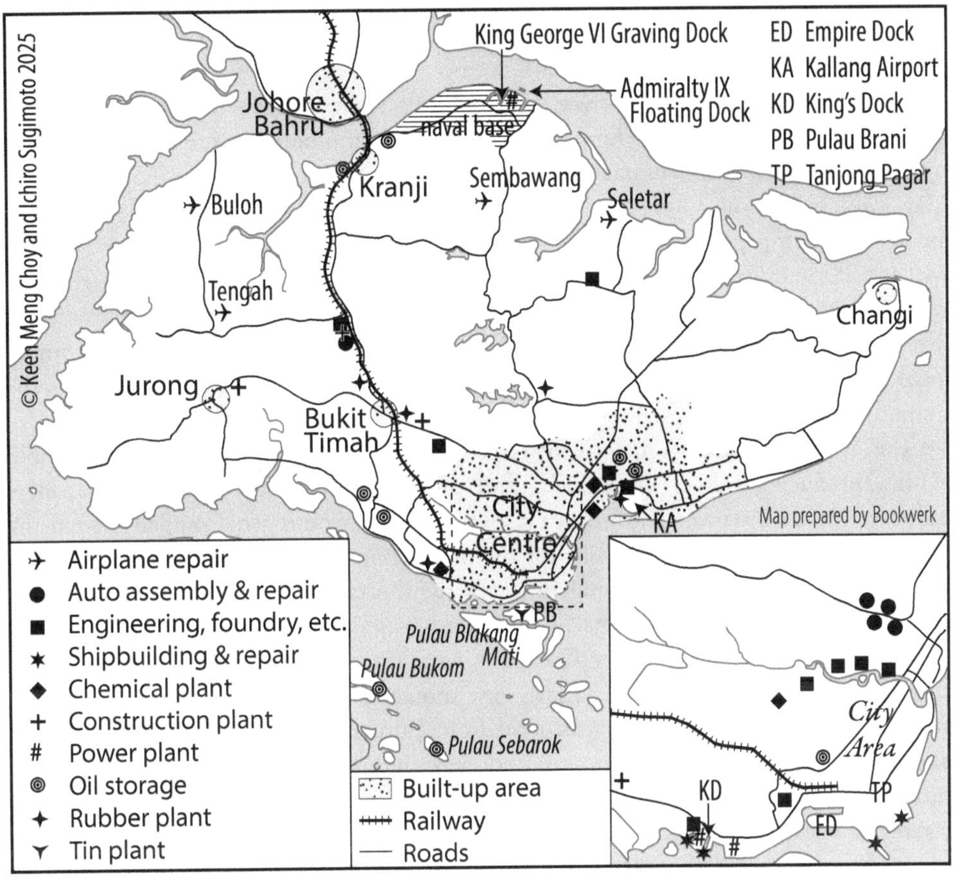

Map 6. Singapore Industrial Facilities, 1944.

Sources: Based on the 1944 OSS map, "Industrial Facilities in Malaya" (Washington, DC: Office of Strategic Services, R&A 2137, 15 May 1944) and on a declassified 1945 British map of Singapore courtesy Wikimedia.

The rubber mills and pineapple canning factories were however of no utility to the Japanese military. The STC's damaged smelting plant at Pulau Brani was refitted for the manufacture of sulphuric acid and the melting of spent cartridge cases; part of it also served as a printing works. Later on, the plant produced metals such as copper, lead and antimony.[72] In the middle of 1943, an ambitious plan was conceived to build industries for manufacturing steel, chemicals, car tyres and electric bulbs in Syonan.[73] However, the scheme eventually failed because of a shortage of imported equipment and skilled labour. Although several

[71] *Chōsabu Reports*, pp. 22, 305–6.

[72] Shimizu and Hirakawa, *Japan and Singapore in the World Economy*, pp. 130, 131–5.

[73] Huff, *World War II and Southeast Asia*, pp. 216–7.

Japanese concerns produced rolled steel, steel bars, submarine cables and bulbs, other firms merely assembled or repaired machinery, wireless and telephonic equipment, and motor vehicles—activities which could hardly qualify as heavy industry.[74] The company sanctioned by the military administration to undertake the assembly, repair and trading of vehicles was Nissan, which was located at the modern Ford factory in Upper Bukit Timah Road. Subsequently, it made lorries from imported knockdown parts with the aid of Japanese engineers and local workers.

A greater measure of success was achieved with light industry, not least because of factories that already existed in Singapore. The Japanese promoted its further development by encouraging the local manufacture of a wide range of goods for daily use.[75] Starting from May 1943, exhibitions were occasionally held to showcase new products, which included an assortment of paper, cardboard, oil and grease, disinfectants, toothbrushes, ironware, as well as toilet and washing soap.[76] Most of the new industries were in Malai, though some were situated in Syonan, for example a Japanese company that took over the Malayan Paint Works and renamed it Dai-Nippon Toryo Kabushiki Kaisha. Another company, Nippon Yusai Kabushiki Kaisha, built a paint factory using equipment transferred from Japan, the output of which was intended for the hulls of ships.

The Yokohama Rubber Company took over the Dutch-owned Singapore Rubber Works, producing rubber hoses, belts and pneumatic tyres for use by the Japanese military.[77] In an instance of a forced takeover, the Japan Nitrogen Company seized the Chinese-owned Ho Hong Oil Mills for the production of soap.[78] Another type of light manufacturing undertaken to compensate for the shortage of steel was the construction of wooden boats fitted with diesel or marine engines.[79] This enterprise was undertaken by the Japan Outfitting Industry Company with the assistance of skilled shipbuilders from Japan, altogether employing nearly one thousand workers.[80] However, production was hampered by a shortage of teakwood from Burma, although Malayan timber was also used.[81] Intermediate between light and heavy industry, the Syonan Oxygen Factory produced oxygen and acetylene, mainly for the military. To achieve self-sufficiency in cigarettes, Shiroki Sangyo Kabushiki Kaisha converted a bakery into a tobacco factory.[82] As a small comfort during the war, tasty beer continued to be produced by the Dai-Nippon and Kirin Beer Companies after they took over the erstwhile Archipelago Breweries and Malayan Breweries, respectively, both established in the early 1930s and owned by Fraser & Neave.[83] And unsurprisingly, a Japanese firm bought out a Chinese factory to produce Japanese soy sauce and miso.

---

74 *Syonan Shimbun*, 30 Sept. 1943.

75 Kratoska, *Japanese Occupation*, p. 180; *Syonan Shimbun*, 27 Mar. 1944.

76 *Syonan Shimbun*, 18 Apr. 1943, 19 Feb. 1944, 20 Apr. 1945.

77 Kratoska, *Japanese Occupation*, pp. 308–9.

78 Shimizu and Hirakawa, *Japan and Singapore in the World Economy*, pp. 129–30, 131–9, 315–6.

79 Chin, *Malaya Upside Down*, p. 188; *Chōsabu Reports*, p. 22.

80 *Syonan Shimbun*, 15 Nov. 1942.

81 *Syonan Shimbun*, 30 Jan. 1943.

82 *Syonan Shimbun*, 22 June 1944.

83 *Chōsabu Reports*, pp. 22, 311–4, 318–9; *Syonan Shimbun*, 5 Dec. 1942.

However, despite the best efforts of the Japanese military and civil administrations to stabilise production, the situation on the ground deteriorated so rapidly that by early 1943, the Syonan economy was on the brink of collapse. This was because imports of raw materials were choked off by the shortage of shipping and at the same time, Japan could not provide sufficient goods and equipment as it had little to spare after satisfying its own war needs.[84] Although the Japanese Navy managed to salvage close to 100 of the vessels sunk by the British, merchant shipping capacity was extremely tight.[85] Japanese shipping tonnage fell from 5,421,000 tonnes at the end of 1941 to 4,171,000 tonnes at the end of 1943 as vessels were sunk by the Allied forces, with a corresponding reduction in the number of serviceable ships. Local shipping came to a standstill as the fleets of the SSC and KPM were impounded. Meanwhile, public transport deteriorated to the extent that only a third of the trams and buses in the city were operating in the latter part of 1944, forcing residents to return to rickshaws and the obsolete horse carriages and bullock carts for transport.[86] Buses, taxis and some automobiles had to run on charcoal.[87]

With imports shut out, businesses in Syonan could depend only on stocks of goods accumulated before the war; these had however effectively run out by the end of 1942.[88] Trade statistics were not collected for Syonan but obviously, whatever commerce existed took place only with Malai and Japan. Even the trade with Malai was retarded by a lack of rail and lorry transport.[89] Nevertheless, Syonan could actually have increased its trade with Japan during the war years even though imports of cotton goods into the island were likely to have shrunk drastically, given a sharp decline in Japan's production. In contrast, Malai's exports to Japan collapsed in 1942 but recovered in 1943 and reached a high of ¥83,019,000 in the following year.[90] The commodities siphoned off from the country were tin, rubber, bauxite and iron, mostly shipped through Syonan.

Left only with Japanese custom, the production of rubber dropped to insignificance as estates reduced their output or stopped operating altogether.[91] In 1943, rubber exports from Malai were only 17 per cent of their level in the previous year and they stayed the same in 1944.[92] Large stocks were left unsold in Syonan. Tin production similarly fell in 1942 to less than a third of its 1939 level, partly because the British had deliberately sunk dredges as they retreated. Production would have declined by even more if Japanese technicians had not repaired the bulk and handed their control over to Japanese mining firms. The macroeconomic contraction that resulted was the worst in Malaya's history. In the absence of GDP estimates, it has been conjectured that aggregate output contracted by

---

84 *Chōsabu Reports*, p. 328; Huff and Huff, "The Second World War Occupation of Singapore", pp. 5–6.

85 Kratoska, *Japanese Occupation*, pp. 167, 170. Shimizu and Hirakawa, *Japan and Singapore in the World Economy*, pp. 121, 123; *Syonan Shimbun*, 2 Sept. 1942.

86 *Chōsabu Reports*, pp. 7, 27.

87 Chin, *Malaya Upside Down*, p. 178; *Syonan Shimbun*, 2 Aug. 1942.

88 Kratoska, *Japanese Occupation*, p. 165; Huff, *World War II and Southeast Asia*, p. 124.

89 Huff, *World War II and Southeast Asia*, pp. 197–8, 201, 217; *Chōsabu Reports*, p. 328.

90 Huff and Huff, "The Second World War Occupation of Singapore", pp. 248–50. The Malayan dollar was fixed on par value with the yen.

91 Kratoska, *Japanese Occupation*, p. 186.

92 Huff, *World War II and Southeast Asia*, pp. 117, 125, 127, 141–3, 146, 217.

one-half to two-thirds. Given Syonan's economic dependence on Malai, the outcome for the city was probably similar or worse. Manufacturing output fell drastically, crippled by shortages of machinery, spare parts, fuel, lubricants, power and transport. Furthermore, as the sector was made up to a large extent of tin processing and rubber milling activities, its value-added slumped, with the smelter down and the cutback in rubber output. Combined with the loss of external and internal trade, the end result was economic collapse.

Population and Labour Supply

In November 1943, Japanese administrators conducted a comprehensive census of Syonan's population that included information on occupation, employment status and households.[93] After the brutal purge of civilian Chinese known as "sook ching" (cleansing by elimination) that took the lives of at least 25,000 people, only 675,726 were left in the community.[94] However, they still formed 78.8 per cent of the total population, higher than the ratio in the previous 1931 census.[95] The Hokkiens were the most numerous dialect group, followed by the Teochews, the Cantonese, the Hakkas and the Hainanese. The increase in the Chinese presence in Syonan is partly explained by labourers thrown out of work in Malai migrating to the city.[96] Indians made up 9.1 per cent of the Syonan population, the same as before, while the proportion of Malays fell to 10.7 per cent. The latter had always engaged in agricultural activity as a means of living and it is therefore plausible that the decrease in their representation was due to some moving up-country. The number of Europeans also declined as the British withdrew from Singapore after their crushing defeat, although a few engineers and health officers were retained by the Japanese administration. The remaining British and Allied troops were interned as prisoners of war at Changi Prison and the less fortunate among them were sent to Thailand to build the infamous "Death Railway", from which many did not return.[97]

The overall net population of Syonan rose to 855,679 in 1943 as a result of rapid growth after the Great Depression.[98] There were 509,032 adult males and 346,647 females as well as 324,000 old people and children. Hence, the sex ratio had improved considerably as a result of female immigration and rising birth rates. The population was made up of 195,824 households, implying that the average household size was 4.4 persons. In 170,874 households, the head—overwhelmingly male—was employed. He and the other working members of the household supported on average 2.5 persons while

[93] *Chōsabu Reports*, pp. 133–4; *Syonan Shimbun*, 1 Apr. 1943.

[94] Frost and Balasingamchow, *Singapore*, p. 290; Akashi, "Japanese Policy", pp. 66–9. The Chinese themselves claimed that around 50,000 died.

[95] *Chōsabu Reports*, pp. 12–14, 68, 136.

[96] Kratoska, *Japanese Occupation*, pp. 186–7, 195; Huff and Huff, "The Second World War Occupation of Singapore", pp. 251, 267–8. The number of rubber estate labourers in Malai were reduced from 148,000 to 70,000, of which 28,000 grew their own food.

[97] Turnbull, *History of Modern Singapore*, p. 214; Frost and Balasingamchow, *Singapore*, pp. 280–4; Huff, *World War II and Southeast Asia*, pp. 345, 348, 350. The number of prisoners of war has been estimated at about 100,000 to 130,000. Lee, "Wartime Victuals", p. 29.

[98] *Chōsabu Reports*, pp. 135–6, 137–8, 149–50. The figure excludes police officers lodging in dormitories, prisoners and Japanese inhabitants.

in households where the head was unemployed, he and the other unemployed members were supported by 1.2 persons.

With the increase in population, the labour supply grew *pari passu* to 530,942 persons in 1943 from 394,302 in 1931.[99] In 1942, the Labour Office found jobs for 120,000 labourers and 3,500 skilled artisans, practically all of whom were employed in the reconstruction of Syonan.[100] However, the labour force participation rate still declined from 69.5 per cent to 62 per cent over the same period. One explanation for the decline is that the residents of Syonan were unwilling to work for their Japanese masters or found other activities such as standing in queues for food rations, hawking and casual employment more rewarding. A second reason was the relatively low participation rate of women of 17.2 per cent, as opposed to 91.9 per cent for men. Consequently, the dependency ratio was close to 40 per cent. In the population as a whole, the employment rate was 39.9 per cent; the rate for males was 60.3 per cent and that for females was just 9.6 per cent.[101] Leaving aside enumeration errors, these low employment rates were a consequence of the dearth of jobs as well as the sex and age structure of the Syonan population. Ethnic groups with a preponderance of males and more people of working age (from 15 to 50 years old) tended to show higher employment rates, as in the case of Indians, many of whom were working-age men, and Europeans, who had a lower dependency ratio. In contrast, the other communities' lower employment rates reflected more balanced sex ratios and a larger number of elderly people and children. The flipside of low employment, especially of women, was a high unemployment rate of 35.7 per cent in November 1943, which was higher than during the Great Depression because economic conditions were more dire and redundant immigrants were not repatriated.

The need for the working population to support the unemployed might not have been as great as suggested by the overall dependency ratio because of an enlarged informal sector, consisting mainly of hawkers. That hawking was a form of forced employment and that hawkers would change their occupation if they were able to find better jobs was admitted by the Japanese.[102] A survey carried out in 1944 reported that there were 12,136 licensed hawkers and street vendors in Syonan selling cooked food, vegetables and fruits, second-hand goods and sundries; this figure still missed a large number of itinerant and stall hawkers. It was observed that they "increased by the thousands, and they glutted highways and byways".[103] As these hawkers and vendors were allowed to peddle only unrationed foods, the higher market prices that had to be paid for them were passed on to their customers, who ironically enough were in the main coolies and low-wage workers.

---

[99] Ibid., pp. 14–17.

[100] *Syonan Shimbun*, 17 July 1942, 29 Mar. 1943.

[101] *Chōsabu Reports*, pp. 19, 152–4. Unlike the participation rate, which is calculated as the percentage of economically active persons in the working-age population, the employment rate is the number of persons employed as a percentage of the total population.

[102] *Chōsabu Reports*, pp. 18, 90–1.

[103] Chin, *Malaya Upside Down*, p. 69.

In enumerating the population by occupation, the Japanese census of 1943 was more detailed than the one conducted by the British in 1931, with finer occupational sub-categories, even though statistics on construction were missing.[104] Notwithstanding wartime conditions, the sectoral distribution of jobs was not radically altered. Including hawkers and stall keepers, commerce was still the largest sector, employing 29 per cent of productive labour, compared to 25.9 per cent in 1931. Within the sector, traders, shopkeepers, shop assistants, salespeople and restaurateurs made up the biggest group, at 52,995 persons. The next largest sub-category comprised hawkers and street vendors, with 38,402 individuals, far higher than the 1944 survey count and the 1931 figure of 28,873. Employment in the financial sector retreated with the exit of the British and foreign banks although there were still 3,242 moneylenders and brokers. Farming and fishing encompassed agricultural labourers and vegetable and fruit growers, representing 9.1 per cent of employment. The share of manufacturing jobs remained relatively stable at 17.2 per cent but there were notable increases in the number of mechanics, electrical machinery workers and blacksmiths. About 9,000 people were employed in cottage industries such as textiles, dyeing and book- and hat-making. In the transport sector could be found 9,419 rickshaw pullers, 7,750 car drivers and 3,905 boatmen.

In the civil service, the number of government servants, police officers and army personnel dropped dramatically to 3,532 from the 52,823 who were classified as being engaged in public administration and defence in 1931. (Japanese administrators and police officers living in dormitories were not included in the census.) Similarly, only 7,816 professionals were left in 1943. Despite the disappearance of the pre-war trade, there were still 69,219 coolies in Syonan, contributing fully one-fifth of employment. Presumably, construction labourers were included in this sub-category; another 3,238 building workers were counted in manufacturing. As noted by the census takers, many of the coolies worked in Japanese manufacturing factories while there also existed a large reserve of unattached labourers. Finally, 21,576 domestic servants and 14,818 clerks were classified as being in "other" occupations. Nearly half of household servants were females, who also took up jobs as shop assistants, street vendors and coolies.

More than a century after the phenomenon first appeared in Singapore, the Japanese discovered that the association between dialect or ethnic group and occupation remained more or less intact. It was reported that in Syonan, there was a high concentration of Chinese occupied in commerce—mostly Hokkiens who were known for their business ability—as well as in agriculture and manufacturing, but lower in other sectors such as transport, the public service and the professions.[105] In particular, the Chinese continued to be under-represented in the police force. Over two-fifths of the Teochews were engaged in commercial work, banking and finance and together with Malays, they dominated fishing. In the manufacturing sector, the Cantonese were the largest ethnic group and they also made up the bulk of mechanics and carpenters. A large proportion of Hakkas were merchants and shop assistants, though a substantial number also toiled in the manufacturing sector. As in the 19th century, the Hainanese were distinguished by their role as domestic servants although many now also worked in sales and as shop assistants.

---

[104] *Chōsabu Reports*, pp. 139–41, 142–3, Table A.3.4, p. 159, Table A.3.7, pp. 164–6.

[105] Ibid., pp. 144–6, 148, 256, Table A.3.7, pp. 164–6.

Transport sector jobs were mostly filled by Malay and Indian car drivers, Malay sailors and Hokkien boatmen. Rickshaw pulling was an almost exclusively Chinese profession, with the Hokkiens (inclusive of Hockchius, Henghuas and Foochow people) and Teochews being the main dialect groups involved. As for the Indians, a class distinction continued to separate the better educated from the menial labourers. The former were traders, merchants and professionals whereas the latter were employed as coolies and in land transport. The largest ethnic group serving as security guards were also Indians, including Sikhs. Lastly, the Eurasians were typically office workers, especially clerks, many of whom lost their jobs when the war started.[106]

Some of the above jobs entailed working for the Japanese, which Singaporeans were generally loath to do after the cruel repression and atrocities inflicted on them. The military administration therefore had no choice but to resort to forced labour, firstly for agricultural pursuits in order to supply food for the population and secondly, to carry out war-related construction work.[107] In August 1943, an attempt was made to relocate labour from Syonan to the Malay Peninsula (and from the city centre to the rural districts) for the first of these purposes, with the resettlement of about 12,000 Chinese in Endau in northeastern Johor.[108] The collective farm scheme implemented in "New Syonan", as the settlement was called, was located on a huge tract of fertile agricultural land that was suitable for growing rice and other crops, and for poultry raising.[109] It did attract some unemployed Chinese labourers and artisans, who were each given four acres of land, agricultural implements and seeds as well as a hut to live in.[110] New Syonan was provided with a post office, a bank, a school, a polytechnic school and a cinema along with a few factories and sawmills.[111] A second farm colony with over 300 families was also initiated in Bahau in Negri Sembilan with the aim of establishing a Catholic community there and enticing Eurasians to migrate.[112] Although the land was hilly and many settlers died of malaria, it produced tapioca and vegetables that were sent to Syonan.[113]

To undertake military construction projects, some men were drafted into the "Seicho" or Labour Service Corps to perform assigned tasks such as digging ditches and building air raid shelters during their non-working hours and sometimes for longer periods.[114] The need for labour had become more acute in mid-1943 even as the Japanese perceived

---

[106] *Syonan Shimbun*, 17 Apr. 1944.

[107] *Chōsabu Reports*, pp. 19, 20; Kratoska, *Japanese Occupation*, p. 192.

[108] Turnbull, *History of Modern Singapore*, p. 215; *Syonan Shimbun*, 15 Feb. 1944, 19 Apr. 1944, 13 June 1945. After the city was occupied, the Japanese had ordered war refugees from Malaya to return to their hometowns. *Syonan Shimbun*, 9 Mar. 1942.

[109] *Syonan Shimbun*, 6 Dec. 1943, 15 Dec. 1943.

[110] *Syonan Shimbun*, 7 Jan. 1944.

[111] *Syonan Shimbun*, 1 Dec. 1943, 29 Feb. 1944, 20 May 1944, 14 Dec. 1944, 11 Apr. 1945, 12 Apr. 1945, 9 June 1945.

[112] *Syonan Shimbun*, 4 Dec. 1943, 3 Jan. 1944, 6 Mar. 1944, 14 Dec. 1944.

[113] Lee, "Wartime Victuals", p. 27; *Syonan Shimbun*, 14 Feb. 1945, 11 Apr. 1945.

[114] Huff, *World War II and Southeast Asia*, pp. 332–3, 336; *Syonan Shimbun*, 8 Apr. 1944. For every 250 inhabitants, 20 males aged 15 to 45 were selected together with government employees.

that a considerable pool of unemployed and underemployed workers existed.[115] Javanese labourers known as *romusha* who were brought into Singapore to provide labour for public works were insufficient and in any event, many of them died from illness and inadequate nutrition.[116] An official report accordingly recommended that marginal workers such as hawkers should be mobilised for more productive undertakings. It also attributed the excess employment in the commercial sector to the Chinese penchant for business pursuits and urged that some of the workers there be transferred into the industrial sector. At the end of 1944, the Japanese authorities began to implement these recommendations by compelling people to change jobs so as to work in agriculture, to man war establishments and produce essential goods like soap and paper.[117] A target was set to close 60 per cent of the shops in Syonan so as to free employees in the commercial sector; from April 1945, men were no longer allowed to work in a variety of service occupations such as clerks, shop assistants, hotel and restaurant staff, telephone operators and hawkers.[118] Youths were encouraged to be mechanics and skilled labourers after being trained at technical institutes set up by the Japanese authorities.[119] Even women were not exempted from the campaign: jobs vacated by men were often filled by them and they were encouraged to participate in the workforce. In addition to the jobs mentioned earlier, many worked in factories, offices, restaurants and cafes while others volunteered for the Medical Auxiliary Services.[120]

Another form of forced labour was aimed at securing manpower for Japanese-managed factories. The Japanese were able to conscript a substantial number of residents to "voluntarily" work in their industrial enterprises by offering food rations as an incentive even though the nominal wage was low.[121] To the extent that these workers could have earned more in alternative occupations, coerced labour effectively amounted to the implicit taxation of work effort.[122] Payment in rice was the surest method of securing workers as the commodity was "the infallible draw...people who had vowed never to work under the Japanese had to swallow their pride and give way" or face starvation.[123] About 70,000 people, including the 25,000 employed by the Japanese Navy, worked for the administration, accounting for more than a fifth of total employment.[124] As the war turned in favour of the Allies, priority rice rations plus some other controlled foods and a small money wage were instituted early in 1944 for employees of Japanese firms and the military forces to make them more productive.[125] From the Japanese point of view, the high proportion of illiterate and unskilled workers in Syonan was an obstacle to factory work.

---

115 *Chōsabu Reports*, pp. 19, 21, 74–5.

116 Thio, "The Syonan Years", p. 106; Frost and Balasingamchow, *Singapore*, pp. 309–10.

117 Kratoska, *Japanese Occupation*, pp. 192–4; *Syonan Shimbun*, 9 Aug. 1944, 7 Sept. 1944.

118 Chin, *Malaya Upside Down*, p. 48; *Syonan Shimbun*, 8 Jan. 1944, 29 Mar. 1945.

119 *Syonan Shimbun*, 13 Jan. 1943, 7 Jan. 1944, 17 Apr. 1944, 6 Oct. 1944, 7 Oct. 1944, 29 Mar. 1945.

120 *Syonan Shimbun*, 18 Jan. 1944, 15 Feb. 1944.

121 *Chōsabu Reports*, p. 21.

122 Huff, *World War II and Southeast Asia*, pp. 332–3.

123 Chin, *Malaya Upside Down*, p. 60.

124 Huff, *World War II and Southeast Asia*, pp. 336, 344–5.

125 Huff and Huff, "The Second World War Occupation of Singapore", p. 265.

Moreover, inadequate nutrition lowered the effort and efficiency of industrial workers while long periods of time taken to travel to work on the dilapidated public transport system resulted in chronic absenteeism.[126]

The deficiency in labour supply was noted in a research report written in October 1944 on Japanese-run factories in Syonan Municipality, which also contained some interesting findings on the workforce, wages and worker welfare. These enterprises employed 42,841 workers, a quarter of whom were females.[127] As evidence of the strong demand for labour at the time, the report pointed out that an estimated 21,100 additional workers were needed to fill vacancies, especially in the woodworking, metal working and chemical industries. Elsewhere in the economy, at least 6,500 maritime workers, dock labourers and land transport staff were required. The Japanese army and navy also demanded about 40,000 workers. Due to the shortage, labour turnover was relatively high, as shown by a recruitment rate of 10.2 per cent and a discharge rate of 6.1 per cent in 45 factories surveyed. As a remedy, factories were asked to draw up plans to recruit more female workers but, in the meantime, the hiring of temporary workers was resorted to. The research report also recommended that a centralised administrative department for labour management be set up to arbitrate between the competing demands of the military and the private sector.

Japanese establishments were notorious for paying low wages when compared to locally managed factories, a situation worsened by slightly longer daily working hours (8½ hours).[128] While local firms paid an average daily male wage of $5.43, the Japanese factories offered only $1.79, with the highest being $3.00 and the lowest $1.30. The wage disparity was even more glaring in view of the fact that the local factories were mainly light industries. Only workers in the transport sector earned a lower average wage, of $1.38 a day, excepting trishaw drivers who took in $10–20. However, some Japanese firms paid special allowances to workers with families or to cover transport costs and reward good attendance.[129] The factories also provided rice rations ranging from 4 to 12 katis per month, although some of them made these conditional on attendance at work.[130] Local companies mostly supplied 5 katis and sometimes also cigarettes, but a few replaced the rations with three meals a day. A minority of Japanese companies provided housing for staff and a majority used lorries to transport workers to factories.

Food Shortages, Rationing and Malnutrition

Instead of the affluence promised by the Greater East Asia Co-Prosperity Sphere, the Japanese brought misery and privation to millions of Southeast Asians during their three-and-a-half year reign. Famines broke out in Cochin-China and the Dutch East Indies, though Syonan and Malai escaped such a fate.[131] But the collapse of their economies and

---

126 *Chōsabu Reports*, pp. 20–1, 279–82.

127 Ibid., pp. 251, 256, 259–60, 264, 265–7, 293, 299.

128 Ibid., pp. 268–74, 278–9.

129 A handful of factories also paid an overtime daily rate of $2.00.

130 *Chōsabu Reports*, pp. 274–7, 283–5. When priority rations were introduced, an extra 5 and later 9 katis were given.

131 Huff, *World War II and Southeast Asia*, p. 247.

the Allied blockade of Southeast Asia resulted in widespread food shortages and hunger.[132] Consumer goods were also in demand as pre-war stocks ran out. Right from the start, however, Japan had no intention of supplying such goods to Syonan and the rest of the region; what they envisaged was self-sufficiency in the conquered territories and the one-way flow of primary commodities from them.[133] The exception to this dictate was a large shipment of machinery in 1944 as part of the effort to industrialise Syonan. Basic consumer items sent from Japan such as textiles and clothing tapered off to ¥310,000 and ¥568,000 respectively in 1942 from ¥24.9 million and ¥7.1 million in 1937.

Curiously enough, there had been a spurious surfeit of every imaginable type of consumer good in the immediate weeks after the fall of Singapore. These were plundered when the British opened up rice godowns, oil stores and liquor shops to the public to deny Japanese access to them.[134] In those chaotic last days, looting added rice, sugar, flour, milk, canned foods, cigarettes, electrical appliances and sundry goods to the supply as individuals and gangs ransacked business premises, warehouses, shops, medical stores and even residential homes. Abandoned vehicles were stripped of their tyres, batteries and headlamps. The pillage ceased when the Japanese army moved into the city, but not before the looted goods were sold for a song.[135] The wiser ones kept their plunder hidden and waited until the time came to sell at a high price. After the stocks of goods were exhausted, improvisation was the order of the day: the ingenuity of Singaporeans and Malayans produced new ways of making things—noodles from tapioca flour, fishing nets from pineapple fibres, paper from bamboo, medicine from shark oil, greases and lubricants from palm oil, varnishes and paints from rubber seed oil and more.[136]

The principle of self-sufficiency in food was implemented with zeal by Japanese officials, despite its obvious infeasibility for Syonan and Malai. Both were specialised in the production and export of raw commodities and therefore highly dependent on imports of foodstuffs and rice, the staple of the countries' diet.[137] Malaya had obtained more than three-quarters of the rice it consumed from external sources before the war while Singapore was totally reliant on imports, as padi had never been planted in any significant quantity there since the earliest times.[138] The insistence on autarky resulted in the most serious rice shortage since the crisis of 1919–20 as supplies from the three principal producers of Siam, Burma and Cochin-China were progressively reduced after August 1942. The reduction in Burmese rice was especially sharp due to continued warfare in the country while Siam experienced floods and bad harvests.[139] The imports of rice by

---

[132] Chin, *Malaya Upside Down*, p. 34.

[133] Huff and Huff, "The Second World War Occupation of Singapore", pp. 244–7.

[134] Chin, *Malaya Upside Down*, pp. 18–21, 29–32.

[135] Turnbull, *History of Modern Singapore*, p. 207.

[136] Chin, *Malaya Upside Down*, p. 162; Huff and Huff, "The Second World War Occupation of Singapore", p. 250; Turnbull, *History of Modern Singapore*, p. 208; Lee, "Wartime Victuals", p. 24.

[137] Huff and Huff, "The Second World War Occupation of Singapore", pp. 250–1.

[138] In 1940, Malaya imported 646,076 tonnes of rice, 91,243 tonnes of wheat flour and prepared cereals, 36,304 tonnes of pulses and 113,935 tonnes of sugar. L. Nicholls, "The State of Nutrition in Singapore Before, During, and After the Japanese Occupation", *The British Medical Journal* 1, 4548 (1948): 37.

[139] *Chōsabu Reports*, pp. 434–5, 440, 444. A relatively small amount of rice came from Cochin-China.

Mitsubishi Corporation into Syonan fell from 11,000 tonnes per month in late 1942 to 4,400 tonnes in early 1944.

In April 1944, however, the Japanese authorities abruptly reversed their policy and allowed the private import of rice into Syonan from southern Siam.[140] An officially sponsored Syonan Rice Import Association was set up to handle logistical arrangements.[141] The Chinese were only too glad to avail themselves of the opportunity to make windfall profits and were soon building new wooden junks to transport the rice. By the end of July, the membership of the association had risen to 181, comprising mostly Hokkiens and Teochews. As in the past, these traders relied on their close connections with Chinese rice exporters in Bangkok for their supplies. In a matter of four months from April to July 1944, 28,270 tonnes of rice were made available to Syonan's residents. Before that turnaround, smuggling of foodstuffs from nearby areas had helped the city's residents avert starvation. Some rice was conveyed by land over the borders of Siam or from Kedah state in northern Malai and stocks were also brought in from elsewhere in small coastal craft.[142] As rice fetched a high price on the black market compared to the ration price, the availability of these illicit supplies was another reason why regulated imports declined. One of the Karimun Islands became the centre of the smuggling trade in rice with over one hundred Syonan Chinese traders operating from it and making profits of 50 per cent.[143] Increasingly however, rather than cash, the Siamese wanted daily necessities such as clothing, soap and matches in payment for the rice or better still, gold, diamonds, jewellery, American dollars, rubber oil and machinery.[144]

The long tradition of the Chinese keeping market gardens in the rural parts of the island also contributed in no small way. Notwithstanding limited land, the area devoted to this enterprise increased from 1,500 acres in 1938 to 7,000 acres in 1944, with the growing of table vegetables, tapioca and sweet potatoes—promoted as cheap and easily grown substitutes for rice—supplemented by the rearing of chickens and ducks.[145] Japanese administrators supported the effort by organising "grow-your-own-food" campaigns, granting loans to smallholders and giving away seeds for free.[146] School fields were transformed *en masse* into vegetable plots and even the Padang opposite City Hall was planted with root crops![147] The "back-to-the-land" scheme discussed earlier was a related initiative, attracting altogether 35,000 people to become farmers in Geylang

---

140 Huff and Huff, "The Second World War Occupation of Singapore", p. 252; *Chōsabu Reports*, p. 70; *Syonan Shimbun*, 18 Sept. 1944.

141 *Chōsabu Reports*, pp. 35–6, 437, 444–6, 449–51, 454–6.

142 Ibid., pp. 28, 29, 70, 446–8; Nicholls, "The State of Nutrition in Singapore", p. 37.

143 Kratoska, *Japanese Occupation*, pp. 175–6; *Chōsabu Reports*, pp. 34–5.

144 Chin, *Malaya Upside Down*, p. 59; Huff, *World War II and Southeast Asia*, p. 230.

145 Huff and Huff, "The Second World War Occupation of Singapore", pp. 251–2; Chin, *Malaya Upside Down*, p. 55; *Syonan Shimbun*, 25 Sept. 1943, 21 Jan. 1944.

146 Lee, "Wartime Victuals", p. 26; Turnbull, *History of Modern Singapore*, p. 208; *Syonan Shimbun*, 10 July 1942, 7 Aug. 1942, 9 Aug. 1942, 24 June 1943, 11 Aug. 1943, 26 May 1944, 10 June 1944. Apart from the crops named above, the growing of yam, maize and ragi was also encouraged. Chin, *Malaya Upside Down*, p. 46.

147 *Syonan Shimbun*, 15 May 1944, 24 May 1944.

Serai, Yio Chu Kang and Pasir Panjang, among other areas.[148] Except for vegetables, however, these efforts cannot be considered successful as Syonan still had to import large quantities of tapioca, sweet potatoes and fruits from Johor and Negri Sembilan to meet daily consumption needs.[149] These foods reached consumers mostly through the city's street hawkers.

As a consequence of the shortages, black markets for food and consumer goods sprouted up all over Syonan. As usual, these were inseparable from speculative activities and hoarding.[150] Participation in black markets was not confined to greedy and unethical individuals but extended to corrupt Japanese officials and soldiers, rikenyas as well as kumiais, the trade guilds that were avowedly set up to ensure an equitable allocation of commodities to the populace.[151] As soon as a kumiai was formed for a foodstuff or good, the product disappeared into the black market and then reappeared later, only to be sold at an exorbitant price.[152] The authorities turned a blind eye to this malpractice as the kumiais ensured that supplies were first distributed to the military establishment, the *kempeitai* (the dreaded Military Police) and Japanese officials and civilians. Black and grey markets for food, including that smuggled into Syonan, were particularly important for supplementing the meagre rations handed out by the administration.[153] Estimates showed that 30 per cent of the rice consumed was supplied by the black market. The flipside of black markets comprised clandestine markets for gold, jewellery, furniture and anything of value that could be sold to pay for food purchases.[154]

The black markets however had some redeeming features. They allowed coffee shop operators and hawkers who acted as *de facto* retailers of black market food to proliferate in Syonan.[155] Moreover, they offered informal employment to a horde of speculators, profiteers and racketeers, not a few of whom became millionaires.[156] Coupled with information asymmetries, the inherent risk of being caught trading illicitly also spawned an army of runners or brokers who matched buyers to sellers for a commission.[157] Less productive was the new wartime occupation of standing in queues for rationed goods to sell at enhanced prices on black markets, a pastime taken up by those who had no work or a low opportunity cost of time.[158] Perhaps most importantly, black markets enabled those

---

148 *Syonan Shimbun*, 30 July 1942, 24 Sept. 1942, 23 Aug. 1943.

149 *Chōsabu Reports*, pp. 27–8, 405, 422–3. In 1944, 55 tonnes of tapioca and sweet potatoes, 14.5 tonnes of fruit and 0.5 tonnes of other vegetables were imported daily.

150 Turnbull, *History of Modern Singapore*, p. 207; *Syonan Shimbun*, 23 Aug. 1943.

151 Lee, "Wartime Victuals", p. 25; Kratoska, *Japanese Occupation*, pp. 174, 175–6, 177; Chin, *Malaya Upside Down*, pp. 61, 65, 86–7; Akashi, "Japanese Policy", p. 82.

152 *Syonan Shimbun*, 24 Apr. 1942.

153 *Chōsabu Reports*, pp. 29, 330; *Syonan Shimbun*, 30 July 1943. Grey markets refer to transactions by employees of the military and kaishas who sold part of their food rations.

154 Huff and Huff, "The Second World War Occupation of Singapore", p. 253.

155 Kratoska, *Japanese Occupation*, pp. 174, 175; *Chōsabu Reports*, p. 18.

156 Turnbull, *History of Modern Singapore*, pp. 207–8; *Syonan Shimbun*, 15 July 1943.

157 Lee, "Wartime Victuals", pp. 25, 26; Chin, *Malaya Upside Down*, pp. 40–3.

158 *Chōsabu Reports*, p. 17. Among those who stood in queues were former domestic servants. Huff, *World War II and Southeast Asia*, p. 236.

really in need of certain goods such as medicines, tinned milk for babies or railway tickets to procure them—at a price. In a sense, the free-wheeling economy that the British nurtured in Singapore persisted during the Second World War through the opportunities offered by these markets.

Black markets were also the consequence of the inadequate rationing system put in place after the Japanese army occupied the city.[159] Rationing was not new to residents as some foods and petrol had been rationed by the authorities just before the city capitulated.[160] Under the Japanese, the basic objective of rationing as implemented through price and quantity controls was to guarantee a minimum standard of living; it failed however to do this.[161] In a directive issued in late February 1942, the public was notified of the maximum prices at which key foods—rice, meat, poultry, fish, eggs, vegetables, fruits, sugar and salt—could be bought and sold.[162] This was followed by fixed prices for textiles, clothing and apparel in September 1943 and restrictions on their distribution.[163] Sales had to be made through exclusive dealers authorised by the government and existing distributors were forced to surrender their stocks to it at a discount. As shortages became more widespread, even the substitute foods of tapioca and sweet potatoes, as well as a few vegetables and fruits, were rationed in October 1944. Earlier on, coffee beans had been rationed, forcing most coffee shops in the city to close.[164]

Together with price control, a rice ration of 20 katis (12 kg) was issued to each person every month, somewhat short of the pre-war level of consumption, which averaged 36 katis per male, 27 katis per female and 18 katis per child.[165] The sugar allotment was one kati per person per month and the salt ration one-third kati.[166] The meat and fish ration was 2.6 katis for each person.[167] Cloth rations were three yards of fabric and three pieces of clothing a year for a family of eight people.[168] Many other goods were irregularly rationed, for example cigarettes, charcoal and firewood.[169] In November 1942, as stocks became depleted and transport bottlenecks increased, the rice ration was reduced to 17 katis per person each month and early in 1943, to 14 katis with the addition of 3 katis of bread made from sago and tapioca flour to make up for the loss in calories.[170] By then, Malaya as a whole was importing only 34,000 tonnes of rice per month owing to a shortage of shipping

---

159 *Chōsabu Reports*, p. 31.

160 Liew and Wilson, *A History of Money*, pp. 142, 153.

161 Huff, *World War II and Southeast Asia*, pp. 234, 236.

162 *Chōsabu Reports*, p. 29; *Syonan Shimbun*, 27 Feb. 1942, 2 July 1942.

163 Kratoska, *Japanese Occupation*, pp. 198–9; *Syonan Shimbun*, 19 Sept. 1943.

164 Frost and Balasingamchow, *Singapore*, p. 307.

165 Huff and Huff, "The Second World War Occupation of Singapore", pp. 263–4; *Chōsabu Reports*, pp. 346, 359–60, 373, 384; *Syonan Shimbun*, 17 Mar. 1942.

166 *Syonan Shimbun*, 26 Jan. 1943.

167 The priority ration was 5 katis per person.

168 Huff, *World War II and Southeast Asia*, p. A239.

169 *Syonan Shimbun*, 2 June 1943, 13 July 1943. A tax was imposed on locally manufactured cigarettes. *Syonan Shimbun*, 14 Apr. 1944.

170 *Syonan Shimbun*, 15 Nov. 1942, 2 Feb. 1943.

tonnage.[171] At the end of the year, the monthly rice ration was again cut to 12 katis for males, 9 katis for females and 6 katis for each child.[172] Finally in February 1944, the rice rations were slashed to 8, 6 and 4 katis, respectively, supplemented by smaller amounts of tapioca, sweet potatoes and vegetables. From November 1943 onwards however, extra rice was distributed to labourers doing essential or heavy manual work and from October 1944, every male over 20 years old received a monthly ration of 20 cigarettes.[173] Furthermore, the public was allowed to purchase limited amounts of rice at free market prices following the liberalisation of the policy on imports in 1944.[174]

Nevertheless, apart from the rich and middle class, most people could not afford to pay the prices demanded by black marketeers, so they had to live with the meagre food rations. Malnutrition among a large portion of the masses and children was the consequence.[175] Although Japanese planners vigorously promoted the planting of padi in Malai, rice output fell because of the deterioration of drainage and irrigation systems, displacement of the population due to forced labour and the cultivation of a rice variant that was not suited to the country's climatic conditions ("Taiwan-padi").[176] Even if the livestock had been maintained and the fish supply kept up, the per capita calorie intake would have been lower than the pre-war norm of 2,562 calories; given the reduction of livestock, this intake would have fallen below the minimum daily requirement of 2,000–2,400 calories.[177] In fact, the food intake for those on general rations was only 905 calories and even workers who received priority rations obtained fewer than 2,000 calories. The consumption of staple foods, meat, fish, vegetables and fruits fell to between 29 per cent and 59 per cent of their pre-war levels.[178]

During the Syonan years, the natural increase in population was negative because more people died from a lack of medical care.[179] Health services were disrupted as the General Hospital was taken over by the military to treat wounded Japanese soldiers and medicines including quinine and hospital supplies were in short supply.[180] Births too fell from the very high rates of the late thirties.[181] From 59,361 in the four years prior to the occupation, the number of deaths more than doubled to 130,382 during 1942–45. Over half of the deaths were due to beri-beri, which spiked between 1944 and 1945 and included cases of

---

[171] *Chōsabu Reports*, pp. 69, 334, 368, 369–70, 376, 378, 381.

[172] *Syonan Shimbun*, 15 Nov. 1942, 2 Nov. 1943.

[173] *Syonan Shimbun*, 22 Jan. 1944, 16 May 1944, 24 Sept. 1944. The extra rice rations varied from 5 to 11 katis.

[174] *Chōsabu Reports*, pp. 36–7.

[175] Huff and Huff, "The Second World War Occupation of Singapore", p. 266.

[176] Chin, *Malaya Upside Down*, pp. 38, 58.

[177] Nicholls, "The State of Nutrition in Singapore", p. 37; *Syonan Shimbun*, 23 May 1942. The livestock was reduced by at least 40 per cent and the fish supply by possibly more.

[178] *Chōsabu Reports*, pp. 69, 334.

[179] Shimizu and Hirakawa, *Japan and Singapore in the World Economy*, p. 129.

[180] Kratoska, *Japanese Occupation*, p. 195; Huff, *World War II and Southeast Asia*, p. 327; Huff and Huff, "The Second World War Occupation of Singapore", pp. 266–8.

[181] Nicholls, "The State of Nutrition in Singapore", pp. 38–9.

general malnutrition.[182] Cirrhosis of the liver resulting from low-protein diets claimed a small but increasing number of lives while the other deaths were classified mostly as being due to tuberculosis, pneumonia and dysentery.[183] Infant mortality rates also increased as a result of malnutrition of mother or child. At the other end of the age spectrum, deaths among old people increased threefold from the yearly average before the war.

This summary of the state of malnutrition indicates that living standards in Syonan fell drastically as the Japanese occupation went on. Since the quantities of food consumed were below subsistence levels, black markets flourished as people turned to them for additional calories.[184] But while war normally serves as an economic leveller, black markets exacerbated pre-war social inequalities because of the differential access to them by rich and poor.[185] Furthermore, people who worked for the Japanese and received priority rations were better off, though some sold their rations to buy non-food necessities. A household expenditure survey carried out by Japanese researchers in October 1943 also revealed variations between races and occupations in Syonan.[186] The survey was careful to elucidate the diets and consumption patterns of each race, and to focus on low-income groups like farmers, fishermen, plantation workers, coolies, hawkers and rickshaw pullers. These people had always led a precarious existence in Singapore; during the occupation, they represented the minimum standard of living for each of their respective ethnicities. Separate lists of food and clothing budgets included in the survey show that some Chinese substituted sweet potatoes for rice and others consumed beancurd, pork and opium. Malays supplemented their diet with tapioca, sweet potatoes, pepper, belacan and coconuts. Indians ate maize, tapioca, sweet potatoes and ragi as staple foods while using pepper and curry as seasoning. It is telling that none of the survey respondents had been able to buy new clothing since the start of the occupation and were forced to wear old clothes and sarongs.

Actual spending patterns were dictated to a large extent by incomes. Being dependent on farming and fishing for a living, Malays in the fringe areas of Syonan had significantly lower incomes than the other races. The households surveyed earned between $15 and $40 per month and spent this, within their means, solely on food and lamp oil for lighting.[187] Indian rubber plantation coolies were in the same boat, earning 40–45 cents a day, lower than farmers and fishermen and less than before the war. However, the situation might not have been as dire as it appeared since they grew their own food and also received rice, sugar and salt rations from their employers. Indian road construction workers were provided with tenements by the Municipality but had to buy coconut oil for lighting. They spent more than the monthly income derived from their daily wages of 60 cents to $1, about $15 if they worked 25 days a month.[188] Among the

[182] *Syonan Shimbun*, 7 June 1943.

[183] Tapioca and sweet potatoes are almost devoid of protein, so a reliance on them as food sources was a cause of malnutrition. Huff, *World War II and Southeast Asia*, pp. 275–6.

[184] Huff, *World War II and Southeast Asia*, p. 69.

[185] *Chōsabu Reports*, pp. 31, 39, 350.

[186] Ibid., pp. 37–8, 486–506.

[187] Ibid., pp. 506–16. They built their own houses and obtained firewood for fuel from the surrounding countryside.

[188] How they financed their excess spending is unclear.

low-income groups, the Chinese were the best off. On average, their monthly wages were $39, whereas the spending of their families was $72, with the deficit covered by other working members of their households. Rather surprisingly, the hawkers among them received the highest income of $50–70 a month while harbour coolies and rubber factory workers got less. As they lived in the town area, all had to pay house rent ranging from around $3 to $10.

Inflation, Seigniorage and Financial Repression

Following the conquest of Malaya and Singapore by the Japanese Imperial Army, a new currency was introduced as legal tender. Often referred to as "military scrip", it was in fact nothing more than unbacked dollar notes, with the only difference being that they were issued on behalf of the Nippon Government and bore pictures of the banana and other fruit trees instead of the British King's portrait on the obverse.[189] This earned them the appellation "banana notes", an apt enough name when they became valueless in the later stages of the war. At first, only unnumbered 1, 5 and 10 dollar notes as well as subsidiary notes for 1, 5, 10 and 50 cents were printed.[190] Later on, 100 and 1,000 dollar notes were also issued.

The Japanese made the shrewd decision to retain the existing Straits currency and Malayan dollar notes and allow them to be circulated at par value side-by-side with the banana notes.[191] But they did not foresee that their prudent attempts to replace these with military dollars would eventually lead to the uncontrolled printing of money as the cost of financing the war escalated. Rather than depend on seigniorage from the outset, they initially opted for non-inflationary if devious means of raising funds, which helped to reduce the stock of British currency to half of its pre-war level.[192] After that, the old notes disappeared from circulation in accordance with Gresham's Law.[193] Lotteries were launched in both Syonan and Malai although the amount of money collected was relatively small.[194] The first government lottery was held in September 1942 with one million tickets put up for sale at $1 each.[195] Another one, known as Konan Saiken, was started in August 1943 and held regularly every month.[196] To raise more funds and in part as an anti-inflationary measure, savings campaigns were initiated and people were required to put money in the

---

[189] Huff, *World War II and Southeast Asia*, pp. 87–8.

[190] Liew and Wilson, *A History of Money*, pp. 146–7. It came to light later that notes with serial numbers had been printed as part of war preparations and distributed to Japan's invading forces.

[191] Ibid., pp. 143, 147; *Syonan Shimbun*, 30 Oct. 1942. There were about $200 million in Straits and Malayan currency notes in circulation, an amount that was bloated by the wages and bonuses paid by British employers as they departed from Singapore, and by fund withdrawals from banks by the public. Kratoska, *Japanese Occupation*, pp. 211–4; *Syonan Shimbun*, 23 Mar. 1942.

[192] Kratoska, *Japanese Occupation*, p. 214; *Syonan Shimbun*, 19 May 1942, 9 Sept. 1942.

[193] Huff, *World War II and Southeast Asia*, p. 88. The law states that bad money will drive out good money.

[194] Liew and Wilson, *A History of Money*, pp. 148–9; Chin, *Malaya Upside Down*, pp. 52–3.

[195] *Syonan Shimbun*, 29 May 1942, 5 Sept. 1942, 13 Sept. 1942. After deducting the prize monies, the net receipts from this draw were only $700,000. Liew and Wilson, *A History of Money*, p. 148.

[196] *Syonan Shimbun*, 19 Feb. 1943, 9 Apr. 1943, 1 Jan. 1945, 1 June 1945, 16 July 1945. The funds collected were utilised for the relief of the poor and the improvement of sanitary conditions.

Post Office Savings Bank.[197] These postal savings were meant for those who were not well-off and they amounted to $7.7 million. In addition, Japanese officers, civil servants and staff doing menial work had to make monthly contributions to a savings fund.[198] The savings drives, of which there were three in 1944, seemed to have been much more effective in soaking up excess liquidity than the lotteries—if official figures are to be believed—with the amount of fixed deposits attracted in Syonan reaching $281 million in March 1945.[199]

Taxation was also a means to pay for government spending. Unlike the British, the Japanese had no qualms about legalising gambling at the end of 1943 and farming it out.[200] About 300 gambling houses opened and their proceeds were taxed, as were the revenues of amusement parks, brothels, restaurants and coffee shops.[201] Of all the methods used to transfer resources from private hands to the government, the most unscrupulous was the demand for a $50 million "gift" from the Chinese in Syonan and Malai.[202] This was supposed to be for the purpose of paying military administrative expenses but was actually a disguised form of extortion intended to cow the Chinese into submission to Japanese rule and to punish them for their past anti-Japanese activities.[203] In Syonan, the committee formed to raise the money decided to collect $10 million from the public by imposing levies on individuals, properties worth more than $3,000 and company assets, while the remainder was to be contributed by the states in Malai.[204] Despite a claim by the official press that the Chinese were happily making donations to show their loyalty to the Japanese regime, only slightly over half of the scheduled amount was raised and the rest had to be borrowed from the Yokohama Specie Bank after collateral was duly provided.[205] The Chettiars were also targeted by the Japanese and some had their Straits currency confiscated, although they got away with a donation of only $100,000.[206]

As the Japanese suffered one military setback after another in the later part of the war, the need to obtain financing on a larger scale became evident. They threw caution to the wind and turned to the printing presses at will. Seigniorage was the easiest and most convenient method of paying for additional spending but it was also the surest way to engineer hyperinflation.[207] Over the entire occupation period, it was estimated that a total

197 Huff and Huff, "The Second World War Occupation of Singapore", p. 253; *Syonan Shimbun*, 6 May 1944, 30 May 1944, 18 Sept. 1944, 30 Nov. 1944, 13 Feb. 1945.

198 Kratoska, *Japanese Occupation*, pp. 221–2.

199 Chin, *Malaya Upside Down*, pp. 50–2; Liew and Wilson, *A History of Money*, pp. 157–8; *Syonan Shimbun*, 7 Feb. 1944, 25 Oct. 1944, 19 Feb. 1945.

200 Turnbull, *History of Modern Singapore*, p. 208; Huff and Huff, "The Second World War Occupation of Singapore", p. 254.

201 Kratoska, *Japanese Occupation*, pp. 214–5; Chin, *Malaya Upside Down*, pp. 53–4.

202 Liew and Wilson, *A History of Money*, pp. 147–8.

203 Akashi, "Japanese Policy", pp. 70–5; Huff and Huff, "The Second World War Occupation of Singapore", p. 253; Tan, *A Very Short History*, pp. 65–6.

204 Turnbull, *History of Modern Singapore*, p. 203.

205 Chin, *Malaya Upside Down*, pp. 70–3; *Syonan Shimbun*, 16 Apr. 1942.

206 Huff, *World War II and Southeast Asia*, pp. 94–5.

207 Huff, *World War II and Southeast Asia*, pp. 95, 97, 99, 100–5, 108.

of $7–8 billion in currency was printed.[208] The expansion of the money supply together with a worsening of goods shortages led to increases in the prices of goods and a fall in the value of the banana notes.[209] As prices rose, people refrained from holding money and at the same time, the fall in the economy's output reduced transactions and the demand for cash. The amount of seigniorage fell as a result, compelling the Japanese to print ever greater quantities of money and causing inflation to accelerate.[210] In Syonan and Malai as a whole, seigniorage declined from $23.2 million in 1942 to $4.8 million in 1945 as inflation outstripped the pace of money creation. If the authorities had not banned the use of pre-war currencies after the first year of the occupation, the decline would have been worse.

The price level increased by eight times between February 1942 and January 1944 and by March, it was rising at 25 per cent a month, or 1,355 per cent a year at a compound annualised rate (Figure 19).[211] If this could not be labelled as hyperinflation, then the average rate of 86.8 per cent during the last two months of the occupation certainly would. Price increases were across the board and affected all the major categories of consumer spending: from July 1942 to February 1944, food inflation was 550 per cent, household necessities 960 per cent and clothing 308 per cent.[212] Transport charges increased nearly sixfold and fuel and water costs also rose, albeit by less.[213] Rents more than doubled as property values inflated. Overall, the cost of living increased by six times; from February 1944 to May 1945, it went up by another nine times. Some representative prices can give a sense of what hyperinflation meant in practice.[214] White rice from Siam that was retailed at 6 cents a kati in December 1941 was priced at $75 in August 1945. Pork went from 48 cents a kati to $280 while an egg that cost 3 cents fetched a price of $35. The sugar price jumped from 8 cents a kati to $120.[215] The increases in the prices of goods were even more overwhelming, with a bottle of brandy selling for $26,000 and a tin of fifty cigarettes for $2,500. Basic necessities like a bar of soap costing only 12 cents before the war could only be had for $35 and an aspirin pill for $8. A cloth shirt worth $1.50 could now be exchanged for $1,000 and leather shoes were offered for sale at $2,500 a pair.

In all cases, the price rises were the combined outcomes of shortages, black markets and the printing of money, the respective individual influences of which are impossible to disentangle. Moreover, every time Japanese forces were defeated, prices jumped: "Every Allied victory...and every visit of B-29s over Malaya, caused spurts of prices in

[208] Liew and Wilson, *A History of Money*, p. 147. A more conservative estimate was $4 billion. H.R. Hone, *Report on the British Military Administration of Malaya, September, 1945, to March, 1946* (Singapore, 1946), p. 105.

[209] Kratoska, *Japanese Occupation*, p. 218.

[210] Huff and Huff, "The Second World War Occupation of Singapore", p. 256.

[211] Huff, *World War II and Southeast Asia*, pp. 99–100.

[212] *Chōsabu Reports*, p. 357; *Syonan Shimbun*, 27 July 1943.

[213] Kratoska, *Japanese Occupation*, pp. 206–7.

[214] Chin, *Malaya Upside Down*, pp. 192–5. The prices quoted were for the black markets in Ipoh, a relatively large town in Malai. Prices were higher in Syonan although the trends over time should be similar.

[215] Tan, *A Very Short History*, p. 66.

foodstuffs".[216] People therefore tried to get rid of banana money as soon as they received it by buying goods and, if they were wealthy, properties.[217] As a consequence, shophouses that used to cost $5,000 to $6,000 sold for $160,000 to $250,000. Barter transactions became increasingly common.[218] The groups in the Syonan population that were the worst hit by inflation were the poor and those on fixed incomes such as government servants and pensioners.[219]

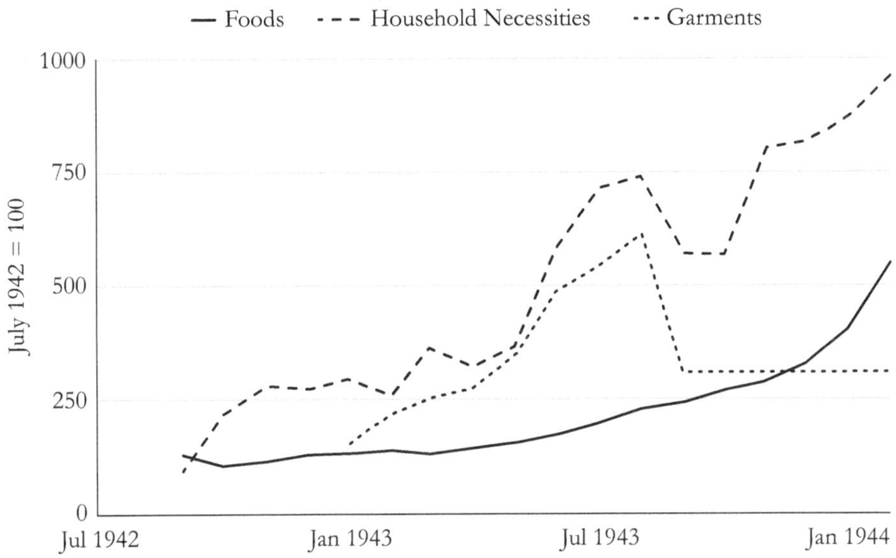

Figure 19. Price Indices in Syonan, July 1942–February 1944
Source: *Chōsabu Reports*, p. 357.

The Japanese appeared not to have recognised that the main cause of inflation was money creation and referred to it only obliquely.[220] They argued that price increases occurred at different rates for individual commodities rather than in a generalised manner. The reasons given for inflation were instead the shortages arising from insufficient local production and a lack of transport. Hoarding of stocks by Chinese merchants and black marketeers was also blamed. At the same time, several measures were proposed to forestall social disorder.[221] First, they called for more unused land to be brought under cultivation to grow food crops. Second, efficient use had to be made of transport facilities, particularly oxcarts. Third, measures were required to absorb the excess currency held by merchants and rich people. The policy of allowing Chinese traders to import rice was also viewed as necessary. However, the move by the military administration in May 1944 to lower the black market prices of meat, fish and vegetables by abolishing official prices had only

216 Chin, *Malaya Upside Down*, pp. 43–4, 45; *Syonan Shimbun*, 28 Jan. 1945.

217 Huff and Huff, "The Second World War Occupation of Singapore", pp. 254, 256.

218 Liew and Wilson, *A History of Money*, p. 157.

219 Kratoska, *Japanese Occupation*, p. 204.

220 *Chōsabu Reports*, pp. 27–8, 327–9, 330.

221 Ibid., pp. 27, 73, 331–4, 336, 339, 348.

a temporary effect.[222] The administration was forced to open public canteens across the island to cater to office and factory workers.

Along with dirigiste economic policies, the Japanese administration kept a tight control over the financial system. The three great British banks—the Hong Kong and Shanghai Bank, the Chartered Bank of India, Australia and China and the Mercantile Bank of India—were closed and eventually liquidated.[223] Other Western banks, the Bank of China, the Bank of Canton and the Kwangtung Provincial Bank were similarly treated.[224] Before that transpired however, these banks were canny enough to transfer all their assets and Straits currency to their headquarters in London or elsewhere. The postal savings banks in Syonan and Malai emptied their vaults and invested most of their deposits and assets in the London financial markets.[225] The colonial government had also taken financial precautions before the surrender: bearer bonds were called in, currency stocks were burnt or shipped to India and coins were dumped into the sea.[226] Nonetheless, Japanese divers managed to recover approximately one million dollars.[227]

Five local Chinese banks—Lee Wah, Ban Hin Lee, Sze Hai Tong, United Chinese and Oversea-Chinese—were permitted to reopen in April 1942, followed later by the China and Southern Bank and Kwong Yik Bank.[228] In addition, three Indian banks also resumed operations.[229] Given the Japanese stranglehold on the economy, these banks transacted little business apart from accepting deposits.[230] As for Japanese banks, the Yokohama Specie Bank was appointed as the cash custodian of the Syonan military administration, while the much smaller Bank of Taiwan served the navy and Japanese clients.[231] A third Japanese bank was established in March 1942 with capital of ¥100 million and named Nanpo Kaihatsu Kinko or Southern Regions Development Bank, in accordance with its main function of providing long-term development loans and special loans to Japanese firms.[232] It issued banknotes on behalf of the military and at the beginning of 1943 was made the administration's banker, at which point it also started to give short-term loans to Japanese companies.

At the end of August 1943, the total deposits lodged at the commercial banks amounted to $164 million; Japanese banks had the largest deposit base of $79 million, followed by

---

222 *Syonan Shimbun*, 28 Oct. 1944, 31 Oct. 1944.

223 Huff, *World War II and Southeast Asia*, p. 86.

224 Shimizu and Hirakawa, *Japan and Singapore in the World Economy*, pp. 116–7; *Syonan Shimbun*, 18 Mar. 1943.

225 Liew and Wilson, *A History of Money*, pp. 139–40; *The Straits Times*, 15 Jan. 1942.

226 Kratoska, *Japanese Occupation*, p. 212.

227 *Syonan Shimbun*, 15 May 1942.

228 *Syonan Shimbun*, 30 Apr. 1942, 24 Nov. 1942.

229 *Syonan Shimbun*, 6 Sept. 1942.

230 Huff, *World War II and Southeast Asia*, pp. 86, 88; Liew and Wilson, *A History of Money*, pp. 149–50.

231 Shimizu and Hirakawa, *Japan and Singapore in the World Economy*, pp. 117–8; Kratoska, *Japanese Occupation*, pp. 219–21. The Yokohama Specie Bank subsequently opened twelve offices in Malai.

232 *Syonan Shimbun*, 8 June 1942, 30 June 1942, 1 Jan. 1943. The bank also served as the agent for the Bank of Japan and had branches in Batavia and Manila.

Chinese banks at $72 million and Indian banks at $13 million.[233] These deposits were received after the Chinese and Indian banks were authorised to gradually release to former depositors funds that were initially blocked.[234] The interest rate on fixed deposits was 3 per cent per annum and that on savings deposits, 2 per cent. The subsidiary status of the Chinese banks was reflected in a $10 million loan extended by the two Japanese commercial banks to enable them to provide overdrafts backed by securities.[235] In all, loans made by the banks were $237 million, with most of them going to industrial enterprises.[236] About $80 million of this amount took the form of long-term loans issued by the Nanpo Kaihatsu Kinko for the exploitation of the region's natural resources and for financing industrial development. The savings deposits belonging to 27,237 account holders at the Post Office Savings Bank in Syonan declined to slightly over $1 million in August 1944.[237] The interest rate offered on these deposits by the bank was 3 per cent per annum, higher than the rest, although limits were imposed on withdrawals.[238] Another bank set up by the Japanese administration in September 1942 for the middle class and the poor was the People's Bank, partly with the intention of supplanting moneylenders and pawnbrokers.[239] By the time of its first anniversary, it had lent $91,660 at an interest rate of 5 per cent per annum to residents who wanted to refurbish damaged homes, those looking to start small businesses and farmers.[240] These loans, like the others made by the commercial banks in Syonan, were not backed by reserves at a central bank or any other institution. They were underwritten only by deposits, which had increased to $407 million at the end of February 1945.[241]

A further aspect of financial repression during the period of Japanese rule was in fact an inherited legacy from the British. When the Second World War started in Europe in 1939, foreign exchange controls were instituted in Singapore.[242] Anyone wishing to send more than $100 abroad had to state the reason and the purchase of $500 or more had to be sanctioned by the authorities. Moreover, overseas remittances were limited to $50 per person.[243] The Japanese maintained the controls and added more restrictions.[244] In January 1942, the decision had already been that the military notes would be valued at par

[233] *Syonan Shimbun*, 7 Oct. 1943. Before the war, total deposits in the banking system were $450 million. Kratoska, *Japanese Occupation*, p. 221.

[234] Liew and Wilson, *A History of Money*, pp. 149–50; *Syonan Shimbun*, 10 Nov. 1942, 29 Nov. 1942, 19 July 1943. Depositors of liquidated banks also received a small refund in 1944. Kratoska, *Japanese Occupation*, pp. 224–5.

[235] Kratoska, *Japanese Occupation*, p. 220; *Syonan Shimbun*, 15 May 1942.

[236] *Syonan Shimbun*, 19 Oct. 1943.

[237] Kratoska, *Japanese Occupation*, pp. 225–6; *Syonan Shimbun*, 13 May 1944.

[238] *Syonan Shimbun*, 12 Dec. 1942, 15 Dec. 1942, 21 Oct. 1944. The initial amount that could be withdrawn was $100, followed by $50 at intervals of six months.

[239] Kratoska, *Japanese Occupation*, pp. 226–7; *Syonan Shimbun*, 30 July 1942, 20 Aug. 1943.

[240] Liew and Wilson, *A History of Money*, pp. 150–1; *Syonan Shimbun*, 28 Aug. 1942, 2 Sept. 1942.

[241] Kratoska, *Japanese Occupation*, p. 224.

[242] Liew and Wilson, *A History of Money*, p. 135.

[243] *Syonan Shimbun*, 12 Dec. 1942.

[244] *Syonan Shimbun*, 9 July 1942.

not only with the Straits dollar, but also with the Japanese yen.[245] Thus, the yen had been deliberately overvalued, since in 1937 ¥100 exchanged for only $54.55, so that it could be used to pay more cheaply for commodities from Southeast Asia.[246] To facilitate these purchases and create a *de facto* monetary union within the Greater East Asia Co-Prosperity Sphere, it was declared that the Japanese military dollar would also be interchangeable with the Netherlands Indies guilder on a one-to-one basis. This was accompanied by regulations and the establishment of clearing houses to govern the conversion of currencies between Syonan (and Malai) and Sumatra for trade, travel and remittance purposes.[247] The amount of currency that travellers in the occupied territories could carry with them was however restricted. In late 1942, money remittances from Syonan to Hong Kong and Shanghai were enabled through the newly established Overseas Chinese Commercial and Industrial Bank but were limited in the case of Hong Kong to $50 per month for each family.[248] In the following year, Malai, Sumatra, Java, North Borneo, the Philippines, Siam, Burma and other destinations in China were added.[249] The same year saw 34 private remittance houses restart their businesses.[250]

The British Military Administration

After the Japanese surrender to the Allied forces in August 1945, the British returned to Singapore to find the population reeling from the deleterious effects of the occupation. While the British were drawing up grand schemes for the political reorganisation of Singapore and Malaya even before the war ended, most ordinary people were more concerned about the shortage of food and getting back to a normal life.[251] In a repetition of what had happened in the early days after Singapore fell, looting took place before the British arrived and there was a sudden temporary abundance of commodities as the Japanese released hoarded stocks. But the continued scarcity of food soon sent prices soaring again as controls collapsed.[252]

Worse, corruption and black markets persisted, if with a different cast of actors in the British Military Administration (BMA), derisively labelled the "Black Market Administration".[253] As in other British colonies, the BMA served as an interim government to ease the transition to civilian rule and it governed Singapore and Malaya only for a short time, from September 1945 to April 1946. It was headed by a Chief Civil Affairs Officer

---

[245] Shimizu and Hirakawa, *Japan and Singapore in the World Economy*, p. 116.

[246] Huff, *World War II and Southeast Asia*, p. 85; Liew and Wilson, *A History of Money*, pp. 151–2.

[247] *Syonan Shimbun*, 25 Sept. 1942, 20 Oct. 1942.

[248] *Syonan Shimbun*, 13 Oct.1942, 11 Dec. 1942.

[249] *Syonan Shimbun*, 11 Mar. 1943, 29 Mar. 1943, 2 Apr. 1943, 14 Apr. 1943, 27 Sept. 1943. North Borneo included Sarawak and British North Borneo.

[250] *Syonan Shimbun*, 28 Aug. 1943.

[251] Turnbull, *History of Modern Singapore*, pp. 220–1, 225–6, 228–9; M. Rudner, "Organization of the British Military Administration in Malaya, 1946–48", *Journal of Southeast Asian History* 9, 1 (1968): 95–6.

[252] Frost and Balasingamchow, *Singapore*, p. 325.

[253] Ibid., pp. 326–7.

and his deputy, who had 274 officers under them in departments responsible for finance, trade and industry, supplies, public works, labour and the police force, to mention only a few key areas.[254] Since these officers had almost total control of supplies and resources, they exploited their position by requesting kickbacks from local businessmen and black market dealers. An Advisory Council made up of 17 nominated representatives from the various communities was set up to voice local interests, but it ended up criticising the BMA's management.[255]

The BMA provided jobs for about 50,000 labourers each month in late 1945 and doubled that in early 1946. It also took on the unenviable tasks of getting the market economy to function again and providing relief supplies to the population.[256] In this it did not fully succeed, in part because of war damage from Allied bombing and the disruption of production facilities.[257] To some extent, the failures of the BMA arose because men without administrative experience or knowledge of the region were appointed to staff it, since the seasoned personnel who were interned by the Japanese had been sent home on recuperative leave.[258] The more pertinent reason however was the delegation of economic management to extra-governmental agencies, which offered scope for inefficiencies and corruption. For example, the vital task of distributing rice supplies was mismanaged because it was handed over to a Special Commissioner while oversight of the rubber industry was assigned to a Buying Unit.

As wartime conditions prevailed at the time of liberation, it is to be expected that the basic issues calling for the immediate attention of the BMA were the same as those with which the Japanese had had to grapple. Apart from rice, domestic distribution of foodstuffs was entrusted to selected British firms, leading to discrimination against Chinese entrepreneurs and supplies being channelled into black markets.[259] In the same vein, several leading companies from the pre-war days were favoured in the distribution of relief goods like clothing, footwear, soap and medical supplies.[260] The result was profiteering, continued inflation and an inequitable allocation of goods to consumers.[261] While the task of actually delivering these goods was performed by the Supplies Department on a Pan-Malayan basis, from the very beginning it was compromised by a lack of staff and transport.[262] Ration cards and application forms for rice, salt, sugar, flour and milk were also not printed in time, forcing the BMA to reuse the Japanese versions.[263] The first thing

---

254 Turnbull, *History of Modern Singapore*, p. 228; Rudner, "Organization of the British Military Administration", pp. 97–100; Hone, *Report on the British Military Administration*, pp. 6, 10, 86.

255 F.S.V. Donnison, *British Military Administration in the Far East 1943–46* (London, 1956), pp. 160, 163.

256 Rudner, "Organization of the British Military Administration", pp. 96, 101–3, 104–5.

257 Turnbull, *History of Modern Singapore*, pp. 228, 229–30.

258 *The Straits Times*, 23 Oct. 1945.

259 Rudner, "Organization of the British Military Administration", pp. 102, 105, 107–8.

260 Hone, *Report on the British Military Administration*, pp. 12–14, 41–4.

261 Liew and Wilson, *A History of Money*, pp. 172–3; *Straits Chronicle*, 3 Oct. 1945.

262 Donnison, *British Military Administration in the Far East*, pp. 156–7.

263 Petrol was also rationed out to people who were engaged by sponsored industries or who were performing essential services. *Malaya Tribune*, 1 Nov. 1945.

it did was to top up the inadequate quantities given by the Japanese. During the month of September 1945, an additional rice ration of 2½ katis, two-thirds kati of salt and 6 tahils of sugar were provided free of charge.[264] Price ceilings were reimposed on the rationed foods in the following month but as stocks improved in 1946, they were progressively lowered.[265] In the meantime, the administration subsidised rice imports and when this failed to keep prices down, it temporarily increased the wages of all employees earning $100 or less per month from their pre-occupation levels.[266] Permanent government servants and those with over ten years of service also received rehabilitation grants of three months' salary.[267]

The BMA had other achievements to show for the seven months it existed. The port of Singapore was handed back to civilian control under the Harbour Board.[268] However, the public utilities and essential engineering services were found to be in a neglected state and buildings and warehouses had been damaged by Allied bombing. The BMA had almost all services running again by March 1946, a remarkable achievement in view of the slow delivery of key machinery. In particular, water, electricity and gas supplies were restored to pre-war norms and the charges for them reduced to one third of the rates prevailing then.[269] Fortunately, the roads and bridges were in good condition, although maintenance and repair work still had to be carried out. In contrast, the condition of the police force was dismal: officers were lowly paid, corrupt and untrained, equipment was damaged and there was a lack of working vehicles.[270] The Sikhs could not be re-employed due to their collaboration with the Japanese during the war and some detectives were similarly tainted. The situation was slowly relieved only with the arrival of more officers, helped by a recruitment drive.[271]

There was not a need to do anything about the commercial system which functioned much as during the occupation.[272] Private traders and dealers had concealed stocks of consumer goods from the Japanese and these together with new imports were put on the free market for sale. Local industry was kickstarted by eight prominent firms that were given priority in obtaining supplies and, after a slow start, the light industries mainly owned by the Chinese were producing import substitutes to full capacity.[273] On the other hand, the machinery and equipment at Japanese factories could not be utilised as they were geared mostly to war production; whatever was usable was sold to suitable buyers. The wooden vessels built during the occupation turned out to be useful in reviving Singapore's

[264] *The Straits Times*, 10 Sept. 1945, 17 Sept. 1945.

[265] Liew and Wilson, *A History of Money*, p. 172.

[266] *Malaya Tribune*, 17 Oct. 1945, 12 Dec. 1945; *Straits Chronicle*, 13 Dec. 1945.

[267] *The Straits Times*, 20 Sept. 1945.

[268] Hone, *Report on the British Military Administration*, pp. 85, 87–8, 96–8.

[269] *The Straits Times*, 2 Oct. 1945.

[270] Turnbull, *History of Modern Singapore*, p. 229.

[271] Donnison, *British Military Administration in the Far East*, p. 161.

[272] Hone, *Report on the British Military Administration*, pp. 108–10.

[273] The eight companies were Malayan Collieries, United Engineers, Hume Pipe Company, Cold Storage, Wearne/Borneo Motors, Fraser & Neave, Singapore Traction Company and Far Eastern Oxygen Company.

trade in foodstuffs with the neighbouring islands.[274] The BMA helped the process along by provisioning additional vessels and in some cases making cash loans.[275] Trade with the West and India was still held back by shipping difficulties and controls imposed by several countries, but in January 1946 produce started to flow from Australia again. The export of commodities was delayed by a lack of staff in the merchant houses, as the available manpower had been seconded to the BMA.

Socio-economic rehabilitation work proved to be more challenging. In healthcare, the population was seriously undernourished, malaria and beri-beri were rampant and tuberculosis had spread unchecked as preventive health services were almost completely neglected by the Japanese.[276] During the re-occupation period, the General Hospital continued to be used by military patients although Tan Tock Seng Hospital, Kandang Kerbau Hospital and Middleton Hospital were immediately filled to capacity. Clinics, welfare centres to dispense medical treatment and advice, and a travelling dispensary were established.[277] Public health services were resumed with special attention paid to cleansing, scavenging, hygiene, sanitation and anti-malarial work. The sewerage system required a complete overhaul, which was attended to.[278] Although hamstrung by an inadequate supply of drugs and equipment, the medical authorities did much to improve the dire conditions prevailing at the end of the war. Milk feeds were given to infants and soup meals to children of preschool age; in the schools, free meals were provided to students. As a result, the number of deaths fell dramatically to reach pre-war figures in the first quarter of 1946.[279]

A similarly uphill task was faced by the BMA in restarting schools, which had been converted to military and other uses by the Japanese. It had to reinstate the old British curriculum that had been suppressed during the war in favour of the learning of the Japanese language and the inculcation of Japanese values.[280] When the schools reopened, they were overwhelmed by the great demand from both new students and overaged children who had not attended school in previous years or whose education had been interrupted by the war. In October 1945, 61 English government and government-aided schools as well as Malay and Chinese schools began classes and by March the following year, enrolment had increased to 62,000, compared with 73,000 before the war.[281] The King Edward VII College of Medicine took back former students and Raffles College admitted a new intake; these two institutions merged in 1949 to form the University of Malaya.[282]

This review of the aftermath of war would be incomplete without a discussion of the British decision to demonetise the Japanese banana notes. At the outset of re-occupation,

---

274 *The Straits Times*, 5 Oct. 1945, 8 Oct. 1945.

275 *The Straits Times*, 7 Oct. 1945.

276 Hone, *Report on the British Military Administration*, pp. 91–3; Tan, "Health and Welfare", p. 345.

277 *The Straits Times*, 26 Sept. 1945.

278 Donnison, *British Military Administration in the Far East*, p. 161.

279 Nicholls, "The State of Nutrition in Singapore", p. 38.

280 Hone, *Report on the British Military Administration*, pp. 102–3.

281 *The Straits Times*, 24 Sept. 1945.

282 Turnbull, *History of Modern Singapore*, pp. 230, 242–3; *The Singapore Free Press*, 3 May 1948.

these notes were declared valueless and the BMA proceeded to introduce a new issue of British currency backed by sterling in London.[283] The notes had actually been printed before the war but not circulated and a small amount of pre-war currency was also in the hands of the public.[284] All outstanding debts incurred before and during the war were proclaimed void. Needless to say, this destruction of the monetary system caused considerable confusion, chaos and hardship as savings were wiped out, even though the policy had been announced in air-dropped pamphlets before the war ended. The administration mitigated the situation through various means of putting the new currency into circulation: for instance, payment for the goods and services required by the forces was quickly made in the new notes.[285] The same was done with the wages of workers, rehabilitation grants, pay arrears and pensions. By the end of the BMA's tenure, close to $179 million had been injected into the economy and the amount of currency in circulation had increased to $422 million.[286] To facilitate the distribution of the new notes, the local banks in Singapore were allowed to reopen their doors within a fortnight of the return of the British so long as they were solvent and after enemy assets were blocked. Some were given loans by the BMA with property and government securities as collateral.[287] The British and European banks reopened slightly later, at the start of September 1945. Despite the moratorium on debt, they allowed depositors to withdraw their pre-occupation balances.[288] This was not the case with the Chinese and Indian banks, the earlier deposits into which were not recognised even if withdrawals in excess of deposits were. The Post Office Savings Bank adopted the same policy, which was a source of grievance to its customers.[289]

As the end of military rule approached, the BMA began to prepare for the handover to a civilian government. In all, 36 departments covering a whole range of government responsibilities were ready to be transferred to form the nucleus of the incoming administration, although some were organised on a Pan-Malayan basis and had to be split.[290] An adequate distribution machinery for supplies had also been built up. Meanwhile, the British government took the political decision to merge the Federated and Unfederated Malay States, Penang and Melaka into a Malayan Union. Against the opposition of interested observers, Singapore was to be a separate entity ruled directly by Britain.[291] The handover was effected on the first day of April 1946 and two days later, a new Governor of the Colony of Singapore was sworn in.

---

283 Hone, *Report on the British Military Administration*, pp. 105–6; Liew and Wilson, *A History of Money*, pp. 164–7; *The Straits Times*, 10 Sept. 1945.

284 Donnison, *British Military Administration in the Far East*, pp. 220, 222, 223, 225. The pre-war currency was demonetised in 1948. P.H. Kratoska, "Banana Money: Consequences of the Demonetization of Wartime Japanese Currency in British Malaya", *Journal of Southeast Asian Studies* 23, 2 (1992): 330, 331.

285 *The Straits Times*, 11 Sept. 1945.

286 Drake, "The Evolution of Money", pp. 13–14.

287 Kratoska, "Banana Money", pp. 333, 336–7.

288 The moratorium was finally removed in 1949.

289 Liew and Wilson, *A History of Money*, pp. 167–8.

290 Donnison, *British Military Administration in the Far East*, pp. 168–9.

291 Turnbull, *History of Modern Singapore*, pp. 226–8.

Chapter 10 Post-War Industrialisation, 1947–65

The legacies of the Second World War remained in Singapore until the late 1940s, when price controls and rationing were finally relaxed. It was business as usual again as the staple and entrepôt trades revived. But these trades were on the decline and Singapore as a separate colony on its own had to embark on modern economic growth based on industrialisation. However, the colonial export economy had not developed an economic infrastructure that was conducive to the process. Moreover, the city was confronted with socio-economic and political problems that required urgent attention. Unemployment and a lack of housing were exploited by leftists to create labour unrest and strikes, stymying efforts to industrialise. An attempt to merge with Malaya failed, leaving Singapore with a bleak and uncertain economic future.

The End of the Staple Trade

The staple trade had served Singapore well for more than 70 years. But as with all industries, there came a time when it was superseded because of the exhaustion of resources, new sources of supply and technological progress. So it was with tin and rubber in Malaya. Tin mining had started to decline when surface deposits were exhausted in the early part of the 20th century. With the phasing out of open cast mining, employment in the industry peaked in 1913 and fell continuously thereafter.[1] Annual output stabilised at about 500,000 tonnes in spite of the use of tin dredges to mine deeper deposits and Bolivia emerged as a rival producer.[2] Rubber production in estates reached a high in 1949 and then fell in the 1950s, though employment started to decline only in the 1960s.

Initially however, a worldwide recovery in the demand for tin and rubber after the war brought about increases in prices and output levels.[3] The rebound in rubber production was more rapid than in tin; it surpassed the 1940 level of output by 1947 whereas tin output reached two-thirds of its earlier level only in 1949.[4] More damage had been inflicted on the Malayan tin industry during the war and the delivery of new mining equipment from

---

[1] Jomo, *A Question of Class*, pp. 176, 181–2.

[2] Lim, *Economic Development of Modern Malaya*, pp. 56–7, Appendix 4.3, pp. 328–9; Yip, *The Development of the Tin Mining Industry*, Appendix 1, pp. 392–3.

[3] *The Straits Times*, 30 Mar. 1947; *The Singapore Free Press*, 31 Dec. 1947, 3 Apr. 1948.

[4] Drabble, *Economic History of Malaysia*, pp. 155–6.

Britain was also delayed.[5] This partly explains the slow recovery in Singapore's per capita GDP—in 1960, the level was still below that in 1939 although this was to some extent also caused by the rapid population growth resulting from the baby boom of the 1950s.[6] Nonetheless, the Korean War of 1950–53 resulted in a temporary upswing in the rubber industry.[7] Estate production increased by 10 per cent from the first to the second half of 1950 and smallholders raised their output by 25 per cent.[8] Thereafter however, the global consumption of natural rubber went on a secular decline as countries increasingly switched to synthetic rubber as a substitute.[9] The United States had been spurred to develop a synthetic rubber industry because of shortages during the war and by 1950, the new industry was meeting over two-fifths of the country's rubber demand.[10] As a result, Malaya's export markets became more diversified, with lower shares for the United States and Britain and higher shares for smaller consuming countries such as those in Europe where automobile and tyre production expanded.[11]

Being still highly dependent on staple commodities, Singapore's trade was affected by these developments. Moreover, its nationalistic neighbours wanted to bypass the port and establish direct maritime links with Western markets.[12] Still, overall exports continued to grow in the 1950s, albeit at a slower pace than before the war and alongside fluctuations in export earnings caused mainly by volatile rubber prices.[13] Rubber was the major commodity in the category of food and primary products and it accounted for more than half of total exports. Consequently, trade fluctuations corresponded to the ups and downs in the rubber industry, with further cycles after the Korean War occurring in 1955–56 and 1959–60. More than half of the rubber imports came from non-Malayan territories; of these, Indonesia was the biggest supplier and in 1953 became Singapore's main source of imports.[14] A significant portion of the wet rubber (and tropical produce) from this country was smuggled by Chinese middlemen into the island in exchange for manufactured products because of restrictions imposed by the Indonesian government and

---

[5] Lim, *Economic Development of Modern Malaya*, pp. 61, 86–7, 90, 322, 323; *The Singapore Free Press*, 10 Jan. 1948.

[6] Maddison Project database, Version 2020.

[7] *Singapore Standard*, 23 July 1950; *The Singapore Free Press*, 30 Dec. 1950. The United States was also adding to its strategic stockpile. Yip, *The Development of the Tin Mining Industry*, pp. 309–10.

[8] P. Meek, "Malaya: A Study of Governmental Response to the Korean War Boom", in *Readings in Malayan Economics*, ed. T.H. Silcock (Singapore: Eastern Universities Press, 1961), pp. 209–11.

[9] *The Straits Budget*, 5 July 1956, 13 May 1959.

[10] Lim, *Economic Development of Modern Malaya*, pp. 84–5, 87, 93–4, Appendix 4.2, p. 327; *The Singapore Free Press*, 18 May 1948; *The Straits Budget*, 22 Oct. 1953.

[11] Huff, *The Economic Growth of Singapore*, p. 281.

[12] *10 Years that Shaped a Nation*, p. 66.

[13] Huff, *The Economic Growth of Singapore*, pp. 278–81, 286–7, Appendix Table A.1, pp. 372–7; United Nations Commission for Asia and the Far East, "Export Instability in the Primary Exporting Countries", in *Readings in Malayan Economics*, ed. Silcock, pp. 119–20.

[14] Cheng Siok Hwa, "Economic Change in Singapore, 1945–1977", *Southeast Asian Journal of Social Science* 7, 1/2 (1979): 85.

low official export prices.[15] North Borneo and Sarawak were the other sources.[16] Indonesia's rubber production had increased substantially from the pre-war period, stimulated by high world prices and the absence of international restriction schemes. Furthermore, a larger proportion of the production—particularly smallholder output—was sent to Singapore for remilling prior to 1955; in that year, the amount was cut by more than half due to the establishment of new mills in Indonesia. The decline of the staple trade in rubber was therefore also due to the loss of the processing industry in Singapore.

There was great divergence in the fortunes of other export commodities in the fifties. Singapore's exports of tin hardly grew over the decade.[17] On the contrary, when the STC (Straits Trading Company) transferred all its operations to enlarged smelters in Penang in 1959, tin exports fell from an average of 25,000 tonnes in the preceding eight years to a mere 667 tonnes, after which the trade faded away in the late sixties.[18] Petroleum exports however continued to expand throughout the 1950s and 1960s, especially after the first oil refinery opened in Singapore in 1960. Palm oil exports to Britain and Western Europe grew tremendously in value in response to the demand for vegetable oils although in volume terms, they did not increase until the late 1960s.[19] This relatively new industry dated from the 1930s as the result of an attempt by the agency houses to diversify away from rubber, since palm oil earned a return of over 20 per cent on capital.[20] Like rubber, the initial cost of starting plantations in Malaya was met by the flotation of new companies; the estates were therefore predominantly owned by Europeans. While in 1939, the land area devoted to palm oil had been 76,000 acres, about half of which was in Johor, by the end of 1954, it had grown to over 109,000 acres. The expansion was in part stimulated by the provision of bulk shipment facilities at Singapore's port and the construction of specialised vessels by the SSC (Straits Steamship Company) to transport the palm oil.[21] Nevertheless, the rise of the palm oil industry could not compensate sufficiently for the decline of the "sunset" tin and rubber industries.

Following the structural changes experienced in the 1930s, the trade in Straits produce diminished in volume after the Second World War.[22] However, the rice business revived and reverted to Chinese traders in the late 1950s, who re-established their connections with producers in Siam and Burma. Foodstuffs like condensed milk, canned fish, beverages and cigarettes, and manufactured goods such as textiles and machinery continued to thrive in the fifties as re-export demand from the region grew, notwithstanding the efforts to

---

[15] The produce was more or less the same as that traded before the war, namely, pepper, copra, sago and coffee.

[16] *Annual Report of the Division of Commerce and Industry 1959*, p. 5.

[17] Huff, *The Economic Growth of Singapore*, Appendix Table A.2, pp. 378–83.

[18] *Annual Report of the Division of Commerce and Industry 1959*, p. 7.

[19] Huff, *The Economic Growth of Singapore*, pp. 76–7, 148, 188–9, Appendix Table A.1, pp. 372–7, Appendix Table A.2, pp. 378–83; Lim, *Economic Development of Modern Malaya*, pp. 130–2, 133–5; *The Straits Times*, 28 Apr. 1959. Palm oil is also used in making soap.

[20] Allen and Donnithorne, *Western Enterprise in Indonesia and Malaya*, pp. 54–5, 142–5.

[21] Tregonning, *Home Port Singapore*, pp. 83–4.

[22] Cheng, "Economic Change in Singapore", p. 82.

by-pass Singapore through direct trade with the developed countries.[23] The most vibrant trade in manufactures was that of textiles made in the United Kingdom, which were sent to Malaya and, owing to import restrictions, to a lesser extent Indonesia.[24] The dominance of English cloth could be attributed to quotas on imports from Japan into these countries and a ban on textile exports imposed by the Indian government.[25] Machinery, equipment and electrical appliances from West Germany, Japan and the United States also featured prominently in the redistribution trade. In spite of war memories and textiles quotas, Japanese enterprise was resuscitated in Singapore, backed by the government-sponsored Japan External Trade Organization (JETRO).

Labour Unrest and Strikes

When the Second World War ended, Singapore was inundated by migrants and refugees from Peninsula Malaya who came to the city in search of jobs.[26] Given the stricter immigration rules put in place since the 1930s, inward migration from British Malaya rather than the traditional sources of China and India accounted for a net migration gain.[27] Moreover, the birth rate was high, which led to a ballooning of the population. With the settling down of local Chinese and Indian families, the natural increase between 1947 and 1957 was 395,600, resulting in a rise in the proportion of the population under 15 years of age to 43 per cent.[28] That brought Singapore's population in 1957 to 1,445,929 or nearly three times the figure in 1931, implying an annual growth rate of about 3.8 per cent. Although most migrants were Chinese, their proportion in the population fell back to three-quarters, with a corresponding increase in the Malay share.[29]

The population explosion resulted not only in a high dependency burden but also unemployment, the mushrooming of squatter settlements and poverty. An International Bank for Reconstruction and Development (the precursor to the World Bank) mission to Singapore in 1955 noted that the potential problem facing the future rise of living standards was the fast rate of population growth, as employment would have to be found for the burgeoning labour force.[30] The colonial government would also be hard-pressed to provide education, health and housing facilities for the youthful population. In 1957, the unemployment rate was 5 per cent, which was not high by any standards, although a later estimate put the rate at 10 per cent in 1959. Whichever was the case, these statistics

[23] Huff, *The Economic Growth of Singapore*, pp. 281–6, Appendix Table A.4, pp. 388–94.

[24] *Annual Report of the Division of Commerce and Industry 1959*, p. 11.

[25] *The Straits Budget*, 17 Jan. 1952, 9 July 1953; *The Singapore Free Press*, 7 Mar. 1952; *Singapore Standard*, 22 Oct. 1952.

[26] Saw, *Population of Singapore*, pp. 9, 14–15.

[27] Turnbull, *History of Modern Singapore*, pp. 237–8; Lee, *From Colony to Nation*, p. 15.

[28] Lee Soo Ann, *Industrialization in Singapore* (Singapore: Longman, 1973), p. 10; Huff, *The Economic Growth of Singapore*, pp. 292–3.

[29] Saw, *Population of Singapore*, p. 29.

[30] Lee, *Industrialization*, pp. 11, 15–16.

concealed widespread underemployment, as witnessed by numerous casual workers, hawkers and trishaw riders.[31]

Squatter colonies on the fringes of Singapore island had sprung up during the Japanese occupation and in 1947, they housed 20,000 families in shacks made of attap, planks and corrugated zinc, with no basic amenities or modern sanitation.[32] The rest of the population lived mainly in shophouses and attap dwellings, accommodating mostly Chinese and Malays, respectively.[33] Just like in the 1930s, the Singapore Improvement Trust (SIT) attempted to build new satellite towns outside the city but it was overwhelmed by the rise in population even though the government increased loans to the Trust to construct new houses.[34] The shortage of housing was aggravated by the Rent Control Ordinance of 1946, which was intended to protect tenants from unreasonable landlords but resulted in buildings deteriorating since their owners had no incentive to renovate them and property developers were similarly discouraged from building new homes.[35]

A comprehensive social survey carried out in Singapore in 1953–54 found that living conditions in the town remained as dismal as they had been in the early part of the century. Almost a quarter of households shared a dwelling with 11 or more families, especially in shophouses.[36] In Chinatown and the city centre, overcrowding was so bad that more than half the households were crammed into one or two rooms—the bigger the household, the more people shared the space.[37] Cubicles of nine square metres (known as "black holes") were rented out as accommodation to labourers; the number of cubicles per floor in a shophouse could be as few as six or as many as 24.[38] Another quarter of households, made up of single persons, slept on wooden bunks or even on the floors in shophouses let out at a very low monthly rental. These sordid living conditions explain why in the late 1940s, the average population density of Chinatown was 200,000 persons per square mile.

Poverty went hand-in-hand with these conditions, afflicting one in five households and one in four individuals.[39] The criterion for poverty adopted in the above survey was that a household's income was insufficient to provide for minimum physical needs and conventional necessities.[40] The usual causes of poverty were interruption of earnings due

---

[31] Huff, *The Economic Growth of Singapore*, pp. 291–2; *The Straits Times*, 4 Jan. 1956.

[32] Huff, *The Economic Growth of Singapore*, p. 294; Huff and Huff, "The Second World War Occupation of Singapore", pp. 251–2; Teo and Savage, "Singapore Landscape", p. 326; Choe, "The Early Years of Nation-Building", p. 3.

[33] Goh Keng Swee, *Urban Incomes and Housing: A Report on the Social Survey of Singapore, 1953–54* (Singapore: Government Printing Office, 1956), pp. 61–7.

[34] Liew and Wilson, *A History of Money*, pp. 190–2; *The Straits Budget*, 24 June 1948; *The Singapore Free Press*, 30 Dec. 1948.

[35] Teo and Savage, "Singapore Landscape", p. 325.

[36] Goh, *Urban Incomes and Housing*, pp. 61–71.

[37] *Malaya Tribune*, 18 Mar. 1947; *The Singapore Free Press*, 17 Aug. 1948. In nine-person households for example, the average number of occupants per room was 5.1.

[38] Savage, *Lion City Narratives*, p. 193.

[39] Huff, *The Economic Growth of Singapore*, pp. 291–2.

[40] Food, clothing, housing, transport and miscellaneous items were included in the consumption of households but the cost of educating children was not. Goh, *Urban Incomes and Housing*, pp. 87, 98–100, 113–29, 130–4.

to a variety of reasons and large family sizes.[41] Average household income was $168 per month although its distribution was uneven, with three-fifths of households earning less than $100. The percentage of resident households who earned $400 or more each month was 11 per cent. Households living in poverty numbered 1,284 and there were 413 among them who received less than half the income corresponding to the poverty line (about $25). Conversely, one half of survey respondents had incomes twice or more the amount needed to live on minimum standards.

The wretched socio-economic conditions in post-war Singapore and high living costs provided fertile ground for labour unrest, which the Malayan Communist Party exploited.[42] Founded in 1930, this band of revolutionaries had won the respect and support of Singapore Chinese by fighting in the Malayan People's Anti-Japanese Army during the occupation.[43] After the war, the army was dissolved and its leaders furthered their Communist cause by working through front organisations in the trade unions and infiltrating clubs, associations and the press. The most prominent of these organisations was the General Labour Union (GLU) based in Singapore with branches in Malayan towns.[44] It solicited workers' support by advocating better working conditions and shorter hours. As early as October 1945, the first strike by dock labourers occurred, followed by workers in other industries.[45] With more than 60 trade unions under its umbrella, the GLU could easily mobilise workers to protest and it did so again in January 1946 with a massive strike involving 173,000 transport union members that paralysed the city.[46] This action inspired others to do the same, including factory workers, hospital attendants, firemen and even cabaret girls.[47]

In 1948, the Communists halted their activities in urban Singapore to focus on an armed struggle in Malaya, prompting the British colonial government to declare a state of emergency.[48] The Emergency was extended to Singapore in the form of restrictions on meetings, associations, trade unions and strikes, coupled with increased surveillance and the arrests of leftists.[49] Peace prevailed for a few years but the respite did not last long. Following the formation by English-speaking trade unionists of the Singapore Trades Union Congress (STUC) to replace the GLU in 1951, the authorities wanted to encourage an orderly and responsible trade unionism and guide it, to prevent it from being hijacked

---

41 Lee, "The Colonial Legacy", pp. 37–8.

42 Frost and Balasingamchow, *Singapore*, pp. 327–8.

43 Turnbull, *History of Modern Singapore*, pp. 144, 232–3.

44 *The Singapore Free Press*, 5 Dec. 1946.

45 *Chronology of Trade Union Development in Singapore 1940–1985* (Singapore: National Trades Union Congress, 1986), p. 2; *Malaya Tribune*, 22 Oct. 1945; *The Straits Times*, 2 Nov. 1945.

46 *The Straits Times*, 30 Jan. 1946; *Malaya Tribune*, 31 Jan. 1946.

47 Loh Oun Hean, *Industrial Relations in Singapore: Practice and Perspective* (Singapore: World Scientific, 2018), p. 14.

48 Turnbull, *History of Modern Singapore*, pp. 239–40, 245–7, 251–4.

49 *Annual Report of the Labour Department 1955*, pp. 11–12, 21; *The Singapore Free Press*, 24 June 1948; *Malaya Tribune*, 14 July 1948. A period of 14 days' notice was made compulsory before a strike or lock-out could be called in the essential services.

by subversive elements.[50] In this respect, their apprehension was justified. The Communists went underground, operating covertly until 1954 when they were ready to harness workers' simmering dissent again by capitalising on labour issues, winning for the first time, through stoppages and wildcat strikes, higher wages and improved working conditions.[51] Two pro-Communist umbrella unions, the Singapore Bus Workers' Union (SBWU) and the Singapore Factory and Shop Workers' Union (SFSWU), were formed in that year. At the same time, the 11,000 students in the Chinese middle schools and undergraduates at the newly established Chinese-medium Nanyang University became the target of recruitment into a militant campaign to capture power through protests, strikes and violence.[52]

Although nominal wages increased by 11 per cent in 1955 and average weekly hours worked fell slightly to 50 hours, there were a record 275 strikes and lockouts that year, many of them fomented by Communist cells in the labour movement and Chinese schools.[53] Trade union membership shot up from 76,452 workers in 1954 to 139,317 workers. In 1955, the Labour Front government that came into office in elections for partial self-government had promised a better deal for workers and this emboldened the unions—only a third of industrial disputes were motivated by claims over wages and conditions of employment. The worst incident happened in May 1955 when, supported by Chinese school students and the SBWU, employees of the Hock Lee Bus Company picketed to protest poor working conditions and the formation of an in-house "yellow union" sponsored by management, which escalated into a deadly riot that killed four people and injured many more.[54] Apart from bus workers, factory labourers, City Council workers and clerical staff of the Singapore Harbour Board also stopped work in sympathy strikes.[55]

The frequency and intensity of strikes in Singapore were irregular during the fifties and early sixties (Figure 20). In 1951, only five strikes took place and in 1954, eight.[56] The number of industrial stoppages shot up in 1955 before declining later in the decade. Correspondingly, the number of man-days lost was 946,354 in 1955 and 26,588 in 1959. Most strikes lasted from one to seven days, though a substantial number stretched on for one to two weeks.[57] The exception was the strike by bus workers of the Singapore

---

[50] *Reunion* (Singapore: National Trades Union Congress, 2019); Loh, *Industrial Relations in Singapore*, pp. 13, 17; Pang Eng Fong, "Changing Patterns of Industrial Relations in Singapore", in *Studies in ASEAN Sociology: Urban Society and Social Change*, ed. Peter S.J. Chen and Hans-Dieter Evers (Singapore: Chopmen Enterprises, 1978), p. 423.

[51] *Sunday Standard*, 21 July 1953; *The Straits Times*, 11 Nov. 1954.

[52] Turnbull, *History of Modern Singapore*, pp. 249–50, 276–7; *Department of Education Annual Report 1955*, p. 29; *The Straits Budget*, 26 May 1955. Nanyang University was set up in 1956 using funds donated by both rich and poor Chinese in Singapore and Malaya.

[53] Turnbull, *History of Modern Singapore*, pp. 262–4; *Annual Report of the Labour Department 1955*, pp. 2, 6, 8–11, 32.

[54] Frost and Balasingamchow, *Singapore*, pp. 359–61; *Chronology of Trade Union Development in Singapore*, p. 9; *Annual Report of the Labour Department 1955*, pp. 12–15; *The Straits Times*, 15 May 1955; *The Straits Budget*, 19 May 1955.

[55] *The Straits Budget*, 8 Sept. 1955.

[56] Huff, *The Economic Growth of Singapore*, pp. 295–6.

[57] *Annual Report of the Labour Department 1955*, p. 70.

Traction Company in 1955, which lasted for 142 days and crippled the public bus system.[58] The decline in strikes after 1956 could be attributed to the arrest in that year of prominent leftists and the dissolution of the SFSWU by the Registrar of Societies after the union instigated Chinese middle school students to riot.[59] In 1961, the number of strikes increased again to 116, resulting in 410,889 man-days lost. The disturbances persisted until 1963 and then tapered off.

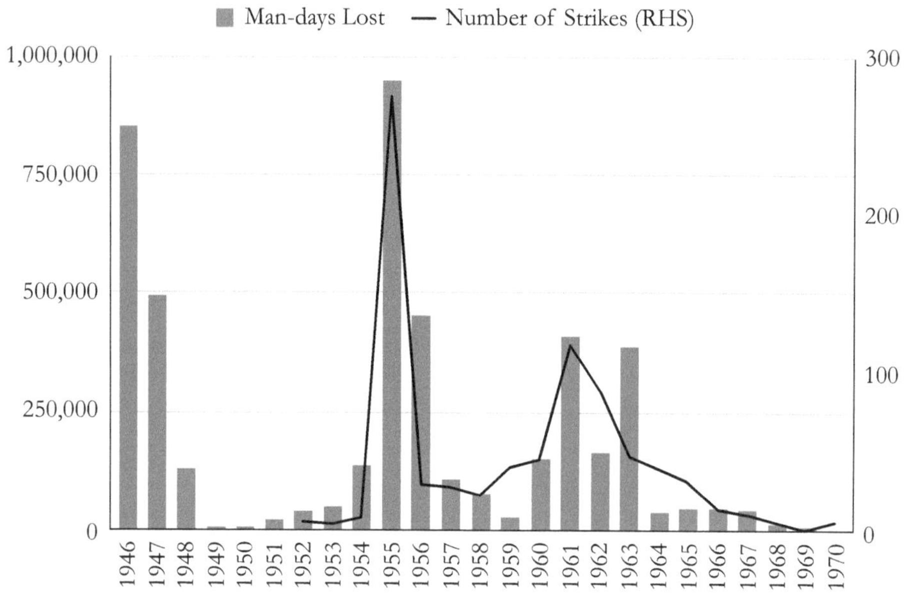

Figure 20. Strikes in Singapore, 1946–70

Sources: Huff, *The Economic Growth of Singapore*, Table 10.7, p. 295; *Annual Report of the Labour Department 1955*, p. 9.

Key political events were behind these incidents. In the later part of 1961, the pro-Communist and Democratic Socialist factions within the People's Action Party (PAP) led respectively by Lim Chin Siong and Lee Kuan Yew openly split, with the former group leaving the party to establish the Barisan Sosialis.[60] Since the founding of the PAP in 1954, there had been an inherent tension between these two camps.[61] For the pro-Communists, the party provided a convenient cover for subversive activities; for the non-Communists, it was a marriage of convenience to allow them to reach out to Chinese voters in Singapore. The political schism that opened up in 1961 was reflected in a parallel break in the STUC, the Communists forming the Singapore Association of Trade Unions (SATU) and the non-Communists, the National Trades Union Congress (NTUC).[62] The contest for worker

[58] Choi Chik Cheong and Nadiah Loh, "Singapore's Bus Reform Experience", *Journeys* (May 2015): 19.

[59] Turnbull, *History of Modern Singapore*, pp. 265–6.

[60] Ibid., pp. 277–80, 286.

[61] Albert Lau, "The Battle for Merger—The Historical Context", in Lee Kuan Yew, *The Battle for Merger* (Singapore: National Archives of Singapore), pp. xvii–xviii.

[62] Pang, "Changing Patterns", p. 426; *Chronology of Trade Union Development in Singapore*, pp. 13–17.

allegiance that followed led to industrial unrest orchestrated by the Barisan Sosialis, since it controlled two-thirds of organised labour. By 1964 however, the moderate faction in the PAP had won the battle for political leadership in a general election, SATU had been refused registration, and workers had coalesced around the NTUC.

Industrialisation Policies

The immediate period after the civilian administration took over from the BMA saw a proliferation of plans to improve social amenities and public utilities in the fields of education, healthcare, housing, water supply and town planning. The education plan aimed, over a ten-year period, at the expansion of existing schools and the building of new ones, provision of free primary education and the establishment of a Teacher Training College.[63] In health services, $50 million was earmarked for the development of the General Hospital, other hospitals and clinics over a period of 10 to 15 years, as well as the provision of medical care for all.[64] Given the dire housing situation, a crash programme for 1948–50 was drawn up by the SIT to provide housing for 36,000 people in 4,366 dwellings at a total cost of $32 million.[65] As for public utilities, Singapore's reservoirs and filtration plants were rehabilitated and a $3 million water scheme was to be undertaken in Johor which would add ten million gallons a day to Singapore's water supply.[66] The sewerage system was also to be extended to more areas.

In late 1950, an ambitious blueprint that encompassed all of the above areas was drawn up by the colonial government, namely, the Six-Year Development Plan for Singapore, budgeted at $454 million.[67] While nominally an economic development plan, housing topped the list of priorities with an allocation of $191 million, followed by $40 million for the construction of an international airport at Paya Lebar.[68] The plan also provided for a power station at Pasir Panjang, new port and harbour facilities including the Queen's Dock, completed in 1956, roads and telecommunications. Educational, medical and social welfare schemes were estimated to cost a combined total of $183 million. The projects were to be funded by the government, the City Council (which replaced the Municipal Council), the SIT, the Singapore Harbour Board, a Colonial Development Fund and loans.

In view of the imperative for economic diversification and the need to develop the manufacturing sector to generate jobs for school leavers, it is somewhat surprising that industrialisation was not given more attention in the development plan.[69] Apart from stating that the Colonial Development Corporation, set up by the British government

---

63 Liew and Wilson, *A History of Money*, pp. 189–90; *The Singapore Free Press*, 14 July 1947; *Morning Tribune*, 29 Aug. 1947; *The Straits Times Annual*, 1 Jan. 1952; *Singapore Standard*, 15 Oct. 1952.

64 *The Singapore Free Press*, 20 May 1948, 13 Oct. 1948; *The Straits Budget*, 15 Apr. 1954.

65 *50,000 Up: Homes for the People*, p. 20.

66 *10 Years that Shaped a Nation*, p. 39; *The Straits Budget*, 13 Nov. 1947; *The Straits Times*, 29 June 1948.

67 *Singapore Standard*, 6 Oct. 1950, 25 Oct. 1950, 2 Dec. 1950, 22 Jan. 1952; *Sunday Standard*, 15 July 1951.

68 Huff, *The Economic Growth of Singapore*, pp. 289–90; *The Straits Times*, 14 Aug. 1955.

69 Cheng, "Economic Change in Singapore", pp. 83–4; *Singapore Standard*, 6 Sept. 1951.

in Singapore and other colonies, would build new industrial estates equipped with water and electricity supplies in satellite towns, the plan referred vaguely to the "encouragement of manufacturing industries" financed by the infusion of foreign private capital.[70] The first concrete step to promote industrial development was taken only in 1954 with the establishment of a 50-acre industrial town in Alexandra Road housing factory sites to be leased to entrepreneurs.[71] The colonial government also launched estates for light industries at Redhill and Tanglin Halt, which obtained their workforce from nearby residential areas.[72] In 1957, the Industrial Promotion Board was created by the Labour Front government to promote and develop industries in the Colony with a revolving fund of $1 million.[73] Two years later, tax concessions were given to companies through the Pioneer Industries Bill and the Industrial Expansion Bill, respectively offering income tax relief to new industries for five years and tax allowances on a sliding scale for new capital spending by existing firms. The second bill was enacted partly to prevent industries from moving to Malaya, which had the advantages of lower production costs as well as its own pioneer incentives and industrial zone at Petaling Jaya on the outskirts of Kuala Lumpur.[74] The lack of industrial training facilities was remedied with the establishment of the Singapore Polytechnic in 1954.[75]

In 1959, the colonial government went a step further with the publication of an officially sponsored report dealing specifically with industrial development in Singapore by a Colombo Plan Industrial Development Adviser, F.J. Lye.[76] The Report began by pointing out that an industrialisation programme in Singapore could advance rapidly because of a relatively high level of consumption of imported manufactured goods, and since Singapore and Malaya combined provided a market of eight million consumers.[77] It therefore recommended that Singapore enter into a common market with Malaya to enlarge its customer base and that the same tariff protection be given to firms in the two territories. The report then noted that Hong Kong had solved its China refugee problem through industrialisation and Singapore could embark on a similar undertaking to tackle its unemployment predicament, as it could no longer rely on the entrepôt trade to generate sufficient jobs.[78] Overall world trade was expected to grow at only

[70] *Malaya Tribune*, 17 Sept. 1950; *The Straits Budget*, 19 Oct. 1950; *Singapore Standard*, 21 Oct. 1950, 29 Nov. 1950; *The Singapore Free Press*, 25 Oct. 1950; *The Straits Times*, 17 July 1952.

[71] *The Singapore Free Press*, 4 Jan. 1954.

[72] Loh Kah Seng, "Imaginaries of Jurong Industrial Estate, Singapore", *International Institute of Asian Studies*, Newsletter 81 (2018): 6.

[73] Lee, *Industrialization*, pp. 22–5; *The Straits Budget*, 15 Nov. 1956.

[74] Lee, *From Colony to Nation*, p. 17; Kwa, Heng and Tan, *Singapore: A 700-Year History*, p. 163; Cheng, "Economic Change in Singapore", p. 86; Lee Soo Ann, *Singapore Chronicles: Economy* (Singapore: Institute of Policy Studies and Straits Times Press, 2018), p. 26; *The Straits Budget*, 16 Apr. 1958, 28 Jan. 1959; *The Straits Times*, 15 Nov. 1958.

[75] Huff, *The Economic Growth of Singapore*, p. 289; *The Straits Times*, 4 Nov. 1958.

[76] F.J. Lyle, *An Industrial Development Programme* (Singapore: Legislative Assembly of Singapore, 1959).

[77] Ibid., pp. 3, 6, 12–14.

[78] Lim Chong Yah, *Economic Development in Singapore* (Singapore: Federal Publications, 1980), pp. 10–12.

2 per cent per annum and buyers in the region were increasingly opting for direct trade with sellers in the West. Other than making these points, the Lye Report stopped short of picking suitable industries for development.[79] Instead, it suggested wooing not only foreign firms that were already exporting goods to Singapore to establish manufacturing plants on the island, but also other companies that might be interested in entering into partnerships with local firms.[80] Since the Industrial Promotion Board had failed in its mission of attracting foreign investment due to operational issues, the report delineated the organisation of a new body.

One should not infer from the foregoing that industrialisation took great strides during the 1950s and early 1960s. By and large, the industries in Singapore were based on the processing of the primary resources of rubber, tin and copra.[81] When rubber prices were high, remilling and smoking activities on the island were boosted, leading to increases in manufacturing output. There were also engineering and machinery workshops that catered to these processing industries.[82] Except for a steel and iron rolling mill, a factory making bus and truck bodies and a vehicle assembly plant, there were hardly any heavy industries. The new enterprises that appeared after the war were geared mostly towards domestic demand although they employed modern production methods. In 1960, nine out of ten firms manufactured for the domestic market.[83] Examples of goods produced for local consumption were husked rice, noodles, biscuits, soft drinks, cigarettes, clothing and shoes, the last of these manufactured by the well-known firm of Bata. As a result of the post-war building boom, the production of all sorts of building materials was stimulated.[84] Cottage industries also proliferated, making things like mosquito nets, mattresses, cushions, ironing boards and wooden ladders, desks and chairs.[85] In the mid-1960s, they were joined by factories producing simple items like baby napkins, carbon paper, matches, fertilisers and mothballs.[86]

In 1957, the manufacturing sector employed 16.6 per cent of the workforce, about the same as in 1931.[87] The majority of firms hired a relatively small labour force of 50 to 100 persons; industries that offered employment to more than 1,500 people were those manufacturing food and beverages, rubber and rubber products, chemicals and chemical products, metal products, wood products and non-electrical machinery.[88] One reason for Singapore's failure to industrialise stayed the same as in the 1930s—comparatively high wages.[89] Factory workers earned at least $2 a day and most industries actually paid more

[79] Lye, *An Industrial Development Programme*, pp. 15–17, 26.

[80] Cheng, "Economic Change in Singapore", p. 87.

[81] Huff, *The Economic Growth of Singapore*, pp. 286–7; *The Singapore Free Press*, 20 Jan. 1962.

[82] Cheng, "Economic Change in Singapore", p. 85.

[83] Linda Lim and Pang Eng Fong, *Trade, Employment and Industrialisation in Singapore* (Geneva: International Labour Organization, 1986), pp. 7–8.

[84] Lee, "The Colonial Legacy", p. 12.

[85] Savage, *Lion City Narratives*, p. 218.

[86] *10 Years that Shaped a Nation*, p. 73.

[87] Huff, *The Economic Growth of Singapore*, Appendix Table A.10, p. 407.

[88] *Annual Report of the Division of Commerce and Industry 1959*, pp. 18–19, 22.

[89] Huff, *The Economic Growth of Singapore*, pp. 293, 322.

than that while the daily wage rates of mechanics, machine operators and artisans were $5 or higher.[90] Moreover, meals and housing were provided by many employers. A second factor that held back industrialisation was the small scale of operation and limited financial resources of the Industrial Promotion Board.[91] In its first year, only about $300,000 in long-term loans were approved. But arguably the strongest deterrent to domestic and foreign investment was the uncertainty created by political trade unionism.[92]

Following a general election in May 1959 that conferred internal self-government to Singapore, the PAP became the government of the day and Lee Kuan Yew was appointed the Prime Minister.[93] During its campaign, the party had pledged to transform Singapore from a trading nation into an industrial society and this it set out to do. Before that, it dissolved the City Council and the Rural Board so as to govern the whole island as one entity.[94] Then it adopted wholesale the policies of the preceding administration except for the recommendations of the Lye Report on economic union with Malaya. Instead, the PAP government requested help from a United Nations Technical Assistance team to advise it on industrialisation.[95] In 1961, it replaced the Industrial Promotion Board with the Economic Development Board (EDB) and empowered it to attract and finance new manufacturing enterprises, build industrial estates, and give management and technical advice to companies.[96]

Headed by a Dutch economist, Albert Winsemius, the United Nations team visited Singapore in October 1960, with a follow-up mission in March 1961.[97] Winsemius was to become a long-time adviser to the Singapore government until his retirement in 1984 but on his maiden trip, he prescribed two prerequisites for economic development: the suppression of the Communists and their influence over the labour unions, and the preservation of Stamford Raffles' statue near the Singapore River as a signal to foreign investors that they were welcomed.[98] The report submitted by the team recognised that industrialisation was going to be a long-term process and that shorter-term measures were needed to alleviate the unemployment problem. Among them was the immediate establishment of labour-intensive industries, the obvious ones being clothing, textiles and leather products, and a building materials industry that could benefit from the construction

[90] *Annual Report of the Labour Department 1955*, pp. 58–67.

[91] Cheng, "Economic Change in Singapore", p. 86.

[92] Turnbull, *History of Modern Singapore*, p. 276.

[93] Ibid., pp. 270–1, 276, 281.

[94] Lee, *Singapore Chronicles: Economy*, pp. 18–19.

[95] Lee, *From Colony to Nation*, p. 16.

[96] Cheng, "Economic Change in Singapore", pp. 88–9; *Annual Report of the Division of Commerce and Industry 1959*, pp. 19–20; *The Straits Times*, 25 May 1961.

[97] United Nations Industrial Survey Mission, *A Proposed Industrialization Programme for the State of Singapore* (New York, 1963); hereafter, *Industrialization Programme*; *The Straits Budget*, 12 Oct. 1960, 10 May 1961.

[98] Euston Quah with Luke Nursultan Iuldashov and Zach Lee, *Albert Winsemius and Singapore: Here It is Going to Happen* (Singapore: World Scientific, 2022).

programme of the public sector.[99] With regard to other activities, those identified by the United Nations experts eventually took hold on the island and formed the mainstay of Singapore's manufacturing sector: ship repair and shipbuilding, metal engineering, chemicals, and electrical equipment and appliances.[100] Another study mission from the United Nations proposed in addition an iron and steel mill complex, which subsequently became the National Iron and Steel Mills.[101]

Several other observations made by the United Nations team were to shape the policies of the PAP. In contrast to the Lye Report, it pointed out that Singapore had the human resources necessary for industrialisation on its own rather than jointly with Malaya, but industrial peace had first to be achieved between employers and workers.[102] Apart from political instability, earlier efforts had not succeeded because of stormy industrial relations and competition from the Federation of Malaya—the political entity that succeeded the Malayan Union. In line with the economic orthodoxy of the time, the advisers recommended continued import protection of selected industries. However, the need to attract foreign manufacturers and managers was also stressed. This recommendation had been made earlier by both the International Bank for Reconstruction and Development and the Lye Report.[103] Anticipating an action the Singapore government would take later, the United Nations team suggested that a large industrial estate be developed on the swampland at Jurong in the western part of the island.[104] Minor proposals by the team were the signing of avoidance of double taxation treaties with foreign countries, the expansion of the Singapore Polytechnic and the establishment of an engineering faculty in one of the universities. A second polytechnic conferring diploma degrees, Ngee Ann Polytechnic, was opened in 1963.[105] All in, the capital requirements of a ten-year industrialisation programme were calculated at $813 million, to be expended on land and buildings, machinery and working capital.[106] Of this total, $393 million would come from foreign investment. The direct and indirect employment created by the programme was projected at 236,000 jobs, with

---

99 Lee, *Industrialization*, pp. 29, 32, 39; *Industrialization Programme*, pp. 156, 171–5, 180–4. In addition, the mission saw economic potential in developing the tourism and fishery industries, which was partially realised later through government efforts to nurture tourism as another pillar of the Singapore economy. R. Le Blanc, *Singapore: The Socio-Economic Development of a City-State, 1960–80* (Cranendonck Coaching, Netherlands, 2008), p. 15; *10 Years that Shaped a Nation*, p. 66.

100 *Industrialization Programme*, pp. 133–55; *The Singapore Free Press*, 8 Dec. 1961, 11 Dec. 1961, 20 Jan. 1962.

101 Lee, *Industrialization*, pp. 53–4; *The Straits Times*, 8 Feb. 1961, 16 Dec. 1961, 16 Sept. 1962.

102 Lee, *Industrialization*, pp. 25–8; *Industrialization Programme*, pp. xxiii, 115–7, 195–201.

103 Cheng, "Economic Change in Singapore", p. 86.

104 Lee, *Industrialization*, pp. 30, 31, 32–4. Japanese experts also had a key role in the physical planning of Jurong Industrial Estate as the location for heavy industry in Singapore. Loh, *Imaginaries*, p. 7.

105 Chan Lee Mun, "Polytechnic Education", in *Toward a Better Future: Education and Training for Economic Development in Singapore since 1965*, ed. Lee Sing Kong, Goh Chor Boon, F. Birger and Tan Jee Peng (World Bank Publications, 2008), p. 136; *The Straits Times*, 20 Mar. 1982. The polytechnic was previously known as Ngee Ann Technical College. Lim and Pang, *Trade, Employment and Industrialisation*, p. 80.

106 Lee, *From Colony to Nation*, p. 19; *Industrialization Programme*, pp. 61–5.

84,000 of them in the manufacturing sector. The commercial sector and other service industries would also generate a substantial number of jobs.

Many of the prescriptions and recommendations of the United Nations team were incorporated into the State Development Plan for 1961–64, the coordination of which was undertaken by the newly formed EDB.[107] However, while the United Nations' report focussed on the types of industrial activity to be undertaken, the plan emphasised the financing and public investment aspects of the industrialisation programme.[108] Specifically, it laid out ways of obtaining the necessary funds within the limited financial means of the government. The key suggestion was for the Minister for Finance, Dr Goh Keng Swee, to raise loans for a Development Fund. This was necessary because the state planners allocated, in addition to economic development, about two-fifths of total public sector expenditure, or $337 million, to schools, health facilities, housing and community services based on the projected future demand for them.[109] Some of the projects such as public utilities and housing were self-funding, thus reducing the call on government resources. The balance of $494 million was earmarked for development spending proper, with a major portion to be invested in land and industrial estate development at the colonial industrial hub of Kallang and in Jurong.[110]

Although not directly generating revenue in most cases, the implementation of economic development schemes by the EDB was expected to increase national income through multiplier effects.[111] The annual rate of increase in investment was targeted at 20 per cent which in turn would result in a 3 per cent increase per annum in per capita income.[112] Over the four-year period 1961 to 1964, it was envisaged that the plan would generate 55,000 jobs directly and 59,000 jobs indirectly, thereby helping to attain full employment. These beneficial effects were significant because by increasing economic activity, they would lead to an expansion of the tax base and hence, government revenue. The Labour Front government had been profligate in its spending, leaving the PAP when it came into office with the lowest level of government reserves since the end of the war.[113] It was forecast that government revenue would exceed expenditure during the plan period and yield a surplus of $207 million, which could be used to finance further development spending.

Nonetheless, there was still a need to borrow a large sum of $500 million from domestic and foreign sources. The Central Provident Fund (CPF) would subscribe to $120 million of government bonds, the public another $110 million and $100 million would come from the World Bank.[114] Contrary to expectations, however, the financial position of the

---

[107] *State of Singapore Development Plan 1961–64* (Singapore, Ministry of Finance, 1961), pp. 47–8.

[108] Lee, *Industrialization*, pp. 35–9.

[109] *State of Singapore Development Plan*, pp. 1–8, 34, 39.

[110] Ibid., pp. 69–73.

[111] Lee, *Industrialization*, pp. 39–41, 43–5. Only about one-fifth of development expenditure was revenue generating, such as rents from industrial estates and charges on posts and telecommunications. Lee, *From Colony to Nation*, pp. 27–8.

[112] *State of Singapore Development Plan*, pp. 53–4.

[113] Lee, *Industrialization*, pp. 22, 45–6, 48–9; Liew and Wilson, *A History of Money*, pp. 188–9.

[114] The Central Provident Fund is a social security scheme started by the colonial government in 1955, to which all employers and employees are required to contribute a portion of the employee's monthly salary.

Singapore government had improved considerably by 1964. A higher than anticipated budgetary surplus of $343 million had been accumulated in the previous four years and a part of it was transferred to the Development Fund. Loans floated locally added $257 million and external loans brought the total to $710 million. Since actual development expenditure was only $353 million, the government could lend money not only to the EDB for industrial development but also to the Housing and Development Board (HDB), which had succeeded the SIT, for housing construction.

The success of the state development plan can be gauged in terms of gross capital formation and economic growth. Overall investment increased at an average annual rate of 23.8 per cent from 1960 to 1965, higher than the target.[115] Total private investment rose to $249 million in 1965 while the number of firms given pioneer status reached close to 100, partly in anticipation of a common market with Malaya.[116] By that year, the manufacturing sector had generated 19,000 new jobs. The rate of increase in per capita income averaged 2.25 per cent per annum although this was pulled down by the Indonesian Confrontation in 1964, which caused a contraction in trade.[117] Against the United Nations' projection, the contribution of foreign capital to domestic investment turned out to be an overwhelming 70 per cent.[118] Economic growth was stimulated by the public sector's land development and residential construction activities. In Jurong, 749 hectares of land were prepared for industrial purposes, ready with utilities, roads, railway and a port. Smaller estates in other parts of Singapore were also built. The HDB stepped up its housing construction programme, building 13,028 dwelling units in 1964. The expansion of public housing led to an increase in retail trades that in turn created employment opportunities. Even so, the number of unemployed persons stood at 52,700 in 1966.[119] It can therefore be concluded that while the result of the post-war industrialisation effort was not stellar, the progress in building up economic and social infrastructure was laudable.

Merger and Separation

Singapore's merger with the Federation of Malaya and subsequent separation have generated considerable controversy and an even larger literature. The following discussion, as befits the title of this book, will however be confined to the economic aspects of this event. Right from the time when the Malayan Union was conceived without Singapore's participation, many quarters had believed that, ultimately, the two territories would be unified again.[120] In the 1950s, Singapore politicians courted Malaya with a view to a merger of the two territories, albeit without success.[121] As mentioned in the preceding

115 Le Blanc, *Singapore*, Table 1.4, p. 109.

116 Lee, *Industrialization*, pp. 41–3.

117 Ibid., p. 92; Sugimoto, *Economic Growth of Singapore*, p. 185; Saw, *Population of Singapore*, p. 14.

118 Lim and Pang, *Trade, Employment and Industrialisation*, p. 12.

119 Lim, *Economic Development in Singapore*, p. 7.

120 Albert Lau, *A Moment of Anguish: Singapore in Malaysia and the Politics of Disengagement* (Singapore: Times Academic Press, 1998), pp. 4, 10; N.M. Fletcher, *The Separation of Singapore from Malaysia*, Data Paper No. 73, Southeast Asia Program, Cornell University, 1969, p. 4.

121 Tan, *A Very Short History*, p. 104.

section, the Lye Report had thought that industrial progress could not be achieved if Singapore were to go at it on its own.[122] These sentiments found their most manifest expression in the political vision of the PAP and especially of Lee Kuan Yew.

Before a narrative assessment of the period, a review of Pan-Malayan monetary developments which presaged the merger may be helpful. In 1934, the Blackett Report had recommended the creation of a common currency for Singapore, Malaya and Brunei.[123] The proposal was implemented four years later with the issue of the Malayan dollar (in place of the Straits dollar) and the establishment of the Board of Commissioners of Currency, Malaya. The Malay states, Brunei, the British North Borneo territory of Sabah as well as Sarawak had been using the Straits dollar since the currency notes were issued in 1899 but did not bear the costs of note issuance and were not entitled to a share of the profits earned by the Currency Guarantee Fund and the seigniorage from issuing currency.[124] In any event, the assets of the Fund began to exceed the liabilities only beginning from 1917.[125] The participating states in the common currency agreed that with the issue of the new Malayan dollar, these gains were to be distributed in accordance with currency use per head of population: the Straits Settlements and the Federated Malay States were each given 37 per cent ownership of the assets, liabilities and profits of the Currency Guarantee Fund while the other Malay states and Brunei were jointly allocated 26 per cent. The new notes and coins were circulated only in 1940–41 due to production delays. In 1952, Sabah and Sarawak joined the scheme, necessitating the issue of a new Malayan and North Borneo dollar and an alteration in the formula for distributing the profits of a reconstituted Board of Commissioners of Currency, Malaya and British Borneo.[126] With this change, the Federation of Malaya would receive 65 per cent, Singapore 29 per cent and the remainder was to be divided among the others.

In the late fifties, a merger with Malaya to bring about a common market had become an even more urgent task for Singapore. Without it, the city would lose its economic hinterland and the industrialisation drive would make no sense given the tiny domestic population.[127] The proposal was endorsed by a World Bank Commission that visited Malaya in 1962.[128] Besides, for Singapore a merger was the route to obtaining full independence from Britain and failure to merge would put the PAP's political survival at risk.[129] The PAP called a national referendum to decide on the issue in September 1962, as the Barisan Sosialis had distanced itself from the proposition since, if implemented, it would lead

[122] Lye, *An Industrial Development Programme*, pp. 6–12.

[123] Liew and Wilson, *A History of Money*, pp. 127–33; *Malaya Tribune*, 30 July 1934.

[124] Drake, "The Evolution of Money", pp. 7–8. The Currency Guarantee Fund was at the heart of the currency board system and was topped up whenever Straits dollar notes or coins were issued. Its assets were invested in overseas securities to earn a rate of return.

[125] Lee, *The Monetary and Banking Development*, pp. 15–16.

[126] Liew and Wilson, *A History of Money*, pp. 182–6.

[127] N.J. White, "The Economics of Singapore's Exit from Malaysia", in *Singapore—Two Hundred Years of the Lion City*, ed. Webster and White, p. 99; *The Straits Times*, 8 Feb. 1962.

[128] Fletcher, *The Separation of Singapore from Malaysia*, pp. 12–13.

[129] Lau, *A Moment of Anguish*, p. 10; Turnbull, *History of Modern Singapore*, pp. 275, 280–1.

to their elimination by an anti-Communist government under Malaya's control.[130] In an astute move, the people of Singapore were asked to vote on the form of merger but merger itself was taken as a foregone conclusion.[131]

In a series of radio broadcasts aptly dubbed the "Battle for Merger", Lee Kuan Yew set out in detail the rationale for merger with Malaya and the ways in which the Communists were obstructing it.[132] He also exposed the Communist conspiracy within the PAP and the key figures involved.[133] The Prime Minister began by asserting that merger was as inevitable as "the rising and setting of the sun" because Singapore and Malaya "are so intertwined and interwoven in their economic, political and military complex that no man can keep up the artificial barrier at the Causeway for long".[134] He then repeated the argument in the Lye Report that were there to be no merger, the Federation, instead of co-operating with Singapore, would compete with it for industrial capital. By contrast, merger would bring about political certainty and encourage investment. Without merger, there would be a wasteful duplication of facilities such as the international airport, the rubber market and, one might add, the port.[135] Singapore could not survive economically alone and if merger was delayed, half of the city's population who had migrated from Malaya would drift back. The radio broadcasts and publicity campaigns mounted by the PAP were effective in achieving their aim: 71 per cent of voters supported the PAP's form of merger although 25 per cent cast blank ballots as instructed by the Barisan Sosialis.[136]

In the hard negotiations over the terms of Singapore's entry into the Federation, the Malayan government felt that it held the upper hand. Despite overtures by Singapore, Malaya had initially been reluctant to contemplate a merger since the city's majority Chinese population would upset the delicate racial and political balance in Malaya.[137] What made Tunku Abdul Rahman, the Malayan premier, change his mind was the spectre of a Communist Singapore in his country's backyard.[138] The terms eventually arrived at in July 1963 were therefore not in Singapore's favour. The Federation would bear responsibility for external affairs, defence and internal security although the city would retain local autonomy on matters of education, health and labour.[139] Moreover, while Singaporeans

---

130 Kwa, Heng and Tan, *Singapore: A 700-Year History*, pp. 164–5; *The Straits Times*, 1 Feb. 1962, 14 Feb. 1962.

131 The alternatives presented to the public were either for Singapore to have some autonomy or a full merger (that is, Singapore becoming a state of Malaya). The first option was espoused by the PAP while the second option was supported by the Barisan Sosialis. Tan, *A Very Short History*, pp. 108–9, 111–2.

132 Lee, *The Battle for Merger*; *The Straits Times*, 12 Sept. 1961.

133 Lau, "Battle for Merger", pp. xxv–xxvi.

134 Lee, *The Battle for Merger*, pp. 4–8, 40–1.

135 Malaya had decided to establish its own rubber market and international airport. E. Sadka, "Singapore and the Federation: Problems of Merger", *Asian Survey* 1, 11 (1962): 21.

136 Lau, "Battle for Merger", pp. xxv–xxx; *The Straits Times*, 3 June 1963.

137 Lau, "Battle for Merger", pp. xii–xvii; Sadka, "Singapore and the Federation", pp. 21–2, 23–5.

138 Fletcher, *The Separation of Singapore from Malaysia*, pp. 8–9. The Tunku envisaged Singapore as the "New York rather than the Cuba of Malaya". Linda Lim, Pang Eng Fong and R. Findlay, "Singapore", in *Five Small Open Economies*, ed. R. Findlay and S. Wellisz (Washington, DC: The World Bank, 1993), p. 95.

139 Lau, *A Moment of Anguish*, pp. 14–16; *The Straits Times*, 10 Dec. 1961.

would automatically become Malaysian citizens, they could vote for their representatives only in the state to the new Federation Parliament, the number of whom would be less than would be justified by the size of the island's population.[140]

The haggling over the economic terms of merger was particularly contentious, even though there were no substantial differences in economic policy between the two governments—for instance, both were committed to the free market, private enterprise and import substitution as the means to industrialise.[141] These early disagreements were a portent of future troubles. Malaya insisted on having control over all taxation matters but this would mean that Singapore would not have the autonomy to conduct its own affairs. In the end, it was agreed that Singapore would hand over a hefty lump sum payment to Malaya equivalent to 40 per cent of the revenue it collected every year. In addition, it offered to give a $150 million loan to Sabah and Sarawak for economic development, of which two-thirds would be interest-free for five years.[142] Furthermore, the merchants and businessmen in the city wanted to keep the island as a free port—as it had been for the previous 150 years—but a common market implied that import tariffs had to be enacted.[143] A compromise was therefore reached that the common market would be progressively introduced over 12 years.[144]

And so, on 16 September 1963, Singapore became a part of the Federation of Malaysia that had obtained its independence earlier in 1957. Sabah and Sarawak with their indigenous peoples were also incorporated into the Federation to reduce Chinese dominance in Singapore. However, during the tumultuous two years when Singapore was in Malaysia, disagreement over fundamental political ideology came to the fore, aggravated by ethnic tensions.[145] Whatever goodwill that had existed was nullified when each side contested elections in the other's territory.[146] To counter the PAP's espousal of a multiracial Malaysia, the governing political parties in the Federation whipped up racial sentiment amongst the Malays and Chinese. In July 1964, racial riots erupted during a procession in Singapore to celebrate Prophet Muhammad's birthday, causing the loss of 23 lives.

But the worst quarrels were again over economic and financial issues, which were not helped by personal animosities between Dr Goh Keng Swee and the Malaysian Finance Minister Tan Siew Sin. Industrial progress in Singapore was stunted by the hostile policies of the Malaysian government.[147] Since pioneer certificates for firms intending to set up

---

140 Instead of 25 seats, only 15 seats were allocated to Singapore. Tan, *A Very Short History*, pp. 109–10.

141 Sadka, "Singapore and the Federation", p. 20; *The Straits Times*, 17 Apr. 1963, 14 May 1963, 1 June 1963.

142 Tan, *A Very Short History*, p. 116.

143 Lee, *Battle for Merger*, p. 79; Turnbull, *History of Modern Singapore*, p. 287; White, "The Economics of Singapore's Exit", pp. 100–1.

144 *The Straits Times*, 15 July 1963.

145 White, "The Economics of Singapore's Exit", p. 96. The PAP government championed a "Malaysian Malaysia" where all the races were equal while the Malaysian government insisted on the political dominance of, and special rights for, the Malays. Edwin Lee, *The Unexpected Nation* (Singapore: Institute of Southeast Asian Studies, 2008), pp. 239–40, 258.

146 Tan, *A Very Short History*, pp. 119–26.

147 Turnbull, *History of Modern Singapore*, pp. 289–91.

in Singapore had to be vetted by Malaysia, the latter took the opportunity to turn most of them down.[148] Understandably, the prompt implementation of the agreement on the common market was Singapore's top priority following the merger. This was supposed to be effected through the establishment of a Tariff Advisory Board to recommend the products to be covered but it came into being only almost a year later and no steps were taken to harmonise duties and establish common external tariffs. The common market seemed not to matter at all for Malaysia since it had nothing to gain from it; rather, it was envious of Singapore sucking in the bulk of foreign investment since the city's industries were more developed.[149] All sorts of pretexts were given to explain the delay—that it would hurt Singapore by interfering with the entrepôt trade, that Singapore would have to accept all import duties then in effect in Malaysia, and so on.[150]

When the financial arrangements of merger came up for review at the end of 1964, another dispute took place.[151] Presenting the Federal Budget in Parliament, Tan Siew Sin demanded that Singapore contribute a higher percentage of revenue to Malaysia in view of the increased defence spending made necessary by the Indonesian Confrontation.[152] He claimed that $147 million had to be raised in new taxes to close the budget deficit and proposed a turnover tax on businesses of 0.5 per cent and a 2 per cent payroll tax.[153] Taxes were also imposed on diesel oil and sugar for the first time in Singapore. Knowing that these levies would hit merchants in the city hard and discourage hiring by firms, the Singapore leaders charged that the proposed taxes were both repressive and regressive. Dr Goh Keng Swee calculated that Singapore would end up paying nearly 40 per cent of the revenue collected from the new taxes even though its population was only 17 per cent of the total population of Malaysia. He argued that 30 per cent of Singapore's revenue was sufficient to meet Federal expenditures in Singapore and pointed out that its autonomy required substantial spending which other states in the Federation did not have to incur. As a tit for tat for not honouring the agreement on the common market, Singapore refused to disburse the loan to the Borneo states. There were other less major economic issues over which the two sides clashed but these were ultimately irrelevant.

The Singapore and Malaysia governments were on a collision course. Their leaders met in December 1964 to discuss the possibility of a looser constitutional arrangement that would give Singapore complete autonomy except in foreign affairs and defence.[154] In return, it would have to give up all its seats in the Federal Parliament, a condition that was not acceptable to Lee Kuan Yew. After mulling over alternative arrangements, the Tunku decided that the best course of action was to make a clean cut. On 9 August 1965, Singapore was ejected from Malaysia to become an independent nation.[155] It had wasted

[148] Kwa, Heng and Tan, *Singapore: A 700-Year History*, pp. 175–8; Fletcher, *The Separation of Singapore from Malaysia*, pp. 12–16, 20–1.

[149] White, "The Economics of Singapore's Exit", pp. 99–101.

[150] *The Straits Times*, 15 Feb. 1965, 18 July 1965.

[151] Fletcher, *The Separation of Singapore from Malaysia*, pp. 16–25.

[152] *The Straits Times*, 3 Dec. 1964.

[153] Lau, *A Moment of Anguish*, pp. 214–7; *The Straits Times*, 26 Nov. 1964.

[154] Turnbull, *History of Modern Singapore*, p. 291.

[155] *The Straits Times*, 10 Aug. 1965.

two years in the Federation, with the only consolation being the neutralisation of the Communist threat once and for all. Pending the merger but prior to it in February 1963, the authorities had mounted "Operation Coldstore" to arrest and detain without trial more than 100 left-wing and anti-Malaysia political, trade union and student leaders including Lim Chin Siong and his cabal in the Barisan Sosialis.[156] But the time would come when Singapore could look back and conclude that it was its good fortune to be evicted from Malaysia and to be left to pursue its own economic policy.

[156] Turnbull, *History of Modern Singapore*, pp. 281–2; Tan, *A Very Short History*, pp. 112–5.

Chapter 11 Export-Led Growth and Manufacturing, 1966–85

Singapore was in a dire situation after it left Malaysia in 1965. The economic picture looked grim and the newly independent city-state had to confront the issue of how it was going to earn a living. Fortunately, it had laid the foundations for industrialisation in the early 1960s prior to the merger with Malaysia and this groundwork was to stand it in good stead. Economic survival demanded that Singapore industrialise somehow and given the loss of the Malaysian market, there was no choice but to produce for the world. This was indeed the strategy adopted and, rather unexpectedly, it led to spectacular economic success. In spite of the withdrawal of the British armed forces from the island, initially announced in 1967, export-oriented industrialisation solved both the growth and unemployment problems and made possible unprecedented improvements in education, healthcare and housing, leading to a significant increase in the population's economic and social well-being.

By the early 1970s, full employment had effectively been achieved with an attendant rise in wages. As an interim measure, the government permitted workers from Malaysia to join Singapore's labour force. The longer-term solution was to restructure the economy, a policy that was pursued at the end of the decade when wage growth was allowed to outpace productivity growth. Although progress in upgrading manufacturing industries was made, it came at the cost of a loss in export competitiveness and the first classical recession since independence. Fiscal and monetary policies were loosened in response, thereby facilitating a quick economic recovery. Apart from smoothing business cycles, the prudent fiscal policy practised by the Singapore government provided the necessary conditions for economic growth while monetary policy helped to maintain a low inflation rate.

Export-Oriented Industrialisation

In export-oriented industrialisation, the manufacturing industries in a developing country make products for the world market. These are typically semi-manufactures or manufactured goods to replace the traditional primary commodity exports. An export strategy has some distinct advantages over the alternative policy of import substitution.[1] It enables the absence of economies of scale associated with a narrow domestic market to be overcome and allows

[1] G.M. Meier, "Industrialization via Export Substitution—Note", in G.M. Meier, *Leading Issues in Economic Development* (Singapore: Oxford University Press, 1984), pp. 394–5.

the country to benefit from learning effects and the increase in efficiency that accrues from competition in global markets. Since it usually involves labour-intensive products, it absorbs more manpower than import substitution and concurrently, the skills of workers are upgraded. Despite these merits, import substitution rather than export orientation had been prescribed by economists for post-colonial nations wishing to industrialise, as the latter strategy was viewed as a form of continued economic colonisation.[2] Singapore had in fact gone through such an import-replacing phase in the early 1960s and during the Malaysia interlude, after the World Bank recommended industrialisation based on the protection of "infant" industries.[3] Tariffs on products were raised and fiscal subsidies given to both domestic and foreign firms.[4] These companies were further protected by quantitative import restrictions on goods which competed with their products.

Nevertheless, several small economies in East Asia—Hong Kong, Taiwan and South Korea—implemented the export strategy, followed by Singapore.[5] In Singapore's case, the reason for its adoption at the time of independence is patently clear in view of the closing of the Malaysian market and the small size of the domestic market. What is not obvious and differentiates Singapore from the other countries was the flipside of this policy—the attraction of foreign direct investment, a strategy that was also unorthodox in the 1960s. Indeed, the entire industrialisation process in Singapore was synonymous with large inflows of capital to spearhead growth in major manufacturing industries.[6] The industries targeted were both export-oriented and labour-intensive in order to generate jobs and resolve the unemployment problem. Relying on foreign capital had the advantages of bringing with it state-of-the-art technology, managerial expertise and markets—a package deal. Given its long history of specialisation in commerce and finance and a concomitant lack of industrial entrepreneurs, Singapore did not possess these prerequisites in the sixties.

From a financial standpoint, Singapore's policy of attracting foreign investment was a strategy for augmenting domestic savings resources.[7] The national savings rate was only 11.4 per cent of GDP in 1960 but for industrial take-off, a higher rate of investment was required. In 1963, Dr Goh Keng Swee had noted that a high investment ratio of 20 per cent or more was to be aimed at in an economy which wanted to expand its basic wealth at a fast rate.[8] Hence, the gap had to be plugged by net inflows of foreign capital, which mostly took the form of direct investment rather than foreign debt or official development assistance. From the point of view of the current account in the balance of

---

[2] Tan, *A Very Short History*, p. 145.

[3] H. Hughes, "Growth of Singapore: An External View", Working Paper No. 91/13 (Canberra: National Centre for Development Studies, 1991), pp. 3–5.

[4] Soon Teck Wong and W.A. Stoever, "Foreign Investment and Economic Development in Singapore: A Policy-Oriented Approach", *The Journal of Developing Areas* 30, 3 (1996): 319–20.

[5] Hughes, "Growth of Singapore", pp. 5, 6.

[6] Keen Meng Choy, "Foreign Direct Investment in the Manufacturing Sector in Singapore", in Keen Meng Choy, *Studies on the Singapore Economy* (Singapore: World Scientific, 2012), p. 19; Lim and Pang, *Trade, Employment and Industrialisation*, pp. 11–12.

[7] Choy, "Foreign Direct Investment", pp. 20–1, 23.

[8] W.G. Huff, "The Developmental State, Government, and Singapore's Economic Development since 1960", *World Development* 23, 8 (1995): 1426.

payments, these fund inflows financed the imports of machinery and equipment needed for expanding the manufacturing and other sectors of the economy. During the period from 1965 to 1970, nearly $1 billion in foreign investment flowed into mainly labour-intensive and relatively low value-added industries in Singapore, in stark contrast to just $157 million during the 1960–65 period. These inflows raised the domestic investment rate to 21.9 per cent of GDP in 1965 and further to 38.7 per cent in 1970.[9] Earlier in the decade, the public sector share of gross capital formation was high on account of the building of socio-economic infrastructure but the private share rose to 80 per cent in 1970, reflecting the huge investments in industry. The average annual growth rate of overall investment over the latter half of the 1960s was 45 per cent.[10]

The EDB was key to Singapore's early industrialisation effort and within it, two divisions played a critical role. One was the Projects Division whose job was to conduct the technical and economic evaluation of projects as well as feasibility studies, starting from a list of industries drawn up by Albert Winsemius and his team.[11] Apart from screening potential investments to assess their suitability for loans and pioneer status, this division's work need not concern us here. More directly relevant is the Investment Promotion Division, whose functions were to sell Singapore as an ideal site for locating manufacturing industries and to reach out to foreign investors. This was done through the setting up of representative offices around the world, including importantly in London, New York, Tokyo and Hong Kong.[12] In addition, the division received trade and industrial delegations from Western countries. Large multinational corporations (MNCs) with established markets were actively wooed by the EDB to set up factories in Singapore.[13] In this task, the division was immensely successful, as indicated by the increase in the number of inquiries from potential investors to 1,300 in 1968 from 300 in 1964.[14] The EDB acted as a "one-stop shop" for foreign investors as all the necessary requirements for setting up industries—land, buildings, labour force and taxation—were well-taken care of by it and production could be up and running in a matter of weeks.[15] From an *ex-post* perspective, its success could be attributed to the ability to "pick winners" or thriving industries that fitted Singapore's comparative advantages.

Initially, the EDB was also responsible for industrial estate development and the financing of manufacturing enterprises, tasks it accomplished with much greater efficiency than its predecessors, the Industrial Promotion Board and Colonial Development Corporation, had done. By the end of 1965, $71 million had been disbursed for the first purpose.[16] A year later demand had accelerated for the subsidised industrial sites at Jurong,

[9] Wong Kum Poh, "Saving, Capital Inflow and Capital Formation", in *Singapore: Resources and Growth*, ed. Lim Chong Yah and P.J. Lloyd (Singapore: Oxford University Press, 1986), pp. 48–51.

[10] Chia Siow Yue, "Direct Foreign Investment and the Industrialization Process in Singapore", in *Singapore*, ed. Lim and Lloyd, p. 89.

[11] Lee, *Industrialization*, pp. 48–52, 61–4; Cheng, "Economic Change in Singapore", p. 91.

[12] *The Straits Times*, 29 Sept. 1966.

[13] *The Straits Times*, 3 Jan. 1967.

[14] *The Straits Times*, 5 Aug. 1967.

[15] Hughes, "Growth of Singapore", pp. 12, 13, 14.

[16] Lee, *Industrialization*, pp. 52–3, 56–8, 74–7.

with the number of applications for factory space rising to 190 and more than 809 hectares of industrial land being prepared, of which 496 hectares were allocated.[17] When space ran out at Jurong, the EDB began to build flatted factories in 1966, first at Tanglin and then at Kallang, while Tanjong Rhu, Geylang, Balestier and Macpherson were slated for development as light industry zones.[18] For financing, the government gave a $100 million capital grant to the EDB, intended for underwriting the issue of stocks and bonds by enterprises, making loans to or investing in industry and providing technical assistance to firms.[19] At end-1965, $39 million in loans at an interest rate of 6–7 per cent had been disbursed and another $14 million was invested in equity stakes, the first being that of the National Iron and Steel Mills.[20] In August 1968, the loan figure reached $66 million while the paid-up equity in various ventures totalled $28.9 million.[21]

At about that time, the estate development function was taken over by the Jurong Town Corporation (JTC), a newly established statutory board, and its mandate broadened to include the provision of amenities for people living and working in industrial estates.[22] To this end, Jurong was transformed into a self-contained town. In 1970, there were 271 factories in the area and pioneer status had been awarded to 281 firms.[23] The JTC's principal sources of income were land leases, tenancies of industrial land and rentals from housing. The financing function was similarly spun off from the EDB in July 1968 and handed to the state-sponsored Development Bank of Singapore (DBS), which sourced its funds from both the government and private sector.[24] By the end of 1970, DBS had made financial commitments of $339 million to 127 companies, mostly in the form of long-term loans. In addition, the bank provided trade financing in the form of export credits and guarantees.[25] Another government agency, Intraco, was formed for the purpose of conducting trade with the Communist countries, which was accompanied by the signing of trade pacts between Singapore and Russia, Bulgaria and Poland.[26]

Institutions aside, the success of the industrialisation drive in Singapore hinged on a highly liberal and business-friendly policy on foreign investment, with no restrictions on the entry of foreign companies, no excluded sectors and no requirements on local content

[17] H. Hughes, "From Entrepot Trade to Manufacturing", in *Foreign Investment and Industrialization in Singapore*, ed. H. Hughes and You Poh Seng (Canberra: Australian National University Press, 1969), p. 29; Soon and Stoever, "Foreign Investment and Economic Development", p. 322; *The Straits Times*, 6 Sept. 1967.

[18] *10 Years that Shaped a Nation*, p. 71.

[19] Cheng, "Economic Change in Singapore", pp. 88–9, 91.

[20] Lee, *Industrialization*, p. 30.

[21] Chia Siow Yue, "Growth and Pattern of Industrialization", in *The Singapore Economy*, ed. You Poh Seng and Lim Chong Yah (Singapore: Eastern Universities Press, 1971), p. 209.

[22] Lee, *Industrialization*, pp. 101–10; *The Straits Times*, 12 May 1968, 22 May 1968. A statutory board is an autonomous government agency established by an Act of Parliament to perform specific operational functions and deliver public services.

[23] Chia, "Growth and Pattern", p. 192.

[24] *The Straits Times*, 7 Oct. 1968.

[25] Le Blanc, *Singapore*, p. 95.

[26] Turnbull, *History of Modern Singapore*, p. 310; Lee, *Industrialization*, p. 99; *10 Years that Shaped a Nation*, p. 77.

or domestic sourcing of inputs.[27] Since protective tariffs and import quotas had been gradually dismantled by the late 1960s with the switch to an export-oriented development strategy, foreign firms could import machinery and intermediate inputs at competitive world prices.[28] Importantly, full foreign ownership of manufacturing ventures was allowed, profits, dividends, royalties and capital could be freely repatriated to home countries and there were no stipulations on technology transfer. The Singapore government also provided new industrial investment incentives other than pioneer status.[29] In 1967, it announced that profits from approved exports would be taxed at a concessionary rate of 4 per cent (instead of the usual 40 per cent) for a period of five years and that this period could be extended if certain conditions were fulfilled.[30] Moreover, an investment tax allowance for new spending on machinery and factory buildings was given to firms that did not qualify for pioneer status or the export incentive. These tax holidays were the principal incentives, though land and training subsidies were also given to some corporations.[31]

Innovative labour legislation was as important as these subventions, if not more so. It was remarked earlier that the trade union movement had been brought under control by the time of independence. The PAP government entrenched this accomplishment with two laws that ensured a disciplined workforce and harmonious industrial relations: the Employment Act and the Industrial Relations Amendment Act, both of 1968.[32] The first standardised the terms and conditions of employment by extending working time to 44 hours a week, reducing the number of paid holidays and annual leave, and restricting the payment of retrenchment benefits and bonuses.[33] The second created an Industrial Arbitration Court to resolve wage disputes and removed recruitment, promotion and dismissal issues from collective negotiations.[34] Essentially, the new legislation transferred bargaining power from workers to employers, helped to contain labour costs and improved the investment climate.[35] As a result, man-days lost through strikes were negligible after 1968, which was also due in part to a law passed in 1966 requiring a secret ballot with a majority of union members in favour before a strike could be called. Above all,

---

[27] Choy, "Foreign Direct Investment", pp. 24–5, 39; Chia, "Direct Foreign Investment", p. 81.

[28] "Foreign Investment Policy", in Lim Chong Yah and Associates, *Policy Options for the Singapore Economy* (Singapore: McGraw-Hill, 1988), p. 256; Hughes, "Growth of Singapore", pp. 6–7. Initially however, tariff and quota protection was maintained and even increased in an effort to create jobs in local industries. Lim, Pang and Findlay, "Singapore", pp. 102–3.

[29] *The Straits Times*, 15 Nov. 1967.

[30] Lim and Pang, *Trade, Employment and Industrialisation*, p. 19.

[31] Hughes, "Growth of Singapore", p. 14.

[32] Lim and Pang, *Trade, Employment and Industrialisation*, p. 11.

[33] T. Geiger and F.M. Geiger, *Tales of Two City-States: The Development Progress of Hong Kong and Singapore* (National Planning Association, 1973), p. 163.

[34] Peter S.J. Chen, "Singapore's Development Strategies: A Model for Rapid Growth", in *Singapore Development Policies and Trends*, ed. Peter S.J. Chen (Singapore: Oxford University Press, 1983), p. 12; Turnbull, *History of Modern Singapore*, p. 310; Lee, *Singapore Chronicles: Economy*, p. 33.

[35] Pang Eng Fong and Linda Lim, "Labor, Productivity and Singapore's Development Model", *The Singapore Economic Review* 60, 3 (2015): 1550033-4.

Singapore had achieved political stability by the mid-1960s and it had a government free of corruption.[36]

Singapore was fortunate that as a result of rising labour costs in the industrialised countries, there was a spread of worldwide sourcing of products by MNCs from low-wage locations. At the same time, manufacturers of electrical and electronic goods in the 1960s developed an international division of labour whereby the labour-intensive assembly of components and finished goods was undertaken in low-cost developing countries and research and other skill-intensive operations continued to be carried out in the advanced economies.[37] These developments were both facilitated by and contributed to the buoyant global trade that resulted from a relatively free world trading system unfettered by restrictions on investment.[38] Furthermore, when the UNCTAD/GATT Generalized System of Preferences (GSP), which gave developing countries preferential access to markets in the industrial countries, started in 1971, Singapore was admitted.[39]

Foreign manufacturing investment showed a wide sectoral distribution during the 1965–70 period. In addition to the petroleum refining industry which had garnered substantial investments since 1960 as global oil companies such as Shell, Esso and British Petroleum (BP) located their refineries in Singapore to be nearer to markets, the segments that received the most investment were electrical machinery and electronics, chemicals and chemical products, metals and precision engineering, transport equipment, and textiles and garments.[40] Capital intensity and hence labour productivity were highest in the petroleum and chemical industries and relatively low in the electronics, transport equipment, textiles and footwear industries.[41] The late sixties also saw the rapid development of an old and familiar industry in Singapore—ship repair and shipbuilding. As in the past, the island's location gave it an edge, with the business almost doubling between 1966 and 1968 and the number of firms increasing to 45.[42] These companies were the modern successors to the small shipyards that were located at Tanjong Rhu during the colonial period.[43] The biggest firm in the industry was Jurong Shipyard, a

---

36 Hughes, "Growth of Singapore", p. 7.

37 Lee, *Industrialization*, pp. 87, 95.

38 Pang Eng Fong and Linda Lim, "Rapid Growth and Relative Price Stability in a Small Open Economy: The Experience of Singapore", in *Export-Oriented Development Strategies: The Success of Five Newly Industrialising Countries*, ed. V. Corbo, A.O. Krueger and F. Ossa (Boulder and London: Westview Press, 1985), p. 81; Chia, "Growth and Pattern", p. 203. Between 1963 and 1973, world manufactured exports grew at an average rate of 11.5 per cent per year. Huff, *The Economic Growth of Singapore*, p. 302; Hughes, "Growth of Singapore", p. 8.

39 Wong Kum Poh, *Essays on the Singapore Economy* (Singapore: Federal Publications and Nanyang Siang Pau, 1982), p. 6.

40 Chia, "Direct Foreign Investment", pp. 84–5, 91; Pang and Lim, "Rapid Growth", pp. 94–5; Lee, *Industrialization*, p. 82; *The Straits Times*, 6 Aug. 1967, 19 Feb. 1971.

41 Lim and Pang, *Trade, Employment and Industrialisation*, pp. 40, 44; Lee Sheng-Yi, "Some Basic Problems of Industrialization in Singapore", *The Journal of Developing Areas* 7, 2 (1973): 188–94; Lim Chong Yah and Ow Chwee Huay, "The Economic Development of Singapore in the Sixties and Beyond", in *The Singapore Economy*, ed. You and Lim, pp. 32–4.

42 Turnbull, *History of Modern Singapore*, pp. 310, 311.

43 *10 Years that Shaped a Nation*, pp. 86–7.

joint venture between the EDB and Ishikawajima Harima from Japan.[44] Oil exploration activities in the waters of Indonesia also attracted more than one hundred consulting, diving, engineering and supply firms to Singapore.

Among the different industries, electrical and electronics and textiles and garments had the highest employment generation capacities. In 1965, the electrical industry in Singapore produced lower-end goods such as television sets, tape recorders, radio kits and electric fans, but by 1968, semiconductor firms from the United States had established a foothold on the island, followed by European and Japanese MNCs.[45] Names like Texas Instruments, Hewlett Packard, Fairchild, Philips, Siemens, Hitachi, Toshiba and Sanyo began to crop up in Jurong and elsewhere.[46] From 1968 to 1970, the electronics industry was the most rapidly growing industry in terms of value-added and by 1973, it was employing 44,483 workers.[47] In contrast, the textile and garments industry started as a local industry of cottage-like outfits manufacturing for the domestic market. During the period of merger with Malaysia, there was an influx of investments from Hong Kong entrepreneurs eager to avoid restrictions imposed by Britain on the city's textile exports.[48] When the common market failed to materialise, the firms began to market their goods overseas by making use of the Multi-Fibre Arrangement (MFA).[49] In 1973, the industry provided jobs for 35,012 workers.

After 1968, Singapore became the preferred venue for American corporations seeking an offshore production base for electronic components. It is therefore not surprising that the United States was the second most important source of foreign investment in 1970, just behind Europe and ahead of Japan.[50] Other American companies in Singapore produced a wide range of manufactured goods, including petroleum, motor vehicles, batteries, photographic products and cosmetics.[51] European investments originated mainly from the United Kingdom and the Netherlands and were predominantly in the petroleum industry. However, British firms also manufactured brake fluid, lubricants and a wide range of industrial and electrical products.[52] From 1970 onwards, West German investment became more conspicuous, especially in precision engineering and photographic

---

44 Lee, *Industrialization*, pp. 83, 84; Loh Kah Seng and Tammy Chandra, "Albert Winsemius Heritage Trail", in Quah with Iuldashov and Lee, *Albert Winsemius and Singapore*, pp. 696–8; Le Blanc, *Singapore*, p. 36.

45 *The Straits Times*, 4 July 1969.

46 Another memorable name was Rollei, the German camera maker that came to Singapore in 1971 but went bankrupt a decade later, one of the few failures of the industrialisation effort. Loh Kah Seng, "Memories of Rollei Singapore", *Berita Newsletter* (Winter 2018/2019): 6–8.

47 Soon and Stoever, "Foreign Investment and Economic Development", p. 323.

48 Huff, *The Economic Growth of Singapore*, p. 322; Lee, *Industrialization*, pp. 81–2.

49 The MFA governed the world trade in textiles and garments between developing and developed countries.

50 Pang and Lim, "Rapid Growth", pp. 92–3.

51 P.H. Lindert, "United States Investment", in *Foreign Investment and Industrialization*, ed. Hughes and You, pp. 154–5.

52 G. Davies, "United Kingdom Investment", in *Foreign Investment and Industrialization*, ed. Hughes and You, p. 50.

and optical products.[53] Japan's manufacturing investment was at first concentrated in the metals and engineering industries but it started to invest in electronics, textiles and shipbuilding and repair in the late 1960s.[54] Family-owned businesses from Hong Kong and Taiwan which were the earlier focus of the EDB also invested in Singapore to avoid the political risk posed by the Cultural Revolution in China.[55] In 1973, the United States overtook Europe to become the top investor while Japan increased its share of inward investment. Given these sources, most of Singapore's domestic exports of manufactured goods went to North America, Europe and Japan.[56] However, Malaysia remained the largest overall export market (even though trade barriers reduced its import of industrial goods from Singapore) and Hong Kong was also a major destination.[57]

In 1970, there were 967 wholly foreign or majority foreign-owned companies in Singapore, most to be found in manufacturing and financial services.[58] These firms accounted for 54 per cent of gross fixed assets in manufacturing, 55 per cent of the sector's output, 49 per cent of value-added and 34 per cent of workers employed.[59] In comparison, locally owned firms accounted for only 25 per cent of manufacturing value-added but employed 40 per cent of the workers in the sector. In 1977, the contribution to the direct exports of the manufacturing sector was 56 per cent for wholly foreign-owned firms and 26 per cent for joint venture companies, resulting in direct exports accounting for 65 per cent of total manufacturing output.[60] In 1973, domestic manufactured exports (that is, excluding re-exports) made up more than half of total exports, exceeding non-oil primary commodity exports for the first time; they had grown at an annual rate of 31 per cent from 1967, another indication of the leading role of foreign firms.[61]

The foregoing narrative of Singapore's industrial development would seem to suggest that it was achieved via pragmatic economic policies and free market forces—"pragmatism in pursuit of growth".[62] Such a conclusion would be consonant with conventional accounts of the economic philosophy underlying government intervention that emphasise its roles as supporting and supplementing the workings of the market mechanism, developing infrastructure or investing in enterprises which could not or would not be established

---

[53] Lee, "Some Basic Problems", pp. 206, 207.

[54] R. Hirono, "Japanese Investment", in *Foreign Investment and Industrialization*, ed. Hughes and You, p. 91; Cheng, "Economic Change in Singapore", p. 108.

[55] Lim and Pang, *Trade, Employment and Industrialisation*, p. 86; Lee, *Singapore Chronicles: Economy*, pp. 30–1; Lee, *The Unexpected Nation*, p. 271.

[56] Lim and Pang, *Trade, Employment and Industrialisation*, pp. 35–6.

[57] Lee, *Industrialization*, pp. 83–4; Chia, "Growth and Pattern", p. 202.

[58] "Foreign Investment Policy", pp. 247–9, 252–4.

[59] Chia, "Direct Foreign Investment", pp. 95, 96, 103, 105; Lee, "Some Basic Problems", pp. 206, 210.

[60] K. Grice and D.W. Drakakis-Smith, "The Role of the State in Shaping Development: Two Decades of Growth in Singapore", *Transactions of the Institute of British Geographers* 10, 3 (1985): 353.

[61] Huff, *The Economic Growth of Singapore*, pp. 312, 318, 320; Geiger and Geiger, *Tales of Two City-States*, p. 175.

[62] Tan Kim Song and Manu Bhaskaran, "The Role of the State in Singapore: Pragmatism in Pursuit of Growth", *The Singapore Economic Review*, 60, 3 (2015).

by the private sector, ranging from shipyards to banking.[63] However, it has been pointed out that the "long arm of the state" rather than the "invisible hand" of the free market is the reason for the city-state's outstanding economic success.[64] The PAP itself considered Singapore to be a "socialist economy that works".[65]

Yet another influential and more general explanation of the "miracle" economies of Hong Kong, Taiwan, Korea and Singapore is the East Asian developmental state. According to this interpretation, strategic state intervention facilitated industrial transformation and economic growth in these countries.[66] Thus, the state was the *primum movens* of socio-economic progress; by the same token, the ideology of developmentalism necessitated government intervention in a dirigiste economy.[67] Unlike in capitalist free market economies where the political leadership made the decisions, policies to guide economic development in such states were formulated and implemented by a relatively autonomous bureaucratic elite (including the senior staff of statutory boards in Singapore). This observation resonates with the label of "administrative state" that has been applied to the Singapore polity.[68] Compared with the other East Asian countries, the Singapore government's intervention in the economy was in fact both more pervasive and intrusive.[69]

Marxian political economists do not subscribe to any of these views. To them, Singapore succeeded by being co-opted into an emerging new international division of labour that exploited developing countries in the manufacturing production of labour-intensive goods.[70] Its incorporation into the world capitalist system came at a time of opportune historical conditions and entailed the state's cooperation with international capital, whereby the state accommodated the requirements of such capital as economic circumstances evolved. Specifically, the PAP provided the preconditions for international capital to produce in Singapore for the world market, of which the key elements were the provision of industrial infrastructure and politically docile labour. The Marxian view therefore grants primary significance to the role of the state in the industrialisation process;

---

63 Ow Chin Hock, "The Role of Government in Economic Development: The Singapore Experience", in *Singapore*, ed. Lim and Lloyd, p. 236; "The Role of Government", in Lim and Associates, *Policy Options*, pp. 51, 61.

64 Linda Lim, "Singapore's Success: The Myth of the Free Market", *Asian Survey* 23, 6 (1983): 755–8, 760.

65 Goh Keng Swee. "A Socialist Economy that Works", in *Socialism that Works … the Singapore Way*, ed. C.V. Devan Nair (Singapore: Federal Publications, 1976), pp. 77–85; Lee, *Singapore Chronicles: Economy*, pp. 20–1.

66 Joseph Wong, "The Adaptive Developmental State in East Asia", *Journal of East Asian Studies* 4, 2 (2004): 350–2. Huff, "The Developmental State", pp. 1421–2.

67 G. White and R. Wade, "Developmental States and Markets in East Asia: An Introduction", in *Developmental States in East Asia*, ed. G. White (Palgrave Macmillan, 1988), pp. 1–2.

68 Chan Heng Chee, "Political Developments", in *A History of Singapore*, ed. Chew and Lee, p. 170; Regnier, *Singapore*, pp. 233–4. Some observers viewed the manner and style of government as Confucianist. Geiger and Geiger, *Tales of Two City-States*, p. 216.

69 Tan and Bhaskaran, "The Role of the State in Singapore", p. 1550030-3.

70 G. Rodan, *The Political Economy of Singapore's Industrialization: National State and International Capital* (Basingstoke: Macmillan Press, 1989), pp. 1, 17–19, 23, 25, 26, 98. Related to this view is that which denounces Singapore as an instrument of the contemporary neo-colonialism of the Western industrial countries. Regnier, *Singapore*, p. 39.

more than that, it places great importance on the social and political conditions within which industrial policy choices were made.

Along with international capital, the state's deployment of its monopoly capital was critical. In addition to the iron and steel mill, the Singapore government in 1963 established enterprises for the manufacture of sugar, textiles, polymers and ceramics.[71] To reduce the cost of exporting, the state in 1969 set up a shipping line which it fully owned, Neptune Orient Lines (NOL), and broke up the shipping conference cartel that dated from colonial days.[72] Other productive investments were in Sembawang and Keppel Shipyards, Singapore Airlines (SIA), the Singapore Petroleum Company (SPC), the Public Utilities Board (PUB), the Telecommunications Authority of Singapore (TAS), the Port of Singapore Authority (PSA) and the Post Office Savings Bank (POSB), the last two being the successors to the erstwhile Singapore Harbour Board and Postal Savings Bank, respectively.[73] Taking the cue from the government, the NTUC also established cooperatives to run supermarket, life insurance and taxi transport businesses, with many more ventures in subsequent years.

In addition to the above entities, there were numerous firms with equity participation by the state, which were later categorised as "government-linked companies" (GLCs) after some of them were corporatised.[74] By the mid-1980s, there were nearly 500 of these, accounting for an estimated 10 per cent of GDP and one-fifth of labour force employment.[75] By contrast, most business establishments in Singapore were small and medium-sized enterprises (SMEs), employing the bulk of the local workforce but accounting for disproportionately less of the economy's output. Run as private enterprises, the GLCs spanned diverse facets of economic activity in the city-state, extending to gambling (Singapore Pools), tourism and leisure (Singapore Zoological Gardens and Jurong Bird Park). Another group of government enterprises met defence and security needs, for example the Chartered Industries of Singapore (CIS) for arms manufacture and the Singapore Mint for coin minting.[76] What is unusual about these public enterprises is that most of them made profits.[77] Therefore, the foreign MNCs, like the colonial agency houses before them, occupied the commanding heights of the Singapore economy; below them were the GLCs and at the bottom, the SMEs. Squeezed and crowded out by international and state capital, the local bourgeoisie harboured the resentment that they were not able to partake fully of the industrialisation process.[78] Local companies also could not avail themselves of the managerial and technical talent in the country since they were

---

[71] Rodan, *The Political Economy of Singapore's Industrialization*, pp. 77–8, 109–10.

[72] Turnbull, *History of Modern Singapore*, p. 310. NOL was sold to a French shipping firm in 2016 after incurring losses. Tan, *A Very Short History*, pp. 147–8.

[73] Lee, *Singapore Chronicles: Economy*, pp. 33–4, 51.

[74] Ow, "The Role of Government", pp. 243, 259–62.

[75] Huff, *The Economic Growth of Singapore*, pp. 331–2; Grice and Drakakis-Smith, "The Role of the State", p. 354.

[76] Cheng, "Economic Change in Singapore", p. 111; *The Straits Times*, 27 Apr. 1968.

[77] Lim, *Free Market*, p. 756.

[78] Rodan, *The Political Economy of Singapore's Industrialization*, pp. 109–10; Ow, "The Role of Government", p. 245.

creamed off by the MNCs and GLCs. Nevertheless, these companies were not crowded out in the capital market since the others obtained their funds mainly from home country head offices or from the Singapore government.

Economic Restructuring and Recession

Export-oriented industrialisation reduced the unemployment rate in Singapore from 8.1 per cent in 1967 to 4.5 per cent in 1973—effectively full employment. The incipient labour shortages that resulted led in turn to wage rises, job-hopping and labour poaching among factories.[79] The government responded to the situation with three sets of policies.[80] First, it allowed the importation of foreign workers both skilled and unskilled to make up for the shortfall in domestic labour supply.[81] Second, in order to raise productivity and incomes, it tightened the investment incentives then existing with the objective of encouraging more capital and skill-intensive as well as higher value-added manufacturing production.[82] Third, the government established a tripartite National Wages Council (NWC) in 1972 with representatives from the government, labour unions and employers' associations to ensure orderly wage increases so as not to jeopardise Singapore's export competitiveness.[83]

Following the liberalisation of immigration rules in 1973, over 100,000 foreign workers entered the labour force, most of them from Peninsular Malaysia.[84] A dependence on foreign labour was of course not new to Singapore as, for most of its history, it had relied on immigrants to achieve economic growth. During the mid-seventies, some migrant workers were retrenched due to a slowdown in the economy, but their numbers were up again in 1978, when the government started a work permit scheme to allow the entry of labourers from Thailand, the Philippines, Indonesia, India, Bangladesh and Sri Lanka, in addition to the Malaysians.[85] The two sectors in which most foreign workers were found were manufacturing—especially the textiles, garments, leather and wood products industries—and construction.[86] In addition to these short-term manual workers, Singapore also welcomed skilled workers, professionals and entrepreneurs on a longer-term basis, as it was thought that they would uplift the quality of labour and increase the stock of human capital in the economy.

In the early 1970s, the qualifying amount of investment required for pioneer status was raised to $1 million and investment allowances for expanding production were restricted

---

79 Lee, "Some Basic Problems", pp. 197–8.

80 *The Straits Times*, 10 May 1972.

81 Lim and Pang, *Trade, Employment and Industrialisation*, pp. 11–12, 18.

82 Chia, "Growth and Pattern", p. 194.

83 Huff, *The Economic Growth of Singapore*, p. 332; *The Straits Times*, 9 Feb. 1972.

84 Pang Eng Fong and Linda Lim, "Foreign Labor and Economic Development in Singapore", *International Migration Review* 16, 3 (1982): 548–50.

85 *The Straits Times*, 2 Dec. 1978.

86 Lim and Pang, *Trade, Employment and Industrialisation*, pp. 61–2.

to new capital outlays of at least $10 million.[87] Accelerated depreciation allowances, allowing losses to be carried forward, were also reserved for larger pioneer firms with fixed investments of at least $1 billion. The export tax incentive was made more stringent, with a reduction in the concessionary term from 15 years to eight years for pioneer enterprises and five years for the rest. Enterprises with large investments in skill-intensive and more technologically advanced industries were given pioneer status for up to ten years. In 1975, a capital assistance scheme was started, with a budget of $100 million, to provide loan and equity financing to investors with specialised projects that would benefit Singapore economically and technologically. The EDB also made available a finance scheme at low interest rates for small firms to upgrade their operations.[88]

As for the NWC, its specific roles were to formulate annual wage guidelines for the labour force based on the tripartite consensus, recommend wage structure adjustment and advise on incentive systems.[89] Of these, the first function was the most important, entailing the consideration of prevailing macroeconomic conditions—inflation, unemployment and productivity growth among other factors—in deciding on the quantum of wage increases in any one year.[90] While the wage guidelines were not mandatory, they strongly influenced actual wage changes in the public service and private companies. In order to maintain international competitiveness in labour-intensive exports, the wage increases recommended by the NWC during the 1970s were modest, less than 10 per cent per annum for most years except in 1974 when the recommendation was 20 per cent to offset high inflation, largely the result of the 1973–74 oil crisis triggered by the Organisation of Petroleum Exporting Countries (OPEC)'s oil price hike. Wage increases had to be kept in check, especially after the global stagflation (a recession accompanied by high inflation) brought on by these price increases. The differential in the manufacturing wage rate between the higher level in Singapore and those in Hong Kong, Taiwan and Korea therefore narrowed.[91]

As a consequence, however, firms in Singapore were not induced to use labour efficiently or to upgrade their production processes, thus worsening labour shortages and keeping manufacturing productivity low.[92] Foreign investment fell during and immediately after the oil shock, rebounding only in 1978 (Figure 21).[93] During this interlude, the government refrained from upgrading policies but took the opportunity to promote local manufacturing enterprises by giving them financial and product development assistance.[94] In 1979, a second oil price increase again led to a curtailment of investment inflows, but these recovered to increase to a record $1.9 billion in 1981 despite gloomy predictions.[95]

[87] Chia, "Direct Foreign Investment", p. 83; K. Yoshihara, *Foreign Investment and Domestic Response: A Study of Singapore's Industrialization* (Singapore: Eastern Universities Press, 1976), pp. 25–7.

[88] Lim and Pang, *Trade, Employment and Industrialisation*, pp. 19–20; *The Business Times*, 3 Oct. 1979.

[89] Pang and Lim, "Labor, Productivity", pp. 1550033-4–1550033-5.

[90] Lim Chong Yah, *Singapore's National Wages Council: An Insider's View* (Singapore: World Scientific, 2014), pp. 24–31.

[91] "Wage Policy", in Lim and Associates, *Policy Options*, pp. 184–5; Lee, "Some Basic Problems", p. 204.

[92] *The Business Times*, 26 June 1979.

[93] Chia, "Direct Foreign Investment", pp. 88–9.

[94] Le Blanc, *Singapore*, p. 26.

[95] Lim and Pang, *Trade, Employment and Industrialisation*, p. 19.

Local investments in the following year also surged to account for a third of all new commitments.[96] Hence, the JTC increased the amount of land allocated for industrial purposes and established new industrial estates in outlying areas, for example at Sungei Kadut and Kranji.[97]

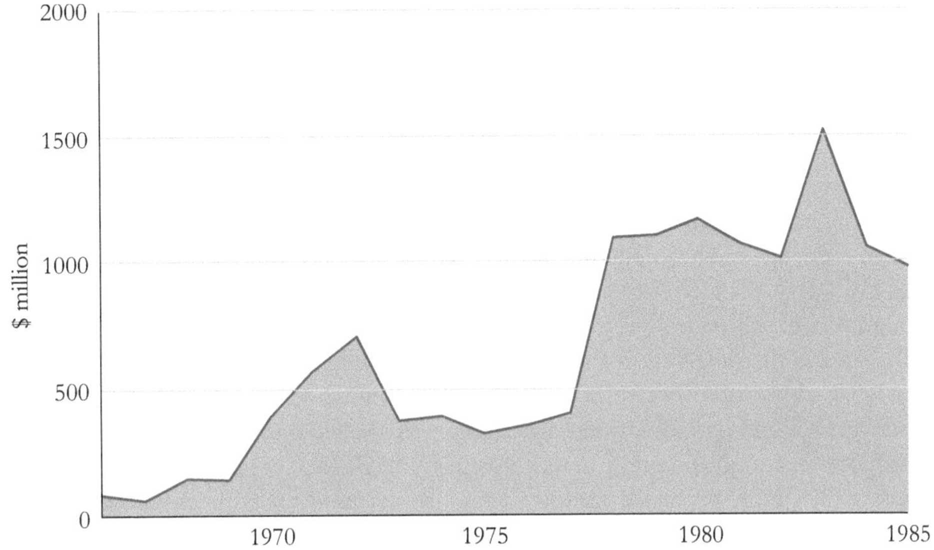

Figure 21. Foreign Investment in Singapore's Manufacturing Sector, 1966–85
Sources: Chia, "Direct Foreign Investment", Table 4.1, p. 89; Soon and Stoever, "Foreign Investment and Economic Development", Table 1, p. 321.

Concerned that orderly and gradual wage increases were leading to a low-wage equilibrium trap, in 1979 the Singapore government through its newly formed Ministry of Trade and Industry embarked on a plan to restructure the economy—the so-called "Second Industrial Revolution". Its centrepiece was the implementation of a wage correction policy to return wages to market levels and force firms to move upmarket.[98] At the broader macroeconomic level, it also entailed substantial increases in government expenditure to expand and improve physical and social infrastructure and thus facilitate economic restructuring.[99] The wage catch-up policy had in fact been recommended by Albert Winsemius earlier, who regretted that his advice to the NWC to institute wage increases and reduce dependency on foreign workers went unheeded after the mid-seventies oil crisis.[100] For three years from 1979 to 1981, the NWC issued guidelines for wages to rise on average by close to

96 *The Business Times*, 31 Dec. 1980.

97 Centre for Liveable Cities, *Industrial Infrastructure: Growing in Tandem with the Economy* (Singapore: Cengage Learning Asia, 2013), p. 12.

98 Lim and Pang, *Trade, Employment and Industrialisation*, pp. 11–2; J. Rigg, "Singapore and the Recession of 1985", *Asian Survey* 28, 3 (1988): 343.

99 Rodan, *The Political Economy of Singapore's Industrialization*, pp. 151–2.

100 Sng Hui Ying, "Albert Winsemius and Wage Policy in Singapore", in Quah with Iuldashov and Lee, *Albert Winsemius and Singapore*, pp. 431–5, 441; *The Business Times*, 23 July 1980.

20 per cent each year.[101] The goal was attained in the first two years but it was exceeded in 1981, with labour costs going up by 28 per cent.

The economic restructuring policy can be seen as an attempt to move away from labour-intensive production and carve out a comparative advantage in more capital-intensive and higher productivity activities, since wage costs in Singapore were rising relative to other developing countries that were also beginning to industrialise and protectionism was on the increase in the developed economies.[102] The aim of the policy was to ease out highly labour-intensive, low-wage and low productivity economic activities—not only in manufacturing but also in the service sector.[103] It sought to achieve these objectives by increasing the relative price of labour so that capital would be substituted for it through automation and computerisation, which were also encouraged through fiscal incentives.[104] As part of this policy, in 1982 the government tightened the rules for the importation of unskilled workers from non-Malaysian sources and imposed a levy on foreign workers hired by domestic firms, but eased controls on immigration of skilled and professional personnel.[105] A Skills Development Fund (SDF) was created with contributions by employers amounting to 4 per cent of the wages of their lower-paid employees, to be used for enhancing worker skills through subsidised training programmes.[106] To improve productivity, a Mechanisation Scheme for firms was introduced.[107] Complementing these measures, the EDB scouted overseas for foreign investment in more advanced industries such as machine tools, precision engineering products and components, electronic instrumentation, optical instruments, computers and peripherals, and chemical products.[108]

The restructuring effort appears to have been relatively successful in upgrading manufacturing production in Singapore. Employment creation slowed while the intake of foreign workers moderated after the wage increases.[109] Net investment commitments averaged $1.7 billion per year from 1980 to 1984, which were channelled mainly into the electronics and information technology industries.[110] Productivity gains doubled to about 5 per cent per annum in the last two years of the restructuring plan and remained

---

101 The guidelines were in the form of a dollar quantum plus a percentage quantum. Together with increases in the employer CPF contribution rate, the Skills Development Fund levy and a payroll tax, they amounted to 20 per cent per year. Lim Chong Yah, *Economic Restructuring in Singapore* (Singapore: Federal Publications, 1984), pp. 34–5.

102 *Wage Policy*, p. 194; *New Nation*, 8 Sept. 1980.

103 Lim, *Singapore's National Wages Council*, p. 117.

104 Soon and Stoever, "Foreign Investment and Economic Development", pp. 326–7.

105 Pang and Lim, "Labor, Productivity", p. 1550033-6; Rigg, "Singapore and the Recession of 1985", p. 343; Linda Lim, *Business, Government and Labor: Essays on Economic Development in Singapore and Southeast Asia* (Singapore: World Scientific, 2018), p. 110.

106 Lim and Pang, *Trade, Employment and Industrialisation*, p. 21; *The Straits Times*, 11 Oct. 1980.

107 Regnier, *Singapore*, p. 86.

108 Rodan, *The Political Economy of Singapore's Industrialization*, pp. 147–8.

109 *The Straits Times*, 22 June 1980, 3 Nov. 1980, 28 Nov. 1980.

110 Soon and Stoever, "Foreign Investment and Economic Development", p. 327; Regnier, *Singapore*, pp. 94–5. The amount represented nearly half of all the foreign investment that went to Asia during that period. Lim, Pang and Findlay, "Singapore", p. 127.

relatively high at 4 per cent in 1983.[111] The average number of workers per establishment declined, accompanied by a greater export orientation and higher capital expenditure and value-added per worker.[112] Labour-intensive industries' contributions to manufacturing output were reduced: textiles, garments and wearing apparel from 4.3 per cent in 1970 to 3.6 per cent in 1981, printing and publishing from 2.5 per cent to 1.8 per cent and fabricated metal products from 5.6 per cent to 4 per cent.

The share of lower value-added industries making jewellery, toys and umbrellas also decreased from 3 per cent to 1.3 per cent over the 1970–81 period. In addition, rubber processing factories and sawmills were shut down; three car assembly plants and a tyre factory were also closed.[113] Higher value-added industries increased their share of output, with petroleum refining rising from 31.4 per cent to 39 per cent and electrical machinery and electronics from 7.2 per cent to 18 per cent. Some electronics manufacturers phased out their lower-end products and moved into higher value goods while others relocated production elsewhere.[114] Hence, the manufacturing sector changed structurally between the late 1960s and the early 1980s, with the production of simple goods giving way to more sophisticated and higher technology products. New industries included those producing automotive components, non-electrical machinery, precision optical instruments, as well as industrial electronics products such as industrial control equipment, electronic measuring equipment, communication equipment and electronic calculators.[115]

Notwithstanding the need for economic restructuring, its execution via a high wage policy exacted a cost on the economy. The rapidity with which the policy was implemented, in particular, is recognised as a major cause of the classical recession that Singapore experienced in 1985–86—the first since independence.[116] Specifically, the severe erosion of export competitiveness resulting from excessive wage increases that outstripped productivity gains was exacerbated by hikes in the contribution rates to the CPF and the SDF levy as well as the imposition of a payroll tax.[117] Between 1978 and 1982, average

---

[111] Lim and Pang, *Trade, Employment and Industrialisation*, pp. 8, 18–19, 25–6, 54, 56; *The Straits Times*, 3 Nov. 1980.

[112] Value-added per worker rose dramatically by 85 per cent between 1980 and 1981. Rigg, "Singapore and the Recession of 1985", p. 343.

[113] Arthur Lim Joo-Hock, "Singapore in 1980: Management of Foreign Relations", in *Southeast Asian Affairs 1981* (Singapore: Institute of Southeast Asian Studies, 1981), pp. 276–7; Rodan, *The Political Economy of Singapore's Industrialization*, pp. 146–7.

[114] *The Straits Times*, 3 Nov. 1980. Both Hewlett Packard and National Semiconductors shifted part of their production to Penang. Rodan, *The Political Economy of Singapore's Industrialization*, pp. 119–20.

[115] Rodan, *The Political Economy of Singapore's Industrialization*, pp. 119, 180–1.

[116] "From Recession to Recovery", in Lim and Associates, *Policy Options*, pp. 35–6; *The Business Times*, 27 July 1985. A classical recession occurs when the level of economic activity falls whereas a growth recession takes place when the rate of GDP growth declines.

[117] L.B. Krause, Koh Ai Tee and Lee (Tsao) Yuan, *The Singapore Economy Reconsidered* (Singapore: Institute of Southeast Asian Studies, 1987), pp. 149, 155. The payroll tax paid by firms was 2 per cent while the increase in the combined CPF contribution rate of employers and employees to 50 per cent in 1984 was partly intended to mop up the excess liquidity created by the wage rises. Lim Chong Yah, "Singapore's Economic Development: Retrospect and Prospect", in *Singapore Development Policies and Trends*, ed. Chen, p. 98.

wages in manufacturing rose by 81 per cent.[118] At the same time, there were increases in the fees and charges levied by statutory boards.[119] The appreciation of the Singapore dollar by the monetary authority to counter inflationary pressures in the early eighties had a similar effect on competitiveness.[120] These combined developments raised relative unit labour costs in Singapore to a level above those in Taiwan and South Korea.[121]

The inadvertent outcome of economic restructuring interacted with other factors to exacerbate the recession's severity. On the external front, there was a downturn in the region precipitated by falling oil and commodity prices, coupled with a slowdown of economic growth in the United States, a key market for Singapore, which reduced export growth significantly.[122] Entrepôt trade with, and tourism from, Indonesia and Malaysia were badly hit.[123] The slump in oil prices also adversely affected oil exploration and oil rig construction activities in Singapore. Quite apart from cyclical events, a few local manufacturing industries were plagued by structural problems. The most badly affected was the oil and marine-related sector, which suffered from the excess capacity resulting from a drop in world oil shipments. Indonesia and Middle Eastern countries were also processing their own oil and South Korean shipyards were offering stiff competition to Singapore.[124] Capacity utilisation rates in shipbuilding and ship repair fell to 60–70 per cent.[125]

An early sign of impending recession appeared in the fourth quarter of 1984 when economic growth slowed to below 6 per cent.[126] In the following year, the economy's output contracted for four consecutive quarters before a mild recovery began in the first three months of 1986, after which growth picked up. For 1985 as a whole, GDP growth was -0.6 per cent but in 1986, it turned positive to 1.9 per cent. Thus, the recession was short-lived but while it was going on, manufacturing output shrank throughout 1985, resulting in negative growth of 7.3 per cent for the whole year.[127] Electronics demand from the United States fell, leading to a slowdown in Singapore's exports.[128] Among the other sectors, wholesale and retail trade experienced negative growth in the last two quarters of 1985 and the first six months of 1986. The worst performer was the construction sector, which contracted in both years, with the fall in output in 1986

---

118 Grice and Drakakis-Smith, "The Role of the State", p. 356.

119 Soon and Stoever, "Foreign Investment and Economic Development", p. 327.

120 Teh Kok Peng and Tharman Shanmugaratnam, "Exchange Rate Policy: Philosophy and Conduct Over the Past Decade", in *Public Policies in Singapore: Changes* in *the 1980s and Future Signposts*, ed. Linda Low and Toh Mun Heng (Singapore: Times Academic Press, 1992), pp. 297–300.

121 *Wage Policy*, pp. 187–9; *The Singapore Economy: New Directions* (Singapore: Ministry of Trade and Industry, 1986), pp. 4, 38, 41–4.

122 Rigg, "Singapore and the Recession of 1985", p. 345.

123 Lim Chong Yah, "From High Growth Rates to Recession", in *Management of Success*, ed. Sandhu and Wheatley, pp. 209, 212.

124 Grice and Drakakis-Smith, "The Role of the State", pp. 355–6.

125 Lim, "From High Growth Rates to Recession", p. 212.

126 "From Recession to Recovery", pp. 23–34; Rigg, "Singapore and the Recession of 1985", p. 345.

127 *The Business Times*, 28 Nov. 1985.

128 Teh and Shanmugaratnam, "Exchange Rate Policy", p. 299.

being a staggering 25.3 per cent. It was a case of a boom-and-bust cycle in the sector: during 1982 and 1983, the industry had expanded at high double-digit rates owing to an accelerated public housing programme and the construction of commercial properties, but once these activities were completed, demand collapsed amidst an oversupply.[129] Cyclical unemployment followed in the trail of these developments, with the loss of 96,000 jobs and the overall rate rising from 4.3 per cent in June 1985 to 6.5 per cent in June 1986 before falling to 5.4 per cent in September.[130] From 1984 to early 1986, 90,000 foreign labourers were sent back to their home countries to ease the burden on local workers, a move reminiscent of the action taken by the colonial government to repatriate immigrant coolies during the Great Depression of the 1930s.[131]

The importation of foreign workers was eased after the recession, although the authorities were aware that this was a temporary measure and reliance on them still had to be reduced in the longer term.[132] The government also responded by lowering business and labour costs in order to relieve the squeeze on companies' profitability. In this regard, the most decisive actions were a cut in the employer CPF contribution rate to 10 per cent from 25 per cent and a reduction in the corporate tax rate from 40 per cent to 33 per cent.[133] A one-off 25 per cent rebate on personal income tax was given to encourage consumption spending. Tax rebates were also offered to tenants of state-owned industrial and commercial properties and reductions in various government and statutory board charges and fees were announced, such as those for port services, warehousing and telecommunications.[134] Electricity and gas charges were lowered by the PUB. The NWC wage guidelines and payroll tax were suspended, the SDF levy was reduced and efforts were made to decentralise wage bargaining and introduce a more flexible wage system, including adding a variable bonus to salaries.[135] Wage restraint was urged upon workers in an effort to cap salary increases. The resulting deflation allowed the monetary authority to lower the exchange rate of the Singapore dollar even though the government had ruled out devaluation as a panacea for the recession.[136] This policy provided the impetus for an economic recovery that was helped along by a fortuitous revival of foreign demand and, after the appreciation of the yen in 1985, a large inflow of Japanese investments.[137]

---

129 *The Singapore Economy*, pp. 38, 44; *The Business Times*, 6 Nov. 1985.

130 Regnier, *Singapore*, p. 58; *The Straits Times*, 26 July 1986.

131 *The Business Times*, 29 Mar. 1985.

132 Pang and Lim, "Labor, Productivity", p. 1550033-6. This was the second time that the foreign worker policy was eased, the first occurring in 1982 to relieve a chronic labour shortage caused in part by the booming construction industry. Le Blanc, *Singapore*, pp. 28–9.

133 "From Recession to Recovery", pp. 46–7; *The Singapore Economy*, pp. 51–3; *The Business Times*, 27 Feb. 1986.

134 Rigg, "Singapore and the Recession of 1985", p. 350.

135 Krause, Koh and Lee, *The Singapore Economy Reconsidered*, p. 149; Lim, Pang and Findlay, "Singapore", p. 105.

136 *The Straits Times*, 28 Jan. 1986.

137 Soon and Stoever, "Foreign Investment and Economic Development", pp. 328–9; *The Straits Times*, 9 Aug. 1986.

Growth, Employment and Structural Change

We now come to a review of the outcomes of export-oriented industrialisation in Singapore with respect to the growth of the economy and manufacturing output, employment, wages and the associated changes in economic structure. In this regard, there is evidence of a causal nexus between foreign direct investment, output growth and employment.[138] Moreover, the structural changes associated with the industrialisation process were the embodiment of the process of modern economic growth—the use of advancing technology to increase a country's capacity to supply goods.[139] This process is typified by three interrelated characteristics: (i) high rates of growth of per capita income and of the population; (ii) a high rate of productivity increase; and (iii) a fast pace of structural transformation. In the middle of the 1980s, these characteristics were clearly visible in Singapore. From $1,299 in 1960, per capita GDP had risen to $6,565 in 1984—the second highest in East and Southeast Asia—while the population had increased from 1.6 million to 2.5 million.[140] Productivity also rose, especially during the economic restructuring phase of growth. The output per worker in manufacturing, for example, increased from $17,000 in 1960 to $130,600 in 1981.

From 1966 to 1970, average annual real GDP growth accelerated to 16.1 per cent from 5.5 per cent in the first half of the decade, reflecting both continued infrastructural development by the Singapore government and foreign investment in export-oriented manufacturing industries.[141] The subsequent performance of the economy during the seventies and early eighties remained good except for the downturn in the mid-seventies, which caused GDP growth to moderate to 8.6 per cent in 1971–82. In terms of sectoral production, these outcomes were driven mainly by the expansion of the manufacturing and financial sectors, which grew by 16 per cent and 20 per cent per annum respectively between 1966 and 1982. The transport and communications industries also expanded at a brisk pace of 14 per cent, the former largely due to growth in sea and air transportation.[142] Growth in the construction sector was robust at 12 per cent, as a result of heavy government spending on housing and social amenities. In contrast, the trade and other services sectors that had been the mainstay of the colonial economy expanded by only 8 per cent, vindicating the government's anticipation that the staple and entrepôt trades were on the decline.[143] Nonetheless, tourism and the hotel and restaurant business within the commercial sector thrived.[144]

In 1981, the rankings of the manufacturing industries by value of output produced were in the following descending order: petroleum refining and petroleum products; electrical and electronic products; shipbuilding and oil rig construction; food and beverages;

---

[138] Choy, "Foreign Direct Investment", pp. 35–7.

[139] S. Kuznets, "Modern Economic Growth: Findings and Reflections", *The American Economic Review* 63, 3 (1973): 247–9, 254, 256–7.

[140] "Development of Singapore: Retrospective Overview", in Lim and Associates, *Policy Options*, p. 8; Chen, "Singapore's Development Strategies", p. 3.

[141] Lim and Pang, *Trade, Employment and Industrialisation*, pp. 22–3.

[142] Le Blanc, *Singapore*, p. 33.

[143] Soon and Stoever, "Foreign Investment and Economic Development", p. 319.

[144] Wong, *Essays*, p. 93.

fabricated metal products; textiles, footwear and wearing apparel; printing and publishing; and paints, pharmaceutical and other chemical products.[145] In terms of growth rates in the decade from 1971 to 1981, petroleum, electrical machinery, industrial machinery (inclusive of refrigerators and air-conditioners) and cement and concrete products were the fastest expanding industries.[146] From 1966 to 1970, the chemical, ship repair and shipbuilding, textiles, garments, leather and engineering industries had grown rapidly.[147]

The dominance in the economy of companies with foreign equity participation had become even more pronounced by 1981. About four-fifths of the gross output during the 1971–81 period was accounted for by wholly foreign-owned companies, while locally-owned firms were more prominent in the shipyards, food and beverage, and production of fabricated metal products, garments and building materials.[148] In all, there were more than 3,000 manufacturing enterprises in Singapore, of which 1,257 were foreign establishments that together owned a capital stock equal to $8.2 billion.[149] Compared to 1970, majority foreign-owned firms accounted for 73 per cent of manufacturing output, 66 per cent of value-added, 83 per cent of direct exports and 55 per cent of employment (Figure 22).[150] Of the 275,000 persons employed in manufacturing, 152,000 were working for foreign companies. These companies were generally larger than local firms, more capital-intensive, had higher productivity and paid higher wages. Majority locally owned companies contributed 33 per cent of value-added and 44 per cent of employment. For all firms, exports rose from 39 per cent of sales in 1970 to 60 per cent in 1982—68 per cent for foreign companies and 36 per cent for local establishments. Overseas shipments of manufactured goods continued to increase at an average rate of 28 per cent a year in the seventies, resulting in a tenfold rise between 1970 and 1981.[151]

Employment in manufacturing grew by 8.2 per cent on average each year between 1966 and 1970 and 8.5 per cent in the 1970s, faster than overall employment growth of 4.4 per cent and 5.2 per cent in the two periods, respectively.[152] Total employed persons in the economy increased roughly twofold from 519,000 in 1966 to 1,018,000 in 1979 but manufacturing employment increased fourfold.[153] The other sectors created jobs at slower rates. The labour-intensive nature of the industrialisation process in Singapore is shown by the fact that the employment growth generated by output growth increased in the seventies. In 1970, the largest employers were the transport equipment (ship repair, shipbuilding and oil rig construction), electrical and electronics and the textiles and garments industries. However, employment in the textiles industry declined in the latter half of the 1970s and by 1981, electrical and electronics firms employed the most workers, numbering 85,499 in all.

---

145 Chia, "Direct Foreign Investment", pp. 97–9.

146 *The Straits Times*, 4 Aug. 1968; *The Business Times*, 28 Sept. 1977.

147 Lee, "Some Basic Problems", p. 186.

148 Cheng, "Economic Change in Singapore", p. 109.

149 Le Blanc, *Singapore*, p. 35, Table 2.3, p. 112; "Foreign Investment Policy", pp. 252–4, 266–7.

150 Chia, "Direct Foreign Investment", pp. 94, 95, 96, 99–101, 103.

151 Lim and Pang, *Trade, Employment and Industrialisation*, pp. 28, 32–3.

152 Ibid., pp. 23, 28, 29–31; *The Straits Times*, 6 Sept. 1970; *New Nation*, 15 Sept. 1971.

153 Pang Eng Fong, "Economic Development and the Labor Market in a Newly Industrializing Country: The Experience of Singapore", *The Developing Economies* 19, 1 (1981): 4, 5.

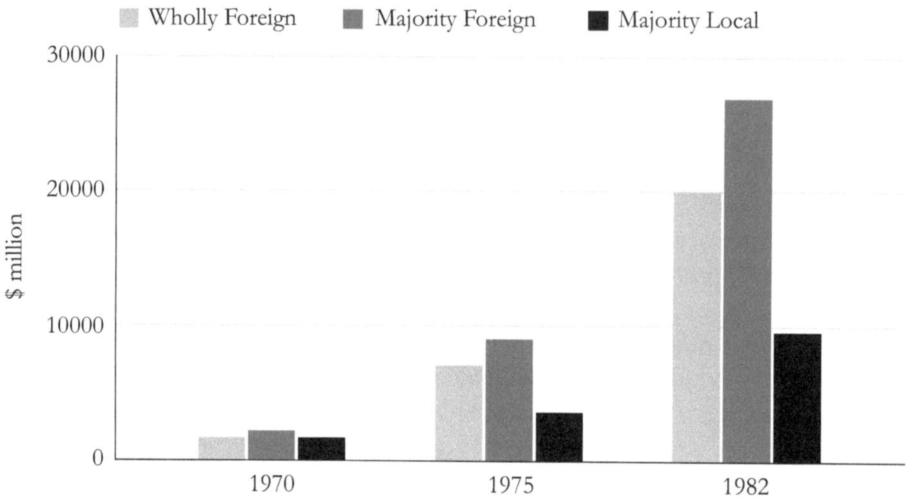

Figure 22. Contribution of Singapore Firms to Manufacturing Output, Various Years
Source: Chia, "Direct Foreign Investment", Table 4.4, p. 95.

As for wages, the average nominal weekly wages of blue-collar workers rose by 2 per cent a year in the 1960s. With inflation at about 1 per cent, real earnings would have increased by only 1 per cent per year.[154] This meagre rate of growth could be attributed to excess labour supply and the government's policy of wage restraint in the second half of the sixties. In the 1970s, the attainment of full employment would have caused wages to rise faster if the NWC had not intervened; in the event, nominal wages in the economy as a whole rose by an average of 10 per cent a year between 1972 and 1979 but real wages increased by just 2 per cent per annum due to the high inflation caused by the oil crises. Inter-industry differences in the growth of nominal earnings were small in the key economic sectors despite variations in their rates of output expansion and demand for labour. Nominal wages in manufacturing increased by 13 per cent per annum while commercial sector wages grew by 14 per cent. Wages in the other service sectors, including financial and business services, all expanded at broadly the same rates, reflecting the uniform nature of the NWC guidelines.

In terms of pay levels, manufacturing workers were paid the least owing to the industry's labour intensity as well as the influx of unskilled workers from Malaysia. The financial and business services sector paid the highest salaries.[155] In 1982, the mean monthly income for all employees was $739, compared with the median monthly income of $180 for men and $115 for women in 1966.[156] Wage differentials based on differences in educational achievements were wider than industry differences: salaries of primary school leavers were $335, secondary school leavers $421 and tertiary graduates $1,690. Classified by occupational status, professional, technical, administrative and

---

154 Pang Eng Fong and Greg Seow, "Labour, Employment and Wage Structure", in *Singapore Development Policies and Trends*, ed. Chen, p. 165.

155 Lim and Pang, *Trade, Employment and Industrialisation*, pp. 66, 69–71.

156 D.H. Clark, "Labour Market and Industrial Relations", in *The Singapore Economy*, ed. You and Lim, pp. 318–9.

managerial staff earned $1,400–$2,200, clerical, sales and service workers $600–$800 and production operators $525. Moreover, the proportion of professional, technical, administrative, managerial and clerical workers in the labour force rose while that of sales, service and production workers declined.[157]

The male–female pay differential was large, with women in general being paid only three-quarters of men's salaries; the gap was widest, at three-fifths, among tertiary educated workers.[158] The difference persisted despite (or because of) an unprecedented increase in the participation of women in the workforce, due to the more permanently settled post-war population and high birth rates as well as a change in the social attitudes of women towards work.[159] The co-location of labour-intensive industries in public housing estates further encouraged females to take up jobs, thus supplementing household incomes. They first entered the labour force in large numbers in the late 1960s and early 1970s when export manufacturing industries that entailed simple assembly or related tasks were set up. Hence, they were most widely employed in the textiles, leather, electrical and electronics factories and tended to occupy the lower value-added jobs and lower-income tiers within occupational categories.[160] However, many were also service providers, for instance teachers and nurses.[161] As a result of these trends, the female labour force participation rate increased from 19.8 per cent in 1966 to 45.2 per cent in 1982, being highest for the unmarried age group of 20–24 years and those with a tertiary qualification. In the case of males, the participation rate was 81.5 per cent in the latter year but it peaked for workers aged 35–39 years. Of a total pool of 1,167,000 workers in 1982, there were 750,000 males and 417,000 females.

Arguably, the cheap labour supplied by female and foreign workers was essential to the success of industrialisation in Singapore as they accounted for 55 per cent of the growth in the labour force during the period 1970–80.[162] With regard to the earnings differentials of foreign versus local workers, expatriates at the high end of the wage scale earned more than their local counterparts since a higher proportion had a tertiary education and they were also over-represented in administrative and managerial positions.[163] These observations are consistent with the "U-shaped" distribution of foreign worker skills whereby professionals were hired for higher level work and menial labourers were brought into the country to perform jobs shunned by Singaporeans. And though the Singapore government has never said so in public, the other important contributions of foreign labourers were to ameliorate cost increases that would otherwise be passed on to consumers and to act as a buffer to unemployment during downturns.

---

[157] Pang, "Economic Development and the Labor Market", pp. 8–9.

[158] Pang and Seow, "Labour, Employment and Wage Structure", pp. 166–7.

[159] *The Straits Times*, 16 Feb. 1976.

[160] Lim, *Business, Government and Labor*, pp. xii–xiv; *New Nation*, 11 Oct. 1975.

[161] Clark, "Labour Market and Industrial Relations", pp. 313–4.

[162] "Manpower Policy", in Lim and Associates, *Policy Options*, pp. 141–2, 144; Lim and Pang, *Trade, Employment and Industrialisation*, pp. 59–61.

[163] Pang and Lim, "Foreign Labor", pp. 560, 561–4.

So far as structural change is concerned, Singapore differed from other countries in that it had never had the burden of modernising a large and backward agricultural sector.[164] The industrious Chinese farmers of the colonial era were quickly relocated to public housing estates after independence and it was only much later that the country developed a small primary sector producing eggs, orchids and ornamental fish.[165] The main structural change that took place in Singapore was its transformation from a trade-based economy in the 1960s into a manufacturing and financial hub by the 1980s, a trajectory very much like Hong Kong's.[166] These two city-states were distinguished from other developing countries in their pattern of growth, wherein productive resources moved from the traditional services sector to the industrial sector rather than from agriculture to industry. As a result of this reallocation, manufacturing and finance emerged as the leading sectors of the economy.[167] While manufacturing constituted only 11.9 per cent of GDP in 1960, its contribution rose to 26.4 per cent in 1982 (Table 13). The next most important sector, the financial and business services industries, contributed 21.9 per cent in the later year. The GDP share of the traditionally prominent entrepôt trade sector was 21.9 per cent, followed by transport and communications at 13.4 per cent. Hence, the non-financial services provided by the combined commerce, transport and communications, and other service sectors like tourism still accounted for a significant 46.5 per cent of GDP. Owing to the building boom in the early eighties, the construction sector's contribution to overall output in 1982 was substantial, at 9.7 per cent.

Table 13. Structural Change in Singapore, 1960–82

	Output (%)			**Employment (%)**		
	1960	**1970**	**1982**	**1957**	**1970**	**1982**
Agriculture, Mining and Quarrying	4.1	2.9	1.6	7.2	3.8	1.2
Manufacturing	11.9	19.7	26.4	14.3	22.0	29.5
Construction	3.6	7.3	9.7	5.2	6.6	6.3
Commerce	35.9	30.2	21.9	27.8	23.5	22.2
Transport and Communications	14.2	11.2	13.4	10.7	12.1	11.4
Financial and Business Services	11.3	14.2	21.9	4.3	3.5	7.9
Other Services	18.2	13.8	11.2	29.1	27.2	20.7

Sources: Lim, *Economic Restructuring in Singapore*, Statistical Appendix 2, p. 111; Lim and Pang, *Trade, Employment and Industrialisation*, Table 38, p. 64.

Of course, the decline of the trade sector was only relative. The nature of the trade also altered, the main structural change being a shift from entrepôt trade to the export of manufactures and services. In a reflection of this, the share of non-oil primary commodities in merchandise exports (and imports) fell steeply to 14 per cent in 1982 from 73 per cent

164 H.B. Chenery, "Growth and Structural Change", *Finance and Development* 8, 3 (1971).

165 P. Mukhopadhaya, G. Shantakumar and B. Rao, *Economic Growth and Income Inequality in China, India and Singapore* (Routledge, 2011), pp. 130, 163.

166 Lim and Pang, *Trade, Employment and Industrialisation*, p. 22; Lee, "Some Basic Problems", pp. 185, 187.

167 Lim, *Economic Restructuring in Singapore*, pp. 7, 10, Statistical Appendix 2, p. 111.

in 1960.[168] Concurrently, the share of Southeast Asia in overall imports fell dramatically as the importance of the entrepôt commerce diminished and neighbouring countries resorted to direct trade. In absolute terms however, the volume of the re-export business was still substantial and Singapore stayed as one of the world's leading markets for rubber and pepper.[169] The major destinations of entrepôt exports were Malaysia and the United States, followed by Japan, Hong Kong and the United Kingdom. Petroleum exports also received a boost from Singapore's role as a supply centre for American troops engaged in the war in Vietnam during the late sixties.[170] From 0.8 per cent in 1960, Vietnam's share in total trade increased to 4.1 per cent in 1969.[171] Owing to industrialisation, domestic exports made in Singapore, namely electrical products and electronic components, petroleum, and machinery and transport equipment, expanded by 23.3 per cent per annum on average up to 1984, constituting nearly two-thirds of overall exports in that year.[172] Including imports, total external trade increased to $104 billion in 1982, a multiple of GDP.[173]

The employment structure that resulted from Singapore's economic development up to the early eighties mirrored that of total output. As industrialisation proceeded, it marginalised the primary activities of agriculture, mining and quarrying, which engaged only 14,106 persons or 1.2 per cent of total employment in 1982, compared to 24,626 persons in 1970.[174] The manufacturing sector was the largest employer in 1982 with a share of 29.5 per cent in total employment while 6.3 per cent worked in the construction industry. Within manufacturing, a majority of workers were still employed in labour-intensive and export-oriented industries like electrical machinery and electronics, ship repair and shipbuilding, and textiles and wearing apparel. These accounted for 62 per cent of all manufacturing workers in 1981. The commercial sector (inclusive of hotels and restaurants) became the second largest employer with a share of 22.2 per cent. Next was the transport and communications sector with a contribution of 11.4 per cent. By virtue of the capital-intensive nature of traded services, the finance, insurance and business services industries absorbed only 7.9 per cent of the workforce.[175]

The British Military Withdrawal

After separating from Malaysia, the Singapore government not only had to ensure the country's survival but also to deal with the threat of large-scale unemployment arising

---

168 Lee Soo Ann, "Trade and Shipping Growth", in *Singapore in the International Economy, Symposium Papers*, ed. Wong Kum Poh and Maureen Tan (Singapore: Singapore University Press, 1972), pp. 74–5; Regnier, *Singapore*, pp. 36–8.

169 Le Blanc, *Singapore*, p. 47, Appendix 6, p. 150; Geiger and Geiger, *Tales of Two City-States*, pp. 16, 176.

170 Turnbull, *History of Modern Singapore*, p. 304; Chia, "Growth and Pattern", p. 197.

171 Lim and Ow, "The Economic Development of Singapore", pp. 10–11.

172 "Development of Singapore: Retrospective Overview", pp. 14, 15; Huff, *The Economic Growth of Singapore*, pp. 312–3; *New Nation*, 19 Aug. 1978.

173 The ratio of international trade to GDP was 200–300 per cent.

174 Lim and Pang, *Trade, Employment and Industrialisation*, pp. 64–6.

175 Huff, *The Economic Growth of Singapore*, pp. 303, 305.

from the accelerated withdrawal of the British armed forces in the late 1960s.[176] At the time, this was made to be a crisis by the PAP leaders but it subsequently turned out to be a non-event.[177] Mounting economic problems had compelled Britain to decide on the policy of withdrawing its military presence "east of Suez", leading to the announcement in early 1968 that its forces would all leave from the island in three years. This came as a shock because the original intention had been for British troops to leave the bases in the middle of the 1970s.

In the late sixties, Singapore remained the main British military base in Southeast Asia, the establishment there consisting of all three forces—army, navy and air force—as well as extensive land and property.[178] These included two infantry battalions and an armoured car regiment, in all over 34,000 men.[179] The assets owned by the military and spread out over one-tenth of the island's land area were the naval dockyard, airbases, planes, helicopters, defence installations, buildings, workshops, a fuel depot, schools and hospitals.[180] Most of the land, facilities and equipment, estimated to be worth £19 million, were handed over without charge to the Singapore government by 1970. The economic contribution of the forces was substantial: 12.7 per cent of GDP in 1967 and employment for 30,000 people, not including jobs created indirectly.[181] By including such occupations as barbers, shopkeepers and domestic service workers, the figure would increase to 38,000.[182] Hence, after entrepôt trade, the British naval base was the next most important pillar of the economy in sustaining incomes and employment.[183] In absolute terms, annual military spending came up to between $550 and $900 million.[184] After the British forces commenced their withdrawal, the contribution of military services to overall output fell to 8.6 per cent in 1969.[185]

The military pull-out created not just an unemployment problem but also a defence vulnerability as Singapore's armed forces were hardly ready to take over.[186] The Prime Minister pleaded Singapore's case for a delayed withdrawal vigorously but unsuccessfully with British leaders, and obtained only a token postponement of the final withdrawal date

---

176 Lee, *Industrialization*, p. 100; *The Straits Times*, 24 Nov. 1974.

177 Turnbull, *History of Modern Singapore*, pp. 304–10; Loh Kah Seng, "The British Military Withdrawal from Singapore and the Anatomy of a Catalyst", in *Singapore in Global History*, ed. Derek Heng and Syed Muhd Khairudin Aljunied (Amsterdam University Press, 2011), pp. 195–6.

178 Lee Soo Ann, *Singapore Chronicles: Economy*, pp. 41–2.

179 Central Intelligence Agency (US), *Singapore: Some Economic Implications of the UK Military Withdrawal*, Intelligence Memorandum (1968), p. 5.

180 Lee, *From Colony to Nation*, pp. 64–6; *The Straits Times*, 5 Feb. 1969.

181 Ow, "The Role of Government", p. 229. The official sources show considerable variation in the estimates of the economic contribution; another document claims that it was a fifth of GDP and one-sixth of the labour force. Loh, "British Military Withdrawal", p. 197.

182 A different source stated the number of jobs at 50,000. Geiger and Geiger, *Tales of Two City-States*, p. 165.

183 Regnier, *Singapore*, p. 100.

184 Lee, *Industrialization*, pp. 96, 97.

185 Lim and Ow, "The Economic Development of Singapore", p. 5.

186 Murfett, Miksic, Farrell and Chiang, *Between Two Oceans*, pp. 323–4.

from March to December 1971.[187] However, they offered a £50 million interest-free loan repayable over 25 years of which one quarter was an outright grant and agreed to retrain civilian employees who were retrenched from the bases and give some of them redundancy payments.[188] In view of the lack of air defence expertise in Singapore, the British were also willing to help with the operation of the facilities, including surface-to-air missiles and aircraft. This apparent generosity prompted a British official to remark that "it was not even a sell-out: it was a handout, with virtually nothing demanded or even bargained for in return".[189] The special aid was viewed as a sweetener and the Singapore government used the money to develop the manufacturing and tourism industries, including setting up the Singapore Tourist Promotion Board (STPB) and converting Sentosa island into a tourist resort.[190] The result was a rise in the contribution of tourism to national income to 4.7 per cent in 1969, making up to some extent for reduced military spending and absorbing some of the slack in the service industry that catered to British personnel.[191] In addition, defence expenditure was tripled, reaching 10 per cent of the gross national product (GNP).

Turning adversity to advantage, the government decided to maximise the commercial potential of the transferred assets and set up a Bases Economic Conversion Unit to do so. Some of the installations were taken over by Singapore's own armed forces, the naval dockyard was converted into Sembawang Shipyard to handle ship repair and shipbuilding, and buildings were turned into government and private offices. Kent Ridge in the western part of the island, which used to be the habitat of British officers, was to become the new location of the University of Singapore. Various services provided to the military forces were carried on by newly formed GLCs (government-linked companies) and statutory boards, such as the maintenance of electronics and communications equipment and the servicing and repair of aircraft, both at the Seletar Airbase.[192] Furthermore, the former British army depot at Telok Blangah was converted into a vocational institute for retraining workers while another depot at Changi was made into a base for offshore oil drilling.[193] Thus, the withdrawal actually helped Singapore to build up its shipping, aviation and manufacturing industries.[194]

Concurrently, the Finance Minister announced a programme of accelerated public expenditure to compensate for the loss of British military spending. The package of measures, amounting to $400 million, entailed a rapid programme of urban renewal,

---

[187] Loh, *British Military Withdrawal*, pp. 199, 200, 203–4.

[188] Central Intelligence Agency, *UK Military Withdrawal*, p. 13; *The Straits Times*, 3 June 1968; *New Nation*, 17 June 1971; *The Business Times*, 11 Jan. 1978.

[189] Loh, "British Military Withdrawal", p. 195.

[190] Ibid., pp. 199–200; Lim and Ow, "The Economic Development of Singapore", pp. 12–13; *The Straits Times*, 11 Dec. 1967.

[191] Central Intelligence Agency, *UK Military Withdrawal*, p. 2.

[192] Loh, "British Military Withdrawal", pp. 201–2, 204.

[193] *The Straits Times*, 24 Nov. 1974.

[194] Murfett, Miksic, Farrell and Chiang, *Between Two Oceans*, pp. 327–8.

road network improvement and land reclamation, among other things.[195] There were also additional defence expenditures of $300 million, mainly on the wages of the local armed forces and government purchases of supplies and services. A portion of the funds required for this extra spending was to come from increased employer and employee contributions to the CPF and the rest from domestic and international loans as well as a draw on foreign reserves.[196] In consequence of the actions taken by the Singapore government and the robust growth of the manufacturing sector, the increase in industrial employment was particularly rapid during the 1968–70 period and there were enough new jobs created to replace the loss due to the British withdrawal.[197] In a way, the pull-out was a blessing in disguise for it galvanised Singaporeans to strive for survival.

Education, Manpower, Health and Housing

The imperative of industrialisation changed the direction of education policy in independent Singapore. First and foremost, education was to serve as the handmaiden to the new economic milieu—the need for an educated workforce and skilled manpower to perform industrial labour. To this end, the government placed great emphasis on technical and vocational schooling and the training of engineers, scientists and business managers.[198] In colonial times, the British had provided technical education in selected schools, including Balestier Junior School and St. Joseph's Trade School, but there was little need for extensive vocational education.[199] More than just manpower, however, education policy in the modern period was geared towards forging a national consciousness and moulding the fledgling nation. It would inculcate values of loyalty, unity and racial harmony in young schoolchildren. This social objective was fraught with difficulties in view of the multiracial and multilingual population and the preponderance of Chinese in the population with their different dialects in a region where Malay was the native language and English was the language of modernisation.

The compromise solution to this conundrum was to designate all language streams as official languages—English, Chinese (Mandarin), Malay and Tamil. In addition, a policy of bilingualism was adopted whereby every student was required to study his or her mother tongue as a second language in secondary school, in addition to English.[200] Thus, English was considered a utilitarian tool for economic survival while the other Asian languages

---

[195] Loh, "British Military Withdrawal", p. 201; Lee, *Industrialization*, pp. 95–101; *The Straits Times*, 1 July 1968.

[196] Central Intelligence Agency, *UK Military Withdrawal*, p. 14.

[197] Loh, "British Military Withdrawal", pp. 198, 208; Lee, *Industrialization*, p. 84; Lim and Ow, "The Economic Development of Singapore", pp. 29–30.

[198] Turnbull, *History of Modern Singapore*, pp. 313–4; *The Straits Times*, 11 Dec. 1965.

[199] Gopinathan, "Education", pp. 271–82; *Technical Education and Industrial Training in Singapore: A Review of the Achievements of the Technical Education Department, 1968–1973* (Singapore: Technical Education Department, 1973), p. 1.

[200] *The Straits Times*, 15 May 1968.

were seen to be providing cultural ballast.[201] Perhaps because of this policy, English medium schools continued to be the most favoured option of parents, with an enrolment of more than 300,000 pupils in 1968, a big jump from the 84,418 in 1954 under the Ten-Year Education Plan implemented in 1948.[202] In these schools, moreover, there was a new orientation towards the study of science, mathematics and technical subjects. Some Chinese parents nonetheless preferred a traditional Chinese education for their children, which swelled the number enrolled in Chinese medium schools to 135,000. Despite their official status, vernacular Malay and Tamil schools fell in popularity.

As compared to the colonial period when education was left largely to the ethnic communities and religious organisations, save for Malay vernacular schooling, the post-independence education system in Singapore was highly centralised.[203] All schools came under the purview of the Ministry of Education, shared a common curriculum and were funded by the government. Students enrolled in English medium schools underwent six years of primary education, four years of secondary education and two or three years of pre-university education before entering either tertiary institutions or the labour market.[204] Universal primary education was already attained in 1965 but by 1970, all students were expected to complete a lower secondary education.[205] In the latter year, enrolment in secondary and post-secondary schools rose to 145,740, resulting in large classes.[206] In tandem with the rise in student numbers, the number of trained and qualified school teachers rose.[207] In 1967, 23 per cent of state expenditure was allocated to education, with a significant portion devoted to building new schools and teacher training.[208]

The focus on quantity rather than quality and the strain of having to learn two languages resulted however in a large number of dropouts and a low literacy level.[209] Therefore, coinciding with the economic restructuring drive, the national education system was revamped in 1979 with the objective of achieving greater efficiency and reducing attrition.[210] The new system allowed students to progress at a pace more suited

---

201 Goh Chor Boon and S. Gopinathan, "Education in Singapore: Developments since 1965", in *An African Exploration of the East Asian Education Experience*, ed. B. Fredriksen and Tan Jee Peng (Washington, DC: The World Bank, 2008), p. 83; Gopinathan, "Education", pp. 278–9.

202 Turnbull, *History of Modern Singapore*, pp. 314–7; Gopinathan, "Education", p. 273; Loh Ai, *A Historical Study of Changes in Vocational and Technical Education and Training in Singapore: 1961–1981*, Honours Thesis (Department of History, National University of Singapore, 1982/1983), p. 4.

203 Chen, "Singapore's Development Strategies", p. 17; Gopinathan, "Education", pp. 268–9, 274.

204 *Education in Singapore* (Singapore: Ministry of Education, 1984), pp. 11–13, 17, 21; Chan, "Polytechnic Education", pp. 135–6.

205 Goh and Gopinathan, "Education in Singapore", pp. 84–6, quoting the *Straits Times*, 26 Sept. 1965; *The Straits Times*, 25 Nov. 1965.

206 S. Gopinathan, *Education and the Nation State: The Selected Works of S. Gopinathan* (Routledge, 2013), p. 6; *10 Years that Shaped a Nation*, p. 27.

207 *The Straits Times*, 26 Jan. 1966.

208 Lim and Pang, *Trade, Employment and Industrialisation*, p. 79; *The Straits Times*, 24 Jan. 1965, 21 Dec. 1965.

209 Seah Chee Meow and Linda Seah, "Education Reform and National Integration", in *Singapore Development Policies and Trends*, ed. Chen, pp. 241–2; Tan, *A Very Short History*, pp. 159–60.

210 *Education in Singapore*, p. 5; *The Straits Times*, 14 Mar. 1979; *New Nation*, 28 Dec. 1979.

to their individual abilities. Those who needed more time to reach their educational goals were given up to eight years to complete primary education and five years for secondary education. To implement this scheme, streaming was introduced at primary grade three and secondary grade two, whereby students were put into different tracks based on their examination results.[211]

Chinese schools in Singapore had a similar hierarchical structure as the English institutions but their graduates typically chose to study at Nanyang University.[212] However, employers tended to favour those graduating from the English medium University of Singapore, until 1962 known as the University of Malaya, and itself constituted from the amalgamation of the King Edward VII College of Medicine and Raffles College in 1949.[213] Owing to this tendency, the demand for Chinese education decreased over time and English schools eventually became the norm by the mid-1980s, at which point all classes had been converted to English medium.[214] In a final blow to Chinese schools, the University of Singapore was merged with Nanyang University in 1980 to form the National University of Singapore (NUS).[215] The job discrimination problem was thus overcome but only after generating much controversy and unhappiness in the Chinese community.

Technical and vocational schools were first established in 1961 to take in less academically inclined students from primary schools for two-year or four-year courses.[216] From this point to 1968, the number of secondary technical and vocational schools proliferated and increased to 21. In 1963, the Balestier Junior School was transformed into the Singapore Vocational Institute offering full and part-time courses and four more vocational institutes were built in 1968.[217] Aiming to equip graduates with occupational skills for industry, the curriculum at these schools consisted of subjects such as woodwork, metalwork, technical drawing, radio and television servicing, electrical fitting and installation, domestic science and art and crafts.[218] In 1969, the Singapore Technical Institute was established to provide two-year bridging courses for students proceeding from vocational institutes to polytechnics. But once industrialisation was under way, it became evident that the output of vocationally trained workers was neither sufficient nor were the schools popular with students.[219] In 1968, only 18,000 pupils attended vocational institutions. The Singapore government therefore decided to make technical

---

211 Streaming in secondary schools was abolished in 2019. Tan, *A Very Short History*, pp. 160–1.

212 Seah and Seah, "Education Reform and National Integration", p. 241. Prior to 1961, Chinese secondary education consisted of three years each of middle and high school. Gopinathan, *Education*, pp. 274, 282.

213 Lee, *From Colony to Nation*, pp. 52–4.

214 *Education in Singapore*, p. 6.

215 *The Straits Times*, 6 Apr. 1980, 13 Apr. 1980.

216 Goh and Gopinathan, "Education in Singapore", pp. 87–8; Loh Ai, *A Historical Study*, pp. 14–15, 16–17; *Technical Education and Industrial Training in Singapore*, pp. 2–4.

217 *The Straits Times*, 25 Mar. 1964, 21 Dec. 1965, 13 Dec.1966.

218 Law Song Seng, "Vocational Technical Education and Economic Development—The Singapore Experience", in *Toward a Better Future*, ed. Lee, Goh, Birger and Tan, p. 114.

219 Gopinathan, *Education and the Nation State*, pp. 9–10.

education more widely available by making it compulsory for all boys in lower secondary schools to take technical subjects and girls to attend home economics classes.

Having done this, in the early seventies the government devoted further resources to the development of technical manpower by creating industrial training centres in collaboration with large MNCs, namely Tata, Rollei, Philips and Brown-Boveri.[220] In addition, two more centres were established with the cooperation of the Japanese and French governments.[221] Administered by the EDB, the centres eventually supplanted vocational schools in directly training skilled labourers such as welders and machinists for the rapidly growing shipbuilding, oil refining, electrical, precision engineering, metalworking and woodworking industries. With on-the-job training provided, those graduating from the centres could go straight into factories to work, therefore shortening the time it took to produce technicians. In 1969, a Faculty of Engineering was established at the University of Singapore; the Nanyang Technological University (NTU), located at the campus of the former Nanyang University, was inaugurated in 1981 with the sole purpose of producing practice-oriented engineers.[222]

In 1979, the Vocational and Industrial Training Board (VITB) was created as an addition to the formal education system so as to open an alternative pathway for secondary school leavers who decided not to move on to the pre-university stage.[223] The VITB institutes also enrolled adults who had not obtained a secondary education.[224] In 1980, more than ten vocational institutes had been set up by the board to cater to about 11,500 students. The wide range of courses offered included electronics, vehicle maintenance and repair, refrigeration and air conditioning, carpentry, masonry and plumbing. In the early 1980s, the EDB again set up more technologically advanced institutes jointly with foreign governments: the German-Singapore Institute of Production Technology, the French-Singapore Institute of Electrotechnology and the Japan-Singapore Institute of Software Technology. These provided specialised training in tools and die design, production processes, robotics and computer software and applications.[225]

---

220 Law, "Vocational Technical Education", pp. 118–9; David Ng Foo Seong, "Strategic Management of Educational Development in Singapore (1965–2005)", in *Toward a Better Future*, ed. Lee, Goh, Birger and Tan, pp. 47–8; Lim and Pang, *Trade, Employment and Industrialisation*, p. 21; *The Straits Times*, 19 Mar. 1973; *New Nation*, 18 June 1973.

221 *The Straits Times*, 7 Apr. 1967.

222 Lim and Pang, *Trade, Employment and Industrialisation*, pp. 13–15; Goh Chor Boon and Leo Tan Wee Hin, "The Development of University Education in Singapore", in *Toward a Better Future*, ed. Lee, Goh, Birger and Tan, pp. 150–2; *The Business Times*, 20 Aug. 1981; *The Straits Times*, 6 July 1982.

223 Gopinathan, *Education and the Nation State*, p. 9; *The Straits Times*, 3 Apr. 1979. The VITB was formed from the merger of the Industrial Training Board and the Adult Education Board, both of which were set up earlier.

224 Ng, "Strategic Management of Educational Development", pp. 54–5.

225 Lim and Pang, *Trade, Employment and Industrialisation*, p. 21; *The Straits Times*, 29 Nov. 1979, 14 Jan. 1981, 29 Sept. 1982; *New Nation*, 29 Feb. 1980; *Singapore Monitor*, 15 Feb. 1985. The three institutes were combined to form the country's fourth polytechnic, Nanyang Polytechnic, in 1992.

The education and training infrastructure was further enhanced in the 1980s with emphasis placed on science and technology education at the tertiary level, the objective being to improve the quality of labour and the level of skills in the economy.[226] There had arisen a shortage of engineers, technicians, accountants and managers in the late 1970s.[227] Moreover, Singapore lagged behind Japan and Taiwan in secondary and especially tertiary education.[228] The government's efforts were synchronised with economic restructuring to supply the required manpower for new industries such as precision engineering, computer peripherals and software manufacturing.[229] By 1985, 47,296 students were undergoing training at the EDB institutes (2,267), VITB (22,276), polytechnics (21,610) and university engineering faculties (1,143). The government was then spending nearly $1.7 billion on education; annual state expenditure on education per student was $1,619 at the primary level, $2,515 at the secondary level and $9,885 at the tertiary level.[230] Enrolment in tertiary institutions for the cohort aged 20–24 years doubled from 6.7 per cent in 1970 to 13.9 per cent in 1985 while the proportion of workers in the labour force with a secondary education rose to 29.3 per cent.

Manpower development was also given increased attention by the Singapore government in the 1980s. A Council on Professional and Technical Education (CPTE) with representatives from the private sector was formed in 1979 to provide forecasts of manpower requirements, make recommendations and set targets.[231] Based on the expected economic growth rate for the 1980s, the CPTE projected that Singapore would still have a shortfall of 400 engineers, 1,050 other graduates, 900 technicians and 2,000 skilled workers.[232] Concurrently, skills training for existing and older workers assumed greater importance. In addition to the SDF scheme already mentioned, there was also a Basic Education for Skills Training (BEST) programme aimed at imparting literacy and numeracy skills to workers who had only a primary education so that they could operate sophisticated machinery.[233] In 1982, the Institute of Systems Science at the National University of Singapore was set up with the help of IBM to provide computer training to postgraduates, followed two years later by the Construction Industry Training Centre to train local skilled construction

---

226 Law, "Vocational Technical Education", p. 116; Ng, "Strategic Management of Educational Development", pp. 49–51.

227 Lee, *The Unexpected Nation*, p. 274.

228 *The Singapore Economy*, pp. 113–4. It has been contended that due to a conservative view of education in Singapore as being reserved for the gifted, many young people in the years up to the 1980s did not get an opportunity for a tertiary education. Hence, a preference for elite education in Singapore might be a reason why it lagged behind the other two countries. A. Booth, "Education and Development in Southeast Asia: Myths and Realities", *ASEAN Economic Bulletin* 16, 3 (1999): 290–306.

229 *The Business Times*, 26 Sept. 1980.

230 Lim, *Business, Government and Labor*, pp. 26–7.

231 *The Straits Times*, 22 Mar. 1983.

232 G. Shantakumar, "Human Resource Development in Singapore", in *Twenty-five Years of Development*, ed. You and Lim, pp. 170–1, 175–6.

233 Lim and Pang, *Trade, Employment and Industrialisation*, p. 21.

workers.[234] These initiatives resulted in the share of skilled labour in total employment doubling from 11 per cent in 1979 to 22 per cent in 1985.

It was noted earlier that the earning capacities of workers were partly determined by educational attainment. From the economic point of view, these variations can be attributed to different rates of return to education. Such an approach treats education as an investment in human capital that generates lifetime benefits for both the individual and society. In Singapore, as a result of the government's heavy subsidies on education, private returns on schooling were higher than social returns. In general, returns were correlated with the level of education: the better educated workers derived larger income streams over their lifetimes. For instance, the social rate of return to a university education after adjusting for ability was 12 per cent in 1980 whereas that for primary education was 4.8 per cent.[235] The private rates were 19.6 per cent and 6.4 per cent respectively. The difference in average wages between a secondary and polytechnic education was $284 while the gap between a secondary and university education was $1,569.[236]

As with education, the Singapore government's philosophy towards public health was to regard it both as a social good and as an investment in human capital with wider benefits to the economy and society.[237] As in advanced nations, the public healthcare system is broadly universal in coverage. Even so, the Minister for Health declared after independence that "health would rank, at the most, fifth in priority of funds—after national security, job creation, housing and education, in that order".[238] This statement explains the relative lack of development in physical medical infrastructure in the immediate years after 1965. The focus in the 1960s was instead on providing basic healthcare to meet the needs of a rapidly growing population—much as the British had done—and controlling infectious diseases such as tuberculosis and smallpox through mass inoculation programmes.[239] School dental clinics also received much attention and in view of the industrialisation effort, medical officers began to be trained in occupational health. In 1970, the government started to push for medical specialisation and tertiary healthcare in such fields as radiotherapy,

---

[234] Shantakumar, "Human Resource Development", pp. 174–5; Lai Si Tsui-Auch, Sherwin Ignatius Chia and Anica Liu, "Putting Singapore on the Global Innovation Map: The Shifting Role of the State in the Rapidly Changing Environment", in *The Routledge Handbook of Politics and Technology*, ed. U. Hilpert (Routledge, 2015), p. 195; *The Business Times*, 16 Dec. 1981, 16 Nov. 1983; *The Straits Times*, 1 Mar. 1984.

[235] Toh Mun Heng and Wong Chai Shing, "Rates of Return to Education in Singapore", *Education Economics* 7, 3 (1999): 238–9, 241–3.

[236] In 1980, a secondary school leaver earned $547, a polytechnic graduate $831 and a university graduate $2,116. Ibid., p. 242.

[237] Lim, *Business, Government and Labor*, pp. 18–19. In Singapore, social goals had not been divorced from the larger economy but were integrated with economic development. S. Vasoo and James Lee, "Singapore: Social Development, Housing and the Central Provident Fund", *International Journal of Social Welfare* 10, 4 (2001): 276.

[238] J.S. Thomas, Ong Suan Ee, Chia Kee Seng and Lee Hin Peng, "A Brief History of Public Health in Singapore", in *Singapore's Health Care System: What 50 Years Have Achieved*, ed. Lee Chien Earn and K. Satku (Singapore: World Scientific, 2016), pp. 37–9.

[239] Tan, "Health and Welfare", pp. 347, 348, 349.

neurosurgery and cardiac surgery while research collaborations with foreign institutions made headway.[240]

A few years later, a university hospital was developed with various specialities for teaching medicine and dentistry and conducting research.[241] In the 1980s, the government embarked on an ambitious 20-year National Health Plan covering hospital and clinic expansion, and the establishment of medical facilities for eye, heart, cancer, skin, dentistry, blood and neuroscience.[242] In 1985, there were ten government hospitals all over the island, including in Toa Payoh, Changi and Woodlands.[243] The bed-to-population ratio was 1 to 259 persons and the doctor-to-population ratio 1 per 972 persons.[244] A new Singapore General Hospital was opened in 1981 at the Sepoy Lines site it had occupied since the 19th century.[245] At the time, it was the most modern in Singapore, built at a cost of $180 million with another $90 million spent on the latest medical equipment. The other two major hospitals, Tan Tock Seng and Kandang Kerbau, did not shift into new buildings until the late nineties. Tan Tock Seng Hospital had been taken over by the Singapore government in 1961 and had been in the forefront of the successful battle against tuberculosis in the 1960s.[246] In the 1970s, it became a general hospital and in 1985, it absorbed Middleton Hospital which had treated infectious diseases like cholera and typhoid during the colonial period.[247] Kandang Kerbau Hospital was converted into an obstetrics and gynaecological hospital after the war and as a result of the baby boom, became the world's busiest maternity hospital from the 1950s until the early 1970s, witnessing a record 39,856 births in 1966.[248] In contrast to hospital services, primary healthcare was provided by private general practitioners, a network of government polyclinics and maternal and child health clinics.[249]

From 1959 onwards, the PAP government instituted population control measures with increasing vigour until the early eighties.[250] In 1966, it set up the Singapore Family Planning and Population Board with the aim of achieving zero population growth and

---

240 Lim Meng-Kin, "Health Care Systems in Transition II. Singapore, Part I. An Overview of Health Care in Singapore", *Journal of Public Health Medicine* 20, 1 (1998), pp. 17–18; *10 Years that Shaped a Nation*, p. 116.

241 Tan, "Health and Welfare", p. 349.

242 *The Straits Times*, 11 Aug. 1981, 3 Feb. 1983.

243 *The Straits Times*, 27 July 1971.

244 Lim, *Business, Government and Labor*, pp. 20–1.

245 *The First General Hospital*, pp. 84–5; *The Straits Times*, 12 Sept. 1981; *New Nation*, 13 Sept. 1981.

246 *150 Years of Caring: The Legacy of Tan Tock Seng Hospital*, pp. 35, 51–2, 55; *The Straits Times*, 21 Nov. 1960.

247 *The Straits Times*, 15 Feb. 1966, 14 Mar. 1985.

248 *150 Years of Caring: KK Women's and Children's Hospital (1858–2008)* (Singapore: KK Women's and Children's Hospital, 2008), pp. 45, 57; *The Straits Times*, 1 Dec. 1958.

249 Adeline Seow and Lee Hin-Peng, "From Colony to City State: Changes in Health Needs in Singapore from 1950 to 1990", *Journal of Public Health Medicine* 16, 2 (1994): 150; Tan, "Health and Welfare", p. 348.

250 Saw Swee-Hock, *Population Control for Zero Growth in Singapore* (Singapore: Oxford University Press, 1980), p. 37.

embarked on the first phase of a plan to get women to accept family planning.[251] Publicity was disseminated at maternity and child health centres and at hospitals to encourage the use of contraception by women. At the same time, policies were formulated to discourage large families, such as an amendment to the Employment Act of 1968 restricting paid maternity leave to at most three births and lower priority for public housing for those with more children. In the 1970s, the slogan of family planning was "Stop At Two" and voluntary sterilisation was actively promoted and made readily available to both men and women.[252] These measures were accompanied by further economic incentives and disincentives: priority for primary school registration was given to children one of whose parents had undergone sterilisation while income tax relief was reduced after the fourth child. The delivery fees at hospitals were also raised as the number of births increased.[253] Abortion was legalised in 1969 and completely liberalised in 1974 by allowing pregnant women to abort their child at government and private hospitals without informing the family planning board.

The consequence of the family planning policy was a quicker demographic transition in Singapore from mid-range crude birth and death rates in the 1950s to low levels in the 1970s (Figure 23).[254] In the earlier period, the birth rate hovered at 44 per 1,000 and then fell gradually to around 18 in the mid-seventies when it stabilised.[255] Since 1968, the population had been growing at under 2 per cent per annum, reaching 2.1 million people in 1972.[256] Corresponding to these changes, the fertility rate declined from 3.0 in 1970 to 2.1 in 1975, slightly below the replacement level.[257] It continued to fall after that, no doubt due to the government's population control policy and the greater participation of women in the labour force; hence, the objective of a two-child family on average was attained. In the early 1980s, however, the low fertility rate prompted the government to make a U-turn and promote a pro-natalist policy starting from 1986.[258]

The crude death rate (Figure 23) followed a similar trajectory as the birth rate, declining from just below 10 per 1,000 of population in the 1950s to around 5 in the 1970s due to further improvements in healthcare and sanitation alongside advances in medical science. Further evidence of the effectiveness of health services in Singapore is provided by the decline in the infant mortality rate to 11.8 per 1,000 births in 1976 and then to 9.8 in

---

251 "Population Policy", in Lim and Associates, *Policy Options*, pp. 111–3; Wan Fook Kee and Margaret T.F. Loh, "Fertility Policies and the National Family Planning and Population Programme", in *Public Policy and Population Change in Singapore*, ed. Peter S.J. Chen and J.T. Fawcett (New York: The Population Council, 1979), p. 99; *The Straits Times*, 29 Sept. 1965; *The Straits Budget*, 18 Jan. 1967.

252 Saw, *Population Control*, pp. 72–5, 78–9, 102–3, 124–5; *The Straits Times*, 23 Feb. 1972; *New Nation*, 5 Nov. 1974, 19 Mar. 1975.

253 Wan and Loh, "Fertility Policies", pp. 102–3; *The Straits Times*, 24 July 1973.

254 Seow and Lee, "From Colony to City State", p. 149.

255 Saw, *Population Control*, pp. 156, 159.

256 Geiger and Geiger, *Tales of Two City-States*, p. 166.

257 Wan and Loh, "Fertility Policies", p. 99.

258 *10 Years that Shaped a Nation*, p. 129.

the early 1980s.[259] Improving healthcare also led to longer lives—life expectancy at birth in 1985 rose to 70 years for men and 75 for women.[260] Owing to the lifestyle changes associated with modernisation, disease patterns had altered as well: instead of infectious and parasitic diseases, cancer and heart disease were the main killers in the later period. Deaths due to diseases of the circulatory system had also been steadily increasing over the years, as had those caused by strokes.[261]

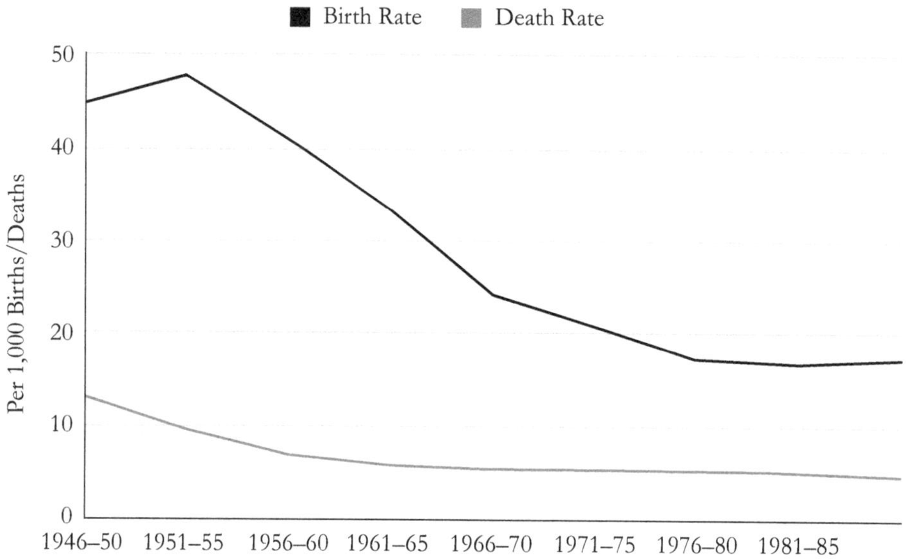

Figure 23. Crude Birth and Death Rates in Singapore, 1946–90
Source: Saw, *Population of Singapore*, pp. 82, 153.

Singapore's low mortality rate compared well with other countries (for example, Japan, Sweden and Switzerland), though it was reached in a shorter time. Indeed, the various indicators cited here suggest that Singaporeans enjoyed a standard of health comparable to people in the developed world.[262] Moreover, this was achieved in a cost-effective manner, as national health expenditure (including on private healthcare) amounted to only 2.5–3.5 per cent of GDP in the 1980s.[263] As a proportion of government expenditure, healthcare spending was 3–4 per cent, or $195 per person in 1985. Therefore, improved health outcomes and economic development were mutually reinforcing: healthier workers by being more productive contributed to economic growth but rapid economic development and rising incomes led to better health standards too.

259 Ho Guan Lim, "Health Services and Population", in *Public Policy and Population Change in Singapore*, ed. Chen and Fawcett, p. 221; Saw, *Population of Singapore*, pp. 84–6; *New Nation*, 2 Oct. 1979.

260 Lim, *Business, Government and Labor*, p. 17.

261 Saw, *Population of Singapore*, pp. 94–7.

262 Lim, *Business, Government and Labor*, pp. 17, 18–19, 20, 21, 22.

263 *The Business Times*, 30 Oct. 1984.

The last of the trio of social welfare services provided by the Singapore government to the population was public housing, which is widely acknowledged to be an outstanding achievement.[264] After unemployment, the acute shortage of housing in 1959 was the most intractable political problem facing the newly elected PAP government.[265] Like education and healthcare, housing functions as social overhead capital with a strong consumption element.[266] In Singapore, furthermore, the ownership of public flats was viewed as helping the cause of nation-building by giving homeowners a stake in the country.[267] A key reason for the housing success lies in the government's compulsory acquisition of privately-owned land for public housing at below market values through the Lands Acquisition Act of 1966. Anecdotal evidence suggests that the owners were compensated by less than one-fifth of the market assessments of their land.[268] The outcome of this quasi-expropriation measure was that the state's ownership of land in Singapore rose from 44 per cent in 1960 to 67 per cent in 1979.[269]

Mention has been made of the Housing and Development Board's (HDB) early success after its formation in 1960 in building modern and comfortable accommodation that low-income families could afford.[270] In 1965, one-quarter of the population was already living in public flats.[271] After that year and with the full backing of the Singapore government, the board continued to construct housing at a breakneck speed and by 1969, it had built another 62,073 units, making a total of 106,418 units since it had been formed.[272] In contrast, the SIT had managed to build only 23,019 units in its 32 years of existence, which housed 8.8 per cent of the city's population.[273] Owing to the low land cost and subsidies from the government, the HDB could rent out or sell its finished units at affordable prices. Rentals were $20 per month for a one-room unit, $40 for a two-room and $60 for a three-room flat, all intended to take up not more than 15–20 per cent of the average wage earner's income. These rates were adjusted upwards over the years as labour and building materials costs increased.[274] For flats that were sold after a home ownership scheme was started in 1964, the estimated subsidies on their prices were 44 per cent for

264 *New Nation*, 8 Aug. 1975.

265 Chen, "Singapore's Development Strategies", pp. 14, 15; Choe, "The Early Years of Nation-Building", p. 8; *Urban Redevelopment: From Urban Squalor to Global City* (Singapore: Centre for Liveable Cities, 2016), p. 7.

266 Stephen H.K. Yeh, "Some Trends and Prospects in Singapore's Public Housing", *Ekistics* 33, 196 (1972): 183.

267 Yeung Yue-Man and D.W. Drakakis-Smith, "Comparative Perspectives on Public Housing in Singapore and Hong Kong", *Asian Survey* 14, 8 (1974): 765.

268 *The Straits Times*, 30 Mar. 1979, 11 Apr. 1979, 16 May 1980.

269 *The Straits Times*, 19 Apr. 1979.

270 *The Straits Times*, 30 June 1971.

271 *10 Years that Shaped a Nation*, p. 30.

272 Teo and Savage, "Singapore Landscape", pp. 329, 330.

273 Geiger and Geiger, *Tales of Two City-States*, pp. 160, 210; *The Straits Times*, 17 Dec. 1973. Like the Industrial Promotion Board, the SIT was hobbled by a lack of funds and legal powers to deal with public housing.

274 *The Business Times*, 31 May 1979. The rise in costs was particularly steep from 1970 to 1974. Wong Kum Poh, *Essays*, pp. 27–9.

a three-room flat, 33 per cent for a four-room and 27 per cent for a five-room unit (the last two types were introduced in the 1970s).[275] The prices charged by the HDB were therefore lower than those for private flats and within the reach of most people.[276] These dwellings could be paid for by monthly instalments deducted from the buyer's CPF savings, after a loan was taken from the HDB at a relatively low interest rate with a repayment period of 20 years.

The HDB carried on with its five-year building programmes into the 1970s and by 1985 it had constructed 551,767 high-rise flats, which accommodated more than four-fifths of the population.[277] Three-quarters of households staying in public flats owned them. For both owners and renters, the improvement in physical living conditions from colonial days cannot be overstated: the average household size in public flats was just 5.7 persons in 1973 and even lower at 4.8 persons in 1981.[278] The residential density of HDB flats on average was then 875 people per hectare. This should be contrasted with the density of 2,500 persons per hectare in the city centre during the 1950s. Household income tended to increase with the size of flats, although this was due in part to income ceilings on the purchase of different types of units: in 1981, the average monthly income was $623 for those living in one-room units, $842 in two-room units, $1,113 in three-room units, $1,522 in four-room flats and $2,168 in five-room flats.

Public housing estates were initially built in the outlying districts of the city, in Queenstown, Toa Payoh, Bukit Ho Swee (built after a huge fire burnt down a squatter settlement there) and Telok Blangah.[279] These self-sufficient high-rise "new towns" had their own schools, markets, hawker centres, shops, clinics, parks and playgrounds, and places of worship to minimise travel outside the neighbourhood.[280] In the 1970s, new-generation and better quality HDB flats with access to more public amenities such as sports complexes and swimming pools were constructed in districts even further out from the city, for example at Ang Mo Kio, Bedok and Clementi. After the back of the housing problem had been broken, the government set up the Housing and Urban Development Company (HUDC) in 1975 to build more upmarket flats for middle-income families that resembled private housing in some respects.[281] By 1981, 2,600 such units with more attractive designs had been completed in choice locations. Meanwhile, the Jurong Town Corporation (JTC) built and managed 24,000 dwelling units between 1963 and 1979 based on the same designs as the HDB.[282] By contrast, private housing as it developed in

---

275 Stephen H.K. Yeh, *Households and Housing*, Census Monograph No. 4 (Singapore: Department of Statistics, 1984), p. 89; Yeh, "Some Trends and Prospects", pp. 182–3; *The Straits Times*, 24 Feb. 1975, 30 May 1980.

276 Liu Thai-Ker, *A Review of Public Housing in Singapore* (Singapore: National Trades Union Congress, 1983), pp. 15–17.

277 Lim, *Business, Government and Labor*, pp. 31, 32.

278 Liu, *A Review of Public Housing*, pp. 2, 11–12.

279 *The Straits Times*, 3 May 1969.

280 Liu, *A Review of Public Housing*, pp. 3–5; Teo and Savage, "Singapore Landscape", pp. 329, 330–2, 335.

281 *New Nation*, 9 Apr. 1974, 18 June 1979; *The Straits Times*, 19 Oct. 1977, 27 Aug. 1985.

282 *The Straits Times*, 4 June 1977.

the post-independence years was focused on the construction of terrace and semi-detached houses, bungalows and condominiums to meet the needs of a more affluent minority of the population.

The economic impact of the public housing programme was notable. Government expenditure on housing as a proportion of development expenditure was 20.5 per cent in 1969, contributing 1.6 per cent point to GDP growth.[283] The ratio subsequently increased to between 24 per cent and 33 per cent in the early 1980s. In the 1960s, more than two-fifths of fixed capital formation was accounted for by construction activity, a large part of which was on housing. As the building industry is highly labour-intensive and requires both unskilled and skilled manpower, the HDB also created substantial employment—about 7 per cent of the non-professional labour force was deployed in the sector during the late 1960s.[284] By subsidising housing, the government reduced the cost of labour, thus further stimulating employment creation.[285] Backward and forward linkages were also established with the building materials and transportation industries. Not less important was the siting of light manufacturing industries and workshops in the vicinity of housing estates to provide jobs for the people living in them.

In the 1950s, the colonial government had drafted a Master Plan for Singapore grounded on British planning concepts but with its narrow focus on land redevelopment and population distribution in the central area, it could hardly be called a blueprint for the urban renewal of a rapidly growing city.[286] The task of urban renewal of the independent city-state of Singapore was initiated in 1966 by a department of the HDB; this remained the case until 1974 when the Urban Redevelopment Authority (URA) was formed.[287] In 1971, a long-term Concept Plan based on UN recommendations was drawn up to guide urban development and land use throughout Singapore via a dense network of transportation and communication lines.[288] Instead of a piecemeal and *ad hoc* approach, the plan adopted a strategic and integrated framework.[289] It was therefore the HDB and the URA that jointly transformed the physical landscape of the city by replacing the erstwhile two- and three-storey shophouses with imposing skyscrapers, offices, banks, hotels, shopping centres and public flats. The eventual result was to produce one of the most striking skylines in the world and elevate Singapore to the status of a most liveable metropolitan city.

---

283 Yeh, "Some Trends and Prospects", p. 184; *The Straits Times*, 25 June 1968.

284 *New Nation*, 29 Oct. 1973.

285 Lim, *Business, Government and Labor*, pp. 31, 35.

286 Wong Tai-Chee, "The Transformation of Singapore's Central Area: From Slums to a Global Business Hub?", *Planning Practice & Research* 16, 2 (2001): 157–8, 160; *Living the Next Lap: Towards a Tropical City of Excellence* (Singapore: Urban Redevelopment Authority, 1991), p. 8.

287 Teo and Savage, "Singapore Landscape", pp. 329, 331, 335–6; Alan F.C. Choe, "Urban Renewal", in *Public Housing in Singapore: A Multi-Disciplinary Study*, ed. Stephen H.K. Yeh (Singapore: Singapore University Press, 1975), pp. 98–9; *New Nation*, 26 Feb. 1973, 9 Feb. 1974.

288 *Urban Redevelopment*, pp. 17, 25; *The Straits Times*, 23 Mar. 1970.

289 Choe, "The Early Years of Nation-Building", pp. 3, 15–17.

Apart from making land available for new development, urban renewal in the early years was concerned with resettling the city population in the new towns and clearing slums in order to revitalise the city centre.[290] Three-quarters of a million inhabitants living in Chinatown, the central area and its fringes required rehousing while family-based small industries had to be removed to flatted factories in the outskirts of the city.[291] Since the government's policy was to pay compensation and also provide alternative subsidised accommodation for the people affected, the processes of resettlement, slum clearance and public housing construction were interrelated, especially in the initial stage of urban renewal.[292] Concomitant to these efforts, rent decontrol in the city allowed landlords to sell or redevelop their properties for other uses and the affected shopkeepers were given priority in renting HDB shops at reduced rates.[293] In the city core, while the state's responsibility was to provide public housing, schools, hawker centres, landscaping and parks, the actual task of developing economically viable projects was carried out by the private sector on amalgamated land parcels sold by the government.[294] To encourage private participation, down payments on the land purchased were kept at 20 per cent, the property tax was reduced from 36 per cent to 12 per cent and the development charge was waived. In total, more than 121 hectares of land in the city centre were cleared and redeveloped during the decade from 1965.

Another aspect of urban renewal was the relocation of 30,000 street hawkers in the city to hawker centres with improved hygiene; these centres were spread all over the island and their rental of stalls was subsidised.[295] The Singapore River was cleaned up by clearing the bumboats and removing debris, bringing to a close its long commercial history. Godowns and warehouses along the river banks were relocated to a new complex in Pasir Panjang and the premises taken over by upmarket eateries.[296] The area adjacent to the river was converted into a modern Central Business District (CBD) consisting of Raffles Place, Cecil Street, Robinson Road and Shenton Way while land was reclaimed from the sea for the new Marina Centre.[297] Farther away, the Orchard Road corridor was turned into a tourist and shopping belt. Amidst this massive urban renewal project, conservation of the city's physical and cultural heritage was not forgotten; the ethnic enclaves of Chinatown, Little India and Kampong Glam as well as historical landmarks were preserved.[298]

---

[290] Wong, "The Transformation of Singapore's Central Area", pp. 158–60; *The Straits Times*, 21 July 1965, 18 Apr. 1967, 13 Oct. 1967; *New Nation*, 2 Apr. 1973.

[291] Chew Chee Sun, "Key Elements in the Urban Renewal of Singapore", in *Planning in Singapore: Selected Aspects and Issues*, ed. Chua Peng Chye (Singapore: Chopmen Enterprises, 1973), pp. 35, 36–9.

[292] Choe, "Urban Renewal", pp. 104–6; Geiger and Geiger, *Tales of Two City-States*, p. 211; *The Straits Times*, 29 Jan. 1967; *New Nation*, 23 Sept. 1971.

[293] *The Straits Times*, 2 Mar. 1970.

[294] Choe, "The Early Years of Nation-Building", pp. 14–15; *The Straits Times*, 2 May 1969, 15 Apr. 1984.

[295] *Urban Redevelopment*, pp. 31, 33; *The Straits Times*, 7 May 1978.

[296] *The Straits Times*, 13 Sept. 1970, 3 Mar. 1977, 9 July 1982, 3 May 1983.

[297] Wong, "The Transformation of Singapore's Central Area", pp. 159–62.

[298] Choe, "Urban Renewal", pp. 106–7; *The Straits Times*, 13 Aug. 1973.

Fiscal and Monetary Policies

The pervasive role played by the Singapore government in industrialisation, manpower training, healthcare and housing warrants a review of its fiscal policy. If there is one word to describe the policy, it is "prudent". In expatiating on this subject, we would do well to remember that the state of government finances had been in disarray when the PAP took over from the previous administration in 1959. To reduce expenditure, the allowances of political officeholders and civil servants were immediately cut.[299] Within a decade, however, the government began to run budget surpluses year after year, adding to the nation's reserves. This outcome was unanticipated even though it was a continuation of a long-standing feature of the colonial state. Specifically, the principle of "living within one's means" was not only upheld in the modern era but became more entrenched despite a shift from a night watchman state with minimal government responsibilities to a developmental state with heavy intervention.[300]

Prior to PAP rule, the main sources of revenue of the Colony of Singapore were duties on petroleum and tobacco, income tax and company tax. The last two had been introduced at long last in 1947 after the revenue from opium sales ceased completely due to a total ban on the drug during the Second World War.[301] As in past abortive attempts to introduce income taxation permanently, it faced strong opposition by European and Chinese business interests on the grounds that an income tax would bear heavily on the recovering rubber and tin industries and that the tax would be inequitable due to evasion.[302] Nevertheless, the Governor was steadfast in his decision and went ahead using his veto power. The tax on personal incomes was progressive—though only moderately so—in order not to blunt work incentives. Tax rates started at 5 per cent (for incomes of $1,500) and rose to 55 per cent for the top income bracket (incomes in excess of $100,000), although personal and family allowances reduced the net liability to pay tax and only a small segment of the population actually did so. The corporate income tax was levied on the profits of private and public limited companies at the uniform rate of 20 per cent.[303] In the first year of assessment, 1948, about 40,000 individual returns and 1,000 corporate returns brought in a total income of $33.2 million.[304] By 1956, income taxes were responsible for 29.6 per cent of colonial revenue while import duties contributed 26.4 per cent. At the lower levels of government, collections by the Municipality of Singapore added 12.4 per cent and the Rural Board just 1.7 per cent.

After self-government was attained, income and corporate taxes continued to be a major source of revenue. Their contribution in 1960 of 24.4 per cent was however overshadowed by the 33.1 per cent of import and excise duties—the result of the import substitution

299 Liew and Wilson, *A History of Money*, p. 197; *The Straits Times*, 24 June 1959.

300 Sugimoto and Tan, "Government Fiscal Behavior", pp. 21, 24–5.

301 *The Straits Times*, 17 Mar. 1947, 21 Aug. 1947, 21 Oct. 1948; *The Straits Budget*, 15 May 1947, 8 Jan. 1948, 19 Feb. 1948; *The Singapore Free Press*, 1 July 1948.

302 C.T. Edwards, *Public Finances in Malaya and Singapore* (Canberra: Australian National University Press, 1970), pp. 65–8, 140–2, 148–9, 153; *The Straits Budget*, 19 Dec. 1946, 27 Nov. 1947, 4 Dec. 1947.

303 The corporate income tax rate was later raised to 30 per cent and subsequently to 40 per cent in 1959. Liew and Wilson, *A History of Money*, pp. 196–7.

304 Liew and Wilson, *A History of Money*, p. 193.

regime put in place during the 1950s (Table 14).[305] By 1975, the former had surpassed the latter, which declined to 12.9 per cent as duties were levied only on petroleum, perfumes, liquor and tobacco. In 1985, when the corporate tax was cut in the aftermath of recession, 28.1 per cent of revenue was accounted for by direct taxes, 11.1 per cent by the tax levied on the annual value of properties and 6.4 per cent by taxes on imported motor vehicles.[306] Over the period, revenue from other sources included taxes on selected goods and services as well as entertainment and gambling duties.[307] The largest item was the non-tax revenue, with a contribution of 36.6 per cent, from the sales and leases of land, fees and fines, and interest earnings on the official reserves.[308]

Table 14. Sources of Singapore Government Revenue, 1960–85

	1960	**1965**	**1970**	**1975**	**1980**	**1985**
Income and corporate taxes (%)	24.4	20.7	20.8	36.0	33.2	28.1
Import and excise duties (%)	33.1	29.8	23.6	12.9	11.7	9.2
Property tax (%)	3.2	12.2	9.0	9.8	9.7	11.1
Motor vehicle tax (%)	2.3	5.5	4.9	4.8	8.5	6.4
Stamp duty (%)	1.3	1.2	1.9	1.5	2.8	2.9
Others (%)	8.0	6.9	10.6	5.1	5.5	5.6
Non-tax revenue (%)	27.7	23.7	29.2	29.9	28.6	36.6

Source: Sugimoto and Tan, "Government Fiscal Behavior", Table 2, p. 26.

Owing to the transition from a night watchman state to a developmental state, the relative magnitudes of government expenditure in the pre-war and post-war periods show a divergence.[309] Whereas state spending as a percentage of GDP averaged 10.3 per cent during 1900–39 and stayed low, at 9.6 per cent, in the 1950s, it increased to 19.2 per cent from the 1960s onwards, although this was still low by the standards of developed economies mainly because social welfare programmes involving state transfers to citizens in Singapore were restricted to the elderly poor, the handicapped and the destitute.[310] In fact, if not for the state's development spending which increased tremendously, public expenditure as a proportion of GDP would have been lower. The rise in public spending was observed in both government consumption and investment and could be traced largely to the PAP's pro-active role in providing economic infrastructure and social services, compared to

[305] Sugimoto and Tan, "Government Fiscal Behavior", pp. 24–6; *The Straits Budget*, 17 Nov. 1965.

[306] Mukul G. Asher and Amina Tyabji, "Trends in Government Revenue and Expenditure, 1966–1977", in *Issues in Public Finance in Singapore*, ed. Mukul G. Asher and Susan Osborne (Singapore: Singapore University Press, 1980), pp. 12–14, 20–2. The property tax was levied at rates ranging from 12 per cent to 36 per cent of assessed values; in addition, an estate duty was payable on properties valued at more than $25,000. However, there are no capital gains or wealth taxes in Singapore. Geiger and Geiger, *Tales of Two City-States*, p. 181.

[307] *The Straits Budget*, 13 Apr. 1960.

[308] Geiger and Geiger, *Tales of Two City-States*, p. 180.

[309] Sugimoto and Tan, "Government Fiscal Behavior", pp. 26–9.

[310] Donald Low, "Fiscal Policy: Discipline with Discretion", Mimeograph, pp. 11–12; *The Straits Times*, 22 Mar. 1971.

the benign neglect of the colonial authorities.[311] Spending on defence, justice and the police force was the largest current expenditure category and rose to 5.1 per cent of GDP for the independent republic.[312] Spending on education increased from 0.3 per cent to 4.3 per cent, on health from 1.1 per cent to 1.4 per cent and on social welfare from 0.3 per cent to 0.9 per cent, all these expenditures being in the form of subsidies.[313]

In spite of these increases in expenditure, fiscal conservatism and strong economic growth resulted in the aforementioned current budget surpluses starting in the late sixties and they grew much larger in the early eighties (Figure 24). Furthermore, by virtue of conservative budgeting, the realised surpluses tended to be higher than forecast as a result of spending falling short of, and revenue exceeding, the estimated amounts.[314] These surpluses included the income of major statutory boards such as the HDB, JTC, PUB and PSA, which were substantial at $3.5 billion in 1983 and arose from the monopoly profits made by pricing services, such as utilities and port charges, above cost.[315] However, if the boards' development expenditures were taken into account, they would have incurred deficits continually except in 1984 and 1985, though the government sector would still be in surplus because of the fiscal discipline it exercised in spending.[316] In 1983, for example, the overall government surplus was $4.1 billion.[317] The surpluses were achieved notwithstanding the fact that the level of expenditure had risen and the tax burden had been kept low, which would seem to suggest that the government was committed to a minimalist role in the economy.[318] Yet it has been said that the government's intervention in the economy was pervasive; the paradox is resolved when one recognises that a large part of government activity was mediated by the statutory boards and GLCs.

The persistent budget surpluses accumulated by the government meant not only that the revenue system in Singapore was adequate but also that it did not need to resort to overseas borrowing to finance spending.[319] External debt consisting of loans from international agencies and foreign governments had been relatively small even in the earlier years when the nation embarked on large-scale industrialisation and it shrunk to $596 million in 1985.[320] Domestic borrowing figured more prominently, particularly from the CPF and POSB, wherein the contributions of members and private savings were invested in government

---

311 *New Nation*, 13 Oct. 1971.

312 Mukul G. Asher, "The Fiscal System of Singapore", in *The Singapore Economy*, ed. You and Lim, p. 90; *The Straits Times*, 9 Mar. 1971.

313 Ow Chin Hock, "The Role of Government", pp. 236–8, 258; *The Straits Times*, 14 Dec. 1965.

314 *The Straits Times*, 30 Mar. 1976.

315 Pang and Lim, "Rapid Growth", p. 101; *The Business Times*, 4 Mar. 1980.

316 "Fiscal Policy", in Lim and Associates, *Policy Options*, pp. 362–3, 383–4; Asher and Tyabji, "Trends in Government Revenue and Expenditure", pp. 26–8.

317 Krause, Koh and Lee, *The Singapore Economy Reconsidered*, p. 137.

318 Mukul G. Asher, A.S. Bali and Chang Yee Kwan, "Public Financial Management in Singapore: Key Characteristics and Prospects", *The Singapore Economic Review* 60, 3 (2015): 1550032-7–1550032-8.

319 "Fiscal Policy in Singapore", IPS-ESS Workshop (Singapore, May 2004), pp. 1–3; Asher and Tyabji, "Trends in Government Revenue and Expenditure", pp. 12, 14, 34; Asher, "The Fiscal System", p. 90; *The Straits Times*, 30 Mar. 1976.

320 "Fiscal Policy", pp. 363–8, 370–1; Geiger and Geiger, *Tales of Two City-States*, pp. 179, 182.

registered stocks and were used to pay for public housing and infrastructure building. Furthermore, treasury bills and bonds were issued not for the purpose of borrowing but to fulfil financial institutions' need to hold liquid assets and to deepen the local money and capital markets. In any event, more funds were borrowed from the CPF than necessary for national development and the excess was simply transferred to the Government of Singapore Investment Corporation (GIC) set up in 1981 by Dr Goh Keng Swee.[321]

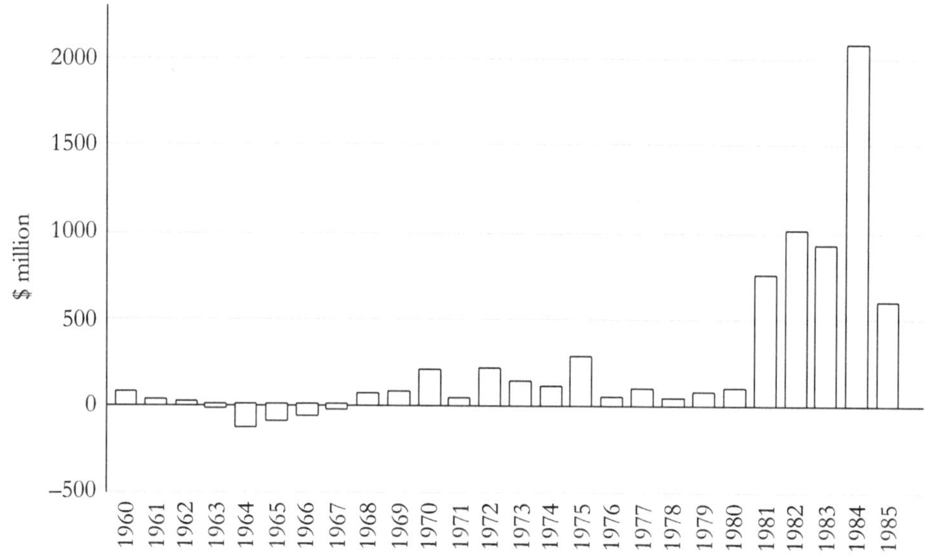

Figure 24. Singapore Government Budget Balance, 1960–85
Note: The figures do not include the statutory boards.
Source: Authors' calculations.

Like sovereign wealth funds in other countries, GIC aims to maximise returns by long-term overseas investments in all types of financial instruments and real estate.[322] Linked to this objective is its mission of preserving the purchasing power of the national reserves for future generations and by doing so secure the stability of the Singapore dollar and act as insurer of last resort in underwriting the financial system. From a precautionary point of view, the reserves were money set aside for "rainy days", that is, for use in the event of contingencies, which did occur in later years.[323] In 1985, the total amount of foreign reserves held by the government was $27 billion, most of which was invested by GIC. On the other hand, the establishment of GIC's sister organisation, Temasek Holdings, in 1974

[321] Krause, Koh and Lee, *The Singapore Economy Reconsidered*, p. 140; Liew and Wilson, *A History of Money*, p. 301; Freddy Orchard, *Safeguarding the Future: The Story of How Singapore Has Managed Its Reserves and the Founding of GIC*, e-book (2016), pp. 7–16.

[322] Henry Wai-Chung Yeung, "From National Development to Economic Diplomacy? Governing Singapore's Sovereign Wealth Funds", *The Pacific Review* 24, 5 (2011): 630–5; *The Business Times*, 28 Feb. 1981, 13 June 1981.

[323] Low, "Fiscal Policy", p. 15.

was for the purpose of holding the government's assets in the GLCs.[324] The equity stakes taken by the EDB in the 1960s were also transferred to Temasek Holdings, whose role was to manage and monitor the entities in its stable on a market-oriented basis. In the early 1980s, this state-owned investment holding company began to seek out new investments and mergers of its companies with others in the private sector. By 1983, it had accumulated a portfolio of 58 diverse companies with a total paid-up capital of $2.9 billion, which in turn owned some 490 firms in Singapore and provided direct employment for 24,000 people. Some of these companies are world-class leaders in their respective industries: Singapore Telecom (Singtel) in telephony, Keppel Corporation and SembCorp Industries in shipyard and marine ventures, DBS in banking and SIA in aviation.

It is perhaps evident from the above account that the primary role of fiscal policy in Singapore had been to create conditions that were conducive to long-term economic growth, that is, the enhancement of physical infrastructure and human capital.[325] In fact, it was used for macroeconomic stabilisation only during the growth slowdowns of 1973–75 and 1981–82, when public housing construction and spending on civil works such as the MRT system were stepped up to boost economic activity.[326] Even when such counter-cyclical Keynesian policies were used, the increase in government spending was expended on projects that improved the productive capacity of the economy.[327] To some extent, the infrequent resort to government pump-priming was because the fiscal multiplier in Singapore is low due to leakages abroad from imports.[328] Besides, the economy enjoyed full employment for most of the time except during the mid-eighties' recession, implying that the need to stimulate growth through activist fiscal policy was limited. The policy has occasionally been used to achieve social objectives instead, for example in raising the fertility rate through the award of pecuniary benefits to families.

In the same way that they had influenced the conduct of fiscal policy, historical circumstances and Singapore's small open economy shaped the *modus operandi* of monetary policy. Before describing the regime, we will first take up the narrative where it had broken off in the early fifties. During the time Singapore was part of Malaysia, the common currency that circulated was still the Malayan and North Borneo dollar issued by the Board of Commissioners of Currency, even though the Federation had established its central bank, Bank Negara, in 1959.[329] When they parted ways in 1965, the authorities in both countries immediately began negotiations on sharing the currency but the talks ran into problems very quickly. In 1966, one year after separation from Malaysia, the historic

---

[324] *The Straits Times*, 16 Feb. 1977.

[325] "Fiscal Policy", pp. 361–2; Low, "Fiscal Policy", p. 2.

[326] Krause, Koh and Lee, *The Singapore Economy Reconsidered*, pp. 143–4, 148–9; Pang and Lim, "Rapid Growth", p. 92; *The Straits Times*, 12 July 1975, 30 Mar. 1976; *The Business Times*, 6 May 1978.

[327] Asher, "The Fiscal System", p. 95.

[328] Tilak Abeysinghe and Keen Meng Choy, *The Singapore Economy: An Econometric Perspective* (Routledge, 2007), pp. 126–9.

[329] Lee, *The Monetary and Banking Development*, pp. 22–3, 53–7; P.J. Drake, *Financial Development in Malaya and Singapore* (Canberra: Australian National University Press, 1969), p. 83.

monetary union between Singapore and the Malayan territories broke down as a result of disagreement between the two sides on a host of issues and conflicting objectives.[330]

The nub of contention was the ownership of the currency reserves and this was aggravated by political animosity and distrust between the two governments.[331] Each had erected tariff walls against the other's goods, an action, amongst others, that bedevilled the currency negotiations. On the issue of who owned the currency assets, Singapore wanted to be assured that in the event of a breakup of the monetary union, it would have immediate access to the reserves and was not convinced by Malaysia's counter-proposal of maintaining two separate accounts, whereby the ultimate ownership of the reserves would still legally rest with Bank Negara.[332] The two parties also disagreed on the issue of whether the currency reserve ratio—the amount of foreign assets required to back the domestic currency—should be 100 per cent or another percentage. Singapore had insisted on this and the continuation of the currency board system to ensure that there would be no over-issue of currency to finance government deficits that would result in inflation.[333] Its leaders' vision was for the city-state to be a regional commercial and financial centre, which would require a stable and strong currency to instil confidence. Malaysia flatly rejected the proposition as being too inflexible and, in contrast to Singapore, wanted more scope for monetary expansion to stimulate domestic production and employment.

A final issue on which they differed was the constitution and powers of the central bank. While the Malaysians favoured the extension of Bank Negara's jurisdiction and currency issuing power to the island via a branch office, the Singaporeans preferred a joint central bank.[334] In fact, the idea of a joint central bank went back to 1956 with the Watson-Caine Report strongly recommending its formation, though nothing came out of it.[335] Singapore eventually gave way on the last two issues but the talks were unravelled by the impasse over the currency reserves. As in the case of the common market, underlying these disputes was Malaysia's perception that a joint currency held little benefit for the country while the cost in terms of tying Bank Negara's hands in monetary policy was substantial.

Given the extensive economic links between Singapore and Malaysia, most people, particularly the business community, on both sides of the Causeway would have preferred a common currency to facilitate commercial transactions and the remittance of funds. But although the International Monetary Fund (IMF) acted as a mediator, negotiations broke down. The hope for a common currency was dashed and the only option left for the two governments was to issue their own currencies.[336] On 12 June 1967, the Singapore dollar was introduced by the Board of Commissioners of Currency, Singapore (BCCS) while

---

[330] Drake, "The Evolution of Money", p. 18.

[331] Liew and Wilson, *A History of Money*, pp. 219, 220–3.

[332] Drake, *Financial Development*, pp. 84–91; *The Straits Times*, 27 Aug. 1966.

[333] C.R. Schenk, "The Dissolution of a Monetary Union: The Case of Singapore and Malaysia 1963–1974", *The Journal of Imperial and Commonwealth History* 41, 3 (2013): 505–8; Liew and Wilson, *A History of Money*, pp. 216, 217, 218–9, 228.

[334] Schenk, "Dissolution", pp. 503–4, 505–6, 507–8.

[335] Lee, *The Monetary and Banking Development*, pp. 20–2, 53–4, 58–9; Drake, *Financial Development*, pp. 64–5; *The Straits Budget*, 12 Jan. 1956, 5 July 1956.

[336] Liew and Wilson, *A History of Money*, pp. 218, 219; *The Straits Times*, 18 Aug. 1966, 27 Aug. 1966.

the Malaysian ringgit had been issued by Bank Negara in the previous year.[337] The former currency was fully backed by gold and foreign exchange and convertible to sterling on demand.[338] Singapore therefore had the distinction of being the only post-colonial state that adhered to the relic of a currency board system.[339]

Being *de facto* pegged through their common link to the pound sterling, the two countries agreed that the dollar and ringgit should be interchangeable at par value and circulated freely in both territories as if they were legal tender, that is, as "customary tender".[340] This arrangement minimised financial disruption and included Brunei; each monetary authority collected the notes and coins of the others for physical exchange and repatriation periodically, with settlement in sterling or another agreed currency.[341] This somewhat cumbersome procedure was replaced in 1968 by a system through which banks could clear their balances across the three countries directly. In May 1973, however, Malaysia unilaterally terminated the currency interchangeability arrangement, purportedly to encourage the development of its own financial markets and institutions.[342] It also announced that the Malaysian stock exchange would henceforth sever its link with the Singapore exchange and that the country would promote its own rubber exchange. However, the impact of Malaysia's actions on Singapore was minimal since the latter had reduced its dependence on entrepôt trade by then.[343] Interchangeability between the Singapore and Brunei currencies continues to this day.[344]

In retrospect, it was beneficial that Singapore issued its own dollar, for the next few years were tumultuous ones for the global monetary system. The first strain occurred with the devaluation of the pound sterling in November 1967. As the move was widely expected due to the United Kingdom's balance of payments difficulties, Singapore had the foresight to freeze its sterling currency assets held in London and invest newly acquired reserves in US dollars and other non-sterling currencies, thereby minimising the loss in value of the sterling assets.[345] Not taking the same measures, Malaysia stood to lose $250 million, although it was quick to react to the situation by deciding not to devalue the ringgit.[346] Singapore followed suit by not devaluing the dollar partly because it desired to maintain parity between the two currencies. However, another consideration was involved: a decline in the dollar exchange rate in sterling terms would lower the prices of Singapore's exports in

337 *The Straits Times*, 15 Mar. 1967.

338 Schenk, "Dissolution", pp. 511–2.

339 Goh Keng Swee, "Why A Currency Board?", in *Prudence at the Helm, Board of Commissioners of Currency Singapore 1967–1992* (Singapore: Board of Commissioners of Currency, 1992), pp. 31–2.

340 Liew and Wilson, *A History of Money*, pp. 241–4, 269–74; *Macroeconomic Review* (Singapore: Monetary Authority of Singapore, April 2017), pp. 73–4; *The Straits Times*, 6 June 1967.

341 *The Straits Times*, 9 June 1967.

342 *The Straits Times*, 9 May 1973; *New Nation*, 9 May 1973.

343 Liew and Wilson, *A History of Money*, p. 273; *The Straits Budget*, 18 Aug. 1965.

344 *The Straits Times*, 23 May 1973.

345 Lee, *The Monetary and Banking Development*, pp. 60–4; Liew and Wilson, *A History of Money*, pp. 244–7, 251–2; *The Straits Times*, 24 Nov. 1967.

346 *The Straits Times*, 20 Nov. 1967.

world markets, thereby stimulating demand for them.[347] However, imports from countries that did not devalue against sterling would be more expensive, thus raising the cost of living and leading to demands for higher wages by workers. The end result would be inflation in the prices of goods and services. For Singapore, the second effect was likely to outweigh the first, since its manufacturing and export sector was still relatively small and it imported a large proportion of goods consumed locally.

Although the decision not to devalue the Singapore dollar was in accordance with economic logic, the announcement that the old Malayan dollar notes would be devalued along with sterling was not.[348] To be sure, this decision was taken by the Malaysian government, with the lame reason that the dollar was fixed in value against the pre-devaluation sterling currency, which meant that it would now be at a discount to the new currencies.[349] Singapore therefore had no choice but to renege on its promise that the old note would exchange one-for-one with the new note; this change of policy caused untold suffering to the poorer classes who had held on to the defunct currency.[350] It was estimated that the amount of old Malayan dollars still circulating in Singapore was $110 million, now worth only $93 million. The blow was hardly softened by allowing five and ten cent coins to be redeemed at par value.

The next series of turbulent monetary events came in rapid succession from 1971 to 1973.[351] In August 1971, following large outflows of funds from the United States to Europe and Japan that were precipitated by trade deficits arising from the Vietnam War and heavy social spending, the United States suspended the convertibility of the US dollar to gold; it was later devalued by raising the official price of gold from $35 per ounce to $38.[352] The European and Japanese currencies were devalued accordingly although the British pound was not, causing it to appreciate against the US dollar. In response, the Singapore and Malaysian authorities also maintained their gold parities; hence, their currencies were revalued in terms of US dollars. Then in February 1973, the US dollar was devalued for a second time after it came under severe pressure and this time, its fixed parity to gold was abandoned, making it a free-floating currency.[353] Since the other major currencies like the Deutsche Mark and yen were no longer tied to the greenback, they floated as well. A few months later, to stop the unwanted accumulation of the US dollar and the losses incurred from intervention to support it, Singapore also floated its dollar after having enjoyed a stable currency for more than 70 years.[354] The Bretton Woods system of fixed exchange rates for world currencies, named after the conference held in the US state of New Hampshire in 1944 and fully inaugurated after the Second World War, had collapsed.

---

347 *The Straits Times*, 21 Nov. 1967.

348 Lee, *The Monetary and Banking Development*, pp. 64–6; Drake, *Financial Development*, pp. 232–4.

349 *The Straits Times*, 20 Nov. 1967.

350 Liew and Wilson, *A History of Money*, pp. 248–51; *The Straits Times*, 24 Nov. 1967; *The Straits Budget*, 13 Dec. 1967.

351 Lee, *The Monetary and Banking Development*, pp. 67–70.

352 Liew and Wilson, *A History of Money*, pp. 262–4, 274–5; *New Nation*, 18 May 1971; *The Straits Times*, 17 Aug. 1971, 17 Sept. 1971, 20 Dec. 1971.

353 *The Straits Times*, 14 Feb. 1973, 6 Apr. 1973; *New Nation*, 15 Feb. 1973.

354 *The Straits Times*, 21 June 1973.

An increase in international financial flows had rendered capital controls ineffective, giving rise to speculation in foreign exchange markets that ultimately undermined the system.

In June 1972, the United Kingdom triggered a minor crisis when it floated the pound to stem an outflow of gold and foreign exchange.[355] As a result, Singapore and Malaysia began to peg their currencies to the US dollar instead of the pound sterling, in part to safeguard the value of their reserve assets.[356] That also meant changing their main reserve currency to the dollar, bringing the countries closer to the practice of other countries. These developments signalled the end of the Sterling Area, the bloc of countries that had shared a common currency peg to the pound sterling during the colonial period.[357] While it operated during the heyday of the British Empire, its members had been well served by having access to sterling reserves in London and the ability to settle intra-area payments in sterling. In the post-war era however, it increasingly lost relevance and usefulness as ex-colonies diversified their trade and investment links. The frequent crises of confidence affecting the pound made it even less attractive as an anchor currency.

Amidst these crises, the Monetary Authority of Singapore (MAS) was founded in 1971—not a moment too soon—to perform all central banking functions except for the issue of currency.[358] This last important task was deliberately left to the BCCS to preclude the government from printing money to pay for its spending.[359] At first, there was some hesitancy to establish a *de facto* central bank in view of the continuation of the currency board system and the absence of a money market in Singapore, although the idea was recommended by the IMF. Nevertheless, the financial structure of the economy had developed sufficiently by the early 1970s to warrant a single regulatory authority. MAS took over the functions of bank and finance company supervision, including monitoring cash reserve and liquid asset ratios, as well as administering exchange control, previously discharged by different government departments.[360] The bulk of Singapore's foreign reserve assets was transferred to the central bank for management from the Ministry of Finance. MAS also acted as the banker for the government and the commercial banks' bank; in 1972, legislation was introduced to allow it to be the lender of last resort.[361]

When it was first established, MAS was assigned the dual mandate of achieving monetary and price stability while promoting the sustained growth of the Singapore economy.[362] If Singapore did not have a monetary policy before its formation, it did now. In colonial times, the currency board had only to issue the notes and coins while the

---

355 Liew and Wilson, *A History of Money*, pp. 265–7; *The Straits Times*, 24 June 1972.

356 Peter Wilson, "Monetary Policy and Financial Sector Development", *The Singapore Economic Review* 60, 3 (2015): 1550031-3; *The Straits Times*, 26 June 1972.

357 *The Straits Times*, 16 Aug. 1972.

358 *The Straits Times*, 3 Sept. 1970.

359 Wilson, "Monetary Policy and Financial Sector Development", p. 1550031-4.

360 Monetary Authority of Singapore, *Sustaining Stability, Serving Singapore* (Singapore: Straits Times Press, 2012), p. 14.

361 Lee Sheng-Yi, *Financial Structure and Monetary Policy*, Occasional Paper No. 35 (Singapore: Institute of Economics and Business Studies, Nanyang University, 1979), pp. 4–7, 95–7; Liew and Wilson, *A History of Money*, pp. 259–60; *The Straits Times*, 27 Oct. 1972.

362 Monetary Authority of Singapore, *Sustaining Stability, Serving Singapore*, p. 35.

British Crown Agents carried out the function of exchanging the Malayan dollar for the pound sterling. After MAS was formed, the system worked in such a way that a balance of payments surplus would automatically induce an increase in the money supply and vice versa. Hence, the foreign exchange earnings from the export of goods and services, interest on investments abroad and capital inflows were exchanged for Singapore dollars through the banks and BCCS, thereby expanding the domestic stocks of currency and loans.[363] In general, the amount of currency in circulation rose with higher incomes: for example, narrow money (that is, reserves held by banks and currency and notes in circulation) increased by 17.3 per cent in 1970 and 35.5 per cent in 1972, when economic growth was faster (Figure 25).

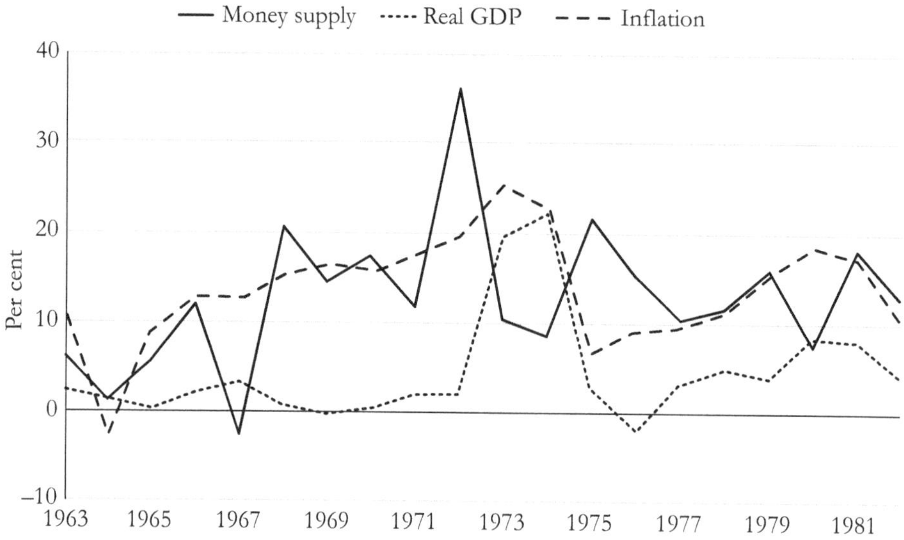

Figure 25. Money Supply Growth, Output Growth and Inflation in Singapore, 1963–82
Source: *Economic and Social Statistics of Singapore 1960–1982*, Singapore: Department of Statistics, 1983, pp. 57–8, 170, 213–14.

Following its formation, MAS had to create new financial instruments and institutions such as treasury bills, discount houses and acceptance houses to implement monetary policy.[364] After the Singapore dollar was floated in 1973, it occasionally intervened in the foreign exchange market to maintain a desired exchange rate, that is, one that was not so high as to hinder exports and not so low as to increase the cost of imports.[365] Furthermore, since public sector surpluses and CPF contributions withdrew liquidity from the financial system, MAS had to intervene to reinject the funds into the economy by selling Singapore dollars. Thus, the dollar was not on a clean float, but a managed one.

[363] Geiger and Geiger, *Tales of Two City-States*, p. 189.

[364] Liew and Wilson, *A History of Money*, p. 280; *The Straits Times*, 19 Apr. 1972, 19 Jan. 1973.

[365] Lee, *Financial Structure and Monetary Policy*, pp. 97, 99, 101–2, 107; Lee, *The Monetary and Banking Development*, pp. 135–7; *New Nation*, 22 May 1973; *The Straits Times*, 6 July 1973.

In view of strong economic growth, rising inflation, large capital inflows, a buoyant stock market and a boom in construction in the early seventies, MAS took steps to restrain the expansion of money and credit by allowing interest rates to rise in tandem with global rates. The prime rate (the minimum lending rate of banks) was raised to 7.5 per cent in 1972 and to 8 per cent in 1973.[366] In 1974 after the first global oil price hike caused consumer price inflation to rise to 22.3 per cent from an average of 1.2 per cent in the 1960s, the rate was first increased to 9.25 per cent and further to 11.28 per cent.[367] This rise in interest rates was accompanied by an increase in the cash reserve ratio of banks, the imposition of a special deposit ratio on net borrowed funds from abroad and credit allocation.[368] The reserve ratio was increased from 3.5 per cent to 5 per cent in August 1972 and to 9 per cent in March 1973.[369] After 1975, the prime rate was determined by market forces instead of being set by a cartel of banks in consultation with MAS. It was lowered to 9.5 per cent in January 1975 and then to 8 per cent in March as inflationary pressures began to ease.

The subsequent period up to 1979 was characterised by slow growth rather than inflation and so liquidity was pumped into the economy by allowing the money supply and bank credit to grow at a faster rate than real income, even though MAS was careful not to reignite inflation.[370] More often than not, the money supply tended to rise in line with output growth and also to presage it. To guide policy formulation, a range of monetary, interest rate and exchange rate indicators were monitored. There was also a discernible shift to influencing interest rates through money market operations, specifically by varying the official discount rate and the volume of treasury bills to be tendered.[371] Beginning from the early 1980s, MAS used foreign exchange swaps to regulate the level of liquidity in the banking system.

In 1980, Dr Goh Keng Swee became the MAS chairman and promptly engaged in an exercise to restructure the organisation and trim its staff strength.[372] Since central banks typically held their reserves in short-term and lower-yield instruments such as cash, bonds and gold, part of the investment function involving long-term reserve assets was transferred to the newly established GIC. The top MAS management was also replaced

366 Liew and Wilson, *A History of Money*, pp. 280, 282; Wong, *Essays*, pp. 22–4; *The Straits Times*, 7 Feb. 1973, 26 Apr. 1973, 24 Dec. 1973.

367 Pang and Lim, "Rapid Growth", pp. 99–100; *Economic and Social Statistics of Singapore 1960–1982* (Singapore: Department of Statistics, 1983), pp. 57–8, 170, 213–4; *The Straits Times*, 18 July 1974. The rise in inflation was aggravated by a hefty jump in the price of imported rice from Thailand. Le Blanc, *Singapore*, p. 30.

368 *The Straits Times*, 19 Dec. 1973.

369 *The Straits Times*, 14 Feb. 1973, 19 Dec. 1973.

370 Wilson, "Monetary Policy and Financial Sector Development", pp. 1550031-6, 1550031-8; *Monetary Authority of Singapore Annual Report 1979/80* (Singapore: Monetary Authority of Singapore, 1980), p. 22; *The Straits Times*, 21 Apr. 1975; *The Business Times*, 15 Feb. 1977.

371 *Monetary Authority of Singapore Annual Report 1976/77* (Singapore: Monetary Authority of Singapore, 1977), p. 13; *Monetary Authority of Singapore Annual Report 1977/78* (Singapore: Monetary Authority of Singapore, 1978), pp. 10–11; *The Business Times*, 15 Feb. 1977.

372 Monetary Authority of Singapore, *Sustaining Stability, Serving Singapore*, pp. 15, 17; Liew and Wilson, *A History of Money*, pp. 261, 298–9, 300; *The Straits Times*, 2 Aug. 1980; *The Business Times*, 3 Dec. 1980.

but the most significant change was the switchover to an exchange rate-centred monetary policy framework in 1981.[373] Instead of relying on a checklist of indicators and using an eclectic set of measures to conduct monetary policy, MAS henceforth focused on just one indicator—the Singapore dollar exchange rate.[374] This policy stance was epitomised by Dr Goh's famous statement that "the MAS is probably the only central bank that does not watch the Ms" (the different measures of money supply).[375] The implication is that the money supply is determined by the demand for it. The external backdrop to this policy shift was the second oil price increase in 1979, which together with wage hikes caused inflation to spike to 8.5 per cent in 1980.[376] However, the increase in prices this time was less severe than in the previous episode, thanks to the appreciation of the Singapore dollar.[377] The strengthening of the currency also had the beneficial effect of helping the economic restructuring drive by forcing producers to switch to higher value-added goods, since cheaper products would not be competitive any more.

The monetary regime that evolved after 1981 has a few distinguishing features.[378] First, MAS targets a composite exchange rate of the Singapore dollar against a basket of currencies of its major trading partners and competitors rather than the Singapore rate against the US dollar, although intervention in the foreign exchange market is effected through the latter. This is to reflect the nation's varied trading patterns with different countries and sources of imported inflation. Second, rather than remaining fixed in value, the trade-weighted exchange rate fluctuates within an undisclosed band that was first introduced in 1975 to allow room for market forces to influence it, although its fundamental value is ultimately determined by MAS based on long-term considerations of growth and productivity. In the event, the Singapore dollar appreciated over the long term. An important implication of the exchange rate-centred monetary policy is that MAS loses control over domestic interest rates (and the money supply), which are determined by the trends in world rates, particularly that in the United States. Any discrepancy between domestic and foreign rates would cause capital funds to flow in or out.[379]

The economic rationale for choosing the exchange rate as the instrument of monetary policy is easily comprehended. Singapore is not just a small economy, but also an extremely open one in terms of its exposure to trade; hence, it depends heavily on imports for the bulk of the requirements for production and consumption.[380] Managing the exchange rate is therefore the most efficacious way of securing price stability, since its level has a

---

373 *The Straits Times*, 15 Jan. 1981, 17 Jan. 1981; *New Nation*, 28 Feb. 1981.

374 Monetary Authority of Singapore, *Sustaining Stability, Serving Singapore*, pp. 33, 35–7.

375 *The Straits Times*, 25 Aug. 1984.

376 *The Business Times*, 5 Mar. 1981.

377 Teh and Shanmugaratnam, "Exchange Rate Policy", p. 298; Liew and Wilson, *A History of Money*, pp. 303, 304.

378 *Singapore's Exchange Rate Policy* (Singapore: Monetary Authority of Singapore, 2001), p. 2.

379 Edward Robinson, "Monetary Policy: Anchor of Stability and Confidence", Mimeograph, pp. 7–8.

380 Teh and Shanmugaratnam, "Exchange Rate Policy", pp. 289–90; Wilson, "Monetary Policy and Financial Sector Development", p. 1550031-8. It has been estimated that three-fifths of domestic expenditure was spent on imports.

powerful influence on domestic prices.[381] Specifically, the exchange rate can be allowed to appreciate to neutralise imported foreign inflation. Concurrently, changes in the value of the exchange rate also affect export competitiveness and allow MAS to regulate overseas demand for Singapore's goods and services, even though the scope to do so is limited since world economic conditions are the primary determinant of export demand.[382] For instance, a weakening of the exchange rate would stimulate external demand and raise economic growth—as happened during the mid-eighties' recession—but at the cost of a rise in inflation. In the short run, this trade-off between growth and inflation presents a policy dilemma for MAS. Nevertheless, changes in the exchange rate tend to be moderate as it is primarily intended to be an anti-inflation tool. The burden of engineering economic recoveries has fallen instead on the lowering of domestic business and labour costs or fiscal policy. In sum, the exchange rate is used to maintain price stability, while wage and fiscal policies are aimed at economic growth.[383]

---

381 Liew and Wilson, *A History of Money*, pp. 303, 304–5.

382 To the extent that the raw materials and capital equipment used in production are imported, the competitiveness effect will be blunted. Wilson, "Monetary Policy and Financial Sector Development", p. 1550031-9.

383 W.M. Corden, "Macroeconomic Targets and Instruments for a Small Open Economy", *The Singapore Economic Review* 29, 2 (1984): 32; "Exchange Rate Policy", in Lim and Associates, *Policy Options*, pp. 315, 318.

Chapter 12

The Service Economy, 1986–99

This chapter continues the economic narrative of Singapore's modern era with a consideration of the last fifteen years of the 20th century. Like the decades before them, this period witnessed changes in the country's political, economic and social environments, although they were not quite as dramatic as in the immediate years after independence. We begin with a review of economic policy changes in the 1980s and 1990s, which had long-term effects on the functioning of the economic system. This is followed by an analysis of national savings and investment and their impact on Singapore's current account—a subject that was not adequately treated in the previous chapter. The government's efforts to add an "external wing" to the economy are also discussed in this connection. Next, the evolution of the manufacturing sector and the ascendance of the service economy are dealt with. Industrial policy during this period was focused on the nurturing of a knowledge-based economy through investment in skills and know-how. Finally, the chapter reviews the debate over the sources of Singapore's long-run economic growth and its productivity performance.

Economic Policy Changes in the 1980s and 1990s

As the world entered the 1980s, the political economy of the industrialised countries underwent a paradigm shift. In the United Kingdom and the United States especially, the idea of relying on the free market and competition to allocate resources gained currency while the role of government was seen to be intrusive and in need of drastic reduction. At the same time, the momentum for a crusade in support of privatisation picked up in many countries.[1] Singapore was not insulated from the influences of these developments and began to rethink its economic policies, particularly after the watershed recession in 1985–86.[2] The Economic Committee convened by the government to help the economy recover stated then that changing circumstances meant that there was a need to reduce the state's role in the economy and to ease the regulatory environment in Singapore.[3]

[1] Linda Low, *The Political Economy of Privatisation in Singapore: Analysis, Interpretation and Evaluation* (Singapore: McGraw-Hill, 1991), pp. 23, 25–8.

[2] Ng Chee Yuen, "Privatization in Singapore: Divestment with Control", *ASEAN Economic Bulletin* 5, 3 (1989): 298–9, 300; *The Business Times*, 23 Apr. 1992.

[3] Rigg, "Singapore and the Recession of 1985", p. 351; Regnier, *Singapore*, p. 59.

Motivated by pragmatism and this desire to shift the engine of economic growth to the private sector, the changes that were subsequently implemented moved the nominally leftist PAP government to the right of the political spectrum.[4] These changes were effected in three key areas under the blanket term "privatisation": divestment of state ownership of GLCs (government-linked companies) and statutory boards, industry deregulation and the financing of social services.

The government's actions in the first of these areas were not in the main motivated by considerations of efficiency, as most public enterprises were well run.[5] Instead, privatisation of GLCs was an end in itself as the government wanted to reduce the state's involvement in business and withdraw from commercial activities which could be carried out by the private sector. A secondary objective was to develop the scope and depth of the local stock market; possibly the government wanted Singaporeans to share in the profits of successful public enterprises.[6] The report by the Public Sector Divestment Committee, formed in 1986 to identify public sector investments to privatise, stated in addition that privatisation was intended to reduce the state's competition with the private sector, an often heard complaint by business and industry leaders.[7] Hence, the privatisation movement represented a retreat of the state from market activity and a downsizing of its direct public role in the nation's economic life.

The committee recommended that as many GLCs as possible should be privatised but it recognised that statutory boards needed to be treated with caution as most were monopolies providing essential services. The sensitivity of the issue was shown by the fact that the largest seven statutory boards had capital and reserves of $13.2 billion and employed over 36,000 people.[8] Furthermore, defence-related GLCs were to stay in government hands for national security reasons. There were also large GLCs which any single group of investors was unlikely to want to take over, so it was suggested that the state reduce its stakes in them gradually over a number of years to about 30 per cent. These included SIA, DBS, Keppel Corporation, Sembawang Shipyard and NOL. The other GLCs that could be floated on the Stock Exchange of Singapore (SES) were Resources Development Corporation (RDC, granite production), Singapore National Printers (SNP, government printer), Singapore Pools (lottery), Jurong Shipyard (ship repair) and three other smaller concerns. The privatisation of these GLCs was to be carried out through offering primary and secondary shares to the public and by private placement. To ease the process, CPF members were allowed to invest up to 20 per cent of their funds in the shares.

---

[4] Phua Kai Hong, *Privatization and Restructuring of Health Services in Singapore*, IPS Occasional Paper No. 5 (Singapore: The Institute of Policy Studies, 1991), p. 6; Lim, *Business, Government and Labor*, pp. 11–14, 15, 25.

[5] L. Heracleous, "State Ownership, Privatization, and Performance in Singapore: An Exploratory Study from a Strategic Management Perspective", *Asia Pacific Journal of Management* 18 (2001): 75–6; Ng, "Privatization in Singapore", p. 292.

[6] Lo Yen Lee, *Privatisation in Singapore: Policy and Impact on Labour Relations* (Singapore: Singapore Institute of Labour Studies, 1995), p. 6.

[7] *Report of the Public Sector Divestment Committee* (Singapore: Ministry of Finance, 1987), pp. 1–5; Tan Chwee Huat, "Singapore Telecom: From Public to Private Sector", *International Journal of Public Sector Management* 5, 4 (1992): 4; *The Straits Times*, 14 Mar. 1987.

[8] Ng, "Privatization in Singapore", pp. 292, 308.

In all, 41 GLCs were identified for partial or total privatisation, with 17 companies in the latter category.[9] Another 15 were to be listed on the SES for public subscription, eight would see the government reduce its shareholding and nine would be wound up.[10] Between 1985 and 1990, 36 GLCs were divested, with the initial public offerings among them grossly oversubscribed.[11] The ownership of the local newspapers had been transferred earlier from a GLC to the private sector and in 1994, the national broadcasting authority, Singapore Broadcasting Corporation (SBC), was corporatised.[12] The government also lowered its shareholding in SIA to 63 per cent, thus still retaining control over it; other privatised GLCs in which the government retained majority ownership are Keppel Corporation, Sembawang Shipyard, Singapore Aerospace and SNP.[13] In 1993, the government announced its plan to divest another eight companies, amongst which were Pidemco Land, Raffles City Pte Ltd, Singapore Technologies Industrial Corporation and the government ordnance firm CIS, the last against the divestment committee's advice.[14] In 1997, CIS and other defence-related companies merged to form ST Engineering, also a GLC.[15] Despite the divestment measures, however, GLCs were still estimated to contribute 12.9 per cent to GDP in 1998.[16]

The divestment committee advised that the Civil Aviation Authority of Singapore (CAAS), responsible for aviation and airport management, and PSA, PUB and Singtel, as statutory boards, be considered for privatisation but in the event only the last two recommendations were initially acted on by the government.[17] Even then, the progress in implementing the recommendations was slow—only Singtel and the Mass Rapid Transit Corporation (MRTC) had been privatised as of 1995.[18] Singtel was the first profit-making statutory board to be privatised through the offering of its shares in the stock market in 1993, said to be worth $10 billion, although the government remains the majority shareholder.[19] This privatisation was in line with the trend in advanced countries such as the United Kingdom, Spain and Japan. The telecommunications equipment market was partially liberalised in 1989, allowing suppliers to sell directly to consumers and bringing

---

[9] Lo, *Privatisation in Singapore*, p. 6.

[10] Tan Chwee Huat, "Public Enterprises and Privatization: The Experience of Singapore", *Annals of Public and Cooperative Economics* 63, 1 (1992): 128.

[11] Low, *Political Economy of Privatisation*, pp. 194–5; Ng, "Privatization in Singapore", p. 315; *The Business Times*, 20 July 1989.

[12] *The Straits Times*, 19 Dec. 1991; *The Business Times*, 1 Oct. 1994.

[13] *The Business Times*, 15 Nov. 1985.

[14] *The Straits Times*, 12 Mar. 1993, 11 Mar. 1994.

[15] *The Straits Times*, 30 Dec. 2007.

[16] Linda Low, "Rethinking Singapore Inc. and GLCs", in *Southeast Asian Affairs 2002* (Singapore: Institute of Southeast Asian Studies, 2002), pp. 286, 287.

[17] *Report of the Public Sector Divestment Committee*, pp. 45–7; *The Straits Times*, 14 Mar. 1987, 8 Mar. 1989; *The Business Times*, 19 Mar. 1993.

[18] Lo, *Privatisation in Singapore*, pp. 8, 10–12.

[19] Tan, "Singapore Telecom", pp. 5–6; *The New Paper*, 10 Nov. 1989; *The Straits Times Weekly Overseas Edition*, 24 Feb. 1990; *The Straits Times*, 21 July 1993. Every Singaporean CPF account holder was given $200 to purchase shares in Singtel. *The Straits Times*, 12 Mar. 1993.

down prices.[20] Further liberalisation took place later in 1997, when a private sector entrant into the telecommunications industry, Starhub, started to compete with Singtel and gained a significant share of the market; it was followed by another private firm, M1.[21] The liberalisation of the telecommunications industry delivered great benefits to consumers, as the three companies also competed in broadband services. After the move, the regulatory function was handed over to TAS (the Telecommunications Authority of Singapore), which provided postal services in Singapore until Singapore Post (SingPost) was created as a subsidiary of Singtel in 1992.[22]

A GLC, Singapore Power (SP), took over the PUB's electricity and gas departments and undertook the distribution of electricity; SP was corporatised in 1995.[23] Jumping ahead in time, it may complete this part of the story to mention that Temasek Holdings' stakes in domestic electricity supply companies were gradually divested to the private sector starting from 2005. By 2014, there were six private companies which between them constituted a fully competitive market in wholesale and retail power generation and were regulated by the Energy Market Authority (EMA).[24] The PUB retains control of water supply, including that sourced from Malaysia. The supply of alternative sources of water, both recycled sewerage water (known locally as NEWater) and desalinated water, is undertaken by the PUB, two former GLCs (SembCorp and Keppel) and a private company, Hyflux. Another new infrastructural service to homes in Singapore, namely cable television channels, started in 1995, when a GLC, Singapore CableVision, was formed as a subsidiary of the SBC.[25]

Port services continued to be provided by PSA, a statutory board turned GLC, although some operations such as the leasing of mobile cranes and bunkering were spun off to the private sector.[26] Planning and regulation were vested in the newly formed Maritime and Port Authority (MPA). Paralleling this arrangement is Changi Airport Group (CAG), the GLC that operates Changi Airport, which was formerly the domain of CAAS. The latter is now a regulatory statutory board providing air traffic control services and negotiating aviation agreements with foreign states. On the other hand, land transport, including the MRT system, was put under the purview of the Land Transport Authority (LTA), a statutory board under the Ministry of Transport, which is also responsible for building new train lines and the construction of roads and expressways. The LTA owns most of the rail lines and operating assets, including train coaches. The day-to-day operation of the

---

20 *The Business Times*, 21 Feb. 1989.

21 Heracleous, "State Ownership, Privatization, and Performance", pp. 75–6; *The Straits Times*, 9 June 1997.

22 *The Straits Times*, 31 Mar. 1992, 2 Apr. 1992. TAS merged with the National Computer Board in 1999 to form the Infocomm Development Authority, which became the Infocomm Media Development Authority in 2016.

23 *The Straits Times*, 14 July 1995.

24 D.S. Jones, "Infrastructure Management in Singapore: Privatization and Government Control", *Asian Education and Development Studies* 4, 3 (2015): 302, 303–6; *The Business Times*, 13 Jan. 2001; *The Straits Times*, 17 Mar. 2001.

25 *The Straits Times*, 17 Sept. 1993; *The Business Times*, 24 Dec. 1993, 6 May 1996; *The New Paper*, 18 July 1994, 23 Sept. 1998.

26 Ng, "Privatization in Singapore", p. 316.

MRT system is divided between two private companies, SMRT and SBS Transit; these companies together with Tower Transit also run the domestic bus network.

In the financing of social services, there was a policy change in the healthcare arena with the adoption of the general principle that wherever possible, people should pay for healthcare provided by the state. Beginning in the early 1980s, the government increasingly took the stance that health services should be funded by user fees and that subsidies should be differentiated according to the ability to pay.[27] The change in policy was a consequence of the rising costs of medical care and the state's unwillingness to bear them, as well as to prevent overconsumption by making healthcare a good to be sold for profit, including to foreigners, or to be paid for by companies.[28] Whatever the reasons, it meant that the government had abandoned its earlier view of healthcare as an investment good and embraced the opposite position that it was a consumption good. Several methods were used to recover the costs of healthcare from consumers. The first is the principle of co-payment which was already implemented in 1960 when 50 cents was charged for a visit to an outpatient clinic.[29] In 1984, the government took a different tack by implementing Medisave, a savings scheme to allow CPF funds to be utilised for the hospitalisation expenses of contributors and their immediate family members.[30]

Medisave was complemented by Medishield, a voluntary low-cost (and hence low payout) catastrophic illness co-insurance scheme started in 1990 that deducted premiums from Medisave to cover the costs of hospitalisation, surgery and outpatient treatment.[31] Under the scheme, beneficiaries still had to make some cash payment, thereby minimising the risk of moral hazard. In addition, Medifund was set up in 1993 as a social safety net for those who could not afford to pay their medical bills.[32] This is an endowment fund with an initial capital of $200 million, growing by $100 million each year.[33] As a result of these initiatives, often referred to as the "3M system", the government's portion of national healthcare expenditure fell from 51 per cent in 1965 to 34 per cent in 1984 and to 20 per cent in 1995. Furthermore, the three schemes together paid only for a relatively small proportion of total healthcare spending while the out-of-pocket expenses of users contributed close to one-half, a ratio that was much higher than in the rich countries.[34]

---

[27] Lim, *Business, Government and Labor*, pp. 23, 25; Lim Meng-Kin, "Transforming Singapore Health Care: Public-Private Partnership", *Annals-Academy of Medicine Singapore* 34, 7 (2005): 462.

[28] Low, *Political Economy of Privatisation*, p. 163; Phua, *Privatization and Restructuring*, p. 16.

[29] Lim, "Health Care Systems", pp. 18–19.

[30] M. Ramesh and Azad Singh Bali, "The Remarkable Healthcare Performance in Singapore", in *Great Policy Successes*, ed. M. Compton and P.T. Hart (Oxford University Press, 2019), pp. 45–6; *The Straits Times*, 4 Feb. 1983, 4 Mar. 1984, 22 June 1984, 1 Sept. 1984, 2 Nov. 1985; *Singapore Monitor*, 7 July 1983; *The Business Times*, 13 July 1984, 21 Mar. 1985. Contributors had to put aside 6 per cent of their monthly incomes for this purpose.

[31] Low, *Political Economy of Privatisation*, p. 166; *The Business Times*, 26 Feb. 1990, 5 July 1990; *The Straits Times*, 25 Apr. 1990, 5 July 1990, 21 Mar. 1991; *The New Paper*, 3 May 1990, 25 May 1990, 13 Dec. 1990.

[32] *The Straits Times*, 17 Nov. 1992, 19 Jan. 1993, 31 Mar. 1993; *The Business Times*, 19 Jan. 1993, 17 Mar. 1994.

[33] *The Straits Times*, 19 May 1993.

[34] Ramesh and Bali, "The Remarkable Healthcare Performance", pp. 43–4.

Despite the cutback in government spending on healthcare, Singapore was still ranked sixth in the world for the overall performance of its health system and the best in Asia.[35] As already noted previously, this was achieved at relatively low costs, with national healthcare spending at only 3 per cent of GDP in 1989.[36]

A related aspect of the healthcare policy changes implemented in the eighties was the restructuring of public hospitals, though this did not count as privatisation since the ownership of the institutions remained with the government.[37] The aim was to grant greater autonomy to these hospitals with the intention of improving efficiency and quality of care through corporatisation and the adoption of business and financial discipline.[38] This move was similar to the way in which statutory boards were run, with the decentralisation of operational matters such as staff recruitment and strategic planning. Nonetheless, the government ensured that the hospitals continued to fulfil their social mission by requiring its approval for increases in charges and by providing subsidies according to income levels, particularly for lower-class wards.[39] For example, the subsidy to the Singapore General Hospital increased from $40 million before the restructuring to $72 million in 1990.[40] The restructuring process started with the newly built National University Hospital in 1985, which commercialised its services and began to charge fees equal to those in the private sector.[41] The outcome of restructuring was improved facilities and services, but also increased costs.[42] By the late nineties, almost all public hospitals had been restructured, therefore blurring the line between public and private healthcare.[43]

As the government also held the longer-term objective of sharing the burden of providing healthcare with the private sector in a "public-private partnership", the number of private hospitals in Singapore had increased under its encouragement.[44] The first two—Parkway East Hospital and Gleneagles Hospital—had actually been founded during the colonial period.[45] The next two, Mount Elizabeth Hospital and Thomson Medical Centre, had both been established in 1979, followed by Raffles Hospital in 2002. In addition, a not-for-profit institution, Mount Alvernia Hospital, was opened in 1961. Together, they

---

35 *The World Health Report 2000—Health Systems: Improving Performance* (Geneva: World Health Organization, 2000).

36 Low, *Political Economy of Privatisation*, p. 162.

37 *The Straits Times*, 13 Dec. 1990.

38 Lim, "Health Care Systems", pp. 19–20; Ramesh and Bali, "The Remarkable Healthcare Performance", pp. 45, 51–2; *The Business Times*, 30 Mar. 1989.

39 *The Straits Times*, 30 Mar. 1989, 13 Dec. 1990. The wards are different classes of hospital accommodation that vary according to the level of comfort ("A" class being the most costly and "C" class the least expensive).

40 "Singapore Restructured", *BMJ: British Medical Journal* 300, 6734 (1990): 1223.

41 Ng, "Privatization in Singapore", p. 316.

42 Phua, *Privatization and Restructuring*, pp. 28–30; *The Straits Times*, 30 May 1990, 23 June 1991, 19 Jan. 1996.

43 Low, *Political Economy of Privatisation*, pp. 164–5; *The Straits Times Weekly Overseas Edition*, 2 Aug. 1997.

44 Lim, "Transforming Singapore Health Care", p. 461.

45 Gary Ang Yee, "Development of the Private Hospitals in Singapore from 1983 to 2022", *Journal of Hospital Management and Health Policy* 7, 11 (2023): 3.

provided 1,631 beds and generally had better facilities and the latest medical technology compared to those of government hospitals. They therefore attracted patients from neighbouring countries (especially Indonesia) to seek tertiary healthcare in Singapore.

A similar approach to healthcare was taken in the reform of education services. Carried out in the late 1980s and early 1990s, the privatisation of schools was not mainly intended to reduce the government's financial burden but rather to give more autonomy and flexibility to some schools by allowing them to design their own curricula and choose their own textbooks, as well as giving teachers the freedom to innovate and principals the prerogative to appoint staff.[46] Accordingly, the best schools in Singapore became "independent" schools, such as Raffles Institution, Anglo-Chinese School, St. Joseph's Institution and Chinese High School, as well as a few girls' schools like the Raffles Girl School and Methodist Girls School.[47] These schools are individually managed by their respective Board of Governors who in turn have the power to appoint principals, dismiss teachers and set fees.[48] They can introduce innovative programmes and acquire extra resources so as to provide a more rounded education for their pupils.[49] Although the independent schools were expected to be self-reliant and raise their own funds, including by charging higher student fees, they continued to receive government financial support in the form of grants and $1 million each to start endowment funds.[50] In addition, the government provided financial aid and bursaries to students who were unable to pay fees.

To ensure that students in non-independent government schools did not lose out to those in independent schools, a subsidy scheme called Edusave was initiated by Singapore's second Prime Minister Goh Chok Tong in 1993.[51] Backed by an endowment fund, the $1 billion plan was aimed at maximising and equalising opportunities for all students regardless of family background by enabling their parents to pay for textbooks, miscellaneous fees, private tuition and extracurricular activities, among other things.[52] It was implemented by giving $50 to every student from the ages of 6 to 16 in special Edusave accounts and $100,000 grants to secondary schools to be used for educational or enrichment programmes.[53] The grants were later extended to primary schools and post-secondary institutions other than polytechnics and universities. The credit in the accounts was also subsequently increased by adding the interest income from the endowment fund once it

---

[46] Low, *Political Economy of Privatisation*, pp. 167–70; *The Straits Times*, 30 May 1985; *The Business Times*, 21 Nov. 1989; *The Straits Times Weekly Overseas Edition*, 9 Mar. 1991.

[47] *The Straits Times*, 18 May 1988, 3 Sept. 1989, 28 Apr. 1991.

[48] David Chan and Jason Tan, "Privatization and the Rise of Direct Subsidy Scheme and Independent Schools in Hong Kong and Singapore", *International Journal of Educational Management* 22, 6 (2008): 471.

[49] *The Straits Times*,14 Dec. 1994.

[50] *The Straits Times*, 1 Sept. 1987, 22 Sept. 1993.

[51] *The Business Times*, 18 Dec. 1990; *The Straits Times*, 19 Dec. 1990.

[52] Jason Tan and S. Gopinathan, "An Innovation in Educational Financing: The Edusave Scheme in Singapore", *Change: Transformations in Education* 2, 2 (1999): 68, 70–3, 78.

[53] *The New Paper*, 5 Apr. 1991; *The Straits Times*, 8 Jan. 1992.

was topped up to $5 billion.[54] By the mid-2010s, the Edusave subsidy had been increased to $200 for each student. Nevertheless, the usage of the funds by students was probably less than the government anticipated even though it increased over the years—in 1997, only four out of ten students had withdrawn money from their accounts. A more targeted initiative came in the form of the scholarships and merit awards given to the top 25 per cent and 10 per cent of students in independent and government schools, respectively.[55] In 1993, about six out of ten students who received the scholarships and awards came from families living in HDB flats while only three in ten came from well-to-do families. A further Edusave bursary scheme was introduced in 1995 to help bright students from lower-middle and low-income families who excelled in their studies.[56] Good progress awards were also given to students who had improved in their studies.

In housing, the Singapore government's policy moved in an opposite direction to that of healthcare and education. In a politically motivated initiative, the HDB in 1989 embarked on a massive plan to rejuvenate housing estates and upgrade public flats over a period of years.[57] It began with the older flats built in the 1960s and 1970s, providing them with new facilities such as toilets, balconies, upgraded lifts, linkways and car drop-off porches, thereby enhancing their market value.[58] Through the upgrading scheme, older residential neighbourhoods acquired the modern facilities and amenities provided in newer housing estates. Along with the upgrading policy, the HDB housing market was deregulated through the relaxation of rules governing the resale of public flats.[59] For the first time, permanent residents and singles above the age of 35 were allowed to purchase flats in the secondary market. Meanwhile, government land sales to developers resulted in an increase in the supply of private houses, including condominiums. It is therefore no surprise that the housing market boomed in the first half of the 1990s, forcing the government to implement prudential measures—such as imposing a tax on capital gains—to cool the market.[60]

During the early nineties, important changes were made to the institutional underpinnings of Singapore's fiscal policy. First, constitutional safeguards were put in place to protect Singapore's official reserves.[61] Rather than by appointment, the President of the nation was to be elected by the populace to provide for a "two-key" safeguard mechanism whereby he or she would act as the second key in agreeing to Parliament's decision to

---

54 Pundarik Mukhopadhaya, "Education Policies as Means to Tackle Income Disparity: The Singapore Case", *International Journal of Sociology and Social Policy* 20, 11/12 (2000): 61, 62–4, 65–6; *The Business Times*, 18 Dec. 1992; *The Straits Times*, 31 Oct. 1993.

55 *The Business Times*, 30 May 1992.

56 *The Straits Times*, 30 Aug. 1995, 15 Dec. 1996; *The Straits Times Weekly Overseas Edition*, 2 Sept. 1995.

57 Tay Kim Poh, "The Twin Pillars of Estate Rejuvenation", *Ethos* (June 2008): 32–8; *The Straits Times*, 12 July 1989, 17 Oct. 1989, 7 Mar. 1992, 11 Apr. 1992; *The Business Times*, 20 Oct. 1989. The upgrading programme was restricted to precincts that had voted for the PAP in general elections.

58 In some cases, residents could also opt for additional space or a room.

59 Phang Sock-Yong, "Singapore's Housing Policies: Responding to the Challenges of Economic Transitions", *The Singapore Economic Review* 60, 3 (2015): 1550036-10–1550036-13; *The Business Times*, 28 Oct. 1992, 31 Aug. 1993.

60 Lee, *The Unexpected Nation*, pp. 567–9.

61 *The Straits Times*, 3 Oct. 1990; *The Business Times*, 30 Nov. 1991.

draw on the reserves for government spending in times of crisis. The President also has the power to veto any large item of expenditure by a statutory board or a GLC. As such, he or she had to be a person of high calibre and have the administrative experience needed for the task. A Presidential Council comprising between three to five members would be appointed to advise the President on decisions related to drawing on the reserves.[62] Since the government of the day could not do this without the approval of the elected President, it would be compelled to balance the budget within its political term in office, thus putting a constraint on fiscal policy.[63]

In a second major innovation, in 1994 the government decided to introduce the Goods and Services Tax (GST) in order to shift the burden of public financing from direct to indirect taxation so as to keep Singapore's income tax regime internationally competitive.[64] The GST is a tax on domestic consumption and was initially calibrated at 3 per cent of the value of purchases but the rate was gradually raised over the years to 9 per cent. To blunt the regressive impact of the GST, the government exempted businesses with an annual turnover of less than $1 million from the tax and increased education and healthcare subsidies to offset its effects on these services. Further help for lower-income groups was given through rebates for rentals of HDB flats and service and conservancy charges as well as through direct offsets in the form of government transfers. Together with changes to the income tax structure, the GST reform reduced the proportion of individuals paying income tax to one-quarter.[65]

Savings, Investment and the Current Account

This section takes a closer look at the mobilisation of the domestic savings needed to finance investment in Singapore and the effect of the interaction between savings and investment on the current account. Traditional theories of economic development typically posit that investment has a catalytic effect in a country embarking on modern economic growth. In these accounts, a rise in the rate of productive investment to over 10 per cent of national income is required to achieve an economic take-off into self-sustained growth.[66] Empirically, it has also been suggested that high savings and investment rates were a key factor behind the economic success of the newly industrialised economies of East Asia.[67]

---

[62] Linda Low and Toh Mun Heng, *The Elected Presidency as a Safeguard for Official Reserves: What is at Stake?* IPS Occasional Paper No. 1 (Singapore: Institute of Policy Studies, 1989), p. 26.

[63] Low, "Fiscal Policy", pp. 19–20; Jón R. Blöndal, "Budgeting in Singapore", *OECD Journal on Budgeting* 6, 1 (2006): 51–2.

[64] *The Goods and Services Tax* (Singapore: Ministry of Trade and Industry and Ministry of Finance, 1993). In 1993, the government reduced the corporate tax rate from 30 per cent to 27 per cent. Soon and Stoever, "Foreign Investment and Economic Development", p. 331.

[65] G. Jenkins and R. Khadka, "Tax Reform in Singapore", Discussion Paper no. 644 (Harvard Institute for International Development, 1998), pp. 6–7.

[66] Meier, *Leading Issues in Economic Development*, p. 40; W. Easterly, "Reliving the '50s: the Big Push, Poverty Traps, and Takeoffs in Economic Development", Working Paper Number 65 (Center for Global Development, 2005), p. 5.

[67] The World Bank, *The East Asian Miracle: Economic Growth and Public Policy* (Oxford University Press, 1993), pp. 40–3, 221.

These assertions have certainly been borne out by the experience of Singapore.[68] As the previous chapter has emphasised, investment and capital accumulation—expenditure on machinery, equipment, buildings and infrastructure—were the basic drivers of industrialisation and economic growth. While private domestic and foreign investment stayed robust in the 1980s, public construction and works declined as Singapore's physical infrastructure was largely in place. Consequently, the share of public sector investment in total gross capital formation shrunk to an average of 29 per cent.[69] The significant investment projects left in the 1980s were Changi Airport, Marina Centre reclamation, expressways and the MRT system.[70]

From 1965 onwards, both gross national savings and investment as ratios of GNP had shown rising but erratic trends (Figure 26). While in 1970 domestic savings amounted to half of total investment, this ratio rose to two-thirds in 1981.[71] In 1980, the savings ratio reached 34 per cent of GNP and the investment ratio, 48 per cent.[72] These were extremely high rates by any standard, with the latter exceeding the former over the entire period. During the 1985–86 recession, the investment ratio fell to about 40 per cent. After the downturn, the savings rate picked up and continued to rise to a peak of 54 per cent in 1999 before levelling off. However, investment declined steadily to 30 per cent in the same year. The trends in these two ratios meant that the difference between savings and investment was negative up to 1985 but thereafter, it turned positive and increased over time.[73] That resulted in Singapore incurring deficits in its merchandise trade balance and hence in the current account in the first period, since the surpluses in services trade and net factor income from GIC's investments abroad were not large enough to offset the trade deficits. The deficits had to be funded by capital inflows in the form of foreign direct investment, as a substitute for domestic savings, resulting in overall balance of payments surpluses and the accumulation of foreign reserves.[74] They reflected imports of raw materials and capital equipment for industrialisation; on the other hand, the surpluses were generated from the export of services such as tourism and ship repair.[75]

Since 1987, current account surpluses had been registered continuously and they grew to an annual average of $33 billion in the last years of the century. Hence in principle, domestic gross capital formation could have been internally financed, even while external funds continued to flow into Singapore. The excess savings were channelled into overseas investments by GIC. A less desirable consequence of the surpluses in the late eighties was the accusation by the United States that Singapore and other East Asian countries had undervalued their exchange rates and engaged in unfair trade practices, and that

[68] Henri Ghesquiere, *Singapore's Success: Engineering Economic Growth* (Singapore: Thomson Learning, 2007), pp. 27–8.

[69] Huff, *The Economic Growth of Singapore*, p. 337, Appendix Table A.14, p. 414.

[70] Wong, "Saving, Capital Inflow and Capital Formation", p. 49.

[71] Le Blanc, *Singapore*, pp. 33–4.

[72] G. Peebles and P. Wilson, *Economic Growth and Development in Singapore* (Cheltenham: Edward Elgar, 2002), pp. 77–9, Appendix Table A.2, pp. 274–5.

[73] *The Straits Times*, 28 Feb. 1984; *The Business Times*, 25 Feb. 1993.

[74] "Savings Policy", in Lim and Associates, *Policy Options*, pp. 219–20.

[75] Wong, "Saving, Capital Inflow and Capital Formation", pp. 67–9.

their macroeconomic policies had artificially increased savings rates.[76] Even though the Americans said in closed meetings that they understood Singapore's position and the charges had no basis in its case, the United States withdrew the country's Generalized System of Preferences (GSP) privileges although it did not name it as a currency manipulator. In more recent decades and in spite of predictions to the contrary, the current account surplus has been close to 20 per cent of GDP and sometimes even more, which raised suspicion of a mercantilist policy.[77]

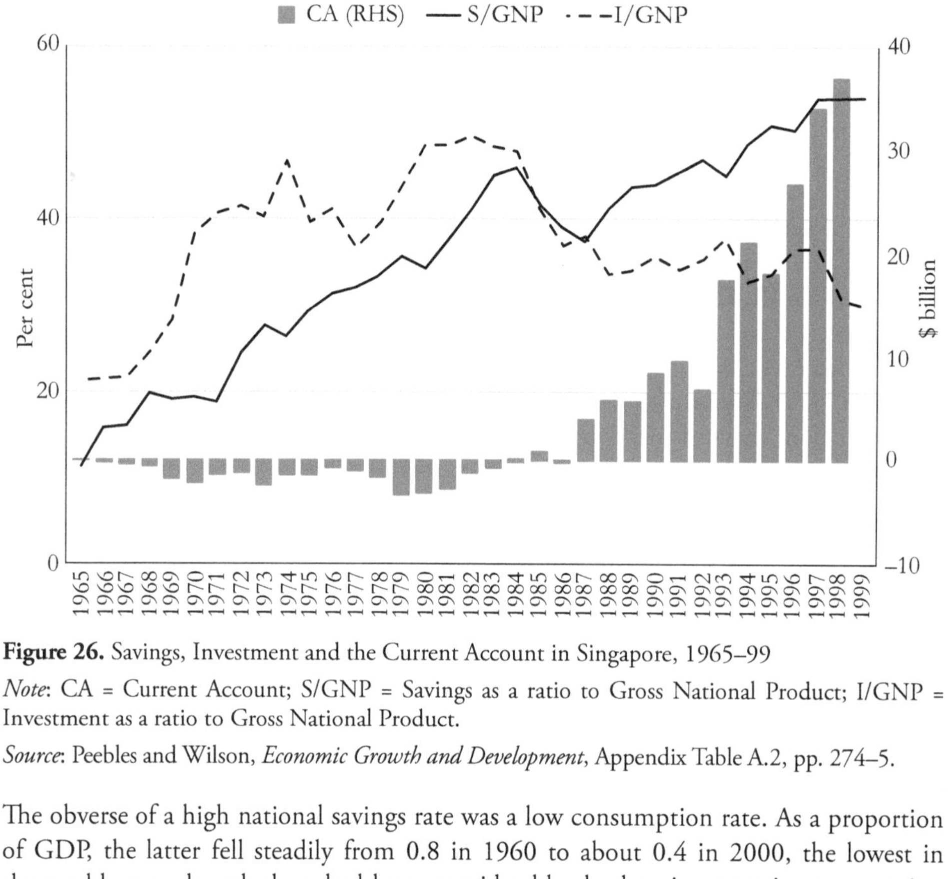

Figure 26. Savings, Investment and the Current Account in Singapore, 1965–99

Note: CA = Current Account; S/GNP = Savings as a ratio to Gross National Product; I/GNP = Investment as a ratio to Gross National Product.

Source: Peebles and Wilson, *Economic Growth and Development*, Appendix Table A.2, pp. 274–5.

The obverse of a high national savings rate was a low consumption rate. As a proportion of GDP, the latter fell steadily from 0.8 in 1960 to about 0.4 in 2000, the lowest in the world, even though there had been considerable absolute increases in consumption expenditure on housing, food, beverages, clothing, footwear and leisure.[78] The usual attempt to explain this phenomenon attributes it to demographic change, since the sustained growth of the economy coincided with a fall in the dependency ratio, which

[76] Liew and Wilson, *A History of Money*, pp. 324–32; *The Straits Times Weekly Overseas Edition*, 12 Dec. 1987; *The Straits Times*, 30 Jan. 1988, 31 Jan. 1988, 5 Feb. 1988.

[77] Ghesquiere, *Singapore's Success*, pp. 29, 30; *The Straits Times*, 22 Aug. 1996.

[78] Tilak Abeysinghe and Keen Meng Choy, "The Aggregate Consumption Puzzle in Singapore", *Journal of Asian Economics* 15, 3 (2004): 564, 569–70; Peebles and Wilson, *Economic Growth and Development*, p. 78.

caused savings to rise.[79] In addition, income growth also raised the level of savings in Singapore.[80] However, demography can account for the decline in the consumption ratio only up to the mid-1980s, as the proportion of the working population had stabilised to about 70 per cent then.[81] A more plausible explanation for the low consumption ratio is that the high prices of physical assets like houses and cars in Singapore exerted a dampening effect on consumption spending because potential buyers have to save more to purchase them.[82] The evidence for this was shown in the declines in the consumption ratio both in the early 1980s and during the first half of the 1990s when there were sharp increases in property prices.

There are two other features peculiar to Singapore that explain the high savings rates: public savings resulting from government budget surpluses and the earnings of statutory boards on the one hand and mandatory contributions to the CPF on the other.[83] With respect to the first, it has been contended that the surpluses recorded actually underestimated the role of public savings when receipts from leasing and selling land are taken into account.[84] Measured correctly, the surpluses resulting from the government budget and the profits of statutory boards were more than half of national savings, making them the principal source.[85] It is necessary to include the revenue of statutory boards in the consolidated accounts of the public sector because the charges for the services they rendered and receipts from selling goods had constituted an increasing proportion of total public savings in the early 1980s.

The other major source of savings was derived from the contributions of employers and employees to the CPF, which had risen over time to more than one quarter of total savings in the 1980s.[86] Through these forced savings and domestic borrowing, the government determined the division of the economy's resources between consumption and investment.[87] The rates of contribution to the CPF by employers and employees were gradually raised in the seventies and eighties until they reached a high of 25 per cent each in 1984. Since it is reasonable to assume that these contributions had reduced the ability and need for members to save voluntarily, it can be concluded that the mobilisation of funds by the CPF had been a second major source of national savings despite withdrawals

---

[79] A.M. Husain, "Determinants of Private Saving in Singapore", in *Singapore: A Case Study in Rapid Development*, IMF Occasional Paper No. 119, ed. K. Bercuson (Washington, DC: International Monetary Fund, 1995); Monetary Authority of Singapore, *Annual Report 1993/1994* (Singapore: Monetary Authority of Singapore, 1994); *The Straits Times*, 11 Dec. 1987.

[80] "Savings Policy", in Lim and Associates, *Policy Options*, pp. 218–9.

[81] Ghesquiere, *Singapore's Success*, p. 31.

[82] Abeysinghe and Choy, "The Aggregate Consumption Puzzle", pp. 571–2; Phang Sock Yong, "House Prices and Aggregate Consumption: Do They Move Together? Evidence from Singapore", *Journal of Housing Economics* 13, 2 (2004): 101–19.

[83] The World Bank, *The East Asian Miracle*, pp. 207–10; *The Business Times*, 3 Jan. 1992.

[84] Peebles and Wilson, *Economic Growth and Development*, pp. 81–3, 87–90; Low, "Fiscal Policy", p. 12.

[85] Huff, *The Economic Growth of Singapore*, pp. 332–4; Wong, "Saving, Capital Inflow and Capital Formation", pp. 54–6, 59–62; "Savings Policy", pp. 223–4.

[86] Krause, Koh and Lee, *The Singapore Economy Reconsidered*, pp. 83–5, 86–7.

[87] Geiger and Geiger, *Tales of Two City-States*, p. 18.

to pay for housing, healthcare and education.[88] Indeed, it is likely that Singapore had oversaved and also overinvested, particularly in housing in view of the ease with which house buyers could finance their purchases with CPF savings.[89] Other policies that were conducive to a high savings rate were the tax exemption given to POSB deposits, gradual abolition of the capital gains tax and the absence of a social safety net, which could have encouraged precautionary savings.[90] Given the dominance of public and CPF savings, the share attributed to the combined corporate sector and households fell to an estimated 16–22 per cent.[91]

In relation to the current account, it is convenient here to remark on the Singapore government's efforts to encourage GLCs and private sector firms (including MNCs) to venture overseas for business expansion in the early 1990s.[92] This was an ambitious multi-pronged strategy that was spearheaded by the EDB and aimed at making Singapore's presence felt in the region and the world at large.[93] It sought to emulate the example of those East Asian countries which had all developed an external or second wing. The initiative was also partly intended to cultivate a larger pool of local entrepreneurs by giving them opportunities to grow their businesses abroad.[94] To begin, companies making low-end labour-intensive goods were persuaded to establish business operations in nearby countries where land and labour costs were lower. The key initiative was directed at developing a "Growth Triangle" between Singapore, Johor (Malaysia) and the Riau Islands (Indonesia) to exploit complementarities in factor endowments.[95] Thus, high-tech and other companies from the city-state as well as MNCs based there set up manufacturing operations in Johor while retaining managerial and research and development (R&D) functions on the island.[96] Meanwhile, two GLCs from Singapore in partnership with Indonesian firms established an industrial park in Batam, the nearest and one of the largest of the Riau Islands, followed by another in Bintan.[97] Consequently, electronics firms were induced to invest in production facilities at the sites. Bintan Island also became an offshore resort island, with hotels, a golf

[88] "Savings Policy", pp. 220–2, 223; The World Bank, *The East Asian Miracle*, p. 242; *The Straits Times*, 23 July 1983.

[89] Huff, "The Developmental State", p. 1428. One indication of this was the fall in the return to private capital in the first half of the 1980s. Lim, Pang and Findlay, "Singapore", p. 101.

[90] Huff, *The Economic Growth of Singapore*, p. 336; Ghesquiere, *Singapore's Success*, pp. 59–60.

[91] Monetary Authority of Singapore, "Singapore's Balance of Payments, 1965–2003: An Analysis", Staff Working Paper No. 33 (Singapore: Monetary Authority of Singapore, 2004).

[92] Ghesquiere, *Singapore's Success*, pp. 28–30; *The Straits Times*, 16 Nov. 1992, 25 Aug. 1993; *The Business Times*, 20 May 1993.

[93] Cassey Lee and Chew Ging Lee, "Determinants of Singapore's Outward FDI", ISEAS Economics Working Paper No. 2016-2 (Singapore: ISEAS-Yusof Ishak Institute, 2016), pp. 3–4.

[94] P. Regnier, "Spreading Singapore's Wings Worldwide: A Review of Traditional and New Investment Strategies", *The Pacific Review* 6, 4 (1993): 308–9.

[95] S.M. Okposin, *The Extent of Singapore's Investments Abroad* (Abingdon: Routledge, 1999), pp. 112–4; *The Business Times*, 20 Dec. 1989; *The Straits Times*, 24 May 1990. Even before the initiative was launched, firms in the city-state had invested in Johor and Batam Island. Regnier, *Singapore*, pp. 72–4, 75–80.

[96] *The Business Times*, 5 Oct. 1992.

[97] Ooi Giok-Ling, "The Indonesia-Malaysia-Singapore Growth Triangle: Sub-Regional Economic Cooperation and Integration", *GeoJournal* 36, 4 (1995): 341; *The New Paper*, 29 Aug. 1990.

course and other amenities built by Singaporean firms.[98] By the mid-nineties, government and business interests in Singapore had investments of $2 billion in Johor and $500 million in the Riau Islands.

Under a broader regionalisation initiative, firms were asked to focus their expansion moves on Southeast and East Asia as Singaporeans knew these countries well and the region was undergoing tremendous economic growth.[99] To help firms which were strapped for finance to go overseas, the government provided loans and equity financing through an expanded Local Enterprise Finance Scheme in 1992 as well as tax incentives such as corporate tax exemptions of income and dividends for up to 10 years and double tax deduction of expenses for overseas investment.[100] These measures were designed to lower start-up costs and facilitate the repatriation of earnings to Singapore. Nevertheless, the regionalisation efforts of SMEs as compared to those of MNCs were hampered by a lack of managerial manpower and the reluctance of Singaporeans to work overseas. In this respect, the GLCs were better placed and had the benefit of brand name, besides enjoying the backing of the Singapore government. The GLCs that successfully regionalised included Singtel, DBS and the property developer CapitaLand. The government initially aided the process by seconding public sector officials for specific projects and by building Singapore schools abroad for the children of staff posted overseas. To overcome the lack of knowledge and experience of foreign markets, the Trade Development Board (TDB) and Singapore International Foundation (SIF) gathered and supplied strategic information to the local business community.[101]

Complementing the regionalisation drive, the government initiated efforts to build joint industrial and information technology parks in China, India and Vietnam.[102] The flagship investments in China were the development of the Singapore–Suzhou Township, modelled after the HDB new towns in Singapore, and the Wuxi–Singapore Industrial Park.[103] The first of these projects began in 1994 when a consortium of 19 Singapore companies led by Keppel Corporation was formed to develop the township in collaboration with companies from China.[104] Costing US$30 billion to build, the township and associated industrial park with ready-built factories, commercial centres and social amenities covered a total area of 70 square km. The official support given by the Singapore and Chinese governments attracted firms from Singapore making all sorts of products. Consortia to develop utility installations for the town were also established,

---

98 J.C. Perry, *Singapore: Unlikely Power* (Oxford University Press, 2017), p. 229.

99 Arun Mahizhnan, "Developing Singapore's External Economy", *Southeast Asian Affairs 1994* (Singapore: Institute of Southeast Asian Studies, 1994), pp. 285–6, 293–6; *The Business Times*, 7 Sept. 1992, 22 May 1993.

100 Tan Chwee Huat, *Venturing Overseas: Singapore's External Wing* (Singapore: McGraw-Hill, 1995), pp. 24–5; Regnier, "Spreading Singapore's Wings Worldwide", p. 308; *The Business Times*, 26 Aug. 1992, 27 Feb. 1993; *The Straits Times*, 21 June 1993, 20 Aug. 1993.

101 *The Business Times*, 25 Aug. 1993.

102 Peebles and Wilson, *Economic Growth and Development*, pp. 188–90.

103 Tan, *Venturing Overseas*, pp. 64–70; *The Straits Times*, 28 Apr. 1993, 12 May 1993; *The Business Times*, 16 Dec. 1997.

104 *The Business Times*, 11 Aug. 1993.

led again by Keppel Corporation and Sembawang Resources, including the construction of a US$3 billion electricity plant and water and sewerage treatment plants.[105] Singapore's premier taxi company Comfort also started operating in the town with a fleet of 50 taxis. By contrast, the Wuxi–Singapore Industrial Park was a much smaller project, although by 1994, it had attracted 1,300 foreign enterprises with investment of US$125 million in its first phase.[106] Conceived as a high-tech park, it managed to entice manufacturers of microelectronics, telecommunications equipment, precision engineering products and pharmaceuticals as well as GLCs from Singapore and companies from Japan.

In India, an information technology park was developed with Singapore's help in Bangalore, the "Silicon Valley" of the country.[107] The companies responsible for the project were a consortium from Singapore and the Tata Group of India, which also clinched a deal to construct an international airport in the same city.[108] Other Singapore enterprises were also involved in joint ventures with Indian firms to develop LPG terminals, provide banking services and build an office complex and warehousing facility, among other projects.[109] In Vietnam, Singapore investors constructed international class hotels, offices and residences in addition to the Vietnam–Singapore Industrial Park.[110] The shipping company NOL built and operated a container port, United Overseas Bank opened a branch office and Cold Storage managed the first Western-style supermarket in Ho Chi Minh City.[111]

In terms of portfolio investment overseas, major GLCs under the label of "Singapore Inc." bought banks and other companies in Thailand, Indonesia, the Philippines and Hong Kong.[112] Leading the way was Singtel, which acquired stakes in telecommunications companies in Southeast Asia, India and Australia. The deal which generated the most publicity was its purchase of a large stake in Cable and Wireless Optus, as approval by the Australian government had to be obtained after the transaction raised sensitive security issues.[113] DBS bought Dao Heng Bank and Kwong On bank, both in Hong Kong, as well as the Thai Danu Bank.[114] Another GLC that sought to increase revenues and profits through regionalisation was SIA, which took stakes in Virgin Atlantic and Air New Zealand but was unsuccessful in attempting to do the same with other airlines.[115] It was not smooth sailing either for Singtel which failed in two bids in Malaysia and Hong Kong because it was perceived to be controlled or influenced by the Singapore state. Similarly, the Suzhou

---

105 *The New Paper*, 12 May 1993.

106 *The Straits Times*, 18 Dec. 1993, 4 Apr. 1994.

107 Tan, *Venturing Overseas*, pp. 88–9, 91–3, 112, 119–23; *The Business Times*, 7 June 1993; *The Straits Times Weekly Overseas Edition*, 22 Apr. 1995.

108 *The Straits Times*, 2 Nov. 1993; *The Business Times*, 6 Jan. 1995.

109 *The Straits Times*, 7 Sept. 1994; *The Business Times*, 10 Sept. 1994, 24 Jan. 1995, 31 Jan. 1997.

110 *The Business Times*, 3 Sept. 1991, 14 Apr. 1993, 23 July 1993, 25 Aug. 1995; *The Straits Times*, 2 Sept. 1994, 5 June 1999; *The New Paper*, 11 Oct. 1995, 13 May 1996, 27 Nov. 1996.

111 *The Business Times*, 17 Nov. 1990, 14 Oct. 1994; *The Straits Times*, 18 July 1995.

112 Low, "Rethinking Singapore Inc.", pp. 288, 292–7.

113 *Today*, 27 Mar. 2001, 28 Aug. 2001.

114 Lee, *The Unexpected Nation*, pp. 562–3; *The Straits Times*, 16 July 1999; *Today*, 2 July 2001.

115 *The Business Times*, 1 Apr. 2000.

project in China ran into problems when the town's municipality started heavily promoting a rival park to compete with it by offering cheaper land rates to investors.

The end result of the second wing movement was a rapid increase in Singapore's stock of outward direct investment to $92 billion in 2000, which constituted 42 per cent of total investments abroad.[116] Portfolio investments (both debt and equity securities) and foreign assets held by the government through GIC made up the rest.[117] As a percentage of domestic equity capital in Singapore, direct investment abroad was about 12 per cent, giving an indication of the size of the second wing.[118] The direct investments were made in 8,600 overseas affiliates, spread all around the world. In terms of geographical distribution, the lion's share went to Asia, with China as the most important destination, accounting for 16 per cent. This trend began in the late 1990s and became more pronounced later.[119] As the factory of the world, China attracted mostly manufacturing investments. In line with the government's exhortation to regionalise, the Association of Southeast Asian Nations (ASEAN) region took 25 per cent of outward investment, with the largest share in Malaysia, followed by Indonesia—an outcome that can be traced to the Growth Triangle. The newer member countries of ASEAN like Vietnam and Myanmar too received investments from Singapore.[120] Most of these were in manufacturing and financial services, with only a sprinkling in commerce. The other host countries were mainly in Europe, where the United Kingdom headed the list, and the United States. In these two regions and in Hong Kong, Singapore's investments were concentrated in the financial sector, but this was due to a preponderance of holding companies and did not necessarily indicate actual economic activity.

The current account surpluses discussed above imply that Singapore from the mid-1980s became a net creditor, exporting capital to the rest of the world instead of being a net debtor as before.[121] In the early 1990s, the surpluses were bolstered by the income from overseas investments, which amounted to $12.6 billion or 16 per cent of GNP. By contrast, between 1985 and 1992, about one-third of Singapore's GDP accrued to foreign firms and individuals.[122] By the later years of the decade, income receipts from overseas investments had burgeoned to $23.1 billion although they remained the same as a ratio to GNP.[123] As a consequence, GNP exceeded GDP, as reflected in net factor income from

116 *Singapore's Investment Abroad, 1999–2000* (Singapore: Department of Statistics, 2001), pp. 1–11.

117 *Today*, 22 Aug. 2002.

118 Hans C. Blomquist, "Extending the Second Wing: The Outward Direct Investment of Singapore", Mimeograph, 2002, pp. 6–7. In 1994, it was estimated that the contribution of firms' overseas operations to value-added in the Singapore economy was also 12 per cent. Toh Mun Heng, "Savings, Capital Formation, and Economic Growth in Singapore", in *Population Change and Economic Development in East Asia: Challenges Met, Opportunities Seized*, ed. A. Mason (Redwood City, CA: Stanford University Press, 2001), p. 197.

119 Lee and Chew, "Determinants of Singapore's Outward FDI", pp. 5, 6, 8.

120 Wong Poh-Kam and Ng Chee Yuen, "Singapore's Industrial Policy to the Year 2000", in *Industrial Policies in East Asia*, ed., S. Masuyama, D. Vandenbrink and Chia Siow Yue (Nomura Research Institute and Institute of Southeast Asian Studies, 1997), pp. 129–31.

121 Ghesquiere, *Singapore's Success*, pp. 28, 30.

122 Huff, "The Developmental State", p. 1426.

123 *Economic Survey of Singapore*, various years (Singapore: Ministry of Trade and Industry).

abroad of $7.9 billion, compared with an average of $844.5 million in the earlier period. While this demonstrated the success of the second wing policy, net factor income was to turn negative in the 2000s because of profit repatriation by foreign companies in Singapore and increased remittances by foreign workers.

Twin Engines of Growth: Manufacturing and Services

Among its many recommendations, the Economic Committee of 1985 had emphasised the continued importance of the manufacturing sector.[124] This strategy was later formalised in a plan called Manufacturing 2000, which aimed to sustain the share of manufacturing output in GDP at 25 per cent and its employment share at 20 per cent.[125] These objectives were to be achieved by upgrading capabilities across the entire industrial value chain, including research, product development, engineering, production and marketing. A distinct shift in policies towards the promotion of technology-intensive and research-oriented industries was noticeable, as part of the transition to a knowledge-based economy.[126] The new emphasis is reflected in efforts to develop high value-added production of electronics, precision equipment, chemicals, biotechnology and information technology (IT) in the late 1980s and 1990s. Consequently, the manufacturing sector grew at an average rate of 7.2 per cent per annum in the nineties and accounted for 25.9 per cent of GDP in 2000.[127] By and large, MNCs spearheaded the investments in new industries, with net commitments crossing the $3 billion mark in 1992 and accounting for four-fifths of the total.[128]

The expansion was accompanied by significant skill upgrading and increased capital intensity, which were due in part to measures taken to improve the technological capabilities of firms and develop indigenous technology, rather than merely absorbing technology from MNCs, as in the earlier phase of development.[129] Accompanying these changes was a new focus not only on R&D but also on product design and development. Early in the 1990s, the National Science and Technology Board (NSTB) was formed to provide direction, tax incentives and financial assistance to the R&D activities of companies while a Science Park was opened in 1980 to encourage high-technology MNCs to locate such activities

---

124 *The Singapore Economy*, pp. 147–9; *The Straits Times*, 6 May 1992.

125 Wong and Ng, "Singapore's Industrial Policy", pp. 125–6; *The Straits Times*, 8 Aug. 1993, 7 Oct. 1996; *The Business Times*, 9 Sept. 1993; *The New Paper*, 30 Nov. 1994.

126 K. Ali Akkemik, *Industrial Development in East Asia: A Comparative Look at Japan, Korea, Taiwan and Singapore* (Singapore: World Scientific, 2009), pp. 32, 47–8, 72. A knowledge-based economy can be defined as an economy in which the production, distribution and use of knowledge compose the main driver of growth, wealth creation and employment across all industries. "Mapping Singapore's Knowledge-Based Economy", *Quarterly Economic Survey of Singapore Third Quarter 2002* (Singapore: Ministry of Trade and Industry), p. 57.

127 Wong Poh-Kam, "The Role of the State in Singapore's Industrial Development", in *Industrial Policy, Innovation and Economic Growth: The Experience of Japan and the Asian NIEs*, ed. Wong Poh-Kam and Ng Chee Yuen (Singapore: Singapore University Press, 2001), pp. 524–8.

128 Regnier, "Spreading Singapore's Wings Worldwide", p. 306.

129 *The Straits Times*, 24 Sept. 1991, 19 Sept. 1992.

in Singapore.[130] Companies that did so included Apple Computer, Motorola, ATT and Matsushita.[131] Science- and technology-based manufacturing industries therefore began to emerge in the 1990s, facilitated by the state's further investments in tertiary education and scientific research.[132] For instance, two more polytechnics were established and an Institute of Microelectronics, a Data Storage Institute and an Institute for Molecular and Cell Biology were formed.[133] These endeavours were buttressed by a National Technology Plan launched in 1991 for which the government allocated R&D funding of $4 billion, with the objectives of raising R&D expenditures to 2 per cent of GDP by 1995 and increasing the number of research scientists and engineers in Singapore.[134] The goals were partially achieved by importing foreign research workers.[135]

The above combination of industrial and technology policies laid the basis for the electronics industry to stay as the dominant activity within the manufacturing sector, accounting for nearly 10 per cent of Singapore's GDP and three-fifths of its domestic exports in 1999.[136] As of 2000, the manufacturing sector was concentrated in just a handful of industries, namely, electronics, precision engineering, petroleum and chemicals. In electronics, MNCs shifted their production to higher value-added products like hard disk drives, printed circuit boards, computers and related peripherals, semiconductors, data storage devices, telecommunications equipment, industrial electronic equipment and consumer electronics.[137] Productivity in the industry increased rapidly in the 1990s, led by the computer segment, with the result that the return on investment for foreign companies reached 19–32 per cent.[138] Given the higher risks and large capital commitments required in advanced electronics manufacturing, the EDB initiated a co-investment programme with leading companies in the industry.[139]

---

130 Wong, "The Role of the State", pp. 545–7; Chau Leung-Chuen, Francis T. Lui and Larry D. Qiu, "Comparison Among Singapore, Taiwan and South Korea in Industrial Development", in *Industrial Development in Singapore, Taiwan and South Korea*, ed. Kwong Kai-Sun, Chau Leung-Chuen, Francis T. Lui and Larry D. Qiu (Singapore: World Scientific, 2001), p. 206; *The Straits Times Weekly Overseas Edition*, 3 Oct. 1987, 4 Aug. 1990; *The Business Times*, 5 Oct. 1988, 10 Sept. 1991; *The Straits Times*, 11 Apr. 1992, 15 Oct. 1993, 1 Sept. 1994, 1 Sept. 1998.

131 Regnier, "Spreading Singapore's Wings Worldwide", p. 307.

132 Hughes, "Growth of Singapore", p. 11; *The Straits Times Weekly Overseas Edition*, 30 Dec. 1995.

133 Kwong Kai-Sun, "Singapore: Dominance of Multinational Corporations in Industrial Development", in *Industrial Development*, ed. Kwong, Chau, Lui and Qiu, pp. 16–19, 30, 41; *The Business Times*, 6 Jan. 1990, 5 Oct. 1990, 19 Feb. 1991, 21 Mar. 1992, 29 Sept. 1997; *The Straits Times*, 15 May 1992.

134 *The Business Times*, 16 Jan. 1991, 29 Sept. 1997; *The Straits Times*, 17 Sept. 1991, 8 Sept. 1996, 18 Dec. 1996.

135 The number of research personnel doubled to 8,340 but R&D spending was only slightly over 1 per cent of GDP in 1995.

136 Wong Poh-Kam, "Singapore: Electronics and Shipbuilding/Repair Industry Case Studies", in *Industrial Policy, Innovation and Economic Growth*, ed. Wong Poh-Kam and Ng Chee Yuen, pp. 581, 583–96; *The Straits Times*, 22 May 1987.

137 D. Beane, A. Shukla and M. Pecht, *The Singapore and Malaysia Electronics Industries* (CRC Press, 1997), pp. 9, 12, 20; *The Straits Times*, 4 Mar. 1993.

138 Kwong, "Singapore: Dominance of Multinational Corporations", p. 47.

139 Wong and Ng, "Singapore's Industrial Policy", p. 136; *The Straits Times*, 7 Jan. 1997; *The Business Times*, 7 Jan. 1997.

In 1993, Singapore manufactured 23.3 million disk drives, which constituted more than two-fifths of global output and made it the largest producer in the world.[140] In the semiconductors sub-sector were found companies engaged in wafer fabrication, assembly and testing, and integrated circuit design.[141] The JTC developed three wafer fabrication parks in Woodlands, Pasir Ris and Tampines with specialised infrastructures and environments.[142] In the 1990s, almost every international electronics producer was present in Singapore: Seagate, IBM, Western Digital and Conner Peripherals (disk drives); Texas Instruments, NEC, Toshiba, STMicroelectronics and National Semiconductor (semiconductors); Sony (colour picture tubes); Matsushita, Sony, Philips and Thomson (consumer electronics appliances such as audio equipment, colour TVs and video cassette recorders); Apple, Compaq, IPC and Hewlett-Packard (desktop and notebook computers, motherboards, printers and servers); and Motorola and Philips (pagers and telephones).[143] In addition, many MNCs established design laboratories in Singapore to undertake electronics design and research.

Large MNCs were therefore the major producers in the upgraded electronics industry, following a wave of investment in the second half of the 1980s.[144] About 56 per cent of the firms and 85 per cent of equity investment in the industry were partially or wholly foreign-owned. These companies were supported by a multitude of local enterprises and suppliers providing precision engineered parts, components, moulds and electroplating services. Creative Technology, a home-grown leading global supplier of sound cards, was one of them.[145] It is notable that local SMEs became more visible only from the mid-1980s, when, after such enterprises had been largely neglected by the government, various initiatives were made to assist and integrate them with MNCs.[146] Under the Local Industry Upgrading Programme, the EDB linked specific MNCs with local suppliers to improve their efficiency and technical capabilities.[147] Thus, the electronics industry stimulated growth in related activities through backward linkages and also enabled local companies

---

140 *The Straits Times*, 20 Apr. 1994, 24 Sept. 1994.

141 Beane, Shukla and Pecht, *The Singapore and Malaysia Electronics Industries*, pp. 45–8, 50–6.

142 Thompson S.H. Teo and James S.K. Ang, "Singapore's Manufacturing Sector as Engine for Economic Growth: Past, Present and Future", *Science and Public Policy* 28, 5 (2001): 365. The JTC also developed Loyang in the eastern part of Singapore into a centre for aviation industries and an engineering base for offshore oil and mineral exploration. Rodan, *The Political Economy of Singapore's Industrialization*, p. 151.

143 *The Straits Times*, 19 Apr. 1981, 24 Feb. 1990, 19 Oct. 1991, 22 May 1992, 24 Aug. 1993, 9 June 1994, 31 Oct. 1994, 19 July 1995, 26 July 1995, 2 Aug. 1996, 9 Nov. 1996; *The Business Times*, 5 Nov. 1985, 14 May 1994, 19 July 1995, 19 Jan. 1996, 8 Nov. 1996; *The Straits Times Weekly Overseas Edition*, 17 Aug. 1991.

144 Wong, "Singapore: Electronics and Shipbuilding/Repair", pp. 581, 586–94.

145 *The Straits Times*, 26 Aug. 1992, 21 Sept. 1993.

146 Chau, Lui and Qiu, "Comparison", p. 213. A Small Enterprise Bureau was set up in 1986 as an operating unit within the EDB to focus on the development of SMEs in part through loans and grants; prior to its formation, there had been constant calls for the government to assist SMEs to overcome managerial and financial problems. *The Business Times*, 13 Nov. 1985, 24 Feb. 1986.

147 Chia Siow Yue and Jamus Jerome Lim, "Singapore: A Regional Hub in ICT", in *Towards a Knowledge-based Economy: East Asia's Changing Industrial Geography*, ed. S. Masuyama and D. Vandenbrink (Singapore: Institute of Southeast Asian Studies, 2003), p. 277; Teo and Ang, "Singapore's Manufacturing Sector", p. 364.

to benefit from technological spillovers by the MNCs. In terms of forward linkages, the industry contributed to growth in marketing activity as well as seaborne and airborne cargo for the transportation of electronics products to overseas destinations.

During the 1990s, many MNCs set up international purchasing offices in Singapore to source products, parts and components for their worldwide operations.[148] Concurrently, foreign companies also used Singapore as a regional logistics hub to integrate the flow of manufacturing products and components in the Asian region. Furthermore, the city-state was home to Original Equipment Manufacturers (OEMs) specialising in the outsourcing of electronics production, like local companies Aztech Systems, Flextronics and Natsteel Electronics.[149] There were a number of other indigenous electronics firms, including GLCs, that emerged in the late 1990s, particularly in the computer-related segments but also in semiconductors and the manufacture of assembly equipment. Prominent among them was Chartered Semiconductor Manufacturing, which grew to be the third largest semiconductor foundry in the world.[150]

Another pre-existing industry that underwent considerable restructuring into higher value-added products in the eighties and nineties was the petroleum and petrochemicals industry. In the late seventies, after the oil majors on the island were joined by Exxon and Mobil, oil refining reached its high point, making up 6 per cent of GDP, nearly two-fifths of manufacturing exports and eclipsing electronics.[151] The locally-owned Singapore Petroleum Company (SPC) was established and later went into a partnership with Caltex and BP.[152] As the swing producer in the Asian region satisfying unfulfilled demand for oil from elsewhere, Singapore was known as the "Houston of Asia".[153] Most of the crude oil sent for processing on the island came from the OPEC countries in the Middle East.[154] As in the early 20th century, refined petroleum and derivative products like diesel, jet fuel, kerosene and lubricants were exported to Japan, Hong Kong, Australia as well as the immediate region.

In the mid-1980s, the petroleum industry experienced a downturn due to a sharp decline in world oil prices and also because Indonesia stopped processing crude oil in Singapore after opening its own refineries.[155] Fortunately, China stepped in to take up the idle capacity.[156] The 1990s became a period of consolidation in the industry that saw

[148] Chia Siow Yue, "Singapore: Towards a Knowledge-based Economy", in *Industrial Restructuring in East Asia: Towards the 21st Century*, ed. S. Masuyama, D. Vendenbrink and Chia Siow Yue (Nomura Research Institute and Institute of Southeast Asian Studies, 2001), p. 180.

[149] *The Business Times*, 31 Dec. 1992, 16 Apr. 1994, 8 Jan. 1996; *The Straits Times*, 30 Jan. 1998.

[150] *The Straits Times*, 8 Nov. 1995, 4 Apr. 1997; *The Business Times*, 5 June 1998.

[151] Ng Weng Hoong, *Singapore, The Energy Economy: From the First Refinery to the End of Cheap Oil, 1960–2010* (Abingdon: Routledge, 2012), pp. 8, 9, 17–22; *The Straits Times*, 10 Dec. 1978.

[152] *The Business Times*, 1 June 1978.

[153] F. Fesharaki, "Singapore as an Oil Centre", in *Management of Success*, ed. Sandhu and Wheatley, pp. 301, 302; T. Doshi, *Houston of Asia: The Singapore Petroleum Industry* (Singapore: Institute of Southeast Asian Studies, 1989).

[154] *New Nation*, 28 Jan. 1977.

[155] *The Straits Times*, 9 Aug. 1987, 24 Oct. 1988.

[156] *The Business Times*, 21 Nov. 1984, 11 Feb. 1985.

the exit of BP from Singapore, the merger of Exxon and Mobil, and the emergence of South Korea as a competitive rival to Singapore.[157] All the refining companies in Singapore not only produce and export refined oil but are also involved in marketing, distribution and trading of crude and petroleum products.[158] Oil trading had of course been a long-standing activity in Singapore; in 1989, at least 32 traders were attracted to the city by the tax breaks offered by the government.[159] On a related note, Singapore not only marketed oil exploration and exploitation equipment for use in Southeast Asia but was the second largest builder of offshore drilling rigs in the world in the early 1980s.[160] Moreover, it became the largest bunkering port in 1987.[161]

The diversification of the oil industry into more lucrative petrochemical production took place in the early 1980s, at which juncture the Singapore government identified chemicals as a strategic cluster with low employment but high productivity.[162] Speciality chemicals in particular have very high value-added per worker and there were more than 50 companies producing them.[163] The petrochemical industry was inaugurated when the Petrochemical Corporation of Singapore—a joint venture between the government, DBS and a consortium of Japanese companies led by Sumitomo Chemical—constructed the first naphtha cracker plant in 1984 in a petrochemical complex located on one of the offshore islands.[164] To complement the complex, Dutch MNC Royal Van Ommeren NV, with the government as a partner, built a chemical storage facility and terminal on Pulai Sebarok.[165] Confronted by increasing competition in the petroleum refining industry, the state actively promoted petrochemical projects and before long, the petrochemical complex was fully occupied.[166] This was when the EDB and JTC were spurred into embarking on a bold plan to amalgamate and enlarge seven southwestern islands (a few of which hosted oil refineries) with an area of 1,000 hectares into a single landmass of 3,000 hectares called Jurong Island, which became synonymous with the oil and chemical industry.[167] Built at a cost of $7 billion, the island is conveniently linked to the neighbouring Jurong Industrial Estate via a causeway.[168] The infrastructural facilities on the island include utilities, jetties,

157 Ng, *Singapore, The Energy Economy*, pp. 22–3, 25; *The Business Times*, 27 Nov. 1998.

158 S. Sharma, "The Changing Structure of the Oil Market and Its Implications for Singapore's Oil Industry", *ASEAN Economic Bulletin* 4, 3 (1988): 275, 276.

159 Fesharaki, "Singapore as an Oil Centre", pp. 303, 305–6; *The New Paper*, 20 Sept. 1988.

160 Regnier, *Singapore*, p. 84; *The Business Times*, 28 May 1981.

161 *The Straits Times*, 11 May 1988.

162 Hing Ai Yun and Lee Kiat Jin, "Evolution of the Petrochemical Industry in Singapore", *Journal of the Asia-Pacific Economy* 14, 2 (2002): 117–20; Monetary Authority of Singapore, *The Petrochemical Industry in Singapore*, Occasional Paper No. 14 (Singapore: Monetary Authority of Singapore, 1999), pp. 8, 9; *The Business Times*, 5 Dec. 1981, 10 Nov. 1984.

163 *The Business Times*, 27 Dec. 1984, 28 Dec. 1984.

164 *The Straits Times*, 31 Oct. 1983, 16 Feb. 1984; *The Business Times*, 10 Nov. 1983, 18 Feb. 1984.

165 *The Business Times*, 5 Feb. 1981, 12 Mar. 1983, 1 Sept. 1983, 15 May 1987, 24 Apr. 1995.

166 Ng, *Singapore, The Energy Economy*, pp. 61–2, 69–70.

167 *The Making of Jurong Island: The Right Chemistry* (Singapore: Jurong Town Corporation, 2000), pp. 19, 32–5, 38, 61; *The Straits Times*, 27 July 1992; *The New Paper*, 18 May 1995.

168 *The New Paper*, 7 Apr. 1997.

storage tanks, pipelines, chemical warehouses and waste treatment facilities, which are shared by the companies there to minimise overhead costs. Food and beverage outlets, stores, a clinic and recreational facilities are also provided for staff working on the island.[169]

The cluster concept underlying the plan was to build a complex that could house upstream plants using naphtha from local refineries to produce ethylene, propylene and acetylene gases.[170] These in turn are used symbiotically as feedstock by downstream companies manufacturing petrochemicals, speciality chemicals and plastics. To start the ball rolling, the EDB took an equity stake in Teijin Polycarbonates.[171] The idea worked and attracted the leading petrochemical companies of the world such as DuPont, Chevron and Mitsui Chemical to site their plants on the island, with Japanese firms as the largest group of investors.[172] In 2000, five years after land reclamation started, there were 60 companies operating in Jurong Island with an investment total of $21 billion. In addition, Exxon and Mobil continued to pour money into billion-dollar projects to produce new chemical products and the Singapore Refining Company invested in a second cracker, as rapid economic growth in the region led to a boom in the demand for petrochemicals.[173] By the late nineties however, the Asian petrochemical industry was faced with a problem of overcapacity as a result of the financial crisis and an increase in supply as oil-rich Malaysia and Indonesia set up their own petrochemical plants.

The last foray of the Singapore government into the manufacturing industry was into biomedical sciences; this enterprise generated some controversy as it seemed a highly risky undertaking.[174] As a leading example of a knowledge-based industry, it required highly qualified manpower and long gestation periods before research could be commercialised.[175] In the event, the EDB during the 1990s was able only to bring in companies producing pharmaceuticals and medical equipment, some in joint ventures with local enterprises.[176] A Pharmaceutical Zone was created on reclaimed land in Tuas to accommodate these companies but there was no real biotechnology research to speak of until the year 2000, when the government decided to commit greater resources to the endeavour.[177] Since then, the EDB and the Agency for Science, Technology and Research (A*STAR), established in 2001, have been charged with promoting the industry.[178] In another example of the

---

169 Teo and Ang, "Singapore's Manufacturing Sector", p. 365.

170 *The Business Times*, 19 May 1981.

171 *The Business Times*, 8 Nov. 1997.

172 Monetary Authority of Singapore, *The Petrochemical Industry*, pp. 2–3, 7, 12, 19–21; *The Business Times*, 24 Jan. 1989, 24 Apr. 1995, 10 Nov. 1997, 26 Jan. 1999.

173 Ng, *Singapore, The Energy Economy*, pp. 70, 71; *The Straits Times*, 22 May 1996.

174 *Today*, 9 Dec. 2006, 8 Feb. 2007, 16 Mar. 2007.

175 Lee Yong-Sook and Tee Ying-Chian, "Reprising the Role of the Developmental State in Cluster Development: The Biomedical Industry in Singapore", *Singapore Journal of Tropical Geography* 30, 1 (2009): 86, 90–2.

176 *The Business Times*, 11 Apr. 1992; *The Straits Times*, 26 May 1993.

177 *Singapore's Biomedical Cluster: Lessons from Two Decades of Innovation and Manufacturing Policy*, Cambridge Industrial Innovation Policy, 2021, p. 15; *The Straits Times*, 28 Jan. 1997; *The Business Times*, 28 Jan. 1997, 8 Oct. 1998; *Today*, 5 Nov. 2002.

178 A*STAR is the successor to the NSTB.

industry cluster approach, the government spent a large sum to build the Biopolis hub that houses biotechnology research institutes, incubator centres and R&D laboratories located in One-North, a work, life and play concept town in Buona Vista that also caters to the infocommunications and media industries.[179] Next to Biopolis is Fusionopolis, a science park opened in 2008 (Phase 1) by the JTC. As in Jurong Island, tenants of Biopolis have access to common facilities and equipment.[180] The advantages that Singapore enjoyed in developing the biomedical sector are its strong intellectual property protection regime, more liberal ethical limits on biomedical research and the possibility of testing medical innovations in the local healthcare industry. However, the country's base in university education in biology and chemistry was weaker than in engineering and electronics.[181]

A $1.2 billion venture fund, Bio*One Capital, was set up to undertake the initial investments in the industry and provide seed money for start-ups.[182] Apart from exemption from corporate tax on profits for five to ten years, other incentives and grants were also extended to the industry: for instance, investors who committed a minimum of $100,000 in start-ups received a 50 per cent tax deduction while investment allowances and subsidies were available to help defray upfront R&D costs.[183] A vigorous recruitment campaign was also carried out to attract foreign research scientists and engineers to work in Singapore, including some of the best in the world. The manpower shortage was simultaneously addressed by sending local students on scholarships to study abroad in renowned universities.[184]

These efforts yielded results: in 2005, there were 172 companies in the biomedical industry producing about 9 per cent of manufacturing output and employing 10,200 workers.[185] A few of the better known companies producing pharmaceuticals in Singapore are GlaxoSmithKline, Pfizer, Beecham, Fisons, Procter & Gamble, Novartis, Merck and Schering-Plough.[186] In 2010, the Swiss multinational biomedical firm Roche established a centre for research into diagnostics and pharmaceuticals to cater to the Asia Pacific region, which was followed by others.[187] In the much smaller medical technology industry, one of the companies was CIBA Vision, the contact lens maker. Another was Siemens Medical Instruments, which manufactured digital hearing aids.[188] The medical equipment industry also has a strong backward linkage to the local precision engineering cluster, which supplies it with plastic, rubber, silicon and metal parts as well as mould design and tooling services. To obtain the necessary manpower for this segment of the industry, both NUS and NTU began to offer bioengineering degrees.

---

179 *Today*, 7 Dec. 2001, 15 Jan. 2003, 24 Oct. 2003, 11 Jan. 2005.

180 *Asian Chemical News* (2–8 June 2003): 12, 14.

181 Kwong, "Singapore: Dominance of Multinational Corporations", pp. 48, 49.

182 Lee and Tee, "Reprising the Role of the Developmental State", pp. 90, 93; *Today*, 20 Jan. 2006.

183 *Today*, 5 Nov. 2003.

184 *SMA News* 36, 11 (2004): 10–11, 12; *Today*, 22 July 2004.

185 *Asia-Pacific Biotech News* 10, 1 (2006): 44–7.

186 *Singapore's Biomedical Cluster*, pp. 10, 13, 16, 20; *The Business Times*, 19 Apr. 1990, 12 June 1998; *The Straits Times*, 15 June 1991, 1 July 1995, 7 May 1998, 8 Sept. 1998; *Today*, 16 Mar. 2001, 6 Nov. 2002.

187 *Asia-Pacific Biotech News* 14, 2 (2010): 34.

188 *The Business Times*, 9 Feb. 1996; *Today*, 21 June 2002.

While emphasising the primacy of the manufacturing sector, the Economic Committee in its report in 1985 added services as a second engine of growth for the Singapore economy. It pointed out that the city-state had a greater comparative advantage in exporting services rather than goods and that services would be a leading growth sector in the years to come.[189] Henceforth, the new development plan was to make Singapore a strategic node for global companies in the Asia-Pacific region.[190] Specifically, the city was envisaged to be a "total business centre" serving as the gateway for foreign companies to venture into Southeast Asia (including through the regionalisation initiative), therefore reprising its colonial role as the conduit for Western firms to penetrate commercially and financially into the region. The committee also proposed that Singapore offer itself as the regional operational headquarters (OHQs) of MNCs that had located their production facilities and business activities in nearby countries.[191] In response to special tax incentives for OHQ status, 3,000 MNCs had opened offices on the island by 1991, including business giants like Exxon, General Electric, IBM and Citibank.[192]

According to the committee, some of the services in which Singapore could excel were banking and finance, business consultancy and the professions, warehousing and distribution, information technology, engineering, healthcare, education, and leisure and entertainment services. The recommendations were subsequently followed up in 1991 by the Goh Chok Tong government with a Strategic Economic Plan, which essentially reiterated a similar vision for the Singapore economy and added the objective for the city-state to become a developed nation by the year 2000. To give some teeth to the proposals, the government extended to the service sector the concessionary tax rates, allowances and grants that applied to manufacturing.[193] The EDB was assigned the additional mission of attracting international corporations to Singapore in order to promote financial, education, medical and lifestyle services.

Even before the recommendations were made, the service sector had not been neglected. While industrialisation was still deemed paramount, planners recognised Singapore's expertise in trade and finance throughout the colonial period. In absolute terms, services output doubled between 1966 and 1973, although its share in GDP declined, and again between 1974 and 1985.[194] The expansions could be attributed to newer services like financial and business services, transportation and communications. Tourism experienced robust growth, boosting the retail, hotel and restaurant industries as well as the transport sector.[195] In 1984, productivity in services (especially the modern activities) was more than twice that in manufacturing. Moreover, services generated more output for a given

---

189 *The Singapore Economy*, pp. 61, 79–81, 141–2; *The Straits Times*, 18 Jan. 1986, 18 Feb. 1986; *The Business Times*, 18 Jan. 1986, 15 Feb. 1986.

190 Wong, "The Role of the State", pp. 512–5; *The Straits Times*, 26 Oct. 1988.

191 *The Business Times*, 21 June 1986.

192 Soon and Stoever, "Foreign Investment and Economic Development", p. 330.

193 Toh Mun Heng and Linda Low, "Singapore's Service Development in the ASEAN Context", *ASEAN Economic Bulletin* 6, 1 (1989): 12; *The Business Times*, 18 Feb. 1986, 24 June 1986.

194 Lee Soo Ann, "Expansion of the Services Sector", in *Management of Success*, ed. Sandhu and Wheatley, pp. 281, 284, 286–7.

195 Peebles and Wilson, *Economic Growth and Development*, p. 103.

increase in final demand.[196] Exportable services also paid workers more, benefitting from Singapore's emerging hub status in the seventies and eighties.

Singapore's specialisation in financial services had begun in 1968 and a retrospective review may be appropriate here. In that year, Albert Winsemius formed the opinion that, due to the time zone difference with America and Europe, Singapore could occupy a niche in the 24-hour provision of global financial services.[197] Thus the Asian Dollar Market (ADM) was born in 1968 and Singapore became a regional and eventually global financial centre.[198] The ADM is an international money and capital market in which commercial and merchant banks borrow and lend currencies other than Singapore dollars—initially the US dollar but later also the Deutsche Mark (and after 2002, the euro) and yen—to finance activities outside of Singapore.[199] It is essentially a wholesale interbank market serving as a funding centre for international banks and a place for the deployment of surplus funds, that is, for accepting deposits and making loans to both banks and non-bank customers.[200] The enforced partitioning of local and foreign currencies is captured by the accounting terms Asian Currency Unit (ACU) and Domestic Banking Unit (DBU), in reference to the offshore and onshore banking systems respectively; the division was carried out to insulate the latter from the vagaries of the former.[201] Regulation and intervention by MAS are light and there are no reserve requirements or liquidity ratio on ACUs. The Singapore government fostered the market by exempting withholding tax on deposit interest income (giving Singapore an edge over Hong Kong which had such a tax), a special 10 per cent concessionary tax rate on ACU offshore income, tax exemptions on income from bonds as well as estate and stamp duty waivers.[202] Perhaps the most important measure making for the success of the ADM was the progressive liberalisation of foreign exchange controls and their total abolition in 1978.[203] These controls had been in place since after the war but were clearly incompatible with the free flow of funds into and out of the ADM. After the controls were removed, Singapore residents were allowed currency transactions in ACUs.[204]

In the early years after the inception of the ADM, growth in aggregate assets was very rapid but it slowed down subsequently, partly because of the global recession in the mid-1970s but also due to the international debt problem caused by some Latin American countries which defaulted on their loans in the early 1980s.[205] Still, the compounded

---

[196] Toh and Low, "Singapore's Service Development", pp. 14, 18.

[197] Monetary Authority of Singapore, *Sustaining Stability, Serving Singapore*, pp. 143–5, 149–50.

[198] *The Straits Times*, 16 May 1969, 7 Feb. 1971, 27 Apr. 1973.

[199] J.R. Hewson, "The Asian Dollar Market and Monetary Policy", in Monetary Authority of Singapore, *Papers on Monetary Economics*, pp. 167–70.

[200] *The Straits Times*, 15 July 1970.

[201] Z. Hodjera, "The Asian Currency Market: Singapore as a Regional Financial Center", *IMF Staff Papers* 25, 2 (1978): 221, 223–4, 225.

[202] Lee, *The Monetary and Banking Development*, pp. 98–101, 103; *The Straits Times*, 13 Oct. 1972; *The Business Times*, 21 Feb. 1978.

[203] *The Straits Times*, 1 May 1973.

[204] Wilson, "Monetary Policy and Financial Sector Development", pp. 1550031-4–1550031-5.

[205] Hodjera, "The Asian Currency Market", pp. 226, 228, 229; *New Nation*, 5 Oct. 1973; *The Straits Times*, 14 June 1975; *The Business Times*, 19 Jan. 1983, 18 Sept. 1984.

annual growth rate over this period was 26.6 per cent, faster than the growth in the Eurodollar market and the domestic banking system. In 1989, total assets amounted to US$289 billion and the number of ACUs had increased to 194 in line with steady growth in international finance and banking.[206] The sources of funds in the market were London, New York and the Middle East while the users were predominantly Southeast and East Asian borrowers who tapped the funds in Singapore for development and manufacturing projects.[207] Deposits by MNCs, private corporations and individuals in Asia were also important and so were loans to governments and public agencies.

Over four-fifths of the assets and liabilities in the ADM were denominated in US dollars, reflecting its role as the vehicle currency for trade and financial transactions in the region. As such, interest rates took their cue from the Eurodollar market in London and the most common loan maturity period in the ADM was between 3 and 12 months. But existing side-by-side with the ADM and performing a complementary function to it was the capital market, also known as the Asian Bond Market (ABM). This market was launched in 1971–72 with bond issues by the Singapore government and DBS, followed by POSB, CPF, SIA, Keppel Shipyard and other authorities.[208] The ABM handled long-term loan syndication with maturities of three to seven years for Asian countries such as Indonesia and Brunei, which used the funds for the exploration and production of oil and natural gas.[209] Therefore, Singapore continues to function as a modern entrepôt for the net transfer of savings from the rest of the world to Southeast Asia.[210]

The government had also been active in the development of financial institutions in Singapore from soon after the colonial period. In the mid-1960s, there were 34 licensed banks in the city operating 132 offices, ten of which were local institutions. The foreign banks were as dominant as before in services such as financing trade and dealing in foreign exchange. Apart from the local commercial banks, the POSB and a large number of finance companies were also active in collecting savings and time deposits to make loans, especially for house purchases. However, savings and time deposits earned at these institutions were paid lower interest rates and loans were made at higher rates.[211] In the 1970s, the government adopted an explicit policy of promoting the growth of financial activities and the development of new financial instruments.[212] Nevertheless, to avoid undue competition with local banks, the categories of "restricted" and "offshore" banking licences were created in 1971 and 1973, respectively, to regulate the entry of foreign banks into Singapore.[213] These came with restrictions on domestic banking business like deposit collection, although

---

206 Liew and Wilson, *A History of Money*, pp. 277, 278.

207 *The Straits Times*, 26 Aug. 1976; *The Business Times*, 8 Nov. 1977, 16 June 1978.

208 *The Straits Times*, 23 Oct. 1972; *The Business Times*, 5 Oct. 1976.

209 *The Straits Times*, 7 Dec. 1971.

210 R.C. Bryant, "The Evolution of Singapore as a Financial Centre", in *Management of Success*, ed. Sandhu and Wheatley, pp. 337–42, 348–9, 355–8.

211 Lee, *The Monetary and Banking Development*, pp. 81–5, 92–3; Peebles and Wilson, *Economic Growth and Development*, p. 117; *New Nation*, 6 Aug. 1974, 26 Jan. 1977; *The Straits Times*, 17 Jan. 1975; *The Business Times*, 24 Dec. 1976, 21 July 1979.

212 *The Straits Times*, 6 May 1972, 28 June 1972.

213 *The Straits Times*, 16 July 1974; *New Nation*, 24 Sept. 1974.

the banks were allowed to operate in the ADM and foreign exchange market.[214] Merchant banks made their debut in 1970 and more finance companies sprang up.[215] The other group of new institutions were discount houses which acted as intermediaries in the local money market by obtaining funds from commercial banks to invest in bills of exchange and short-term government securities.[216] They also dealt in negotiable certificates of deposits, which were introduced in 1975 as a means of interbank lending and borrowing.[217]

By the early 1980s, most global banks from the United States, Europe, Asia and Malaysia had established a Singapore branch or subsidiary and, in some cases, also a merchant bank offshoot. This had the effect of encouraging MNCs to set up their regional treasury and funding headquarters in Singapore which by that time had also become a centre for the collection of funds and booking of credits on offshore transactions.[218] In the late eighties, there were altogether 137 commercial banks in Singapore with 412 branches (35 full licence, local and foreign; 14 restricted licence; and 88 offshore banks).[219] Bank assets amounted to $127.2 billion in 1989 and accounted for more than half of the assets of all financial intermediaries.[220] Partly because of mergers, the number of finance companies was reduced to 28, while that of merchant banks was 67 after increasing rapidly in the 1980s. The former specialised in car and house financing while the latter were engaged in wholesale banking, corporate finance and bond issuance.[221] From 1968 to 1984, the total assets of all institutions inclusive of ACUs grew at an average annual rate of 31 per cent and this was reflected in a similar expansion of loans and advances to non-bank customers. The biggest borrowers were the general commerce, manufacturing and construction and housing sectors.[222] Indicative of the fast growth was the increase in the savings deposits of the POSB, from $91 million in 1971 to $6.2 billion in 1983, enabled in part by tax-free interest on deposits that were guaranteed by the government.[223] Over roughly the same period, the share of financial and business services in GDP rose from about 13–14 per cent to 22 per cent. In this connection, it is interesting to note that the stock of ACUs reached about seven times the flow of GDP and domestic financial assets about three times.

Another significant service industry that should be mentioned here is transportation. Following the introduction of containerisation in 1972, earlier than in many countries, Singapore became the second busiest port in the world after Rotterdam, with shipping tonnage doubling in the 1970s and container cargo handled rising to 104 million feet in

---

214 Monetary Authority of Singapore, *Sustaining Stability, Serving Singapore*, pp. 150–1; *The Straits Times*, 23 Mar. 1973.

215 *The Straits Times*, 9 Feb. 1970, 17 June 1970, 23 Sept. 1970, 8 Oct. 1970; *New Nation*, 18 Apr. 1972.

216 *New Nation*, 25 Oct. 1972; *The Straits Times*, 26 Nov. 1974; *The Business Times*, 24 Feb. 1978.

217 *The Straits Times*, 30 Mar. 1975, 1 May 1975, 17 May 1975; *New Nation*, 30 June 1975.

218 Regnier, *Singapore*, p. 124.

219 Lee, *The Monetary and Banking Development*, pp. 73–4, 77–81, 85–9; *The Business Times*, 11 May 1988.

220 *Economic Survey of Singapore 1990* (Singapore: Ministry of Trade and Industry); Bryant, "Evolution", pp. 342–7.

221 *The Business Times*, 11 May 1988.

222 Le Blanc, *Singapore*, p. 40, Table 2.13, p. 119.

223 *The Straits Times*, 13 Nov. 1983; *Singapore Monitor*, 28 Apr. 1984.

1984.[224] Bulk-handling trade especially for mineral fuels took on much greater importance owing to the development of large crude carriers which allowed more cargo to be carried over longer distances.[225] The city's simultaneous metamorphosis into the premier air hub of Southeast Asia providing airport as well as aircraft maintenance and repair services began with the expansion of SIA following the split with Malaysia-Singapore Airlines in 1972.[226] A decade later in 1981, the number of passengers passing through the newly opened Changi Airport—the largest in Asia at the time—was 4.3 million.[227] Singapore became a tourist destination with the construction of new attractions, hotels and shopping centres.[228] In 1982, three million tourists visited the island, some of whom used the city as a base for exploring the region. Improvements in land transport were also not neglected. In 1965, an extensive transportation plan was proposed to connect the major housing estates and city area.[229] The plan entailed building new roads and expressways, which laid the foundation for the extensive system existing today. Planning of a Mass Rapid Transit (MRT) system also began in the late sixties but the first trains began running only in 1987.

During the 1990s, the Singapore government intensified and diversified its efforts to promote the growth of services.[230] Apart from further measures to develop the financial sector, Singapore's planners hoped to make the city-state a tourism hub and a media and telecommunications hub for the Asia-Pacific region.[231] In 1995, a plan was formulated by the STPB to develop tourism related not only to leisure but also to business.[232] To this end, Singapore was promoted as a MICE (meetings, incentives, conventions and exhibitions) destination and the EDB at the same time encouraged the growth of the leisure and lifestyle industry.[233] It also produced a blueprint to boost creative services like advertising, design, public relations, music recording, the movie industry, entertainment and fashion.[234] In 1990, the government announced that a new Institute of Communicative Arts was to be established to train the needed workers in these activities.[235] After establishing satellite communications, Singapore did indeed become a media and broadcasting hub with the entry of leading US companies in business and sports news channels, cable programming

224 Lee, *Singapore Chronicles: Economy*, p. 34; Huff, *The Economic Growth of Singapore*, pp. 305–6.

225 Lee, "Trade and Shipping Growth", pp. 79–80.

226 Lee, *From Colony to Nation*, pp. 50–2.

227 Lee Soo Ann, "Patterns of Economic Structure in Singapore", in *Singapore: Twenty-five Years of Development*, ed. You and Lim, p. 16. Changi Airport replaced the commercial airport in Paya Lebar which had taken over from Kallang Airport in 1955.

228 *The Straits Times*, 15 Sept. 1967.

229 *10 Years that Shaped a Nation*, pp. 93, 99–101.

230 *The Business Times*, 12 Nov. 1998.

231 Hing Ai Yun, "The Singapore State Takes Charge: Strategizing for the New Hi-Tech Service Society", *European Planning Studies* 7, 2 (1999): 191, 192, 193; *The Business Times*, 4 Jan. 1996, 8 June 1998; *The Straits Times*, 12 Mar. 1997, 9 July 1997.

232 *The Straits Times*, 15 Mar. 1995, 5 Jan. 1996, 25 July 1996; *The Business Times*, 15 Mar. 1995, 25 July 1996.

233 *The Business Times*, 22 Dec. 1990, 12 Nov. 1992; *The Straits Times*, 21 Jan. 1998.

234 *The Straits Times*, 21 Jan. 1990; *The Straits Times Weekly Overseas Edition*, 20 Oct. 1990.

235 *The Straits Times*, 8 May 1990.

and TV subscription services (for example, HBO, ESPN and Disney).[236] Growth in these areas was driven by the increasing convergence of telecommunications, broadcasting and computing technologies.[237] The related publishing and printing industry flourished as leading publishers in the world such as Springer Verlag, Pearson, McGraw-Hill and Imperial College Press made Singapore their base for satisfying the region's demand for the commoditisation of information and knowledge.[238] In the printing industry, the city-state held on to its leading position in Southeast Asia, which it had maintained since the colonial era, with companies like Tien Wah Press and Times Printers offering high-quality services.[239]

The Singapore government also reconstituted the country's human and infrastructural resources to support the emergence of an information and communications technology (ICT) industry. In addition to developing manpower skills in computer programming, a National IT Plan was launched in 1985 to promote the diffusion and adoption of information technology and computerisation in the trading, legal and healthcare sectors.[240] To show the way, the government set up the National Computer Board (NCB) in 1981 as the coordinating agency to implement IT initiatives and embarked on computerisation and the use of electronic means to provide public services (that is, e-government). Together with the nurturing of a local IT industry encompassing computer-related manufacturing, software development and IT services, this was intended to turn Singapore into an "intelligent island", with the government, firms and households connected by a nationwide high-speed network.[241] In the late eighties and early nineties, this local IT industry grew rapidly from the impetus of growing overseas demand.[242] Under a revised IT 2000 plan conceived in 1992, the NCB targeted the development of computing, cable and wireless networks across the entire island. A nationwide broadband network called Singapore ONE was launched commercially in 1998 to enable a wide range of multimedia applications; this was subsequently upgraded to an optical fibre network, thus increasing the speed of information transmission.[243] At the regional level, Singapore adopted a strategy to position itself as an ICT hub in order to facilitate the export of high value-added infocommunications, telecommunications and multimedia services.[244] In 1999, the output of the ICT sector amounted to $20 billion, or 6 per cent of GDP, and in 2000, it employed over 100,000 people. As a hub, Singapore also marketed and distributed office machinery and telecommunications equipment to Southeast Asia.

---

236 Wong and Ng, "Singapore's Industrial Policy", pp. 127–8; *The Business Times*, 20 Nov. 1993, 4 June 1996; *The Straits Times*, 28 Aug. 1995, 29 Dec. 1995, 19 May 1996.

237 *The Straits Times*, 3 June 1996.

238 *The Business Times*, 3 Feb. 1990, 28 Apr. 1992; *The Straits Times*, 29 Nov. 1991, 18 Mar. 1992.

239 Regnier, *Singapore*, p. 114.

240 Wong, "The Role of the State", pp. 515–6; *The Business Times*, 27 Mar. 1986, 4 Dec. 1986, 2 Apr. 1992; *The Straits Times*, 4 Dec. 1986.

241 *The New Paper*, 7 Sept. 1995; *The Straits Times*, 9 June 1997.

242 *The Straits Times*, 11 Dec. 1990; *The Business Times*, 14 Oct. 1996.

243 *The Straits Times*, 19 Nov. 1997, 3 June 1998; *The Business Times*, 26 July 1999.

244 Chia and Lim, "Singapore: A Regional Hub in ICT", pp. 259, 276, 289; *The Straits Times*, 9 June 1997.

As a cumulative result of these longer-term developments and initiatives, the structure of economic activity shifted during the 1990s to one in which the service sector was dominant (Figure 27).[245] The sector grew by 8.2 per cent per annum in the 1990s before the Asian Financial Crisis broke out in 1997; this rate was faster than that of the manufacturing sector.[246] Exports of services increased from $2.3 billion in 1990 to $44.8 billion in 1997, catapulting Singapore into its ranking as the twelfth largest services exporter in the world.[247] The ratio of services exports to total exports (including merchandise) increased accordingly to 19.5 per cent. When the economy recovered from the crisis in 1999, the output of the service sector represented two-thirds of GDP whereas manufacturing contributed only one-quarter. The number of people working in the sector was 1.3 million, or 71 per cent of total employment. These increases in the shares of the service sector in the economy were consistent with the experience of developed countries, which had seen the demand for services expand with rising incomes. That experience also reinforces the view that as a country develops and its stock of human capital rises, it shifts from being a net importer of technology and skills to a net exporter.[248]

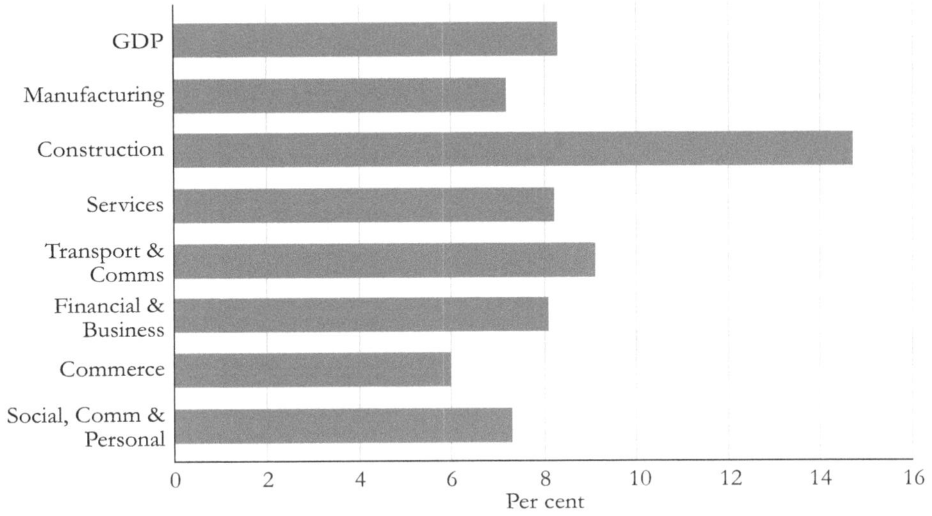

Figure 27. Sectoral Growth Rates of the Singapore Economy, 1990–99
Note: Social, Comm & Personal = Social, Community and Personal Services.
Source: *Economic Survey of Singapore*, various issues. Singapore: Ministry of Trade and Industry.

245 S. Kumar, "Singapore 1991: Towards New Horizons", in *Southeast Asian Affairs 1992* (Singapore: Institute of Southeast Asian Studies, 1992), p. 282.

246 *Economic Survey of Singapore*, various issues (Singapore: Ministry of Trade and Industry). Of the major sectors, construction experienced the highest growth of 14.7 per cent owing to the property boom in the early half of the 1990s and a healthy pipeline of government projects.

247 *The Straits Times*, 28 July 1997.

248 H. Hill and Pang Eng Fong, "Technology Exports from a Small, Very Open NIC: The Case of Singapore", *World Development* 19, 5 (1991): 553.

Among the sub-sectors, the financial and business services industries grew at a rapid pace—8.1 per cent on average each year—in the 1990s, as new financial institutions such as investment banks and reinsurance companies set up in Singapore.[249] Business services are made up of diverse industries like real estate, the legal profession, accounting and business consultancy services, architectural and engineering services and business representative offices, almost all of which, especially the knowledge-intensive activities, reward their employees with high earnings.[250] Financial and business services combined were responsible for generating 23 per cent of GDP in 1999, with the output shares between them almost equally divided. The exports of these services and those relating to insurance, telecommunications and advertising grew at an annual rate of 9.2 per cent in the 1990s. Meanwhile, the creative industries expanded at an average rate of 17.2 per cent between 1986 and 1990 and contributed 3.2 per cent of GDP.[251]

Transport and communications was the fastest growing service sub-sector and it also had the highest value-added per worker as it benefitted from the liberalisation of the telecommunications industry. Following average growth of 9.1 per cent per annum in the 1990s, its share of the economy's output was 14.1 per cent in 1999. Sea and air cargo handled rose by 8.3 per cent and 11.2 per cent respectively. These traditional services, based on locational advantages as well as container and warehousing services, were modernised through automation and computerisation.[252] In the late 1980s, Singapore was a staging-post for 700 shipping lines from all over the world, linking 500 different ports.[253] The growth of the air transportation sector created further spin-offs for the aerospace repair and overhaul industry, which received new investments from foreign companies.[254] In logistics and supply chain management, large companies such as DHL and FedEx together with local firms like ST Logistics had built up regional operation bases in Singapore, making it the top logistics hub in Asia.[255] With the rise in cargo throughput at the seaport and airport, the demand for warehousing services increased correspondingly, which resulted in strong growth in the construction of "distriparks", the modern version of the godowns of old but now also offering distribution, repacking and labelling services.[256]

---

249 Monetary Authority of Singapore, *Singapore's Services Sector in Perspective: Trends and Outlook*, Occasional Paper No. 5 (Singapore: Monetary Authority of Singapore, 1998), pp. 3–4, 9; *The Straits Times*, 2 Mar. 1990, 30 Apr. 1992, 15 Aug. 1992, 8 June 1998. Foreign direct investment inflows into financial and business services had exceeded those into manufacturing since the 1980s; in 1993, the stock of foreign investment in the sector was about equal to that in manufacturing. Toh, "Savings, Capital Formation, and Economic Growth", p. 196.

250 "Overview of Singapore's Business Services Sector", *Economic Survey of Singapore 2007* (Singapore: Ministry of Trade and Industry), pp. 122, 126.

251 "Economic Contributions of Singapore's Creative Industries", *Economic Survey of Singapore First Quarter 2003* (Singapore: Ministry of Trade and Industry), pp. 51–5.

252 Toh and Low, "Singapore's Service Development", p. 13.

253 Regnier, *Singapore*, pp. 101–2.

254 *The Straits Times*, 14 Jan. 1993.

255 *The Business Times*, 18 Sept. 1991, 10 July 1992, 8 Jan. 1993, 16 Feb. 1993, 20 Jan. 1994; *The Straits Times*, 29 Oct. 1997.

256 *The Business Times*, 7 Feb. 1990, 22 July 1994.

Putting aside the smaller but vital social, community and personal services sub-sector which covers government employment and trades like barbers, tailors and plumbers, the laggard was still the commerce sector. It expanded only by 6 per cent per annum and accounted for 15.9 per cent of overall output, despite wholesale and entrepôt trade rising at the rate of 12 per cent a year in the early 1990s. The increases in wholesale trade were in line with the Economic Committee's exhortation to enter into the trading of high-value commodities like electrical and electronics products, pharmaceuticals and office and photographic equipment.[257] The slower overall rate of expansion was due to the more subdued growth of the retail trade. Within the commercial sector, the value-added of hotels and restaurants was boosted by the spending not only of visitors but also of locals. During the period between the Gulf War in early 1991 and the currency crisis in 1997, tourist arrivals increased by an average of 6.2 per cent per annum and reached a record of 7.7 million visitors in 2000, out of which 22 per cent were business-related travellers. The number of hotel rooms available in Singapore increased from 22,080 in 1986 to 30,469 in 2000.

A few final remarks on the relationship between the manufacturing and service sectors are in order. First, it should be pointed out that the gains in services output and employment had been at the expense of the manufacturing industry.[258] As manufacturing productivity increased, the sector shed workers, who then joined the ranks of those employed in service industries. This phenomenon explained the faster growth seen in employment in the service sector—in fact, the sector had accounted for the bulk of jobs created since 1991. Many of these jobs requiring a high level of skill and competence were performed by administrative, managerial, professional and technical staff. Second, except for commerce, the service industries still paid workers more on average than the manufacturing sector. Third, the service sector was less cyclically sensitive and hence it experienced less volatility; while being labour-intensive, it generated more jobs for the economy. Fourth, the interdependencies between manufacturing and services had increased: manufacturing firms increasingly outsourced their marketing, computing, accounting, auditing and logistics needs to the business services industry. A good example is found in IT services, which enhanced manufacturing competitiveness by cutting operational costs, shortening product life cycles and increasing value-added.[259] Furthermore, manufacturing services had grown to include R&D, product design and development, process engineering and testing services.[260] The deployment of ICT blurred the lines between the two sectors as the provision of services increasingly required advanced manufacturing technologies. In this sense, manufacturing and services are indeed the twin engines of economic growth in Singapore.

The Great Productivity Debate

Singapore's journey from rags to riches within one generation has been the envy of many a developing nation. Yet in the 1990s, some observers began to question the country's

[257] *The Business Times*, 19 Feb. 1986.

[258] Monetary Authority of Singapore, *Singapore's Services Sector*, pp. 1, 7–8, 10–12, 14–15.

[259] Teo and Ang, "Singapore's Manufacturing Sector", p. 364.

[260] *The Straits Times Weekly Overseas Edition*, 20 June 1998.

sterling record of economic growth and, in particular, how it had been achieved. A debate was sparked off in 1994 when the prominent American economist Paul Krugman wrote an article maintaining that Singapore's spectacular performance was due entirely to increases in factor inputs, rather than increases in efficiency.[261] Singapore had succeeded based on "perspiration rather than inspiration", through a massive mobilisation of resources, just as the former Soviet Union had done. In a similar vein, a study by Alwyn Young, cited by Krugman, had suggested slightly earlier that the factors of production in Singapore had been inefficiently used.[262] His view was that the country's industrial targeting policies and state intervention in the form of continual economic restructuring had forced workers to move into new industries prematurely, thus not giving them the time to learn by doing.[263] The economic prognosis was therefore gloomy, as input-driven growth would inevitably run into diminishing returns. While Krugman may have sparked the debate, these observations had in fact been pre-empted by an earlier study. In 1986, a local economist had already found that there was little evidence of efficiency improvements in Singapore's economy.[264]

The disputations spawned a whole host of further studies that examined the issue in great detail; more than that, the debates, unusually, attracted the attention of the national and international authorities.[265] The gauge of efficiency used in all these studies is total factor productivity (TFP), rather than the measure of labour productivity defined as output per worker. Increases in TFP result from the efficiency with which factor inputs are utilised and are often traced to technological progress or the adoption of new production methods. The measure's importance lies in the fact that TFP increases are the only source of sustained improvements in living standards. In accounting for Singapore's economic growth between 1970 and 1990, it was estimated that one-quarter of the increase in GDP was due to increases in labour inputs or the number of working persons, and the remainder was attributed to increases in capital inputs. The contribution of TFP was slightly negative, meaning that it actually fell during the period concerned. In terms of output per worker, all the increases in labour productivity were accounted for by capital deepening, or the fact that workers had more capital equipment to work with. These findings hold even after making allowances for the improving educational profile of the labour force and differentiated types of capital inputs. They are also consistent with the real rate of return to capital in Singapore falling from 36 per cent in 1965 to 12 per cent in 1989.

---

261 P. Krugman, "The Myth of Asia's Miracle", *Foreign Affairs* 73, 6 (November/December 1994): 67, 69–73; *The Business Times*, 14 Sept. 1995.

262 A. Young, "A Tale of Two Cities: Factor Accumulation and Technical Change in Hong Kong and Singapore", *NBER Macroeconomics Annual* 7 (1992): 30–43.

263 *The Straits Times*, 28 Aug. 1992. Young made the point at a lunch meeting of the MIT Club in Singapore on 27 Aug. 1992.

264 Tsao Yuan, "Sources of Growth Accounting for the Singapore Economy", in *Singapore*, ed. Lim and Lloyd, pp. 20–6.

265 Krugman's criticism drew the following retort in 1995 from then Senior Minister Lee Kuan Yew: "you're right so far, but our total factor productivity growth will be much higher in the future because of the investments we're making in education". Peebles and Wilson, *Economic Growth and Development*, p. 61. Table 15 gives an overview of the relevant literature presented in this section.

Table 15. Studies of the Sources of Economic Growth in Singapore

Study	Period	Output Growth (%)	Labour Input (%)	Capital Input (%)	TFP (%)
Young, "Tyranny" (1995)	1966–90	8.7	5.7	11.5	0.2
Tsao, "Sources"(1986)	1966–72 1972–80	12.5 8.0	2.7 2.1	9.3 6.8	0.6 –0.9
van Elkan, "Accounting for Growth" (1995)	1960–91	8.0	1.9	4.3	1.8
Department of Statistics, Singapore, *Multifactor Productivity Growth* (1997)	1973–80 1980–85 1985–90 1990–96	6.8 5.8 8.2 7.9	1.5 0.7 1.3 2.1	5.8 5.7 3.1 4.0	-0.5 -0.6 3.8 1.8
Wong and Gan, "Total Factor Productivity" (1994)**	1981–85 1986–90	1.3 12.1	-0.1 0.7	2.1 1.9	–0.8 4.0
Rao and Lee, "Sources of Growth" (1995)	1966–73 1976–84 1987–94	12.7 8.5 8.6	2.3 2.1 1.9	8.5 5.6 3.6	1.9 0.8 3.1
Hsieh, "Productivity Growth" (1999)	1972–90	–	–	–	1.9
Sarel, "Growth and Productivity" (1997)*	1978–96	5.1	1.1	6.5	2.2
Koh, Rahman and Tan, "Growth and Productivity" (2002)**	1975–98	11.5	0.5	0.7	2.7
Nomura and Amano, "Labour Productivity" (2012)	1974–2010	6.8	2.8	4.3	–0.3
Monetary Authority of Singapore (MAS) "Sources" (2010)	1990–99 2000–09	7.6 4.9	2.2 2.4	4.5 2.3	0.9 0.2

* In per capita terms

** Manufacturing sector

When the investigation of TFP was extended to the other East Asian economies of Hong Kong, Taiwan and South Korea, productivity growth in these countries was found to be higher than in Singapore but it still contributed a relatively small fraction (one-quarter to one-third) of their rapid economic growth, implying that a substantial portion of it was also due to factor accumulation.[266] In Singapore's case, and extending back to the period from 1966 to 1990, out of the average GDP growth rate of 8.7 per cent per annum, growth in TFP accounted for only 0.2 per cent, with the remainder again attributable to additions of labour and capital. Although productivity gains were made in the late 1960s, they were negated in the following decades. Surprisingly also, TFP growth in the manufacturing sector was negative.

266 A. Young, "The Tyranny of Numbers: Confronting the Statistical Realities of the East Asian Growth Experience", *The Quarterly Journal of Economics* 110, 3 (1995): 656–64.

Lest these results be doubted, research by the International Monetary Fund (IMF) concluded that at best, around one-fifth (1.6 per cent of 8 per cent) of growth during the even longer period from 1960 to 1991 was due to TFP improvements.[267] Given very high investment rates, most of the expansion in output was accounted for by a larger capital stock; labour supply increases and land reclamation played smaller roles. The Singapore government itself produced research in 1997 that collaborated these findings: TFP growth was generally low in the 1970s and early 1980s but it picked up after that before slowing again in the 1990s.[268] A 1994 study also arrived at the conclusion that manufacturing TFP growth fell in the first half of the 1980s, although it rebounded later in the decade because of a change in the composition of industrial output towards higher productivity activities.[269] Taking all the work reviewed so far into account, it seems to be the case that TFP growth in Singapore was meagre or non-existent in the earlier years of economic development, but improved after the recession in 1985–86. That is precisely what another study in 1995 found: in 1976–84, TFP accounted for only 7 per cent of the annual growth of GDP but it increased to 30 per cent in 1987–94.[270] The increase in the later period reflected in part the improved performance of the manufacturing sector. Moreover, the Singapore government had placed greater emphasis on R&D and efficiency improvements since the late eighties.

All the TFP growth studies mentioned above have been confounded by the lack of officially published data on the capital stock in Singapore. Demonstrating the dependence of the findings also on the methodology used, new evidence cropped up in the late 1990s to suggest that the behaviour of the empirically observed return to capital was not consistent with the claim that Singapore's long-term growth was driven solely by capital accumulation.[271] In particular, measures of TFP based on factor prices showed that productivity growth in Singapore was stronger than earlier thought. Similarly, another study by the IMF overturned the earlier results and found that significant contributions were made by productivity growth even in the first two decades after independence.[272]

---

[267] R. van Elkan, "Accounting for Growth in Singapore", in *Singapore*, ed. Bercuson, pp. 4, 5–6, 7, 8–10. The higher TFP estimate was most likely due to the fact that the factor inputs are not adjusted for changes in input quality, for example when foreign investment brought with it improvements in technology embodied in imported capital goods.

[268] Department of Statistics, *Multifactor Productivity Growth in Singapore: Concept, Methodology and Trends*, Occasional Paper Series (Singapore: Department of Statistics, 1997); M. Renuka, "Total Factor Productivity Growth in Singapore: A Survey", *ASEAN Economic Bulletin* 16, 1 (1999): 59–60, 62; Peebles and Wilson, *Economic Growth and Development*, pp. 62–4; *The Straits Times*, 28 Oct. 1997; *The Business Times*, 28 Oct. 1997.

[269] Wong Fot Chyi and Gan Wee Beng, "Total Factor Productivity in the Singapore Manufacturing Industries during the 1980s", *Journal of Asian Economics* 5, 2 (1994); *The Straits Times*, 15 July 1993; *The Business Times*, 15 July 1993.

[270] V.V. Bhanoji Rao and Christopher Lee, "Sources of Growth in the Singapore Economy and Its Manufacturing and Service Sectors", *The Singapore Economic Review* 40, 1 (1995): 86; Peebles and Wilson, *Economic Growth and Development*, pp. 60–1.

[271] Chang-Tai Hsieh, "Productivity Growth and Factor Prices in East Asia", *The American Economic Review* 89, 2 (1999): 136–7.

[272] M. Sarel, "Growth and Productivity in ASEAN Countries", IMF Working Paper 97/97 (Washington, DC: International Monetary Fund, 1997), pp. 12, 14–17, 19–23, 25, 27, 29, 37.

Unlike the other studies, this investigation relied much less on (possibly flawed) national accounts data. This feature led to the result that the return on investment—as measured by the marginal product of capital—had not declined over the years. That in turn implied that TFP growth had been strong during the period 1978–96, accounting for more than two-fifths of the growth in output per person. The basic reason for the reversal of findings is a lower estimate of the capital share in national income, at one-third.[273]

A 2002 article gives a further example of how investigation outcomes could be affected by the data used. This study, introducing a reclassification of manufacturing industries to account for definitional changes and structural change, also came to a markedly different conclusion from the seminal papers.[274] As a result of the government's economic restructuring policies to move Singapore up the technology ladder, the rate of structural change had been very rapid, with new industries created over time and obsolete ones disappearing. Such a reallocation of resources would lead to TFP gains and, without any adjustments being made, would result in misleading findings. The study introduced two novel features into the growth accounting exercise: first, raw materials and energy inputs were considered together with labour and capital inputs; second, industry-specific output price deflators and materials deflators were used to derive manufacturing output in real terms. With these refinements in place, two-thirds of the average output growth of 11.5 per cent per annum in manufacturing between 1975 and 1998 were accounted for by raw materials and one-quarter by increases in TFP, which amounted to 2.7 per cent per annum. This long-term estimate could be broken down into 4.6 per cent productivity growth in 1975–80, 0.7 per cent in 1981–85, 2 per cent in 1986–90 and 3.1 per cent in 1991–95. The authors of the article interpreted the slowdown in the early eighties as an interregnum during which economic restructuring got underway and the increases experienced after that as a result of the establishment of technology-intensive industries.

Our review of the productivity debate in Singapore would not be complete without discussing other studies that appeared after 1999. Of these, the most carefully executed constructed a new labour dataset in order to obtain more accurate measures of both aggregate labour input and labour quality change for the period 1974–2010.[275] Labour input was measured in terms of total number of hours worked and workers were differentiated according to gender, age, educational attainment, employment status and residency. Capital input originated from two sources, IT and non-IT. Over the four decades examined, both Singapore's economic growth and labour productivity growth had been predominantly capital-driven, explaining from two-thirds to three-quarters of overall growth respectively. The rest of output growth resulted from the increase in the number of workers employed multiplied by their average hours worked and improvements in the quality of labour.[276] In

273 Another reason could be the use of homogeneous capital and labour inputs. However, the latter were adjusted for age differences and made an allowance for the presence of foreign workers in Singapore.

274 Koh Soo Wei, Shahidur Rahman and Randolph G.K. Tan, "Growth and Productivity in Singapore Manufacturing Industries: 1975–1998", *Asian Economic Journal* 16, 3 (2002): 252–65. In total, 18 industries within the manufacturing sector are examined using annual data.

275 K. Nomura and T. Amano, "Labour Productivity and Quality Change in Singapore: Achievements in 1974–2011 and Prospects for the Next Two Decades", KEO Discussion Paper No. 129 (2012), pp. 6–11.

276 The higher educational attainment of the labour force and work experience were the main causes of labour quality improvement.

a vindication of the earlier findings of Young and Krugman, TFP growth detracted from output growth by declining 0.3 per cent on average every year. Looking at sub-periods, the study also confirmed that TFP growth was negative except for the late 1980s, the early 1990s and the 2000s.

The last piece of research on Singapore's historical sources of economic growth to be considered here is an article by MAS that focused on the later period, that between 1990 and 2009.[277] Noting the reliance of many sectors and industries on ICT, it explicitly appraised the impact of such investments in equipment and software. This type of investment contributed to GDP growth through capital deepening as well as to TFP by increasing firms' efficiency in combining labour and capital inputs. Like the other studies, the article also took account of investment in human capital by estimating the labour inputs of different worker groups classified by gender and education level. The measure of labour quality that resulted from this adjustment showed a significant rise after 2000 as the proportion of workers with a tertiary education rose and the influx of skilled foreign workers increased. From 1990 to 2009, non-ICT capital continued to be the most important determinant of GDP growth, followed by labour input and ICT capital. The residual TFP growth was positive over the whole period, although it decreased in the 2000s. There was also a shift in growth drivers from capital to labour during this period, attesting to better labour quality.

After all is said and done, what does one make of the productivity debate? Is it a case of "much ado about nothing" as argued by some analysts?[278] They pointed out that all the attempts to estimate TFP growth were methodologically flawed because underlying the calculations is the income accounting identity that relates factor payments to GDP. The differences in the empirical results were therefore the consequences of making wrong assumptions such as constant returns to scale and fixed factor shares in national income, or the result of data mismeasurement. At the common sense level, the critique of the above studies is that it makes no difference whether TFP growth is positive or negative, as long as the policies adopted by the Singapore government led to higher standards of living. This is especially the case with the heavy investment in housing stock, which might have been low yielding but had vastly improved living conditions. Moreover, efforts on the ground to promote productivity consciousness among workers had already begun in 1972 with the establishment of the National Productivity Board (NPB) and were continued with the setting up of the National Productivity Council in 1982. Thus, TFP investigations are an arcane project in which economists delight but may not matter much in practical terms.

Another way to view long-term economic growth in Singapore would be to assess it in terms of the idea of catching up to the advanced nations (Figure 28). Starting from a relatively backward position in 1965, the city-state was able to absorb and assimilate knowledge and technologies imported from the West which raised productivity and living standards. This catching-up process means that countries that lag behind can grow

---

[277] Monetary Authority of Singapore, "Sources of Singapore's Economic Growth 1990–2009", *Macroeconomic Review* (Singapore: Monetary Authority of Singapore, April 2010), pp. 66–73.

[278] J. Felipe and J. McCombie, "The Debate About the Sources of Growth in East Asia After a Quarter of a Century", ADB Economics Working Paper Series No. 512 (Manila: Asian Development Bank, 2017), pp. 7–10, 29–30.

at a rapid pace in the early stages of economic development. Furthermore, they can exploit the advantages of economic backwardness to leapfrog in a shorter time to the status of developed nations.[279] In Singapore's case, the process was achieved through a massive influx of foreign direct investment, which brought with it advanced technology embodied in capital equipment, modern production processes and managerial best practices. The technological gap as measured by the difference in productivity with the industrialised nations was initially wide. By 1999, however, Singapore had reached 79 per cent of the US level.[280] At $35,156, the country's per capita GDP in that year was one of the highest in the world. Therefore, it had effectively become a developed country, joining the ranks of the mature economies with a commensurately high living standard.[281] By virtue of this fact, economic growth had to slow down—a more intuitive explanation than diminishing returns.[282]

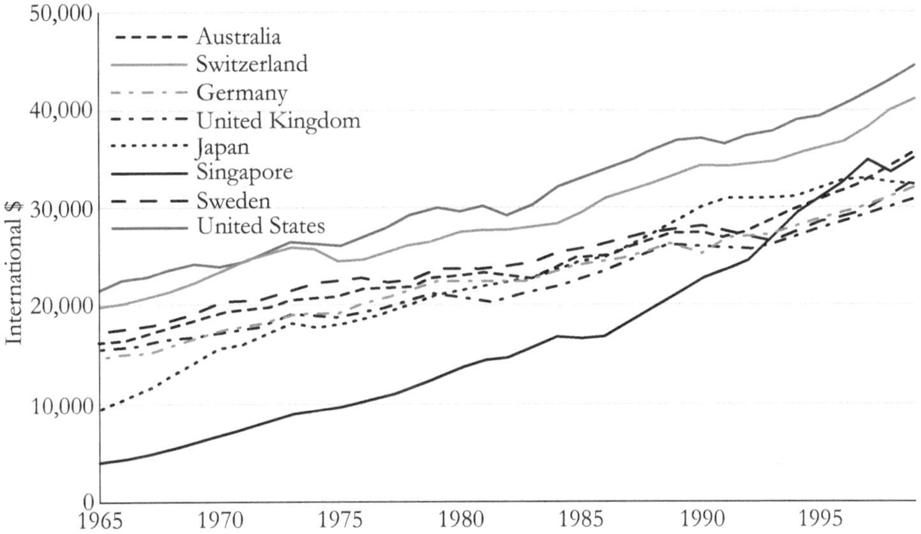

Figure 28. GDP Per Capita in Various Countries, 1965–99

Note: The international dollar is based on the exchange rates of countries with the US dollar after adjusting for purchasing power parity. An international dollar would buy in the cited country a comparable amount of goods and services a dollar would buy in the United States.

Source: Maddison Project Database, Version 2023.

---

279 Huff, *The Economic Growth of Singapore*, p. 301; A. Gershenkron, *Economic Backwardness in Historical Perspective: A Book of Essays* (Belknap Press of Harvard University Press, 1962).

280 The GDP per capita data were retrieved from the Maddison Project database and are in purchasing power parity terms.

281 This assertion is reinforced by the following statistics for the 1990s: apart from near universal ownership of televisions, refrigerators and washing machines, 65 per cent of households in Singapore owned air-conditioners and 77 per cent owned a video cassette recorder. *Singapore: The Last 10 Years*, Supplement to Prime Minister Goh Chok Tong's National Day Rally Speech 2001, p. 22.

282 B. Heitger, "Comparative Economic Growth: Catching Up in East Asia", *ASEAN Economic Bulletin* 10, 1 (1993): 68–9.

Nevertheless, not all developing countries catch up; technology transfer and adaptation can take place only if there are no barriers placed against them. Conversely, certain conducive factors or preconditions must be present as were in place with regard to export-oriented industrialisation in Singapore. Many were not economic in nature, such as good governance.[283] The most crucial ones—more so than tax incentives—probably related to a politically stable and business-friendly environment that attracted MNCs to produce in Singapore for the world market.[284] Even as the inflow of foreign investment facilitated technological diffusion from abroad and resulted in learning effects, higher demand for workers led to a fall in the unemployment rate and wage increases across the board. At the same time, the technologies brought by the MNCs spurred capital accumulation. As wages and the amount of capital per worker rose, Singapore found its relative comparative advantage shifting to the production of higher value-added goods, which was part and parcel of the process of catching up with the industrialised countries.

The other receptive factors pertain to the labour force and physical infrastructure. Foreign investors were willing to come to Singapore in the first place because of a hardworking and cooperative workforce. Over the years, the increase in the average number of years of schooling of the population and the acquisition of higher skills enabled workers to perform progressively more sophisticated tasks. This in turn was due in no small measure to the government's heavy investments in education and manpower training. Finally, companies that set up bases in Singapore were partly induced to do so by the excellent transport and communications infrastructure, as testified to by the port, airport, roads and extensive telecommunications links with the world.

[283] Tilak Abeysinghe, "Lessons of Singapore's Development for Other Developing Economies", *The Singapore Economic Review* 60, 3 (2015): 155029-3–155029-5, 155029-6–155029-8.

[284] Hoon Hian Teck, *Economic Dynamism, Openness, and Inclusion* (Singapore: World Scientific, 2019), pp. 43–6, 49–51, 57–8, 76, 78–9, 92–4, 101–4.

Chapter 13 Global City, 2000–Present

This chapter brings the narrative on the modern period to a close by reviewing economic developments in the new millennium. Under the stewardship of its third Prime Minister, Lee Hsien Loong, Singapore's ambitious goal was to be a "global city". But in fact, in the sense of being integrated into the international economy through trade and investment, Singapore had been such a global city since Raffles founded the settlement. However, the new era differs from the colonial period, with unprecedented globalisation, the rise of China, the Digital Revolution and a skill-intensive bias to jobs. As a global city, Singapore had to transit from investment-driven economic development in the earlier period to an innovation-driven economy. In this fast-changing environment, domestic economic volatility heightened as the nation confronted more frequent and deeper recessions, financial crises and epidemics. Despite these setbacks, Singapore achieved its objective of becoming a global city, even if new economic and social challenges appeared. A key preoccupation of policymakers in this changed world was the worsening of income distribution and poverty, compelling them to take remedial measures.

Singapore: The Global City

Already in 1972, Singapore was imagined as a "global city" by S. Rajaratnam, the nation's Foreign Minister.[1] This meant that the country needed to expand its political and economic horizons to encompass the whole world so that it could overcome the constraints of its immediate geography, thus by-passing its regional trading partners and escaping from its traditional hinterland. The term was also construed in terms of the small city-state forging economic linkages with the rest of the world.[2] This attempt to attain global reach was motivated by the desire to articulate Singapore into, benefit from, and achieve security through participation in the global economy.[3] Indeed, Singapore's economic success since

[1] *The Straits Times*, 7 Feb. 1972, 6 Feb. 2012.

[2] M. Leifer, "The Conduct of Foreign Policy", in *Management of Success*, ed. Sandhu and Wheatley, p. 969; K.S. Sandhu and P. Wheatley, "Challenges of Success", in *Management of Success*, ed. Sandhu and Wheatley, p. 1068.

[3] Henry Yeung Wai-Chung, "Globalising Singapore: One Global City, Global Production Networks and the Developmental State", in *Singapore Perspectives 2010*, ed. Tarn Tan How (Singapore: World Scientific, 2010), pp. 109–10.

independence and its developmental trajectory present the epitome of global city status, if one views such a city as a place in which "a quite disproportionate part" of the world's business and value creation is conducted.[4] Global cities like Singapore are therefore key nodal points in the international economy, sites where large flows of capital, labour and technology come together.

In more recent times, the aspiration to be a global city can be traced to a document which laid out the state's economic plan for Singapore with a 15-year timeframe—the report of the Economic Review Committee (ERC) issued in 2003, with the subtitle "Towards A Dynamic Global City".[5] The chief stated priority for becoming a globally connected city was to expand external ties with both the developed economies and new growth engines like China and India.[6] Singapore companies were exhorted to tap the opportunities presented by these two countries through increased trade and investment links. Furthermore, the nation needed to increase the number of Free Trade Agreements (FTAs) with its current and potential trade partners. Although it continued to support multilateral initiatives, bilateral FTAs were Singapore's preferred trade strategy for boosting the country's international trade after the World Trade Organisation (WTO) round of trade negotiations in 1999 failed to secure agreement from participating countries.[7] A further motivation was frustration over the slow progress in forming an ASEAN Free Trade Area (AFTA), an ambitious regional tariff liberalisation scheme by Southeast Asian countries that was launched in 1992.[8] Hence, Singapore's FTAs are the 21st century embodiment of the free trade principle it had upheld for two centuries.

The FTA initiative was given a huge fillip by the conclusion of the landmark Singapore–US FTA in 2004, the first for an Asian country.[9] Importantly, reductions of tariffs by the United States included the exports of electronics products, chemicals and precision engineering products not only from Singapore but also those produced in the Riau Archipelago, which had become for the city-state an offshore components source in the Growth Triangle.[10] In return for access to the American market, Singapore had to open its service industries such as banking and legal services. By 2023, the country had signed a total of 27 bilateral and regional FTAs, including with key trading partners such as the European Union, Japan and China, and extending to South Korea, India, Australia and

---

[4] Peter Hall, quoted in N. Oswin, *Global City Futures: Desire and Development in Singapore* (The University of Georgia Press, 2019), p. 6; *The Straits Times*, 31 May 2014.

[5] *The Straits Times Weekly Overseas Edition*, 8 Dec. 2001; *The Straits Times*, 7 Feb. 2003; *Today*, 8 Feb. 2003.

[6] *New Challenges, Fresh Goals—Towards A Dynamic Global City* (Singapore: Ministry of Trade and Industry, 2003), pp. 51–2.

[7] Peebles and Wilson, *Economic Growth and Development*, pp. 195–7, 199–200.

[8] *The Straits Times*, 28 Jan. 1992; *The Business Times*, 20 July 1992, 11 Dec. 1995; *Today*, 4 Jan. 2003.

[9] *Today*, 16 Jan. 2003; *The New Paper*, 7 May 2003.

[10] Chia Siow Yue, "Singapore", in *Asia's Free Trade Agreements: How Is Business Responding?*, ed. M. Kawai and G. Widnaraja (Cheltenham: Edward Elgar, 2011), pp. 163–4; Kwa, Heng and Tan, *Singapore: A 700-Year History*, p. 210; *The Business Times*, 7 Feb. 2003.

New Zealand.[11] In the region, the ASEAN Economic Community (AEC) that succeeded AFTA was conceived with the intention to achieve a free flow of goods, services and investment.[12] While this did not fully materialise, its coming into being in 2015 benefitted services exporters through reduced barriers to services trade, the liberalisation of more service sectors and an increase in foreign equity limits.

In 2020, Singapore signed the Regional Comprehensive Economic Partnership (RCEP) agreement, the world's largest FTA, that covers a bloc of 15 nations in the Asia-Pacific region and produces 30 per cent of global output.[13] It built on existing free trade deals among members and would ease trade in goods and services, facilitate the flow of foreign investments, and enhance protection in areas such as e-commerce and intellectual property.[14] Apart from the ASEAN countries, the agreement brought together as a group the key Asian economies of China, Japan and Korea as well as Australia and New Zealand. The countries in East Asia had assumed a new importance for Singapore as the direction of its trade altered in favour of them. In 2013, trade with China, Hong Kong and Japan amounted to 28 per cent of the total, surpassing the 20.8 per cent with the Western economies, while the ASEAN economies accounted for 26.4 per cent.[15] In that year, the share of FTA partners in domestic exports was 62.1 per cent.

Singapore's primary motivation in signing FTAs was economic. Apart from preferential access to markets and reinforcement of its status as a regional services hub, an additional benefit to the country from the agreements is the legal protection given to its investments. However, the advantages in practice might be less than those indicated in some empirical studies because of the low utilisation of FTA tariff preferences. For example, although it was found that FTAs resulted in tariff savings of over $1.1 billion in 2010 for Singapore-based companies, this estimate did not take account of a utilisation rate of only 17 per cent.[16] Since Singapore's free trade policy allowed almost all goods, except for perfumes and alcoholic beverages, to enter the country duty-free, consumers had little to gain. However, the liberalisation of the service sector as a reciprocal condition for the FTAs did lead to more foreign providers, thereby increasing the range and quality of the domestic services available.

In the 2003 ERC report, the essence of the global city vision for Singapore was to turn it into an international hub for science, technology, finance, arts and education by capitalising on the island's advantageous location; in this light, global connections were

---

[11] Chia Siow Yue, "Globalization and Regionalisation: Singapore's Trade and FDI", *The Singapore Economic Review* 60, 3 (2015): 1550034-4–1550034-8; *The Straits Times*, 3 Nov. 2002; *The Business Times*, 25 Dec. 2002, 4 Dec. 2008; *Today*, 4 Aug. 2005.

[12] M.G. Plummer, *ASEAN Economic Integration: Trade, Foreign Investment, and Finance* (Singapore: World Scientific, 2019), pp. 22–3, 78–83; *Today*, 26 July 2012, 23 Nov. 2015; *The Straits Times*, 22 Nov. 2015, 31 Dec. 2015.

[13] *Today*, 16 Aug. 2014, 7 Feb. 2017.

[14] *The Straits Times*, 16 Nov. 2020; *The Business Times*, 16 Nov. 2020.

[15] Chia, "Globalization and Regionalisation", pp. 155034-10–155034-11, 155034-13–155034-14.

[16] "Do Trade Agreements Matter? Evaluating the Impact of FTAs on Singapore's Domestic Exports of Goods", *Economic Survey of Singapore Second Quarter 2011* (Singapore: Ministry of Trade and Industry).

deemed to be the key to progress.[17] Moreover, there was a need to remake the city-state into a vibrant, cosmopolitan hub filled with "buzz", akin to London and New York, and into one of the best places in the world to live and work.[18] Towards this objective, Singapore was cultivated as a global city for the arts with the opening of the Esplanade-Theatres by the Bay in 2002 and the National Art Gallery at the former City Hall and Supreme Court buildings in 2015. The vision of the island as a "City in a Garden" that evolved from the earlier "Garden City" concept was realised with the creation of the Gardens at the Bay in 2011.[19] Other iconic buildings that enhanced the city's architectural appeal are the HDB's seven 50-storey tower residential development, the Pinnacle@Duxton (2009) in Tanjong Pagar and the iconic Marina Bay Sands hotel complex (2010). Significant changes were made to the urban landscape, including notably the new downtown financial hub.[20]

At the core of the ERC's post-industrial vision was an innovation-based growth strategy for Singapore that focused on investments in R&D and the creation of new technologies. This called for a new type of worker and a critical mass of creative talent, which the government sought to obtain both domestically and through an open-arms "foreign talent" policy designed to attract highly skilled professionals and entrepreneurs in all fields to work in Singapore.[21] At the same time, funding for basic research at the universities and public research institutions was significantly increased.[22] The ERC also recommended that both the corporate and highest marginal personal income tax rates be lowered to 20 per cent to compete with other cities for foreign investment and global talent, which were necessary for Singapore to be a hub of enterprise and innovation.[23] The recommendation was implemented by the government and for good measure, the overseas earnings of companies in Singapore were exempted from tax.[24]

The committee also stressed the need to promote an entrepreneurial mindset in Singaporeans, especially among the young, to take advantage of new global markets, ideas and businesses. It therefore tried to address a long-standing problem in Singapore—the dearth of entrepreneurship, which had been partly blamed on the secure jobs offered by

---

17 I.P. Austin, "Singapore as a 'Global City': Governance in a Challenging International Environment", in *A New Paradigm for International Business, Proceedings of the Conference on Free Trade Agreements and Regional Integration in East Asia*, ed. Hadrian Geri Djajadikerta and Zhang Zhaoyong (Singapore: Springer, 2015), p. 173; N. Oswin and Brenda S.A. Yeoh, "Introduction: Mobile City Singapore", *Mobilities* 5, 2 (2010): 168.

18 Tan, *A Very Short History*, p. 150; *Today*, 4 Feb. 2010.

19 Lim Tin Seng, "From Botanic Gardens to Gardens by the Bay: Singapore's Experience in Becoming a Garden City", *BiblioAsia* 8, 2 (2012): 24–31.

20 Ching Tuen Yee and Benjamin Ng, "Realising the Marina Bay Vision", *Skyline* (July–August 2008): pp. 16–18.

21 Tan and Bhaskaran, "The Role of the State", pp. 1550030-17–1550030-18; *The Straits Times*, 21 Mar. 1999.

22 Winston T.H. Koh, "Singapore's Transition to Innovation-based Economic Growth: Infrastructure, Institutions and Government's Role", *R&D Management* 36, 2 (2006): 144.

23 *New Challenges, Fresh Goals*, pp. 63, 65–6, 67, 117, 123, 125–6, 127–8, 129.

24 Low, "Fiscal Policy", pp. 7–8.

the MNCs and GLCs.[25] The Ministry of Education played its part in this endeavour by realigning the focus of education and revising the school curriculum to develop students' creativity and critical thinking.[26] As the state's pervasive role in the economy could also have stifled the entrepreneurial spirit, the ERC called for less government intervention, just like the Economic Committee had done in the 1980s. In the event, a coordinated liberalisation in business regulations across different government agencies was undertaken.[27] To fuel entrepreneurship, there was a need to develop different types of risk capital, for example venture funds, cash-flow financing and private equity. A first step had been taken in 1999 when the government established a US$1 billion fund to attract venture capital companies to Singapore.

The ERC envisaged that Singapore would play its roles both as a host country for MNCs, in order to upgrade to higher value-added activities, and as a platform for startup companies to launch their products. In 2015, the country hosted over 7,000 MNCs, with a total employment of 110,000 expatriates; there were also more than 5,000 startups in the technology sector.[28] Local firms were expected to become major international players in their respective business lines; to facilitate this, GLCs which had succeeded in overseas markets could lead clusters of SMEs to venture abroad. With the help of government assistance schemes, these suggestions bore fruit, as seen in the fact that in 2009, about two-thirds of all SMEs had an overseas presence.[29] To encourage the formation of startups, the nexus between academia and technology-based companies needed to be strengthened and the regulatory landscape had to be revamped. In this connection, the ERC made the novel recommendation of enacting a competition framework and law to prevent price fixing and other cartel practices by firms; this framework was subsequently implemented through the establishment of the Competition Commission of Singapore in 2005.[30] By the 2010s, it was projected, Singapore would be a knowledge-based and innovation-driven economy, with a society that was both creative and entrepreneurial.

Echoing the economic committees that came before it, the ERC stated categorically its intention to preserve the manufacturing sector as a growth driver and suggested that Singapore focus on and strengthen the four key pillars of electronics, chemicals, precision and transport engineering, and biomedical sciences.[31] In 1999, a ten-year plan named Industry 21 had set as its goals for manufacturing activities to contribute a quarter of

[25] T.K. Ti and Edward S.W. Ti, *Singapore and Asia: Celebrating Globalisation and an Emerging Postmodern Asian Civilisation* (Xlibris, 2012), p. 186.

[26] Tan and Bhaskaran, "The Role of the State", p. 1550030-15.

[27] Koh, "Singapore's Transition to Innovation-based Economic Growth", p. 157.

[28] Sarah Cheah, Ho Yuen Ping and Philip Lim, "Role of Public Science in Fostering the Innovation and Startup Ecosystem in Singapore", *Asian Research Policy* 7, 1 (2016): 79; *Living in Singapore: Key Information for Expatriates Living or Relocating to Singapore* (Singapore: Ministry of Manpower, 2015).

[29] Ti and Ti, *Singapore and Asia*, pp. 187, 189.

[30] *The Straits Times*, 6 Apr. 2005, 30 July 2005. The commission was renamed the Competition and Consumer Commission of Singapore in 2018.

[31] *New Challenges, Fresh Goals*, pp. 56–8, 66; *The Business Times*, 7 Feb. 2003.

GDP, increasing the share of manufacturing services and creating 15,000 jobs each year.[32] There would be no hollowing out of industry, as had happened in Hong Kong.[33] With respect to the type of industries, the value proposition was that Singapore would strive to be a global leader in high value-added manufacturing activities with an emphasis on technology, innovation and capabilities. Potential new growth niches were industrial IT, micro-electromechanical systems, nanotechnology, photonics and niche engineering.[34] Apart from continuing to rely on MNCs for access to technology, management know-how and markets, Singapore should aim to be a creator of new products through R&D. A good way to do this was by building cluster-focused infrastructure as in Jurong Island and Biopolis, since it would lead to economies of scale and attract agglomerations of firms in new industries. In 2006, the National Research Foundation (NRF), a sister body of A*STAR, was established with the mission of funding strategic initiatives, building R&D capabilities by nurturing local and international research talent, and commercialising ideas and inventions.[35] In 2003, A*STAR launched a PhD scholarship scheme to expand the local pool of Singaporeans who could conduct high-end research.[36]

True to the intention of the ERC, the manufacturing sector in Singapore continued to grow over the 2000s and 2010s at 4.8 per cent and 5.7 per cent per annum, respectively. In 2010, manufacturing accounted for 21 per cent of GDP and the ratio stayed more or less the same in 2020. However, the employment share fell to 9.6 per cent in the later year. An upgrading of production took place in several industries alongside an increase in the number of research scientists and engineers from 40 per 10,000 of the labour force in 1993 to 73 in 2002, about half of whom belonged to the private sector.[37] After the NRF's budget for research was doubled to $13 billion, expenditure on R&D as a proportion of GDP reached 3 per cent in 2010, with about two-thirds being spent by private firms.[38] In semiconductors, new products such as NAND flash and DRAMs were manufactured, thereby increasing their importance in the manufacturing sector; in the data storage segment, the production of disk drives made way for high-end server drives and disk media.[39] The precision engineering industry diversified into the production of modules, components, machinery, industrial equipment and plastic components. In transport engineering, marine and offshore activities (ship repair, shipbuilding and oil rig fabrication) and aerospace overhaul (aircraft maintenance and repair) contributed 10–15 per cent of

---

32 *The New Paper*, 13 June 1998; *The Straits Times Weekly Overseas Edition*, 20 June 1998; *The Straits Times*, 21 Jan. 1999. The broader vision of Industry 21 was to make Singapore a vibrant hub of knowledge-driven industries in both manufacturing and services, with the ICT and media sectors providing support.

33 *The Straits Times*, 19 Oct. 2002.

34 *New Challenges, Fresh Goals*, pp. 138–40, 144, 151, 154–7.

35 Woon Kin Chung and Loo Ya Lee, *50 Years of Singapore's Productivity Drive* (Singapore: World Scientific, 2018), pp. 272–3; *Today*, 18 Jan. 2006.

36 Goh Chor Boon, *From Traders to Innovators: Science and Technology in Singapore Since 1965* (Singapore: ISEAS–Yusof Ishak Institute, 2016), p. 117.

37 *Economic Survey of Singapore*, various years (Singapore: Ministry of Trade and Industry).

38 Ti and Ti, *Singapore and Asia*, pp. 183, 190–1; "City State Hopes Research Cash Will Buy Global Status", *Nature* 442 (13 July 2006): 118–9.

39 "Singapore's Electronics Cluster", *Economic Survey of Singapore First Quarter 2008* (Singapore: Ministry of Trade and Industry), p. 9; *Today*, 8 Nov. 2006, 22 Apr. 2011.

manufacturing output. In 2010, the aerospace sector received a significant boost when Rolls-Royce opened a $700 million facility at the Seletar Aerospace Hub to make engine fan blades for large aircraft, the first outside the United Kingdom; subsequently, the plant also built aircraft engines.[40] Employment in the biomedical manufacturing industry encompassing pharmaceuticals, medical devices and biotechnology more than doubled from 6,000 in 2000 to 13,000 in 2009.[41] Singapore was also successful in attracting drug companies to set up biologics production plants on the island.[42]

During the 2010s, the major innovation in Singapore's manufacturing sector was the advent of "factoryless" goods producing firms, an extreme form of the international fragmentation of production activities.[43] These are firms that do not directly engage in manufacturing but nonetheless perform pre-production activities of R&D, design and engineering. The manufacturing process itself is outsourced or offshored to contract manufacturers. Two such well-known companies in Singapore are Dyson and Apple, though factoryless companies are more widely represented in the semiconductor industry as "fabless" firms that engaged in the design of chips and outsourced production to other firms.[44] They provided mostly skilled jobs and had higher productivity than the average manufacturing firm. Furthermore, they stimulated the growth of local companies by subcontracting production to foundries and assembly and testing firms, and post-production tasks like marketing, logistics and distribution to service firms.

With regard to the service sector, the ERC reiterated that established industries such as financial and business services, international trading, ICT, logistics and tourism as well as services like education, healthcare and lifestyle activities should be promoted further. All of these are exportable and can leverage the growing size of the regional and global markets. Given its location and excellent physical infrastructure, Singapore could also supply manufacturing-related and headquarters services to the Asian region, an idea that was first mooted in the late 1980s. The committee noted the growing affluence of consumers in that region, which would provide an important source of demand. Unlike in manufacturing, however, there were more regulatory impediments in the service sector—particularly in healthcare and education—that ought to be reviewed and removed. Singapore should also market its services overseas more aggressively and build up its branding as a world-class service hub. The manufacturing and service sectors were expected to be more interdependent, knowledge-based and research-intensive in the new millennium. This "servicisation" of manufacturing was envisaged to speed up in new growth areas such as advanced manufacturing and the Internet of Things (IoT).

---

40 *The Straits Times*, 29 July 2009; *Today*, 7 Sept. 2012. In 2016, aircraft engine maker Pratt Whitney also opened a manufacturing plant, the first outside the United States. *The Straits Times*, 1 Feb. 2013; *The Business Times*, 16 Feb. 2016.

41 Goh, *From Traders to Innovators*, p. 118.

42 Biologics companies use living organisms and plants to produce pharmaceuticals and biomaterials.

43 A.B. Bernard and T.C. Fort, "Factoryless Goods Producing Firms", *The American Economic Review, Papers & Proceedings* 105, 5 (2015): 518–9.

44 "Economic Contribution of Factoryless Goods Producing Firms in Singapore", *Economic Survey of Singapore Second Quarter 2018* (Singapore: Ministry of Trade and Industry), pp. 36, 37–8; *Today*, 2 July 2014. Dyson built a facility in Singapore to manufacture next generation batteries and Apple partnered with the Singapore government and a local company to build solar energy systems.

Due to these interlinkages, the advances in manufacturing facilitated steady growth in the service sector, averaging 6.1 per cent per annum in the first decade of the new century and 5.1 per cent in the second.[45] Financial services performed especially well with an annual rate of expansion of 8.2 per cent before the Global Financial Crisis of 2008–09 and 7.8 per cent after it. The continued development of these services began with wide-ranging reforms instituted by MAS starting in 1997 in banking supervision, the consolidation of local banks and the liberalisation of foreign competition, the last partly to fulfil FTA obligations.[46] Financial regulation shifted from a stringent "one-size-fits-all" approach to systemic risk-focused supervision with a lighter touch, thus allowing individual banks to take calculated risks and to provide new, innovative financial products.[47] In commercial banking, a plan was formulated to divest the non-core assets of local banks, strengthen their corporate governance and encourage them to merge, resulting in the acquisition of POSB by DBS in 1998 and the takeover of Overseas Union Bank by the United Overseas Bank in 2001.[48] Although the acquired banks had been profitable, they were less efficient because they were shielded from foreign competition; after the consolidation wave, only three local banks remained from the original seven. POSB was also to lose its privileges of tax-free interest and government guarantee.

In 1999, MAS began a five-year process of banking liberalisation by creating a new category, "Qualifying Full Bank", for foreign banks. This designation gave them access to the domestic retail banking sector through the opening of more branches and installation of automated teller machines (ATMs).[49] An important consideration in the liberalisation exercise was to ensure the continued survival of the local banks by allowing them sufficient time to adjust to the new competition. Following liberalisation, there were in 2005 about 700 local and foreign financial institutions in Singapore offering a wide range of financial services and products.[50] They included firms that traded in the securities and futures markets, the latter activity beginning in 1984 with the establishment of the Singapore International Monetary Exchange (SIMEX), thus pioneering futures trading in Asia. The exchange was linked to the Chicago Mercantile Exchange to provide a global round-the-clock futures trading platform; it initially traded in Eurodollar and Euroyen interest rate

---

45 For every $1 million of value-added generated in the manufacturing sector, $0.29 million was produced in the service sector, particularly in professional services. "Manufacturing and Services in Singapore's Economy: Twin Engines of Growth and Their Asymmetric Dependencies", *Economic Survey of Singapore Third Quarter 2017* (Singapore: Ministry of Trade and Industry), p. 52.

46 *The Business Times*, 16 Apr. 1999, 5 June 2001; *The New Paper*, 9 May 1999; *The Straits Times*, 8 July 1999; *Today*, 12 Oct. 2004.

47 Monetary Authority of Singapore, *Sustaining Stability, Serving Singapore*, pp. 119–22, 166–71.

48 Peebles and Wilson, *Economic Growth and Development*, p. 117; Tan Chwee Huat, *Financial Services and Wealth Management in Singapore* (Singapore: Ridge Books, 2011), pp. 6–7; *The Straits Times*, 8 Aug. 1998, 31 Dec. 2001, 10 May 2002; *The Business Times*, 16 Nov. 1998, 27 Mar. 1999, 17 June 2002.

49 Ngiam Kee Jin, "Financial Sector Reforms in Singapore", in *The International Handbook on Financial Reform*, ed. M.J.B. Hall (Cheltenham: Edward Elgar, 2003), pp. 192, 198–201, 202–3; *The Straits Times*, 3 Aug. 2002; *The Business Times*, 18 June 2004. The ATMs first made their appearance in 1979. Liew and Wilson, *A History of Money*, pp. 188–90.

50 Tan Chwee Huat, *Financial Markets and Institutions in Singapore*, 11th Edition (Singapore: Singapore University Press, 2005), pp. 27, 28, 244, 248, 249–50.

futures, stock index futures of Asian countries, and gold futures.[51] The Stock Exchange of Singapore (SES) was gradually opened to foreign participation in the 1990s and secondary listing of foreign shares was introduced. This followed the establishment in 1987, at the SES, of a second board, called Sesdaq, for the listing and trading of shares in smaller local companies.[52] In 1999, SIMEX was merged with SES to become the Singapore Exchange (SGX) and with this move, a wider choice of derivative products was traded, including not only Singapore stock index and interest rate futures but also options.[53] Following the commodity exchange established in 1992 to trade in rubber futures contracts, the Singapore Mercantile Exchange (SMX) was opened in 2010 to deal in futures for a wide range of commodities such as crude oil, precious metals, agricultural products and currencies.[54]

Singapore emerged as the premier wealth management centre of Asia—the "Zürich of the East"—after MAS introduced in the 1990s incentives for global asset management companies to operate in the city and permitted the liberal immigration of foreign personnel.[55] To give the industry a head start, MAS and GIC placed out some of their funds for investment by the companies.[56] Private banks, boutique fund managers and hedge funds sprouted up to serve the financial needs of the rising number of high net worth individuals in the Asia-Pacific region. From $150 billion in 1998, the amount of funds managed in Singapore increased to $4.7 trillion in 2020.[57] Well-known asset managers like BlackRock, Fidelity International, Schroders, BNP Paribas and Fullerton are among the 962 fund managers with offices in Singapore. Nearly four-fifths of funds were sourced from outside Singapore while two-thirds were invested in countries in the Asia Pacific. Furthermore, the super-rich in Asia and elsewhere were given incentives to settle in Singapore and make it their playground. A residential enclave (Sentosa Cove) was created on Sentosa island to cater for the housing and leisure of these wealthy individuals.[58]

The modern wholesale trade sector, with its roots in the erstwhile entrepôt trade, expanded with renewed vigour starting from 2000. As the larger part of the wholesale and retail trade sector, it grew by 8.7 per cent per annum before the 2008–09 recession, the fastest rate among all sectors of the economy, and accounted for 17 per cent of GDP and about 250,000 mostly skilled jobs.[59] These outcomes were facilitated by the large number of international trading companies that were incentivised to set up operations in Singapore, the successors to the agency houses of old.[60] Another major development that imparted a

---

[51] Peebles and Wilson, *Economic Growth and Development*, p. 115; *Singapore Monitor*, 25 Jan. 1984; *The Business Times*, 20 June 1984; *The Straits Times*, 30 Aug. 1984.

[52] *The Straits Times*, 12 Mar. 1987.

[53] *The Business Times*, 12 Nov. 1998, 8 July 1999; *The Straits Times*, 25 Sept. 1999.

[54] Tan Chwee Huat, *Financial Services*, pp. 149–51, 222–3; *The Business Times*, 16 June 2010.

[55] Austin, "Singapore as a 'Global City'", pp. 183–4; *The Business Times*, 19 Nov. 2005; *Today*, 22 June 2011; *The Straits Times*, 12 Mar. 2013.

[56] Monetary Authority of Singapore, *Sustaining Stability, Serving Singapore*, pp. 161–3.

[57] *2020 Singapore Asset Management Survey* (Singapore: Monetary Authority of Singapore), pp. 2–4, 7.

[58] Tan, *A Very Short History*, pp. 151, 152.

[59] "Overview of Singapore's Wholesale Trade Sector", *Economic Survey of Singapore 2008* (Singapore: Ministry of Trade and Industry), pp. 51, 52–4.

[60] *The Straits Times*, 6 July 1995; *The Business Times*, 18 Aug. 2003.

stimulus to the sector was China's entry into the WTO in 2001, which led to a flourishing intraregional trade in electronics components.[61] In this supply chain, Singapore served as a node for dispatching parts and components produced in Southeast Asia to factories in the Pearl River Delta in China for assembly, thus once again integrating the economies of these two regions, as during the 14th century. These re-exports as well as offshore trade were responsible for the rapid growth seen in the wholesale sector.[62] The products were diversified, although they were dominated by industrial and construction equipment, computers, telecommunications and office equipment, petroleum and related products, and chemical products. The importance of oil products and electronics could be attributed to Singapore's position as a global oil trading centre and electronics distribution hub, respectively. Major companies in these two industries such as Shell, Petrobras, Glencore, Seagate, Texas Instruments, Qualcomm, Dell and Infineon had set up regional trading and distribution bases in the city.

Fuelled by new technologies and the full liberalisation of the telecommunications industry which resulted in lower costs of mobile subscriptions and cheaper international phone call rates, the transport and communications sector grew at a pace of 5.1 per cent per annum during the non-recession years from 2000 to 2020 (that is, excluding 2008–09).[63] Mobile phone subscriptions multiplied rapidly to reach 1.4 per person in 2010 and Internet broadband subscriptions rose to 1.9 per household. Driven by strong demand from Asia, the export of IT and communications services increased at an even faster pace owing partly to the presence of technology giants such as Google, Microsoft and Amazon that had made Singapore their Asia-Pacific headquarters. In 2010, the IT industry drew revenue of $70 billion, of which two-thirds were generated outside of the country.[64] The expansion was stimulated by an official blueprint announced in 2000 to develop a vibrant ICT industry and grow e-commerce, resulting in the latter increasing at an annual rate of 20 per cent in the three-year period 2016–18.[65] Singapore companies like Lazada and Shopee took advantage of government inducements to set up regional e-commerce trading centres in the city-state.[66]

The digital economy, encompassing the production and consumption of products and services as well as business activities that are enabled by digital technologies, became pervasive.[67] By the mid-2010s, consumers were increasingly performing more of their shopping and financial transactions online while a bigger share of enterprises were

---

[61] "Overview of Singapore's Wholesale Trade Sector", *Economic Survey of Singapore First Quarter 2011* (Singapore: Ministry of Trade and Industry), pp. 12, 13, 14, 15–17.

[62] Offshore trade is defined as transactions in which the goods are not exported from or imported into Singapore.

[63] "The Information & Communications Sector—Trends, Drivers and Opportunities", *Economic Survey of Singapore Second Quarter 2009* (Singapore: Ministry of Trade and Industry), pp. 13–18.

[64] Tsui-Auch, Chia and Liu, "Putting Singapore", p. 195.

[65] "Trends in E-commerce in the Services Sector", *Economic Survey of Singapore 2019* (Singapore: Ministry of Trade and Industry), pp. 81, 86.

[66] Chia, "Singapore: Towards a Knowledge-based Economy", p. 190; *The Business Times*, 4 June 2014; *The Straits Times*, 3 Sept. 2019, 11 Apr. 2022.

[67] "The Digital Economy in Singapore", *Economic Survey of Singapore Third Quarter 2017* (Singapore: Ministry of Trade and Industry), pp. 18–20.

adopting digital tools such as mobile services, e-payment systems and cloud services in their business. Data centres also proliferated as firms' data storage requirements increased. The government therefore rolled out the "Smart Nation" initiative in 2014 to reinforce these trends by encouraging Singaporeans to leverage digital technologies to transform their lives.[68] It also turned its attention to promoting interactive digital media, with the intention of making Singapore a testbed for new products. These developments resulted in the infocommunications and media industry contributing 8.3 per cent to GDP in 2015 and 200,000 workers to employment.

In sea transport, Singapore became the busiest port in the world in terms of shipping tonnage and was consistently ranked as the best seaport in Asia.[69] The number of vessels calling at the harbour in a year came close to the 150,000 mark as shippers flocked to the city in response to incentives offered by the government to make it an international maritime centre. In 2000, the gross tonnage of these ships was over 900 million tonnes and they carried more than 300 million tonnes of cargo.[70] As for air transport, a free trade Airport Logistics Park was officially opened in 2003, thereby entrenching Singapore's status as a logistics and air cargo hub.[71] The new Terminal 3 at the internationally acclaimed Changi Airport commenced operations in early 2008; passenger traffic had hit a record 36.7 million people in the previous year.[72] In 2007, the airport had connections to over 50 countries and close to 200 capital cities, and Singapore welcomed 10.3 million visitors, who spent $13.8 billion in total. About three-quarters of them originated from Asia, with Indonesia, China and Malaysia topping the list.

Singapore was ranked third in the world as a venue for convening international conferences and the top in Asia.[73] The inauguration in the city centre of Formula One's first night race against the backdrop of a lit-up skyline in 2008 gave business and leisure travel a further boost.[74] In 2010, two world-class casinos euphemistically labelled "integrated resorts" were opened in downtown Singapore and the recreational island of Sentosa respectively to cater to the tourist traffic, particularly from China.[75] Apart from high-end shopping, these resorts featured a wide array of amenities and attractions such as celebrity chef restaurants, Universal Studios and a theatre.[76] Between them, 22,000 new jobs were created but to minimise the adverse social impact of gambling on the domestic population, Singaporeans are charged a fee for each visit to the casinos. In 2011, a huge cruise terminal in Marina South was constructed and in 2019, a sprawling shopping

[68] *The Business Times*, 3 June 2005, 25 Nov. 2014; *The Straits Times*, 21 Feb. 2017, 7 Mar. 2017.

[69] *Economic Survey of Singapore*, various years (Singapore: Ministry of Trade and Industry); *The Straits Times*, 5 Nov. 2000; *Today*, 16 Apr. 2005, 11 Jan. 2008.

[70] Chia and Lim, "Singapore: A Regional Hub in ICT", p. 269.

[71] *The Business Times*, 21 Mar. 2003.

[72] *Today*, 26 Oct. 2007; *The Straits Times*, 10 Oct. 2008; *The Business Times*, 10 Oct. 2008.

[73] *Streats*, 24 June 2004; *The Business Times*, 1 Feb. 2008; *The Straits Times*, 22 May 2013.

[74] Ti and Ti, *Singapore and Asia*, pp. 228–9; Tan, *A Very Short History*, p. 150; *Today*, 12 Jan. 2007; *The Business Times*, 25 Sept. 2008, 27 Sept. 2008.

[75] *Today*, 31 Oct. 2008; *The Straits Times*, 12 Feb. 2009, 27 Apr. 2010; *The Business Times*, 6 Jan. 2010, 24 June 2010.

[76] "Integrated Resorts" (Singapore: Ministry of Trade and Industry, 2012).

mall at Changi Airport, Jewel, opened with 280 retail and dining outlets.[77] These new attractions and infrastructure helped to cement Singapore's reputation as a top tourist destination and duty-free port.[78] In the late 2000s, tourism accounted for 3–3.5 per cent of GDP and more than 100,000 jobs. Spending on accommodation, food, beverages and shopping was the most important contributor, rising by an overall 4 per cent on average during good years.

In the education field, measures were taken by the government to make Singapore an international education hub by opening new universities, expanding existing ones and providing incentives to foreign institutions to establish branch campuses in Singapore. For example, the Singapore Management University opened in 2000 and a fifth polytechnic was started in 2002.[79] Under the Global Schoolhouse scheme initiated by the EDB, foreign universities with teaching and research facilities attracted to Singapore included MIT, INSEAD, Johns Hopkins University and the University of Chicago Booth School of Business.[80] These institutions added to the significant number of foreign students at local universities. Collaborations with renowned foreign universities expanded diversity and quality—examples from the field of medical education were the NUS joint MD-PhD programme with Duke University in the United States and NTU's joint PhD degree with the Karolinska Institut in Sweden.[81] Funding for arts education by the state increased at world-class establishments such as LASALLE College of the Arts (a constituent of the University of the Arts from 2024), the pre-tertiary School of the Arts and the Yong Siew Toh Conservatory of Music at NUS, in addition to the existing Nanyang Academy of Fine Arts.[82] Even the sporting arena was not neglected, as could be seen by the construction of the Singapore Sports Centre (the new National Stadium) at Kallang and the Singapore Sports School.

In healthcare, specialised centres for the treatment of and research on eye, skin, heart, brain and cancer problems were established.[83] Although Singapore could not compete with Malaysia and Thailand as a regional medical hub in terms of costs, its selling point remains a reputation for offering state-of-the-art medical and surgical care. In 2004, more than 320,000 tourists came to Singapore for medical treatment. In the same year, the EDB, Singapore Tourism Board (the successor to the STPB) and International Enterprise Singapore (IE Singapore, the successor to the TDB and charged with enhancing international access for Singapore-based firms) launched Singapore Medicine, a joint initiative aimed at developing Singapore into a leading destination for healthcare services in the region.[84]

---

[77] *The Straits Times*, 5 Mar. 2012, 7 Mar. 2019, 11 Apr. 2019, 18 Oct. 2019; *The Business Times*, 8 June 2012.

[78] "The Contribution of Tourism to the Singapore Economy", *Economic Survey of Singapore 2010* (Singapore: Ministry of Trade and Industry), pp. 71–7.

[79] Turnbull, *History of Modern Singapore*, p. 364; *The Straits Times*, 20 Mar. 2002, 9 July 2002; *The New Paper*, 23 May 2015.

[80] Chia, "Singapore: Towards a Knowledge-based Economy", p. 188.

[81] *The New Paper*, 31 Jan. 2005; *Today*, 15 Apr. 2005; *The Straits Times*, 28 Sept. 2009.

[82] Ti and Ti, *Singapore and Asia*, pp. 252, 265–6, 275–6, 279.

[83] *The Straits Times*, 25 July 1997, 24 Jan. 2003; *The Business Times*, 27 Sept. 2005, 11 Nov. 2015.

[84] Lim Meng-Kin, "Transforming Singapore Health Care", p. 464.

Besides healthcare, the accumulated expertise gained in building and managing physical infrastructure in Singapore in areas such as housing, urban facilities, water recycling, seaport and airport operations and even e-government services was exported to other countries.[85] For instance, PSA Corporation operates numerous ports all over the world, Sembawang Shipyard opened yards in China and the Karimun Islands, and the water recycling conglomerate Hyflux exported its technology by building 1,000 plants in over 300 locations around the world.[86]

The above developments accounted for the robust growth of services exports from Singapore, which increased by 9.4 per cent a year during the 2010s and constituted about one-third of total exports.[87] Compared to merchandise exports, services exports generate more value-added for the economy due to their higher domestic content.[88] In 2013, exports of services were valued at $163 billion and imports were about the same, resulting in a balanced services trade account. The leading export items were transport, travel, financial services and business services, which accounted for 84 per cent of total services exports. Sea and air transport services rose by 8.1 per cent and 4 per cent per annum on average in the 2010s, respectively. Travel services expanded at the rate of 8.8 per cent per annum due to robust growth in tourist arrivals. Spurred partly by activities in the ADM, financial services exports grew at an annual rate of 11 per cent. Within the business services category, telecommunications, computer, information, professional and management consulting services expanded by over 16 per cent a year, in a reflection of Singapore's development as a global business hub. Health services expanded at a pace of 21.4 per cent while education services grew at an even faster rate of 31.1 per cent. The major imported services were transport and travel (reflecting outward tourism), charges for the use of intellectual property and business services. While the bulk of exports were to Southeast and East Asia, imports were to a large extent sourced from Europe and the United States (Table 16).

Given the expansions in both the manufacturing and service sectors, overall GDP grew by 5.4 per cent per annum in the 2000s and 5 per cent in the 2010s. While commendable, it is unusual for a developed country like Singapore to grow at such high rates. The anomaly is explained by a massive increase in employment, especially during the first of the two decades—precisely the contention of the productivity critics. Following that debate, the government had been quite serious about getting productivity up and had formed a statutory board in 1996, the Singapore Productivity and Standards Board (PSB), to do so, by merging the NPB and the Singapore Institute of Standards and Industrial Research (SISIR).[89] The aim was to achieve 2 per cent growth a year in TFP, a target it failed

---

85 *The Straits Times*, 2 May 2016.

86 Ti and Ti, *Singapore and Asia*, pp. 106–7, 187, 193, 195–6, 226, 249, 273–4; Perry, *Singapore*, p. 231; *The Business Times*, 2 Nov. 1988, 24 Jan. 2007; *The Straits Times*, 11 Jan. 1989, 27 Apr. 2007, 5 Nov. 2014, 27 Apr. 2015.

87 *Economic Survey of Singapore*, various years (Singapore: Ministry of Trade and Industry). The year 2019 was excluded from the growth rate calculation in view of the outbreak of the COVID-19 pandemic.

88 "Rising Contribution of Services Exports to the Singapore Economy", *Economic Survey of Singapore Second Quarter 2014* (Singapore: Ministry of Trade and Industry), pp. 13–14.

89 *The Business Times*, 31 Oct. 1995; *The Straits Times*, 6 Dec. 1995.

to achieve in the first decade of the new century with an increase of only 1.1 per cent.[90] Labour productivity growth was also relatively weak at 1.5 per cent per annum and even turned negative during the 2008–09 recession.

Table 16. Geographical Distribution of Singapore's Trade in Services, 2012

	Exports (%)	Imports (%)
Southeast and East Asia	44.5	31.3
East Asia	22.1	19.0
China and Hong Kong	11.4	9.5
Japan	6.7	5.5
South Korea	2.3	2.1
Taiwan	1.8	2.0
ASEAN	13.5	7.0
Malaysia	3.8	2.2
Indonesia	3.6	1.7
Thailand	2.8	1.2
India	3.8	2.6
Europe	23.8	27.6
United States	16.4	21.5

Source: Chia, "Globalization and Regionalisation", pp. 1550034-12–1550034-13.

Why was productivity growth low? One explanation could be because the government steered its focus to innovation and entrepreneurship. But the basic reason was the large intake of foreign workers in the 2000s. In the three-year period 2006 to 2008, foreign employment increased at an average rate of 18.4 per cent each year. As a consequence, the proportion of foreigners in the labour force—both white-collar and blue-collar workers—of 2.9 million persons rose to 35.2 per cent in 2009, or more than 1 million workers (including domestic helpers). On average, foreign labour increased by 1.6 per cent per annum during the decade, while employment of locals grew by 2.7 per cent; together, they accounted for three-quarters of economic growth.[91] In the four years from 2004 to 2007, GDP grew on average at an unsustainable rate of 7.6 per cent per year and the unemployment rate fell to 2.7 per cent in 2006 as the Singapore government pursued a growth maximisation policy.[92] The skilled foreigners were mostly employed as computer analysts, engineers, scientists, financial specialists and consultants, a large number of whom became permanent residents. Low-skilled foreign workers could be found in all the major economic sectors, with the highest concentration in the construction industry. In 2004, even mid-skilled migrant workers were allowed into Singapore as the government accommodated the short-term needs of businesses.

As stated previously, there had indeed been a long-standing policy of reducing the size of the foreign workforce, but when economic growth was strong and firms lobbied for more

---

[90] *The Business Times*, 27 Jan. 2010.

[91] Hui Weng Tat and Ruby Toh, *Growth with Equity in Singapore: Challenges and Prospects*, Conditions of Work and Employment Series No. 48 (Geneva: International Labour Office, 2014), pp. 1, 3, 5.

[92] Austin, "Singapore as a 'Global City'", pp. 179–80.

workers, the government backtracked on its policy.[93] Deviations from the stated policy were often justified by extraneous reasons, like rising costs amidst increasing international competition. The government also claimed that foreigners complemented the local workforce and helped Singaporeans to keep their jobs. Although one could argue that the reluctance of locals to take on jobs in lower-skilled occupations was partly to be blamed, the point remains that the availability of abundant and cheap foreign labour discouraged investment in productivity-enhancing machinery and innovation by firms. The quality of labour inputs also deteriorated because of the lower educational levels and skills of foreign workers.[94] Furthermore, the large foreign population occasionally gave rise to socio-political frictions and problems, with Singaporeans perceiving that jobs were being taken away from them. In 2010, out of a total population of 5.1 million people, the proportion that were neither citizens nor permanent residents was 26 per cent.[95] Aggravated by rising housing, healthcare and transportation costs, congestion and overcrowding, the concern over jobs led to a swing against the ruling party (the PAP) in the 2011 general election. There was a palpable sense of displacement amongst citizens who felt that being a global city had exacted costs in terms of greater inequality and a decline in living standards. That finally forced the government to change course, with the Minister for Finance declaring in 2012 that Singapore had to decisively reduce its dependence on foreign labour. Accordingly, the inflow of foreign workers was tightened by increasing the levies on them that businesses had to pay, restricting the proportion of foreign staff in firms and raising the minimum qualifying salaries on higher-skilled workers, thus slowing its growth to 8.8 per cent in 2011 and just 1 per cent in 2014.

In 2009, another economic planning committee, the Economic Strategies Committee (ESC), was formed in the wake of the Global Financial Crisis with representatives from the government, labour movement and private sector. It had the aims of maximising Singapore's opportunities in the new world environment with the rise of China and India and achieving sustained and inclusive growth.[96] Its report, released in early 2010, continued to emphasise the goal of being "a vibrant and distinctive global city" with a unique Asian cultural diversity.[97] Attracting high-quality foreign talent remained paramount but,

---

[93] Pang and Lim, "Labor, Productivity", p. 1550033-16.

[94] Nomura and Amano, "Labour Productivity and Quality Change", p. 10. This statement applies only to unskilled labour as the contribution to economic growth of foreign talent (that is, professionals and skilled workers) has been found to be relatively high. "Has Foreign Talent Contributed to Singapore's Economic Growth? An Empirical Assessment", *Economic Survey of Singapore Third Quarter 2001* (Singapore: Ministry of Trade and Industry), pp. 39–43.

[95] Mukhopadhaya, Shantakumar and Rao, *Economic Growth and Income Inequality*, p. 125. Singapore citizens comprised only 3.2 million while another 540,000 were permanent residents. Faizal bin Yahya, "Singapore in 2010: Rebounding from Economic Slump, Managing Tensions between a Global City and a Fledgling Nation State", in *Southeast Asian Affairs 2011* (Singapore: Institute of Southeast Asian Studies, 2011), p. 258.

[96] *Report of the Economic Strategies Committee: High Skilled People, Innovative Economy, Distinctive Global City* (Singapore, 2010), pp. 3–5, 6, 7, 9, 14–19, 20, 24–5, 30–1; *The Straits Times*, 28 May 2009, 2 Feb. 2010; *The Business Times*, 9 July 2009, 2 Feb. 2010; *Today*, 2 Feb. 2010, 3 Feb. 2010.

[97] *Report from the Economic Strategies Committee Subcommittee on Making Singapore a Leading Global City*, Press Release (Singapore: Ministry of Finance, 2010), pp. 1, 2.

reflecting the political environment at the time, growth had to benefit Singaporeans and the supply of foreign workers had to be managed.[98] The report restated goals that had been formulated earlier, the foremost being the need to anchor Singapore as a "Global-Asia" hub by getting MNCs and Asian firms to use the city-state as a launching pad for operations across Asia and the globe.[99] The other key objectives were to retain a globally competitive manufacturing sector and strengthen Singapore as not only a financial and business services hub but also a consumer business centre offering marketing, branding and research services.

The policy emphasis on productivity came across strongly in the report: "We must shift to achieving GDP growth by expanding productivity rather than the labour force...we can achieve productivity growth of 2 to 3 per cent per year over the next 10 years". The report noted that due to the low (below replacement level) fertility rate, the workforce would be growing at a slower pace; there was therefore an even greater need to raise productivity growth. With such growth at 2–3 per cent per year, GDP was envisaged to expand by 3–5 per cent per annum. It was also pointed out that there was significant room to improve the economy's productivity as Singapore's level was only 55–65 per cent that in the US or Japan. Productivity in the construction sector was especially low compared with other countries. The ESC proposed to boost productivity by deepening the skills and expertise in every sector of the economy and improving the quality of the foreign workforce. A high-level national council, the National Productivity and Continuing Education Council (NPCEC), was appointed to oversee and drive efforts to boost productivity at the industry, enterprise and worker levels through a National Productivity Fund.[100] The council was also responsible for improving the skills of workers in the labour force and of new job entrants. A Workforce Training Scheme (WTS) would provide employers with almost full funding to send their workers for training.[101] A further initiative called the Productivity and Innovation Credit (PIC) costing $480 million a year was introduced for a period of seven years from 2011 to give companies tax deductions or cash grants when they undertook activities that boost productivity.[102] In addition, sectoral roadmaps for raising productivity in individual industries were rolled out in 2010 for the next ten years. In all, 16 sectors covering more than half of the economy's output and employment were included, with the EDB or SPRING Singapore (the successor to the PSB) made responsible for each sector.

By mid-decade, these efforts seemed to have paid off. Overall productivity grew on average by 2.5 per cent per annum in the 2010s, in the middle of the government's target range.[103] However, there were significant differences in sectoral performances.

---

[98] Yahya, "Singapore in 2010", p. 259.

[99] *The Straits Times*, 2 Feb. 2010.

[100] Woon and Loo, *50 Years of Singapore's Productivity Drive*, pp. 322–3, 325–30, 338–51, 356–8; *The Business Times*, 2 Feb. 2010, 17 Sept. 2010; *The Straits Times*, 1 May 2010; *Today*, 17 Sept. 2010, 19 Feb. 2011.

[101] Yahya, "Singapore in 2010", p. 259.

[102] *The Business Times*, 23 Feb. 2010; *Today*, 23 Feb. 2010, 5 Mar. 2010, 22 Jan. 2014; *The Straits Times*, 20 Mar. 2010.

[103] *The Straits Times*, 22 Oct. 2013, 21 Feb. 2015.

Manufacturing productivity rose by an average of 6.5 per cent per annum during the decade and services performed decently with growth of 2 per cent but construction lagged at 1.3 per cent. The industries that experienced productivity increases at a faster rate than the average were financial and insurance services, wholesale and retail trade, and arts, entertainment and recreation. Rather unexpectedly, productivity in transport and communications grew by less than 2 per cent per year. The worst performances were seen in business services—most likely due to domestic real estate services—and the food and beverages industry, in both of which annual productivity rose by less than 0.5 per cent. Between the different sources of economy-wide productivity growth, capital deepening was the most important, although improvements in labour quality and TFP increases both contributed positively. It was also found that intangible assets such as computer software, R&D, intellectual property and branding contributed substantially to capital deepening.[104] In 2019, such assets amounted to 16 per cent of the total capital stock in Singapore.

Not coincidentally, the industries with weak productivity growth were also the ones that hired a large number of foreign workers. Lacklustre productivity growth was also attributed to SMEs, which had been reluctant or were slow to change their operating model, notwithstanding increasing levels of support from the government; for instance, the EDB had earlier implemented a scheme to cultivate 100 local enterprises with annual turnover of $100 million.[105] The SMEs were mostly to be found in the sectors catering to the local population; indeed, a government study showed that the movement of workers from the export-oriented sectors such as manufacturing, financial services and wholesale trade to the domestically-oriented sectors like food and real estate services dampened overall productivity growth.[106]

The productivity drive of the 2010s culminated in two plans. The first, launched in 2014, was a scheme called SkillsFuture that gave every Singaporean aged 25 and above an initial $500 which would be topped up regularly for attending skills upgrading courses.[107] In addition, there were sub-schemes under the programme like mid-career subsidies and study awards.[108] At the sectoral level, manpower plans were developed to identify future skills requirements and map out career progression plans for individuals. Altogether, five sectors were involved—hotel, retail, construction, bus services and food services. As of 2016, the SkillsFuture credit had been utilised by over 126,000 Singaporeans. The second plan was also sector-based, namely, the Industry Transformation Maps (ITMs) announced in 2016 with the integrated objectives of productivity improvement, skills development,

[104] "The Contribution of Intangible Assets to Labour Productivity Growth in Singapore, 2009–2019", *Economic Survey of Singapore First Quarter 2022* (Singapore: Ministry of Trade and Industry), pp. 61–2, 63–5, 70.

[105] Chia, "Singapore: Towards a Knowledge-based Economy", pp. 188–9.

[106] "Drivers of Labour Productivity Growth in Singapore 2009–2019", *Economic Survey of Singapore Third Quarter 2020* (Singapore: Ministry of Trade and Industry), pp. 43, 46–52.

[107] Pang and Lim, "Labor, Productivity", pp. 1550033-8–1550033-9, 1550033-15; *The New Paper*, 24 Feb. 2015, 9 Apr. 2015; *The Business Times*, 26 Feb. 2015, 15 Feb. 2016; *Today*, 9 Jan. 2017; *The Straits Times*, 19 Feb. 2017, 15 Sept. 2017.

[108] Woon and Loo, *50 Years of Singapore's Productivity Drive*, pp. 360–3, 391.

innovation and internationalisation.[109] Every ITM involved government agencies, employers and unions in a collective effort to increase productivity. The various strategies driving the ITMs included moving to higher value-added activities, creating a system for skills development and lifelong learning, and leveraging on technology to spur innovation and access global markets.

The two plans described above were followed by the 2017 release of the report of the Committee on the Future Economy (CFE), convened the year before to build on the ESC's work and address the new challenges facing Singapore.[110] The CFE's assessment was that good progress had been made thus far, including in growing an innovative economy, developing higher skills in the workforce and in becoming a distinctive global city.[111] However, the report took a different tack from those of previous restructuring committees in not "picking winners", as the decade ahead would witness structural changes and unexpected events in the world economy.[112] Instead, Singapore could continue to prosper by staying open, building deep capabilities and being innovative, bold and willing to change. In other words, the country had to stay nimble, flexible and agile in responding to changes.[113] The CFE's vision of the future economy was that of a vibrant global city which was connected to the world and continually renewing itself. This vision was to be realised by implementing the following mutually reinforcing strategies: deepen and diversify international connections, acquire and utilise "deep skills", strengthen enterprise capabilities to "partner each other", innovate and create value, and build strong digital networks—all not new, as we have seen from previous plans.

Although future GDP growth was projected to be 2–3 per cent—lower than the ESC's target—there was not much mention of productivity; rather, the existing ITMs were to be used as platforms to integrate planning and implementation in industries that were facing restructuring challenges.[114] In their new phase, a cluster-based approach was to be taken to maximise synergies across industries, for which purpose the government provided an additional $1 billion. New industries were also added to the ITM list, including marine and offshore engineering, real estate services, professional services and education. But the major theme of the CFE report was once again innovation. In 2016, a record $19 billion plan called Research, Innovation and Enterprise 2020 (RIE 2020) spelled out the directions for R&D efforts up to the year 2020. It was more selective and targeted in its support, focusing on industries in which Singapore had a competitive advantage: advanced manufacturing and engineering, health and biomedical sciences, digital economy and services, and urban solutions.[115] Under RIE 2020, three programmes were given attention:

---

[109] *The Straits Times*, 29 Mar. 2016.

[110] *The Straits Times*, 3 Oct. 2015, 19 Dec. 2016, 10 Feb. 2017, 15 Mar. 2017; *The Business Times*, 15 Jan. 2016; *Today*, 10 Feb. 2017.

[111] *Report of the Committee on the Future Economy, Pioneers of the Next Generation* (Singapore, 2017), pp. 1–15.

[112] *Today*, 11 Feb. 2017.

[113] Tan, *A Very Short History*, p. 154.

[114] Woon and Loo, *50 Years of Singapore's Productivity Drive*, pp. 359, 363–71, 401–5; *Today*, 10 Feb. 2017.

[115] *Today*, 8 Jan. 2016; *The Business Times*, 21 July 2017.

academic research and excellence, manpower and talent development, and innovation and enterprise. In the first two years of the plan, it is estimated that a $1 increase in the R&D stock raised a median firm's productivity by 28 cents.[116] The implementation of the CFE recommendations was overseen by a newly formed Future Economy Council (FEC).[117] At the same time, a new government agency, Enterprise Singapore, was established by merging SPRING Singapore and IE Singapore, whose enterprise development functions had converged. With that, the productivity movement became a thing of the past.

In concluding this section, we provide an assessment of Singapore's success in its latest, 21st century phase of growth, based on the global city paradigm and the ability to be innovative in new growth industries. Singapore won numerous accolades as a global city in the first decade of the new century: it was ranked by various organisations as Asia's leading city and one of the top cities in the world across different dimensions such as connectivity, competitiveness and ease of doing business.[118] At the start of the new millennium, Singapore had also successfully projected itself as a high-tech city with advanced IT infrastructure, science parks and technology corridors, cutting-edge research institutes and foreign technology leaders in their respective fields.[119] Basic science research at NUS, NTU and the research institutes under A*STAR is gaining respect in the world scientific community. In the startup scene and, relatedly, the cultivation of "technopreneurs" (that is, technological entrepreneurs), Singapore had also achieved a measure of success. With the government taking the lead by co-investing in early stage startups, the number of venture capital deals grew encouragingly from just eight in 2007 to 73 in 2013; venture capital investment in Singapore-based companies by both local and foreign funds increased to $4.9 billion in 2018.[120] The Ayer Rajah Industrial Estate is now home to more than 800 startups, venture capital firms and tech incubators.

However, Singapore had performed less well in the innovation sphere. Heavy government spending on R&D had mostly benefitted foreign companies while successful indigenous enterprises were much slower to develop.[121] Furthermore, R&D outlays had not led to much higher productivity growth in the economy. And, as often pointed out, the city-state has not produced any global champions. The reality in Singapore is that the ability to conduct world-class R&D had eluded it so far while the government had not yet succeeded in building a domestic "ecosystem of innovation". It has also yet to develop

[116] "Returns to Research and Development (R&D) Among Firms in Singapore", *Economic Survey of Singapore Third Quarter 2019* (Singapore: Ministry of Trade and Industry), p. 48.

[117] *The Straits Times*, 2 May 2017.

[118] Heng Yee-Kuang, *Managing Global Risks in the Urban Age: Singapore and the Making of a Global City* (Farnham: Ashgate, 2015), pp. 33–5; *The New Paper*, 19 June 2011, 14 Mar. 2012. The *Foreign Policy* journal and A.T. Kearney rankings placed Singapore as the world's most globalised country for the three consecutive years from 2005 to 2007. Ti and Ti, *Singapore and Asia*, p. 19.

[119] Goh, *From Traders to Innovators*, pp. xviii, 175–6, 177.

[120] Cheah, Ho and Lim, "Role of Public Science", p. 82; N. Pangarkar and P. Vandenberg, *Singapore's Ecosystem for Technology Startups and Lessons for Its Neighbors*, Country Report No. 2, Ecosystems for Technology Startups in Asia and the Pacific (Manila: Asian Development Bank, 2022), pp. 7, 10–11.

[121] J. Powers, "Singapore's Economic Development: The Dilemma of Managing Success", in *Planning Singapore: The Experimental City*, ed. S. Hamnett and Belinda Yuen (Abingdon: Routledge, 2019), pp. 71–6.

an indigenous, self-reliant technological base capable of producing innovations that can be marketed and only a small percentage of startups have been engaged in cutting-edge manufacturing research.[122] In terms of manpower, the country lacks a critical mass of local R&D personnel with the appropriate qualifications. Tellingly, Singapore's world ranking in innovation has been much lower than that as a competitive global city. In 2014 for example, the city-state ranked highly in innovation inputs but abysmally in innovation outputs and efficiency.[123] It would appear that the city-state had achieved more success as a high value-added services hub than as a high-technology manufacturing centre.

Business Cycles, Financial Crises and Epidemics

As we approach the end of the narrative on Singapore's modern economic history, a retrospective survey of the recurrent fluctuations along the long-run growth path taken over the past 60 years can serve as a timely reminder both of the nation's vulnerability and resilience to external shocks. Indeed, these business cycles became more amplified in the new millennium as growth slowed, with the volatility imparted to all facets of domestic economic activity. Furthermore, financial crises broke out in the last years of the 20th century and again late in the first decade of the new century. Deadly epidemics due to new disease variants (SARS and COVID-19) in the first and second decades respectively wreaked havoc on the economy. In all the episodes to be described below, the economic shock originated elsewhere in the world but was quickly transmitted to Singapore because of the country's position as a manufacturing and services hub. This vulnerability to external events and the lack of control over them came as a price to be paid for thriving as an open, global city-state.

In all, there were seven major cycles, crises and epidemics from 1960 to 2023, in each case giving rise to recessionary economic conditions or an outright contraction in total output (Figure 29).[124] Although these events were distinct phenomena, common general features can be discerned. First of all, the average duration of a cycle was slightly over three years from peak to peak (or trough to trough) as gauged by movements in real GDP; the periods coincide therefore with what have been called "Kitchin cycles". However, they were asymmetrical in the sense that the expansion phases typically lasted longer than the recession phases, at about two years and one-and-a-half years respectively.[125] As true of all business cycles in capitalist free market economies, many economic activities went through the upturn and downturn phases of a business cycle synchronously, or nearly so.[126] These co-movements form a second set of stylised features. Chief among them was the strong procyclicality of private consumption, investment, productivity, employment, wages and inflation; that is to say, they changed in the same direction as aggregate output, though the

---

[122] Goh, *From Traders to Innovators*, pp. xii, xix.

[123] Tan and Bhaskaran, "The Role of the State", pp. 1550030-21–1550030-22.

[124] "Singapore's Growth Cycle Chronology, Coincident and Leading Indicators", *Economic Survey of Singapore Second Quarter 2004* (Singapore: Ministry of Trade and Industry), pp. 47, 48–9.

[125] "Singapore's Growth Cycle Chronology, Coincident and Leading Indicators", *Statistics Singapore Newsletter Issue 2* (Singapore: Department of Statistics, 2023), p. 8.

[126] A.F. Burns and W.C. Mitchell, *Measuring Business Cycles*, NBER Studies in Business Cycles No. 2 (New York: Columbia University Press, 1946).

last three did so only with a time lag.[127] Moreover, exports were strongly correlated with imports due to Singapore's dependence on re-exports, imported raw materials, intermediate inputs and capital goods.[128]

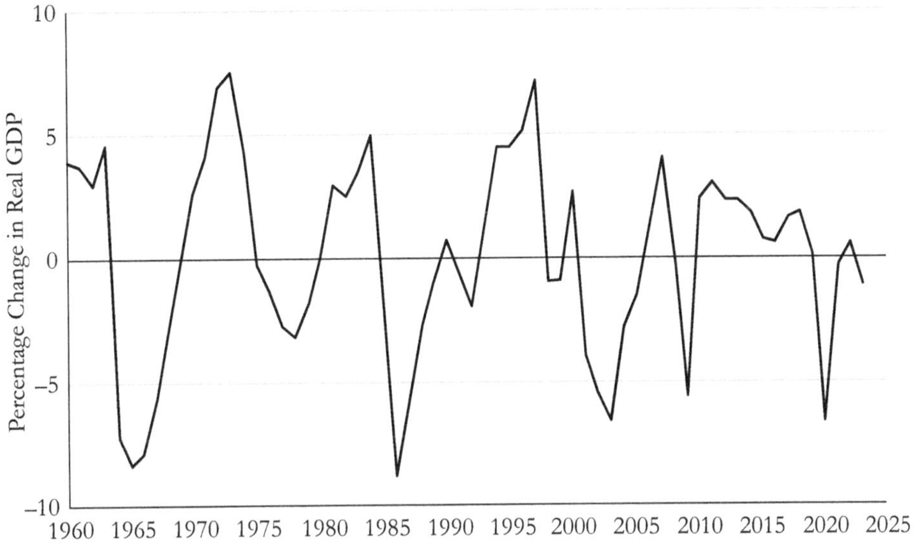

Figure 29. Business Cycles in Singapore, 1960–2023
Source: Department of Statistics, Singapore.

The procyclical properties extended to the outputs of the manufacturing, commerce and transport and communications sectors.[129] These sectors fluctuated in tandem with changes in global economic conditions and world semiconductor sales, owing to the importance of electronics goods in both domestic exports and re-exports. The other industries moved in a desynchronised manner to GDP; this was especially the case with construction as it depended mainly on the cycles in property prices. Employment fluctuations in the individual sectors tracked one another fairly well, again with the exception of construction. The short-run cycles in GDP, its components and the economic sectors were congruent with a Keynesian explanation of business cycles—they originated largely from aggregate demand shocks. Aggregate supply shocks such as increases in labour supply had long-term effects instead while global oil price increases caused domestic output growth to decline, although their impact was partially offset by higher margins for the refined oil products exported from Singapore.[130]

---

[127] Keen Meng Choy, "Business Cycles in Singapore: Stylised Facts for a Small Open Economy", *Pacific Economic Review* 16, 1 (2011): 27–31.

[128] Keen Meng Choy, "Trade Cycles in a Re-Export Economy", *International Economic Journal* 26, 2 (2012): 189–91, 198–9.

[129] "Sectoral, Industry and Employment Business Cycles in Singapore", *Macroeconomic Review*, (Singapore: Monetary Authority of Singapore, April 2009), pp. 203–11.

[130] Keen Meng Choy, "Singapore Business Cycles: A Supply-Side Analysis", *ASEAN Economic Bulletin* 20, 1 (2003): 171–4.

The first business cycle in Singapore's modern economic history occurred before independence, from 1963 to 1966, and was politically induced. It was precipitated by the Indonesian Confrontation, an undeclared war waged by President Sukarno of Indonesia against Malaysia and Singapore. The grounds for the Confrontation grew from the claim that the formation of Malaysia was a British "neo-colonialist plot" to maintain their rule over Southeast Asia and foil Indonesia's dream of uniting the Malay world.[131] A series of bombings by saboteurs at several places in Singapore damaged properties and claimed several lives, including the most serious incident in March 1965 at MacDonald House in Orchard Road.[132] Indonesian gunboats also seized Singapore fishing craft.[133] As a result of the Confrontation, some foreign investors became wary of establishing manufacturing plants in Jurong and trade with Indonesia came to an abrupt stop.[134] In 1964, Singapore's GDP fell by 3.1 per cent, with the wholesale trade, hotels and restaurants, and transport sectors being the most affected.[135] Slightly more than half of the workers in the rubber processing, sago, rattan, coffee, coconut oil and pepper industries were made redundant and had to be supported by the government. Trade with Indonesia resumed only in 1966 after President Sukarno was deposed and the Confrontation ended.[136]

After a long stretch of robust and uninterrupted growth in the late 1960s and early 1970s, the next cycle was brought on by the oil shock of October 1973, when the global oil price quadrupled as a result of supply restrictions engineered by the OPEC cartel. The situation was worsened by high world food prices due to weather disruptions, resulting in stagflation in many countries.[137] Singapore was not an exception, although growth merely slowed to 6.1 per cent in 1974 and 4 per cent in 1975 from the double digits that had prevailed since 1966.[138] However, manufacturing output contracted in 1975.[139] According to the official growth cycle chronology, economic activity peaked in May 1974 but the slow growth that followed lasted only until December of the same year. The government implemented some anti-recessionary measures such as allocating more funds for development and activating public sector construction projects while MAS reduced the cash reserve ratio and cut the rediscount rate.[140]

In 1976, the Singapore economy commenced a recovery as external demand picked up, benefitting the manufacturing sector and entrepôt trade.[141] Following a minor cycle

---

131 Turnbull, *History of Modern Singapore*, pp. 282, 290, 329.

132 Alvin Tan, "Konfrontasi: Singapore's Experience of an Undeclared War", *BiblioAsia* 19, 4 (2024): 24–31; *The Straits Times*, 20 Apr. 1964, 11 Sept. 1964, 11 Mar. 1965, 6 Oct. 1966.

133 *The Straits Times*, 2 Feb. 1963, 2 Nov. 1963.

134 *The Straits Times*, 27 Sept. 1963, 14 Nov. 1963, 8 Apr. 1964, 15 Sept. 1967.

135 Cheng Siok Hwa, "Economic Change in Singapore", p. 92; *The Straits Budget*, 17 June 1964.

136 *The Straits Times*, 14 Sept. 1966.

137 "Revisiting the 1970s Inflation Shocks", *Macroeconomic Review* (Singapore: Monetary Authority of Singapore, April 2022), pp. 61–3.

138 *New Nation*, 26 Nov. 1973; *The Straits Times*, 8 Aug. 1974, 11 Nov. 1974, 9 Aug. 1975.

139 Rodan, *The Political Economy of Singapore's Industrialization*, p. 115.

140 Pang Eng Fong and Linda Seah, "The Singapore Economy in 1975: Stagnation and Recovery", in *Southeast Asian Affairs 1976* (Singapore: Institute of Southeast Asian Studies, 1976), pp. 341–4.

141 *The Straits Times*, 9 Aug. 1976.

between 1976 and 1978, the economy was buffeted by the second oil shock of the early eighties, in part triggered by the Iran-Iraq war of 1980.[142] Again, large increases in oil prices sent the industrialised economies into recession. In the United States and United Kingdom, the downturn was made worse by tight monetary policies implemented by the governments of Reagan and Thatcher respectively. Economic growth in Singapore slackened correspondingly to 7.1 per cent in 1982 while trade-related activities such as industrial production and non-oil domestic exports fell.[143] However, the oil refining margins of companies in Singapore rose due to the destruction of refining capacity in the Middle East.[144] Pump-priming in the form of public works again helped the economy bottom out in December 1982. Subsequently, a rebound in the US economy contributed to a recovery in the manufacturing sector and GDP growth while the domestic property market experienced a boom that stimulated residential and commercial building projects.

We have earlier described the classical recession in the mid-eighties in which Singapore's GDP contracted, and the measures taken to counteract it. Led by the manufacturing sector, the economy rebounded strongly in 1987 and 1988. The resulting build-up of inflationary pressures following a bout of deflation in 1986 prompted MAS to appreciate the exchange rate in mid-1988.[145] It had to act, as the unemployment rate had fallen to a historically unprecedented level of below 2.5 per cent, causing wages and unit labour costs to rise and threaten Singapore's competitiveness again. Economic growth moderated as a consequence until another cycle materialised in the early 1990s. This time, a confluence of events—the Gulf War in Kuwait, a slowdown in the US economy and a downturn in the global electronics cycle—operated simultaneously to drag Singapore's GDP growth down to 6.7 per cent in 1991.[146] At the industry level, there was a cutback in disk drive production and a fall in visitor arrivals.[147] Nevertheless, support for growth was provided by the construction sector which received more building contracts from the public sector.[148]

That brings us to the Asian Financial Crisis. In July 1997, speculators in the foreign exchange markets attacked the Thai baht and forced the central bank to abandon its peg to the US dollar.[149] The speculators factored in a weakening economy, a property bubble, a growing current account deficit and high short-term foreign indebtedness. Through a process of currency contagion, the speculators then turned their attention to other economies in Asia that were believed to be suffering from the same symptoms. Before long, these currencies had depreciated by 40–80 per cent against the US dollar while stock and property markets collapsed as capital flowed out.[150] The financial turmoil unleashed in the second half of 1997 quickly led to severe recessions in Thailand, Malaysia, Indonesia and

---

142 *The Business Times*, 10 Oct. 1980; *The Straits Times*, 12 Aug. 1982.

143 *The Straits Times*, 9 Aug. 1982, 1 Mar. 1983; *Singapore Monitor*, 28 Mar. 1983.

144 Lim, "Singapore in 1980", p. 275.

145 Teh and Shanmugaratnam, "Exchange Rate Policy", pp. 299–301.

146 *The Business Times*, 4 Dec. 1990, 21 June 1991, 8 Nov. 1991; *The Straits Times*, 1 Jan. 1991, 31 Mar. 1992; *The Straits Times Weekly Overseas Edition*, 19 Jan. 1991, 26 Jan. 1991; *The New Paper*, 18 May 1991.

147 *The Business Times*, 18 Feb. 1991, 30 Aug. 1991.

148 Kumar, "Singapore 1991", p. 286.

149 Liew and Wilson, *A History of Money*, pp. 337–44; *The Straits Times*, 7 Dec. 1997.

150 *The Straits Times*, 23 Nov. 1997, 1 Jan. 1998.

South Korea.[151] Spiralling debt burdens, corporate bankruptcies with knock-on effects on banking, and a plunge in trade followed in 1998. Singapore for the most part escaped the carnage because of its prudent policies and strong macroeconomic position.[152] To some extent, demand from the United States and European Union cushioned the impact of the downturn in regional demand, which affected exportable services more adversely than manufacturing exports.[153]

However, the city-state still slipped into a recession in the second half of 1998 owing to its extensive trade and financial linkages with the Asian economies, resulting in negative growth of 2.2 per cent for the whole year. Non-oil exports and re-exports shrank by 10 per cent and 13 per cent respectively. Singapore's total trade declined by 7.5 per cent while private investment expenditure fell by 9.9 per cent as business confidence waned. The sharp depreciation of the regional currencies exacerbated the situation by eroding Singapore's export competitiveness.[154] Meanwhile, overcapacity in the global electronics industry caused a decline in manufacturing sector output of 0.5 per cent. The commerce sector with its large regional exposure contracted by 4 per cent in 1998 as it was badly hit by weak wholesale trade and tourist arrivals.[155] In the financial sector, offshore lending in the Asian Dollar Market (ADM) was curtailed. The balance sheets and profitability of Singapore's banks weakened somewhat due to non-performing loans to the region but overall, the banks weathered the crisis well.[156] The same cannot be said of the asset markets—over approximately a one-year period from the beginning of the crisis, the stock and property markets dropped by 60 per cent and 40 per cent respectively.[157] As a consequence, the financial services sub-sector contracted by 8.8 per cent in 1998. Furthermore, the crisis led to some consolidation in the industry and a protracted decline in regional lending activities until the affected economies recovered in the early 2000s.[158]

Given the country's large foreign exchange reserves and a few remaining restrictions on lending by domestic banks to foreigners, the currency speculators had not attempted to attack the Singapore dollar. Nonetheless, MAS allowed the exchange rate to depreciate by up to 20 per cent against the US dollar; to accommodate market volatility, the policy band was also widened.[159] Fortuitously, Singapore had just launched another review of

---

[151] *The Straits Times*, 3 June 1998.

[152] Peebles and Wilson, *Economic Growth and Development*, pp. 244–6; *The Straits Times Weekly Overseas Edition*, 3 Jan. 1998.

[153] Chia, "Singapore: Towards a Knowledge-based Economy", p. 185; *Economic Survey of Singapore*, various years (Singapore: Ministry of Trade and Industry); *The Straits Times*, 8 Dec. 1997.

[154] Ngiam Kee Jin, "Coping with the Asian Financial Crisis: The Singapore Experience", ISEAS Working Papers (Singapore: Institute of Southeast Asian Studies, 2000), pp. 1–2, 5–8, 15–18.

[155] *The Straits Times*, 24 Dec. 1997; *The Business Times*, 24 Mar. 1998.

[156] *The Straits Times Weekly Overseas Edition*, 2 May 1998; *The Business Times*, 16 Sept. 1998.

[157] Chia Siow Yue, "The Asian Financial Crisis: Singapore's Experience and Response", *ASEAN Economic Bulletin* 15, 3 (1998): 302–6; *The Straits Times*, 13 Jan. 1998, 18 Oct. 1998, 30 Oct. 1998; *The Straits Times Weekly Overseas Edition*, 2 Jan. 1999; *The Business Times*, 1 Apr. 1999.

[158] Chia and Lim, "Singapore: A Regional Hub in ICT", p. 272.

[159] *The Straits Times*, 8 Jan. 1998. The restrictions on the non-internationalisation of the Singapore dollar were eased in August 1998. *The Business Times*, 14 Aug. 1998, 8 July 1999.

long-term economic strategies by the Committee on Singapore's Competitiveness in May 1997, and so its recommendations broadened to include short-term economic recovery measures.[160] In this regard, the government initially made adjustments to lower business costs and provide financial assistance to individuals and households. This was followed by two off-budget packages worth $2 billion and $10.5 billion in June and November 1998 respectively.[161] The measures in the packages were aimed at minimising company lay-offs by further reducing business costs, wages, property taxes, rentals, utilities as well as government fees and charges. Public infrastructure projects were brought forward, particularly the construction of schools.[162]

In the November 1998 measures were included a 10 percentage point reduction in employers' CPF contributions, a 5 per cent cut in the variable component of wages and a corporate tax rebate of 10 per cent. These had the effect of lowering unit labour costs, thus partly offsetting the loss in competitiveness due to the relative appreciation of the Singapore dollar against the Asian currencies. On account of these policies and in tandem with an incipient recovery in the crisis-hit Asian economies, Singapore's economy showed growth of 5.7 per cent in 1999 and the unemployment rate was contained at 3.6 per cent.[163] However, 28,200 workers were still retrenched in 1998, the highest number since the 1985 recession.[164] Further impetus for the expansion came from a recovery in global electronics demand and an improvement in domestic consumption spending.[165] External trade rebounded sharply by 8.1 per cent and foreign investment recovered, bringing them back to their pre-crisis levels.[166]

In 2001, just two years after the economy recovered from the Asian currency crisis, another recession took hold. This later prompted the Prime Minister to allude to the biblical parable of "seven fat years followed by seven lean years".[167] In the second half of the 1990s, US businesses had overinvested in computers, communications equipment and software, occasioning a boom in technology-related stocks as an irrational exuberance came over the market.[168] The crunch came inevitably in 2001 when global electronics demand suffered a total collapse and the technology bubble burst, which ended the longest economic expansion in US history.[169] This unravelling of the industry was aggravated by the September 11 2001 terrorist attacks in New York City. In the early

---

160 Tan, *A Very Short History*, pp. 148–9; Chia, "Singapore: Towards a Knowledge-based Economy", p. 184.

161 *The Straits Times*, 24 June 1998, 1 July 1998, 29 Oct. 1998; *The Business Times*, 12 Nov. 1998.

162 *The New Paper*, 30 June 1998.

163 *The Business Times*, 25 June 1999; *The Straits Times*, 16 Oct. 1999, 22 Nov. 1999.

164 *Economic Survey of Singapore 1997* (Singapore: Ministry of Trade and Industry), pp. 21, 24.

165 *The Straits Times*, 12 July 1999.

166 Simon S.C. Tay, "Island in the World: Globalization and Singapore's Transformation", in *Southeast Asian Affairs 2001* (Singapore: Institute of Southeast Asian Studies, 2001), p. 279.

167 Lee, *The Unexpected Nation*, p. 571.

168 *The Straits Times*, 9 Feb. 2000; *The Business Times*, 17 Apr. 2000, 15 Mar. 2002; *Today*, 15 Dec. 2000.

169 "Special Feature on Comparing Present and Past Recessions", *MAS ED Quarterly Bulletin* (Singapore: Monetary Authority of Singapore, October 2001), pp. 70–2, 81–2; *The Straits Times*, 21 Sept. 2001; *The Business Times*, 1 Oct. 2001.

nineties, government planners in Singapore had noted that the country's heavy reliance on the competitive and volatile electronics (and pharmaceuticals) industry would be a source of vulnerability, but, when the downturn did come, it proved to be a severe one. In 2000, even if there had been some diversification into other industries, over half of manufacturing exports were still accounted for by electronics. Global semiconductor sales—a good indicator of the electronics cycle—plunged by 32 per cent in 2001 and industrial production in Singapore declined by 11.5 per cent.[170] There was a fall in the output of the electronics and other supporting industries in the manufacturing sector, while sea and air freight shipments were also adversely affected. These effects combined to cause the economy's growth rate to swing to −1.1 per cent in 2001 from 9 per cent in the preceding year. Furthermore, some electronics MNCs abandoned production in the city-state and moved to cheaper locations elsewhere.[171]

The government was forced to intervene again in 2001 by carrying over some of the measures promulgated during the Asian crisis, such as delaying the full restoration of the employer CPF contribution rate, extending the earlier reduction in the foreign worker levy and awarding property tax and rental rebates to companies.[172] As part of a $2.2 billion off-budget stimulus, more money was allocated to worker retraining for the elderly and unemployed and spending on selected infrastructural projects was brought forward.[173] In further actions taken later in the year, income tax rebates were given to individuals and households while the salaries and allowances of political appointees and senior civil servants were cut.[174] On top of these measures, "New Singapore Shares" amounting to $2.7 billion were distributed to citizens, with the less well-off getting more.[175] The government also offered help to lower-income households and the unemployed through the disbursement of $200 per month for three months to tide them over the hardship.[176]

Barely a year after the economy reached a trough in October 2001, a further shock struck, resulting in a "double-dip" recession.[177] The November 2002 outbreak in China of a zoonotic disease called Severe Acute Respiratory Syndrome (SARS), which had its epicentre in Hong Kong, took a heavy toll on the Singapore economy in the second quarter of 2003. From Hong Kong, the highly infectious disease was transmitted to the country and by late March 2003, there were 44 cases.[178] The government immediately took prevention and control measures to reduce infections and fatalities, such as imposing border controls on

[170] *The Business Times*, 11 Apr. 2001, 12 July 2001; *The Straits Times*, 27 Apr. 2001, 11 July 2001, 18 Sept. 2001.

[171] Austin, "Singapore as a 'Global City'", p. 178.

[172] *The Business Times*, 26 July 2001.

[173] *The Straits Times*, 26 July 2001; *The Business Times*, 26 July 2001.

[174] *The Business Times*, 13 Oct. 2001.

[175] Lee, *The Unexpected Nation*, p. 578; *The Straits Times*, 1 Nov. 2001.

[176] Gillian Koh and Ooi Giok-Ling, "Singapore: A Home, A Nation?", in *Southeast Asian Affairs 2002* (Singapore: Institute of Southeast Asian Studies, 2002), p. 268; *The Straits Times*, 13 Oct. 2001.

[177] *Macroeconomic Review* (Singapore: Monetary Authority of Singapore, October 2003), pp. 6–7, 9–11, 12–13, 15.

[178] J.J. Woo, *Building Immunity: Crisis and Contagion in the City State* (Singapore: World Scientific, 2022), pp. 63–9; *Today*, 26 Mar. 2003.

both inbound and outbound travellers, screening them for symptoms of the disease, and contact tracing of those who had been in close proximity with SARS patients in order to quarantine them.[179] Schools, junior colleges and childcare centres were closed for three weeks and confirmed cases of infection were sent to Tan Tock Seng Hospital, the designated SARS hospital, for isolation and treatment.[180]

The impact of SARS on the Singapore economy was most visible in the industries related to tourism. About half of the contraction in GDP of 11.4 per cent in the second quarter of 2003 was due to sharp declines in the affected segments of the service sector, namely hotels, restaurants, retail trade, and air and land transport, as people stayed at home.[181] Visitor arrivals fell by 62 per cent and hotels' average occupancy rate dropped to 30 per cent.[182] Travel agents saw their business plunge by 70–80 per cent.[183] The service industries registered employment losses and some workers were put on a shorter work week. Furthermore, the valuations of private properties fell by 38 per cent compared to their peak in 1996, resulting in some homeowners going into negative equity.[184] On the government's part, apart from the strenuous measures taken to contain the epidemic, a $230 million relief package to help the worst hit sectors and individuals was announced. The financial assistance included a rebate on aircraft landing fees at Changi Airport, property tax rebates and diesel tax rebates for taxis.[185] A fund was also started to provide relief to healthcare workers who fell sick and the families of SARS patients.[186] Following the quicker than expected containment of the pandemic in May 2003, the economy began a tentative recovery in the third quarter.[187] By the end of September, tourist arrivals had recovered to about 90 per cent of their pre-SARS level. Retail sales also picked up, especially as stores offered large price discounts. Nonetheless, GDP growth was still weak at 4.5 per cent for 2003 as a whole and due to the delayed impact of the epidemic on the labour market, the unemployment rate spiked up to 5.9 per cent in September.

Following the SARS crisis, Singapore experienced a few years of strong economic growth up to 2008 when the worst financial catastrophe since the Great Depression swept through

---

179 *The Straits Times*, 3 Apr. 2003, 11 May 2003; *Today*, 24 Apr. 2003, 2 May 2003, 2 June 2003.

180 *The New Paper*, 23 Mar. 2003; *The Business Times*, 27 Mar. 2003; *Today*, 27 Mar. 2003, 5 Apr. 2003; *The Straits Times*, 22 July 2003.

181 *Economic Survey of Singapore*, various issues (Singapore: Ministry of Trade and Industry); *The Business Times*, 29 Mar. 2003, 9 Apr. 2003, 20 May 2003.

182 "The Impact of SARS on the Singapore Economy and Action Taken in Response", *Asia Pacific Biotech News* 8, 12 (2004): 672–3, 677.

183 "Impact of Severe Acute Respiratory Syndrome (SARS) on the Singapore Economy", *Economic Survey of Singapore First Quarter 2003* (Singapore: Ministry of Trade and Industry), p. 46; *Streats*, 26 Mar. 2003.

184 Lee, *The Unexpected Nation*, p. 574.

185 *The Business Times*, 17 Apr. 2003, 18 Apr. 2003; *Today*, 22 Apr. 2003; *The Straits Times*, 24 Apr. 2003.

186 *The Straits Times*, 12 Apr. 2003; *The New Paper*, 14 Apr. 2003.

187 *Today*, 31 May 2003, 5 Sept. 2003; *The New Paper*, 31 May 2003; *Streats*, 4 June 2003, 30 July 2003; *The Business Times*, 11 June 2003, 12 June 2003, 4 July 2003, 21 July 2003, 9 Aug. 2003, 16 Dec. 2003; *The Straits Times*, 14 July 2003, 23 Aug. 2003, 1 Nov. 2003.

the world, almost exactly ten years after the Asian crisis.[188] Initially a sub-prime mortgage problem in the United States, it erupted into the Global Financial Crisis of 2008–09.[189] The US banks had lent indiscriminately to house buyers of all stripes when the housing market boomed from 2003 to 2005 in an environment of low interest rates ("sub-prime"), abundant liquidity and lax supervision by the Federal Reserve Board. These mortgage loans were then bundled and repackaged into high yielding and highly rated mortgage-backed securities (MBSs) and collateralised debt obligations (CDOs)—subsequently referred to as "toxic assets"—that were sold to investment banks and individuals.[190] The housing price bubble was pricked when the Federal Reserve raised interest rates in 2006 amid signs of rising inflation, causing sub-prime borrowers to default on their mortgages. The crash of the housing market set off a chain reaction in the financial sector. First, the investment bank Bear Stearns failed, then mortgage lenders Freddie Mac and Fannie Mae went bankrupt and had to be nationalised.[191] The tipping point came when the US government refused to rescue financial services firm Lehman Brothers in September 2008, although it bailed out the giant American Insurance Group (AIG).[192] Once the panic had started and spread to Europe, central banks had to step in to restore confidence by injecting liquidity into financial systems.

The Global Financial Crisis hit Singapore unexpectedly and severely. According to the official business cycle chronology, the city-state had already entered into a recession in the second quarter of 2008, as GDP had fallen by 7.7 per cent. Worse was to come after the Lehman Brothers debacle, with the economy contracting by 2.1 per cent in the third quarter, 16.4 per cent in the fourth quarter and 11 per cent in the initial quarter of 2009.[193] Over this period, the manufacturing sector shrank by a cumulative 26.1 per cent and the service sector by 5.2 per cent. Every major industry declined except for construction, information and communications, and business services. The financial services industry was badly affected as the trading of stocks and bonds, foreign exchange dealing and fund management activities were cut back.[194] These declines made the recession induced by the crisis the most severe to date.[195] Total exports plunged by 12 per cent in the last quarter of 2008, with electronics and pharmaceuticals leading the fall.[196] Cross-border production

---

188 M. Kawai, "Global Financial Crisis and Implications for ASEAN", in *Global Financial Crisis: Implications for ASEAN*, ASEAN Studies Centre, Report No. 6 (Singapore: Institute of Southeast Asian Studies, 2009), pp. 1–3.

189 *The Straits Times*, 6 Apr. 2007, 18 Aug. 2007, 1 Feb. 2008; *The New Paper*, 13 Aug. 2007; *The Business Times*, 10 Sept. 2007, 11 Feb. 2008.

190 Bernard Yeung, "Failures on Many Fronts", in *Financial Crisis 2008*, ed. Ivan Png, Saw Centre Financial Studies No. 5 (Singapore: Saw Centre for Financial Studies, 2008), pp. 11–16.

191 *The Business Times*, 27 June 2007, 31 May 2008, 8 Sept. 2008; *The Straits Times*, 2 June 2008, 8 Sept. 2008; *The New Paper*, 9 Aug. 2008.

192 *The Straits Times*, 13 Sept. 2008, 16 Sept. 2008; *The Business Times*, 13 Sept. 2008, 17 Sept. 2008; *Today*, 16 Sept. 2008, 17 Sept. 2008, 11 Nov. 2008.

193 *The Straits Times*, 6 Oct. 2008, 22 Nov. 2008; *Today*, 21 Nov. 2008; *The New Paper*, 1 Jan. 2009; *The Business Times*, 30 Apr. 2009.

194 Austin, "Singapore as a 'Global City'", p. 184.

195 *Macroeconomic Review* (Singapore: Monetary Authority of Singapore, April 2009), pp. 7, 24–6.

196 *The Straits Times*, 22 Jan. 2009; *The Business Times*, 27 Feb. 2009.

networks and trade flows were disrupted by the worldwide credit crunch. As global demand collapsed from the synchronised recessions in both developed and developing countries, Singapore's non-oil exports recorded another sharp fall of 25.6 per cent in the first quarter of 2009. Shipments to all the major markets plummeted, especially those to the United States and Europe. With the pullback in economic activity, the high inflation in 2008 caused by surging food and energy prices turned into deflation in 2009.[197]

As during the Asian Financial Crisis a decade before, the Straits Times Index of share prices tumbled, from 3,500 points in December 2007 to 1,700 points in the last quarter of 2008.[198] Private residential property prices again dropped, by 40 per cent, after a strong run-up in the preceding years.[199] Among the companies which reported a fall in profits or closed down, the fiasco at Temasek Holdings is worth pointing out.[200] Venturing out of its familiar domestic territory, Temasek had bought large stakes in banks in Indonesia, China, Western Europe and the United States during the months before the global crisis.[201] With the outbreak of the crisis, the holding company began to show losses from its investments in ailing financial institutions. Its stake in the investment bank Merrill Lynch was particularly large; when the bank failed and had to be taken over by the Bank of America in January 2009, Temasek lost US$4 billion. DBS Bank, whose largest shareholder was Temasek Holdings, also suffered a 40 per cent drop in profits in late 2008 and retrenched 900 staff in early 2009.[202] Similarly, GIC sustained a substantial decline in the value of its overseas investments, although its accounts were not fully disclosed.[203] The losses were not restricted to the two funds, as many ordinary Singaporeans, including retirees, had invested in financial products underwritten by Lehman Brothers and lost almost all their savings.[204]

In the initial phase of the financial crisis, 2,000 workers in Singapore were made redundant, mainly from the manufacturing sector. Job retrenchments continued into the last months of 2008 and the resident unemployment rate rose in all the successive quarters of 2009, to a high of 5 per cent in September.[205] Redeployment, job sharing and a reduced work week were implemented at large firms.[206] In response, the government allocated $600 million to enhance the Skills Programme for Upgrading and Resilience (SPUR),

---

197 Sanchita Basu Das, *Road to Recovery: Singapore's Journey through the Global Crisis* (Singapore: Institute of Southeast Asian Studies, 2010), pp. 53–6.

198 *The Straits Times*, 9 Oct. 2008, 11 Oct. 2008.

199 *The Business Times*, 25 Oct. 2008, 23 Jan. 2009.

200 *The Business Times*, 11 Aug. 2008; *Today*, 27 Aug. 2008, 8 Dec. 2009; *The Straits Times*, 30 July 2009; *The New Paper*, 18 Sept. 2009.

201 R. Jordan, "Singapore in Its Worst Recession for Years. The Effects of the Current Economic Crisis on the City-State's Economy", *Journal of Current Southeast Asian Affairs* 28, 4 (2009): 101–3.

202 Austin, "Singapore as a 'Global City'", p. 184.

203 *Today*, 28 Aug. 2008, 30 Sept. 2009; *The Straits Times*, 5 Mar. 2009, 29 Sept. 2009.

204 Tan, *A Very Short History*, p. 151.

205 *The Straits Times*, 16 Aug. 2008, 21 Oct. 2008, 15 Nov. 2008, 31 Jan. 2009. The unemployment rate for residents (that is, Singapore citizens and permanent residents) better captured the condition of the labour market since a large number of foreign workers were deported.

206 P. Warring and J. Lewer, "The Global Financial Crisis, Employment Relations and the Labour Market in Singapore and Australia", *Asia Pacific Business Review* 19, 2 (2013): 221–2.

which provided highly subsidised courses aimed at improving workers' skills during slack periods.[207] The even more critical measure was the Jobs Credit Scheme (JCS) adopted in the 2009 Budget.[208] This was a $4.5 billion wage subsidy paid to companies that employed Singapore citizens and permanent residents. Under the scheme, employers received a 12 per cent subsidy on the first $2,500 of each month's wages for every employee who contributed to the CPF. It was initially to be in effect only in 2009 but was extended until June 2010 with progressively lower subsidy rates. The JCS was credited with preserving a substantial number of jobs, as shown by the fact that retrenchments were fewer than those experienced during the Asian crisis.[209] Notwithstanding these schemes, graduates from the local universities encountered difficulty in getting jobs and it was estimated that a tenth of the workforce had to take unpaid leave or accept lower salaries.

As regards other policies, MAS decided in October 2008 to guarantee all bank deposits until the end of 2010 and in the same month retracted its strong Singapore dollar policy. The Singapore government initially pumped $2.9 billion into the ailing economy.[210] This was followed by a March 2009 Budget of $20.5 billion which was aptly dubbed the Resilience Package. In it, the government announced a plan to create 18,000 new public sector positions in the education, childcare and healthcare sectors over two years.[211] Other financial and economic initiatives were included in the package. For instance, one measure was designed to stimulate bank lending and credit markets, whereby the government shared the risks of commercial banks' bridging and trade financing loans to businesses. More than 13,000 large and small companies benefitted from loans worth $8 billion under this scheme. A slew of tax measures was introduced, including a reduction in the corporate income tax rate to 17 per cent, a one-year income tax rebate of 20 per cent, accelerated capital allowances, the usual property and rental rebates, and an enhanced "loss carry-back scheme" which eased business cashflows by allowing firms to offset losses against past taxable income. To help construction firms survive the recession, $1.3 billion in infrastructure projects was brought forward and a further $1 billion was to be spent on sustainable development and the environment. Since a budget deficit of $8.7 billion was incurred for 2009, the above measures had to be partly financed by drawing on the state's locked-up reserves for the first time since the law was passed in 1991, requiring the consent of the elected President of Singapore to do so, thus setting a precedent for the future.[212]

---

[207] *The Business Times*, 22 Nov. 2008, 23 Feb. 2009; *The Straits Times*, 21 Dec. 2008; *Today*, 23 Feb. 2009, 22 Dec. 2009.

[208] *The Business Times*, 23 Jan. 2009, 9 Feb. 2009, 14 Oct. 2009, 19 Dec. 2009; *The Straits Times*, 25 Jan. 2009, 6 Feb. 2009; *Today*, 25 Mar. 2009.

[209] *The Straits Times*, 16 Feb. 2009; *Today*, 25 Mar. 2009; *The Business Times*, 29 Apr. 2009.

[210] Jordan, "Singapore in Its Worst Recession", pp. 104–6; Tan, *A Very Short History*, p. 151; *Today*, 10 Oct. 2008; *The Straits Times*, 11 Oct. 2008, 21 Oct. 2008, 22 Oct. 2008.

[211] *The Straits Times*, 23 Jan. 2009, 26 Jan. 2009, 9 Feb. 2009; *Today*, 23 Jan. 2009; *The Business Times*, 28 Jan. 2009.

[212] Das, *Road to Recovery*, pp. 72–86; *Today*, 4 Feb. 2009; *The Business Times*, 6 Feb. 2009; *The Straits Times*, 20 Feb. 2009, 13 Mar. 2009.

The amount drawn was relatively small however, at $4.9 billion to fund the JCS and the risk-sharing scheme.[213]

Although the downturn in the Singapore economy caused by the financial crisis was sharp and deep, the recovery from it was rapid. Just as the country was one of the earliest to sink into recession, it was also quick to post positive growth again when global markets started to stabilise and recover.[214] In retrospect, however, it is clear that China's huge fiscal stimulus package of over US$300 billion unveiled in November 2008 was the primary reason for the swift revival in economic activity.[215] The package was focused on increasing state investment in infrastructure projects like the construction of high-speed railways and low-cost housing, thus boosting domestic and import demand. It not only lifted economic growth in China but also generated positive spillover effects onto the Asian region.[216] In Singapore, GDP grew at the pace of 18.5 per cent in the second quarter of 2009, led by a rebound in manufacturing production and exports.[217] During the following two quarters, growth broadened to more sectors of the economy and property prices recovered strongly. For 2009 as a whole however, GDP growth was flat; at the end of the year, the economy had still not regained its pre-crisis level. In contrast, the number of people in employment, at 3 million, had exceeded its previous high, an outcome that could be partly attributed to the JCS.[218] The decisive economic rebound came only in 2010 when a revival of external demand due in part to unprecedented fiscal stimuli in major economies other than China propelled Singapore's GDP growth to 14.5 per cent.[219] Following that, the economy slowed again in 2011 and 2012 because of the European sovereign debt crisis, which dampened business sentiment and investment.

The years after the resolution of the global and European crises saw renewed growth in Singapore, although China's economic slowdown at mid-decade reduced the pace somewhat. Compared to the previous period, the trend expansion was at slower rates that averaged 3.5 per cent per annum between 2013 and 2019 because of household deleveraging and fiscal consolidation in the advanced countries, coupled with restrictions on the entry of foreign workers into Singapore. In 2020 however came the shock of another epidemic, but one with effects that were more deleterious than those of SARS in 2003. China was again the source, which is not surprising given its long history of tolerating markets where live animals were sold for public consumption. The market in this case

---

213 Azhar Ghani, "Singapore in 2009: Braving a Grave New World", in *Southeast Asian Affairs 2010* (Singapore: Institute of Southeast Asian Studies, 2010), pp. 262–4.

214 *The Straits Times*, 7 May 2009.

215 A. McKissack and J. Xu, "Chinese Macroeconomic Management Through the Crisis and Beyond", *Asian-Pacific Economic Literature* 25, 1 (2011): 43–55; *The Business Times*, 8 Apr. 2009, 14 Apr. 2009; *The Straits Times*, 19 Apr. 2009, 30 Aug. 2009.

216 "Singapore's Export Performance", *Economic Survey of Singapore 2009* (Singapore: Ministry of Trade and Industry), pp. 30–2.

217 *The Straits Times*, 17 July 2009; *Today*, 12 Oct. 2009.

218 "Employment Trends During Recessions: A Comparison from Peak to Trough", *Economic Survey of Singapore 2009* (Singapore: Ministry of Trade and Industry), pp. 9, 11.

219 *The Business Times*, 21 May 2010, 7 Feb. 2011.

was situated in Wuhan, an industrial city in central China.[220] From there in December 2019, air passengers travelling out of the country brought the disease to the rest of the world. By March 2020 when the World Health Organization declared that a pandemic had broken out, the disease had taken root in many places. As it was caused by a strain of the coronavirus responsible for SARS (SARSCoV2) and in view of the year of outbreak, it was given the unceremonious name of COVID-19.[221] In only a short while, it became apparent that COVID-19 was a global phenomenon affecting many more people than SARS had done and was equally contagious, although its fatality rate was lower.

In late January 2020, Singapore was one of the first countries outside China to be struck by an imported case; the first deaths occurred in March.[222] In February and March, community transmission multiplied; even worse, many foreign workers living in dormitories across the island contracted the disease because of cramped and unsanitary conditions.[223] Fortunately, the nation was prepared to deal with the pandemic after learning the lessons from the SARS episode.[224] The infrastructure for epidemic management had been enhanced, including the stockpiling of protective equipment, medications and vaccines. More crucially, the National Centre for Infectious Diseases had been opened in 2019 to serve as a disease isolation centre and intensive care facilities at hospitals had been boosted.[225] After the first patient was detected with the disease, the government formed a multi-ministry taskforce, implemented social distancing measures and contact tracing, and distributed surgical masks to all Singaporean households.[226] Events and social gatherings involving large groups were suspended and bars, cinemas and entertainment outlets were closed. Shopping malls and public attractions were required to reduce crowd density.

These measures did not stop the number of COVID-19 cases from increasing exponentially, forcing the authorities to implement the "circuit breaker" lockdown in early April for eight weeks.[227] During the lockdown, significantly stricter measures were imposed and all schools and non-essential workplaces were shut down. Mask wearing was mandatory, employees worked from home and schools conducted home-based classes; on-premises dining was prohibited in food establishments and even religious services moved online. As COVID-19 cases began to stabilise in June 2020, the restrictions were gradually

---

220 *The Straits Times*, 30 Mar. 2020, 18 Dec. 2021.

221 *The Straits Times*, 12 Feb. 2020.

222 J.J. Woo, *Capacity-Building and Pandemics: Singapore's Response to Covid-19* (Palgrave Macmillan, 2021), pp. 67–75, 78–9; *The Straits Times*, 18 Mar. 2021.

223 *White Paper on Singapore's Response to COVID-19: Lessons for the Next Pandemic* (Singapore: Prime Minister's Office, 2023), pp. 6, 14–15, 18–19, 22–3, 26–7; *The Business Times*, 10 Apr. 2020; *The Straits Times*, 21 Apr. 2020, 24 May 2021, 6 Mar. 2022.

224 *Today*, 2 Feb. 2020; *The Straits Times*, 24 May 2021.

225 Chow Hwee Kwan and Ho Kong Weng, "The Case of Singapore", in *Economic Policy and the Covid-19 Crisis: The Macroeconomic Response in the US, Europe and East Asia*, ed. B. Andreosso-O'Callaghan, W. Moon and W. Sohn (Abingdon: Routledge, 2022), p. 204.

226 *The Straits Times*, 20 Mar. 2020, 27 Mar. 2020, 5 Apr. 2020, 12 Nov. 2020, 24 May 2021; *The Business Times*, 20 Mar. 2020; *Today*, 20 Mar. 2020.

227 "Impact of the Circuit Breaker and Budget Measures in Response to COVID-19", *Economic Survey of Singapore Second Quarter 2020* (Singapore: Ministry of Trade and Industry), pp. 44–7; *The Straits Times*, 7 Apr. 2020, 10 Apr. 2020, 22 Apr. 2020, 19 Mar. 2021; *Today*, 14 Apr. 2020, 2 June 2020.

relaxed and a cautious series of reopening measures across a span of three phases was implemented to allow for a controlled return to day-to-day living.[228] But the intermittent outbreak of new clusters of infection or new variants of the disease compelled the authorities to reimpose safe management measures.[229]

This of course proved to be highly disruptive to the economy. Policymakers had to make unpalatable choices between containing the virus and minimising the adverse impact on the economy of restrictions in a trade-off between "lives and livelihoods".[230] By the time the domestic population was almost fully vaccinated against the disease and it had become endemic in 2022, the economic damage done was incalculable. Unlike in past recessions or crises caused by either a demand or supply shock, there were concurrently a fall in consumer spending due to controls on the movement of people and interruptions in the supply of goods and services because of factory and shop closures as well as trade disruptions.[231] One private sector company estimated the direct cost of the pandemic on Singapore's health system to be around $142 million a year and indirect costs due to productivity losses to be $3.4 billion.[232]

It is however more instructive to look at the key economic statistics to gauge the impact of COVID-19 as they accounted for inter-industry linkages and multiplier effects. The cumulative decline of GDP from its peak in October 2019 to its trough eight months later in June 2020 was 14 per cent, and for the full year 2020, aggregate output contracted by 3.9 per cent.[233] Both were unprecedented occurrences. The travel-related and domestically oriented sectors which included accommodation, food services, retail trade, recreation and air transport were harder hit than the manufacturing and other sectors were.[234] Employment in the service sector as a whole fell by 107,200 in the first three quarters of 2020. Apart from the circuit breaker which was estimated to have reduced GDP by 2.2 per cent on an annual basis, the declines seen in these industries were due to border closure measures that barred or restricted the entry of travellers from other countries, or required them to be tested for COVID-19 and complete a two-week quarantine period.[235] These effectively put a stop to

---

228 *The Straits Times*, 21 Oct. 2020, 17 Dec. 2020, 24 Aug. 2021.

229 *The Straits Times*, 8 May 2021, 24 May 2021.

230 Terence Ho, "Supporting Jobs and Livelihoods During the Pandemic", *Ethos*, Issue 22 (2021): 43; *The Straits Times*, 2 June 2020, 2 Nov. 2020, 8 Mar. 2023.

231 Monetary Authority of Singapore, "Background Note on Macroeconomic Policy Responses to Covid-19: The Singapore Experience", *BIS Papers No. 122* (Basel: Bank for International Settlements, 2022), pp. 268–9, 272–3.

232 Merck & Co (MSD), *A Neglected Burden: The Ongoing Economic Costs of COVID-19 in Singapore*, 2023.

233 *The Straits Times*, 12 Aug. 2020, 4 Jan. 2021.

234 "Impact of the COVID-19 Pandemic on the Singapore Economy", *Economic Survey of Singapore First Quarter 2020* (Singapore: Ministry of Trade and Industry), pp. 39–43; *The Straits Times*, 26 Mar. 2020, 24 Nov. 2021.

235 *The Straits Times*, 13 Aug. 2020. Many countries also imposed travel restrictions and border controls, which exacerbated the fall in international travel.

all visitors to Singapore, especially in the early days of the pandemic.[236] The sharp reduction in air travel and consequent grounding of aircraft led in turn to a plunge in the output of the aerospace sector. Furthermore, a steep decline in global demand curtailed the volumes of wholesale trade, seaborne cargo and air cargo handled.[237] Meanwhile, the construction and marine engineering industries were disrupted by the spread of COVID-19 among foreign labourers and the reduced inflow of such workers. The business services and real estate industries were affected by the generalised slowdown in domestic activity.[238]

In light of the severe dislocations to daily economic life, the government realised right from the start that monetary policy would have limited potency as an anti-recessionary tool and the onus of fighting the recession had to be on fiscal policy.[239] Still, MAS shifted the policy band for the Singapore dollar exchange rate downward and adopted a zero appreciation policy in late March 2020.[240] And as the revenue streams of businesses dried up, companies' need to obtain credit from financial institutions became urgent. MAS therefore introduced several measures targeted at firms, particularly SMEs which were badly impacted by the epidemic: first, it took on the same risk-sharing role that it had performed during the Global Financial Crisis; second, SMEs were allowed to defer principal repayment on secured loans; third, a facility was launched to lend Singapore dollars at an interest rate of 0.1 per cent per annum for a two-year period to banks for on-lending to SMEs.[241] As a result, local enterprises were able to obtain $5.7 billion in bridging and working capital loans at lower interest rates than usual. Individuals and households were permitted to defer payments on residential property loans and insurance premiums, as well as convert outstanding credit card balances to lower interest loans.[242]

Faced with the worst recession in the nation's history and the unprecedented nature of the pandemic, the Singapore government responded with the most comprehensive set of fiscal measures to date to alleviate the economic cost of the public health restrictions. In monetary terms, these measures were also the largest on record, amounting to about $71 billion or 14 per cent of GDP.[243] This led to a huge deficit that the government needed to, but could not, finance during its political term in office; about $30 billion had to be drawn from the reserves again. Roughly two-thirds of the direct fiscal injections were devoted to keeping workers employed and minimising firm closures via wage subsidies and cost-saving measures; the rest were for providing financial assistance to

---

236 "Performance of the Singapore Economy in 2020", *Economic Survey of Singapore 2020* (Singapore: Ministry of Trade and Industry), pp. 86–93; *The Straits Times*, 5 June 2020, 1 Feb. 2021; *Today*, 17 July 2020.

237 *The Straits Times*, 27 Dec. 2020.

238 *Macroeconomic Review* (Singapore: Monetary Authority of Singapore, April 2020), p. 61; *The Straits Times*, 6 Aug. 2020, 3 Jan. 2022.

239 Chow and Ho, "The Case of Singapore", pp. 211, 212–4; *The Straits Times*, 31 Mar. 2020.

240 Monetary Authority of Singapore, "Background Note", pp. 273–5; *The Straits Times*, 30 Mar. 2020.

241 *The Straits Times*, 6 Apr. 2020, 20 Apr. 2020; *The Business Times*, 12 Oct. 2020.

242 *The Straits Times*, 1 Apr. 2020; *The Business Times*, 5 Oct. 2020.

243 Another $22 billion was earmarked as capital for the government's loan guarantees. Monetary Authority of Singapore, "Background Note", pp. 275, 276, 277; *The Straits Times*, 9 Apr. 2020, 14 Sept. 2022; *Today*, 26 May 2020.

vulnerable individuals and households. It has been estimated that if these measures and the complementary monetary easing had not been carried out, the contraction in GDP in 2020 would have been more than 10 per cent.[244]

The government's fiscal package was delivered in four budgets in 2020 announced in quick succession that were given the names Unity, Resilience, Solidarity and Fortitude.[245] The first, presented at the usual time of the annual budget in February, featured as its key measure the Jobs Support Scheme (JSS), which will be discussed in detail below. In addition, a Care and Support programme handed out between $100 and $300 to all adult Singaporeans depending on income earned and various tax rebates were extended to companies in the aviation, hospitality, MICE and leisure sectors, in addition to a 25 per cent corporate tax rebate for all firms.[246] A 100 per cent property tax rebate was offered to shops while offices and industrial properties received 30 per cent so that the savings could be passed on to tenants.[247] The occupiers of HDB and other commercial government properties, such as hawkers and stallholders, were granted rental waivers of a half or full month. This first budget was followed by a much larger supplementary budget of $28 billion in March, which enhanced both the JSS and Care and Support schemes, the latter by a tripling of the initial payouts and an extra $300 for all parents and the elderly.[248] The property tax rebates and rental waivers announced earlier were increased.[249] A relief scheme was also announced that paid a monthly sum of $1,000 for nine months (subject to certain criteria) to the approximately 100,000 self-employed persons in Singapore; such persons and companies were allowed to defer income tax payments for three months.[250]

The last two budgets, announced in April and May, essentially extended and expanded the financial assistance provided in the earlier schemes.[251] The former was drawn up to mitigate the economic impact of the circuit breaker and the latter also included a new Jobs and Skills package aimed at creating 40,000 jobs, 25,000 traineeships and 30,000 skills training opportunities.[252] The scheme was intended not only to help redeploy laid-off workers from the worst affected industries through training subsidies but also to boost employability for fresh graduates by co-funding traineeship allowances. Support for households and the less privileged was most extensive. Every Singaporean household was given at least a $100 utilities credit while those living in HDB flats received somewhat more as well as rebates to help pay estate and conservancy charges. Cash grants that provided income support for up to three months were provided to people who had lost their jobs, experienced significant income losses or had gone on no-pay leave.

---

[244] *The Straits Times*, 17 Feb. 2022.

[245] *The Straits Times*, 5 June 2020.

[246] *Macroeconomic Review* (Singapore: Monetary Authority of Singapore, April 2020), pp. 71, 72; *The Straits Times*, 18 Feb. 2020, 19 Feb. 2020, 6 Apr. 2020; *Today*, 19 Feb. 2020.

[247] Alfred M. Wu, "Fiscal Responses to COVID-19 in Singapore and Hong Kong", *Ethos*, Issue 22 (2021): 32, 34–5, 36–8, 39.

[248] *The Straits Times*, 26 Mar. 2020, 28 May 2021; *Today*, 26 Mar. 2020, 3 Apr. 2020.

[249] *Today*, 27 Mar. 2020.

[250] Ho, "Supporting Jobs and Livelihoods", pp. 44–5, 46–9; *The Straits Times*, 28 Apr. 2020, 4 June 2020.

[251] *The Straits Times*, 6 Apr. 2020; *Today*, 6 Apr. 2020, 7 Apr. 2020, 10 Apr. 2020, 21 Apr. 2020.

[252] *The Business Times*, 7 Apr. 2020, 26 May 2020; *Today*, 28 May 2020; *The Straits Times*, 21 Aug. 2021.

Targeted at the labour market, the JSS was modelled after the 2009 JCS (Jobs Credit Scheme); it initially provided a wage subsidy of 8 per cent on the first $3,600 of employees' salaries. This was later enhanced and graduated to give priority to companies in the tourism, hospitality and aviation industries by raising the rate to 75 per cent for them, while a lower rate of 50 per cent was applied to the food services and retail sectors and 25 per cent to the rest.[253] At the same time, the salary ceiling was also increased to $4,600. During the circuit breaker period, the different rates were temporarily increased to 75 per cent for all firms.[254] The scheme was subsequently extended to March 2021 at lower subsidy rates except for the most badly affected sectors, which continued to be covered until September 2021.[255] In all, the JSS cost the government more than $25 billion but benefitted 150,000 employers and prevented the resident unemployment rate from rising above the level of 4.8 per cent registered in September 2020, the highest during the entire crisis. By the same token, resident employment declined in only the first three quarters of the year.[256] An official study found that the JSS had saved 165,000 local jobs over the period of March to December 2020.[257] The Jobs and Skills scheme contributed to these outcomes by placing nearly 76,000 persons in jobs or training programmes. In August 2020, the government separately launched the Jobs Growth Incentive, which provided a wage subsidy for each eligible local hire.[258] The amounts were 25 per cent of the first $5,000 in salary for up to a year for employees aged below 40 and 50 per cent of the first $6,000 for 18 months for employees aged 40 and above. From September 2020 to February 2021, firms in Singapore made use of the incentives to hire an additional 47,000 workers.[259]

As transmission of the virus eased within Singapore, the phased reopening of the economy from June 2020 led to a rebound in GDP in the third and fourth quarters, averaging 6.4 per cent, thus bringing output back to its pre-COVID level.[260] The bounce-back was underpinned by a recovery in private consumption: food, beverage and retail sales recovered with the resumption of dine-in activities and reopening of retail outlets but declined again whenever sporadic outbreaks in 2021 led to a reimposition of safe measures.[261] The outward-oriented sectors like manufacturing and wholesale trade also recovered relatively quickly in the second half of 2020 as major economies around the world emerged from initial lockdowns. Manufacturing output resumed expansion as global

---

[253] *The Straits Times*, 31 Mar. 2020, 7 Sept. 2020; *The Business Times*, 21 Apr. 2020.

[254] *The Straits Times*, 9 Apr. 2020.

[255] *Today*, 24 Aug. 2020; *The Straits Times*, 28 Aug. 2020, 21 Feb. 2021.

[256] "Employment Trends During the COVID-19 Pandemic", *Economic Survey of Singapore Third Quarter 2021* (Singapore: Ministry of Trade and Industry), pp. 21–2. As in past recessions, a fall of 214,000 in the number of migrant workers cushioned the impact on residents. *Assessment of the Impact of Key COVID-19 Budget Measures*, Occasional Paper (Singapore: Ministry of Finance, 2022), p. 26.

[257] "Impact of the Jobs Support Scheme on Labour Market Outcomes", *Economic Survey of Singapore 2021* (Singapore: Ministry of Trade and Industry), pp. 87–8, 91.

[258] *Today*, 19 Aug. 2020; *The Straits Times*, 28 Aug. 2020, 1 Apr. 2021, 15 July 2021.

[259] *Assessment of the Impact*, p. 51.

[260] *The Straits Times*, 23 Nov. 2020; *Today*, 4 Feb. 2021.

[261] "Trends in the Recovery of Retail and Food & Beverage Spending in Singapore", *Economic Survey of Singapore 2022* (Singapore: Ministry of Trade and Industry), pp. 77–8, 79–80.

demand for semiconductors and chemicals strengthened. In contrast, the level of activity in Singapore's tourism and aviation-related sectors stayed depressed as cross-border travel restrictions remained in place.[262] These industries finally commenced a gradual recovery in early 2022 when Singapore allowed vaccinated foreign travellers into the country and worldwide borders reopened; the disruption had lasted seven quarters from the onset of the crisis (in comparison, the recovery from SARS extended over three).[263] The construction, marine and offshore engineering, and aerospace industries similarly languished below their pre-pandemic levels at the end of 2020 and started to grow again only in 2021, thus helping overall GDP to rebound vigorously by 9.7 per cent in that year.

If COVID-19 could be said to have had a brighter side, it could be that the pandemic accelerated the adoption of digitalisation and new business practices such as telecommuting, which would raise productivity in the longer term. The government provided support through various schemes tailored for consumers, firms and financial institutions such as the Digital Resilience Bonus, the SME Go Digital Programme and the Productivity Solutions Grant.[264] Even hawkers and stallholders were given grants to encourage them to migrate to digital payment systems. These initiatives were complemented by the private sector; for example, Visa opened a facility in Singapore for innovation in commerce and payments.[265] The restrictions necessitated by the pandemic also resulted in a shift in consumer spending from physical to online channels, especially for food and beverage purchases, a trend that continued after the crisis was over.[266] This led to growth in food delivery services provided by outfits such as Deliveroo, Food Panda and Grab, the last of which was also dominant in private car hire services.[267] The pandemic-induced leap in digital adoption was perhaps the only good thing that came out of the crisis.

Income Inequality and Poverty

In the initial decades after Singapore embarked on an export-oriented strategy of industrialisation, not only was its economic development remarkable but the strategy also benefitted a wide segment of the local population. Whether one calls this "the trickle-down effect", "a rising tide lifts all boats" or simply "growth with equity" is immaterial; the fact is that strong growth in the early period did not worsen income distribution, and in all likelihood improved it when compared to colonial times. However, according to several measures, income inequality rose from the 1990s due to structural changes in the labour market and government policies. Furthermore, as during the colonial era with its underclass, it is still possible to be poor in rich Singapore. In what follows, we

262 *The Straits Times*, 26 Jan. 2022.

263 "Recovery of Air Travel and Tourism in Singapore", *Economic Survey of Singapore Second Quarter 2022* (Singapore: Ministry of Trade and Industry), pp. 30–6; *The Straits Times*, 7 Mar. 2022, 5 May 2022, 21 Oct. 2022, 17 Jan. 2023.

264 *The Business Times*, 27 May 2020; *The Straits Times*, 19 June 2020, 7 Nov. 2020.

265 "Digital Globalization: How MNCs Must Reinvent to Tap Asia's Growth Story", *Future Ready Singapore*, 2016.

266 *The Straits Times*, 15 Apr. 2020.

267 *The Straits Times*, 29 Mar. 2019, 11 Apr. 2022, 1 Aug. 2023, 2 Feb. 2024.

spell out the changes between the two periods, discuss their causes, and review the policy measures taken to address these issues.

A widely used measure of the size distribution of income, the Gini ratio, shows that inequality among workers decreased from 1966 through to the late seventies, falling from 0.5 in 1966 to 0.41 in 1980.[268] It then increased to 0.47 in 1984, though this was still lower than in 1966.[269] The improvement in income distribution in the early years could be attributed to the massive increase in employment and the induction of youths and females into the labour force—a result of the labour-intensive industrialisation programme pursued by the government.[270] The NWC (National Wages Council) guidelines also recommended a fixed quantum of wage increases, which formed a larger proportion in the income of lower-income groups. Between 1973 and 1979, lower-paid occupations like production operators and service workers experienced higher earnings growth than higher-paid professional and managerial workers. If the progressive tax structure and the extensive social benefits in subsidised public housing, education and healthcare are taken into account, the record for this period seems even better.[271]

The rise in inequality in the early 1980s was manifested in a larger income gap between workers in different occupations and with different levels of education. In 1983, for example, professional and managerial workers' earnings were five times more than those of production and service workers. Similarly, those with a tertiary education earned about six times more than those with only a post-primary education. In this case, the worsening of income distribution was caused by greater human capital formation and economic restructuring into higher value-added industries, which benefitted skilled workers disproportionately. As we have seen, this period was characterised by policies aimed at increasing the supply of skilled and professional manpower while phasing out unskilled labour.[272] The income gap was also noticeable in the increased income differences between the major races in Singapore. In 1991, a survey showed that the proportion of working Malays who earned only between \$200–\$599 per month was higher than that of their Chinese and Indian counterparts.[273]

After the mid-eighties recession, the NWC's central role in the wage-setting process was reduced and the Council stopped issuing quantitative guidelines altogether. Increased

---

268 "Poverty, Income Distribution and the Less Privileged", in Lim and Associates, *Policy Options*, pp. 400–7; V.V.B. Rao and M.K. Ramakrishnan, *Income Inequality in Singapore: Impact of Economic Growth and Structural Change 1966–1975* (Singapore: Singapore University Press, 1980), pp. 23–8, 31–3, 38–9, 45–52, 54–8. The Gini ratios reported here are based on data from the *Labour Force Survey* published by the Singapore government.

269 I. Islam and C. Kirkpatrick, "Export-Led Development, Labour-Market Conditions and the Distribution of Income: The Case of Singapore", *Cambridge Journal of Economics* 10, 2 (1986): 119–23. The rise in inequality was confirmed by survey data which indicated that the proportion of households with below average income increased from 62 per cent in 1977–78 to 68 per cent in 1982–83.

270 *The Straits Times*, 28 Nov. 1974.

271 Lee Sheng-Yi, "Income Distribution, Taxation, and Social Benefits of Singapore", *The Journal of Developing Areas* 14, 1 (1979): 82, 91–7; *The Business Times*, 28 Mar. 1978.

272 Islam and Kirkpatrick, "Export-Led Development", pp. 115, 116, 117.

273 William K.M. Lee, "The Poor in Singapore: Issues and Options", *Journal of Contemporary Asia* 31, 1 (2001): 57–8.

emphasis was given to wage increases decided at the firm or industry level, so as to allow wages to change in line with productivity gains rather than being seniority-based.[274] An annual variable component (AVC) was incorporated into the total wage, thereby giving employers the flexibility to reduce wages in downturns.[275] In 1999, the flexi-wage system was enhanced by introducing a monthly variable component (MVC) of up to 10 per cent of wages, which together with the 20 per cent of AVC allowed firms to further vary total wages according to economic conditions.[276] In and of themselves, more flexible wages could raise earnings inequality between workers by creating a link between wage increases and worker performance, even though companies in Singapore were generally slow in adopting the MVC.

In view of Singapore's rapid economic growth, it could have been expected that the poverty inherited from the colonial regime would be alleviated. This is certainly the conclusion from a carefully crafted poverty line for 1982–83.[277] At $60 per capita per month, it could in fact be surmised that poverty was not only mitigated but completely eradicated.[278] Although it may sound implausible, the absolute poverty level arrived at took only food intake into consideration while the disabled and aged staying in institutional homes were not covered. At most, it could be inferred that no one faced starvation.[279] A revised poverty line that considered lifestyle changes since the 1950s was $120, which had the more plausible implication that the number of households living in poverty in 1982–83 was 7.4 per cent.[280] Going by this figure, the huge reduction in the poverty rate compared to the early 1950s partly reflected smaller household sizes and a lower dependency burden resulting from more women working. As for the profile of poor households, they typically had a single income earner (usually the male) in low-paying manual jobs and lowly-educated or unemployed members who lived in rented one or two-room public flats. Combining these households with the destitute, handicapped and elderly, there were around 200,000 poor persons, but only 65,000 received public assistance or community help.[281] This assistance included homes operated by voluntary, religious and private bodies that were supported by grants from the government.

After increasing in the eighties, the Gini ratio was largely stable right up to the early part of the 2000s, suggesting that the degree of income inequality was more or less

---

[274] Lee, *The Unexpected Nation*, pp. 560, 573.

[275] Mukhopadhaya, Shantakumar and Rao, *Economic Growth and Income Inequality*, pp. 135–6.

[276] *The Straits Times*, 17 Oct. 2020, 18 Oct. 2020.

[277] "Poverty, Income Distribution", pp. 392–5, 399–400, 408–11. The poverty line was based on two sets of least cost food baskets and was robust to different construction methodologies.

[278] *The Business Times*, 17 Nov. 1990.

[279] *The Straits Times*, 21 Apr. 1985, 19 Mar. 1989.

[280] Even among the poorest 5 per cent of households in 1983, 81 per cent had a television, 56 per cent a telephone and 19 per cent a washing machine. Lim, Pang and Findlay, "Singapore", p. 129.

[281] Irene Y.H. Ng, "Being Poor in a Rich 'Nanny State': Developments in Singapore Social Welfare", *The Singapore Economic Review* 60, 3 (2015): 1550038-2, 1550038-5–1550038-6; *The New Paper*, 6 Mar. 1989.

unchanged.[282] This conclusion was corroborated by an official study that found that the proportion of households in absolute poverty had remained at 5 per cent in 1991.[283] From about 2003, however, the ratio started to rise and it reached 0.48 in 2007, much higher than in other developed countries. It should however be recognised that Singapore is a city-state with an urban economy, lacking therefore a rural sector that helps to mitigate income differences.[284] Nonetheless, the structure of the labour market had already fundamentally altered since the 1990s. First, older workers aged 50 and above increasingly made up a larger proportion of the long-term unemployed in Singapore because employers were generally more reluctant to hire and invest in training them, despite the government's concerted efforts to encourage employment of older workers. They were more prone to retrenchment and once unemployed, found it difficult to get another job due to their low educational attainment and skills. As Singapore's population aged, more elderly people with inadequate financial resources slipped into poverty.

Second, a phenomenon known as "job polarisation" had appeared all over the world since the nineties as a result of technological change that favoured highly skilled workers. On the one hand, the proliferation of IT and its applications led to a demand for educated knowledge workers; on the other, the number of mundane and routine tasks was reduced by automation and digitalisation, and of course robots. These transitions reduced the number of middle-paying jobs, forcing such workers to join the lower-educated labourers in performing non-routine manual tasks and service jobs. The consequence is an increasing gulf in earnings between high- and low-wage workers, a trend seen in Singapore as well.

In addition to skill-biased technological advances, wage disparity in Singapore was accentuated by the government's foreign talent and migrant worker policies.[285] By augmenting the size of the labour force, the large influx of low-skilled foreign workers held down economy-wide wage increases. But these workers also depressed earnings at the lower end of the nominal wage scale. At the upper end, the policy of recruiting skilled expatriates to attain global city status and to meet labour shortages raised domestic salaries to the levels prevailing in the industrialised countries.[286] Thus, earnings were stretched at both ends, worsening the income distribution. In the first decade of the 2000s, the median wages of employed residents in the bottom 30 per cent fell in real terms whereas the rest experienced increases, with the rise being particularly steep for the top 20 per cent of income earners.[287] The former were mostly employed as cleaners, security guards, plant and machine operators and the like while the latter were usually professional, managerial and technical staff. Hence,

---

282 P. Mukhopadhaya, *Income Inequality in Singapore* (Abingdon: Routledge, 2014), pp. 64–7; *The Business Times*, 31 May 2000; *The Straits Times*, 21 Feb. 2020.

283 Lee, "The Poor in Singapore", pp. 57, 60.

284 Hui and Toh, *Growth with Equity*, pp. 6–8, 9–13; Nathan Peng, "Inequality and the Social Compact in Singapore", *Journal of Southeast Asian Economies* 36, 3 (2019): 358; *The Straits Times*, 11 Dec. 2010. The long-term trends in the Gini ratio obtained from a different data source were broadly similar except for an increase in the early 1990s. Ng, "Being Poor", pp. 1550038-3, 1550038-4.

285 *Today*, 15 Feb. 2011; *The Straits Times*, 19 Jan. 2016.

286 Islam and Kirkpatrick, "Export-Led Development", p. 124.

287 Jacqueline Poh, "Workfare: The Fourth Pillar of Social Security in Singapore", *Ethos*, Issue 3 (2007): 51; *The Business Times*, 10 Feb. 2001.

a dichotomous economic structure that resembled the dual economy in late colonial times had emerged in which a high-wage sector employing expatriates and oriented to globalised activities co-existed with a low-wage sector that serviced the high-wage earners.[288]

In 2005, the poorest 10 per cent, numbering some 90,000 to 100,000 households, earned around $640 a month for a family of four. In 2012, nearly a quarter of employed residents still earned less than $1,500 a month.[289] This income level could be compared to average household expenditure on basic needs of $1,250 and a guideline of around $1,500 used by many public agencies to indicate the need for social assistance.[290] Alternatively, policymakers defined the low-income group more broadly as people in the bottom 30 per cent of households, although this is by no means an indicator of absolute poverty.[291] Despite this absence of an official poverty line in Singapore, an attempt was made to derive the level of poverty in 2013 using the above thresholds, yielding the conclusion that it was in the vicinity of 10–14 per cent.[292] If the relative poverty level, which takes into account the standard of living in a specific country and is defined as half of median income, is used instead to compare nations, then the rate rises to 20–22 per cent, higher than the OECD countries and East Asia. Wage stagnation apart, poverty had increased in the new century because of two developments in Singapore's labour market. One was the rising number of low-wage workers engaged in part-time work, which offered fewer benefits than full-time occupations in terms of CPF contributions, bonuses and leave. A second reason was an increase in the elderly poor who had to depend on family support, which was not always forthcoming.

A related malaise is the intergenerational transmission of poverty in the form of low social mobility. In the early phase of economic development, upward mobility was high because Singapore started from a largely unskilled workforce and huge public investments were made in education and healthcare. In the first two decades of the new century, however, even though educational attainment and occupation status had further improved further in the general population, social mobility declined to a moderately low level for the cohort of Singaporeans who were in their twenties and thirties.[293] This finding is consistent with the observations that class rather than merit played a key role in admissions to the best primary schools and that university-educated parents were more likely to have children

---

[288] Yahya, "Singapore in 2010", p. 262.

[289] Hui and Toh, *Growth with Equity*, p. 23.

[290] C. Smith et al., *A Handbook on Inequality, Poverty and Unmet Social Needs in Singapore* (Singapore: Lien Centre for Social Innovation, 2015), pp. 14–15, 17; Yeoh Lam Keong, "Rethinking A New Social Compact for Singapore", *Ethos*, Issue 3 (2007): 9; *The Straits Times*, 25 Sept. 2013. The average household expenditure on basic needs is a measure of minimum expenditure on necessities such as food, clothing, and shelter for a household in a one or two-room HDB rental flat.

[291] M.G. Asher and A. Nandy, "Singapore's Policy Responses to Ageing, Inequality and Poverty: An Assessment", *International Social Security Review* 61, 1 (2008): 46.

[292] Ng, "Being Poor", pp. 1550038-5–1550038-7, 1550038-9–1550038-10; *The Straits Times*, 23 Oct. 2013.

[293] Ho Kong Weng and Marcus Tan Kheng Tat, "Challenges to Social Mobility in Singapore: Facilitating Social Mobility", in *The Singapore Economy: Dynamism and Inclusion*, ed. Hoon Hian Teck (Abingdon: Routledge, 2022), pp. 225–9; *The Straits Times*, 14 Aug. 2013.

who qualified for the top secondary schools in Singapore.[294] Studies elsewhere have shown that parental and family background is an important factor determining social mobility or immobility; this is also true in Singapore where parental influence has been found to be a determinant of educational attainment. Skilled parents were usually more educated, earned a higher income and were more capable of coaching their children in their studies.[295] Furthermore, streaming in secondary schools and the existence of independent schools also resulted in greater intergenerational immobility. Taken together with the principle of meritocracy practised in Singapore, low social mobility risked perpetuating a permanent underclass of poor people.[296]

According to official data, the Gini ratio came down slightly to 0.46 in 2013 following its peak in 2007 (Figure 30).[297] The fall in the ratio was reflected in faster real income growth for the lowest two quintiles of households (the bottom 40 per cent) from 2009 to 2014.[298] After accounting for taxes and transfers, the growth was even faster than that of the highest quintile (the top 20 per cent). In monetary terms, the average household incomes of low-wage workers at the bottom 20 per cent increased from $1,500 in 2009 to $1,972 in 2014, a rise of about one-third.[299] Correspondingly, the real wages of individuals in the lowest quintile followed a similar trend. From 2013 onwards, the decline in the Gini ratio accelerated until it reached the level of 0.43 (before taxes and transfers) in 2023. After taking account of taxes and transfers, the downward trend was basically intact, although the degree of inequality was lower. The Gini ratio for this adjusted measure fluctuated around 0.41 and 0.42 until the decline started in 2013, which finally brought it down to an all-time low of 0.37 in 2023. Compared with countries that had higher tax and transfer regimes, the reduction in the adjusted ratio was smaller.[300] Still, Singapore's progressive fiscal system and government transfers had steadily widened the gap between the two Gini measures, since the top quintile paid more than half of taxes while social benefits and transfers favoured the lower-income groups.[301]

---

294 Tan Ern Ser, "Comments on Presentation by Speaker", in *Inequality in Singapore*, ed. Faizal Bin Yahya (Singapore: World Scientific, 2015), p. 43.

295 Ho Kong Weng, "Wage Inequality, Intergenerational Mobility and Education in Singapore", *Ethos*, Issue 3 (2007): 44.

296 Smith et al., *Handbook on Inequality*, pp. 27–30; *The Straits Times*, 3 Mar. 2011.

297 *Income Growth, Inequality and Mobility Trends in Singapore*, Occasional Paper (Singapore: Ministry of Finance, 2015), pp. 4–6, 8; *Key Household Income Trends*, various years (Singapore: Department of Statistics); *Today*, 19 Feb. 2014; *The Straits Times*, 3 Mar. 2014.

298 *The Business Times*, 27 Feb. 2016.

299 N. Ganesan, "Singapore in 2014: Managing Domestic and Regional Concerns and Signalling a New Regional Role", in *Southeast Asian Affairs 2015* (Singapore: Institute of Southeast Asian Studies, 2015), p. 310.

300 Smith et al., *Handbook on Inequality*, p. 7; *The Straits Times*, 19 Mar. 2018.

301 Peng, "Inequality and the Social Compact", p. 359; *The Straits Times*, 18 Mar. 2014.

Figure 30. The Gini Ratio in Singapore, 2000–23
Source: *Key Household Income Trends*, various issues. Department of Statistics, Singapore.

Turning to policies to address income inequality and poverty, it should be stated at the outset that a welfare state is anathema to the Singapore government. Instead, as in other East Asian countries, social policies were geared towards a "productivist" model of welfare with heavy state spending on education, healthcare and housing, as documented in previous chapters.[302] In such regimes, social policy played a supportive role to economic policies while welfare programmes and redistribution policies were typically underdeveloped.[303] However, although this had been generally true for Singapore in earlier times, significant economic and social changes in recent decades—ageing, higher inequality and poverty—had forced the government to reconsider its philosophy.[304] Thus, social policies evolved from a dependence on self-reliance through which individuals and their families were expected to be the first line of support, to a more proactive slant of providing state help to those segments of the population left behind by the vicissitudes of economic change.[305] The policy reorientation could also be interpreted as a shift from a productivist to "protective" model to shield vulnerable workers from enhanced economic risks that had not been

302 Lee Soo Ann and Qian Jiwei, "The Evolving Singaporean Welfare State", *Social Policy and Administration* 51, 6 (2017): 917, 922–7, 932–4.

303 In these countries, social expenditure had generally been oriented towards spending that brought an economic return.

304 In 1995, Singapore's spending on welfare-related programmes made up a mere 2 per cent of total government expenditure. Lee, "The Poor in Singapore", pp. 63–4.

305 *The Straits Times*, 9 Aug. 2013, 15 Aug. 2015.

previously present. The new social welfare regime put in place in the 2000s and 2010s had come an even longer way from the hands-off policy of the British colonialists.[306]

One long-standing pillar of social security in Singapore had remained unchanged amidst all the changes: the CPF. For almost all employed workers, the funds in individual CPF accounts continued to be used for financing expenditures on housing, healthcare, education and approved investments in equities. Realising the CPF's original intention as an old-age retirement scheme, retirement accounts also provide monthly payouts to retirees to partially cover their spending in old age, with the caveat that there is still a group of elderly people with little or no CPF savings due to low-paying jobs or irregular employment.[307] Concern has also arisen that for many Singaporeans, the amount they have in CPF retirement savings is inadequate to finance their pre-retirement lifestyle. In housing, the HDB awarded grants to low-income families and mortgage loans for new buyers of public flats.[308] In 2015, more than 80 per cent of the population still lived in public housing and nine out of ten tenants owned their flats.[309] Rising real estate prices in the 2010s had priced many households out of the private housing market, compelling the government to again mitigate the excessive price increases due to the purchase of private properties by foreign investors by imposing additional stamp duties on them.[310] In addition, various restrictions on housing loans taken by local residents were imposed.[311] Since upon retirement Singaporeans tended to be "asset-rich and cash-poor" with most of their wealth in public housing, a Lease Buyback Scheme (or reverse mortgage scheme) was implemented by the government in 2009 to enable them to monetise their housing assets.[312] The proceeds of the sale to the HDB were then paid as monthly instalments into CPF retirement accounts and the owners could still stay in their flats for another 30 years. Alternatively, the elderly could sell their flat and move into a smaller apartment.

Policy developments in the education sphere also had an impact on trends in income inequality. During the two most recent decades, state spending on Institutes of Technical Education (that is, vocational institutes), polytechnics and universities increased further, in line with higher enrolment. In 2012, the literacy rate among the population had increased to 96 per cent, the mean years of schooling had risen to 10.9 for males and 9.9 for females, and education expenditure used up approximately one-fifth of the government budget. Singapore students consistently ranked among the top in the world in science and mathematics exams (PISA scores). In that year's cohort of Singaporeans, 26 per cent made

---

306 The new regime was described by the Minister for Finance in 2013 as a shift to the left-of-centre of the PAP. Lee and Qian, "The Evolving Singaporean Welfare State", p. 930; Tan, *A Very Short History*, p. 140.

307 Lee, "The Poor in Singapore", pp. 66–8.

308 Phang, "Singapore's Housing Policies", pp. 155036-15–1550036-17.

309 Tan, *A Very Short History*, p. 155.

310 *Macroprudential Policies to Mitigate Housing Market Risks, Country Case Study: Singapore*, CFGS Papers No. 69 (Basel: Bank for International Settlements, 2023).

311 Yahya, "Singapore in 2010", p. 263.

312 *The New Paper*, 1 Sept. 2007, 20 May 2010; *Today*, 25 Oct. 2008; *The Straits Times*, 2 Mar. 2009, 6 Mar. 2010.

it to university and the government announced its intention to raise the rate to 40 per cent by 2020, a goal that was broadly attained.[313]

In contrast, public healthcare spending was only 2 per cent of GDP in 2014 out of total healthcare expenditure of 5 per cent, higher than in the 1980s but still low by world standards, partly because the problems posed by an ageing population had not fully set in. However, 80 per cent of hospital care was provided by the government sector, whereas the proportions were reversed for primary care.[314] As before, government subsidies to public hospitals varied with ward classes, in accordance with the principle that patients who demanded higher levels of service in terms of comfort and amenities (including private facilities) should pay more. Furthermore, subsidies were higher for the lower-income groups; for example, patients whose monthly incomes were below $3,200 received 80 per cent subsidies and patients with monthly incomes of above $5,200 65 per cent. To cope with the ageing population and the concomitant increase in health expenditure, Medishield Life, an enhanced and universal form of health insurance with more generous coverage (including for people with pre-existing conditions) and lower co-payments, was introduced in 2015 to replace the existing Medishield plan.[315] In the new scheme, the government provided subsidies on premiums for lower and middle-income persons as well as the pioneer generation born before 1949. In addition, there is Eldershield, an insurance plan that provides coverage for disabled older Singaporeans.[316]

Despite the policy tilt towards poorer households, the official stance remains that of minimising social hand-outs to avoid the perceived negative effects on the work ethic. Hence, there was neither an unemployment insurance scheme nor a minimum wage law. Nevertheless, the government came up with Singapore's own version of unemployment benefits in the form of the Workfare Income Supplement (WIS).[317] Initially introduced in the 2006 budget as a one-off bonus, Workfare was made permanent a year later.[318] As the name suggests, it aimed to top up the incomes of low-wage workers, on the condition that they engaged in work; the supplement should therefore serve as an incentive to continue working. As long as an individual above 35 years of age had worked in three out of six months over a period of a year, the recipient would be eligible for a payment from the state at varying rates: from $150 for a 35 to 44 year old worker earning $1,600 or less per month to $2,800 for a worker aged 60 years and above earning $1,000 per month.[319] These wage supplements, paid partly in take-home pay and partly in CPF contributions,

---

313 Loke Hoe-Yeong and S. Gopinathan, "The Policy and Politics of the Cohort Participation Rate in Universities: The Case of Singapore and 'SkillsFuture'", *International Journal of Chinese Education* 5, 2 (2016): 218–9.

314 Several new regional hospitals with extensive healthcare services were built: Changi General Hospital, Khoo Teck Puat Hospital and Ng Teng Fong General Hospital.

315 Tan, *A Very Short History*, p. 153; *The Business Times*, 3 Aug. 2015; *The Straits Times*, 30 Aug. 2015.

316 Smith et al., *Handbook on Inequality*, pp. 48–9.

317 *The Straits Times*, 29 Nov. 2010.

318 Irene Y.H. Ng, "Workfare in Singapore", in *Welfare Reform in East Asia: Towards Workfare?*, ed. Chak Kwan Chan and Kinglun Ngok (Abingdon: Routledge, 2011), pp. 137–8; *The Straits Times*, 16 Feb. 2007, 17 Feb. 2007, 2 May 2007; *The Business Times*, 16 Feb. 2007; *Today*, 17 Feb. 2007, 8 June 2009.

319 This is the minimal work criterion to receive half the payout; to obtain the full payout, an individual must have worked for six months during the year.

therefore increased according to age, with the twofold objective of encouraging otherwise unemployed or inactive older workers to work and to increase their savings for retirement needs. However, self-employed workers and those who were informally employed received only two-thirds of the amounts given to the others, and this only if they put some money into a CPF Medisave account. In all, Workfare was expected to benefit more than 400,000 Singaporeans (about a fifth of the local workforce); it was found effective in incentivising less-educated persons, particularly those in the older age groups, to enter and stay in the workforce.[320] Since 2010, both the monthly income cap and payouts have been raised.

Among other measures implemented to narrow income inequality, the Workforce Development Agency (WDA) was set up in 2003 to advance workforce development through adult continuing education and training, and to increase the employability of workers through SkillsFuture.[321] At the same time, the Workforce Skills Qualification (WSQ), a national skills accreditation system, was created to certify standards, courses and qualifications.[322] Its role was to provide pathways for progressive training of individual workers in specific sectors and occupations and help raise the wages and employability of certified trainees.[323] In 2013, a Wage Credit Scheme (WCS) was introduced to induce employers to pay higher wages to local employees with monthly earnings below $4,000.[324] This was effected by the government's co-payment of wage increases of new or existing employees for three years. Together with the policy to limit foreign workers by raising levies and reducing quotas, the WCS appeared to be one of the reasons for the fall in inequality after 2013.

The other reason was the introduction of the Progressive Wage Model (PWM) in 2012 as a pilot scheme that at first covered cleaners but was subsequently extended to security guards and landscaping workers, and then to other occupations.[325] Its basic objective was to increase the wages of these workers through skills upgrading and higher productivity. Specifically, the PWM is an initiative to raise the incomes of lower-wage workers through stipulated wage floors and ladders corresponding to skills and productivity.[326] Companies

---

[320] Poh, "Workfare", p. 54; "The Impact of the Workfare Income Supplement Scheme on Individuals' Labour Outcomes", *Economic Survey of Singapore Second Quarter 2014* (Singapore: Ministry of Trade and Industry), pp. 30–1.

[321] Hui and Toh, *Growth with Equity*, pp. 14, 15, 17, 23–5; *The Straits Times*, 13 Sept. 2003, 17 Sept. 2003; *Today*, 15 Feb. 2007, 17 Sept. 2013, 25 May 2016; *The New Paper*, 13 Dec. 2007; *The Business Times*, 14 Apr. 2010.

[322] *The New Paper*, 24 Apr. 2006; *The Straits Times*, 1 June 2010; *The Business Times*, 16 June 2012; *Today*, 7 June 2013.

[323] Ng, "Workfare", p. 139; "Returns to Singapore Workforce Skills Qualifications (WSQ) Training: Does Training Raise Wages and Employability?", *Economic Survey of Singapore 2018* (Singapore: Ministry of Trade and Industry), p. 97.

[324] Lee and Qian, "The Evolving Singaporean Welfare State", p. 932; *Today*, 26 Feb. 2013; *The Straits Times*, 4 Mar. 2013.

[325] *The Straits Times*, 26 Aug. 2013, 12 Oct. 2013, 9 Jan. 2014, 13 Nov. 2014, 4 Mar. 2016, 12 Aug. 2017, 5 Mar. 2018; *Today*, 4 Nov. 2013, 9 Jan. 2014, 1 Aug. 2014, 30 Oct. 2014; *The Business Times*, 30 Oct. 2014, 25 Apr. 2015.

[326] Terence Ho, "The Growing Scope and Impact of the Progressive Wage Model", *Singapore Labour Journal* (2023): 56, 57–63.

in which the workers are employed have also been obliged to pay them at least $1,000–$1,300 per month, making the PWM effectively an *ad hoc* minimum wage scheme. To address concerns that a wage floor delinked from productivity would erode price competitiveness and distort the market, the firms are expected to prepare progressive wage structure plans mapping onto different levels of skills and job responsibilities as the bases for wage increases.[327] These plans have to be submitted for mediation by the tripartite system of unions, employers and the government. In the event, the median monthly wage of full-time resident cleaners increased from $850 in 2012 to $1,400 in 2021, that of security guards from $800 to $1,600 while the increase for park and garden maintenance workers was more modest, from $1,250 to slightly above $1,400.[328] In 2020, a two-week bonus was made mandatory for cleaners and landscaping workers, and the number of overtime hours for security guards was restricted to 72 a month.[329] In the 2021 round of reviews, more ambitious targets for wage growth were set: by 2028, the monthly wages of cleaners, security guards and landscaping workers were envisaged to reach at least $2,200, $3,500 and $2,400 respectively.[330] In 2021, the PWM was extended to cover other jobs like drivers, food service workers and retail assistants, representing eight in ten low-wage workers.

A few other policies to redistribute income and mitigate poverty are worth pointing out. First, there had been moves to make the income and property tax structures more progressive.[331] The top marginal tax rate of personal income taxes was increased to 22 per cent in 2015 after having been lowered in previous years and later to 24 per cent, while property taxes on higher-value houses as well as taxes on luxury cars were raised in 2010 and 2013.[332] At the other end of the wealth spectrum, the government increased the offsets for GST for lower-income groups through cash payments and utility rebates. To keep the tax burden manageable, half of the interest income from investing the nation's reserves is added to annual budget revenues. Second, assistance to disadvantaged groups was expanded substantially to provide a social safety net as a last resort. Third, for people who are unable to work, earn low incomes and for needy retirees, financial help is offered through the ComCare scheme under a multi-layered approach to the provision of social assistance where different tiers of help are available to Singaporeans—the "many helping hands" approach through which family and community take precedence and the state is a provider of last resort.[333] Finally, a welfare programme known as Silver Support was started to provide supplementary income for up to 30 per cent of the elderly.[334] Whether these measures are sufficient to successfully tackle the problems of income inequality and poverty remains to be seen.

327 Ng, *Being Poor*, p. 1550038-13.

328 *The Straits Times*, 13 Dec. 2016.

329 *Today*, 30 Oct. 2014.

330 *The Straits Times*, 10 June 2021.

331 Peng, "Inequality and the Social Compact", pp. 373, 374–5.

332 *The Business Times*, 23 Feb. 2010, 26 Feb. 2013; *Today*, 26 Feb. 2013, 20 Mar. 2015; *The Straits Times*, 24 Feb. 2015.

333 Ng, "Workfare", p. 136; *The Straits Times*, 15 Nov. 2013, 10 Dec. 2016; *Today*, 18 Dec. 2015.

334 *The Straits Times*, 24 Feb. 2015, 6 Mar. 2015.

Bibliography

Official Reports and Publications

Administration Report on the War Tax Ordinance, 1919.

Annual Departmental Reports of the Straits Settlements for the Year, 1900.

Annual Medical Report on the Civil Hospitals of the Straits Settlements, 1900–39.

Annual Report of the Bankruptcy Department for the Year 1931.

Annual Report of the Department of Excise for the Year 1935.

Annual Report of the Division of Commerce and Industry, 1959.

Annual Report of the Labour Department for the Year, 1913–55.

Annual Report of the Postal and Telegraph Department, 1906.

Annual Report of the Public Works Department, 1906–37.

Annual Report of the Statistical Office for the Year 1927.

Annual Report on Education, 1886–1938.

Annual Report on the Administration of the Straits Settlements During the Year, 1858–60.

Annual Report on Tan Tock Seng's Hospital, 1909–10.

Annual Report on the Chinese Protectorate, Singapore, 1889–1900.

Annual Report on the Registration of Births and Deaths in the Straits Settlements, 1888–1936.

Annual Report on the Straits Settlements Police Force and on the State of Crime, for the Year 1890.

British Malaya Opium Committee. *Proceedings of the Committee Appointed by His Excellency the Governor and High Commissioner to Inquire into Matters Relating to the Use of Opium in British Malaya*. Singapore, 1924.

British Military Administration. *The Entrepôt Trade of Singapore*. Singapore, 1945.

Census of the Straits Settlements 1881.

Department of Education Annual Report 1955.

Economic and Social Statistics of Singapore 1960–1982. Singapore: Department of Statistics, 1983.

Economic Survey of Singapore. Singapore: Ministry of Trade and Industry.

Education in Singapore. Singapore: Ministry of Education, 1984.

Financial Report and Statements 1900.

Goh Keng Swee. *Urban Incomes and Housing: A Report on the Social Survey of Singapore, 1953–54.* Singapore: Government Printing Office, 1956.

Hone, H.R. *Report on the British Military Administration of Malaya, September, 1945, to March, 1946*. Singapore, 1946.

Interim Administration Report on the War Tax Ordinance, 1917.

Key Household Income Trends. Singapore: Department of Statistics.

Lyle, F.J. *An Industrial Development Programme.* Singapore: Legislative Assembly of Singapore, 1959.

Macroeconomic Review. Singapore: Monetary Authority of Singapore.

Monetary Authority of Singapore Annual Report, 1976–93.

New Challenges, Fresh Goals—Towards A Dynamic Global City. Singapore: Ministry of Trade and Industry, 2003.

Proceedings of the Legislative Council of the Straits Settlements, 1868–1940.

Report from the Economic Strategies Committee Subcommittee on Making Singapore a Leading Global City, Press Release. Singapore: Ministry of Finance, 2010.

Report of the Commission appointed by His Excellency the Governor of the Straits Settlements to Enquire into and Report on the Trade of the Colony, vol. 1. Singapore: 1933–34.

Report of the Committee on the Future Economy, Pioneers of the Next Generation. Singapore, 2017.

Report of the Economic Strategies Committee: High Skilled People, Innovative Economy, Distinctive Global City. Singapore, 2010.

Report of the Public Sector Divestment Committee. Singapore: Ministry of Finance, 1987.

Report on Currency Note Issue for the Year 1900.

Report on the Administration of the Straits Settlements During the Year, 1855–59.

Report on the Foreign Trade of Malaya for the Year, 1931–33.

Report on the Government Monopolies Department, 1910–26.

Report on the Working and Effects of Quotas on Cotton and Artificial Silk Piece-Goods in Malaya and Sarawak during the period 1st January to 31st December, 1935.

Report on the Working of the Currency Department for the Year 1926.

Singapore's Exchange Rate Policy. Singapore: Monetary Authority of Singapore, 2001.

Singapore's Investment Abroad, 1999–2000. Singapore: Department of Statistics, 2001.

State of Singapore Development Plan 1961–64. Singapore, Ministry of Finance, 1961.

Straits Settlements Annual Report, ed. R.L. Jarman. Archive Editions, 1998.

Straits Settlements Blue Book, 1868–1939.

Straits Settlements Medical Report, 1924–25.

Straits Settlements Opium Commission. *Proceedings of the Commission Appointed to Enquire Into Matters Relating to the Use of Opium in the Straits Settlements and the Federated Malay States,* vol. I. Singapore: 1909.

Straits Settlements Records, 1819–60.

Technical Education and Industrial Training in Singapore: A Review of the Achievements of the Technical Education Department, 1968–1973. Singapore: Technical Education Department, 1973.

The Goods and Services Tax. Singapore: Ministry of Trade and Industry and Ministry of Finance, 1993.

The Singapore Economy: New Directions. Singapore: Ministry of Trade and Industry, 1986.

2020 Singapore Asset Management Survey. Singapore: Monetary Authority of Singapore.

United Nations Industrial Survey Mission. *A Proposed Industrialization Programme for the State of Singapore.* Singapore, 1963.

White Paper on Singapore's Response to COVID-19: Lessons for the Next Pandemic. Singapore: Prime Minister's Office, 2023.

Yeh, Stephen H.K. *Households and Housing*, Census Monograph No. 4. Singapore: Department of Statistics, 1984.

Newspapers

Eastern Daily Mail and Straits Morning Advertiser
Malaya Tribune
Malayan Saturday Post
Mid-day Herald
Mid-day Herald and Daily
Morning Tribune
New Nation
Pinang Gazette and Straits Chronicle
Singapore Chronicle and Commercial Register
Singapore Daily News
Singapore Daily Times
Singapore Monitor
Singapore Standard
Straits Chronicle
Straits Echo
Straits Times Overland Journal
Streats
Sunday Standard
Syonan Shimbun
Syonan Shimbun Fortnightly
The Business Times
The New Paper
The Singapore Free Press
The Singapore Free Press and Mercantile Advertiser
The Singapore Free Press and Mercantile Advertiser (Weekly)
The Straits Budget
The Straits Independent and Penang Chronicle
The Straits Times
The Straits Times Annual
The Straits Times Weekly Issue
The Straits Times Weekly Overseas Edition
The Sunday Tribune (Singapore)
Today

Books

A Short History of the Port of Singapore with Particular Reference to the Undertakings of the Singapore Harbour Board. Singapore: Fraser and Neave, 1922.

Abdullah, Munshi (A.R. Hill, trans.). *Hikayat Abdullah.* Kuala Lumpur: Malaysian Branch of the Royal Asiatic Society, 2009.

Abeysinghe, Tilak and Keen Meng Choy. *The Singapore Economy: An Econometric Perspective.* Abingdon: Routledge, 2007.

Abshire, J.R. *The History of Singapore.* Santa Barbara, CA: Greenwood, 2011.

Acharya, J.B. *Beyond the Myth: Indian Business Communities in Singapore.* Singapore: Institute of Southeast Asian Studies, 2011.

Akkemik, K. Ali. *Industrial Development in East Asia: A Comparative Look at Japan, Korea, Taiwan and Singapore.* Singapore: World Scientific, 2009.

Allen, G.C. and A.G. Donnithorne. *Western Enterprise in Indonesia and Malaya: A Study in Economic Development.* London: George Allen and Unwin, 1957.

Andaya, B.W. and L.Y. Andaya. *A History of Early Southeast Asia, 1400–1830.* Cambridge, UK: Cambridge University Press, 2015.

Anthonisz, J.O. *Currency Reform in the Straits Settlements.* London: R.W. Simpson, 1913.

Assessment of the Impact of Key COVID-19 Budget Measures, Occasional Paper. Singapore: Ministry of Finance, 2022.

Bauer, P.T. *The Rubber Industry: A Study in Competition and Monopoly.* Cambridge, MA: Harvard University Press, I948.

Beane, D., A. Shukla and M. Pecht. *The Singapore and Malaysia Electronics Industries.* Boca Raton, FL: CRC Press, 1997.

Begbie, P.J. *The Malayan Peninsula: Embracing Its History, Manners and Customs of the Inhabitants, Politics, Natural History, etc. From Its Earliest Records.* Madras: Vepery Mission Press, 1834.

Blythe, W. *The Impact of Chinese Secret Societies in Malaya: A Historical Study.* London: Oxford University Press, 1969.

Bogaars, G. *The Tanjong Pagar Dock Company, 1864–1905*, Memoirs of the Raffles Museum, No. 3. Singapore, 1956.

Braddell, T. *Statistics of the British Possessions in the Straits of Malacca: With Explanatory Notes.* Pinang (Pinang Gazette Printing Office), 1861.

Braudel, F. *The Mediterranean and the Mediterranean World in the Age of Phillip II*, vol. I. Berkeley, CA: University of California Press, 1966.

Buckley, C.B. *An Anecdotal History of Singapore.* Singapore: Fraser and Neave, 1902.

Burnett, I. *East Indies.* Kenthurst, NSW, Australia: Rosenberg, 2013.

Burns, A.F. and W.C. Mitchell. *Measuring Business Cycles*, NBER Studies in Business Cycles, no. 2. New York: Columbia University Press, 1946.

Cameron, J. *Our Tropical Possessions in Malayan India: Being a Descriptive Account of Singapore, Penang, Province Wellesley, and Malacca; Their Peoples, Products, Commerce, and Government.* London: Smith, Elder and Co., 1865.

Campbell, P.C. *Chinese Coolie Emigration to Countries Within the British Empire.* Taipei: Ch'eng Wen Press, 1971.

Cavenagh, O. *Reminiscences of an Indian Official.* London: W.H. Allen, 1884.

Central Intelligence Agency (United States). *Singapore: Some Economic Implications of the UK Military Withdrawal*, Intelligence Memorandum. 1968.

Centre for Liveable Cities. *Industrial Infrastructure: Growing in Tandem with the Economy*. Singapore: Cengage Learning Asia, 2013.

Chee Siew Nim. *Labour and Tin Mining in Malaya*, Data Paper No. 7. Southeast Asia Program, Cornell University, 1953.

Cheng Lim-Keak. *Social Change and the Chinese in Singapore*. Singapore: Singapore University Press, 1985.

Chiang Hai Ding. *A History of Straits Settlements Foreign Trade, 1870–1915*. Singapore: National Museum, 1978.

Chin Kee Onn. *Malaya Upside Down*. Singapore: Jitts, 1946.

Chronology of Trade Union Development in Singapore 1940–1985. Singapore: National Trades Union Congress, 1986.

Clements, B. *The Fatal Fortress: The Guns and Fortifications of Singapore 1819–1953*. Barnsley: Pen and Sword Books, 2016.

Crawfurd, J. *Journal of an Embassy from the Governor-General of India to the Courts of Bangkok and Cochin-China*, vol. 1. London: Colbum, 1828.

Curtin, P.D. *Cross-Cultural Trade in World History*. Cambridge, UK: Cambridge University Press, 1984.

Darwin, J. *Unlocking the World: Port Cities and Globalization in the Age of Steam, 1830–1930*. London: Allen Lane, 2020.

Das, Sanchita Basu. *Road to Recovery: Singapore's Journey through the Global Crisis*. Singapore: Institute of Southeast Asian Studies, 2010.

Davidson, G.F. *Trade and Travel in the Far East; or Recollections of Twenty-One Years Passed in Java, Singapore, Australia, and China*. London: Maiden and Malcolm, 1846.

Department of Statistics. *Multifactor Productivity Growth in Singapore: Concept, Methodology and Trends*, Occasional Paper Series. Singapore: Department of Statistics, 1997.

Derks, H. *History of the Opium Problem: The Assault on the East, ca. 1600–1950*. Leiden: Brill, 2012.

Dobbs, S. *The Singapore River: A Social History 1819–2002*. Singapore: Singapore University Press, 2003.

Donnison, F.S.V. *British Military Administration in the Far East 1943–46*. London: Her Majesty's Stationery Office, 1956.

Doraisamy, T.R. *150 Years of Education in Singapore*. Singapore: Teachers' Training College Publications Board, 1969.

Doshi, T. *Houston of Asia: The Singapore Petroleum Industry*. Singapore: Institute of Southeast Asian Studies, 1989.

Drabble, J.H. *An Economic History of Malaysia, c. 1800–1990*. Basingstoke: Macmillan, 2000.

________. *Malayan Rubber: The Interwar Years*. Basingstoke: Macmillan, 1991.

________. *Rubber in Malaya 1876–1922*. Kuala Lumpur: Oxford University Press, 1973.

Drake, P.J. *Financial Development in Malaya and Singapore*. Canberra: Australian National University Press, 1969.

________. *Merchants, Bankers, Governors: British Enterprise in Singapore and Malaya, 1786–1920*. Singapore: World Scientific, 2018.

Earl, G.W. *The Eastern Seas, or Voyages and Adventures in the Indian Archipelago in 1832–33–34, Comprising A Tour of the Island of Java—Visits to Borneo, the Malaya Peninsula, Siam, &c; Also, an Account of the Present State of Singapore, with Observations of the Commercial Resources of the Archipelago*. London: Wm. H. Allen, 1837.

Edwards, C.T. *Public Finances in Malaya and Singapore.* Canberra: Australian National University Press, 1970.

50,000 Up: Homes for the People. Singapore: Housing and Development Board, 1965.

Fletcher, N.M. *The Separation of Singapore from Malaysia,* Data Paper No. 73. Ithaca, NY: Southeast Asia Program, Cornell University, 1969.

Frost, Mark Ravinder and Yu-Mei Balasingamchow. *Singapore: A Biography.* Singapore: Editions Didier Millet, 2009.

Geiger, T. and F.M. Geiger. *Tales of Two City-States: The Development Progress of Hong Kong and Singapore.* Washington, DC: National Planning Association, 1973.

Gershenkron, A. *Economic Backwardness in Historical Perspective: A Book of Essays.* Cambridge, MA: Belknap Press of Harvard University Press, 1962.

Ghesquiere, Henri. *Singapore's Success: Engineering Economic Growth.* Singapore: Thomson Learning, 2007.

Gipouloux, F. *The Asian Mediterranean: Port Cities and Trading Networks in China, Japan and Southeast Asia, 13th–21st Century.* Cheltenham: Edward Elgar, 2011.

Goh Chor Boon. *From Traders to Innovators: Science and Technology in Singapore since 1965.* Singapore: ISEAS–Yusof Ishak Institute, 2016.

Gopinathan, S. *Education and the Nation State: The Selected Works of S. Gopinathan.* Abingdon: Routledge, 2013.

Greenberg, M. *British Trade and the Opening of China, 1800–1842.* Cambridge, UK: Cambridge University Press, 1951.

Hancock, T.H.H. *Coleman's Singapore.* Royal Asiatic Society in association with Pelanduk Publications, 1986.

Heng Yee-Kuang. *Managing Global Risks in the Urban Age: Singapore and the Making of a Global City.* Farnham: Ashgate, 2015.

Hirschman, A.O. *The Strategy of Economic Development.* New Haven, CT: Yale University Press, 1958.

Holloway, C.P. *Tabular Statements of the Commerce of Singapore during the Years 1823/24 to 1839/40 Inclusive.* Singapore, 1842.

Hoon Hian Teck. *Economic Dynamism, Openness, and Inclusion.* Singapore: World Scientific, 2019.

Huff, W.G. *The Economic Growth of Singapore: Trade and Development in the Twentieth Century.* Cambridge, UK: Cambridge University Press, 1994.

________ [as Gregg Huff]. *World War II and Southeast Asia: Economy and Society Under Japanese Occupation.* Cambridge, UK: Cambridge University Press, 2020.

________ [as Gregg Huff] and S. Majima, ed. and trans. *World War II Singapore: The Chōsabu Reports on Syonan.* Singapore: NUS Press, 2018.

Hughes, H. *Growth of Singapore: An External View,* Working Paper No. 91/13. Canberra: National Centre for Development Studies, 1991.

Hui Weng Tat and Ruby Toh. *Growth with Equity in Singapore: Challenges and Prospects,* Conditions of Work and Employment Series No. 48. Geneva: International Labour Office, 2014.

Hussin, Nordin. *Trade and Society in the Straits of Melaka: Dutch Melaka and English Penang, 1780–1830.* Singapore: NUS Press, 2007.

Income Growth, Inequality and Mobility Trends in Singapore. Occasional Paper. Singapore: Ministry of Finance, 2015.

Innis, H.A. *The Fur Trade in Canada: An Introduction to Canadian Economic History.* 1930; rev. ed. Toronto: University of Toronto Press, 1956.

Jackson, J.C. *Planters and Speculators: Chinese and European Agricultural Enterprise in Malaya*. Kuala Lumpur: University of Malaya Press, 1968.

Jayapal, M. *Old Singapore*. Oxford: Oxford University Press, 1992.

Jomo, K.S. *A Question of Class: Capital, the State and Uneven Development in Malaya*. New York: Monthly Review Press, 1988.

Khoo Kay Kim. *The Western Malay States 1850–1873*. Kuala Lumpur: Oxford University Press, 1972.

Knowles, M.I. *The Expansion of British Influence in the Malay Peninsula, 1867–1885: A Study in Nineteenth Century Imperialism*, Doctoral Thesis. University of Wisconsin, 1935.

Koh Buck Song and Lee Geok Boi. *Brighter: Electricity in Singapore: From Beginning to Beyond*. Singapore: Energy Market Authority, 2011.

Kratoska, P.H. *The Japanese Occupation of Malaya and Singapore, 1941–45: A Social and Economic History*. 1998; 2nd ed. Singapore: NUS Press, 2018.

Krause, L.B., Koh Ai Tee and Lee (Tsao) Yuan. *The Singapore Economy Reconsidered*. Singapore: Institute of Southeast Asian Studies, 1987.

Kwa Chong Guan, Derek Heng, Peter Borschberg and Tan Tai Yong. *Seven Hundred Years: A History of Singapore*. Singapore: National Library Board and Marshall Cavendish Editions, 2019.

Kwa Chong Guan, Derek Heng and Tan Tai Yong. *Singapore: A 700-Year History*. Singapore: National Archives of Singapore, 2009.

Lau, Albert. *A Moment of Anguish: Singapore in Malaysia and the Politics of Disengagement*. Singapore: Times Academic Press, 1998.

Le Blanc, R. *Singapore: The Socio-Economic Development of a City-State, 1960–80*. Maarheeze, NL: Cranendonck Coaching, 2008.

Lee, Edwin. *The British as Rulers Governing Multiracial Singapore 1867–1914*. Singapore: Singapore University Press, 1991.

________. *The Unexpected Nation*. Singapore: Institute of Southeast Asian Studies, 2008.

Lee Kuan Yew. *The Battle for Merger*. Singapore: National Archives of Singapore, 1962.

Lee Sheng-Yi. *Financial Structure and Monetary Policy*. Occasional Paper No. 35. Singapore: Institute of Economics and Business Studies, Nanyang University, 1979.

________. *The Monetary and Banking Development of Singapore and Malaysia*, 3rd ed. Singapore: Singapore University Press, 1990.

Lee Soo Ann. *From Colony to Nation: Continuity and Change in the Singapore Economy 1946–2006*. Singapore: Singapore Heritage Board.

________. *Industrialization in Singapore*. Singapore: Longman, 1973.

________. *Singapore Chronicles: Economy*. Singapore: Institute of Policy Studies and Straits Times Press, 2018.

Lee, Y.K. *The Medical History of Early Singapore*. Tokyo: Southeast Asian Medical Information Center, 1978.

Levathes, L. *When China Ruled the Seas: The Treasure Fleet of the Dragon Throne 1405–1433*. New York: Simon and Schuster, 1994.

Liew, Clement and P. Wilson. *A History of Money in Singapore*. Singapore: Talisman, 2021.

Lim Chong Yah. *Economic Development in Singapore*. Singapore: Federal Publications, 1980.

________. *Economic Development of Modern Malaya*. Kuala Lumpur: Oxford University Press, 1967.

________. *Economic Restructuring in Singapore*. Singapore: Federal Publications, 1984.

________. *Singapore's National Wages Council: An Insider's View*. Singapore: World Scientific, 2014.

Lim Chong Yah and Associates. *Policy Options for the Singapore Economy*. Singapore: McGraw-Hill, 1988.

Lim, Linda. *Business, Government and Labor: Essays on Economic Development in Singapore and Southeast Asia*. Singapore: World Scientific, 2018.

________ and Pang Eng Fong. *Trade, Employment and Industrialisation in Singapore*. Geneva: International Labour Organization, 1986.

Liu Thai-Ker. *A Review of Public Housing in Singapore*. Singapore: National Trades Union Congress, 1983.

Living in Singapore: Key Information for Expatriates Living or Relocating to Singapore. Singapore: Ministry of Manpower, 2015.

Living the Next Lap: Towards a Tropical City of Excellence. Singapore: Urban Redevelopment Authority, 1991.

Lo Yen Lee. *Privatisation in Singapore: Policy and Impact on Labour Relations*. Singapore: Singapore Institute of Labour Studies, 1995.

Loh Ai. *A Historical Study of Changes in Vocational and Technical Education and Training in Singapore: 1961–1981*. Honours Thesis, Department of History, National University of Singapore, 1982/1983.

Loh Oun Hean. *Industrial Relations in Singapore: Practice and Perspective*. Singapore: World Scientific, 2018.

Loh Wen Fong. *The Singapore Houses of Agency, 1819–1900*. Academic Exercise, Department of History, University of Malaya, 1958.

Low, Linda. *The Political Economy of Privatisation in Singapore: Analysis, Interpretation and Evaluation*. Singapore: McGraw-Hill, 1991.

________ and Toh Mun Heng. *The Elected Presidency as a Safeguard for Official Reserves: What is at Stake?* IPS Occasional Paper No. 1. Singapore: Institute of Policy Studies, 1989.

Low Siow Chek. *Gambier-and-Pepper Planting in Singapore, 1819–1860*. Academic Exercise, University of Malaya, 1955.

Luscombe, F.M. *Singapore, 1819–1930*. Singapore: C.A. Ribeiro, 1930.

Macroprudential Policies to Mitigate Housing Market Risks, Country Case Study: Singapore, CFGS Papers No. 69. Basel: Bank for International Settlements, 2023.

Maddison Project database. Groningen, NL: Groningen Growth and Development Centre, Faculty of Economics and Business, Rijksuniversiteit Groningen. Available at https://www.rug.nl/ggdc/historicaldevelopment/maddison/releases/maddison-project-database-2020?lang=en [26 Sept. 2025].

Mak Lau Fong. *The Sociology of Secret Societies: A Study of Chinese Secret Societies in Singapore and Peninsular Malaysia*. Kuala Lumpur: Oxford University Press, 1981.

McCormick, M. *Origins of the European Economy*. Cambridge, UK: Cambridge University Press, 2001.

Merck & Co. (MSD). *A Neglected Burden: The Ongoing Economic Costs of COVID-19 in Singapore*. Rahway, NJ: MSD, 2023.

Miksic, J.N. *Singapore and the Silk Road of the Sea, 1300–1800*. Singapore: NUS Press and National Museum of Singapore, 2013.

Monetary Authority of Singapore. *Singapore's Balance of Payments, 1965–2003: An Analysis*, Staff Working Paper No. 33. Singapore: Monetary Authority of Singapore, 2004.

________. *Singapore's Services Sector in Perspective: Trends and Outlook*, Occasional Paper No. 5. Singapore: Monetary Authority of Singapore, 1998.

________. *Sustaining Stability, Serving Singapore*. Singapore: Straits Times Press, 2012.

________. *The Petrochemical Industry in Singapore*, Occasional Paper No. 14. Singapore: Monetary Authority of Singapore, 1999.

Moor, J.H. *Notices of the Indian Archipelago and Adjacent Countries*. Singapore, 1837.

Moore, D. and J. Moore. *The First 150 Years of Singapore*. Singapore: Donald Moore Press, 1969.

Mukhopadhaya, P. *Income Inequality in Singapore*. Abingdon: Routledge, 2014.

Mukhopadhaya, P., G. Shantakumar and V.V.B. Rao. *Economic Growth and Income Inequality in China, India and Singapore*. Abingdon: Routledge, 2011.

Murfett, M.H., J.N. Miksic, B.P. Farrell and Chiang Ming Shun. *Between Two Oceans: A Military History of Singapore from First Settlement to Final British Withdrawal*. Singapore: Oxford University Press, 1999.

Nagendiram, N. *The Straits Settlements, 1867–1874*. Master's Thesis, Australian National University, 1976.

Neal, S. *Singapore, Chinese Migration and the Making of the British Empire, 1819–67*. Martlesham, Suffolk: Boydell, 2019.

Newbold, T.J. *Political and Statistical Account of the British Settlements in the Straits of Malacca viz., Pinang, Malacca and Singapore; with a History of the Malayan States on the Peninsula of Malacca, in Two Volumes*. London: John Murray, 1839.

Ng Chin Keong. *Boundaries and Beyond: China's Maritime Southeast in Late Imperial Times*. Singapore: NUS Press, 2017.

Ng Weng Hoong. *Singapore, The Energy Economy: From the First Refinery to the End of Cheap Oil, 1960–2010*. Abingdon: Routledge, 2012.

Okposin, S.M. *The Extent of Singapore's Investments Abroad*. Abingdon: Routledge, 1999.

150 Years of Caring: KK Women's and Children's Hospital (1858–2008). Singapore: KK Women's and Children's Hospital, 2008.

150 Years of Caring: The Legacy of Tan Tock Seng Hospital. Singapore: Tan Tock Seng Hospital, 1994.

Orchard, Freddy. *Safeguarding the Future: The Story of How Singapore Has Managed Its Reserves and the Founding of GIC*. e-book. 2016.

Oswin, N. *Global City Futures: Desire and Development in Singapore*. Athens, GA: The University of Georgia Press, 2019.

Pangarkar, N. and P. Vandenberg. *Singapore's Ecosystem for Technology Startups and Lessons for Its Neighbors*. Country Report No. 2, Ecosystems for Technology Startups in Asia and the Pacific. Manila: Asian Development Bank, 2022.

Peebles, G. and P. Wilson. *Economic Growth and Development in Singapore*. Cheltenham: Edward Elgar, 2002.

Perry, J.C. *Singapore: Unlikely Power*. New York: Oxford University Press, 2017.

Phipps, J. *A Practical Treatise on the China and Eastern Trade: Comprising the Commerce of Great Britain and India, Particularly Bengal and Singapore, with China and the Eastern Islands*. London: Wm. H. Allen, 1836.

Phua Kai Hong. *Privatization and Restructuring of Health Services in Singapore*, IPS Occasional Paper No. 5. Singapore: The Institute of Policy Studies, 1991.

Pires, T. (Armando Cortesao, trans.). *The Suma Oriental of Tome Pires: An Account of the East, From the Red Sea to Japan, Written in Malacca and India in 1512–1515*, vol. 1. London: The Hakluyt Society, 1944.

Plummer, M.G. *ASEAN Economic Integration: Trade, Foreign Investment, and Finance*. Singapore: World Scientific, 2019.

Pomeranz, K. *The Great Divergence: China, Europe, and the Making of the Modern World Economy*. Princeton, NJ: Princeton University Press, 2000.

Quah, Euston with Luke Nursultan Iuldashov and Zach Lee. *Albert Winsemius and Singapore: Here It is Going to Happen*. Singapore: World Scientific, 2022.

Raffles, S[ophia]. *Memoir of the Life and Public Services of Sir Thomas Stamford Raffles*. London: John Murray, 1830.

Rai, R. *Indians in Singapore 1819–1945: Diaspora in the Colonial Port City*. New Delhi: Oxford University Press, 2014.

Rao, V.V.B. and M.K. Ramakrishnan. *Income Inequality in Singapore: Impact of Economic Growth and Structural Change 1966–1975*. Singapore: Singapore University Press, 1980.

Regnier, P. *Singapore, City-State in Southeast Asia*. Honolulu: University of Hawaii Press, 1991.

Reid, A. *A History of Southeast Asia: Critical Crossroads*. Malden, MA: Wiley Blackwell, 2015.

Reunion. Singapore: National Trades Union Congress, 2019.

Rodan, G. *The Political Economy of Singapore's Industrialization: National State and International Capital*. Basingstoke: Macmillan Press, 1989.

Ross, J.D. *The Capital of a Little Empire, A Descriptive Study of a British Crown Colony in the Far East*. Singapore: Kelly and Walsh, 1898.

Rubber Growers' Association's Bulletin, Feb. 1931.

Sadka, E. *The Protected Malay States 1874–1895*. Kuala Lumpur: University of Malaya Press, 1968.

Sandhu, K.S. *Indian Migration and Population Change in Malaya, c.100–1957 A.D.: A Historical Geography*. Master of Arts Thesis, Department of Geography, The University of British Columbia, 1961.

________. *Indians in Malaya: Some Aspects of Their Immigration and Settlement (1786–1957)*. Cambridge University Press, 1969.

SarDesai, D.R. *British Trade and Expansion in Southeast Asia, 1830–1914*. New Delhi: Allied, 1977.

Savage, Victor R. *Lion City Narratives: Singapore Through Western Eyes*. Singapore: World Scientific, 2022.

Saw Swee-Hock. *Population Control for Zero Growth in Singapore*. Singapore: Oxford University Press, 1980.

________. *The Population of Singapore*, 3rd ed. Singapore: Institute of Southeast Asian Studies, 2012.

Serangoon Road: A Pictorial History. Singapore: Educational Publications Bureau, 1983.

Shah, Nazrin. *Charting the Economy: Early 20th Century Malaya and Contemporary Malaysian Contrasts*. Oxford University Press, 2017.

Shimizu, H. and H. Hirakawa. *Japan and Singapore in the World Economy: Japan's Economic Advance into Singapore, 1870–1965*. Abingdon: Routledge, 1999.

Singapore Port History. Singapore: Maritime Museum, Port of Singapore Authority, 1982.

Singapore's Biomedical Cluster: Lessons from Two Decades of Innovation and Manufacturing Policy. Cambridge, UK: Cambridge Industrial Innovation Policy, 2021.

Smith, Catherine et al. *A Handbook on Inequality, Poverty and Unmet Social Needs in Singapore*. Singapore: Lien Centre for Social Innovation, 2015.

Song Ong Siang. *One Hundred Years' History of the Chinese in Singapore.* 1923. The Annotated Edition. Singapore: National Library Board and World Scientific, 2020.

Sugimoto, Ichiro. *Economic Growth of Singapore in the Twentieth Century: Historical GDP Estimates and Empirical Investigations.* Singapore: World Scientific, 2011.

Swettenham, F. *British Malaya: An Account of the Origin and Progress of British Influence in Malaya.* London: George Allen and Unwin, 1948.

Tan, Alvin. *Singapore: A Very Short History—From Temasek to Tomorrow.* Singapore: Talisman, 2022.

Tan Chwee Huat. *Financial Markets and Institutions in Singapore,* 11th ed. Singapore: Singapore University Press, 2005.

________. *Financial Services and Wealth Management in Singapore.* Singapore: Ridge Books, 2011.

________. *Venturing Overseas: Singapore's External Wing.* Singapore: McGraw-Hill, 1995.

Tan Gia Lim. *An Introduction to the Culture and History of the Teochews in Singapore.* Singapore: World Scientific, 2018.

Tarling, N. *Singapore Chronicles: Colonial Singapore.* Singapore: Institute of Policy Studies and Straits Times Press, 2015.

10 Years that Shaped a Nation. Singapore: National Archives of Singapore, 2008.

The First General Hospital: 175th Anniversary, 1821–1996. Singapore: Singapore General Hospital, 1996.

The Land Transport of Singapore: From Early Times to the Present, Revised Edition. Singapore: Educational Publications Bureau, 1984.

The Making of Jurong Island: The Right Chemistry. Singapore: Jurong Town Corporation, 2000.

The Ring and the Book. Singapore, 1908.

The Singapore and Straits Directory. Singapore, 1888.

The Straits Settlements and the Colonial System. London: Alfred Boot, 1873.

The World Health Report 2000—Health Systems: Improving Performance. Geneva: World Health Organization, 2000.

Thomson, J.T. *Some Glimpses into Life in the Far East.* London: Richardson, 1864.

Ti, T.K. and Edward S.W. Ti. *Singapore and Asia: Celebrating Globalisation and an Emerging Postmodern Asian Civilisation.* Xlibris, 2012.

Tregonning, K.G. *Home Port Singapore: A History of Straits Steamship Company Limited 1890–1965.* Singapore: Oxford University Press, 1967.

Trocki, C.A. *Opium and Empire: Chinese Society in Colonial Singapore, 1800–1910.* Ithaca, NY: Cornell University Press, 1990.

________. *The Prince of Pirates: The Temenggongs and the Development of Johor and Singapore, 1784–1885.* Singapore: Singapore University Press, 1979.

Turnbull, C.M. *A History of Modern Singapore: 1819–2005.* 1977; Singapore: NUS Press, 2009.

________. *The Straits Settlements, 1826–67: Indian Presidency to Crown Colony.* London: The Athlone Press, 1972.

Urban Redevelopment: From Urban Squalor to Global City. Singapore: Centre for Liveable Cities, 2016.

van der Kraan, A. *Contest for the Java Cotton Trade, 1811–40: An Episode in Anglo-Dutch Rivalry.* University of Hull (UK), Centre for South-East Asian Studies, 1998.

Vaughan, J.D. *The Manners and Customs of the Chinese of the Straits Settlements*. Singapore: Mission Press, 1879.

von Glahn, R. *The Economic History of China: From Antiquity to the Nineteenth Century*. Cambridge, UK: Cambridge University Press, 2016.

Warren, J.F. *Ah Ku and Karayuki-san: Prostitution in Singapore 1870–1940*. Singapore: NUS Press, 2003.

________. *Rickshaw Coolie: A People's History of Singapore 1880–1940*. Singapore: NUS Press, 2003.

Wheatley, P. *The Golden Khersonese: Studies in the Historical Geography of the Malay Peninsula Before A.D. 1500*. Kuala Lumpur: University of Malaya Press, 1961.

Wickizer, V.D. and M.K. Bennett. *The Rice Economy of Monsoon Asia*. Stanford, CA: Stanford University Press, 1941.

Winstedt, R.O. *Malaya and Its History*. London: Hutchinson, 1948; 7th ed., 1966.

Wise, M. *Travellers' Tales of Old Singapore*. Singapore: Marshall Cavendish Editions, 2018.

Wong, Francis H.K. and Gwee Yee Hean, eds. *Official Reports on Education: Straits Settlements and the Federated Malay States, 1870–1939*. Singapore: Pan Pacific Book Distributors, 1980.

Wong Kum Poh. *Essays on the Singapore Economy*. Singapore: Federal Publications and Nanyang Siang Pau, 1982.

Wong Lin Ken. *The Malayan Tin Industry to 1914, with Special Reference to the States of Perak, Selangor, Negri Sembilan and Pahang*. Tucson, AZ: The University of Arizona Press, 1965.

________. *The Trade of Singapore, 1819–1869*. Kuala Lumpur: The Malaysian Branch of the Royal Asiatic Society, 2003.

Woo, J.J. *Building Immunity: Crisis and Contagion in the City State*. Singapore: World Scientific, 2022.

________. *Capacity-Building and Pandemics: Singapore's Response to Covid-19*. Singapore: Palgrave Macmillan, 2021.

Woon Kin Chung and Loo Ya Lee. *50 Years of Singapore's Productivity Drive*. Singapore: World Scientific, 2018.

World Bank. *The East Asian Miracle: Economic Growth and Public Policy*. Oxford University Press, 1993.

Wright, A. and H.A. Cartwright, eds. *Twentieth Century Impressions of British Malaya: Its History, People, Commerce, Industries, and Resources*, Abridged Edition. Singapore: Graham Brash, 1989.

Yen Ching-Hwang. *A Social History of the Chinese in Singapore and Malaya: 1800–1911*. Singapore: Oxford University Press, 1986.

Yeo Eng Leng. *Effects of Great Depression on Singapore*. Academic Exercise, History Department, University of Singapore, 1972.

Yip Yat Hoong. *The Development of the Tin Mining Industry of Malaya*. Kuala Lumpur: University of Malaya Press, 1969.

Yoshihara, K. *Foreign Investment and Domestic Response: A Study of Singapore's Industrialization*. Singapore: Eastern Universities Press, 1976.

Zaini, Shah Alam M. *Metal Finds and Metal-Working at the Parliament House Complex, Singapore*. Ann Arbor, MI: University of Michigan Press, 1997.

Articles

Abdullah, Elinah. "Malay/Muslim Patterns of Settlement and Trade in the First 50 Years", in *Malays/Muslims in Singapore: Selected Readings in History, 1819–1965*, ed. Khoo Kay Kim, Elinah Abdullah and Wan Meng Hao. Subang Jaya: Pelanduk Publications, 2006, pp. 79–111.

Abeysinghe, Tilak. "Lessons of Singapore's Development for Other Developing Economies", *The Singapore Economic Review* 60, 3 (2015): 155029-1–155029-13.

________ and Keen Meng Choy. "The Aggregate Consumption Puzzle in Singapore", *Journal of Asian Economics* 15, 3 (2004): 563–78.

Abraham, A. "The Transfer of the Straits Settlements: A Revisionist Approach to the Study of Colonial Law and Administration", *Journal of the Hong Kong Branch of the Royal Asiatic Society* 42 (2002): 1–33.

"Accounts, Respecting the Annual Revenues and Disbursements, Trade and Sales, of the East India Company", *House of Commons Parliamentary Papers*, 1830.

"Agriculture of Singapore", *The Journal of the Indian Archipelago and Eastern Asia*, ed. J.R. Logan, 3 (1849): 508–11.

Ahmat, S. "American Trade with Singapore, 1819–65", *Journal of the Malaysian Branch of the Royal Asiatic Society* 38, 2 (1965): 241–57.

Akashi, Y. "Japanese Policy Towards the Malayan Chinese 1941–1945", *Journal of Southeast Asian Studies* 1, 2 (1970): 61–89.

Allen, R.C., T. Bengtsson and M. Dribe. "Introduction", in *Living Standards in the Past: New Perspectives on Well-being in Asia and Europe*, ed. R.C. Allen, T. Bengtsson and M. Dribe. Oxford: Oxford University Press, 2005.

Altman, M. "Staple Theory and Export-led Growth: Constructing Differential Growth", *Australian Economic History Review* 43, 3 (2003): 230–55.

Ang Yee, Gary. "Development of the Private Hospitals in Singapore from 1983 to 2022", *Journal of Hospital Management and Health Policy* 7, 11 (2023): 2523–33.

"Annual Remittances by Chinese Immigrants in Singapore to Their Families in China", *The Journal of the Indian Archipelago and Eastern Asia*, ed. J.R. Logan, 1 (1847): 35–7.

Asher, Mukul G. "The Fiscal System of Singapore", in *Singapore: Twenty-five Years of Development*, ed. You Poh Seng and Lim Chong Yah. Singapore: Nan Yang Xing Zhou Lianhe Zaobao, 1984, pp. 78–107.

________ and A. Nandy. "Singapore's Policy Responses to Ageing, Inequality and Poverty: An Assessment", *International Social Security Review* 61, 1 (2008): 41–60.

________ and Amina Tyabji. "Trends in Government Revenue and Expenditure, 1966–1977", in *Issues in Public Finance in Singapore*, ed. Mukul G. Asher and Susan Osborne. Singapore: Singapore University Press, 1980, pp. 11–35.

________, A.S. Bali and Chang Yee Kwan. "Public Financial Management in Singapore: Key Characteristics and Prospects", *The Singapore Economic Review* 60, 3 (2015): 1550032-1–1550032-18.

Austin, I.P. "Singapore as a 'Global City': Governance in a Challenging International Environment", in *A New Paradigm for International Business, Proceedings of the Conference on Free Trade Agreements and Regional Integration in East Asia*, ed. Hadrian Geri Djajadikerta and Zhang Zhaoyong. Singapore: Springer, 2015, pp. 171–92.

Baldwin, R.E. "Patterns of Development in Newly Settled Regions", *Manchester School of Economic and Social Studies* 24, 2 (1956): 161–79.

Balestier, J. "View of the State of Agriculture in the British Possessions in the Straits of Malacca", *The Journal of the Indian Archipelago and Eastern Asia*, ed. J.R. Logan, 2 (1848): 139–50.

Bartley, W. "Population of Singapore in 1819", *Journal of the Malaysian Branch of the Royal Asiatic Society* 42, 1 (1969): 112–3.

________. "Singapore and the Great War", in *One Hundred Years of Singapore,* vol. I, ed. W. Makepeace, G.E. Brooke and R. St.J. Braddell. London: John Murray, 1921, pp. 405–26.

Bassino, J. and Debin Ma. "Japanese Unskilled Wages in International Perspective, 1741–1913", *Research in Economic History* 23 (2005): 229–48.

Bazell, C. "Education in Singapore", in *One Hundred Years of Singapore,* vol. I, ed. W. Makepeace, G.E. Brooke and R. St.J. Braddell. London: John Murray, 1921, pp. 427–76.

Benham, F. "The Rubber Industry", *Economica,* New Series 16, 64 (1949): 355–68.

Bernard, A.B. and T.C. Fort. "Factoryless Goods Producing Firms", *The American Economic Review, Papers & Proceedings* 105, 5 (2015): 518–23.

Bertram, G. "Economic Growth in Canadian Industry, 1870–1915: The Staple Model and the Take-off Hypothesis", *Canadian Journal of Economics and Political Science* 29, 2 (1963): 159–84.

Blagden, C.O. "Singapore Prior to 1819", in *One Hundred Years of Singapore,* vol. I, ed W. Makepeace, G.E. Brooke and R. St.J. Braddell. London: John Murray, 1921, pp. 1–5.

________. "The Foundation of the Settlement", in *One Hundred Years of Singapore,* vol. I, ed. W. Makepeace, G.E. Brooke and R. St.J. Braddell. London: John Murray, 1921, pp. 6–12.

Blomquist, Hans C. "Extending the Second Wing: The Outward Direct Investment of Singapore", Mimeograph, 2002.

Blöndal, Jón R. "Budgeting in Singapore", *OECD Journal on Budgeting* 6, 1 (2006): 45–85.

Blythe, W.L. "Historical Sketch of Chinese Labour in Malaya", *Journal of the Malayan Branch of the Royal Asiatic Society* 20, 1 (1947): 64–114.

Bogaars, G. "The Effect of the Opening of the Suez Canal on the Trade and Development of Singapore", *Journal of the Malaysian Branch of the Royal Asiatic Society* 42, 1 (1969): 208–51.

Booth, A. "Education and Development in Southeast Asia: Myths and Realities", *ASEAN Economic Bulletin* 16, 3 (1999): 290–306.

________. "Measuring Living Standards in Different Colonial Systems: Some Evidence from South East Asia, 1900–1942", *Modern Asian Studies* 46, 5 (2012): 1145–81.

Braddell, R. St.J. "A Short History of the Colony", in *One Hundred Years of Singapore,* vol. I, ed. W. Makepeace, G.E. Brooke and R. St.J. Braddell. London: John Murray, 1921, pp. 12–31.

________. "Crime: Its Punishment and Prevention", in *One Hundred Years of Singapore,* vol. I, ed. W. Makepeace, G.E. Brooke and R. St.J. Braddell. London: John Murray, 1921, pp. 244–90.

________. "The Good Old Days", in *One Hundred Years of Singapore,* vol. II, ed. W. Makepeace, G.E. Brooke and R. St.J. Braddell. London: John Murray, 1921, pp. 465–524.

Braddell, T. "Concerning the Tan Tae Hoey in Singapore", *The Journal of the Indian Archipelago and Eastern Asia,* ed. J.R. Logan, 6 (1852): 545–55.

________. "Notes on Naning, with a Brief Notice of the Naning War", *The Journal of the Indian Archipelago and Eastern Asia,* ed. J.R. Logan, New Series I (1856): 194–232.

Brooke, G.E. "Medical Work and Institutions", in *One Hundred Years of Singapore,* vol. I, ed. W. Makepeace, G.E. Brooke and R. St.J. Braddell. London: John Murray, 1921, pp. 487–519.

________. "Piracy", in *One Hundred Years of Singapore,* vol. I, ed. W. Makepeace, G.E. Brooke and R. St.J. Braddell. London: John Murray, 1921, pp. 290–300.

Brown, I. "The British Merchant Community in Singapore and Japanese Commercial Expansion in the 1930s", in *International Commercial Rivalry in Southeast Asia in the Interwar Period,* ed. S. Shinya and M.C. Guerrero. New Haven, CT: Yale University Southeast Asia Studies, 1994, pp. 111–32.

Brunero, D. "Maritime Goes Global: The British Maritime Empire in Asia", in *Empire in Asia: A New Global History, Volume Two, The Long Nineteenth Century*, ed. D. Brunero and B.P. Farrell. London: Bloomsbury Academic, 2018, pp. 249–80.

Bryant, R.C. "The Evolution of Singapore as a Financial Centre", in *Management of Success: The Moulding of Modern Singapore*, ed. K.S. Sandhu and P. Wheatley. Singapore: Institute of Southeast Asian Studies, 1989, pp. 337–72.

Caves, R.E. "Export-led Growth and the New Economic History", in *Trade, Balance of Payments, and Growth*, ed. J.N. Bhagwati, R.W. Jones, R.A. Mundell and J. Vanek. Amsterdam: North-Holland Publishing, 1971, pp. 403–42.

Chan, David and Jason Tan. "Privatization and the Rise of Direct Subsidy Scheme Schools and Independent Schools in Hong Kong and Singapore", *International Journal of Educational Management* 22, 6 (2008): 464–87.

Chan Heng Chee. "Political Developments", in *A History of Singapore*, ed. Ernest Chew and Edwin Lee. Singapore: Oxford University Press, 1991, pp. 157–81.

Chan Lee Mun, "Polytechnic Education", in *Toward a Better Future: Education and Training for Economic Development in Singapore since 1965*, ed. Lee Sing Kong, Goh Chor Boon, F. Birger and Tan Jee Peng. Washington, DC: World Bank Publications, 2008, pp. 135–48.

Chan, Selina Ching. "Consuming Food: Structuring Social Life and Creating Social Relationships", in *Past Times: A Social History of Singapore*, ed. Chan Kwok Bun and Tong Chee Kiong. Singapore: Times Editions, 2003, pp. 123–35.

Chau Leung-Chuen, Francis T. Lui and Larry D. Qiu. "Comparison Among Singapore, Taiwan and South Korea in Industrial Development", in *Industrial Development in Singapore, Taiwan and South Korea*, ed. Kwong Kai-Sun, Chau Leung-Chuen, Francis T. Lui and Larry D. Qiu. Singapore: World Scientific, 2001, pp. 201–32.

Chaudhuri, K.N. "The World-System East Longitude 20°: The European Role in Asia 1500–1750", *Review (Fernand Braudel Centre)* 5, 2 (1981): 219–45.

Cheah, Sarah, Ho Yuen Ping and Philip Lim. "Role of Public Science in Fostering the Innovation and Startup Ecosystem in Singapore", *Asian Research Policy* 7, 1 (2016): 78–93.

Chen, Peter S.J. "Singapore's Development Strategies: A Model for Rapid Growth", in *Singapore Development Policies and Trends*, ed. Peter S.J. Chen. Singapore: Oxford University Press, 1983, pp. 3–25.

Chen, Z. and K. Peng. "Production, Consumption, and Living Standards", in *The Cambridge Economic History of China*, vol. I, ed. D. Ma and R. von Glahn. Cambridge, UK: Cambridge University Press, 2022, pp. 676–709.

Chenery, H.B. "Growth and Structural Change", *Finance and Development* 8, 3 (1971): 16–27.

Cheng Lim Keak. "*Bang* Specialisation of the Chinese Community in Singapore", in *A General History of the Chinese in Singapore*, ed. Kwa Chong Guan and Kua Bak Lim. Singapore: World Scientific, 2019, pp. 309–18.

Cheng Siok Hwa. "Economic Change in Singapore, 1945–1977", *Southeast Asian Journal of Social Science* 7, 1/2 (1979): 81–113.

Cheng U Wen. "Opium in the Straits Settlements, 1867–1910", *Journal of Southeast Asian History* 2, 1 (1961): 52–75.

Chew Chee Sun. "Key Elements in the Urban Renewal of Singapore", in *Planning in Singapore: Selected Aspects and Issues*, ed. Chua Peng Chye. Singapore: Chopmen Enterprises, 1973, pp. 32–44.

Chew, Ernest. "The Reasons for British Intervention in Malaya: Review and Reconsideration", *The Journal of Southeast Asian History* 6, 1 (1965): 81–93.

Chia Siow Yue. "Direct Foreign Investment and the Industrialization Process in Singapore", in *Singapore: Resources and Growth*, ed. Lim Chong Yah and P.J. Lloyd. Singapore: Oxford University Press, 1986, 79–117.

________. "Globalization and Regionalisation: Singapore's Trade and FDI", *The Singapore Economic Review* 60, 3 (2015): 1550034-1–1550034-23.

________. "Growth and Pattern of Industrialization", in *The Singapore Economy*, ed. You Poh Seng and Lim Chong Yah. Singapore: Eastern Universities Press, 1971, pp. 189–223.

________. "Singapore", in *Asia's Free Trade Agreements: How Is Business Responding?*, ed. M. Kawai and G. Widnaraja. Cheltenham: Edward Elgar, 2011, pp. 159–98.

________. "Singapore: Towards a Knowledge-based Economy", in *Industrial Restructuring in East Asia: Towards the 21st Century*, ed. S. Masuyama, D. Vendenbrink and Chia Siow Yue. Tokyo: Nomura Research Institute and Singapore: Institute of Southeast Asian Studies, 2001, pp. 169–208.

________. "The Asian Financial Crisis: Singapore's Experience and Response", *ASEAN Economic Bulletin* 15, 3 (1998): 297–308.

________ and Jamus Jerome Lim. "Singapore: A Regional Hub in ICT", in *Towards a Knowledge-based Economy: East Asia's Changing Industrial Geography*, ed. S. Masuyama and D. Vandenbrink. Singapore: Institute of Southeast Asian Studies, 2003, pp. 259–98.

Ching Tuen Yee and Benjamin Ng. "Realising the Marina Bay Vision", *Skyline* (July–August 2008): 16–18.

Choe, Alan F.C. "The Early Years of Nation-Building: Reflections on Singapore's Urban History", in *50 Years of Urban Planning in Singapore*, ed. Heng Chye Kiang. Singapore: World Scientific, 2016, pp. 3–21.

________. "Urban Renewal", in *Public Housing in Singapore: A Multi-Disciplinary Study*, ed. Stephen H.K. Yeh. Singapore: Singapore University Press, 1975, pp. 97–116.

Choi Chik Cheong and Nadiah Loh. "Singapore's Bus Reform Experience", *Journeys* (May 2015).

Chow Hwee Kwan and Ho Kong Weng. "The Case of Singapore", in *Economic Policy and the Covid-19 Crisis: The Macroeconomic Response in the US, Europe and East Asia*, ed. B. Andreosso-O'Callaghan, W. Moon and W. Sohn. Abingdon: Routledge, 2022, pp. 204–53.

Choy Keen Meng. "Business Cycles in Singapore: Stylised Facts for a Small Open Economy", *Pacific Economic Review* 16, 1 (2011): 18–35.

________. "Foreign Direct Investment in the Manufacturing Sector in Singapore", in Keen Meng Choy, *Studies on the Singapore Economy*. Singapore: World Scientific, 2012, pp. 19–40.

________. "Singapore Business Cycles: A Supply-Side Analysis", *ASEAN Economic Bulletin* 20, 1 (2003): 1–10.

________. "Trade Cycles in a Re-Export Economy", *International Economic Journal* 26, 2 (2012): 189–201.

________ and Ichiro Sugimoto. "Opium Consumption and Living Standards in Singapore, 1900–39", *Journal of Southeast Asian Studies* 54, 1 (2023): 116–31.

________. "Staple Trade, Real Wages, and Living Standards in Singapore, 1870–1939", *Economic History of Developing Regions* 33, 1 (2018): 18–50.

________. "Trade, the Staple Theory of Growth, and Fluctuations in Colonial Singapore, 1900–39", *Australian Economic History Review* 53, 2 (2013): 121–45.

Chua Ai Lin. "The Story of Singapore Radio, 1924–41", *BiblioAsia* 12, 1 (2016): 22–7.

"City State Hopes Research Cash Will Buy Global Status", *Nature* 442 (13 July 2006): 118–9.

Clark, D.H. "Labour Market and Industrial Relations", in *The Singapore Economy*, ed. You Poh Seng and Lim Chong Yah. Singapore: Eastern Universities Press, 1971, pp. 307–27.

Coclanis, P.A. "Southeast Asia's Incorporation into the World Rice Market: A Revisionist View", *Journal of Southeast Asian Studies* 24, 2 (1993): 251–67.

Comber, L. "Chinese Secret Societies in Malaya; An Introduction", *Journal of the Malayan Branch of the Royal Asiatic Society* 29, 1 (1956): 146–62.

Corden, W.M. "Macroeconomic Targets and Instruments for a Small Open Economy", *The Singapore Economic Review* 29, 2 (1984): 27–37.

Cowan, C.D. "Early Penang & the Rise of Singapore 1805–1832", *Journal of the Malayan Branch of the Royal Asiatic Society* 23, 2 (1950): 2–210.

Crane, T.O. "Remarks on the Cultivation of Cotton in Singapore", *The Journal of the Indian Archipelago and Eastern Asia*, ed. J.R. Logan, 5 (1851): 120–3.

Crawfurd, J. "Remarks on the Excise Revenue", *The Journal of the Indian Archipelago and Eastern Asia*, ed. J.R. Logan, 8 (1854): 408–15.

Darbishire, C.W. "Commerce and Currency", in *One Hundred Years of Singapore*, vol. II, ed. W. Makepeace, G.E. Brooke and R. St.J. Braddell. London: John Murray, 1921, pp. 22–55.

Davies, G. "United Kingdom Investment", in *Foreign Investment and Industrialization in Singapore*, ed. H. Hughes and You Poh Seng. Canberra: Australian National University Press, 1969, pp. 46–61.

"Development of Singapore: Retrospective Overview", in Lim Chong Yah and Associates, *Policy Options for the Singapore Economy*. Singapore: McGraw-Hill, 1988, pp. 1–22.

"Digital Globalization: How MNCs Must Reinvent to Tap Asia's Growth Story", *Future Ready Singapore*, 2016.

"Do Trade Agreements Matter? Evaluating the Impact of FTAs on Singapore's Domestic Exports of Goods", *Economic Survey of Singapore Second Quarter 2011*. Singapore: Ministry of Trade and Industry, pp. 17–26.

Drabble, J.H. "Investment in the Rubber Industry in Malaya c. 1900–1922", *Journal of Southeast Asian Studies* 3, 2 (1972): 247–61.

________. "The Plantation Rubber Industry in Malaya up to 1922", *Journal of the Malaysian Branch of the Royal Asiatic Society* 40, 1 (1967): 52–77.

________ and P.J. Drake. "The British Agency Houses in Malaysia: Survival in a Changing World", *Journal of Southeast Asian Studies* 12, 2 (1981): 297–328.

"Drainage of Singapore Town", *The Journal of the Indian Archipelago and Eastern Asia*, ed. J.R. Logan, 8 (1854): 414–5.

Drake, P.J. "The Evolution of Money in Singapore since 1819", in Monetary Authority of Singapore, *Papers on Monetary Economics*. Singapore: Singapore University Press, 1981, pp. 1–25.

"Drivers of Labour Productivity Growth in Singapore 2009–2019", *Economic Survey of Singapore Third Quarter 2020*. Singapore: Ministry of Trade and Industry, pp. 42–54.

Earl, G.W. "The Kri and Aru Islands", *The Journal of the Indian Archipelago and Eastern Asia*, ed. J.R. Logan, 7 (1853): 64–72.

Easterly, W. "Reliving the '50s: the Big Push, Poverty Traps, and Takeoffs in Economic Development", Working Paper Number 65. Washington, DC: Center for Global Development, 2005.

"Economic Contribution of Factoryless Goods Producing Firms in Singapore", *Economic Survey of Singapore Second Quarter 2018*. Singapore: Ministry of Trade and Industry, pp. 36–9.

"Economic Contributions of Singapore's Creative Industries", *Economic Survey of Singapore First Quarter 2003*. Singapore: Ministry of Trade and Industry, pp. 51–75.

Ee, Joyce. "Chinese Migration to Singapore, 1896–1941", *Journal of Southeast Asian History* 2, 1 (1961): 33–51.

"Employment Trends During Recessions: A Comparison from Peak to Trough", *Economic Survey of Singapore 2009*. Singapore: Ministry of Trade and Industry, pp. 9–11.

"Employment Trends During the COVID-19 Pandemic", *Economic Survey of Singapore Third Quarter 2021*. Singapore: Ministry of Trade and Industry, pp. 18–24.

Erb, M. "Moulding a Nation: Education in Early Singapore", in *Past Times: A Social History of Singapore*, ed. Chan Kwok Bun and Tong Chee Kiong. Singapore: Times Editions, 2003, pp. 17–31.

Estevadeordal, A., B. Frantz and A. M. Taylor. "The Rise and Fall of World Trade, 1870–1939", *The Quarterly Journal of Economics* 118, 2 (2003): 359–407.

"Exchange Rate Policy", in Lim Chong Yah and Associates, *Policy Options for the Singapore Economy*. Singapore: McGraw-Hill, 1988, pp. 301–20.

Federico, G. and A. Tena-Junguito, "World Trade, 1800–1938: A New Synthesis", *Revista de Historia Económica* 37, 1 (2019): 9–41.

Felipe, J. and J. McCombie. "The Debate About the Sources of Growth in East Asia After a Quarter of a Century", ADB Economics Working Paper Series No. 512. Manila: Asian Development Bank, 2017.

Fesharaki, F. "Singapore as an Oil Centre", in *Management of Success: The Moulding of Modern Singapore*, ed. K.S. Sandhu and P. Wheatley. Singapore: Institute of Southeast Asian Studies, 1989, pp. 300–13.

Findlay, R. and M. Lundahl. "Natural Resources, Vent for Surplus, and the Staples Theory", in *From Classical Economics to Development Economics: Essays in Honor of Hla Myint*, ed. G. Meier. New York: St. Martin's Press, 1994, pp. 68–93.

"Fiscal Policy", in Lim Chong Yah and Associates, *Policy Options for the Singapore Economy*. Singapore: McGraw-Hill, 1988, pp. 361–89.

"Fiscal Policy in Singapore", IPS-ESS Workshop. Singapore, May 2004.

"Foreign Investment Policy", in Lim Chong Yah and Associates, *Policy Options for the Singapore Economy*. Singapore: McGraw-Hill, 1988, pp. 247–73.

"From Recession to Recovery", in Lim Chong Yah and Associates, *Policy Options for the Singapore Economy*. Singapore: McGraw-Hill, 1988, pp. 23–49.

Frost, Mark Ravinder. "Emporium in Imperio: Nanyang Networks and the Straits Chinese in Singapore, 1819–1914", *Journal of Southeast Asian Studies* 36, 1 (2005): 29–66.

"Gambling and Opium Smoking in the Straits of Malacca", *The Journal of the Indian Archipelago and Eastern Asia*, ed. J.R. Logan, New Series 1 (1856): 66–83.

Ganesan, N. "Singapore in 2014: Managing Domestic and Regional Concerns and Signalling a New Regional Role", in *Southeast Asian Affairs 2015*. Singapore: Institute of Southeast Asian Studies, 2015, pp. 305–20.

Ghani, Azhar. "Singapore in 2009: Braving a Grave New World", in *Southeast Asian Affairs 2010*. Singapore: Institute of Southeast Asian Studies, 2010, pp. 261–84.

Giacomin, V. "Singapore, Global City Ante Litteram in Early Twentieth Century Southeast Asia", in *Singapore—Two Hundred Years of the Lion City*, ed. A. Webster and N.J. White. Abingdon: Routledge, 2020, pp. 61–79.

Glickman, D.L. "The British Imperial Preference System", *The Quarterly Journal of Economics* 61, 3 (1947): 439–70.

Goh Chor Boon and S. Gopinathan. "Education in Singapore: Developments since 1965", in *An African Exploration of the East Asian Education Experience*, ed. B. Fredriksen and Tan Jee Peng. Washington, DC: The World Bank, 2008, pp. 80–108.

Goh Chor Boon and Leo Tan Wee Hin. "The Development of University Education in Singapore", in *Toward a Better Future: Education and Training for Economic Development in Singapore since 1965*, ed. Lee Sing Kong, Goh Chor Boon, F. Birger and Tan Jee Peng. Washington, DC: World Bank Publications, 2008, pp. 149–66.

Goh Keng Swee. "A Socialist Economy that Works", in *Socialism that Works... the Singapore Way*, ed. C.V. Devan Nair. Singapore: Federal Publications, 1976, pp. 77–85.

________. "Why A Currency Board?", in *Prudence at the Helm, Board of Commissioners of Currency Singapore 1967–1992*. Singapore: Board of Commissioners of Currency, 1992, pp. 31–5.

Gopinathan, S. "Education", in *A History of Singapore*, ed. Ernest Chew and Edwin Lee. Singapore: Oxford University Press, 1991, pp. 268–87.

Goto-Shibata, H. "Empire on the Cheap: The Control of Opium Smoking in the Straits Settlements, 1925–1939", *Modern Asian Studies* 40, 1 (2006): 59–80.

Grice, K. and D.W. Drakakis-Smith. "The Role of the State in Shaping Development: Two Decades of Growth in Singapore", *Transactions of the Institute of British Geographers* 10, 3 (1985): 347–59.

Hack, K. "Framing Singapore's History", in *Studying Singapore's Past: C.M. Turnbull and the History of Modern Singapore*, ed. N. Tarling. Singapore: NUS Press, 2012, pp. 17–64.

Hallifax, F.J. "Municipal Government", in *One Hundred Years of Singapore*, vol. I, ed. W. Makepeace, G.E. Brooke and R. St.J. Braddell. London: John Murray, 1921, pp. 315–40.

Harley, C. Knick. "Ocean Freight Rates and Productivity, 1740–1913: The Primacy of Mechanical Invention Reaffirmed", *The Journal of Economic History* 48, 4 (1988): 851–76.

"Has Foreign Talent Contributed to Singapore's Economic Growth? An Empirical Assessment", *Economic Survey of Singapore Third Quarter 2001*. Singapore: Ministry of Trade and Industry, pp. 39–47.

Heitger, B. "Comparative Economic Growth: Catching Up in East Asia", *ASEAN Economic Bulletin* 10, 1 (1993): 68–82.

Heng, Derek. "Casting Singapore's History in the Longue Durée", in *Singapore from Temasek to the 21st Century: Reinventing the Global City*, ed. K. Hack, J. Margolin with K. Delaye. Singapore: NUS Press, 2010, pp. 55–75.

________. "Economic Networks Between the Malay Region and the Hinterlands of Quanzhou and Guangzhou", in *Early Singapore: 1300s–1819*, ed. J.N. Miksic and Cheryl-Ann Low Mei Gek. Singapore: Singapore History Museum, 2004, pp. 73–85.

________. "Export Commodity and Regional Currency: The Role of Chinese Copper Coins in the Melaka Straits, Tenth to Fourteenth Centuries", *Journal of Southeast Asian Studies* 37, 2 (2006): 179–203.

________. "Reconstructing Banzu, A Fourteenth Century Port Settlement in Singapore", *Journal of the Malayan Branch of the Royal Asiatic Society* 75, 1 (2002): 69–90.

Heracleous, L. "State Ownership, Privatization, and Performance in Singapore: An Exploratory Study from a Strategic Management Perspective", *Asia Pacific Journal of Management* 18 (2001): 69–81.

Hewson, J.R. "The Asian Dollar Market and Monetary Policy", in Monetary Authority of Singapore, *Papers on Monetary Economics*. Singapore: Singapore University Press, 1981, pp. 165–95.

Hill, H. and Pang Eng Fong. "Technology Exports from a Small, Very Open NIC: The Case of Singapore", *World Development* 19, 5 (1991): 553–68.

Hing Ai Yun. "The Singapore State Takes Charge: Strategizing for the New Hi-Tech Service Society", *European Planning Studies* 7, 2 (1999): 189–205.

________ and Lee Kiat Jin. "Evolution of the Petrochemical Industry in Singapore", *Journal of the Asia-Pacific Economy* 14, 2 (2009): 116–22.

Hirono, R. "Japanese Investment", in *Foreign Investment and Industrialization in Singapore*, ed. H. Hughes and You Poh Seng. Canberra: Australian National University Press, 1969, pp. 86–111.

Ho Guan Lim. "Health Services and Population", in *Public Policy and Population Change in Singapore*, ed. Peter S.J. Chen and J.T. Fawcett. New York: The Population Council, 1979, pp. 217–28.

Ho Kong Weng. "Wage Inequality, Intergenerational Mobility and Education in Singapore", *Ethos*, Issue 3 (2007): 43–7.

________ and Marcus Tan Kheng Tat. "Challenges to Social Mobility in Singapore: Facilitating Social Mobility", in *The Singapore Economy: Dynamism and Inclusion*, ed. Hoon Hian Teck. Abingdon: Routledge, 2022, pp. 221–76.

Ho, Terence. "Supporting Jobs and Livelihoods During the Pandemic", *Ethos*, Issue 22 (2021): 42–51.

________. "The Growing Scope and Impact of the Progressive Wage Model", *Singapore Labour Journal* (2023): 56–67.

Hodjera, Z. "The Asian Currency Market: Singapore as a Regional Financial Center", *IMF Staff Papers* 25, 2 (1978): 221–53.

Hsieh, Chang-Tai. "Productivity Growth and Factor Prices in East Asia", *The American Economic Review* 89, 2 (1999): 133–8.

Huff, W.G. "Entitlements, Destitution and Emigration in the 1930s Singapore Great Depression", *The Economic History Review* 54, 2 (2001): 290–323.

________. "The Development of the Rubber Market in Pre-World War II Singapore", *Journal of Southeast Asian Studies* 24, 2 (1993): 285–306.

________. "The Developmental State, Government, and Singapore's Economic Development since 1960", *World Development* 23, 8 (1995): 1421–38.

________ [as Gregg Huff] and G[illian] Huff. "The Second World War Occupation of Singapore", *Journal of Southeast Asian Studies* 51, 1–2 (2020): 243–70.

Hughes, H. "From Entrepot Trade to Manufacturing", in *Foreign Investment and Industrialization in Singapore*, ed. H. Hughes and You Poh Seng. Canberra: Australian National University Press, 1969, pp. 1–45.

Husain, A.M. "Determinants of Private Saving in Singapore", in *Singapore: A Case Study in Rapid Development*, IMF Occasional Paper No. 119, ed. K. Bercuson. Washington, DC: International Monetary Fund, 1995, pp. 42–51.

Hutton, T.A. "The Innisian Core-Periphery Revisited: Vancouver's Changing Relationships with British Columbia's Staple Economy", *BC Studies: The British Columbian Quarterly*, no. 113 (1997).

Hyde, F.E. "British Shipping Companies and East and South-East Asia, 1860–1939", in *The Economic Development of South-East Asia*, ed. C.D. Cowan. 1964; Abingdon: Routledge, 2012, pp. 27–47.

"Impact of Severe Acute Respiratory Syndrome (SARS) on the Singapore Economy", *Economic Survey of Singapore First Quarter 2003*. Singapore: Ministry of Trade and Industry, pp. 45–50.

"Impact of the Circuit Breaker and Budget Measures in Response to COVID-19", *Economic Survey of Singapore Second Quarter 2020*. Singapore: Ministry of Trade and Industry, pp. 42–8.

"Impact of the COVID-19 Pandemic on the Singapore Economy", *Economic Survey of Singapore First Quarter 2020*. Singapore: Ministry of Trade and Industry, pp. 36–44.

"Impact of the Jobs Support Scheme on Labour Market Outcomes", *Economic Survey of Singapore 2021*. Singapore: Ministry of Trade and Industry, pp. 86–93.

"Integrated Resorts". Singapore: Ministry of Trade and Industry, 2012.

Islam, I. and C. Kirkpatrick "Export-Led Development, Labour-Market Conditions and the Distribution of Income: The Case of Singapore", *Cambridge Journal of Economics* 10, 2 (1986): 113–27.

Jackson, J.C. "Chinese Agricultural Pioneering in Singapore and Johore 1800–1917", *Journal of the Malaysian Branch of the Royal Asiatic Society* 38, 1 (1965): 77–105.

Jenkins, G. and R. Khadka. "Tax Reform in Singapore", Discussion Paper no. 644. Harvard Institute for International Development, 1998.

Jones, D.S. "Infrastructure Management in Singapore: Privatization and Government Control", *Asian Education and Development Studies* 4, 3 (2015): 299–311.

Jordan, R. "Singapore in Its Worst Recession for Years. The Effects of the Current Economic Crisis on the City-State's Economy", *Journal of Current Southeast Asian Affairs* 28, 4 (2009): 95–110.

Kamble, A.A. "Indians in the Plantation Industry of Malaya (Mid-19th to 20th Century)", *Proceedings of the Indian History Congress 68, Part Two* (2007): 1168–77.

Kathirithamby-Wells, J. "Early Singapore and the Inception of a British Administrative Tradition in the Straits Settlements (1819–1832)", *Journal of the Malaysian Branch of the Royal Asiatic Society* 42, 2 (1969): 48–73.

Kawai, M. "Global Financial Crisis and Implications for ASEAN", in *Global Financial Crisis: Implications for ASEAN*, ASEAN Studies Centre, Report No. 6. Singapore: Institute of Southeast Asian Studies, 2009, pp. 1–10.

Kawamura, T. "Trade, Finance and the 'Anglo-Dutch' International Order in Southeast Asia: The Case of the British Eastern Exchange Banks, 1870–1890", in *Singapore—Two Hundred Years of the Lion City*, ed. A. Webster and N.J. White. Abingdon: Routledge, 2020, pp. 46–60.

Khoo Kay Kim. "Taiping (Larut): The Early History of a Mining Settlement", *Journal of the Malaysian Branch of the Royal Asiatic Society* 64, 1 (1991): 1–32.

________. "The Great Depression: The Malaysian Context", in *The History of South-East, South and East Asia: Essays and Documents*, ed. Khoo Kay Kim. Kuala Lumpur: Oxford University Press, 1977, pp. 78–94.

________. "The Origin of British Administration in Malaya", *Journal of the Malaysian Branch of the Royal Asiatic Society* 39, 1 (1966): 52–91.

Kindleberger, C.P. "The Rise of Free Trade in Western Europe, 1820–1875", *The Journal of Economic History* 35, 1 (1975): 20–55.

King, A.W. "Plantation and Agriculture in Malaya, with Notes on the Trade of Singapore", *The Geographical Journal* 93, 2 (1939): 136–48.

Kobayashi, A. "International Bimetallism and Silver Absorption in Singapore, 1840–73", *The Economic History Review* 72, 2 (2019): 595–617.

________. "Price Fluctuations and Growth Patterns in Singapore's Trade, 1831–1913", *Australian Economic History Review* 57, 1 (2017): 108–29.

________. "The Origins of Singapore's Economic Prosperity, c. 1800–1874", in *Singapore—Two Hundred Years of the Lion City*, ed. A. Webster and N.J. White. Abingdon: Routledge, 2020, pp. 13–29.

________. "The Role of Singapore in the Growth of Intra-Southeast Asian Trade, c.1820s–1852", *Southeast Asian Studies* 2, 3 (2013): 443–74.

Koh, Denis Soo Jin and K. Tanaka. "Japanese Competition in the Trade of Malaya in the 1930s", *Southeast Asian Studies* 21, 4 (1984): 374–99.

Koh, Gillian and Ooi Giok-Ling. "Singapore: A Home, A Nation?", in *Southeast Asian Affairs 2002*. Singapore: Institute of Southeast Asian Studies, 2002, pp. 255–81.

Koh Soo Wei, Shahidur Rahman and Randolph G.K. Tan. "Growth and Productivity in Singapore Manufacturing Industries: 1975–1998", *Asian Economic Journal* 16, 3 (2002): 247–66.

Koh, Winston T. H. "Singapore's Transition to Innovation-based Economic Growth: Infrastructure, Institutions and Government's Role", *R&D Management* 36, 2 (2006): 143–60.

Kratoska, P.H. "Banana Money: Consequences of the Demonetization of Wartime Japanese Currency in British Malaya", *Journal of Southeast Asian Studies* 23, 2 (1992): 322–45.

________. "Imperial Unity versus Local Autonomy: British Malaya and the Depression of the 1930s", in *Weathering the Storm: The Economies of Southeast Asia in the 1930s Depression*, ed. P. Boomgaard and I. Brown. Singapore: Institute of Southeast Asian Studies, 2000, pp. 271–94.

________. "The British Empire and the Southeast Asian Rice Crisis of 1919–1921", *Modern Asian Studies* 24, 1 (1990): 115–46.

Krugman, P. "The Myth of Asia's Miracle", *Foreign Affairs* 73, 6 (November/December 1994): 62–78.

Kumar, S. "Singapore 1991: Towards New Horizons", in *Southeast Asian Affairs 1992*. Singapore: Institute of Southeast Asian Studies, 1992, pp. 281–98.

Kuo Huei-Ying, "Rescuing Businesses through Transnationalism: Embedded Chinese Enterprise and Nationalist Activities in Singapore in the 1930s", *Enterprise & Society* 7, 1 (2006): 98–127.

Kuznets, S. "Modern Economic Growth: Findings and Reflections", *The American Economic Review* 63, 3 (1973): 247–58.

Kwa Chong Guan. "Jackson Plan", in *On Paper: Singapore Before 1867*. Singapore: National Library Board, 2019, pp. 116–9.

Kwong Kai-Sun. "Singapore: Dominance of Multinational Corporations in Industrial Development", in *Industrial Development in Singapore, Taiwan and South Korea*, ed. Kwong Kai-Sun, Chau Leung-Chuen, Francis T. Lui and Larry D. Qiu. Singapore: World Scientific, 2001, pp. 1–55.

Latham, A.J.H. "The Dynamics of Intra-Asian Trade, 1868–1913: The Great Entrepôts of Singapore and Hong Kong", in *Japanese Industrialization and the Asian Economy*, ed. A.J.H. Latham and H. Kawakatsu. Abingdon: Routledge, 1994, pp. 145–71.

Lau, Albert. "The Battle for Merger—The Historical Context", in Lee Kuan Yew, *The Battle for Merger*. Singapore: National Archives of Singapore, 1962, pp. xii–xxx.

Law Song Seng. "Vocational Technical Education and Economic Development—The Singapore Experience", in *Toward a Better Future: Education and Training for Economic Development in Singapore since 1965*, ed. Lee Sing Kong, Goh Chor Boon, F. Birger and Tan Jee Peng. Washington, DC: World Bank Publications, 2008, pp. 114–34.

Lee, Cassey and Chew Ging Lee. "Determinants of Singapore's Outward FDI", ISEAS Economics Working Paper No. 2016-2. Singapore: ISEAS-Yusof Ishak Institute, 2016.

Lee, Edwin. "The Colonial Legacy", in *Management of Success: The Moulding of Modern Singapore*, ed. K.S. Sandhu and P. Wheatley. Singapore: Institute of Southeast Asian Studies, 1989, pp. 3–5.

Lee Geok Boi. "Wartime Victuals", *BiblioAsia* 15, 1 (2019): 22–9.

Lee Sheng-Yi. "Income Distribution, Taxation, and Social Benefits of Singapore", *The Journal of Developing Areas* 14, 1 (1979): 71–98.

________. "Some Basic Problems of Industrialization in Singapore", *The Journal of Developing Areas* 7, 2 (1973): 185–216.

Lee Soo Ann. "Expansion of the Services Sector", in *Management of Success: The Moulding of Modern Singapore*, ed. K.S. Sandhu and P. Wheatley. Singapore: Institute of Southeast Asian Studies, 1989, pp. 280–99.

________. "Patterns of Economic Structure in Singapore", in *Singapore: Twenty-five Years of Development*, ed. You Poh Seng and Lim Chong Yah. Singapore: Nan Yang Xing Zhou Lianhe Zaobao, 1984, pp. 13–37.

________. "Trade and Shipping Growth", in *Singapore in the International Economy, Symposium Papers*, ed. Wong Kum Poh and Maureen Tan. Singapore: Singapore University Press, 1972.

________ and Qian Jiwei. "The Evolving Singaporean Welfare State", *Social Policy and Administration* 51, 6 (2017): 916–39.

Lee, William K.M. "The Poor in Singapore: Issues and Options", *Journal of Contemporary Asia* 31, 1 (2001): 57–70.

Lee, Y.K. "A Short History of Kandang Kerbau Hospital and the Maternity Services of Singapore", *Singapore Medical Journal* 3 (1990): 599–613.

________. "Private Practitioners and Private Hospitals in Early Singapore (1819–1872)", *Singapore Medical Journal* 46, 9 (2005): 489–503.

________. "Singapore's Pauper and Tan Tock Seng Hospitals, Part Three, The New Hospital, 1860", *Journal of the Malaysian Branch of the Royal Asiatic Society* 49, 2 (1976): 164–83.

________. "The 1926 General Hospital, Singapore", *Annals of the Academy of Medicine, Singapore* 34, 6 (2005): 52C–60C.

________. "The Pauper Hospital in Early Singapore, Part I, 1819–1829", *Singapore Medical Journal* 14, 1 (1973): 49–54.

________. "The Pauper Hospital in Early Singapore, Part II, 1830–1839", *Singapore Medical Journal* 15, 1 (1974): 72–83.

________. "The Pauper Hospital in Early Singapore, Part III, 1840–1849, Section I", *Singapore Medical Journal* 16, 2 (1975): 106–22.

________. "The Pauper Hospital in Early Singapore, Part IV, 1850–1859, Section I", *Singapore Medical Journal* 16, 4 (1975): 269–89.

Lee Yip Lin. "Chinese Junk Trade in Early Singapore", in *A General History of the Chinese in Singapore*, ed. Kwa Chong Guan and Kua Bak Lim. Singapore: World Scientific, 2019, pp. 23–33.

Lee Yong-Sook and Tee Ying-Chian. "Reprising the Role of the Developmental State in Cluster Development: The Biomedical Industry in Singapore", *Singapore Journal of Tropical Geography* 30, 1 (2009): 86–97.

Legge, J. "The Colonial Office and Governor Ord", *Journal of Southeast Asian Studies* 29, 1 (1998): 1–7.

Leifer, M. "The Conduct of Foreign Policy", in *Management of Success: The Moulding of Modern Singapore*, ed. K.S. Sandhu and P. Wheatley. Singapore: Institute of Southeast Asian Studies, 1989, pp. 965–81.

Leong Foke Meng. "Early Land Transactions in Singapore: The Real Estates of William Farquhar (1774–1839), John Crawfurd (1783–1868), and Their Families", *Journal of the Malaysian Branch of the Royal Asiatic Society* 77, 1 (2004): 23–42.

"Letter of Instructions to Mr Crawfurd on Raffles' Departure", *The Journal of the Indian Archipelago and Eastern Asia*, ed. J.R. Logan, 7 (1853): 337–45.

Leung Yuen Sang. "The Economic Life of the Chinese in Late Nineteenth-century Singapore", in *Early Chinese Immigrant Societies: Case Studies from North America and British Southeast Asia*, ed. Lee Lai To. Singapore: Heineman Asia, 1988, pp. 126–55.

Lieberman, V. "Maritime Influences in Southeast Asia, c. 900–1300: Some Further Thoughts", *Journal of Southeast Asian Studies* 41, 3 (2010): 529–39.

Lim, Arthur Joo-Hock. "Geographical Setting", in *A History of Singapore*, ed. Ernest Chew and Edwin Lee. Singapore: Oxford University Press, 1991, pp. 3–14.

________. "Singapore in 1980: Management of Foreign Relations", in *Southeast Asian Affairs 1981*. Singapore: Institute of Southeast Asian Studies, 1981, pp. 273–89.

Lim Chong Yah. "From High Growth Rates to Recession", in *Management of Success: The Moulding of Modern Singapore*, ed. K.S. Sandhu and P. Wheatley. Singapore: Institute of Southeast Asian Studies, 1989, pp. 201–17.

________. "Singapore's Economic Development: Retrospect and Prospect", in *Singapore Development Policies and Trends*, ed. Peter S.J. Chen. Singapore: Oxford University Press, 1983, pp. 89–104.

________ and Ow Chwee Huay. "The Economic Development of Singapore in the Sixties and Beyond", in *The Singapore Economy*, ed. You Poh Seng and Lim Chong Yah. Singapore: Eastern Universities Press, 1971, pp. 1–42.

Lim Guan Hock. "Development of Chinese Education in Singapore (1819–1979)", in *A General History of the Chinese in Singapore*, ed. Kwa Chong Guan and Kua Bak Lim. Singapore: World Scientific, 2019, pp. 419–44.

________. "Gambier and Early Development of Singapore", in *A General History of the Chinese in Singapore*, ed. Kwa Chong Guan and Kua Bak Lim. Singapore: World Scientific, 2019, pp. 35–72.

Lim, Linda. "Singapore's Success: The Myth of the Free Market", *Asian Survey* 23, 6 (1983): 752–64.

________, Pang Eng Fong and R. Findlay. "Singapore", in *Five Small Open Economies*, ed. R. Findlay and S. Wellisz. Washington, DC: The World Bank, 1993, pp. 93–139.

Lim Meng-Kin. "Health Care Systems in Transition II. Singapore, Part I. An Overview of Health Care Systems in Singapore", *Journal of Public Health Medicine* 20, 1 (1998): 16–22.

________. "Transforming Singapore Health Care: Public-Private Partnership", *Annals-Academy of Medicine Singapore* 34, 7 (2005): 461–7.

Lim Peng Han. "English Schools and School Libraries Before the Second World War: A Singapore Perspective", *Singapore Journal of Library & Information Management* 37 (2008): 61–80.

________. "Elementary Malay Vernacular Schools and School Libraries in Singapore Under British Colonial Rule, 1819–1941", *School Libraries Worldwide* 14, 1 (2008): 72–85.

Lim Tin Seng. "Coolies, Triads and Pimps: Chinatown in Former Times", *BiblioAsia* 11, 3 (2015): 2–7.

________. "From Botanic Gardens to Gardens by the Bay: Singapore's Experience in Becoming a Garden City", *BiblioAsia* 8, 2 (2012): 24–31.

Lindert, P.H. "United States Investment", in *Foreign Investment and Industrialization in Singapore*, ed. H. Hughes and You Poh Seng. Canberra: Australian National University Press, 1969, pp. 154–76.

Little, R. "On the Habitual Use of Opium in Singapore", *The Journal of the Indian Archipelago and Eastern Asia*, ed. J.R. Logan, 2 (1848): 1–82.

Logan, J.R. "Sago", *The Journal of the Indian Archipelago and Eastern Asia*, ed. J.R. Logan, 3 (1849): 288–313.

Loh, Francis Kok-Wah. "Chinese Immigration and Tin Mining", in *Early Modern History, 1800–1940, The Encyclopedia of Malaysia*, ed. Cheah Boon Kheng. Singapore: Editions Didier Millet, 2001, pp. 72–3.

________. "Early Malay Tin Mining", in *Early Modern History, 1800–1940, The Encyclopedia of Malaysia*, ed. Cheah Boon Kheng. Singapore: Editions Didier Millet, 2001, pp. 20–1.

Loh Kah Seng. "Beyond Rubber Prices: Negotiating the Great Depression in Singapore", *South East Asia Research* 14, 1 (2006): 5–31.

________. "Imaginaries of Jurong Industrial Estate, Singapore", *International Institute of Asian Studies*, Newsletter 81 (2018): 6–7.

________. "Records and Voices of Social History: The Case of the Great Depression in Singapore", *Southeast Asian Studies* 44, 1 (2006): 31–54.

________. "The British Military Withdrawal from Singapore and the Anatomy of a Catalyst", in *Singapore in Global History*, ed. Derek Heng and Syed Muhd Khairudin Aljunied. Amsterdam: Amsterdam University Press, 2011, pp. 195–213.

________ and Tammy Chandra. "Albert Winsemius Heritage Trail", in Euston Quah with Luke Nursultan Iuldashov and Zach Lee, *Albert Winsemius and Singapore: Here It is Going to Happen*. Singapore: World Scientific, 2022, pp. 691–715.

________ and Nguyen Loc Luu Ly. "Memories of Rollei Singapore", *Berita Newsletter* (Winter 2018/2019): 6–15.

Loke Hoe-Yeong and S. Gopinathan. "The Policy and Politics of the Cohort Participation Rate in Universities: The Case of Singapore and 'SkillsFuture'", *International Journal of Chinese Education* 5, 2 (2016): 209–25.

Lornie, J. "Land Tenure", in *One Hundred Years of Singapore,* vol. I, ed. W. Makepeace, G.E. Brooke and R. St.J. Braddell. London: John Murray, 1921, pp. 301–14.

Low, Donald. "Fiscal Policy: Discipline with Discretion", Mimeograph.

Low, Linda. "Rethinking Singapore Inc. and GLCs", in *Southeast Asian Affairs 2002*. Singapore: Institute of Southeast Asian Studies, 2002, pp. 282–302.

Mackintosh, W.A. "Economic Factors in Canadian History", *Canadian Historical Review* 4, 1 (1923): 12–25.

Mahizhnan, Arun. "Developing Singapore's External Economy", in *Southeast Asian Affairs 1994*. Singapore: Institute of Southeast Asian Studies, 1994, pp. 285–301.

Mak Lau Fong. "Chinese Secret Societies in the Nineteenth-century Straits Settlements", in *Early Chinese Immigrant Societies: Case Studies from North America and British Southeast Asia*, ed. Lee Lai To. Singapore: Heineman Asia, 1988, pp. 230–43.

________ and Him M. Lai. "Occupational Structures of Chinese Immigrants in Early Malaya and North America", *Southeast Asian Journal of Social Science* 20, 1 (1992): 43–66.

Makepeace, W. "Singapore Defences", in *One Hundred Years of Singapore,* vol. I, ed. W. Makepeace, G.E. Brooke and R. St.J. Braddell. London: John Murray, 1921, pp. 377–84.

________. "The Legislative Council", in *One Hundred Years of Singapore,* vol. I, ed. W. Makepeace, G.E. Brooke and R. St.J. Braddell. London: John Murray, 1921, pp. 149–59.

________. "The Machinery of Commerce", in *One Hundred Years of Singapore,* vol. II, ed. W. Makepeace, G.E. Brooke and R. St.J. Braddell. London: John Murray, 1921, pp. 166–234.

"Manpower Policy", in Lim Chong Yah and Associates, *Policy Options for the Singapore Economy*. Singapore: McGraw-Hill, 1988, pp. 139–70.

"Manufacturing and Services in Singapore's Economy: Twin Engines of Growth and Their Asymmetric Dependencies", *Economic Survey of Singapore Third Quarter 2017*. Singapore: Ministry of Trade and Industry, pp. 48–60.

"Mapping Singapore's Knowledge-Based Economy", *Quarterly Economic Survey of Singapore Third Quarter 2002*. Singapore: Ministry of Trade and Industry, pp. 56–75.

Marriott, H. "The Peoples of Singapore: Inhabitants and Population", in *One Hundred Years of Singapore,* vol. I, ed. W. Makepeace, G.E. Brooke and R. St.J. Braddell. London: John Murray, 1921, pp. 341–76.

McIntyre, W.D. "The Strategic Significance of Singapore, 1917–1942. The Naval Base and the Commonwealth", *Journal of Southeast Asian History* 10, 1 (1969): 69–94.

McKissack, A. and J. Xu. "Chinese Macroeconomic Management Through the Crisis and Beyond", *Asia-Pacific Economic Literature* 25, 1 (2011): 43–55.

Meek, P. "Malaya: A Study of Governmental Response to the Korean War Boom", in *Readings in Malayan Economics,* ed. T.H. Silcock. Singapore: Eastern Universities Press, 1961, pp. 201–29.

Meier, G.M. "Industrialization via Export Substitution—Note", in *Leading Issues in Economic Development,* ed. G.M. Meier. Singapore: Oxford University Press, 1984, pp. 394–7.

Middlebrook, S.M., J.M. Gullick and C.A. Gibson-Hill. "Yap Ah Loy (1837–1885)", *Journal of the Malayan Branch of the Royal Asiatic Society* 24, 2 (1951): 1–127.

Miksic, J.N. "14th-Century Singapore: A Port of Trade", in *Early Singapore: 1300s–1819,* ed. J.N. Miksic and Cheryl-Ann Low Mei Gek. Singapore: Singapore History Museum, 2004, pp. 41–54.

________. "Recent Archaeological Excavations in Singapore: A Comparison of Three Fourteenth-Century Sites", *Bulletin of the Indo-Pacific Prehistory Association* 20 (2000): 56–61.

________. "Temasik to Singapura: Singapore in the 14th to 15th Centuries", in *Singapore from Temasek to the 21st Century: Reinventing the Global City,* ed. K. Hack, J. Margolin with K. Delaye. Singapore: NUS Press, 2010, pp. 103–32.

Mills, L.A., C.M. Turnbull and D.K. Bassett. "British Malaya, 1824–67", *Journal of the Malayan Branch of the Royal Asiatic Society,* 33, 3 (1960): 1–424.

Mok Ly Yng. "Plan of Singapore Town and Adjoining Districts", in *On Paper: Singapore Before 1867.* Singapore: National Library Board, 2019, pp. 142–7.

Monetary Authority of Singapore. "Background Note on Macroeconomic Policy Responses to Covid-19: The Singapore Experience", *BIS Papers No. 122.* Basel: Bank for International Settlements, 2022, pp. 267–79.

________. "Sources of Singapore's Economic Growth 1990–2009", *Macroeconomic Review.* Singapore: Monetary Authority of Singapore (April 2010): pp. 66–81.

Morley, J.A.E. "The Arabs and the Eastern Trade", *Journal of the Malayan Branch of the Royal Asiatic Society* 22, 1 (1849): 143–76.

Mukhopadhaya, P. "Education Policies as Means to Tackle Income Disparity: The Singapore Case", *International Journal of Sociology and Social Policy* 20, 11/12 (2000): 59–73.

Myint, H. "The 'Classical Theory' of International Trade and the Underdeveloped Countries", *Economic Journal* 68 (1958): 317–37.

Ng Chee Yuen. "Privatization in Singapore: Divestment with Control", *ASEAN Economic Bulletin* 5, 3 (1989): 290–318.

Ng Chin Keong. "At the Crossroads of the Maritime Silk Route", in *Maritime Heritage of Singapore,* ed. Aileen Lau and Laure Lau. Singapore: Subtree, 2005, pp. 60–79.

________. "The Maritime Chinese and Coloial Singapore 1819–1900", in *Maritime Heritage of Singapore,* ed. Aileen Lau and Laure Lau. Singapore: Subtree, 2005, pp. 102–23.

Ng, David Foo Seong. "Strategic Management of Educational Development in Singapore (1965–2005)", in *Toward a Better Future: Education and Training for Economic Development in Singapore since 1965,* ed. Lee Sing Kong, Goh Chor Boon, F. Birger and Tan Jee Peng. Washington, DC: World Bank Publications, 2008, pp. 39–68.

Ng, Irene Y.H. "Being Poor in a Rich 'Nanny State': Developments in Singapore Social Welfare", *The Singapore Economic Review* 60, 3 (2015): 1550038-1–1550038-17.

________. "Workfare in Singapore", in *Welfare Reform in East Asia: Towards Workfare?* ed. Chak Kwan Chan and Kinglun Ngok. Abingdon: Routledge, 2011, pp. 131–48.

Ng Siew Hoong. "The Chinese Protectorate in Singapore, 1877–1900", *Journal of Southeast Asian History* 2, 1 (1961): 76–99.

Ngiam Kee Jin. "Coping with the Asian Financial Crisis: The Singapore Experience", ISEAS Working Papers. Singapore: Institute of Southeast Asian Studies, 2000.

________. "Financial Sector Reforms in Singapore", in *The International Handbook on Financial Reform*, ed. M.J.B. Hall. Cheltenham: Edward Elgar, 2003, pp. 192–215.

Nicholls, L. "The State of Nutrition in Singapore Before, During, and After the Japanese Occupation", *The British Medical Journal* 1, 4548 (1948): 37–9.

Nicholson, J.R. "The Tanjong Pagar Dock Company", in *One Hundred Years of Singapore,* vol. II, ed. W. Makepeace, G.E. Brooke and R. St.J. Braddell. London: John Murray, 1921, pp. 1–19.

Nomura, K. and T. Amano. "Labour Productivity and Quality Change in Singapore: Achievements in 1974–2011 and Prospects for the Next Two Decades", KEO Discussion Paper No. 129 (2012).

Norruddin, N. "*Sejarah Melayu*: Beginnings of Singapura", in *On Paper: Singapore Before 1867,* Singapore: National Library Board, 2019, pp. 10–19.

"Notes on the Chinese in the Straits", *The Journal of the Indian Archipelago and Eastern Asia*, ed. J.R. Logan, 9 (1855): 109–24.

"Notices of Singapore", *The Journal of the Indian Archipelago and Eastern Asia*, ed. J.R. Logan, 7 (1853): 325–57.

"Notices of Singapore", *The Journal of the Indian Archipelago and Eastern Asia*, ed. J.R. Logan, 8 (1854): 403–14.

"Notices of Singapore", *The Journal of the Indian Archipelago and Eastern Asia*, ed. J.R. Logan, 9 (1855): 442–82.

Nunn, B. "Some Account of Our Governors and Civil Service", in *One Hundred Years of Singapore,* vol. I, ed. W. Makepeace, G.E. Brooke and R. St.J. Braddell. London: John Murray, 1921, pp. 69–148.

Ooi Giok Ling. "British Colonial Healthcare Development and the Persistence of Ethnic Medicine in Peninsular Malaysia and Singapore", *Southeast Asian Studies* 29, 2 (1991): 158–78.

________. "The Indonesia-Malaysia-Singapore Growth Triangle: Sub-Regional Economic Cooperation and Integration", *GeoJournal* 36, 4 (1995): 337–44.

Oswin, N. and Brenda S.A. Yeoh. "Introduction: Mobile City Singapore", *Mobilities* 5, 2 (2010): 167–75.

"Overview of Singapore's Business Services Sector", in *Economic Survey of Singapore 2007*. Singapore: Ministry of Trade and Industry, pp. 122–30.

"Overview of Singapore's Wholesale Trade Sector", in *Economic Survey of Singapore 2008*. Singapore: Ministry of Trade and Industry, pp. 51–6.

"Overview of Singapore's Wholesale Trade Sector", in *Economic Survey of Singapore First Quarter 2011*. Singapore: Ministry of Trade and Industry, pp. 12–18.

Ow Chin Hock. "The Role of Government in Economic Development: The Singapore Experience", in *Singapore: Resources and Growth*, ed. Lim Chong Yah and P.J. Lloyd. Singapore: Oxford University Press, 1986, pp. 221–67.

Oxley, T. "Some Account of the Nutmeg and Its Cultivation", *The Journal of the Indian Archipelago and Eastern Asia*, ed. J.R. Logan, 2 (1848): 641–60.

Pang Eng Fong. "Changing Patterns of Industrial Relations in Singapore", in *Studies in ASEAN Sociology: Urban Society and Social Change*, ed. Peter S.J. Chen and Hans-Dieter Evers. Singapore: Chopmen Enterprises, 1978, pp. 422–36.

________. "Economic Development and the Labor Market in a Newly Industrializing Country: The Experience of Singapore", *The Developing Economies* 19, 1 (1981): 3–16.

________ and Linda Lim. "Foreign Labor and Economic Development in Singapore", *International Migration Review* 16, 3 (1982): 548–76.

________. "Labor, Productivity and Singapore's Development Model", *The Singapore Economic Review* 60, 3 (2015): 1550033-1–1550033-30.

________. "Rapid Growth and Relative Price Stability in a Small Open Economy: The Experience of Singapore", in *Export-Oriented Development Strategies: The Success of Five Newly Industrialising Countries*, ed. V. Corbo, A.O. Krueger and F. Ossa. Boulder and London: Westview Press, 1985, pp. 79–110.

________ and Linda Seah. "The Singapore Economy in 1975: Stagnation and Recovery", in *Southeast Asian Affairs 1976*. Singapore: Institute of Southeast Asian Studies, 1976, pp. 339–47.

________ and Greg Seow. "Labour, Employment and Wage Structure", in *Singapore Development Policies and Trends*, ed. Peter S.J. Chen. Singapore: Oxford University Press, 1983, pp. 160–70.

Parthasarathi, P. "Rethinking Wages and Competitiveness in the Eighteenth Century: Britain and South India", *Past and Present* 158 (1998): 79–109.

Pascali, L. "The Wind of Change: Maritime Technology, Trade, and Economic Development", *The American Economic Review* 107, 9 (2017): 2821–54.

Pearson, H.F. "Lt. Jackson's Plan of Singapore", *Journal of the Malaysian Branch of the Royal Asiatic Society* 42, 1 (1969): 161–5.

Peng, Nathan. "Inequality and the Social Compact in Singapore", *Journal of Southeast Asian Economies* 36, 3 (2019): 355–79.

Pereira, A. "Triads and Riots: Threats to Singapore's Social Stability", in *Past Times: A Social History of Singapore*, ed. Chan Kwok Bun and Tong Chee Kiong. Singapore: Times Editions, 2003, pp. 183–97.

"Performance of the Singapore Economy in 2020", *Economic Survey of Singapore 2020*. Singapore: Ministry of Trade and Industry, pp. 84–95.

Phang Sock-Yong. "House Prices and Aggregate Consumption: Do They Move Together? Evidence from Singapore", *Journal of Housing Economics* 13, 2 (2004): 101–19.

________. "Singapore's Housing Policies: Responding to the Challenges of Economic Transitions", *The Singapore Economic Review* 60, 3 (2015): 1550036-1–1550036-25.

Pickering, W.A. "Chinese Secret Societies and Their Origin", *Journal of the Straits Branch of the Royal Asiatic Society* 1 (1878): 63–84.

"Piracy and the Slave Trade of the Indian Archipelago", *The Journal of the Indian Archipelago and Eastern Asia*, ed. J.R. Logan, 4 (1850): 45–53.

Poh, Jacqueline. "Workfare: The Fourth Pillar of Social Security in Singapore", *Ethos*, Issue 3 (2007): 48–55.

"Population Policy", in Lim Chong Yah and Associates, *Policy Options for the Singapore Economy*. Singapore: McGraw-Hill, 1988, pp. 111–37.

"Poverty, Income Distribution and the Less Privileged", in Lim Chong Yah and Associates, *Policy Options for the Singapore Economy*. Singapore: McGraw-Hill, 1988, pp. 391–424.

Powers, J. "Singapore's Economic Development: The Dilemma of Managing Success" in *Planning Singapore: The Experimental City*, ed. S. Hamnett and Belinda Yuen. Abingdon: Routledge, 2019, pp. 63–81.

Price, H. "Planting in Singapore", in *One Hundred Years of Singapore,* vol. II, ed. W. Makepeace, G.E. Brooke and R. St.J. Braddell. London: John Murray, 1921, pp. 79–84.

"Raffles' Instructions on Formation of Singapore", *The Journal of the Indian Archipelago and Eastern Asia*, ed. J.R. Logan, 7 (1853): 325–57.

Rai, R. "Sepoys, Convicts and the 'Bazaar' Contingent: The Emergence and Exclusion of 'Hindustani' Pioneers at the Singapore Frontier", *Journal of Southeast Asian Studies* 35, 1 (2004): 1–19.

Ramesh, M. and Azad Singh Bali. "The Remarkable Healthcare Performance in Singapore", in *Great Policy Successes*, ed. M. Compton and P.T. Hart. Oxford University Press, 2019, pp. 42–62.

Rao, V.V. Bhanoji and Christopher Lee. "Sources of Growth in the Singapore Economy and Its Manufacturing and Service Sectors", *The Singapore Economic Review* 40, 1 (1995): pp. 83–115.

"Recovery of Air Travel and Tourism in Singapore", *Economic Survey of Singapore Second Quarter 2022*. Singapore: Ministry of Trade and Industry, pp. 30–6.

Regnier, P. "Spreading Singapore's Wings Worldwide: A Review of Traditional and New Investment Strategies", *The Pacific Review* 6, 4 (1993): 305–12.

Reid, A. "An 'Age of Commerce' in Southeast Asian History", *Modern Asian Studies* 24, 1 (1990): 1–30.

________. "Humans and Forests in Pre-Colonial Southeast Asia", in *Nature and the Orient: The Environmental History of South and Southeast Asia*, ed. R.H. Grove, V. Damodaran and S. Sangwan. Delhi: Delhi University Press, 1998.

________. "Southeast Asian Consumption of Indian and British Cotton Cloth, 1600–1850", in *How India Clothed the World: The World of South Asian Textiles, 1500–1850*, ed. G. Riello and Tirtankar Roy. Leiden: Brill, 2009, pp. 29–51.

Renuka, M. "Total Factor Productivity Growth in Singapore: A Survey", *ASEAN Economic Bulletin* 16, 1 (1999): 51–67.

"Returns to Research and Development (R&D) Among Firms in Singapore", *Economic Survey of Singapore Third Quarter 2019*. Singapore: Ministry of Trade and Industry, pp. 42–50.

"Returns to Singapore Workforce Skills Qualifications (WSQ) Training: Does Training Raise Wages and Employability?", *Economic Survey of Singapore 2018*. Singapore: Ministry of Trade and Industry, pp. 92–98.

"Revenues of Singapore", *The Journal of the Indian Archipelago and Eastern Asia*, ed. J.R. Logan, 8 (1854): 415–9.

"Revisiting the 1970s Inflation Shocks", *Macroeconomic Review*, Singapore: Monetary Authority of Singapore (April 2022): 60–5.

Rigg, J. "Singapore and the Recession of 1985", *Asian Survey* 28, 3 (1988): 340–52.

"Rising Contribution of Services Exports to the Singapore Economy", *Economic Survey of Singapore Second Quarter 2014*. Singapore: Ministry of Trade and Industry, pp. 13–19.

Robinson, Edward. "Monetary Policy: Anchor of Stability and Confidence", Mimeograph.

Rönnbäck, K., O. Broberg and S. Galli. "A Colonial Cash Cow: The Return on Investments in British Malaya, 1889–1969", *Cliometrica* 16, 1 (2022): 149–73.

Rudner, M. "The Organization of the British Military Administration in Malaya, 1946–48", *Journal of Southeast Asian History* 9, 1 (1968): 95–106.

Sadka, E. "Singapore and the Federation: Problems of Merger", *Asian Survey* 1, 11 (1962): 17–25.

Sandhu, K.S. and P. Wheatley. "Challenges of Success", in *Management of Success: The Moulding of Modern Singapore*, ed. K.S. Sandhu and P. Wheatley. Singapore: Institute of Southeast Asian Studies, 1989, pp. 1067–106.

Sarel, M. "Growth and Productivity in ASEAN Countries", IMF Working Paper 97/97. Washington, DC: International Monetary Fund, 1997.

"Savings Policy", in Lim Chong Yah and Associates, *Policy Options for the Singapore Economy*. Singapore: McGraw-Hill, 1988, pp. 215–46.

Schenk, C.R. "The Dissolution of a Monetary Union: The Case of Singapore and Malaysia 1963–1974", *The Journal of Imperial and Commonwealth History* 41, 3 (2013): 496–522.

Seah Chee Meow and Linda Seah. "Education Reform and National Integration", in *Singapore Development Policies and Trends*, ed. Peter S.J. Chen. Singapore: Oxford University Press, 1983, pp. 240–67.

"Sectoral, Industry and Employment Business Cycles in Singapore", *Macroeconomic Review*. Singapore: Monetary Authority of Singapore (April 2009): 70–82.

Seow, Adeline and Lee Hin-Peng. "From Colony to City State: Changes in Health Needs in Singapore from 1950 to 1990", *Journal of Public Health Medicine* 16, 2 (1994): 149–58.

Shantakumar, G. "Human Resource Development in Singapore", in *Singapore: Twenty-five Years of Development*, ed. You Poh Seng and Lim Chong Yah. Singapore: Nan Yang Xing Zhou Lianhe Zaobao, 1984, pp. 165–88.

Sharma, S. "The Changing Structure of the Oil Market and Its Implications for Singapore's Oil Industry", *ASEAN Economic Bulletin* 4, 3 (1988): 271–86.

Shinya, S. "The Expansion of Japan's Cotton Textile Exports into Southeast Asia", in *International Commercial Rivalry in Southeast Asia in the Interwar Period*, ed. S. Shinya and M.C. Guerrero. New Haven, CT: Yale University Southeast Asia Studies, 1994, pp. 40–73.

Siah U Chin. "General Sketch of the Numbers, Tribes, and Avocations of the Chinese in Singapore", *The Journal of the Indian Archipelago and Eastern Asia*, ed. J.R. Logan, 2 (1848): 283–90.

"Singapore Restructured". *BMJ: British Medical Journal* 300, 6734 (1990): 1223.

"Singapore's Electronics Cluster", *Economic Survey of Singapore First Quarter 2008*. Singapore: Ministry of Trade and Industry, pp. 9–10.

"Singapore's Export Performance", *Economic Survey of Singapore 2009*. Singapore: Ministry of Trade and Industry, pp. 30–2.

"Singapore's Growth Cycle Chronology, Coincident and Leading Indicators", *Economic Survey of Singapore Second Quarter 2004*. Singapore: Ministry of Trade and Industry, pp. 45–53.

"Singapore's Growth Cycle Chronology, Coincident and Leading Indicators", *Statistics Singapore Newsletter* Issue 2 (2023): 7–10.

Singh, Mohan. "Health and Health Policy in Singapore", *ASEAN Economic Bulletin* 16, 3 (1999): 330–43.

Sng Hui Ying. "Albert Winsemius and Wage Policy in Singapore", in Euston Quah with Luke Nursultan Iuldashov and Zach Lee, *Albert Winsemius and Singapore: Here It is Going to Happen*. Singapore: World Scientific, 2022, pp. 431–62.

Soon Teck Wong and W.A. Stoever. "Foreign Investment and Economic Development in Singapore: A Policy-Oriented Approach", *The Journal of Developing Areas* 30, 3 (1996): 317–40.

"Special Feature on Comparing Present and Past Recessions", *MAS ED Quarterly Bulletin*. Singapore: Monetary Authority of Singapore (October 2001): 70–83.

Stillson, R.T. "The Financing of Malayan Rubber, 1905–1923", *The Economic History Review* 24, 4 (1971): 589–98.

St. John, S. "Piracy in the Indian Archipelago", *The Journal of the Indian Archipelago and Eastern Asia*, ed. J.R. Logan, 3 (1849): 251–60.

Sugihara, K. "The Resurgence of Intra-Asian Trade, 1800–1850", in *How India Clothed the World: The World of South Asian Textiles, 1500–1850*, ed. G. Riello and Tirtankar Roy. Leiden: Brill, 2009, pp. 139–69.

Sugimoto, Ichiro and Keen Meng Choy. "Reconstructing the National Accounts of a British Colony: New GDP Estimates for Singapore, 1870–1900", Mimeograph, 2023.

Sugimoto, Ichiro and Tan Eu Chye. "Government Fiscal Behavior and Economic Growth of Singapore in the Twentieth Century", *The Singapore Economic Review* 56, 1 (2011): 19–40.

Tan, Alvin. "Konfrontasi: Singapore's Experience of an Undeclared War", *BiblioAsia* 19, 4 (2024): 24–31.

Tan Chwee Huat. "Public Enterprises and Privatization: The Experience of Singapore", *Annals of Public and Cooperative Economics* 63, 1 (1992): 119–25.

________. "Singapore Telecom: From Public to Private Sector", *International Journal of Public Sector Management* 5, 4 (1992): 4–14.

Tan Ee-Leong. "The Chinese Banks Incorporated in Singapore and the Federation of Malaya", *Journal of the Malaysian Branch of the Royal Asiatic Society* 42, 1 (1969): 256–81.

Tan Ern Ser. "Comments on Presentation by Speaker", in *Inequality in Singapore*, ed. Faizal Bin Yahya. Singapore: World Scientific, 2015, pp. 42–9.

Tan, Jason and S. Gopinathan. "An Innovation in Educational Financing: The Edusave Scheme in Singapore", *Change: Transformations in Education* 2, 2 (1999): 66–79.

Tan Kim Song and Manu Bhaskaran. "The Role of the State in Singapore: Pragmatism in Pursuit of Growth", *The Singapore Economic Review* 60, 3 (2015): 1550030-1–1550030-30.

Tan, Nalla. "Health and Welfare", in *A History of Singapore*, ed. Ernest Chew and Edwin Lee. Singapore: Oxford University Press, 1991, pp. 339–56.

Tan Tai Yong. "Early Entrepôt Portal—Trade and Founding of Singapore", in *Maritime Heritage of Singapore*, ed. Aileen Lau and Laure Lau. Singapore: Subtree, 2005, pp. 80–101.

________. "The Indian Ocean—Arab and Indian Traders", in *Maritime Heritage of Singapore*, ed. Aileen Lau and Laure Lau. Singapore: Subtree, 2005, pp. 18–29.

Tarling, N. "British Policy in the Malay Peninsula and Archipelago 1824–1871", *Journal of the Malayan Branch of the Royal Asiatic Society* 30, 3 (1957): 3–7, 9–228.

Tay Kim Poh. "The Twin Pillars of Estate Rejuvenation", *Ethos* (June 2008): 32–42.

Tay, Simon S.C. "Island in the World: Globalization and Singapore's Transformation", in *Southeast Asian Affairs 2001*. Singapore: Institute of Southeast Asian Studies, 2001, pp. 279–309.

Teh Kok Peng and Tharman Shanmugaratnam. "Exchange Rate Policy: Philosophy and Conduct Over the Past Decade", in *Public Policies in Singapore: Changes in the 1980s and Future Signposts*, ed. Linda Low and Toh Mun Heng. Singapore: Times Academic Press, 1992, pp. 285–314.

Teo Siew Eng. "Planning Principles in Pre- and Post-Independence Singapore", *The Town Planning Review* 63, 2 (1992): 163–85.

________ and Victor R. Savage. "Singapore Landscape: A Historical Overview of Housing Image", in *A History of Singapore*, ed. Ernest Chew and Edwin Lee. Singapore: Oxford University Press, 1991, pp. 312–38.

Teo, Thompson S.H. and James S.K. Ang. "Singapore's Manufacturing Sector as Engine for Economic Growth: Past, Present and Future", *Science and Public Policy* 28, 5 (2001): 361–70.

The Asiatic Journal and Monthly Register for British India and its Dependencies, 1822–25. London: Black, Parbury and Allen [East India Company booksellers].

"The Contribution of Intangible Assets to Labour Productivity Growth in Singapore, 2009–2019", *Economic Survey of Singapore First Quarter 2022*. Singapore: Ministry of Trade and Industry, pp. 60–75.

"The Contribution of Tourism to the Singapore Economy", *Economic Survey of Singapore 2010*. Singapore: Ministry of Trade and Industry, pp. 71–7.

"The Digital Economy in Singapore", *Economic Survey of Singapore Third Quarter 2017*. Singapore: Ministry of Trade and Industry, pp. 18–29.

"The Impact of SARS on the Singapore Economy and Action Taken in Response", *Asia Pacific Biotech News* 8, 12 (2004): 672–9.

"The Impact of the Workfare Income Supplement Scheme on Individuals' Labour Outcomes", *Economic Survey of Singapore Second Quarter 2014*. Singapore: Ministry of Trade and Industry, pp. 27–36.

"The Information & Communications Sector—Trends, Drivers and Opportunities", *Economic Survey of Singapore Second Quarter 2009*. Singapore: Ministry of Trade and Industry, pp. 13–18.

"The Mineral Oil Trade", in *One Hundred Years of Singapore*, vol. II, ed. W. Makepeace, G.E. Brooke and R. St.J. Braddell. London: John Murray, 1921, pp. 97–101.

"The Role of Government", in Lim Chong Yah and Associates, *Policy Options for the Singapore Economy*. Singapore: McGraw-Hill, 1988, pp. 51–73.

Thio, Eunice. "The Syonan Years, 1942–1945", in *A History of Singapore*, ed. Ernest Chew and Edwin Lee. Singapore: Oxford University Press, 1991, pp. 95–114.

Thomas, J.S., Ong Suan Ee, Chia Kee Seng and Lee Hin Peng. "A Brief History of Public Health in Singapore", in *Singapore's Health Care System: What 50 Years Have Achieved*, ed. Lee Chien Earn and K. Satku. Singapore: World Scientific, 2016, pp. 33–55.

Thomson, J.T. "Account of the Horsburgh Light-house", *The Journal of the Indian Archipelago and Eastern Asia*, ed. J.R. Logan, 6 (1852): 376–498.

________. "General Report on the Residency of Singapore, Drawn up Principally with a View of Illustrating its Agricultural Statistics", *The Journal of the Indian Archipelago and Eastern Asia*, ed. J.R. Logan, 3 (1849): 618–28, 744–55.

________. "General Report on the Residency of Singapore, Drawn up Principally with a View of Illustrating its Agricultural Statistics", *The Journal of the Indian Archipelago and Eastern Asia*, ed. J.R. Logan, 4 (1850): 27–41 ff.

Toh Mun Heng. "Savings, Capital Formation, and Economic Growth in Singapore", in *Population Change and Economic Development in East Asia: Challenges Met, Opportunities Seized*, ed. A. Mason. Redwood City, CA: Stanford University Press, 2001, pp. 185–208.

________ and Linda Low. "Singapore's Service Development in the ASEAN Context", *ASEAN Economic Bulletin* 6, 1 (1989): 8–30.

________ and Wong Chai Shing. "Rates of Return to Education in Singapore", *Education Economics* 7, 3 (1999): 235–52.

Tregonning, K.G. "Straits Tin: A Brief Account of the First Seventy-Five Years of The Straits Trading Company, Limited", *Journal of the Malayan Branch of the Royal Asiatic Society* 36, 1 (1963): 79–152.

"Trends in E-commerce in the Services Sector", *Economic Survey of Singapore 2019*. Singapore: Ministry of Trade and Industry, pp. 80–6.

"Trends in the Recovery of Retail and Food & Beverage Spending in Singapore", *Economic Survey of Singapore 2022*. Singapore: Ministry of Trade and Industry, pp. 76–81.

Trocki, C.A. "The Origins of the Kangchu System 1740–1860", *Journal of the Malaysian Branch of the Royal Asiatic Society* 49, 2 (1976): 132–55.

Tsao Yuan. "Sources of Growth Accounting for the Singapore Economy", in *Singapore: Resources and Growth*, ed. Lim Chong Yah and P.J. Lloyd. Singapore: Oxford University Press, 1986, pp. 17–44.

Tsui-Auch, Lai Si, Sherwin Ignatius Chia and Anica Liu. "Putting Singapore on the Global Innovation Map: The Shifting Role of the State in the Rapidly Changing Environment" in *The Routledge Handbook of Politics and Technology*, ed. U. Hilpert. Abingdon: Routledge, 2015, pp. 191–206.

Turnbull, C.M. "Convicts in the Straits Settlements 1826–1867", *Journal of the Malaysian Branch of the Royal Asiatic Society* 43, 1 (1970): 87–103.

United Nations Commission for Asia and the Far East. "Export Instability in the Primary Exporting Countries", in *Readings in Malayan Economics*, ed. T.H. Silcock. Singapore: Eastern Universities Press, 1961, pp. 106–70.

van Elkan, R. "Accounting for Growth in Singapore", in *Singapore: A Case Study in Rapid Development*, IMF Occasional Paper No. 119, ed. K. Bercuson. Washington, DC: International Monetary Fund, 1995, pp. 4–10.

van Helten, J. and G. Jones. "British Business in Malaysia and Singapore since the 1870s", in *British Business in Asia since 1860*, ed. R.P.T. Davenport-Hines and G. Jones. Cambridge, UK: Cambridge University Press, 1989, pp. 157–88.

van Zanden, J.L. "The Skill Premium and the 'Great Divergence'", *European Review of Economic History* 13, 1 (2009): 121–53.

Vasoo, S. and James Lee. "Singapore: Social Development, Housing and the Central Provident Fund", *International Journal of Social Welfare* 10, 4 (2001): 276–83.

Wade, G. "An Early Age of Commerce in Southeast Asia, 900–1300 CE", *Journal of Southeast Asian Studies* 40, 2 (2009): 221–65.

"Wage Policy", in Lim Chong Yah and Associates, *Policy Options for the Singapore Economy*. Singapore: McGraw-Hill, 1988, pp. 171–213.

Wan Fook Kee and Margaret T.F. Loh. "Fertility Policies and the National Family Planning and Population Programme", in *Public Policy and Population Change in Singapore*, ed. Peter S.J. Chen and J.T. Fawcett. New York: The Population Council, 1979, pp. 97–108.

Warring, P. and J. Lewer. "The Global Financial Crisis, Employment Relations and the Labour Market in Singapore and Australia", *Asia Pacific Business Review* 19, 2 (2013): 217–29.

Waterson, R. "Gathering Speed: Transport and the Pace of Life", in *Past Times: A Social History of Singapore*, ed. Chan Kwok Bun and Tong Chee Kiong. Singapore: Times Editions, 2003, pp. 103–21.

Watkins, M.H. "A Staple Theory of Economic Growth", *Canadian Journal of Economics and Political Science* 29, 2 (1963): 141–58.

Webster, A. "Singapore, the Straits Settlements and the Politics of Imperial Commerce, 1819–1867", in *Singapore—Two Hundred Years of the Lion City*, ed. A. Webster and N.J. White. Routledge, 2020, pp. 119–36.

________. "The Strategies and Limits of Gentlemanly Capitalism: The London East India Agency Houses, Provincial Commercial Interests, and the Evolution of British Economic Policy in South and South East Asia 1800–50", *The Economic History Review*, New Series 59, 4 (2006): 743–64.

White, G. and R. Wade. "Developmental States and Markets in East Asia: An Introduction", in *Developmental States in East Asia*, ed. G. White. London: Palgrave Macmillan, 1988, pp. 1–29.

White, N.J. "The Economics of Singapore's Exit from Malaysia", in *Singapore—Two Hundred Years of the Lion City*, ed. A. Webster and N.J. White. Abingdon: Routledge, 2020, pp. 96–116.

Whittlesey, C.R. "The Stevenson Plan: Some Conclusions and Observations", *Journal of Political Economy* 39, 4 (1931): 506–25.

Wilson, P. "Monetary Policy and Financial Sector Development", *The Singapore Economic Review* 60, 3 (2015): 1550031-1–1550031-25.

Winstedt, R.O. "A History of Malaya", *Journal of the Malayan Branch of the Royal Asiatic Society* 13, 1 (1935): iii–270.

Wisseman-Christie, J. "Money and Its Uses in the Javanese States of the Ninth to Fifteenth Centuries A.D.", *Journal of the Economic and Social History of the Orient* 39, 3 (1996): 243–86.

Wong Fot Chyi and Gan Wee Beng. "Total Factor Productivity in the Singapore Manufacturing Industries during the 1980s", *Journal of Asian Economics* 5, 2 (1994): 177–96.

Wong, Joseph. "The Adaptive Developmental State in East Asia", *Journal of East Asian Studies* 4, 2 (2004): 345–62.

Wong Kum Poh. "Saving, Capital Inflow and Capital Formation", in *Singapore: Resources and Growth*, ed. Lim Chong Yah and P.J. Lloyd. Singapore: Oxford University Press, 1986, pp. 45–78.

Wong Lin Ken. "Commercial Growth Before the Second World War", in *A History of Singapore*, ed. Ernest Chew and Edwin Lee. Singapore: Oxford University Press, 1991, pp. 41–65.

________. "Singapore: Its Growth as an Entrepôt Port, 1819–1941", *Journal of Southeast Asian Studies* 9, 1 (1978): 50–84.

________. "Western Enterprise and the Development of the Malayan Tin Industry to 1914", in *The Economic Development of South-East Asia*, ed. C.D. Cowan. 1964; Abingdon: Routledge, 2012, pp. 127–53.

Wong Poh-Kam. "Singapore: Electronics and Shipbuilding/Repair Industry Case Studies", in *Industrial Policy, Innovation and Economic Growth: The Experience of Japan and the Asian NIEs*, ed. Wong Poh-Kam and Ng Chee-Yuen. Singapore: Singapore University Press, 2001, pp. 580–626.

________. "The Role of the State in Singapore's Industrial Development", in *Industrial Policy, Innovation and Economic Growth: The Experience of Japan and the Asian NIEs*, ed. Wong Poh-Kam and Ng Chee-Yuen. Singapore: Singapore University Press, 2001, pp. 503–79.

________ and Ng Chee Yuen. "Singapore's Industrial Policy to the Year 2000", in *Industrial Policies in East Asia*, ed. S. Masuyama, D. Vandenbrink and Chia Siow Yue. Tokyo: Nomura Research Institute and Singapore: Institute of Southeast Asian Studies, 1997, pp. 121–41.

Wong Tai-Chee. "The Transformation of Singapore's Central Area: From Slums to a Global Business Hub?", *Planning Practice & Research* 16, 2 (2001): 155–70.

Wu, Alfred M. "Fiscal Responses to COVID-19 in Singapore and Hong Kong", *Ethos*, Issue 22 (2021): 28–41.

Faizal bin Yahya. "Singapore in 2010: Rebounding from Economic Slump, Managing Tensions between a Global City and a Fledgling Nation State", in *Southeast Asian Affairs 2011*. Singapore: Institute of Southeast Asian Studies, 2011, pp. 257–70.

Yamada, H. "The Origins of British Colonialization of Malaya with Special Reference to Its Tin", *The Developing Economies* 9, 3 (1971): 225–45.

Yamashita, K. "Residential Segregation of Chinese Dialect Groups in Singapore: with Focus on the Period Before ca. 1970", *Geographical Review of Japan* 59 (Ser. B), 2 (1986): 83–102.

Yeh, Stephen H.K. "Some Trends and Prospects in Singapore's Public Housing", *Ekistics* 33, 196 (1972): 182–5.

Yeoh, Brenda S.A. "Urban Sanitation, Health and Water Supply in Late Nineteenth and Early Twentieth Century Colonial Singapore", *South East Asia Research* 1, 2 (1993): 143–72.

Yeoh Lam Keong. "Rethinking A New Social Compact for Singapore", *Ethos*, Issue 3 (2007): 7–12.

Yeung, Bernard. "Failures on Many Fronts", in *Financial Crisis 2008*, ed. Ivan Png. Saw Centre Financial Studies No. 5. Singapore: Saw Centre for Financial Studies, 2008, pp. 11–16.

Yeung, Henry Wai-Chung. "From National Development to Economic Diplomacy? Governing Singapore's Sovereign Wealth Funds", *The Pacific Review* 24, 5 (2011): 625–52.

________. "Globalising Singapore: One Global City, Global Production Networks and the Developmental State", in *Singapore Perspectives 2010*, ed. Tarn Tan How. Singapore: World Scientific, 2010, pp. 109–21.

Yeung Yue-Man and D.W. Drakakis-Smith. "Comparative Perspectives on Public Housing in Singapore and Hong Kong", *Asian Survey* 14, 8 (1974): 763–75.

Young, A. "A Tale of Two Cities: Factor Accumulation and Technical Change in Hong Kong and Singapore", *NBER Macroeconomics Annual* 7 (1992): 13–54.

________. "The Tyranny of Numbers: Confronting the Statistical Realities of the East Asian Growth Experience", *The Quarterly Journal of Economics* 110, 3 (1995): 641–80.

Index

FSC
www.fsc.org
MIX
Papier | Fördert
gute Waldnutzung
FSC® C083411

Kolibri 360 GmbH
Ferdinand-Jühlke-Straße 7
99095 Erfurt, Deutschland
produktsicherheit@kolibri360.de